VW Transporter (T5) diesel
Owners Workshop Manual

John S. Mead

Models covered

(5743 - 352 - 11AW1)

VW Transporter 'T5' variants with diesel engines and front-wheel-drive
Diesel: 1.9 litre (1896cc) & 2.0 litre (1968cc) 4-cyl and 2.5 litre (2461cc) 5-cyl

Does NOT cover petrol engined models, 'DSG' transmission, twin-turbo diesel engine, all-wheel-drive '4-Motion' models, or interior features specific to Caravelle, California or specialist bodywork/camper conversions

ABCDE

A book in the **Haynes Owners Workshop Manual Series**

ISBN **978 1 78521 420 2**

British Library Cataloguing in Publication Data
A catalogue record for this book is available from the British Library.

Printed in India

Haynes Group Limited
Sparkford, Yeovil, Somerset BA22 7JJ, England

Haynes North America, Inc
2801 Townsgate Road, Suite 340, Thousand Oaks, CA 91361

Contents

Contents

REPAIRS AND OVERHAUL

Engine and associated systems

Transmission

Brakes and suspension

Body equipment

Wiring diagrams

REFERENCE

Index

The VW T5 Transporter covered by this manual was introduced in the UK in July 2003 as a replacement for the T4 model. The range was facelifted in November 2009 with significant mechanical revisions also incorporated. Seemingly innumerable variations of body types and styles are available, in either short or long wheelbase configuration.

The Transporter was originally available with 1.9 and 2.5 litre diesel engines, in a wide range of power outputs. The 2.0 litre diesel engine was introduced in the November 2009 facelift, replacing both of the previous engines. 2.0 and 3.2 litre petrol engines are also available but are not covered by this manual. The 1.9 litre engines are of 4-cylinder SOHC 8-valve configuration with direct diesel injection and turbocharger. The 2.5 litre engines are of 5-cylinder SOHC 10-valve configuration, also utilizing direct diesel injection and a turbocharger. The 2.0 litre engines which replaced the two previous units are of 4-cylinder, DOHC 16-valve configuration, featuring the latest design of direct injection common rail fuel system. A 5- or 6-speed manual transmission is fitted as standard equipment, dependant on engine size and power output, with a 6-speed automatic transmission being optionally available on certain models. The engine is mounted transversely at the front of the vehicle with the transmission mounted on the left-hand side. All models are of front-wheel drive configuration (a 4-wheel drive version is also available but is not covered by this manual).

The front suspension is fully independent using MacPherson struts, transverse lower wishbones and an anti-roll bar. The rear suspension is also fully independent by means of trailing arms, coil springs and telescopic shock absorbers.

The dual-circuit, servo-assisted braking system has discs all round, with ABS, Electronic Stability Program (ESP) Emergency Brake Assist (EBA) and Electronic Brakeforce Distribution (EBD) either fitted as standard, or optionally available, for extra safety when braking in emergency situations.

A wide range of standard and optional equipment is available within the Transporter range, including power steering, air conditioning, remote central locking, electric windows, electronic engine immobiliser and supplemental restraint systems.

For the home mechanic, the Transporter is a relatively straightforward vehicle to maintain, and most of the items requiring frequent attention are easily accessible.

Your VW Transporter Manual

The aim of this manual is to help you get the best value from your vehicle. It can do so in several ways. It can help you decide what work must be done (even should you choose to get it done by a garage). It will also provide information on routine maintenance and servicing, and give a logical course of action and diagnosis when random faults occur. However, it is hoped that you will use the manual by tackling the work yourself. On simpler jobs it may even be quicker than booking the vehicle into a garage and going there twice, to leave and collect it. Perhaps most important, a lot of money can be saved by avoiding the costs a garage must charge to cover its labour and overheads.

The manual has drawings and descriptions to show the function of the various components so that their layout can be understood. Tasks are described and photographed in a clear step-by-step sequence.

References to the 'left' and 'right' of the vehicle are in the sense of a person in the driver's seat facing forward.

Project vehicles

The main vehicle used in the preparation of this manual, and which appears in many of the photographic sequences, was a VW Caravelle with a 2.5 litre engine. Additional work was carried out on a Transporter van with a 2.0 litre engine.

Acknowledgements

Thanks are due to Draper Tools Limited, who provided some of the workshop tools, and to all those people at Sparkford who helped in the production of this manual. Thanks also go to Steve Churchill for the loan of his Caravelle for use in the project and to Darkside Developments for supplying the replacement exhaust manifold.

This manual is not a direct reproduction of the vehicle manufacturer's data, and its publication should not be taken as implying any technical approval by the vehicle manufacturers or importers.

We take great pride in the accuracy of information given in this manual, but vehicle manufacturers make alterations and design changes during the production run of a particular vehicle of which they do not inform us. No liability can be accepted by the authors or publishers for loss, damage or injury caused by any errors in, or omissions from, the information given.

Working on your vehicle can be dangerous. This page shows just some of the potential risks and hazards, with the aim of creating a safety-conscious attitude.

General hazards

Scalding

• Don't remove the radiator or expansion tank cap while the engine is hot.
• Engine oil, transmission fluid or power steering fluid may also be dangerously hot if the engine has recently been running.

Burning

• Beware of burns from the exhaust system and from any part of the engine. Brake discs and drums can also be extremely hot immediately after use.

Crushing

• When working under or near a raised vehicle, always supplement the jack with axle stands, or use drive-on ramps.
Never venture under a vehicle which is only supported by a jack.
• Take care if loosening or tightening high-torque nuts when the vehicle is on stands. Initial loosening and final tightening should be done with the wheels on the ground.

Fire

• Fuel is highly flammable; fuel vapour is explosive.
• Don't let fuel spill onto a hot engine.
• Do not smoke or allow naked lights (including pilot lights) anywhere near a vehicle being worked on. Also beware of creating sparks (electrically or by use of tools).
• Fuel vapour is heavier than air, so don't work on the fuel system with the vehicle over an inspection pit.
• Another cause of fire is an electrical overload or short-circuit. Take care when repairing or modifying the vehicle wiring.
• Keep a fire extinguisher handy, of a type suitable for use on fuel and electrical fires.

Electric shock

• Ignition HT and Xenon headlight voltages can be dangerous, especially to people with heart problems or a pacemaker. Don't work on or near these systems with the engine running or the ignition switched on.

• Mains voltage is also dangerous. Make sure that any mains-operated equipment is correctly earthed. Mains power points should be protected by a residual current device (RCD) circuit breaker.

Fume or gas intoxication

• Exhaust fumes are poisonous; they can contain carbon monoxide, which is rapidly fatal if inhaled. Never run the engine in a confined space such as a garage with the doors shut.
• Fuel vapour is also poisonous, as are the vapours from some cleaning solvents and paint thinners.

Poisonous or irritant substances

• Avoid skin contact with battery acid and with any fuel, fluid or lubricant, especially antifreeze, brake hydraulic fluid and Diesel fuel. Don't syphon them by mouth. If such a substance is swallowed or gets into the eyes, seek medical advice.
• Prolonged contact with used engine oil can cause skin cancer. Wear gloves or use a barrier cream if necessary. Change out of oil-soaked clothes and do not keep oily rags in your pocket.
• Air conditioning refrigerant forms a poisonous gas if exposed to a naked flame (including a cigarette). It can also cause skin burns on contact.

Asbestos

• Asbestos dust can cause cancer if inhaled or swallowed. Asbestos may be found in gaskets and in brake and clutch linings. When dealing with such components it is safest to assume that they contain asbestos.

Special hazards

Hydrofluoric acid

• This extremely corrosive acid is formed when certain types of synthetic rubber, found in some O-rings, oil seals, fuel hoses etc, are exposed to temperatures above 4000C. The rubber changes into a charred or sticky substance containing the acid. *Once formed, the acid remains dangerous for years. If it gets onto the skin, it may be necessary to amputate the limb concerned.*
• When dealing with a vehicle which has suffered a fire, or with components salvaged from such a vehicle, wear protective gloves and discard them after use.

The battery

• Batteries contain sulphuric acid, which attacks clothing, eyes and skin. Take care when topping-up or carrying the battery.
• The hydrogen gas given off by the battery is highly explosive. Never cause a spark or allow a naked light nearby. Be careful when connecting and disconnecting battery chargers or jump leads.

Air bags

• Air bags can cause injury if they go off accidentally. Take care when removing the steering wheel and trim panels. Special storage instructions may apply.

Diesel injection equipment

• Diesel injection pumps supply fuel at very high pressure. Take care when working on the fuel injectors and fuel pipes.

⚠ *Warning: Never expose the hands, face or any other part of the body to injector spray; the fuel can penetrate the skin with potentially fatal results.*

Remember...

DO

• Do use eye protection when using power tools, and when working under the vehicle.
• Do wear gloves or use barrier cream to protect your hands when necessary.
• Do get someone to check periodically that all is well when working alone on the vehicle.
• Do keep loose clothing and long hair well out of the way of moving mechanical parts.
• Do remove rings, wristwatch etc, before working on the vehicle – especially the electrical system.
• Do ensure that any lifting or jacking equipment has a safe working load rating adequate for the job.

DON'T

• Don't attempt to lift a heavy component which may be beyond your capability – get assistance.
• Don't rush to finish a job, or take unverified short cuts.
• Don't use ill-fitting tools which may slip and cause injury.
• Don't leave tools or parts lying around where someone can trip over them. Mop up oil and fuel spills at once.
• Don't allow children or pets to play in or near a vehicle being worked on.

The following pages are intended to help in dealing with common roadside emergencies and breakdowns. You will find more detailed fault finding information at the back of the manual, and repair information in the main chapters.

If your vehicle won't start and the starter motor doesn't turn

☐ If it's a model with automatic transmission, make sure the selector lever is in 'P' or 'N'.
☐ Open the bonnet and make sure that the battery terminals are clean and tight.
☐ Switch on the headlights and try to start the engine. If the headlights go very dim when you're trying to start, the battery is probably flat. Get out of trouble by jump starting (see next page) using a friend's car.

If your vehicle won't start even though the starter motor turns as normal

☐ Is there fuel in the tank?
☐ Is there moisture on electrical components under the bonnet? Switch off the ignition, then wipe off any obvious dampness with a dry cloth. Spray a water-repellent aerosol product (WD-40 or equivalent) on engine and fuel system electrical connectors like those shown in the photos.

1 Check the security and condition of the battery connections.

2 Check all multi-plugs and wiring connectors for security.

3 Check that all fuses are still in good condition and none have blown.

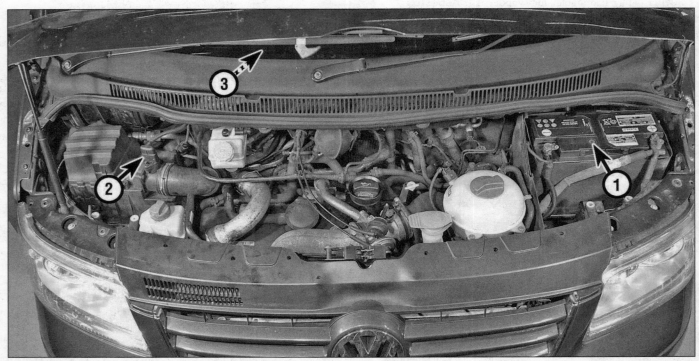

Check that electrical connections are secure (with the ignition switched off) and spray them with a water-dispersant spray like WD-40 if you suspect a problem due to damp.

Jump starting

Jump starting will get you out of trouble, but you must correct whatever made the battery go flat in the first place. There are three possibilities:

1 The battery has been drained by repeated attempts to start, or by leaving the lights on.

2 The charging system is not working properly (alternator drivebelt slack or broken, alternator wiring fault or alternator itself faulty).

3 The battery itself is at fault (electrolyte low, or battery worn out).

When jump-starting a vehicle, observe the following precautions:

✓ Before connecting the booster battery, make sure that the ignition is switched off.

Caution: Remove the key in case the central locking engages when the jump leads are connected

✓ Ensure that all electrical equipment (lights, heater, wipers, etc) is switched off.
✓ Take note of any special precautions printed on the battery case.
✓ Make sure that the booster battery is the same voltage as the discharged one in the vehicle.

✓ If the battery is being jump-started from the battery in another vehicle, the two vehicles MUST NOT TOUCH each other.

✓ Make sure that the transmission is in neutral (or PARK, in the case of automatic transmission).

Budget jump leads can be a false economy, as they often do not pass enough current to start large capacity or diesel engines. They can also get hot.

1 Connect one end of the red jump lead to the positive (+) terminal of the flat battery

2 Connect the other end of the red lead to the positive (+) terminal of the booster battery.

3 Connect one end of the black jump lead to the negative (-) terminal of the booster battery

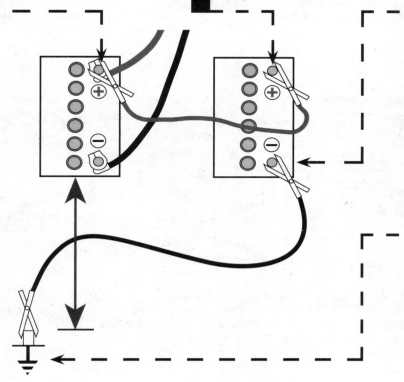

4 Connect the other end of the black jump lead to a bolt or bracket on the engine block, well away from the battery, on the vehicle to be started.

5 Make sure that the jump leads will not come into contact with the fan, drive-belts or other moving parts of the engine.

6 Start the engine using the booster battery and run it at idle speed. Switch on the lights, rear window demister and heater blower motor, then disconnect the jump leads in the reverse order of connection. Turn off the lights etc.

Wheel changing

 Warning: Do not change a wheel in a situation where you risk being hit by other traffic. On busy roads, try to stop in a lay-by or a gateway. Be wary of passing traffic while changing the wheel – it is easy to become distracted by the job in hand.

Preparation

- ☐ When a puncture occurs, stop as soon as it is safe to do so.
- ☐ Park on firm level ground, if possible, and well out of the way of other traffic.
- ☐ Use hazard warning lights if necessary.

- ☐ If you have one, use a warning triangle to alert other drivers of your presence.
- ☐ Apply the handbrake and engage first or reverse gear (or 'P' on automatic transmission models).

- ☐ Chock the wheel diagonally opposite the one being removed – a couple of large stones will do for this.
- ☐ If the ground is soft, use a flat piece of wood to spread the load under the jack.

Changing the wheel

Note: *The following information is mainly applicable to Van models. Some differences in component location will be found on Chassis cab variants, and certain later models.*

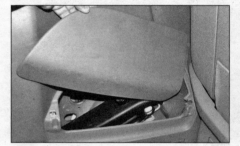

1 The jack, wheelbrace and vehicle tools are located in a stowage compartment at the rear left of the luggage compartment. On some models it may be necessary to take off a removable stowage compartment cover for access.

2 Unscrew the centre fastener and take out the tool kit and the jack.

3 The spare wheel is mounted under the rear of the vehicle. Using the wheelbrace, slacken the folding bracket safety bolt until it turns freely.

4 Undo the folding bracket retaining bolt and allow the bracket to rest on the safety bolt.

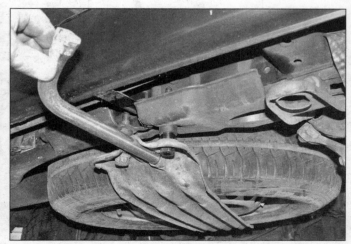

5 Insert the flat end of the wheelbrace into the guide on the folding bracket, up to the stop. Grasp the wheelbrace firmly, lift it slightly and move it to the right until the elongated hole slips over the safety bolt.

6 Lower the folding bracket to the ground, then lift the spare wheel out of the folding bracket.

7 Where applicable, prise off the wheel bolt covers or wheel trim, using the flat end of the wheelbrace, or the removal tool in the tool kit. Slacken each wheel bolt by half a turn.

8 Position the jack under the jacking point nearest the punctured wheel. The jacking points are indicated by depressions in the side sills just to the rear of the front wheels and just to the front of the rear wheels (see *Jacking and vehicle support*).

9 Engage the head of the jack with the jacking point and turn the jack handle clockwise until the wheel is raised clear of the ground. Unscrew the wheel bolts and remove the wheel.

10 Fit the spare wheel and screw on the bolts. Lightly tighten the bolts with the wheelbrace. Lower the vehicle to the ground and fully tighten the wheel bolts in a diagonal sequence. Refit the wheel bolt covers or wheel trim, as applicable.

Finally...

☐ Remove the wheel chocks.

☐ Secure the punctured wheel back under the vehicle, then stow the jack and tools in the stowage compartment.

☐ Check the tyre pressure on the wheel just fitted. If it is low, or if you don't have a pressure gauge with you, drive slowly to the next garage and inflate the tyre to the correct pressure.

☐ Have the damaged tyre or wheel repaired as soon as possible, or another puncture will leave you stranded.

☐ Don't leave the spare wheel folding bracket empty and unsecured – it could drop onto the ground while the vehicle is moving.

☐ Have the roadwheel bolts tightened to the correct torque (see Chapter 10) at the earliest opportunity.

Identifying leaks

Puddles on the garage floor or drive, or obvious wetness under the bonnet or underneath the vehicle, suggest a leak that needs investigating. It can sometimes be difficult to decide where the leak is coming from, especially if an engine undershield is fitted. Leaking oil or fluid can also be blown rearwards by the passage of air under the vehicle, giving a false impression of where the problem lies.

 Warning: Most automotive oils and fluids are poisonous. Wash them off skin, and change out of contaminated clothing, without delay.

 The smell of a fluid leaking from the vehicle may provide a clue to what's leaking. Some fluids are distinctively coloured. It may help to remove the engine undershield, clean the vehicle carefully and to park it over some clean paper overnight as an aid to locating the source of the leak. Remember that some leaks may only occur while the engine is running.

Sump oil

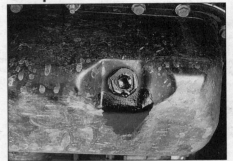

Engine oil may leak from the drain plug...

Oil from filter

...or from the base of the oil filter.

Gearbox oil

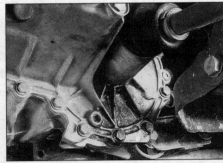

Gearbox oil can leak from the seals at the inboard ends of the driveshafts.

Antifreeze

Leaking antifreeze often leaves a crystalline deposit like this.

Brake fluid

A leak occurring at a wheel is almost certainly brake fluid.

Power steering fluid

Power steering fluid may leak from the pipe connectors on the steering rack.

Towing

When all else fails, you may find yourself having to get a tow home – or of course you may be helping somebody else. Long-distance recovery should only be done by a garage or breakdown service. For shorter distances, DIY towing using another vehicle is easy enough, but observe the following points:

☐ Use a proper tow-rope – they are not expensive. The vehicle being towed must display an ON TOW sign at the rear of the vehicle.

☐ Always turn the ignition key to the 'on' position when the vehicle is being towed, so that the steering lock is released, and the direction indicator and brake lights work.

☐ The towing eye is located in the vehicle tool kit. To fit the eye, remove the trim panel from the front bumper and screw the eye firmly into position. Note that the towing eye has a left-hand thread. The rear towing eye is permanently fixed to the underbody.

☐ Only attach the tow-rope to the towing eyes located below the front and rear bumpers.

☐ Before being towed, release the handbrake and select neutral on the transmission.

☐ Note that greater-than-usual pedal pressure will be required to operate the brakes, since the vacuum servo unit is only operational with the engine running.

☐ Note that greater-than-usual steering effort will also be required.

☐ The driver of the vehicle being towed must keep the tow-rope taut at all times to avoid snatching.

☐ Make sure that both drivers know the route before setting off.

☐ Only drive at moderate speeds and keep the distance towed to a minimum. Drive smoothly and allow plenty of time for slowing down at junctions.

☐ On models with automatic transmission, special precautions apply. If in doubt, do not tow, or transmission damage may result.

Introduction

There are some very simple checks which need only take a few minutes to carry out, but which could save you a lot of inconvenience and expense.

These checks require no great skill or special tools, and the small amount of time they take to perform could prove to be very well spent, for example:

☐ Keeping an eye on tyre condition and pressures, will not only help to stop them wearing out prematurely, but could also save your life.

☐ Many breakdowns are caused by electrical problems. Battery-related faults are particularly common, and a quick check on a regular basis will often prevent the majority of these.

☐ If your vehicle develops a brake fluid leak, the first time you might know about it is when your brakes don't work properly. Checking the level regularly will give advance warning of this kind of problem.

☐ If the oil or coolant levels run low, the cost of repairing any engine damage will be far greater than fixing the leak, for example.

Underbonnet check points

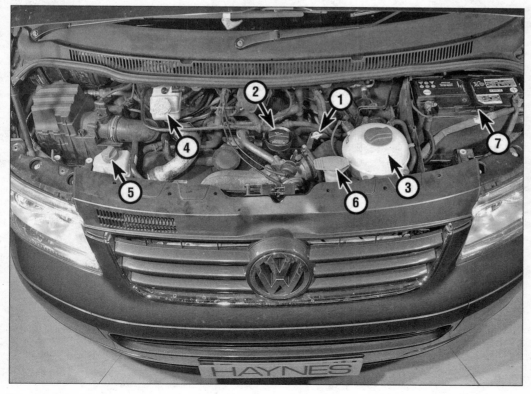

◀ **2.5 litre engine (others similar)**

1 *Engine oil level dipstick*

2 *Engine oil filler cap*

3 *Coolant reservoir (expansion tank)*

4 *Brake and clutch fluid reservoir*

5 *Power steering fluid reservoir*

6 *Washer fluid reservoir*

7 *Battery*

Engine oil level

Before you start

✔ Make sure that the vehicle is on level ground.
✔ The oil level should be checked with the engine at normal operating temperature, however, wait at least 5 minutes after the engine has been switched off..

HAYNES HiNT *If the oil is checked immediately after driving the vehicle, some of the oil will remain in the upper engine components, resulting in an inaccurate reading on the dipstick.*

The correct oil

Modern engines place great demands on their oil. It is very important that the correct oil for your vehicle is used (see *Lubricants and fluids*).

Vehicle care

● If you have to add oil frequently, you should check whether you have any oil leaks. Place some clean paper under the vehicle overnight, and check for stains in the morning. If there are no leaks, the engine may be burning oil.

● Always maintain the level in the dipstick's cross-hatched area (see photo 3). If the level is too low severe engine damage may occur. Oil seal failure may result if the engine is overfilled by adding too much oil.

1 Where applicable, lift up the access panel in the centre of the engine cover.

2 The dipstick is brightly coloured for easy identification (see *Underbonnet check points* on page 0•11 for exact location). Withdraw the dipstick.

3 Using a clean rag or paper towel remove all oil from the dipstick. Insert the clean dipstick into the tube as far as it will go, then withdraw it again.

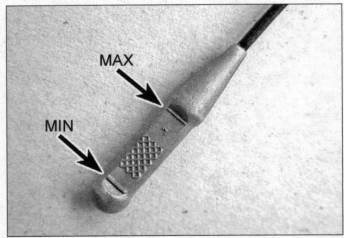

MAX
MIN

4 Note the oil level on the end of the dipstick; it should be in the cross-hatched area – never above the 'MAX' line or below the 'MIN' line. If topping-up is required (only if the level is between the cross-hatched area and the 'MIN' line, or below) add no more than 0.5 litre of oil at a time.

5 Oil is added through the filler cap. Unscrew the cap and top-up the level. A funnel may help to reduce spillage. Add the oil slowly, checking the level on the dipstick frequently. Avoid overfilling (see *Vehicle care*).

Coolant level

 Warning: Do not attempt to remove the expansion tank pressure cap when the engine is hot, as there is a very great risk of scalding. Do not leave open containers of coolant about, as it is poisonous.

Vehicle care

● Adding coolant should not be necessary on a regular basis. If frequent topping-up is required, it is likely there is a leak. Check the radiator, all hoses and joint faces for signs of staining or wetness, and rectify as necessary.

● It is important that antifreeze is used in the cooling system all year round, not just during the winter months. Don't top-up with water alone, as the antifreeze will become too diluted.

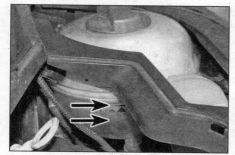

1 The coolant level varies with the temperature of the engine, and is visible through the expansion tank (remove the engine cover if necessary to check the level). When the engine is cold, the coolant level should be between the MAX and MIN marks on the side of the tank. When the engine is hot, the level may rise slightly above the MAX mark.

2 If topping-up is necessary, **wait until the engine is cold**. Slowly unscrew the expansion tank cap, to release any pressure present in the cooling system, and remove it.

3 Add a mixture of water and antifreeze to the expansion tank until the coolant level is halfway between the level marks. Refit the cap and tighten it securely.

Brake and clutch fluid level

Note: *All models have a hydraulically-operated clutch, which uses the same fluid as the braking system.*
Caution:
• *Hydraulic fluid can harm your eyes and damage painted surfaces, so use extreme caution when handling and pouring it.*
• *Do not use fluid that has been standing open for some time, as it absorbs moisture from the air, which can cause a dangerous loss of braking effectiveness.*

Before you start

✔ Make sure that your vehicle is on level ground.
✔ According to model, undo the retaining bolts and rotary fasteners and remove the battery cover and engine covers as applicable, for access to the reservoir.

Safety first!

● If the reservoir requires repeated topping-up this is an indication of a fluid leak somewhere in the system, which should be investigated immediately.
● If a leak is suspected, the vehicle should not be driven until the braking system has been checked. Never take any risks where brakes are concerned.

 The fluid level in the reservoir will drop slightly as the brake pads wear down, but the fluid level must never be allowed to drop below the MIN mark.

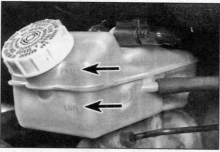

1 The MAX and MIN marks are indicated on the front and sides of the reservoir. The fluid level must be kept between the marks at all times.

3 Unscrew the reservoir cap and remove it. Inspect the reservoir, if the fluid is dirty the hydraulic system should be drained and refilled (see Chapter 1, Section 29).

2 If topping-up is necessary, first wipe clean the area around the filler cap to prevent dirt entering the hydraulic system.

4 Carefully add fluid, taking care not to spill it onto the surrounding components. Use only the specified fluid; mixing different types can cause damage to the system. After topping-up to the correct level, securely refit the cap and wipe off any spilt fluid.

Battery

Caution: Before carrying out any work on the vehicle battery, read the precautions given in 'Safety first!' at the start of this manual. If the battery is to be disconnected, refer to 'Disconnecting the battery' before proceeding.

✔ Make sure that the battery tray is in good condition, and that the clamp is tight. Corrosion on the tray, retaining clamp and the battery itself can be removed with a solution of water and baking soda. Thoroughly rinse all cleaned areas with water. Any metal parts damaged by corrosion should be covered with a zinc-based primer, then painted.

✔ The exterior of the battery should be inspected periodically for damage such as a cracked case or cover.

✔ Periodically (approximately every three months), check the charge condition of the battery, as described in Chapter 5, Section 3.

✔ If the battery is flat, and you need to jump start your vehicle, see *Roadside repairs*.

HAYNES HINT *Battery corrosion can be kept to a minimum by applying a layer of petroleum jelly to the clamps and terminals after they are reconnected.*

1 The battery is located on the left-hand side of the engine compartment. According to model, undo the retaining bolts and rotary fasteners and remove the battery cover.

2 Check the tightness of both clamps to ensure good electrical connections. You should not be able to move them. Also check each cable for cracks and frayed conductors.

3 If corrosion (white, fluffy deposits) is evident, remove the cables from the battery terminals, clean them with a small wire brush, then refit them. Automotive stores sell a tool for cleaning the battery post . . .

4 . . . as well as the battery cable clamps.

Electrical systems

✔ Check all external lights and the horn. Refer to the appropriate Sections of Chapter 12 for details if any of the circuits are found to be inoperative.

✔ Visually check all accessible wiring connectors, harnesses and retaining clips for security, and for signs of chafing or damage.

HAYNES HINT *If you need to check your brake lights and indicators unaided, back up to a wall or garage door and operate the lights. The reflected light should show if they are working properly.*

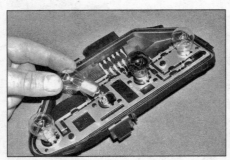
1 If a single indicator light, stop-light or headlight has failed, it is likely that a bulb has blown and will need to be replaced. Refer to Chapter 12, Section 5 for details. If both stop-lights have failed, it is possible that the switch has failed (see Chapter 9, Section 17).

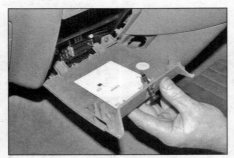
2 If more than one indicator light or headlight has failed, it is likely that either a fuse has blown or that there is a fault in the circuit (see Chapter 12, Section 2). The main fusebox is located under the centre of the facia. To gain access on some models, open the bottle holder, press the two levers together and remove the bottle holder from the facia. Open the transparent cover over the fuses. To gain access on Transporter models, use a screwdriver to turn the retaining catch and open the fusebox cover. Lift the cover up and remove it from the facia.

3 To renew a blown fuse, remove it, where applicable, using the plastic tool provided or needle nosed pliers. Fit a new fuse of the same rating, available from car accessory shops. It is important that you find the reason that the fuse blew (see *Electrical fault finding* in Chapter 12, Section 2).

Power steering fluid level

Before you start

✔ Park the vehicle on level ground.
✔ Set the steering wheel straight-ahead.
✔ The engine should be turned off.
✔ For the check to be accurate, the steering must not be turned once the engine has been stopped.

Safety First!

● The need for frequent topping-up indicates a leak, which should be investigated immediately.

1 The reservoir is mounted at the front right-hand side of the engine compartment. According to model, undo the retaining bolts and rotary fasteners and remove the battery cover and engine covers as applicable, for access to the reservoir.

2 Wipe clean the area around the reservoir filler cap and unscrew the cap. Using a clean rag or paper towel remove all oil from the integral dipstick, refit and tighten the filler cap, then unscrew and remove the cap again.

3 Note the fluid level on the end of the dipstick – if the system is cold the fluid level should be within the cross-hatched area marked 'cool' If the vehicle has just been driven and the system is hot, the fluid level should be within the cross-hatched area marked 'hot'.

4 If topping-up is necessary, use the specified type of fluid and do not overfill the reservoir (check the level on the dipstick after a small amount of fluid has been added). When the level is correct, securely refit the cap.

Screen washer fluid level

● Screenwash additives not only keep the windscreen clean during bad weather, they also prevent the washer system freezing in cold weather – which is when you are likely to need it most. Don't top-up using plain water, as the screenwash will become diluted, and will freeze in cold weather.

 Warning: On no account use engine coolant antifreeze in the screen washer system – this may damage the paintwork.

1 The reservoir for the washer systems is located at the front right of the engine compartment. If topping-up is necessary, open the filler cap.

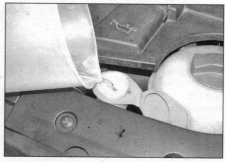

2 When topping-up the reservoir a screenwash additive should be added in the quantities recommended on the bottle.

Tyre condition and pressure

It is very important that tyres are in good condition, and at the correct pressure - having a tyre failure at any speed is highly dangerous. Tyre wear is influenced by driving style - harsh braking and acceleration, or fast cornering, will all produce more rapid tyre wear. As a general rule, the front tyres wear out faster than the rears. Interchanging the tyres from front to rear ("rotating" the tyres) may result in more even wear. However, if this is completely effective, you may have the expense of replacing all four tyres at once!

Remove any nails or stones embedded in the tread before they penetrate the tyre to cause deflation. If removal of a nail does reveal that the tyre has been punctured, refit the nail so that its point of penetration is marked. Then immediately change the wheel, and have the tyre repaired by a tyre dealer.

Regularly check the tyres for damage in the form of cuts or bulges, especially in the sidewalls. Periodically remove the wheels, and clean any dirt or mud from the inside and outside surfaces. Examine the wheel rims for signs of rusting, corrosion or other damage. Light alloy wheels are easily damaged by "kerbing" whilst parking; steel wheels may also become dented or buckled. A new wheel is very often the only way to overcome severe damage.

New tyres should be balanced when they are fitted, but it may become necessary to re-balance them as they wear, or if the balance weights fitted to the wheel rim should fall off. Unbalanced tyres will wear more quickly, as will the steering and suspension components. Wheel imbalance is normally signified by vibration, particularly at a certain speed (typically around 50 mph). If this vibration is felt only through the steering, then it is likely that just the front wheels need balancing. If, however, the vibration is felt through the whole vehicle, the rear wheels could be out of balance. Wheel balancing should be carried out by a tyre dealer or garage.

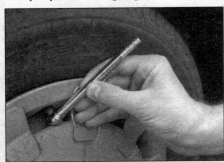

1 Tread Depth - visual check
The original tyres have tread wear safety bands (B), which will appear when the tread depth reaches approximately 1.6 mm. The band positions are indicated by a triangular mark on the tyre sidewall (A).

2 Tread Depth - manual check
Alternatively, tread wear can be monitored with a simple, inexpensive device known as a tread depth indicator gauge.

3 Tyre Pressure Check
Check the tyre pressures regularly with the tyres cold. Do not adjust the tyre pressures immediately after the vehicle has been used, or an inaccurate setting will result.

Tyre tread wear patterns

Shoulder Wear

Underinflation (wear on both sides)
Under-inflation will cause overheating of the tyre, because the tyre will flex too much, and the tread will not sit correctly on the road surface. This will cause a loss of grip and excessive wear, not to mention the danger of sudden tyre failure due to heat build-up.
Check and adjust pressures
Incorrect wheel camber (wear on one side)
Repair or renew suspension parts
Hard cornering
Reduce speed!

Centre Wear

Overinflation
Over-inflation will cause rapid wear of the centre part of the tyre tread, coupled with reduced grip, harsher ride, and the danger of shock damage occurring in the tyre casing.
Check and adjust pressures

If you sometimes have to inflate your car's tyres to the higher pressures specified for maximum load or sustained high speed, don't forget to reduce the pressures to normal afterwards.

Uneven Wear

Front tyres may wear unevenly as a result of wheel misalignment. Most tyre dealers and garages can check and adjust the wheel alignment (or "tracking") for a modest charge.
Incorrect camber or castor
Repair or renew suspension parts
Malfunctioning suspension
Repair or renew suspension parts
Unbalanced wheel
Balance tyres
Incorrect toe setting
Adjust front wheel alignment
Note: *The feathered edge of the tread which typifies toe wear is best checked by feel.*

Wiper blades

✔ Only fit good-quality wiper blades.

✔ When removing an old wiper blade, note how it is fitted. Fitting new blades can sometimes be tricky, and noting how the old blade came off can save time.

✔ While the wiper blade is removed, take care not to knock the wiper arm from its locked position, or it could strike the glass.

✔ Offer the new blade into position the same way round as the old one. Ensure that it clicks home securely, otherwise it may come off in use, damaging the glass.

 HAYNES HiNT *If smearing is still a problem despite fitting new wiper blades, try cleaning the glass with neat screenwash additive or methylated spirit.*

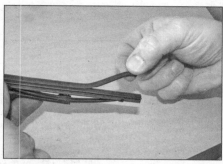

1 Check the condition of the wiper blades; if they are cracked or show any signs of deterioration, or if the glass swept area is smeared, renew them. Wiper blades should be renewed annually.

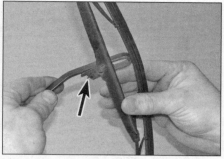

2 To remove a windscreen wiper blade, pull the arm fully away from the windscreen until it locks. Swivel the blade through 90°, then depress the locking tab (arrowed) and push the blade down the arm.

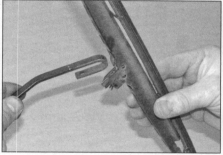

3 Detach the blade from the end fitting on the arm. When fitting the new blade, make sure that the blade locks securely into the arm, and that the blade is orientated correctly.

4 Don't forget to check the rear wiper blade(s) as well (where applicable) which are removed in the same way.

Lubricants and fluids

Engine:

Standard (distance/time) service interval (1.9 and 2.5 litre): . .	Multigrade (high-lubricity) engine oil, viscosity SAE 5W/40 to 20W/50
Standard (distance/time) service interval (2.0 litre):	Multigrade (high-lubricity) engine oil, viscosity SAE 5W/30
Engines without particulate filter	VW 505 01, 507 00 or better
Engines with particulate filter	VW 507 00 or better
LongLife (variable) service interval:	VW LongLife engine oil
Engines without particulate filter	VW 506 01, 507 00 or better
Engines with particulate filter	VW 507 00 or better
Cooling system	Mixture of 40% VW coolant G12 plus plus or higher (to spec TL-VW 774 F or G) and 60% water
Manual transmission	VW synthetic gear oil VW G50 (SAE 75W/90)
Automatic transmission	VW Automatic Transmission Fluid (ATF)
Brake and clutch hydraulic system	Hydraulic fluid to US standard FMVSS 116 DOT 4
Power steering	VW hydraulic fluid G 002 000

Tyre pressures

Note: *Vehicle specific information on tyre pressures and wheel and tyre data is contained on a sticker attached to the driver's side door pillar. Additional information is also contained in the driver's handbook supplied with the vehicle. The pressures and sizes given are for the original-equipment tyres – the recommended pressures may vary if any other make or type of tyre is fitted. Check with the tyre manufacturer or supplier for latest recommendations. The following pressures are typical and shown for a laden vehicle.*

Tyre size	Front	Rear
205/65 x 16 107/105T	4.0 bar (58 psi)	4.4 bar (64 psi)
215/65 x 16 102/100H	3.3 bar (48 psi)	3.3 bar (48 psi)
215/65 x 16 106/104T	3.4 bar (49 psi)	3.7 bar (54 psi)
235/60 x 16 104H.	2.8 bar (41 psi)	2.8 bar (41 psi)
215/60 x 17 104/102T	3.8 bar (55 psi)	4.1 bar (60 psi)
233/55 x 17 103W	3.0 bar (44 psi)	3.1 bar (45 psi)

Chapter 1
Routine maintenance and servicing

Contents

Degrees of difficulty

 Easy, suitable for novice with little experience | **Fairly easy,** suitable for beginner with some experience | **Fairly difficult,** suitable for competent DIY mechanic | **Difficult,** suitable for experienced DIY mechanic | 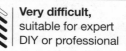 **Very difficult,** suitable for expert DIY or professional

Lubricants and fluids. . . . .   Refer to the end of *Weekly checks* on page 0•18

Capacities – approximate

Engine oil (including oil filter):

1.9 litre engines:
    Engine codes AXB and AXC. . . . .   5.8 litres
    Engine codes BRR and BRS . . . .   6.3 litres
2.0 litre engines . . . .   7.0 litres
2.5 litre engines . . . .   7.4 litres

Cooling system . . . .   N/A*

Manual transmission:

5-speed transmissions. . . . .   2.0 litres
6-speed transmissions. . . . .   2.7 litres

Automatic transmission:

Main transmission unit including final drive . . . .   7.0 litres total

Power-assisted steering system . . . .   1.0 litre

Fuel tank . . . .   80 litres

*Information not available at time of writing. Consult a VW dealer for further details.

Cooling system

	Antifreeze	Water
Antifreeze mixture:		
Protection down to -25°C.	40%	60%
Protection down to -35°C.	50%	50%

Note: *Refer to antifreeze manufacturer's instructions for latest recommendations.*

Braking system

Minimum brake pad lining thickness (excluding back plate) . . . .   2.0 mm

Torque wrench settings

	Nm	lbf ft
Oil filter cap	25	19
Roadwheel bolts.	180	133
Sump drain plug.	30	22

Maintenance schedule

The maintenance intervals in this manual are provided with the assumption that you, not the dealer, will be carrying out the work. These are the minimum intervals recommended by us for vehicles driven daily. If you wish to keep your vehicle in peak condition at all times, you may wish to perform some of these procedures more often. We encourage frequent maintenance, since it enhances the efficiency, performance and resale value of your vehicle.

When the vehicle is new, it should be serviced by a dealer service department (or other workshop recognised by the vehicle manufacturer as providing the same standard of service), in order to preserve the warranty. The vehicle manufacturer may reject warranty claims if you are unable to prove that servicing has been carried out as and when specified, using only original equipment parts or parts certified to be of equivalent quality.

All VW Transporter models are equipped with a service interval display indicator in the instrument panel. Every time the engine is started the panel will illuminate for approximately 20 seconds with service information. With the standard non-variable display, the service intervals are in accordance with specific distances and time periods. With the LongLife display, the service interval is variable according to the number of starts, length of journeys, vehicle speeds, brake pad wear, bonnet opening frequency, fuel consumption, oil level and oil temperature, however the vehicle must be serviced at least every two years. The service reminder is displayed 20 days before the service is due. Once the service interval has been reached, the display will flash 'Service Now' and a spanner symbol will be displayed. Note that if the variable (LongLife) service interval is being used, the engine must only be filled with the recommended long-life engine oil (see *Lubricants and fluids*).

After completing a service, VW technicians use a special instrument to reset the service display to the next service interval, and a print-out is put in the vehicle service record. The display can be reset by the owner as described in Section 5, but note that for models using the 'LongLife' interval, the procedure will automatically reset the display to the 10 000 miles 'distance' interval. To have the display reset to the 'variable' (LongLife) interval, it is necessary to take the vehicle to a VW dealer who will use a special instrument to encode the on-board computer.

Every 250 miles

- ☐ Refer to *Weekly checks*

Every 10 000 miles or 12 months, whichever comes first

- ☐ Renew the engine oil and filter (Section 3)

Note: *Frequent oil and filter changes are good for the engine. We recommend changing the oil at least once a year.*

- ☐ Check the front and rear brake pad thickness (Section 4)
- ☐ Reset the service interval display (Section 5)

Every 20 000 miles or 2 years, whichever comes first

In addition to the items listed above, carry out the following:

- ☐ Check the condition of the exhaust system and its mountings (Section 6)
- ☐ Check all underbonnet components and hoses for fluid and oil leaks (Section 7)
- ☐ Renew the fuel filter* (Section 8)
- ☐ Check the condition of the auxiliary drivebelt (Section 9)
- ☐ Check the coolant antifreeze concentration (Section 10)
- ☐ Check the brake hydraulic circuit for leaks and damage (Section 11)
- ☐ Check the headlight beam adjustment (Section 12)
- ☐ Renew the pollen filter element (Section 13)
- ☐ Check the manual transmission oil level (Section 14)
- ☐ Check the underbody protection for damage (Section 15)
- ☐ Check the condition of the driveshaft gaiters (Section 16)
- ☐ Check the steering and suspension components for condition and security (Section 17)
- ☐ Check the battery condition, security and electrolyte level (Section 18)
- ☐ Lubricate all hinges and locks (Section 19)
- ☐ Check the condition of the airbag unit(s) (Section 20)
- ☐ Check the operation of the windscreen/rear window/headlight washer system(s) (as applicable) (Section 21)
- ☐ Check the engine management self-diagnosis memory for faults (Section 22)
- ☐ Check the operation of the sunroof and lubricate the guide rails (Section 23)
- ☐ Carry out a road test and check exhaust emissions (Section 24)

Only when using diesel fuel not conforming to DIN EN 590 or when using RME fuel (diester)

Every 40 000 miles or 4 years, whichever comes first

Note: *Many dealers perform these tasks at every second service.*

- ☐ Renew the air filter element (Section 25)
- ☐ Renew the fuel filter* (Section 26)
- ☐ Renew the auxiliary drivebelt (Section 27)

Only when using diesel fuel conforming to DIN EN 590

Every 60 000 miles or 4 years, whichever comes first

- ☐ Renew the timing belt and tensioner roller (Section 28)

Note: *VW specify a timing belt renewal interval of approximately 60 000 miles for 1.9 litre models with engine codes AXB and AXC, and 75 000 miles for 1.9 litre models with engine codes BRR and BRS. A renewal interval of approximately 130 000 miles is specified for 2.0 litre models. Timing belt tensioner roller renewal is specified at approximately 112 000 miles for 1.9 litre models with engine codes AXB and AXC, and 150 000 miles for 1.9 litre models with engine codes BRR and BRS. A tensioner roller renewal interval of 130 000 miles is specified for 2.0 litre models. However, if the vehicle is used mainly for short journeys, we recommend that a shorter renewal interval be adhered to. The belt and tensioner renewal interval is very much up to the individual owner but, bearing in mind that severe engine damage will result if the belt breaks in use, we recommend a shorter interval.*

Every 95 000 miles, then every 19 000 miles

- ☐ Check the particulate filter ash deposit mass (Section 31)

Every 2 years

- ☐ Renew the brake (and clutch) fluid (Section 29)
- ☐ Renew the coolant* (Section 30)

*Note: *This work is not included in the VW schedule and should not be required if the recommended VW G12 LongLife coolant antifreeze/inhibitor is used.*

Underbonnet view of a 2.5 litre model (others similar)

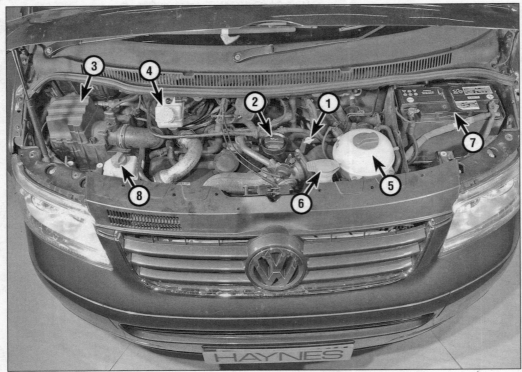

1 Engine oil level dipstick
2 Engine oil filler cap
3 Air cleaner assembly
4 Brake (and clutch) fluid reservoir
5 Coolant expansion tank
6 Screen washer fluid reservoir
7 Battery
8 Power steering fluid reservoir

Front underbody view of a 2.5 litre model (others similar)

1 Engine oil drain plug
2 Air conditioning compressor
3 Front brake calipers
4 Steering track rod ends
5 Lower suspension arms
6 Right-hand driveshaft
7 Front subframe
8 Catalytic converter

1 *Handbrake cables*
2 *Rear silencer*
3 *Shock absorbers*
4 *Trailing arms*
5 *Anti-roll bar*
6 *Brake hydraulic hoses*
7 *Spare wheel*

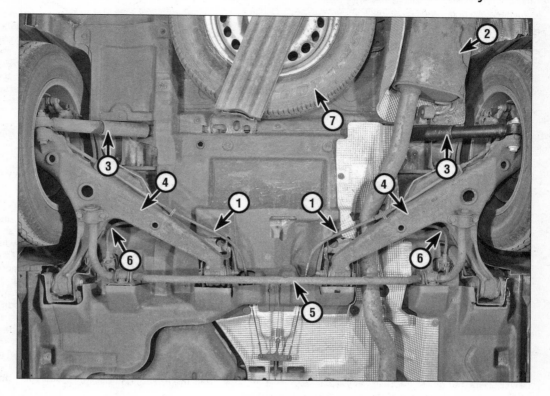

Maintenance procedures

1 General information

This Chapter is designed to help the home mechanic maintain his/her vehicle for safety, economy, long life and peak performance.

The Chapter contains a master maintenance schedule, followed by Sections dealing specifically with each task in the schedule. Visual checks, adjustments, component renewal and other helpful items are included. Refer to the accompanying illustrations of the engine compartment and the underside of the vehicle for the locations of the various components.

Servicing your vehicle in accordance with the mileage/time maintenance schedule and the following Sections will provide a planned maintenance programme, which should result in a long and reliable service life. This is a comprehensive plan, so maintaining some items but not others at the specified service intervals, will not produce the same results.

As you service your vehicle, you will discover that many of the procedures can – and should – be grouped together, because of the particular procedure being performed, or because of the proximity of two otherwise-unrelated components to one another. For example, if the vehicle is raised for any reason, the exhaust can be inspected at the same time as the suspension and steering components.

The first step in this maintenance programme is to prepare yourself before the actual work begins. Read through all the Sections relevant to the work to be carried out, then make a list and gather all the parts and tools required. If a problem is encountered, seek advice from a parts specialist, or a dealer service department.

2 Regular maintenance

1 If, from the time the vehicle is new, the routine maintenance schedule is followed closely, and frequent checks are made of fluid levels and high-wear items, as suggested throughout this manual, the engine will be kept in relatively good running condition, and the need for additional work will be minimised.

2 It is possible that there will be times when the engine is running poorly due to the lack of regular maintenance. This is even more likely if a used vehicle, which has not received regular and frequent maintenance checks, is purchased. In such cases, additional work may need to be carried out, outside of the regular maintenance intervals.

3 If engine wear is suspected, a compression test or leak-down test will provide valuable information regarding the overall performance of the main internal components. Such a test can be used as a basis to decide on the extent of the work to be carried out. If, for example, a compression or leak-down test indicates serious internal engine wear, conventional maintenance as described in this Chapter will not greatly improve the performance of the engine, and may prove a waste of time and money, unless extensive overhaul work is carried out first.

4 The following series of operations are those most often required to improve the performance of a generally poor-running engine:

Primary operations

a) *Clean, inspect and test the battery (See Weekly checks).*
b) *Check all the engine-related fluids (See Weekly checks).*

c) *Check the condition and tension of the auxiliary drivebelt (Section 9).*
d) *Check the condition of the air filter, and renew if necessary (Section 25).*
e) *Check the condition of all hoses, and check for fluid leaks (Section 7).*

5 If the above operations do not prove fully effective, carry out the following secondary operations:

Secondary operations

All items listed under *Primary operations*, plus the following:
a) *Check the charging system (see Chapter 5, Section 5).*
b) *Check the pre/post-heating system (see Chapter 5, Section 12).*
c) *Renew the fuel filter (Section 26) and check the fuel system (see Chapter 4A or 4B).*

Every 10 000 miles or 12 months

3 Engine oil and filter renewal

1 Frequent oil and filter changes are the most important preventative maintenance procedures which can be undertaken by the DIY owner. As engine oil ages, it becomes diluted and contaminated, which leads to premature engine wear.

2 Before starting this procedure, gather all the necessary tools and materials. Also make sure that you have plenty of clean rags and newspapers handy, to mop up any spills. Ideally, the engine oil should be warm, as it will drain better, and more built-up sludge will

be removed with it. Take care, however, not to touch the exhaust or any other hot parts of the engine when working under the vehicle. To avoid any possibility of scalding, and to protect yourself from possible skin irritants and other harmful contaminants in used engine oils, it is advisable to wear gloves when carrying out this work.

3 Access to the underside of the vehicle will be greatly improved if it can be raised on a lift, driven onto ramps, or jacked up and supported on axle stands (see *Jacking and vehicle support*). Whichever method is chosen, make sure that the vehicle remains level, or if it is at an angle, that the drain plug is at the lowest point.

4 Where applicable, undo the retaining bolts

and remove the engine undertray. According to model, undo the retaining bolts and rotary fasteners and remove the battery cover and engine covers as applicable.

5 Slacken the sump drain plug about half a turn. Position the draining container under the drain plug, then remove the plug completely **(see illustrations)**.

6 Allow some time for the old oil to drain, noting that it may be necessary to reposition the container as the oil flow slows to a trickle.

7 After all the oil has drained, wipe off the drain plug with a clean rag, and fit a new sealing washer. Clean the area around the drain plug opening, and refit the plug. Tighten the plug to the specified torque. **Note:** *On some engines, the sealing washer is integral with the drain plug. On these engines, the drain plug must be renewed.*

8 If the filter is also to be renewed, move the container into position under the oil filter, which is located on the front facing side of the cylinder block. Note that access to the filter is extremely limited on 2.5 litre engines but can be improved by undoing the retaining bolt and moving the power steering fluid reservoir to one side. It may also be beneficial to extract the retaining spring clip and detach the intercooler air duct **(see illustrations)**.

9 Fully unscrew the cap from the top of the oil filter and remove it together with the filter element. On 2.5 litre engines it will be necessary to use a long socket extension

3.5a Slacken the sump drain plug...

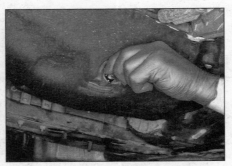

3.5b ...then remove the plug completely...

3.5c ...and allow the oil to drain into the container

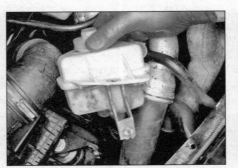

3.8a Improve access to the oil filter on 2.5 litre engines by moving the power steering fluid reservoir to one side...

3.8b ... and detaching the intercooler air duct

bar preferably with a universal joint to reach the filter cap. Unclip the filter element from the cap and dispose of it **(see illustrations)**. Recover the large sealing ring from the cap, and the small sealing ring(s) from the centre rod.

10 Using a clean rag, wipe all oil and sludge from the inside of the filter housing and cap.

11 Fit new sealing rings, then refit the assembly and tighten to the specified torque. Make sure the filter element is engaged with the cap and the correct way up **(see illustrations)**.

12 On 2.5 litre engines, reconnect the intercooler air duct and refit the power steering fluid reservoir.

13 Remove the old oil and all tools from under the vehicle then, where applicable, refit the undertray and lower the vehicle to the ground. Also refit the engine cover and battery cover.

14 Remove the dipstick, and then unscrew the oil filler cap from the cylinder head cover. Fill the engine, using the correct grade and type of oil (see *Lubricants and fluids*). An oil can spout or funnel may help to reduce spillage. Pour in half the specified quantity of oil first, then wait a few minutes for the oil to run to the sump (see *Weekly checks*). Continue adding oil a small quantity at a time until the level is up to the maximum mark on the dipstick. Refit the filler cap.

15 Start the engine and run it for a few minutes; check for leaks around the oil filter cap and the sump drain plug. Note that there may be a few seconds delay before the oil pressure warning light goes out when the

3.9a Withdraw the oil filter and cap...

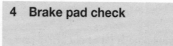

3.9b ...then unclip the filter element from the cap

engine is started, as the oil circulates through the engine oil galleries and the new oil filter before the pressure builds-up.

⚠️ **Warning: Do not increase the engine speed above idling while the oil pressure light is illuminated, as considerable damage can be caused to the turbocharger.**

16 Switch off the engine, and wait a few minutes for the oil to settle in the sump once more. With the new oil circulated and the filter completely full, recheck the level on the dipstick, and add more oil as necessary.

17 Dispose of the used engine oil and filter safely, with reference to *General repair procedures*. Do not discard the old filter with domestic household waste. The facility for waste oil disposal provided by many local council refuse tips and/or recycling centres generally has a filter receptacle alongside.

4 Brake pad check

1 The outer brake pads can be checked without removing the wheels, by observing the brake pads through the holes in the wheels **(see illustration)**. If necessary, remove the wheel trim. The thickness of the pad lining must not be less than the dimension given in the Specifications.

2 If the outer pads are worn near their limits, it is worthwhile checking the inner pads as well. Apply the handbrake then jack up vehicle and support it on axle stands (see *Jacking and vehicle support*). Remove the roadwheels.

3 Use a steel rule to check the thickness of the brake pads, and compare with the

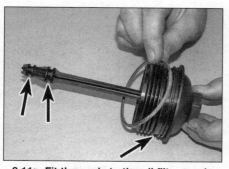

3.11a Fit the seals to the oil filter cap in the positions shown...

3.11b ...then slide the new filter onto the cap...

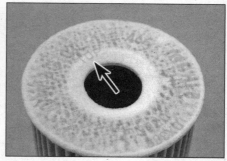

3.11c ...noting 'TOP' on the filter for correct fitting

3.11d Lubricate the O-ring seals with clean engine oil...

3.11e ...then refit to the oil filter housing

4.1 The outer brake pads can be observed through the holes in the wheels

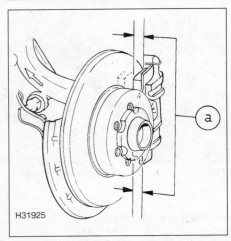

4.3 The thickness (a) of the brake pad linings must not be less than the specified amount

minimum thickness given in the Specifications (see illustration).

4 For a comprehensive check, the brake pads should be removed and cleaned. The operation of the caliper can then also be checked, and the condition of the brake disc itself can be fully examined on both sides. Refer to Chapter 9, Section 4 (front) or Chapter 9, Section 7 (rear).

5 If any pad's friction material is worn to the specified minimum thickness or less, *all four pads at the front or rear, as applicable, must be renewed as a set.*

6 On completion of the check, refit the roadwheels and lower the vehicle to the ground.

5 Resetting the service interval display

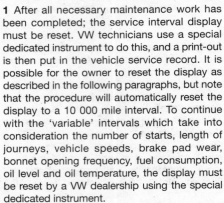

1 After all necessary maintenance work has been completed; the service interval display must be reset. VW technicians use a special dedicated instrument to do this, and a print-out is then put in the vehicle service record. It is possible for the owner to reset the display as described in the following paragraphs, but note that the procedure will automatically reset the display to a 10 000 mile interval. To continue with the 'variable' intervals which take into consideration the number of starts, length of journeys, vehicle speeds, brake pad wear, bonnet opening frequency, fuel consumption, oil level and oil temperature, the display must be reset by a VW dealership using the special dedicated instrument.

2 To reset the standard display (vehicles without text message display), follow the procedures below:

Vehicles with a clock adjusting button and trip reset button on the instrument panel

a) *Switch off the ignition.*
b) *Press and hold down the trip reset button beneath the speedometer.*
c) *Switch the ignition on.*
d) *The display must now show the next SERVICE or SERVICE NOW.*
e) *Turn the adjusting button on the digital clock clockwise (adjusts the hours). The SERVICE text is deleted from the display.*
f) *Release the reset button. The normal display will appear after a short delay.*
g) *Switch off the ignition.*

Vehicles with a function button in the centre of the instrument panel

a) *Switch off the ignition.*
b) *Press and hold down the function button on the instrument panel.*
c) *Switch the ignition on.*
d) *Wait until the message 'Reset oil change service?' or 'Reset inspection service?' appears on the display.*
e) *Release the function button, then briefly press the function button once more. The normal display will appear after a short delay.*
f) *Repeat this procedure if an additional service is to be reset.*
g) *On completion, switch off the ignition.*

Every 20 000 miles or 2 years

6 Exhaust system check

1 With the engine cold, check the complete exhaust system, from its starting point at the engine to the end of the tailpipe. If necessary, raise the front and rear of the vehicle and support it on axle stands (see *Jacking and vehicle support*).

2 Check the exhaust pipes and connections for evidence of leaks, severe corrosion, and

A leak in the cooling system will usually show up as white- or antifreeze-coloured deposits on the area adjoining the leak.

damage. Make sure that all brackets and mountings are in good condition and that all relevant nuts and bolts are tight. Leakage at any of the joints or in other parts of the system will usually show up as a black sooty stain in the vicinity of the leak.

3 Rattles and other noises can often be traced to the exhaust system, especially the brackets and rubber mountings. Try to move the pipes and silencers. If the components are able to come into contact with the body or suspension parts, secure the system with new mountings. Otherwise separate the joints (if possible) and twist the pipes as necessary to provide additional clearance.

7 Hose and fluid leak check

1 Where applicable, undo the retaining bolts and remove the engine undertray. According to model, undo the retaining bolts and rotary fasteners and remove the battery cover and engine cover as applicable.

2 Visually inspect the engine joint faces, gaskets and seals for any signs of water or oil leaks. Pay particular attention to the areas around the camshaft cover, cylinder head, oil filter and sump joint faces. Bear in mind that, over a period of time, some very slight seepage from these areas is to be expected – what

you are really looking for is any indication of a serious leak. Should a leak be found, renew the offending gasket or oil seal by referring to the appropriate Chapters in this manual.

3 Also check the security and condition of all the engine-related pipes and hoses. Ensure that all cable-ties or securing clips are in place and in good condition. Clips which are broken or missing can lead to chafing of the hoses, pipes or wiring, which could cause more serious problems in the future.

4 Carefully check the radiator hoses and heater hoses along their entire length. Renew any hose which is cracked, swollen or deteriorated. Cracks will show up better if the hose is squeezed. Pay close attention to the hose clips that secure the hoses to the cooling system components. Hose clips can pinch and puncture hoses, resulting in cooling system leaks.

5 Inspect all the cooling system components (hoses, joint faces etc.) for leaks. A leak in the cooling system will usually show up as white or rust coloured deposits on the area adjoining the leak **(see Haynes Hint)**. Where any problems of this nature are found on system components, renew the component or gasket with reference to Chapter 3.

6 Where applicable, inspect the automatic transmission fluid cooler hoses for leaks or deterioration.

7 With the vehicle raised, inspect the fuel tank and filler neck for punctures, cracks

and other damage. The connection between the filler neck and tank is especially critical. Sometimes a rubber filler neck or connecting hose will leak due to loose retaining clamps or deteriorated rubber.

8 Carefully check all rubber hoses and metal fuel lines leading away from the fuel tank. Check for loose connections, deteriorated hoses, crimped lines, and other damage. Pay particular attention to the vent pipes and hoses, which often loop up around the filler neck and can become blocked or crimped. Follow the lines to the front of the vehicle, carefully inspecting them all the way. Renew damaged sections as necessary.

9 From within the engine compartment, check the security of all fuel hose attachments and pipe unions, and inspect the fuel hoses and vacuum hoses for kinks, chafing and deterioration. Also check the condition of the power steering fluid hoses and pipes.

10 On completion, refit the engine undertray, engine cover and battery cover as applicable.

8 Fuel filter renewal (vehicles using high sulphur diesel fuel)

Note: Carry out this procedure at this interval only when using diesel fuel not conforming to DIN EN 590 or when using RME fuel (diester) – this fuel is not available in the UK. There is no longer any requirement to drain water from the filter.

Refer to Section 26, for renewal of fuel filter.

9 Auxiliary drivebelt check

1 Apply the handbrake, then jack up the front of the vehicle and support it on axle stands (see *Jacking and vehicle support*).

2 Where applicable, undo the retaining bolts and remove the engine undertray. According to model, undo the retaining bolts and rotary fasteners and remove the battery cover and engine covers as applicable.

3 Using a socket on the crankshaft pulley bolt, turn the engine slowly clockwise so that the full length of the auxiliary drivebelt can be examined. Look for cracks, splitting and fraying on the surface of the belt; check also for signs of glazing (shiny patches) and separation of the belt plies. If damage or wear is visible, or if there are traces of oil or grease on it, the belt should be renewed (see Section 27).

4 On completion, refit the engine undertray, engine cover and battery cover as applicable.

10 Antifreeze check

1 The cooling system should be filled with the recommended antifreeze and maintained at the correct concentration all year round. Over a period of time, the concentration of fluid may be reduced due to topping-up (this can be avoided by topping-up with the correct antifreeze mixture) or fluid loss. If loss of coolant has been evident, it is important to make the necessary repair before adding fresh fluid. The exact mixture of antifreeze-to-water which you should use depends on the relative weather conditions. The mixture should contain at least 40% antifreeze, but not more than 60%. Consult the mixture ratio chart on the antifreeze container before adding coolant. Use antifreeze which meets the vehicle manufacturer's specifications.

2 With the engine cold, carefully remove the cap from the expansion tank. If the engine is not completely cold, place a cloth rag over the cap before removing it, and remove it slowly to allow any pressure to escape.

3 Antifreeze checkers are available from car accessory shops. Draw some coolant from the expansion tank and observe how many plastic balls are floating in the checker. Usually, 2 or 3 balls must be floating for the correct concentration of antifreeze, but follow the manufacturer's instructions.

4 If the concentration is incorrect, it will be necessary to either withdraw some coolant and add antifreeze, or alternatively drain the old coolant and add fresh coolant of the correct concentration.

11 Brake hydraulic circuit check

1 Check the entire brake hydraulic circuit for leaks and damage. Start by checking the master cylinder in the engine compartment. At the same time, check the vacuum servo unit and ABS units for signs of fluid leakage.

2 Raise the front and rear of the vehicle and support it on axle stands (see *Jacking and vehicle support*). Check the rigid hydraulic brake lines for corrosion and damage.

3 At the front of the vehicle, check that the flexible hydraulic hoses to the calipers are not twisted or chafing on any of the surrounding suspension components. Turn the steering on full lock to make this check. Also check that the hoses are not brittle or cracked.

4 Lower the vehicle to the ground after making the checks.

12 Headlight beam adjustment

1 Accurate adjustment of the headlight beam is only possible using optical beam-setting equipment, and this work should therefore be carried out by a VW dealer or service station with the necessary facilities.

2 Refer to Chapter 12, Section 8 for further information.

13 Pollen filter element renewal

1 The pollen filter is located in the heater unit and is accessed from inside the vehicle, on the passenger's side.

2 Undo the three screws securing the top edge of the left-hand footwell trim panel to the facia **(see illustration)**.

3 Lower the panel down, pull it away from the facia to disengage the lower retaining hook, then remove the footwell trim **(see illustration)**.

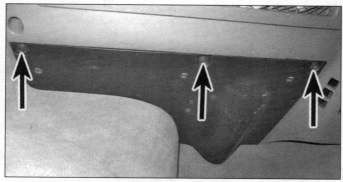
13.2 Undo the three screws (arrowed) securing the left-hand footwell trim panel to the facia

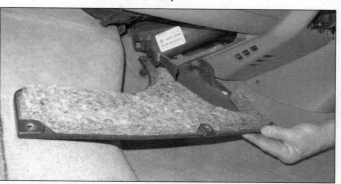
13.3 Lower the panel down and pull it away from the facia to disengage the lower retaining hook

13.4a Undo the two screws (arrowed)...

13.4b ...and remove the pollen filter access cover from the underside of the heater unit

13.5 Slide out the pollen filter element downwards from the heater unit

4 Undo the two screws and remove the pollen filter access cover from the underside of the heater unit **(see illustrations)**.

5 Slide out the pollen filter element downwards from the heater unit **(see illustration)**.

6 Fit the new element then refit the access cover and secure with the two screws

7 Refit the footwell trim panel to the facia.

14 Manual transmission oil level check

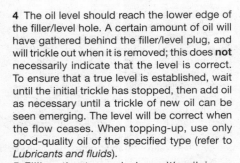

1 Park the vehicle on a level surface. The oil level must be checked before the vehicle is driven, or at least 5 minutes after the engine has been switched off. If the oil is checked just after driving the vehicle, some of the oil will remain distributed around the transmission, resulting in an inaccurate level reading.

2 Where applicable, undo the retaining bolts and remove the engine undertray. According to model, undo the fasteners and remove the sound insulation around the transmission casing.

3 Wipe clean the area around the filler/level plug. On 5-speed transmissions the filler/level plug is located on the left-hand side of the differential housing. On 6-speed transmissions the filler/level plug is located on the front facing side of the transmission housing **(see illustrations)**. Unscrew the filler/level plug and clean it.

4 The oil level should reach the lower edge of the filler/level hole. A certain amount of oil will have gathered behind the filler/level plug, and will trickle out when it is removed; this does **not** necessarily indicate that the level is correct. To ensure that a true level is established, wait until the initial trickle has stopped, then add oil as necessary until a trickle of new oil can be seen emerging. The level will be correct when the flow ceases. When topping-up, use only good-quality oil of the specified type (refer to *Lubricants and fluids*).

5 Filling the transmission with oil is an extremely awkward operation; above all, allow plenty of time for the oil level to settle properly before checking it. If a large amount is added to the transmission, and a large amount flows out on checking the level, refit the filler/level plug and take the vehicle on a short journey so that the new oil is distributed fully around the transmission components, then recheck the level when it has settled again.

6 If the transmission has been overfilled so that oil flows out when the filler/level plug is removed, check that the vehicle is completely level (front-to-rear and side-to-side), and allow the surplus to drain off into a suitable container.

7 When the level is correct, refit the plug, tightening it securely. Wash off any spilt oil, refit the sound insulation and engine undertray (as applicable) then lower the vehicle to the ground.

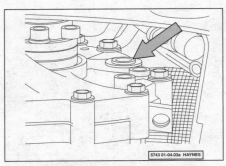

14.3a Transmission oil filler/level plug location (arrowed) on 5-speed transmissions...

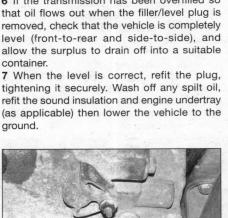

14.3b ...and on 6-speed transmissions

15 Underbody protection check

With the vehicle raised and securely supported, carry out a thorough check of the vehicle underbody sealant for signs of damage. If any area of the underbody sealant shows visible damage, the affected area should be repaired to prevent possible problems with corrosion occurring at a later date.

16 Driveshaft gaiter check

1 The driveshaft rubber gaiters are very important, because they prevent dirt, water and foreign material from entering and damaging the constant velocity (CV) joints. External contamination can cause the gaiter material to deteriorate prematurely, so it's a good idea to wash the gaiters with soap and water occasionally.

2 Firmly apply the handbrake, then jack up the front of the vehicle and support it securely on axle stands (see *Jacking and vehicle support*). Where applicable, undo the retaining bolts and remove the engine undertray.

3 Turn the steering onto full-lock, then slowly rotate each front wheel in turn. Inspect the condition of the outer constant velocity (CV) joint rubber gaiters, squeezing the gaiters to open out the folds **(see illustration)**. Check for signs of cracking, splits, or deterioration of the rubber, which may allow the escape of grease, and lead to the ingress of water and grit into the joint. Also check the security and condition of the retaining clips. Repeat these checks on the inner CV joints. If any damage or deterioration is found, the gaiters should be renewed as described in Chapter 8, Section 3.

4 At the same time, check the general condition of the outer CV joints themselves, by first holding the driveshaft and attempting to rotate the wheels. Repeat this check on the inner joints, by holding the inner joint yoke and attempting to rotate the driveshaft.

16.3 Check the driveshaft gaiters by hand for cracks and/or leaking grease

17.2 Visually inspect the steering rack-and-pinion gaiters for splits, chafing or deterioration

17.3 Checking for wear in the front suspension and hub bearings

5 Any appreciable movement in the CV joint indicates wear in the joint, wear in the driveshaft splines, or a loose driveshaft retaining nut.
6 On completion, refit the engine undertray, then lower the vehicle to the ground.

17 Steering, suspension and roadwheel check

Front suspension and steering

1 Firmly apply the handbrake, then jack up the front of the vehicle and support it securely on axle stands (see *Jacking and vehicle support*). Where applicable, undo the retaining bolts and remove the engine undertray.
2 Visually inspect the balljoint dust covers and the steering rack-and-pinion gaiters for splits, chafing or deterioration **(see illustration)**. Any wear of these components will cause loss of lubricant, together with dirt and water entry, resulting in rapid deterioration of the balljoints or steering gear.
3 Check the power steering fluid hoses for chafing or deterioration, and the pipe and hose unions for fluid leaks. Also check for signs of fluid leakage under pressure from the steering gear rubber gaiters, which would indicate failed fluid seals within the steering gear.
4 Grasp the roadwheel at the 12 o'clock and 6 o'clock positions, and try to rock it **(see illustration)**. Very slight free play may be felt, but if the movement is appreciable, further investigation is necessary to determine the source. Continue rocking the wheel while an assistant depresses the footbrake. If the movement is now eliminated or significantly reduced, it is likely that the hub bearings are at fault. If the free play is still evident with the footbrake depressed, then there is wear in the suspension joints or mountings.
5 Now grasp the wheel at the 9 o'clock and 3 o'clock positions, and try to rock it as before. Any movement felt now may again be caused by wear in the hub bearings or the steering track-rod balljoints. If the inner or outer balljoint is worn, the visual movement will be obvious.

6 Using a large screwdriver or flat bar, check for wear in the suspension mounting bushes by levering between the relevant suspension component and its attachment point. Some movement is to be expected as the mountings are made of rubber, but excessive wear should be obvious. Also check the condition of any visible rubber bushes, looking for splits, cracks or contamination of the rubber.
7 With the vehicle standing on its wheels, have an assistant turn the steering wheel back and forth about an eighth of a turn each way. There should be very little, if any, lost movement between the steering wheel and roadwheels. If this is not the case, closely observe the joints and mountings previously described, but in addition, check the steering column universal joints for wear, and the rack-and-pinion steering gear itself.

Rear suspension

8 Chock the front wheels, then jack up the rear of the vehicle and support securely on axle stands (see *Jacking and vehicle support*).
9 Working as described previously for the front suspension, check the rear hub bearings, the trailing arm mounting bushes and the shock absorber mountings for wear.

Suspension struts/ shock absorbers

10 Check for any signs of fluid leakage around the front suspension struts and rear shock absorbers. Should any fluid be noticed, the suspension strut/shock absorber is defective internally, and should be renewed. **Note:** *Suspension struts/shock absorbers should always be renewed in pairs on the same axle.*
11 The efficiency of the suspension strut/shock absorber may be checked by bouncing the vehicle at each corner. Generally speaking, the body will return to its normal position and stop after being depressed. If it rises and returns on a rebound, the suspension strut/shock absorber is probably suspect. Examine also the shock absorber upper and lower mountings for any signs of wear.

Roadwheels

12 Periodically remove the roadwheels, and

clean any dirt or mud from the inside and outside surfaces. Examine the wheel rims for signs of rusting, corrosion or other damage. Light alloy wheels are easily damaged by 'kerbing' whilst parking, and similarly, steel wheels may become dented or buckled. Renewal of the wheel is very often the only course of remedial action possible.
13 The balance of each wheel and tyre assembly should be maintained, not only to avoid excessive tyre wear, but also to avoid wear in the steering and suspension components. Wheel imbalance is normally signified by vibration through the vehicle's bodyshell, although in many cases it is particularly noticeable through the steering wheel. Conversely, it should be noted that wear or damage in suspension or steering components may cause excessive tyre wear. Out-of-round or out-of-true tyres, damaged wheels and hub bearing wear also fall into this category. Balancing will not usually cure vibration caused by such wear.

18 Battery check

1 The battery is located on the left-hand side of the engine compartment. Where fitted, undo the fasteners and remove the battery cover to gain access to the battery **(see illustration)**.
2 Check that both battery terminals are

18.1 Undo the fasteners and remove the battery cover

18.2 Check that both battery terminals are securely attached and are free from corrosion

18.3 Check that the battery retaining clamp bolt (arrowed) is securely tightened

securely attached and are free from corrosion **(see illustration)**. **Note:** *Before disconnecting the terminals from the battery, refer to 'Disconnecting the battery'.*

3 Check the battery casing for signs of damage or cracking and check the battery retaining clamp bolt is securely tightened **(see illustration)**. If the battery casing is damaged in any way the battery must be renewed (see Chapter 5, Section 4).

4 If the vehicle is not fitted with a sealed-for-life maintenance-free battery, check the electrolyte level is between the MAX and MIN level markings on the battery casing. If topping-up is necessary, remove the battery from the vehicle then remove the cell caps/cover (as applicable). Using distilled water, top the electrolyte level of each cell up to the MAX level mark then securely refit the cell caps/cover. Ensure the battery has not been overfilled then refit the battery to the vehicle (see Chapter 5, Section 4).

5 On completion refit the battery cover.

19 Hinge and lock lubrication

1 Lubricate the hinges of the bonnet, doors and, where fitted, the tailgate with a light general-purpose oil. Similarly, lubricate all latches, locks and lock strikers.

2 Lightly lubricate the bonnet release mechanism and cable with a suitable grease.

22.1 Engine management diagnostic socket location (arrowed)

20 Airbag unit check

Where fitted, inspect the airbag(s) exterior condition checking for signs of damage or deterioration. If an airbag shows signs of damage, it must be renewed (see Chapter 12, Section 19).

21 Windscreen/rear window/headlight washer system(s) check

1 Check that each of the washer jet nozzles are clear and that each nozzle provides a strong jet of washer fluid. The windscreen washer jets should be aimed to spray at a point slightly above the centre of the windscreen. If necessary, adjust the jets upward or downward only (not sideways) using the adjuster on the jet. The rear window jets should be aimed to spray at the centre of the wiped area of the glass. If necessary, adjust the jet using a pin.

2 The headlight inner jet should be aimed slightly above the horizontal centreline of the headlight, and the outer jet should be aimed slightly below the centreline. VW technicians use a special tool to adjust the headlight jet after pulling the jet out onto its stop.

3 Especially during the winter months, make sure that the washer fluid frost concentration is sufficient.

22 Engine management self-diagnosis memory fault check

This work should be carried out by a VW dealer or a diagnostic specialist using special equipment. The diagnostic socket is located below the facia, at the right-hand side above the bonnet release handle **(see illustration)**.

23 Sunroof check and lubrication

1 Slide the sunroof fully backwards to expose the slider rails on either side.

2 Remove all dirt and grime from each slider then lubricate both mechanisms with a silicone-spray type lubricant.

3 Wipe off any excess lubricant then close the sunroof.

24 Road test and exhaust emissions check

Instruments and electrical equipment

1 Check the operation of all instruments and electrical equipment including the air conditioning system.

2 Make sure that all instruments read correctly, and switch on all electrical equipment in turn, to check that it functions properly.

Steering and suspension

3 Check for any abnormalities in the steering, suspension, handling or road 'feel'.

4 Drive the vehicle, and check that there are no unusual vibrations or noises, which may indicate wear in the driveshafts, wheel bearings, etc.

5 Check that the steering feels positive, with no excessive 'sloppiness', or roughness, and check for any suspension noises when cornering and driving over bumps.

Drivetrain

6 Check the performance of the engine, clutch (where applicable), transmission and driveshafts.

7 Listen for any unusual noises from the engine, clutch and transmission.

8 Make sure the engine runs smoothly at idle, and there is no hesitation on accelerating.

9 Check that, where applicable, the clutch action is smooth and progressive, that the drive is taken up smoothly, and that the pedal travel is not excessive. Also listen for any noises when the clutch pedal is depressed.

10 On manual transmission models check that all gears can be engaged smoothly without noise, and that the gear lever action is smooth and not abnormally vague or 'notchy'.

11 On automatic transmission models, make sure that all gearchanges occur smoothly, without snatching, and without an increase in engine speed between changes. Check that all the gear positions can be selected with the vehicle at rest. If any problems are found, they should be referred to a VW dealer.

12 Listen for a metallic clicking sound from the front of the vehicle, as the vehicle is driven slowly in a circle with the steering on full-lock. Carry out this check in both directions. If a clicking noise is heard, this indicates wear in a driveshaft joint, in which case renew the joint if necessary.

Braking system

13 Make sure that the vehicle does not pull to one side when braking, and that the wheels do not lock when braking hard.
14 Check that there is no vibration through the steering when braking.
15 Check that the handbrake operates correctly without excessive movement of the lever, and that it holds the vehicle stationary on a slope.

16 Test the operation of the brake servo unit as follows. With the engine off, depress the footbrake four or five times to exhaust the vacuum. Hold the brake pedal depressed, and then start the engine. As the engine starts, there should be a noticeable 'give' in the brake pedal as vacuum builds-up. Allow the engine to run for at least two minutes, and then switch it off. If the brake pedal is depressed now, it should be possible to detect a hiss from the servo as the pedal is depressed. After about four or five applications, no further hissing should be heard, and the pedal should feel considerably harder.

17 Under controlled emergency braking, the pulsing of the ABS unit must be felt at the footbrake pedal.

Exhaust emissions check

18 Although not part of the manufacturer's maintenance schedule, this check will normally be carried out on a regular basis according to the country the vehicle is operated in. Currently in the UK, exhaust emissions testing is included as part of the annual MOT test after the vehicle is 3 years old. In Germany the test is made when the vehicle is 3 years old, then repeated every 2 years.

Every 40 000 miles or 4 years

25 Air filter element renewal

1 The air filter element is located in the air cleaner housing, which is situated on the right-hand side of the engine compartment. According to model, undo the retaining bolts and rotary fasteners and remove the battery cover and engine cover as applicable.
2 Disconnect the wiring connector from the airflow meter located on the air cleaner cover **(see illustration)**.
3 Release the hose clip and disconnect the air outlet duct from the air cleaner cover **(see illustration)**.

4 Release the two catches securing the air cleaner cover to the housing. Lift the cover up, disengage it from the housing and manipulate it out from the engine compartment **(see illustrations)**.
5 Lift out the element, noting its direction of fitting, and wipe out the housing **(see illustration)**.
6 If carrying out a routine service, the element must be renewed regardless of its apparent condition.
7 If you are checking the element for any other reason, inspect its lower surface; if it is oily or very dirty, renew the element. If it is only moderately dusty, it can be re-used by blowing it clean with compressed air.
8 Fit the new element using a reversal of the removal procedure.

26 Fuel filter renewal (vehicles using standard diesel fuel)

Note: *Carry out this procedure at this interval only when using diesel fuel conforming to DIN EN 590 (standard fuel in the UK).*
1 According to model, undo the retaining bolts and rotary fasteners and remove the battery cover and engine cover as applicable.
2 The fuel filter is mounted on the left-hand side of the engine compartment, adjacent to the battery **(see illustration)**. For improved access, undo the two bolts and move the cooling system expansion tank to one side.
3 Before removing the fuel filter, clean around

25.2 Disconnect the wiring connector from the airflow meter

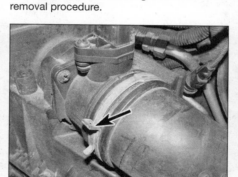

25.3 Release the hose clip (arrowed) and disconnect the air outlet duct from the air cleaner cover

25.4a Release the catch (arrowed) on each side of the air cleaner housing...

25.4b ...then lift the cover up and disengage it from the housing

25.5 Lift out the air cleaner element and wipe out the housing

26.2 The fuel filter is mounted on the left-hand side of the engine compartment, adjacent to the battery

26.4a Depress the tabs on the fuel pipe unions...

26.4b ...and lift the pipes off the filter stubs

26.6 Compress the legs of the retaining clip and lift the filter from its location

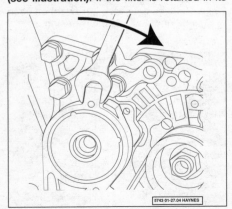

27.4 Turn the tensioner arm clockwise to relieve the tension on the drivebelt – 1.9 litre engines

the fuel pipes on the top of the filter housing to prevent any dirt entering the fuel system. Place some cloth around the filter housing to catch any fuel spillage.

4 Suitably identify the fuel pipes to avoid confusion when refitting, then depress the tabs on the fuel pipe unions and lift the pipes off the filter stubs **(see illustrations)**.

5 Note the installation position of the old filter and in particular the identification and orientation of the pipe stubs.

6 If the filter is retained in its mounting bracket by a large hose clip, compress the legs of the retaining clip using pliers or a hose clip releasing tool, and lift the filter from its location **(see illustration)**. If the filter is retained in its

mounting bracket by a clamp bolt, slacken the clamp bolt and lift the filter from its location.

7 Where applicable, compress the retaining clip legs and locate the new filter into position on the mounting bracket. Position the filter so that it is in the same position as the old filter, as noted during removal. Tighten the clamp bolt, if fitted.

8 Reconnect all the fuel pipes to the filter except the supply hose to the fuel pump (marked VM on the top of the filter).

9 Obtain a suitable length of rubber or plastic hose that is a snug fit on the filter pipe stub. Connect one end of the hose to the pipe stub marked VM and insert the other end of the hose into a jar or container **(see illustration)**.

10 Turn the ignition on for a few seconds, then switch it off again. This will energize the in-tank fuel supply pump and deliver fuel to the filter. The supply pump only runs for a few seconds when the ignition is switched on so it will be necessary to repeat this procedure quite a few times. When fuel emerges from the end of the hose, the filter is full of fuel and the system has been primed.

11 Disconnect the priming hose and reconnect the fuel pipe to the filter.

12 Place the cooling system expansion tank back in position and secure with the two retaining bolts.

13 Start and run the engine at idle, then check around the fuel filter for fuel leaks. *Note: It may take a few seconds of cranking before the engine starts.*

14 On completion, refit the engine cover and battery cover where applicable.

27 Auxiliary drivebelt renewal

Note: An auxiliary drivebelt is only fitted to 1.9 and 2.0 litre engines. On 2.5 litre engines, the engine ancillary components are gear-driven via a rubber coupling from the engine geartrain at the flywheel/driveplate end of the engine. To replace the alternator coupling, refer to Chapter 5, Section 7. For the air conditioning compressor coupling, refer to Chapter 10, Section 22.

1.9 litre engines

1 Firmly apply the handbrake, then jack up the front of the vehicle and support it securely on axle stands (see *Jacking and vehicle support*).

2 Where applicable, undo the retaining bolts and remove the engine undertray. According to model, undo the retaining bolts and rotary fasteners and remove the battery cover and engine covers as applicable.

3 Remove the air duct and hoses between the intercooler and turbocharger.

4 Using a 16 mm spanner on the lug at the top of the tensioner arm turn the tensioner clockwise to relieve the tension on the drivebelt **(see illustration)**. Lock the tensioner in its released position by inserting a locking pin (Allen key or similar) through the lug into the tensioner body.

5 Note how the drivebelt is routed, then remove it from the crankshaft pulley, alternator pulley, and air conditioning compressor pulley (as applicable).

6 Locate the new drivebelt on the pulleys, ensuring that the ribs seat securely in the grooves on the surface of the pulleys. On models without air conditioning, fit the belt over the alternator pulley last. On models with air conditioning, fit the belt over the compressor pulley last.

7 Hold the pressure of the tensioner with the spanner and remove the locking pin. Slowly release the pressure on the spanner so that the tensioner takes up the slack in the belt. Check that the belt is still located correctly in the pulley grooves.

8 Refit the air duct and hoses between intercooler and turbocharger.

9 Refit the engine undertray, engine cover and battery cover as applicable, then lower the vehicle to the ground.

2.0 litre engines

10 Firmly apply the handbrake, then jack up the front of the vehicle and support it securely on axle stands (see *Jacking and vehicle support*).

11 Where applicable, undo the retaining bolts and remove the engine undertray. According to model, undo the retaining bolts and rotary fasteners and remove the battery cover and engine covers as applicable.

27.12a Turn the tensioner clockwise...

27.12b ...and lock the tensioner in position – 2.0 litre engines

12 Use a 16 mm spanner on the centre bolt and turn the tensioner clockwise. Lock the tensioner in its released position by inserting a locking pin (Allen key or similar) through the lug into the tensioner body **(see illustrations)**.

13 Note how the drivebelt is routed, then remove it from the crankshaft pulley **(see illustration)**, alternator pulley, and air conditioning compressor pulley (as applicable).

14 Locate the new drivebelt on the pulleys, ensuring that the ribs seat securely in the grooves on the surface of the pulleys. Fit the belt over the tensioner roller last.

15 Hold the pressure of the tensioner with the spanner and remove the locking pin. Slowly release the pressure on the spanner so that the tensioner takes up the slack in

27.13 Note the fitted position of the belt before removal – 2.0 litre engines

the belt **(see illustration)**. Check that the belt is still located correctly in the pulley grooves.

27.15 With the locking pin removed, slowly take up the slack in the belt – 2.0 litre engines

16 Refit the engine undertray, engine cover and battery cover as applicable, then lower the vehicle to the ground.

Every 60 000 miles or 4 years

28	Timing belt and tensioner roller renewal

Refer to Chapter 2A, Section 7 (1.9 litre engines) or Chapter 2B, Section 7 (2.0 litre engines) for details of timing belt and tensioner roller renewal.

Every 2 years

29	Brake (and clutch) fluid renewal

Warning: Brake hydraulic fluid can harm your eyes and damage painted surfaces, so use extreme caution when handling and pouring it. Do not use fluid that has been standing open for some time, as it absorbs moisture from the air. Excess moisture can cause a dangerous loss of braking effectiveness.

1 The procedure is similar to that for the bleeding of the hydraulic system as described in Chapter 9, Section 2, except that the brake fluid reservoir should be emptied by siphoning, using an old, clean antifreeze tester or similar before starting, and allowance should be made for the old fluid to be expelled when bleeding a section of the circuit. Since the clutch hydraulic system also uses fluid from the brake system reservoir, it should also be bled at the same time by referring to Chapter 6, Section 2.

2 Working as described in Chapter 9, Section 2, open the first bleed screw in the sequence, and pump the brake pedal gently until nearly all the old fluid has been emptied from the master cylinder reservoir.

3 Top-up to the MAX level with new fluid, and continue pumping until only the new fluid remains in the reservoir, and new fluid can be

seen emerging from the bleed screw. Tighten the screw, and top the reservoir level up to the MAX level line.

4 Work through all the remaining bleed screws in the sequence until new fluid can be seen at all of them. Be careful to keep the master cylinder reservoir topped-up to above the MIN level at all times, or air may enter the system and greatly increase the length of the task.

5 When the operation is complete, check that all bleed screws are securely tightened, and that their dust caps are refitted. Wash off all traces of spilt fluid, and recheck the master cylinder reservoir fluid level.

6 On models with manual transmission, once the brake fluid has been changed the clutch

fluid should also be renewed. Referring to Chapter 6, Section 2, bleed the clutch until new fluid is seen to be emerging from the slave cylinder bleed screw, keeping the master cylinder fluid level above the MIN level line at all times to prevent air entering the system. Once the new fluid emerges, securely tighten the bleed screw then disconnect and remove the bleeding equipment. Securely refit the dust cap then wash off all traces of spilt fluid.
7 On all models, ensure the master cylinder fluid level is correct (see *Weekly checks*) and thoroughly check the operation of the brakes and (where necessary) clutch before taking the vehicle on the road.

30 Coolant renewal

Note: *This work is not included in the VW schedule and should not be required if the recommended VW G12 LongLife coolant antifreeze/inhibitor is used. However, if standard antifreeze/inhibitor is used, the work should be carried out at the recommended interval.*

 Warning: *Do not allow antifreeze to come in contact with your skin or painted surfaces of the vehicle. Flush contaminated areas immediately with plenty of water. Don't store new coolant, or leave old coolant lying around, where it's accessible to children or pets – they're attracted by its sweet smell. Ingestion of even a small amount of coolant can be fatal. Wipe up garage-floor and drip-pan spills immediately. Keep antifreeze containers covered, and repair cooling system leaks as soon as they're noticed.*

⚠ **Warning:** *Never remove the expansion tank filler cap when the engine is running, or has just been switched off, as the cooling system will be hot, and the consequent escaping steam and scalding coolant could cause serious injury.*

⚠ **Warning:** *Wait until the engine is cold before starting these procedures.*

30.10 Disconnect the hoses from the coolant circulation pump – 2.0 litre engines

Cooling system draining

1 Firmly apply the handbrake, then jack up the front of the vehicle and support it securely on axle stands (see *Jacking and vehicle support*).
2 Where applicable, undo the retaining bolts and remove the engine undertray.
3 Cover the expansion tank cap with a wad of rag, and slowly turn the cap anti-clockwise to relieve the pressure in the cooling system (a hissing sound will normally be heard). Wait until any pressure remaining in the system is released, then continue to turn the cap until it can be removed.

1.9 and 2.5 litre engines

4 Position a suitable container beneath the left-hand side of the radiator.
5 Pull out the horseshoe shaped retaining clip securing the coolant temperature sensor to the base of the radiator left-hand side tank. Withdraw the coolant temperature sensor from the radiator and allow the coolant to drain into the container.
6 To fully drain the system, also disconnect one of the coolant hoses from the oil cooler which is located at the front of the cylinder block.
7 On completion, check the condition of the coolant temperature sensor O-ring and renew if necessary. Refit the sensor and reconnect the coolant hoses. If the system is not to be flushed, refit the engine undertray and lower the vehicle to the ground.

2.0 litre engines

8 Position suitable containers beneath the left-hand side of the radiator and under the front of the engine.
9 Release the retaining clip and disconnect the bottom hose from the radiator.
10 Release the retaining clips and disconnect the hoses from the electric coolant circulation pump, located at the front of the cylinder block, below the oil cooler (see illustration).
11 To fully drain the system also disconnect one of the coolant hoses from the oil cooler, which is located at the front of the cylinder block.
12 On completion, reconnect the coolant hoses. If the system is not to be flushed, refit the engine undertray and lower the vehicle to the ground.

Cooling system flushing

13 If coolant renewal has been neglected, or if the antifreeze mixture has become diluted, then in time, the cooling system may gradually lose efficiency, as the coolant passages become restricted due to rust, scale deposits, and other sediment. The cooling system efficiency can be restored by flushing the system clean.
14 The radiator should be flushed independently of the engine, to avoid unnecessary contamination.

Radiator flushing

15 Disconnect the top and bottom hoses and any other relevant hoses from the radiator.

16 Insert a garden hose into the radiator top inlet. Direct a flow of clean water through the radiator, and keep flushing until clean water emerges from the radiator bottom outlet.
17 If after a reasonable period, the water still does not run clear, the radiator can be flushed with a good proprietary cooling system cleaning agent. It is important that their manufacturer's instructions are followed carefully. If the contamination is particularly bad, insert the hose in the radiator bottom outlet, and reverse-flush the radiator.

Engine flushing

18 Remove the thermostat as described in Chapter 3, Section 4, then temporarily refit the thermostat cover.
19 With the top and bottom hoses disconnected from the radiator, insert a garden hose into the radiator top hose. Direct a clean flow of water through the engine, and continue flushing until clean water emerges from the radiator bottom hose.
20 On completion, refit the thermostat and reconnect the hoses with reference to Chapter 3, Section 4.

Antifreeze mixture

21 VW state that, if the only antifreeze (coolant) used is VW's own G12 or higher, then it does not need to be renewed. This is subject to it being used in the recommended concentration, unmixed with any other type of antifreeze or additive, and topped-up when necessary using only that antifreeze type, mixed with clean water. If any other type of antifreeze is (or has been) added, the above no longer applies; in this case, the system must be drained and thoroughly flushed before fresh coolant mixture is poured in.
22 If any antifreeze other than VW's is to be used, the coolant must be renewed at regular intervals to provide an equivalent degree of protection. The conventional recommendation is to renew the coolant every two years.
23 If the antifreeze used is to VW's specification, the levels of protection it affords are indicated in the Specifications Section of this Chapter. To give the recommended standard mixture ratio for this antifreeze, 40% (by volume) of antifreeze must be mixed with 60% of clean, soft water. If you are using any other type of antifreeze, follow its manufacturer's instructions to achieve the correct ratio.
24 It is best to make up slightly more than the system's capacity, so that a supply is available for subsequent topping-up. However, note that you are unlikely to fully drain the system at any one time (unless the engine is being completely stripped), any capacity quoted is therefore slightly academic for routine coolant renewal.
25 Before adding antifreeze, the cooling system should be completely drained, preferably flushed, and all hoses checked for condition and security. Fresh antifreeze will rapidly find any weaknesses in the system.

26 After filling with antifreeze, a label should be attached to the expansion tank, stating the type and concentration of antifreeze used, and the date installed. Any subsequent topping-up should be made with the same type and concentration of antifreeze.

27 Do not use engine antifreeze in the washer system, as it will damage the vehicle's paintwork. A screen wash additive should be added to the washer system in its maker's recommended quantities.

Cooling system filling

28 Before attempting to fill the cooling system, make sure that all hoses and clips are in good condition, and that the clips are tight. Note that an antifreeze mixture must be used all year round, to prevent corrosion of the engine components.

29 Remove the expansion tank filler cap, and fill the system by slowly pouring the coolant mixture into the expansion tank.

30 Once the level in the expansion tank starts to rise, squeeze the radiator top and bottom hoses to help expel any trapped air in the system. Once all the air is expelled, top-up the coolant level to the 'MAX' mark and refit the expansion tank cap.

31 Start the engine and run it until it reaches normal operating temperature, then stop the engine and allow it to cool.

32 Check for leaks, particularly around disturbed components. Check the coolant level in the expansion tank, and top-up if necessary. Note that the system must be cold before an accurate level is indicated in the expansion tank. If the expansion tank cap is removed while the engine is still warm, cover the cap with a thick cloth, and unscrew the cap slowly to gradually relieve the system pressure (a hissing sound will normally be heard). Wait until any pressure remaining in the system is released, then continue to turn the cap until it can be removed.

Airlocks

33 If, after draining and refilling the system, symptoms of overheating are found which did not occur previously, then the fault is almost certainly due to trapped air at some point in the system, causing an airlock and restricting the flow of coolant; usually, the air is trapped because the system was refilled too quickly.

34 If an airlock is suspected, first try gently squeezing all visible coolant hoses. A coolant hose which is full of air feels quite different to one full of coolant when squeezed. After refilling the system, most airlocks will clear once the system has cooled, and been topped-up.

35 While the engine is running at operating temperature, switch on the heater and heater fan, and check for heat output. Provided there is sufficient coolant in the system, lack of heat output could be due to an airlock in the system.

36 Airlocks can have more serious effects than simply reducing heater output – a severe airlock could reduce coolant flow around the engine. Check that the radiator top hose is hot when the engine is at operating temperature – a top hose which stays cold could be the result of an airlock (or a non-opening thermostat).

37 If the problem persists, stop the engine and allow it to cool down **completely**, before unscrewing the expansion tank filler cap or loosening the hose clips and squeezing the hoses to bleed out the trapped air. In the worst case, the system will have to be at least partially drained (this time, the coolant can be saved for re-use) and flushed to clear the problem. If all else fails, have the system evacuated and vacuum filled by a suitably-equipped garage.

Every 95 000 miles, then every 19 000 miles

31 Particulate filter ash deposit mass check

On vehicles equipped with a particulate filter, the amount of ash deposited in the particulate filter by the filtration process will eventually cause a blockage, and engine running problems. VW state that the maximum amount of ash is 60g. At this point, the particulate filter must be renewed. Unfortunately, the mass of the ash can only be established using dedicated VW diagnostic equipment, connected to the vehicle through the diagnostic socket under the driver's side of the facia. Consequently, we recommend this task is entrusted to a VW dealer or suitably equipped specialist.

Chapter 2 Part A:
1.9 litre engine in-vehicle repair procedures

Contents

Degrees of difficulty

Easy, suitable for novice with little experience	Fairly easy, suitable for beginner with some experience	Fairly difficult, suitable for competent DIY mechanic	Difficult, suitable for experienced DIY mechanic	Very difficult, suitable for expert DIY or professional

Specifications

General

Engine type.	4-cylinder, in-line, single overhead camshaft
Engine codes:	
77 kW engines	AXB
63 kW engines	AXC
62 kW engines	BRR
75 kW engines	BRS
Capacity.	1896 cc
Bore	79.5 mm
Stroke	95.5 mm
Compression ratio	18 : 1
Compression pressures:	
Minimum compression pressure	Approximately 19.0 bar
Maximum difference between cylinders.	Approximately 5.0 bar
Firing order	1 – 3 – 4 – 2 (No 1 cylinder at timing belt end)
Direction of crankshaft rotation	Clockwise (seen from right-hand side of vehicle)

Camshaft

Camshaft endfloat (maximum)	0.15 mm
Camshaft bearing running clearance (maximum).	0.11 mm
Camshaft run-out (maximum).	0.01 mm

Lubrication system

Oil pump type.	Gear type, chain-driven from crankshaft
Oil pressure (oil temperature 80°C, at 2000 rpm).	2.0 bar

Torque wrench settings

	Nm	lbf ft
Ancillary (alternator, etc) bracket mounting bolts...............	45	33
Auxiliary drivebelt tensioner retaining bolts	25	18
Big-end bearing caps bolts*:		
Stage 1....................................	30	22
Stage 2....................................	Angle-tighten a further 90°	
Camshaft bearing cap bolts*:		
Stage 1....................................	8	6
Stage 2....................................	Angle-tighten a further 90°	
Camshaft cover bolts.......................	10	7
Camshaft sprocket hub centre bolt	100	74
Camshaft sprocket-to-hub bolts	25	18
Crankshaft oil seal housing bolts..................	15	11
Crankshaft pulley bolts:		
Stage 1....................................	10	7
Stage 2....................................	Angle-tighten a further 90°	
Crankshaft speed/position sensor wheel-to-crankshaft bolts*:		
Engine codes AXB and AXC:		
Stage 1....................................	10	7
Stage 2....................................	Angle-tighten a further 90°	
Crankshaft sprocket bolt*:		
Stage 1....................................	120	89
Stage 2....................................	Angle-tighten a further 90°	
Cylinder head bolts*:		
Stage 1....................................	35	26
Stage 2....................................	60	44
Stage 3....................................	Angle-tighten a further 90°	
Stage 4....................................	Angle-tighten a further 90°	
Engine/transmission mountings*:		
Front mounting through-bolt		
Stage 1....................................	90	66
Stage 2....................................	Angle-tighten a further 180°	
Front mounting bracket-to-cylinder block:		
Stage 1....................................	50	37
Stage 2....................................	Angle-tighten a further 90°	
Front mounting-to-subframe bolts:		
Stage 1....................................	20	15
Stage 2....................................	Angle-tighten a further 90°	
Left-hand mounting-to-body bolts:		
Stage 1....................................	50	37
Stage 2....................................	Angle-tighten a further 90°	
Left-hand mounting-to-transmission bolts:		
Stage 1....................................	50	37
Stage 2....................................	Angle-tighten a further 90°	
Right-hand mounting-to-body bolts:		
Stage 1....................................	50	37
Stage 2....................................	Angle-tighten a further 90°	
Right-hand mounting-to-engine bracket bolts:		
Stage 1....................................	50	37
Stage 2....................................	Angle-tighten a further 90°	
Right-hand engine bracket-to-cylinder block:		
Stage 1....................................	40	30
Stage 2....................................	Angle-tighten a further 180°	
Rear mounting through-bolt:		
Stage 1....................................	50	37
Stage 2....................................	Angle-tighten a further 180°	
Rear mounting-to-subframe nuts:		
Stage 1....................................	20	15
Stage 2....................................	Angle-tighten a further 180°	
Rear mounting engine bracket-to-cylinder block:		
Small bolts:		
Stage 1....................................	20	15
Stage 2....................................	Angle-tighten a further 90°	
Large bolt:		
Stage 1....................................	50	37
Stage 2....................................	Angle-tighten a further 90°	
Pump injector rocker shaft bolts*:		
Stage 1....................................	20	15
Stage 2....................................	Angle-tighten a further 90°	

Torque wrench settings (continued)

	Nm	lbf ft
Main bearing cap bolts*:		
Stage 1	65	48
Stage 2	Angle-tighten a further 90°	
Oil cooler securing plate	25	18
Oil filter housing-to-cylinder block bolts*:		
Stage 1	15	11
Stage 2	Angle-tighten a further 90°	
Oil filter cover	25	18
Oil level/temperature sensor-to-sump bolts	10	7
Oil pick-up pipe securing bolts	15	11
Oil pressure warning light switch	20	15
Oil pump chain tensioner bolt	15	11
Oil pump securing bolts	15	11
Oil pump sprocket securing bolt	25	18
Piston oil spray jet bolt	25	18
Roadwheel bolts	180	133
Sump:		
Drain plug	30	22
Sump-to-cylinder block bolts	15	11
Sump-to-transmission bolts	40	30
Timing belt idler pulley nut	20	15
Timing belt cover bolts	10	7
Timing belt tensioner roller securing nut:		
Stage 1	20	15
Stage 2	Angle-tighten a further 45°	

*Note: *Use new bolts*

1 General information

Using this Chapter

Chapter 2 is divided into four Parts; A, B, C and D. Repair operations that can be carried out with the engine in the vehicle are described in Part A (1.9 litre engines), Part B (2.0 litre engines), and Part C (2.5 litre engines). Part D covers the removal of the engine/transmission as a unit, and describes the engine dismantling and overhaul procedures.

In Parts A, B and C, the assumption is made that the engine is installed in the vehicle, with all ancillaries connected. If the engine has been removed for overhaul, the preliminary dismantling information which precedes each operation may be ignored.

Engine description

The engines are water-cooled, single overhead camshaft, in-line four-cylinder units, with cast-iron cylinder blocks and aluminium-alloy cylinder heads. All are mounted transversely at the front of the vehicle, with the transmission bolted to the left-hand end of the engine.

The crankshaft is of five-bearing type, and thrustwashers are fitted to the centre main bearing to control crankshaft endfloat.

The camshaft is driven via a toothed timing belt from the crankshaft. The camshaft is mounted at the top of the cylinder head, and is secured by bearing caps.

The valves are closed by coil springs, and run in guides pressed into the cylinder head.

The camshaft actuates the valves directly, via hydraulic tappets.

The gear-type oil pump is driven via a chain from a sprocket on the crankshaft. Oil is drawn from the sump through a strainer, and then forced through an externally-mounted, renewable filter. From there, it is distributed to the cylinder head, where it lubricates the camshaft journals and hydraulic tappets, and also to the crankcase, where it lubricates the main bearings, connecting rod big-ends, gudgeon pins and cylinder bores. A coolant-fed oil cooler is fitted to the oil filter housing on all engines. Oil jets are fitted to the base of each cylinder – these spray oil onto the underside of the pistons, to improve cooling.

A brake servo vacuum pump, driven by the camshaft, is attached to the transmission end of the cylinder head. The vacuum pump and the fuel injection system fuel pump are combined in one unit, termed a 'tandem pump'.

Engine coolant is circulated by a pump, driven by the timing belt. For details of the cooling system, refer to Chapter 3.

Repairs possible with the engine installed in the vehicle

The following operations can be performed without removing the engine:

a) Compression pressure – testing.
b) Camshaft cover – removal and refitting.
c) Crankshaft pulley – removal and refitting.
d) Timing belt covers – removal and refitting.
e) Timing belt – removal, refitting and adjustment.
f) Timing belt tensioner and sprockets – removal and refitting.

g) Camshaft oil seals – renewal.
h) Camshaft and hydraulic tappets – removal, inspection and refitting.
i) Cylinder head – removal and refitting.
j) Cylinder head and pistons – decarbonising.
k) Sump – removal and refitting.
l) Oil pump – removal, overhaul and refitting.
m) Crankshaft oil seals – renewal.
n) Engine/transmission mountings – inspection and renewal.
o) Flywheel – removal, inspection and refitting.

Note: *It is possible to remove the pistons and connecting rods (after removing the cylinder head and sump) without removing the engine. However, this is not recommended. Work of this nature is more easily and thoroughly completed with the engine on the bench, as described in Chapter 2D.*

2 Compression and leakdown tests – description and interpretation

Compression test

Note: *A compression tester suitable for use with diesel engines will be required for this test.*

1 When engine performance is down, or if misfiring occurs which cannot be attributed to the ignition or fuel systems, a compression test can provide diagnostic clues as to the engine's condition. If the test is performed regularly, it can give warning of trouble before any other symptoms become apparent.

2.3 Disconnect the injector solenoids wiring plug connector (arrowed)

2 The engine must be fully warmed-up to normal operating temperature, the battery must be fully-charged and you will require the aid of an assistant. According to model, undo the retaining bolts and rotary fasteners and remove the battery cover and engine covers as applicable.

3 Disconnect the injector solenoids by disconnecting the wiring connector at the end of the cylinder head **(see illustration)**. **Note:** *As a result of the wiring being disconnected, faults will be stored in the ECU memory. On completion of the test it will be necessary to have the fault codes cleared by a VW dealer or suitably equipped garage, using specialist diagnostic equipment.*

4 Remove the glow plugs as described in Chapter 5, Section 13 then fit a compression tester to the No 1 cylinder glow plug hole.

The type of tester which screws into the plug thread is preferred.

5 Have your assistant, crank the engine for several seconds on the starter motor. After one or two revolutions, the compression pressure should build-up to a maximum figure and then stabilise. Record the highest reading obtained.

6 Repeat the test on the remaining cylinders, recording the pressure in each.

7 The cause of poor compression is less easy to establish on a diesel engine than on a petrol engine. The effect of introducing oil into the cylinders (wet testing) is not conclusive, because there is a risk that the oil will sit in the recess on the piston crown, instead of passing to the rings. However, the following can be used as a rough guide to diagnosis.

8 All cylinders should produce very similar pressures. Any difference greater than that specified indicates the existence of a fault. Note that the compression should build-up quickly in a healthy engine. Low compression on the first stroke, followed by gradually increasing pressure on successive strokes, indicates worn piston rings. A low compression reading on the first stroke, which does not build-up during successive strokes, indicates leaking valves or a blown head gasket (a cracked head could also be the cause).

9 A low reading from two adjacent cylinders is almost certainly due to the head gasket having blown between them and the presence of coolant in the engine oil will confirm this.

10 On completion, remove the compression

tester, and refit the glow plugs, with reference to Chapter 5, Section 13.

11 Reconnect the injector solenoids wiring connector.

Leakdown test

12 A leakdown test measures the rate at which compressed air fed into the cylinder is lost. It is an alternative to a compression test, and in many ways it is better, since the escaping air provides easy identification of where pressure loss is occurring (piston rings, valves or head gasket).

13 The equipment required for leakdown testing is unlikely to be available to the home mechanic. If poor compression is suspected, have the test performed by a suitably-equipped garage.

---

3 Engine assembly and valve timing marks – general information and usage

General information

1 TDC is the highest point in the cylinder that each piston reaches as it travels up-and-down when the crankshaft turns. Each piston reaches TDC at the end of the compression stroke and again at the end of the exhaust stroke, but TDC generally refers to piston position on the compression stroke. No 1 piston is at the timing belt end of the engine.

2 Positioning No 1 piston at TDC is an essential part of many procedures, such as timing belt removal and camshaft removal.

3 The design of the engines covered in this Chapter is such that piston-to-valve contact may occur if the camshaft or crankshaft is turned with the timing belt removed. For this reason, it is important to ensure that the camshaft and crankshaft do not move in relation to each other once the timing belt has been removed from the engine.

Setting TDC on No 1 cylinder

Models up to December 2005

Note: *VW special tool T10050 (or a suitable alternative) is required to lock the crankshaft sprocket in the TDC position.*

4 Remove the auxiliary drivebelt as described in Chapter 1, Section 27.

5 Remove the crankshaft pulley as described in Section 5.

6 Remove the timing belt outer covers as described in Section 6.

7 Remove the glow plugs, as described in Chapter 5, Section 13 to allow the engine to turn more easily.

8 Using a spanner or socket on the crankshaft sprocket bolt, turn the crankshaft in the normal direction of rotation (clockwise) until the alignment mark on the face of the sprocket is almost vertical **(see illustrations)**.

9 The arrow (marked 4Z) on the timing belt rear cover aligns between the two lugs on the rear of the camshaft hub sender wheel **(see illustration)**.

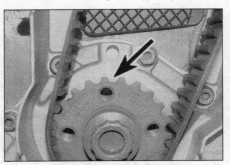

3.8a Position the crankshaft so that the mark on the sprocket is almost vertical (arrowed)...

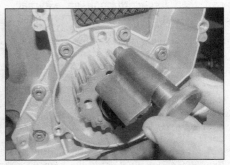

3.8b ...then insert the VW tool T10050...

3.8c ...and align the marks (arrowed) on the tool and sprocket

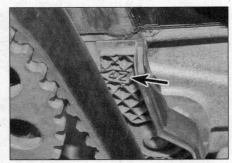

3.9 Align the arrow on the rear of the timing belt cover (arrowed) between the lugs on the rear of the camshaft hub sender wheel

3.10 Insert a 6 mm drill bit (arrowed) through the camshaft hub into the cylinder head to lock the camshaft

4.5 The camshaft cover gasket locates in a groove in the cover

4.7a Apply sealant to the points (arrowed) on the cylinder head

10 While in this position it should be possible to insert VW tool T10050 to lock the crankshaft, and a 6 mm diameter rod to lock the camshaft **(see illustration)**. **Note:** *The mark on the crankshaft sprocket and the mark on the VW tool T10050 must align, whilst at the same time the shaft of tool T10050 must engage in the drilling in the crankshaft oil seal housing.*

11 The engine is now set to TDC on No 1 cylinder.

Models from January 2006

Note: *A modified crankshaft sprocket was progressively introduced from this date. If the later type sprocket is fitted, the alignment mark on the face of the sprocket will be at approximately the 1 o'clock position when the engine is set to TDC on No 1 cylinder. VW special tool (T10100) will be required to lock the crankshaft sprocket in the TDC position.*

12 Remove the auxiliary drivebelt as described in Chapter 1, Section 27.

13 Remove the crankshaft pulley as described in Section 5.

14 Remove the timing belt outer covers as described in Section 6.

15 Remove the glow plugs, as described in Chapter 5, Section 13 to allow the engine to turn more easily.

16 Using a spanner or socket on the crankshaft sprocket bolt, turn the crankshaft in the normal direction of rotation (clockwise) until the alignment mark on the face of the sprocket is at approximately the 1 o'clock position.

17 The arrow (marked 4Z) on the timing belt rear cover aligns between the two lugs on the rear of the camshaft hub sender wheel **(see illustration 3.9)**. If this is not the case, then it is possible that the engine is still fitted with the earlier crankshaft sprocket. If this is the case, use the procedure described in paragraphs 4 to 11 to set the engine to TDC on No 1 cylinder.

18 While in this position it should be possible to insert VW tool T10100 to lock the crankshaft, and a 6 mm diameter rod to lock the camshaft **(see illustration 3.10)**. **Note:** *The mark on the crankshaft sprocket and the mark on the VW tool T10100 must align, whilst at the same time the shaft of tool T10100 must*

engage in the drilling in the crankshaft oil seal housing.

19 The engine is now set to TDC on No 1 cylinder.

4 Camshaft cover – removal and refitting

Removal

1 According to model, undo the retaining bolts and rotary fasteners and remove the battery cover and engine covers as applicable.

2 On engine codes BRR and BRS, remove the EGR valve connecting pipe as described in Chapter 4C, Section 2, and the inlet manifold changeover flap motor as described in Chapter 4A, Section 7.

3 Disconnect the crankcase ventilation hose from the camshaft cover.

4 Unscrew the camshaft cover retaining bolts and lift the cover away. If it sticks, do not attempt to lever it off – instead free it by working around the cover and tapping it lightly with a soft-faced mallet.

5 Recover the camshaft cover gasket **(see illustration)**. Inspect the gasket carefully,

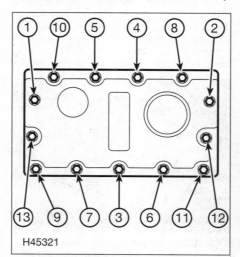

4.7b Camshaft cover tightening sequence

and renew it if damage or deterioration is evident.

6 Clean the mating surfaces of the cylinder head and camshaft cover thoroughly, removing all traces of oil and old gasket – take care to avoid damaging the surfaces as you do this.

Refitting

7 Refitting is a reversal of the removal procedure, bearing in mind the following points:
a) *Apply suitable sealant to the points where camshaft bearing caps No 1 and 5 contact the cylinder head* **(see illustration)**.
b) *Tighten the camshaft cover retaining nuts/bolts progressively to the specified torque, in the sequence shown* **(see illustration)**.
c) *On engine codes BRR and BRS, refit the EGR valve connecting pipe as described in Chapter 4C, Section 2, and the inlet manifold changeover flap motor as described in Chapter 4A, Section 7.*

5 Crankshaft pulley – removal and refitting

Removal

1 Remove the auxiliary drivebelt as described in Chapter 1, Section 27.

2 Prise the cover from the centre of the pulley to expose the securing bolts **(see illustration)**.

5.2 Prising out the crankshaft pulley centre cap

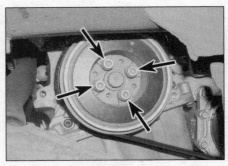

5.3 Crankshaft pulley retaining bolts (arrowed)

3 Unscrew the bolts securing the pulley to the sprocket, and remove the pulley **(see illustration)**. If necessary, the pulley can be prevented from turning by counterholding with a spanner or socket on the crankshaft sprocket bolt.

Refitting

4 Refit the pulley over the locating peg on the crankshaft sprocket, then refit the pulley securing bolts.
5 Prevent the crankshaft from turning as during removal, then fit the pulley securing bolts, and tighten to the specified torque.
6 Refit the auxiliary drivebelt as described in Chapter 1, Section 27.

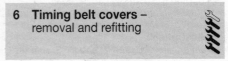

6 Timing belt covers – removal and refitting

Upper outer cover

1 According to model, undo the retaining bolts and rotary fasteners and remove the battery cover and engine covers as applicable.
2 Remove the air duct and hoses between the intercooler and turbocharger.
3 Disconnect the crankcase ventilation hose from the camshaft cover.
4 Release the clips and remove the air duct from the air cleaner and turbocharger.
5 Where applicable, release the retaining clips and remove the air intake hose from across the top of the timing belt cover.
6 Release the uppermost part of the timing belt outer cover by prising open the metal spring clips, then withdraw the cover away from the engine **(see illustration)**.
7 Refitting is a reversal of removal, noting that the lower edge of the upper cover engages with the centre cover.

Centre outer cover

8 Remove the auxiliary drivebelt as described in Chapter 1, Section 27.
9 Remove the upper outer cover as described previously.
10 Unscrew and remove the retaining bolts from the centre cover. Withdraw the centre cover from the engine, noting how it fits over the lower cover.
11 Refitting is a reversal of removal.

6.6 Timing belt upper cover front retaining clip (arrowed)

Lower outer cover

12 Remove the upper and centre covers as described previously.
13 Remove the crankshaft pulley as described in Section 5.
14 Unscrew the remaining bolt(s) securing the lower cover, and lift it out.
15 Refitting is a reversal of removal; locate the centre cover in place before fitting the top two bolts.

Rear cover

16 Remove the upper, centre and lower covers as described previously.
17 Remove the timing belt, tensioner and sprockets as described in Sections 7 and 8.
18 Slacken and withdraw the retaining bolts and lift the timing belt inner cover from the studs on the end of the engine, and remove it from the engine compartment.
19 Refitting is a reversal of removal.

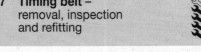

7 Timing belt – removal, inspection and refitting

Removal

1 The primary function of the toothed timing belt is to drive the camshaft, but it also drives the coolant pump. Should the belt slip or break in service, the valve timing will be disturbed and piston-to-valve contact may occur, resulting in serious engine damage. For

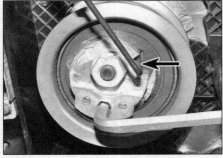

7.9 Rotate the timing belt tensioner hub anti-clockwise until a 2 mm rod/drill bit (arrowed) can be inserted to lock the hub to the pulley

this reason, it is important that the timing belt is tensioned correctly, and inspected regularly for signs of wear or deterioration.
2 Disconnect the battery negative terminal (refer to *Disconnecting the battery*).
3 Remove the auxiliary drivebelt as described in Chapter 1, Section 27.
4 Undo the retaining bolts and remove the auxiliary drivebelt tensioner.
5 Remove the timing belt outer covers, as described in Section 6.
6 Set the engine to TDC on No 1 cylinder as described in Section 3.
7 Remove the complete right-hand engine mounting assembly, with reference to Section 20. Also, unbolt the engine mounting bracket from the cylinder block.
8 Slacken the three camshaft sprocket retaining bolts so that the sprocket is free to move on the hub.
9 Slacken the timing belt tensioner retaining nut and turn the tensioner hub anti-clockwise until it can be locked in place using a 2.0 mm pin/drill bit. The tensioner hub can be turned using circlip pliers inserted in the two holes in the hub face. On later models an Allen key can be inserted into the hole in the hub face **(see illustration)**.
10 Now rotate the tensioner hub clockwise to the stop, and hand-tighten the retaining nut.
11 If the original timing belt is to be refitted, mark the running direction of the belt, to ensure correct refitting.
Caution: If the belt appears to be in good condition and can be re-used, it is essential that it is refitted the same way around, otherwise accelerated wear will result, leading to premature failure.
12 Slide the belt from the sprockets, taking care not to twist or kink the belt excessively if it is to be re-used.

Inspection

13 Examine the belt for evidence of contamination by coolant or lubricant. If this is the case, find the source of the contamination before progressing any further. Check the belt for signs of wear or damage, particularly around the leading edges of the belt teeth. Renew the belt if its condition is in doubt; the cost of belt renewal is negligible compared with potential cost of the engine repairs, should the belt fail in service. The belt must be renewed if it has covered the mileage given in Chapter 1, however, if it has covered less, it is prudent to renew it regardless of condition, as a precautionary measure.
14 If the timing belt is not going to be refitted for some time, it is a wise precaution to hang a warning label on the steering wheel, to remind yourself (and others) not to attempt to start the engine.

Refitting

15 Ensure that the crankshaft and camshaft are still set to TDC on No 1 cylinder, as described in Section 3.
16 Position the camshaft sprocket so that

7.16 Position the camshaft sprocket so that the securing bolts are in the centre part of the elongated holes

7.19 Turn the tensioner clockwise until the pointer (arrowed) is in the middle of the gap in the tensioner backplate

the securing bolts are in the centre part of the elongated holes **(see illustration)**.

17 Loop the timing belt loosely under the crankshaft sprocket. **Note:** *Observe any direction of rotation markings on the belt.*

18 Manoeuvre the belt into position around the tensioner camshaft sprocket, idler pulley and finally around the coolant pump sprocket. Make sure that the belt teeth seat correctly on the sprockets. **Note:** *Slight adjustment to the position of the camshaft sprocket may be necessary to achieve this.* Avoid bending the belt back on itself or twisting it excessively as you do this.

19 Loosen the timing belt tensioner retaining nut, and pull out the tensioner locking pin. Turn the tensioner clockwise using circlip pliers or an Allen key until the pointer is in the middle of the gap in the tensioner backplate **(see illustration)**. With the tensioner held in this position, tighten the securing nut to the specified torque and angle.

20 Counterhold the camshaft sprocket with a homemade tool to prevent any rotation, and then tighten the camshaft sprocket to the specified torque. Remove the sprocket locking tool and the crankshaft locking tool.

21 Using a spanner or wrench and socket on the crankshaft pulley centre bolt, rotate the crankshaft clockwise through two complete revolutions. Reset the engine to TDC on No1 cylinder, with reference to Section 3 and refit the crankshaft locking tool.

22 Check that the tensioner pointer is centred, or within a maximum of 5 mm to the right of the gap in the backplate. If not, hold the tensioner hub stationary with circlip pliers or an Allen key, slacken the retaining nut and position the arm in the centre of the gap. Tighten the retaining nut to the specified torque. Remove the Allen key.

23 Check that the camshaft sprocket locking pin can still be inserted.

24 If the camshaft sprocket locking pin cannot be inserted, pull the crankshaft locking tool slight away from the engine, and rotate the

crankshaft *anti-clockwise* slightly past TDC. Now slowly rotate the crankshaft clockwise until the camshaft sprocket locking tool can be inserted.

25 If the locating pin of the crankshaft locking tool is to the left of the corresponding hole, slacken the camshaft sprocket bolts, slowly rotate the crankshaft clockwise until the locking tool can be fully inserted. Tighten the camshaft sprocket bolts to the specified torque.

26 If the locating pin of the crankshaft locking tool is to the right of the corresponding hole, slacken the camshaft sprocket bolts, rotate the crankshaft *anti-clockwise* slightly until the pin is to the left of the hole, then slowly rotate it clockwise until the locking tool can be fully inserted. Tighten the camshaft sprocket bolts to the specified torque.

27 Remove the crankshaft and camshaft locking tools, then rotate the crankshaft two complete revolutions clockwise and check the locking tools can be reinserted. If necessary, repeat the adjustment procedure described previously.

28 The remainder of refitting is a reversal of removal.

8 Timing belt tensioner and sprockets – removal and refitting

Timing belt tensioner
Removal

1 Remove the timing belt as described in Section 7.

2 Unscrew the timing belt tensioner nut, and remove the tensioner from the engine.

Refitting

3 When refitting the tensioner to the engine, ensure that the lug on the tensioner backplate engages with the corresponding cut-out in the rear timing belt cover, then refit the tensioner nut **(see illustration)**.

4 Refit and tension the timing belt as described in Section 7.

Idler pulley
Removal

5 Remove the timing belt as described in Section 7.

6 Unscrew the idler pulley securing nut, and then withdraw the pulley.

Refitting

7 Refit the pulley and tighten the securing nut to the specified torque.

8 Refit and tension the timing belt as described in Section 7.

Crankshaft sprocket

Note: *A new crankshaft sprocket retaining bolt must be used on refitting.*

Removal

9 Remove the timing belt as described in Section 7.

10 The sprocket retaining bolt must now be slackened, and the crankshaft must be prevented from turning as the sprocket bolt is unscrewed. To hold the sprocket, make up a suitable tool, and bolt it to the sprocket using two bolts inserted into two of the crankshaft pulley bolt holes.

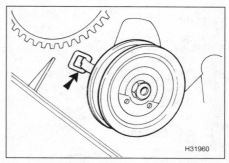

8.3 Ensure that the lug on the tensioner backplate engages with the cut-out in the rear timing belt cover

8.12 Unscrew the bolt, and slide the sprocket from the end of the crankshaft

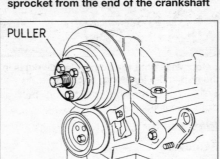

8.23 Attach a three-legged puller to the hub, and evenly tighten the puller until the hub is free of the camshaft taper

11 Hold the sprocket using the tool, then slacken the sprocket securing bolt. Take care, as the bolt is very tight. Do not allow the crankshaft to turn as the bolt is slackened.
12 Unscrew the bolt, and slide the sprocket from the end of the crankshaft, noting which way round the sprocket's raised boss is fitted **(see illustration)**.

Refitting

13 Commence refitting by positioning the sprocket on the end of the crankshaft.
14 Fit a new sprocket retaining bolt, then counter hold the sprocket using the method employed on removal, and tighten the bolt to the specified torque then through the specified angle.
15 Refit the timing belt as described in Section 7.

9.2 Starting with the outer bolts first, carefully and evenly slacken the rocker shaft retaining bolts (arrowed)

8.22 Using a fabricated tool to counterhold the camshaft sprocket hub

8.24 The built in key in the hub taper must align with the key way in the camshaft taper (arrowed)

Camshaft sprocket

Removal

16 Remove the timing belt as described in Section 7, then rotate the crankshaft 90° anti-clockwise to prevent any accidental piston-to-valve contact.
17 Unscrew the three retaining bolts and remove the camshaft sprocket from the sprocket hub.

Refitting

18 Refit the sprocket ensuring that it is fitted the correct way round, as noted before removal, then insert the sprocket retaining bolts, and tighten by hand only at this stage.
19 If the crankshaft has been turned, turn the crankshaft clockwise 90° back to TDC.
20 Refit and tension the timing belt as described in Section 7.

Camshaft sprocket hub

Note: *VW technicians use special tool T10051 to counter hold the hub, however it is possible to fabricate a suitable alternative.*

Removal

21 Remove the camshaft sprocket as described previously in this Section.
22 Engage special tool T10051 with the three locating holes in the face of the hub to prevent the hub from turning. If this tool is not available, fabricate a suitable alternative. Whilst holding the tool, undo the central hub retaining bolt about two turns **(see illustration)**.
23 Slide the hub from the camshaft. If necessary, attach VW tool T10052 (or a similar

three-legged puller) to the hub, and evenly tighten the puller until the hub is free of the camshaft taper **(see illustration)**.

Refitting

24 Ensure that the camshaft taper and the hub centre are clean and dry, locate the hub on the taper, noting that the built-in key in the hub taper must align with the keyway in the camshaft taper **(see illustration)**.
25 Hold the hub in this position with tool T10051 (or similar home-made tool), and tighten the central bolt to the specified torque.
26 Refit the camshaft sprocket as described previously in this Section.

Coolant pump sprocket

27 The coolant pump sprocket is integral with the coolant pump. Refer to Chapter 3, Section 7 for details of coolant pump removal.

9 Pump injector rocker shaft assembly – removal and refitting

Removal

1 Remove the camshaft cover as described in Section 4. In order to ensure that the rocker arms are refitted to their original locations, use a marker pen or paint and number the arms 1 to 4, with No 1 nearest the timing belt end of the engine. If the arms are not fitted to their original locations the injector basic clearance setting procedure must be carried out as described in Chapter 4A, Section 8.
2 Starting with the outer bolts first, carefully and evenly slacken the rocker shaft retaining bolts. Discard the rocker shaft bolts, new ones must be fitted **(see illustration)**.

Refitting

3 Carefully check the rocker shaft, rocker arms and camshaft bearing cap seating surface for any signs of excessive wear or damage.
4 Ensure that the shaft seating surface is clean and position the rocker shaft assembly in the camshaft bearing caps, making sure that, if reusing the original rocker arms, they are in their original locations.
5 Insert the new rocker shaft retaining bolts, and starting with the inner bolts, gradually and evenly tighten the bolts to the specified Stage 1 torque setting.
6 Again, starting with the inner retaining bolts, tighten the bolts through the specified Stage 2 angle.
7 Refit the camshaft cover as described in Section 4.

10 Camshaft and hydraulic tappets – removal, inspection and refitting

Note: *A new camshaft oil seal and new bearing cap retaining bolts will be required for refitting.*

Removal

1 Remove the timing belt as described in Section 7.

2 Remove the camshaft sprocket and hub as described in Section 8.

3 Remove the brake vacuum pump as described in Chapter 9.

4 Remove the injector rocker arms as described in Section 9.

5 Check the camshaft bearing caps for identification markings. The bearing caps are normally stamped with their respective cylinder numbers. If no marks are present, make suitable marks using a scriber or punch. The caps should be numbered from 1 to 5, with No 1 at the timing belt end of the engine. Note on which side of the bearing caps the marks are made to ensure that they are refitted the correct way round.

6 The camshaft rotates in shell bearings. As the camshaft bearing caps are removed, recover the shell bearing halves from the camshaft. Number the back of the bearings with a felt pen to ensure that, if re-used, the bearings are fitted to their original locations. **Note:** *Fitted into the cylinder head, under each camshaft bearing cap, is a washer for each cylinder head bolt.*

7 Unscrew the retaining bolts, and remove Nos 1, 3 and 5 bearing caps. Note that new bearing cap retaining bolts will be required for refitting.

8 Working progressively, in a diagonal sequence, slacken the bolts securing Nos 2 and 4 bearing caps. Note that as the bolts are slackened, the valve springs will push the camshaft up.

9 Once the bolts securing Nos 2 and 4 bearing caps have been fully slackened, remove them, then lift off the bearing caps. Note that new bearing cap retaining bolts will be required for refitting.

10 Carefully lift the camshaft from the cylinder head, keeping it level and supported at both ends as it is removed so that the journals and lobes are not damaged. Remove the oil seal from the end of the camshaft and discard it – a new one will be required for refitting **(see illustration)**.

11 Lift the hydraulic tappets from their bores in the cylinder head, and store them with the valve contact surfaces facing downwards, to prevent the oil from draining out. Make a note of the position of each tappet, as they must be refitted in their original locations on reassembly – accelerated wear leading to early failure will result if the tappets are interchanged.

12 Recover the lower shell bearing halves from the cylinder head; number the back of the shells with a felt pen to ensure that, if re-used, the bearings are fitted to their original locations.

Inspection

13 With the camshaft removed, examine the bearing caps and the bearing locations in the cylinder head for signs of obvious wear or pitting. If evident, a new cylinder head will probably be required. Also check that the oil

supply holes in the cylinder head are free from obstructions.

14 Visually inspect the camshaft for evidence of wear on the surfaces of the lobes and journals. Normally their surfaces should be smooth and have a dull shine; look for scoring, erosion or pitting and areas that appear highly polished, indicating excessive wear. Accelerated wear will occur once the hardened exterior of the camshaft has been damaged, so always renew worn items. **Note:** *If these symptoms are visible on the tips of the camshaft lobes, check the corresponding tappet, as it will probably be worn as well.*

15 If the machined surfaces of the camshaft appear discoloured or blued, it is likely that it has been overheated at some point, probably due to inadequate lubrication. This may have distorted the shaft, so check the run-out as follows: place the camshaft between two V-blocks and using a DTI gauge, measure the run-out at the centre journal. If it exceeds the figure quoted in the Specifications at the start of this Chapter, renew the camshaft.

16 To measure the camshaft endfloat, temporarily refit the camshaft to the cylinder head, then fit Nos 1 and 5 bearing caps and tighten the retaining bolts to the specified torque setting. Anchor a DTI gauge to the timing belt end of the cylinder head **(see illustration)**. Push the camshaft to one end of the cylinder head as far as it will travel, then rest the DTI gauge probe on the end face of the camshaft, and zero the gauge. Push the camshaft as far as it will go to the other end of the cylinder head, and record the gauge reading. Verify the reading by pushing the camshaft back to its original position and checking that the gauge indicates zero again. **Note:** *The hydraulic tappets must **not** be fitted whilst this measurement is being taken.*

17 Check that the camshaft endfloat measurement is within the limit listed in the Specifications. If the measurement is outside the specified limit, wear is unlikely to be confined to any one component, so renewal of the camshaft, cylinder head and bearing caps must be considered.

18 The camshaft bearing running clearance should now be measured. This will be difficult to achieve without a range of micrometers or internal/external expanding calipers, measure the outside diameters of the camshaft bearing surfaces and the internal diameters formed by the bearing caps (and shell bearings where applicable) and the bearing locations in the cylinder head. The difference between these two measurements is the running clearance.

19 Compare the camshaft running clearance measurements with the figure given in the Specifications; if any are outside the specified tolerance, the camshaft, cylinder head and bearing caps and shell bearings should be renewed.

20 Inspect the hydraulic tappets for obvious signs of wear or damage, and renew if necessary. Check that the oil holes in the tappets are free from obstructions.

10.10 Remove the camshaft oil seal

Refitting

21 Smear some clean engine oil onto the sides of the hydraulic tappets, and offer them into position in their original bores in the cylinder head. Push them down until they contact the valves, then lubricate the camshaft lobe contact surfaces.

22 Lubricate the camshaft and cylinder head bearing journals (and shell bearings where applicable) with clean engine oil.

23 Carefully lower the camshaft into position in the cylinder head making sure that the cam lobes for No 1 cylinder are pointing upwards.

24 Fit a new camshaft oil seal on the front of the camshaft. Make sure that the closed end of the seal faces the camshaft sprocket end of the camshaft, and take care not to damage the seal lip. Locate the seal against the seat in the cylinder head.

25 Oil the upper surfaces of the camshaft bearing journals and shell bearings, then fit Nos 2 and 4 bearing caps. Ensure that they are fitted the right way round and in the correct locations (see paragraph 6), then progressively tighten the new retaining bolts in a diagonal sequence to the specified torque. Note that as the bolts are tightened, the camshaft will be forced down against the pressure of the valve springs.

26 Fit bearing caps 1, 3 and 5 over the camshaft and progressively tighten the new bolts to the specified torque. Note that it may be necessary to locate No 5 bearing cap by tapping lightly on the end of the camshaft.

27 Refit the injector rocker arms as described in Section 9.

10.16 Checking camshaft endfloat using a DTI gauge

13.7a Undo the bolt (arrowed) from the inner cover...

28 Refit the camshaft hub and sprocket as described in Section 8.
29 Refit and tension the timing belt as described in Section 7.
30 Refit the brake vacuum pump as described in Chapter 9, Section 20.

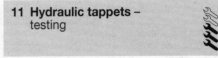

11 Hydraulic tappets – testing

⚠️ **Warning: After fitting hydraulic tappets, wait a minimum of 30 minutes (or preferably, leave overnight) before starting the engine, to allow the tappets time to settle, otherwise the valve heads will strike the pistons.**

1 The hydraulic tappets are self-adjusting, and require no attention whilst in service.
2 If the hydraulic tappets become excessively noisy, their operation can be checked as described below.
3 Start the engine, and run it until it reaches normal operating temperature, increase the engine speed to approximately 2500 rpm for 2 minutes.
4 If any hydraulic tappets are heard to be noisy, carry out the following checks.
5 Remove the camshaft cover as described in Section 4.
6 Using a socket or spanner on the crankshaft sprocket bolt, turn the crankshaft until the tip of the camshaft lobe above the tappet to be checked is pointing vertically upwards.
7 Using feeler blades, check the clearance between the top of the tappet, and the cam

13.8 Using two nuts locked together to unscrew the tensioner mounting stud

13.7b ...and the one (arrowed) on the side of the cover

lobe. If the play is in excess of 0.1 mm, renew the relevant tappet. If the play is less than 0.1 mm, or there is no play, proceed as follows.
8 Press down on the tappet using a wooden or plastic instrument. If free play in excess of 1.0 mm is present before the tappet contacts the valve stem, renew the relevant tappet.
9 On completion, refit the camshaft cover as described in Section 4.

12 Camshaft oil seals – renewal

Right-hand oil seal

1 Remove the timing belt as described in Section 7.
2 Remove the camshaft sprocket and hub, as described in Section 8.
3 Drill two small holes into the existing oil seal, diagonally opposite each other. Take great care to avoid drilling through into the seal housing or camshaft sealing surface. Thread two self-tapping screws into the holes, and using a pair of pliers, pull on the heads of the screws to extract the oil seal.
4 Clean out the seal housing and the sealing surface of the camshaft by wiping it with a lint-free cloth. Remove any swarf or burrs that may cause the seal to leak.
5 Do **not** lubricate the lip and outer edge of the new oil seal, push it over the camshaft until it is positioned in place above its housing. To prevent damage to the sealing lips, wrap

13.10 Unscrew the bolt and remove the camshaft position sensor

some adhesive tape around the end of the camshaft.
6 Using a hammer and a socket of suitable diameter, drive the seal squarely into its housing. **Note:** *Select a socket that bears only on the hard outer surface of the seal, not the inner lip which can easily be damaged.*
7 Refit the camshaft hub and sprocket as described in Section 8.
8 Refit and tension the timing belt as described in Section 7.

Left-hand oil seal

9 The left-hand camshaft oil seal is formed by the brake vacuum pump seal. Refer to Chapter 9, Section 20 for details of brake vacuum pump removal and refitting.

13 Cylinder head – removal, inspection and refitting

Note: *The cylinder head must be removed with the engine cold. New cylinder head bolts and a new cylinder head gasket will be required for refitting, and suitable studs will be required to guide the cylinder head into position – see text.*

Removal

1 Disconnect the battery negative terminal (refer to *Disconnecting the battery*).
2 Drain the cooling system as described in Chapter 1, Section 30.
3 Drain the engine oil as described in Chapter 1, Section 3.
4 Remove the camshaft cover as described in Section 4.
5 Remove the timing belt as described in Section 7.
6 Remove the camshaft sprocket and timing belt tensioner as described in Section 8.
7 Unscrew the bolts securing the rear timing belt cover to the cylinder head **(see illustrations)**.
8 Using two suitable nuts locked together, unscrew the timing belt tensioner mounting stud from the cylinder head **(see illustration)**.
9 If the engine is currently supported using a hoist and lifting tackle attached to the engine lifting brackets on the cylinder head, it is now necessary to attach a suitable bracket to the cylinder block, so that the engine can still be supported as the cylinder head is removed. Alternatively, the engine can be supported using a trolley jack and a block of wood positioned under the engine sump.
10 Remove the bolt securing the camshaft position sensor to the cylinder head. There is no need to disconnect the wiring at this stage **(see illustration)**.
11 Disconnect the charge air pipe from the inlet manifold to the intercooler and place to one side.
12 Disconnect the injector solenoids by disconnecting the wiring connector at the end

of the cylinder head (see illustration). Note: *As a result of the wiring being disconnected, faults will be stored in the ECU memory. On completion of the test It will be necessary to have the fault codes cleared by a VW dealer or suitably equipped garage, using specialist diagnostic equipment.*

13 Undo the two bolts securing the coolant junction to the end of the cylinder head (see illustration). There is no need to disconnect the pipes or wiring plugs at this stage.

14 Unscrew the four retaining bolts and pull the vacuum pump away from the cylinder head without disconnecting the fuel or vacuum hoses (see illustration).

15 Disconnect and remove the hose connecting the upper coolant pipe to the pipe at the end of the cylinder head (see illustration).

16 Remove the turbocharger as described in Chapter 4A, Section 14.

17 Remove the inlet manifold as described in Chapter 4A, Section 9.

18 Slacken and remove the bolt securing the upper metal coolant pipe to the cylinder head.

19 Disconnect the wiring connectors from the glow plugs.

20 Using a multi-splined tool, undo the cylinder head bolts, working from the outside-in, evenly and gradually. Check

13.12 Disconnect the central connector for the injectors

that nothing remains connected, and lift the cylinder head from the engine block. Seek assistance if possible, as it is a heavy assembly.

21 Remove the gasket from the top of the block, noting the locating dowels. If the dowels are a loose fit, remove them and store them with the head for safe-keeping. Do not discard the gasket yet – it will be needed for identification purposes.

Inspection

22 Dismantling of the cylinder head is covered in Chapter 2D, Section 6.

Cylinder head gasket selection

Note: *A dial test indicator (DTI) will be required for this operation.*

23 Examine the old cylinder head gasket for manufacturer's identification markings (see illustration). These will be in the form of holes or notches, and a part number on the edge of the gasket. Unless new pistons have been fitted, the new cylinder head gasket must be of the same type as the old one. In this case, purchase a new gasket, and proceed to paragraph 30.

24 If new piston assemblies have been fitted as part of an engine overhaul, or if a new short engine is to be fitted, the projection of the piston crowns above the cylinder head mating face of the cylinder block at TDC must be measured. This measurement is used to determine the thickness of the new cylinder head gasket required.

25 Anchor a dial test indicator (DTI) to the top face (cylinder head gasket mating face) of the cylinder block, and zero the gauge on the gasket mating face.

26 Rest the gauge probe on No 1 piston crown, and turn the crankshaft slowly by hand until the piston reaches TDC. Measure and record the maximum piston projection at TDC (see illustration).

13.13 Undo the two bolts (arrowed) and remove the coolant outlet from the end of the cylinder head

13.14 Undo the four vacuum pump retaining bolts (arrowed)

13.15 Disconnect the coolant hose from the end of the cylinder head

13.23 The thickness of the cylinder head gasket can be identified by notches or holes

13.26 Measuring the piston projection at TDC using a dial gauge

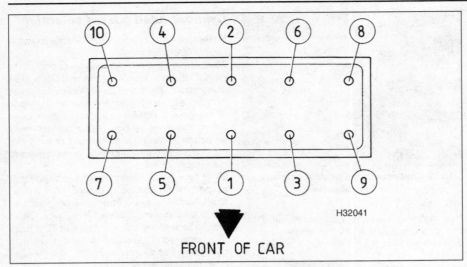

13.42a Cylinder head bolt tightening sequence

27 Repeat the measurement for the remaining pistons, and record the results.

28 If the measurements differ from piston-to-piston, take the highest figure, and use this to determine the thickness of the head gasket required as follows.

Gasket identification

Piston projection	(number of holes/notches)
0.91 to 1.00 mm	1
1.01 to 1.10 mm	2
1.11 to 1.20 mm	3

29 Purchase a new gasket according to the results of the measurements.

Refitting

Note: *If a VW exchange cylinder head, complete with camshaft, is to be fitted, the manufacturers recommend the following:*

a) *Lubricate the contact surfaces between the tappets and the cam lobes before fitting the camshaft cover.*

b) *Do not remove the plastic protectors from the open valves until immediately before fitting the cylinder head.*

c) *Additionally, if a new cylinder head is fitted, VW recommend that the coolant is renewed.*

30 The mating faces of the cylinder head and block must be perfectly clean before refitting the head. Use a scraper to remove all traces of gasket and carbon, also clean the tops of the pistons. Take particular care with the aluminium surfaces, as the soft metal is easily damaged.

31 Make sure that debris is not allowed to enter the oil and water passages – this is particularly important for the oil circuit, as carbon could block the oil supply to the camshaft and crankshaft bearings. Using adhesive tape and paper, seal the water, oil and bolt holes in the cylinder block.

32 To prevent carbon entering the gap between the pistons and bores, smear a little grease in the gap. After cleaning a piston, rotate the crankshaft to that the piston moves down the bore, then wipe out the grease and carbon with a cloth rag. Clean the other piston crowns in the same way.

33 Check the head and block for nicks, deep scratches and other damage. If slight, they may be removed carefully with a file. More serious damage may be repaired by machining, but this is a specialist job.

34 If warpage of the cylinder head is suspected, use a straight-edge to check it for distortion, as described in Chapter 2D, Section 6.

35 Ensure that the cylinder head bolt holes in the crankcase are clean and free of oil. Syringe or soak up any oil left in the bolt holes. This is most important in order that the correct bolt tightening torque can be applied, and to prevent the possibility of the block being cracked by hydraulic pressure when the bolts are tightened.

36 Turn the crankshaft anti-clockwise until all the pistons are at an equal height, approximately halfway down their bores from the TDC position (see Section 3). This will eliminate any risk of piston-to-valve contact as the cylinder head is refitted.

37 To guide the cylinder head into position, screw two long studs (or old cylinder head bolts with the heads cut off, and slots cut in the ends to enable the bolts to be unscrewed) into the cylinder block.

38 Ensure that the cylinder head locating dowels are in place in the cylinder block, then fit the new cylinder head gasket over the dowels, ensuring that the part number is uppermost. Where applicable, the OBEN/TOP marking should also be uppermost. Note that VW recommend that the gasket is only removed from its packaging immediately prior to fitting.

39 Lower the cylinder head into position on the gasket, ensuring that it engages correctly over the guide studs and dowels.

40 Fit the new cylinder head bolts to the eight remaining bolt locations, and screw them in as far as possible by hand.

41 Unscrew the two guide studs from the cylinder block, then screw in the two remaining new cylinder head bolts as far as possible by hand.

42 Working progressively, in sequence, tighten all the cylinder head bolts to the specified Stage 1 torque **(see illustrations)**.

43 Again working progressively, in sequence, tighten all the cylinder head bolts to the specified Stage 2 torque.

44 Tighten all the cylinder head bolts, in sequence, through the specified Stage 3 angle **(see illustration)**.

45 Finally, tighten all the cylinder head bolts, in sequence, through the specified Stage 4 angle.

46 After finally tightening the cylinder head bolts, turn the camshaft so that the cam lobes for No 1 cylinder are pointing upwards.

47 Where applicable, reconnect the lifting tackle to the engine lifting brackets on the cylinder head, then adjust the lifting tackle to support the engine. Once the engine is adequately supported using the cylinder head brackets, disconnect the lifting tackle from the bracket bolted to the cylinder block, and unbolt the improvised engine lifting bracket from the cylinder block. Alternatively, remove the trolley jack and block of wood from under the sump.

48 The remainder of the refitting procedure is a reversal of the removal procedure, bearing in mind the following points.

a) *Refit the inlet manifold as described in Chapter 4A, Section 9.*

b) *Refit the turbocharger as described in Chapter 4A, Section 14.*

13.42b Using a torque wrench to tighten the cylinder head bolts

13.44 Angle-tightening the cylinder head bolts

c) *Refit the vacuum pump as described in Chapter 9, Section 20.*
d) *Refit the timing belt tensioner as described in Section 8.*
e) *Refit the camshaft sprocket as described in Section 8, and refit the timing belt as described in Section 7.*
f) *Refit the camshaft cover as described in Section 4.*
g) *Refill the engine with oil as described in Chapter 1, Section 3.*
h) *Refill the cooling system as described in Chapter 1, Section 30.*

14 Sump –
removal and refitting

Note: *VW sealant (D 176404 A2 or equivalent) will be required to seal the sump on refitting.*

Removal

1 Firmly apply the handbrake, then jack up the front of the vehicle and support it securely on axle stands (see *Jacking and vehicle support*).
2 Where fitted, undo the retaining bolts and remove the engine undertray.
3 Drain the engine oil as described in Chapter 1, Section 3.
4 Where fitted, disconnect the wiring connector from the oil level/temperature sender in the sump **(see illustration)**.
5 Using a wide-bladed scraper or similar tool inserted between the sump and cylinder block, carefully break the joint to release the sump, then manoeuvre the sump out from under the vehicle.
6 If desired, unbolt the oil baffle plate from the cylinder block.

Refitting

7 Begin refitting by thoroughly cleaning the mating faces of the sump and cylinder block. Ensure that all traces of old sealant are removed.
8 Where applicable, refit the oil baffle plate, and tighten the securing bolts.
9 Ensure that the cylinder block mating face of the sump is free from all traces of old sealant, oil and grease, and then apply a 2.0 to 3.0 mm thick bead of silicone sealant (VW D 176404 A2 or equivalent) to the sump **(see illustration)**. Note that the sealant should be run around the inside of the bolt holes in the sump. The sump must be fitted within 5 minutes of applying the sealant.
10 Offer the sump up to the cylinder block, then refit the sump-to-cylinder block bolts, and lightly tighten them by hand, working progressively in a diagonal sequence. **Note:** *If the sump is being refitted with the engine and transmission separated, make sure that the sump is flush with the flywheel end of the cylinder block.*
11 Refit the sump-to-transmission casing bolts, and tighten them lightly, using a socket.
12 Again working in a diagonal sequence,

14.4 Disconnect the wiring connector from the oil level/temperature sender

lightly tighten the sump-to-cylinder block bolts, using a socket.
13 Tighten the sump-to-transmission casing bolts to the specified torque.
14 Working in a diagonal sequence, progressively tighten the sump-to-cylinder block bolts to the specified torque.
15 Refit the wiring connector to the oil level/temperature sender (where fitted), then refit the engine undertray, and lower the vehicle to the ground.
16 Allow at least 30 minutes from the time of refitting the sump for the sealant to dry, then refill the engine with oil, with reference to Chapter 1, Section 3.

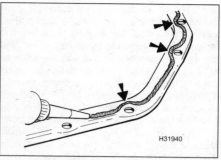

14.9 Apply the sealant around the inside of the bolt holes

15 Oil pump and drive chain –
removal, inspection and refitting

Oil pump
Removal

1 Remove the sump as described in Section 14.
2 Unscrew the securing bolts, and remove the oil baffle from the cylinder block.
3 Unscrew and remove the three mounting bolts, and release the oil pump from the dowels in the crankcase **(see illustration)**.

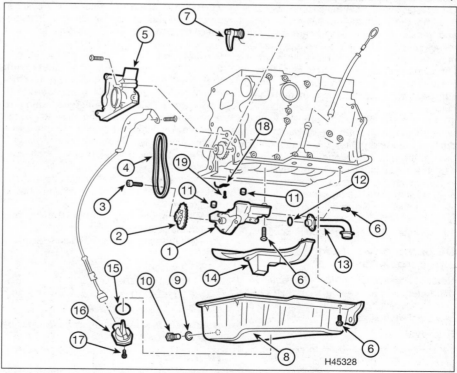

15.3 Sump and oil pump components

1 *Oil pump*	5 *Crankshaft oil seal housing*	9 *Seal*	15 *Seal*
2 *Oil pump sprocket*	6 *Bolt*	10 *Sump drain plug*	16 *Oil level/temperature sender*
3 *Bolt*	7 *Drive chain tensioner*	11 *Dowels*	17 *Bolt*
4 *Oil pump drive chain*	8 *Sump*	12 *O-ring*	18 *Oil spray jet*
		13 *Oil pick-up pipe*	19 *Bolt*
		14 *Oil baffle*	

Unhook the oil pump drive sprocket from the chain and withdraw the oil pump and oil pick-up pipe from the engine. Note that the tensioner will attempt to tighten the chain, and it may be necessary to use a screwdriver to hold it in its released position before releasing the oil pump sprocket from the chain.

4 If desired, unscrew the flange bolts and remove the suction pipe from the oil pump. Recover the O-ring seal. Unscrew the bolts and remove the cover from the oil pump. **Note:** *If the oil pick-up pipe is removed from the oil pump, a new O-ring will be required on refitting.*

Inspection

5 Clean the pump thoroughly, and inspect the gear teeth/rotors for signs of damage or wear. If evident, renew the oil pump.

6 To remove the sprocket from the oil pump, unscrew the retaining bolt and slide off the sprocket (note that the sprocket can only be fitted in one position).

Refitting

7 Prime the pump with oil by pouring oil into the pick-up pipe aperture while turning the driveshaft.

8 Refit the cover to the oil pump and tighten the bolts securely. Where applicable, refit the pick-up pipe to the oil pump, using a new O-ring seal, and tighten the securing bolts.

9 If the drive chain, crankshaft sprocket and tensioner have been removed, delay refitting them until after the oil pump has been mounted on the cylinder block. If they have not been removed, use a screwdriver to press the tensioner against its spring to provide sufficient slack in the chain to refit the oil pump.

10 Engage the oil pump sprocket with the drive chain, then locate the oil pump on the dowels. Refit and tighten the three mounting bolts to the specified torque.

11 Where applicable, refit the drive chain, tensioner and crankshaft sprocket using a reversal of the removal procedure.

12 Refit the oil baffle, and tighten the securing bolts.

13 Refit the sump as described in Section 14.

Oil pump drive chain and sprockets

Note: *VW sealant (D 176404 A2 or equivalent) will be required to seal the crankshaft oil seal housing on refitting, and it is advisable to fit a new crankshaft oil seal.*

Removal

14 Proceed as described in paragraphs 1 and 2.

15 To remove the oil pump sprocket, unscrew the securing bolt, then pull the sprocket from the pump shaft, and unhook it from the drive chain.

16 To remove the chain, remove the timing belt as described in Section 7, then unbolt the crankshaft oil seal housing from the cylinder block. Unbolt the chain tensioner from the

cylinder block, then unhook the chain from the sprocket on the end of the crankshaft.

17 The oil pump drive sprocket is a press-fit on the crankshaft, and cannot easily be removed. Consult a VW dealer for advice if the sprocket is worn or damaged.

Inspection

18 Examine the chain for wear and damage. Wear is usually indicated by excessive lateral play between the links, and excessive noise in operation. It is wise to renew the chain in any case if the engine is to be overhauled. Note that the rollers on a very badly worn chain may be slightly grooved. If there is any doubt as to the condition of the chain, renew it.

19 Examine the teeth on the sprockets for wear. Each tooth forms an inverted V. If worn, the side of each tooth under tension will be slightly concave in shape when compared with the other side of the tooth (ie, the teeth will have a hooked appearance). If the teeth appear worn, the sprocket should be renewed (consult a VW dealer for advice if the crankshaft sprocket is worn or damaged).

Refitting

20 If the oil pump has been removed, refit the oil pump as described previously in this Section before refitting the chain and sprocket.

21 Refit the chain tensioner to the cylinder block, and tighten the securing bolt to the specified torque. Make sure that the tensioner spring is correctly positioned to pretension the tensioner arm.

22 Engage the oil pump sprocket with the chain, then engage the chain with the crankshaft sprocket. Use a screwdriver to press the tensioner against its spring to provide sufficient slack in the chain to engage the sprocket with the oil pump. Note that the sprocket will only fit in one position.

23 Refit the oil pump sprocket bolt, and tighten to the specified torque.

24 Fit a new crankshaft oil seal to the housing, and refit the housing as described in Section 16.

25 Where applicable, refit the oil baffle, and tighten the securing bolts.

26 Refit the sump as described in Section 14.

16 Flywheel – removal, inspection and refitting

Note: *New flywheel securing bolts must be used on refitting.*

Removal

1 Remove the transmission as described in Chapter 7A, Section 6.

2 Remove the clutch assembly as described in Chapter 6, Section 7.

3 The flywheel bolts are offset to ensure correct fitment. Temporarily insert a bolt in the cylinder block, and use a screwdriver to hold the flywheel, or make up a holding tool.

Unscrew the retaining bolts, and remove the flywheel.
Caution: Take care, as the flywheel is heavy.

Inspection

Single-mass (solid) flywheel

4 Either a conventional solid flywheel or a dual-mass flywheel may be fitted according to engine and year of manufacture.

5 Examine the flywheel for wear or chipping of the ring gear teeth. Renewal of the ring gear is not possible and if the wear or chipping is significant, a new flywheel will be required.

6 Examine the flywheel for scoring of the clutch face. If the clutch face is scored significantly, a new flywheel will be required.

7 If there is any doubt about the condition of the flywheel, seek the advice of a VW dealer or engine reconditioning specialist.

Dual-mass flywheel

8 Either a conventional solid flywheel or a dual-mass flywheel may be fitted according to engine and year of manufacture. A dual-mass flywheel has the effect of reducing engine and transmission vibrations and harshness. The flywheel consists of a primary mass and a secondary mass constructed in such a way that the secondary mass is allowed to rotate slightly in relation to this primary mass. Springs within the assembly restrict this movement to set limits.

9 Dual-mass flywheels have earned an unenviable reputation for unreliability and have been known to fail at quite low mileages (sometimes as low as 20 000 miles). As well as the checks described above in paragraphs 5 and 6, some additional checks should be performed as follows.

10 Look through the bolt hole and inspection openings in the secondary mass and check for any visible damage in the area of the centre bearing.

11 Place your thumbs on the clutch face of the secondary mass at the 3 o'clock and 9 o'clock positions and try to rock it. The maximum movement should not exceed 3 mm. Repeat this check with your thumbs at the 12 o'clock and 6 o'clock positions.

12 Rotate the secondary mass clockwise and anti-clockwise. It should move freely in both directions until spring resistance is felt, with no abnormal grating or rattling noises.

13 If there is any doubt about the condition of the flywheel, seek the advice of a VW dealer or engine reconditioning specialist. They will be able to advise if the flywheel is an acceptable condition, or whether renewal is necessary.

Refitting

14 Offer the flywheel to the end of the crankshaft, and align the bolt holes in the crankshaft and flywheel.

15 Coat the threads of the new flywheel bolts with thread-locking compound (note that new bolts may be supplied ready-coated), then fit the bolts and tighten them to the specified

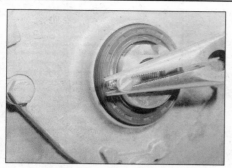

17.2 Removing the crankshaft oil seal using self-tapping screws

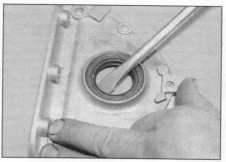

17.3 Prising the oil seal from the crankshaft oil seal housing

17.9 Slide the oil seal housing over the end of the crankshaft

torque, then through the specified angle whilst preventing the flywheel from turning as during removal.

16 Refit the clutch as described in Chapter 6, Section 7 then refit the transmission as described in Chapter 7A, Section 6.

17 Crankshaft oil seals – renewal

Note: *The oil seals are a PTFE (Teflon) type and are fitted dry, without using any grease or oil. These have a wider sealing lip and have been introduced instead of the coil spring type oil seal.*

Note: *If the oil seal housing is removed, suitable sealant (VW D 176 404 A2, or equivalent) will be required to seal the housing on refitting.*

Right-hand oil seal

1 Remove the timing belt as described in Section 7, and the crankshaft sprocket with reference to Section 8.

2 To remove the seal without removing the housing, drill two small holes diagonally opposite each other, insert self-tapping screws, and pull on the heads of the screws with pliers **(see illustration)**.

3 Alternatively, to remove the oil seal complete with its housing, proceed as follows.

  a) *Remove the sump as described in Section 14. This is necessary to ensure a satisfactory seal between the sump and oil seal housing on refitting.*

  b) *Unbolt and remove the oil seal housing.*

  c) *Working on the bench, lever the oil seal from the housing using a suitable screwdriver. Take care not to damage the seal seating in the housing (see illustration).*

4 Thoroughly clean the oil seal seating in the housing.

5 Wind a length of tape around the end of the crankshaft to protect the oil seal lips as the seal (and housing, where applicable) is fitted.

6 Fit a new oil seal to the housing, pressing or driving it into position using a socket or tube of suitable diameter. Ensure that the socket or tube bears only on the hard outer ring of the seal, and take care not to damage the seal

lips. Press or drive the seal into position until it is seated on the shoulder in the housing. Make sure that the closed end of the seal is facing outwards.

7 If the oil seal housing has been removed, proceed as follows, otherwise proceed to paragraph 11.

8 Clean all traces of old sealant from the crankshaft oil seal housing and the cylinder block, then coat the cylinder block mating faces of the oil seal housing with a 2.0 to 3.0 mm thick bead of sealant (VW D 176 404 A2, or equivalent). Note that the seal housing must be refitted within 5 minutes of applying the sealant.

Caution: DO NOT put excessive amounts of sealant onto the housing as it may get into the sump and block the oil pick-up pipe.

9 Refit the oil seal housing, and tighten the bolts progressively to the specified torque **(see illustration)**.

10 Refit the sump as described in Section 14.

11 Refit the crankshaft sprocket with reference to Section 8, and the timing belt as described in Section 7.

Left-hand oil seal

Engine codes AXB and AXC

12 Remove the flywheel as described in Section 16.

13 Remove the sump as described in Section 14. This is necessary to ensure a satisfactory seal between the sump and oil seal housing on refitting.

14 Unbolt and remove the oil seal housing, complete with the oil seal.

15 The new oil seal will be supplied ready-fitted to a new oil seal housing.

16 Thoroughly clean the oil seal housing mating face on the cylinder block.

17 New oil seal/housing assemblies are supplied with a fitting tool to prevent damage to the oil seal as it is being fitted. Locate the tool over the end of the crankshaft **(see illustration)**.

18 If the original oil seal housing was fitted using sealant, apply a thin bead of suitable sealant (VW D 176 404 A2, or equivalent) to the cylinder block mating face of the oil seal housing. Note that the seal housing must be refitted within 5 minutes of applying the sealant.

Caution: DO NOT put excessive amounts of sealant onto the housing as it may get into the sump and block the oil pick-up pipe.

19 Carefully fit the oil seal/housing assembly over the end of the crankshaft, then refit the securing bolts and tighten the bolts progressively, in a diagonal sequence, to the specified torque **(see illustration)**.

20 Remove the oil seal protector tool from the end of the crankshaft.

21 Refit the sump as described in Section 14.

22 Refit the flywheel as described in Section 16.

Engine codes BRR and BRS

Note: *In these engines, the seal, sealing flange and sender wheel are a complete unit. Special tools are required to refit the sealing flange, and press the sender wheel onto the end of the crankshaft. It is not possible to accurately fit these parts without the tools, which may be*

17.17 Locate the crankshaft oil seal fitting tool over the end of the crankshaft – engine codes AXB and AXC

17.19 Fit the oil seal/housing assembly over the end of the crankshaft – engine codes AXB and AXC

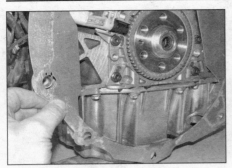

17.23a Remove the intermediate plate from the dowels...

17.23b ...and from behind the top of the crankshaft seal housing – engine codes BRR and BRS

17.24a Undo the crankshaft speed sensor retaining bolt (arrowed) – engine codes BRR and BRS

17.24b Sealing flange bolts (arrowed) – engine codes BRR and BRS

17.25a Screw in three 6 x 35 mm bolts...

17.25b ...and draw off the sealing flange and sender wheel – engine codes BRR and BRS

available from VW (part no. T10134) or from aftermarket automotive tool specialists.
23 Remove the flywheel as described in Section 16, then prise the intermediate plate

from the locating dowels on the cylinder block and unhook it from behind the top of the seal housing (see illustrations).
24 Undo the bolt securing the crankshaft

speed sensor and remove it from the seal housing, then undo the bolts securing the sealing flange to the cylinder block (see illustrations).
25 Insert three 6 x 35 mm bolts into the threaded holes in the sealing flange. Tighten the bolts gradually and evenly, and press the sealing flange, and sender wheel from the crankshaft/cylinder block (see illustrations). The seal, sender wheel and sealing flange are supplied as a complete unit.
26 Ensure the mating face of the cylinder block is clean and free from debris. The new sealing flange/seal/sender wheel assembly is supplied with a sealing lip support ring, which serves as a fitting sleeve, and must not be removed prior to installation. Equally, the sender wheel must not be separated from the assembly.
27 If using the VW tool, proceed as follows. If using an aftermarket tool specialist's product, follow the instructions supplied with the tool. Rotate the large spindle nut until it's level with the end of the clamping surface of the spindle, then clamp the spindle in a vice (see illustrations).
28 Press the tool housing downwards until it rests on the nut and washer. Rotate the nut until the inner part of the tool is at the same height as the housing (see illustrations).
29 Remove the seal securing clip. The hole on the sender wheel must align with the marking on the sealing flange (see illustrations).
30 Place the flange outer side down on a clean, flat surface, then press the seal guide

17.27a Rotate the nut until its level with the end of the flat clamping surface...

17.27b ...then clamp it in a vice – engine codes BRR and BRS

17.28a Rotate the nut until the inner part of the tool...

17.28b ...is flush with the flat surface of the housing – engine codes BRR and BRS

17.29a Remove the securing clip...

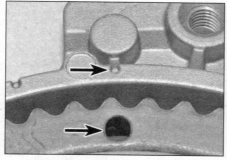

17.29b ...the hole in the sender wheel should align with the marking on the flange (arrowed) – engine codes BRR and BRS

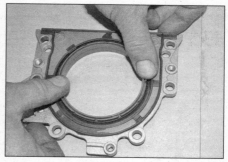

17.30a Press the assembly downwards on a clean, flat surface...

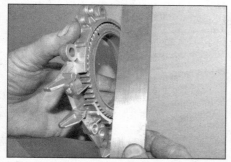

17.30b ...so the upper edge of the sender wheel is level with the edge of the flange – engine codes BRR and BRS

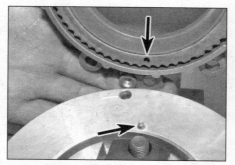

17.31 Fit the flange to the tool, ensuring the pin locates in the hole (arrowed) – engine codes BRR and BRS

17.32 With the pin engaged, tighten the 3 knurled screws to secure the flange to the tool – engine codes BRR and BRS

fitting sleeve (supplied ready fitted), housing, and sender wheel downwards until all the components are flat on the surface. In this position the upper edge of the sender wheel should be level with the edge of the sealing flange (see illustrations).

31 Place the sealing flange on the assembly tool, so the pin locates in the hole in the sender wheel (see illustration).

32 Push the sealing flange and guide fitting sleeve against the tool whilst tightening the 3 knurled screws. Ensure the pin is still located in the sender wheel (see illustration).

33 Ensure the end of the crankshaft is clean, and is locked at TDC on No. 1 cylinder as described in Section 3.

34 Unscrew the large nut to the end of the spindle threads, then press the spindle inwards as far as possible (see illustrations).

35 Align the flat side of the assembly with the sump flange, then secure the tool to the crankshaft using the integral Allen bolts (see illustration). Only hand tighten the bolts.

36 Insert two M7x 35 mm bolts to guide the sealing flange to the cylinder block (see illustration).

37 Using hand pressure alone, push the tool assembly onto the crankshaft until the seal guide fitting sleeve contacts the crankshaft flange, then push the guide pin (black knob) into the hole in the crankshaft. This is to ensure the sender wheel reaches its correct installation position (see illustration).

38 Rotate the large nut until it makes contact with the tool housing, then tighten it to 35 Nm.

After tightening this nut, a small air gap must still be present between the sealing flange and cylinder block (see illustrations).

17.34a Unscrew the nut to the end of the thread...

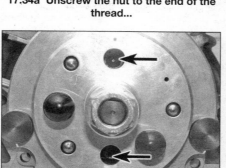

17.35 Hand-tighten the Allen bolts (arrowed), to secure the tool to the crankshaft – engine codes BRR and BRS

39 Unscrew the large nut; the two M7 x 35 mm bolts, the three knurled screws and the Allen bolts securing the tool to the crankshaft.

17.34b ...and push the spindle in as far as possible – engine codes BRR and BRS

17.36 Use two M7 x 35 mm bolts (arrowed) to guide the sealing flange – engine codes BRR and BRS

17.37 Push the black knob into the hole in the crankshaft – engine codes BRR and BRS

17.38a After tightening the spindle nut to 35 Nm...

17.38b ...there should be an air gap between the sealing flange and the cylinder block (arrowed) – engine codes BRR and BRS

Remove the tool, and pull the seal guide fitting sleeve from place (if it didn't come out with the tool) **(see illustration)**.

40 Use a vernier caliper or feeler gauge to measure the fitted depth of the sender wheel in relation to the crankshaft flange **(see illustration)**. The correct depth is 0.5 mm.

41 If the gap is correct, fit the sealing flange bolts and tighten them to the specified torque.

42 If the gap is too small, re-attach the tool to the sealing flange and crankshaft, then refit the two M7 x 35 mm guide bolts to the flange. Tighten the large spindle nut to 40 Nm, remove the tool and re-measure the air gap. If the gap is still too small, re-attach the tool and tighten the spindle nut to 45 Nm. Re-measure the gap. When the gap is correct, refit the flange retaining bolts, and tighten them to the specified torque.

43 The remainder of refitting is a reversal of removal.

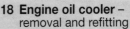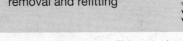

18 Engine oil cooler – removal and refitting

Note: *New sealing rings will be required on refitting.*

Removal

1 The oil cooler is mounted under the oil filter housing on the front of the cylinder block.

2 According to model, undo the retaining bolts and rotary fasteners and remove the battery cover and engine covers as applicable.

17.39 Remove the tool and seal fitting guide sleeve – engine codes BRR and BRS

3 Position a container beneath the oil filter to catch escaping oil and coolant.

4 Clamp the oil cooler coolant hoses to minimise coolant spillage, then remove the clips, and disconnect the hoses from the oil cooler. Be prepared for coolant spillage.

5 Unscrew the oil cooler securing plate from the bottom of the oil filter housing, then slide off the oil cooler. Recover the O-rings from the top and bottom of the oil cooler.

Refitting

6 Refitting is a reversal of removal, bearing in mind the following points:

  a) Use new oil cooler O-rings.
  b) Tighten the oil cooler securing plate to the specified torque.
  c) On completion, check and if necessary top up the oil and coolant levels.

19 Oil pressure warning light switch – removal and refitting

Removal

1 The oil pressure warning light switch is fitted to the side of the oil filter housing. According to model, undo the retaining bolts and rotary fasteners and remove the battery cover and engine covers as applicable.

2 Disconnect the wiring connector and wipe clean the area around the switch.

3 Unscrew the switch from the filter housing

17.40 Measure the fitted depth of the sender wheel in relation to the end of the crankshaft – engine codes BRR and BRS

and remove it, along with its sealing washer. If the switch is to be left removed from the engine for any length of time, plug the oil filter housing aperture.

Refitting

4 Examine the sealing washer for signs of damage or deterioration and if necessary renew.

5 Refit the switch, complete with washer, and tighten it to the specified torque.

6 Securely reconnect the wiring connector then check and, if necessary, top-up the engine oil as described in *Weekly checks*. On completion, refit the engine top cover(s).

20 Engine/transmission mountings – inspection and renewal

Inspection

1 Firmly apply the handbrake, then jack up the front of the vehicle and support it securely on axle stands (see *Jacking and vehicle support*).

2 Where applicable, undo the retaining bolts and remove the engine undertray. According to model, undo the retaining bolts and rotary fasteners and remove the battery cover and engine covers as applicable.

3 Check the mounting blocks (rubbers) to see if they are cracked, hardened or separated from the metal at any point. Renew the mounting block if any such damage or deterioration is evident.

4 Check that all the mounting securing nuts and bolts are securely tightened, using a torque wrench to check if possible.

5 Using a large screwdriver, or a similar tool, check for wear in the mounting blocks by carefully levering against them to check for free play. Where this is not possible, enlist the aid of an assistant to move the engine/transmission unit back-and-forth, and from side-to-side, while you observe the mountings. While some free play is to be expected, even from new components, excessive wear should be obvious. If excessive free play is found, check first to see that the securing nuts and bolts are correctly tightened, then renew any worn components as described in the following paragraphs.

Renewal

Note: *New mounting retaining bolts will be required for refitting.*

Right-hand mounting

6 Disconnect the battery negative terminal (refer to *Disconnecting the battery*).

7 Firmly apply the handbrake, then jack up the front of the vehicle and support it securely on axle stands (see *Jacking and vehicle support*).

8 Where applicable, undo the retaining bolts and remove the engine undertray. According to model, undo the retaining bolts and rotary fasteners and remove the battery cover and engine covers as applicable.

9 Remove the air duct and hoses between the intercooler and turbocharger. For improved access, remove the air cleaner assembly as described in Chapter 4A, Section 2.

10 Position a trolley jack underneath the sump with an interposed block of wood between the jack head and the sump.

11 Raise the jack until it just takes the weight of the engine off the right-hand mounting.

12 Undo the three bolts securing the mounting bracket to the engine bracket **(see illustration)**.

13 Undo the three bolts securing the mounting to the body and remove the mounting and mounting bracket assembly.

14 Refitting is a reversal of removal, tightening the new retaining bolts to the specified torque.

Left-hand mounting

15 Disconnect the battery negative terminal (refer to *Disconnecting the battery*).

16 Firmly apply the handbrake, then jack up the front of the vehicle and support it securely on axle stands (see *Jacking and vehicle support*). Remove the left-hand roadwheel.

17 Where applicable, undo the retaining bolts and remove the engine undertray. According to model, undo the retaining bolts and rotary fasteners and remove the battery cover and engine covers as applicable.

18 Position a trolley jack underneath the transmission with an interposed block of wood between the jack head and the transmission casing. Raise the jack until it just takes the weight of the transmission.

19 Undo the two bolts securing the left-hand mounting to the underbody **(see illustration)**.

20 Undo the three bolts securing the mounting bracket to the transmission. Lower the jack slightly and manipulate the mounting out from under the left-hand wheel arch.

21 Refitting is a reversal of removal, tightening the new retaining bolts to the specified torque.

Front mounting

22 Disconnect the battery negative terminal (refer to *Disconnecting the battery*).

23 Firmly apply the handbrake, then jack up the front of the vehicle and support it securely on axle stands (see *Jacking and vehicle support*).

24 Where applicable, undo the retaining bolts and remove the engine undertray. According to model, undo the retaining bolts and rotary fasteners and remove the battery cover and engine covers as applicable.

25 Undo the front engine/transmission mounting through-bolt **(see illustration)**.

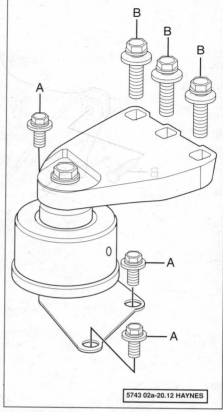

20.12 Right-hand engine/transmission mounting attachments

A Mounting to body retaining bolts
B Mounting bracket to engine bracket retaining bolts

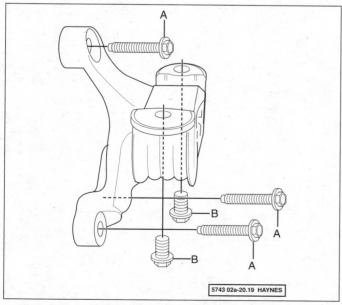

20.19 Left-hand engine/transmission mounting attachments

A Mounting bracket to transmission retaining bolts
B Mounting to underbody retaining bolts

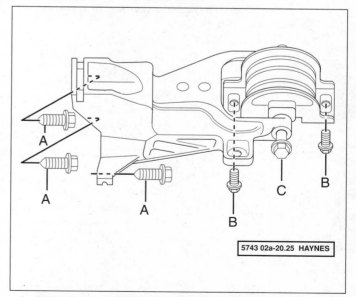

20.25 Front engine/transmission mounting attachments

A Mounting bracket to cylinder block retaining bolts
B Mounting to subframe retaining bolts
C Mounting through-bolt

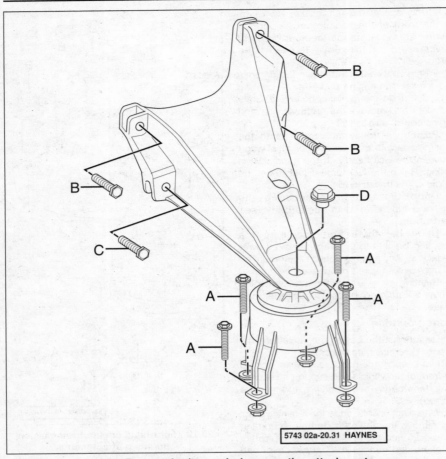

5743 02a-20.31 HAYNES

20.31 Rear engine/transmission mounting attachments

A *Mounting to subframe retaining bolts*
B and C *Engine bracket to cylinder block retaining bolts*
D *Engine bracket to mounting through-bolt*

26 Undo the two bolts securing the mounting to the subframe and remove the mounting from the mounting bracket. If required the mounting bracket can be removed after undoing the three retaining bolts.

27 Refitting is a reversal of removal, tightening the new retaining bolts to the specified torque.

Rear mounting

28 Disconnect the battery negative terminal (refer to *Disconnecting the battery*).

29 Firmly apply the handbrake, then jack up the front of the vehicle and support it securely on axle stands (see *Jacking and vehicle support*). Remove the left-hand roadwheel.

30 Where applicable, undo the retaining bolts and remove the engine undertray. According to model, undo the retaining bolts and rotary fasteners and remove the battery cover and engine covers as applicable.

31 Undo the through bolt securing the engine bracket to the rear mounting **(see illustration)**.

32 Undo the four nuts and remove the bolts securing the mounting 'legs' to the subframe.

33 Undo the four bolts securing the engine bracket to the cylinder block. Remove the engine bracket, then lift the rear mounting off the subframe.

34 Refitting is a reversal of removal, tightening the new retaining bolts to the specified torque.

Chapter 2 Part B:
2.0 litre engine in-vehicle repair procedures

Contents

Degrees of difficulty

Easy, suitable for novice with little experience	Fairly easy, suitable for beginner with some experience	Fairly difficult, suitable for competent DIY mechanic	Difficult, suitable for experienced DIY mechanic	Very difficult, suitable for expert DIY or professional

Specifications

General

Engine type.	4-cylinder, in-line, double overhead camshaft
Engine codes:	
62 kW engines	CAAA
75 kW engines	CAAB
84 kW engines	CAAD
100 kW engines	CAAE and CCHB
103 kW engines	CAAC and CCHA
Capacity.	1968 cc
Bore	81.0 mm
Stroke.	95.5 mm
Compression ratio	16.5 : 1
Compression pressures:	
Minimum compression pressure	Approximately 19.0 bar
Maximum difference between cylinders	Approximately 5.0 bar
Firing order	1 – 3 – 4 – 2 (No 1 cylinder at timing belt end)
Direction of crankshaft rotation	Clockwise (seen from right-hand side of vehicle)

Lubrication system

Oil pump type.	Gear type, chain-driven from crankshaft
Oil pressure (oil temperature 80°C, at 2000 rpm).	1.0 bar (minimum)

Torque wrench settings

	Nm	lbf ft
Ancillary (alternator, etc) bracket mounting bolts:*		
Stage 1	40	30
Stage 2	Angle-tighten a further 90°	
Auxiliary drivebelt tensioner securing bolt:		
Stage 1	20	15
Stage 2	Angle-tighten a further 90°	
Balance shaft drivegear bolts:*		
Stage 1	20	15
Stage 2	Angle-tighten a further 90°	
Balance shaft housing to cylinder block:*		
M7:		
Stage 1	13	10
Stage 2	Angle-tighten a further 90°	
M8:		
Stage 1	20	15
Stage 2	Angle-tighten a further 90°	
Balance shaft idler gear:*		
Stage 1	90	66
Stage 2	Angle-tighten a further 90°	
Big-end bearing caps bolts:*		
Stage 1	30	22
Stage 2	Angle-tighten a further 90°	
Camshaft bearing frame bolts/nut	10	7
Camshaft cover bolts	10	7
Camshaft sprocket hub centre bolt	100	74
Camshaft sprocket-to-hub bolts:*		
Stage 1	20	15
Stage 2	Angle-tighten a further 45°	
Crankshaft oil seal housing bolts	15	11
Crankshaft pulley-to-sprocket bolts:*		
Stage 1	10	7
Stage 2	Angle-tighten a further 90°	
Crankshaft sprocket bolt:*		
Stage 1	180	133
Stage 2	Angle-tighten a further 135°	
Cylinder head bolts:*		
Stage 1	35	26
Stage 2	60	44
Stage 3	Angle-tighten a further 90°	
Stage 4	Angle-tighten a further 90°	
Engine/transmission mountings:*		
Front mounting through-bolt		
Stage 1	90	66
Stage 2	Angle-tighten a further 180°	
Front mounting bracket-to-cylinder block:		
Stage 1	20	15
Stage 2	Angle-tighten a further 900°	
Front mounting-to-subframe bolts:		
Stage 1	20	15
Stage 2	Angle-tighten a further 90°	
Left-hand mounting-to-body bolts:		
Stage 1	50	37
Stage 2	Angle-tighten a further 90°	
Left-hand mounting-to-transmission bolts:		
Stage 1	50	37
Stage 2	Angle-tighten a further 90°	
Right-hand engine bracket-to-cylinder block:		
Stage 1	40	30
Stage 2	Angle-tighten a further 180°	
Right-hand mounting-to-body bolts:		
Stage 1	50	37
Stage 2	Angle-tighten a further 90°	
Right-hand mounting-to-engine bracket bolts:		
Stage 1	50	37
Stage 2	Angle-tighten a further 90°	

Torque wrench settings (continued)

	Nm	lbf ft
Engine/transmission mountings:* (continued)		
Right-hand mounting through-bolt:		
Stage 1	90	66
Stage 2	Angle-tighten a further 90°	
Rear mounting engine bracket-to-cylinder block:		
Small bolt:		
Stage 1	20	15
Stage 2	Angle-tighten a further 90°	
Large bolts:		
Stage 1	50	37
Stage 2	Angle-tighten a further 90°	
Rear mounting-to-subframe nuts:		
Stage 1	20	15
Stage 2	Angle-tighten a further 180°	
Rear mounting through-bolt:		
Stage 1	50	37
Stage 2	Angle-tighten a further 90°	
Flywheel:*		
Stage 1	60	44
Stage 2	Angle-tighten a further 90°	
Fuel pump hub nut	95	70
Fuel pump sprocket bolts:*		
Stage 1	20	15
Stage 2	Angle-tighten a further 90°	
Intermediate gear bolt:*		
Stage 1	90	66
Stage 2	Angle-tighten a further 90°	
Main bearing cap bolts:*		
Stage 1	65	48
Stage 2	Angle-tighten a further 90°	
Oil cooler bolts	11	7
Oil drain plug*	30	22
Oil filter housing-to-cylinder block bolts:*		
Stage 1	14	10
Stage 2	Angle-tighten a further 180°	
Oil filter cap	25	18
Oil level/temperature sensor-to-sump bolts	10	7
Oil pick-up pipe securing bolts	10	7
Oil pressure warning light switch	22	16
Oil pump-to-balance shaft bolts	10	7
Oli pump-to-cylinder block bolts	15	11
Piston oil spray jet bolt	25	18
Roadwheel bolts	180	133
Sump:		
Sump-to-cylinder block bolts	15	11
Sump-to-transmission bolts	40	30
Timing belt outer cover bolts	10	7
Timing belt tensioner roller securing nut:		
Stage 1	20	15
Stage 2	Angle-tighten a further 45°	
Timing belt idler pulleys:		
Lower idler roller nut	20	15
Upper idler roller (small) bolt	20	15
Upper idler roller (large) bolt:*		
Stage 1	50	37
Stage 2	Angle-tighten a further 90°	

*Use new bolts

1 General information

How to use this Chapter

This Part of Chapter 2 describes those repair procedures that can reasonably be carried out on the engine while it remains in the vehicle. If the engine has been removed from the vehicle and is being dismantled as described in Part D, any preliminary dismantling procedures can be ignored.

Note that while it may be possible physically to overhaul certain items while the engine is in the vehicle, such tasks are not usually carried out as separate operations, and usually require the execution of several additional procedures (not to mention the cleaning of components and of oilways); for this reason, all such tasks are classed as major overhaul procedures, and are described in Part D of this Chapter.

Engine description

Throughout this Chapter, engines are

referred to by type, and are often identified and referred to by the manufacturer's code letters. A listing of all engines covered, together with their code letters, is given in the Specifications at the start of this Chapter.

The engines are water-cooled, double overhead camshafts (DOHC), in-line four-cylinder units, with cast-iron cylinder blocks and aluminium-silicon alloy cylinder heads. All are mounted transversely at the front of the vehicle, with the transmission bolted to the left-hand end of the engine.

The crankshaft is of five-bearing type, and thrustwashers are fitted to the centre main bearing to control crankshaft endfloat.

Drive for the exhaust camshaft is by a toothed timing belt from the crankshaft, with the intake camshaft driven by interlocking gears at the left-hand end of both camshafts. The gears incorporate a toothed backlash compensator element. Each camshaft is mounted at the top of the cylinder head, and is secured by a bearing frame/ladder.

The valves are closed by coil springs, and run in guides pressed into the cylinder head. The valves are operated by roller rocker arms incorporating hydraulic tappets.

Engine codes CCHA, CCHB, CFCA and CAAD are equipped with a twin, counter-rotating balance shaft assembly, fitted to the base of the cylinder block. The rearmost balance shaft is driven by a gear on the crankshaft, via an intermediate gear bolted to the balance shaft housing. The two balance shafts are geared together.

On engines without a balance shaft, the gear-type oil pump is driven via a toothed drive belt from a sprocket on the crankshaft. On engines with a balance shaft, the oil pump is driven by the front balance shaft. On all engines, oil is drawn from the sump through a strainer, and then forced through an externally-mounted, renewable filter. From there, it is distributed to the cylinder head, where it lubricates the camshaft journals and hydraulic tappets, and also to the crankcase, where it lubricates the main bearings, connecting rod big-ends, gudgeon pins and cylinder bores. A coolant-fed oil cooler is fitted to the oil filter housing on all engines. Oil jets are fitted to the base of each cylinder – these spray oil onto the underside of the pistons, to improve cooling.

All engines are fitted with a brake servo vacuum pump driven by the camshaft on the transmission end of the cylinder head.

On all engines, engine coolant is circulated by a pump, driven by the timing belt. For details of the cooling system, refer to Chapter 3.

Repairs possible with the engine installed in the vehicle

The following operations can be performed without removing the engine:

a) Compression pressure – testing.
b) Camshaft cover – removal and refitting.
c) Crankshaft pulley – removal and refitting.
d) Timing belt covers – removal and refitting.

e) Timing belt – removal, refitting and adjustment.
f) Timing belt tensioner and sprockets – removal and refitting.
g) Camshaft oil seals – renewal.
h) Camshafts and hydraulic tappets – removal, inspection and refitting.
i) Cylinder head – removal and refitting.
j) Cylinder head and pistons – decarbonising.
k) Sump – removal and refitting.
l) Oil pump – removal, overhaul and refitting.
m) Crankshaft oil seals – renewal.
n) Engine/transmission mountings – inspection and renewal.
o) Flywheel – removal, inspection and refitting.

Note: *It is possible to remove the pistons and connecting rods (after removing the cylinder head and sump) without removing the engine. However, this is not recommended. Work of this nature is more easily and thoroughly completed with the engine on the bench, as described in Chapter 2D.*

2 Compression and leakdown tests – description and interpretation

Compression test

Note: *A compression tester suitable for use with diesel engines will be required for this test.*

1 When engine performance is down, or if misfiring occurs which cannot be attributed to the ignition or fuel systems, a compression test can provide diagnostic clues as to the engine's condition. If the test is performed regularly, it can give warning of trouble before any other symptoms become apparent.

2 The engine must be fully warmed-up to normal operating temperature, the battery must be fully charged, and you will require the aid of an assistant.

3 Remove the glow plugs as described in Chapter 5, Section 13, and then fit a compression tester to the No 1 cylinder glow plug hole. The type of tester that bolts into the plug thread is preferred. **Note:** *Part of the glow plug removal procedure is to disconnect the fuel injector wiring plugs. As a result of the plugs being disconnected and the engine cranked, faults will be stored in the ECU memory. On completion of the test it will be necessary to have the fault codes cleared by a VW dealer or suitably equipped garage, using specialist diagnostic equipment.*

4 Have your assistant crank the engine for several seconds on the starter motor. After one or two revolutions, the compression pressure should build-up to a maximum figure and then stabilise. Record the highest reading obtained.

5 Repeat the test on the remaining cylinders, recording the pressure in each.

6 The cause of poor compression is less easy to establish on a diesel engine than on a petrol engine. The effect of introducing oil into the cylinders (wet testing) is not conclusive, because there is a risk that the oil will sit in the recess on the piston crown, instead of passing to the rings. However, the following can be used as a rough guide to diagnosis.

7 All cylinders should produce very similar pressures. Any difference greater than that specified indicates the existence of a fault. Note that the compression should build-up quickly in a healthy engine. Low compression on the first stroke, followed by gradually increasing pressure on successive strokes, indicates worn piston rings. A low compression reading on the first stroke, which does not build-up during successive strokes, indicates leaking valves or a blown head gasket (a cracked head could also be the cause).

8 A low reading from two adjacent cylinders is almost certainly due to the head gasket having blown between them and the presence of coolant in the engine oil will confirm this.

9 On completion, remove the compression tester, and refit the glow plugs, with reference to Chapter 5, Section 13.

Leakdown test

10 A leakdown test measures the rate at which compressed air fed into the cylinder is lost. It is an alternative to a compression test, and in many ways it is better, since the escaping air provides easy identification of where pressure loss is occurring (piston rings, valves or head gasket).

11 The equipment required for leakdown testing is unlikely to be available to the home mechanic. If poor compression is suspected, have the test performed by a suitably equipped garage.

3 Engine assembly and valve timing marks – general information and usage

General information

1 TDC is the highest point in the cylinder that each piston reaches as it travels up-and-down when the crankshaft turns. Each piston reaches TDC at the end of the compression stroke and again at the end of the exhaust stroke, but TDC generally refers to piston position on the compression stroke. No 1 piston is at the timing belt end of the engine.

2 Positioning No 1 piston at TDC is an essential part of many procedures, such as timing belt removal and camshaft removal.

3 The design of the engines covered in this Chapter is such that piston-to-valve contact may occur if the camshaft or crankshaft is turned with the timing belt removed. For this reason, it is important to ensure that the camshaft and crankshaft do not move in relation to each other once the timing belt has been removed from the engine.

3.7 The alignment mark (arrowed) on the crankshaft sprocket should be almost vertical

3.8a Fit the tool to the hole in the oil seal housing (arrowed)...

3.8b ...so the marks on the tool and sprocket align (arrowed)

Setting TDC on No 1 cylinder

Note: *VW special tool T10050 (or a suitable alternative) is required to lock the crankshaft sprocket in the TDC position.*

4 Remove the auxiliary drivebelt as described in Chapter 1, Section 27.

5 Remove the crankshaft pulley as described in Section 5.

6 Remove the timing belt outer covers as described in Section 6.

7 Using a spanner or socket on the crankshaft sprocket bolt, turn the crankshaft in the normal direction of rotation (clockwise) until the alignment mark on the face of the sprocket is almost vertical, and the hole in the camshaft sprocket hub aligns with the hole in the cylinder head **(see illustration)**.

8 While in this position it should be possible to insert the VW tool T10050 to lock the crankshaft, and a 6 mm diameter rod/drill bit to lock the camshafts **(see illustrations)**. **Note:** *The mark on the crankshaft sprocket and the mark on the VW tool must align, whilst at the same time the shaft of the tool must engage in the drilling in the crankshaft oil seal housing.*

9 The engine is now set to TDC on No 1 cylinder.

4 Camshaft cover – removal and refitting

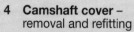

Removal

1 Remove the fuel injectors as described in Chapter 4B, Section 8 and the fuel rail as described in Chapter 4B, Section 11.

2 Remove the timing belt upper cover as described in Section 6.

3 Note their fitted positions, then disconnect the relevant vacuum hoses from the camshaft cover, and release them and the wiring loom from the retaining clips.

4 Squeeze together the sides of the collar, and disconnect the breather hose from the camshaft cover.

5 Detach the coolant hose from the clips on the cylinder head cover.

6 Release the wiring from the clips at the rear

3.8c Insert a 6 mm drill bit/rod to lock the camshaft hub (arrowed)...

of the cover, then unscrew the camshaft cover retaining bolts and lift the cover away. If the cover sticks, do not attempt to lever it off – instead free it by working around the cover and tapping it lightly with a soft-faced mallet.

7 Recover the camshaft cover gasket. Inspect the gasket carefully, and renew it if damage or deterioration is evident – note that the retaining bolts and seals must be pushed fully through the cover **(see illustration)**.

8 Clean the mating surfaces of the cylinder head and camshaft cover thoroughly, removing all traces of oil – take care to avoid damaging the surfaces as you do this.

Refitting

9 Refit the camshaft cover by following the removal procedure in reverse, tightening the cover retaining bolts to the specified torque in a diagonal sequence.

4.7 Renew the cover seal if necessary

3.8d ...with the arrow on the sprocket almost at the 12 o'clock position

5 Crankshaft pulley – removal and refitting

Removal

1 Remove the auxiliary drivebelt as described in Chapter 1, Section 27.

2 Unscrew the bolts securing the pulley to the sprocket, and remove the pulley **(see illustration)**. If necessary, the pulley can be prevented from turning by counterholding with a spanner or socket on the crankshaft sprocket bolt.

Refitting

3 Refit the pulley over the locating peg on the crankshaft sprocket, then refit the pulley securing bolts.

5.2 Undo the pulley bolts, counterholding it with a socket on the centre sprocket bolt

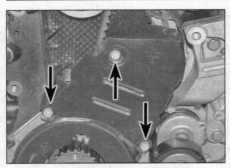

6.9 Centre timing belt cover bolts (arrowed)

4 Prevent the crankshaft from turning as during removal, then fit the pulley securing bolts, and tighten to the specified torque.

5 Refit the auxiliary drivebelt as described in Chapter 1, Section 27.

6 Timing belt covers – removal and refitting

Upper outer cover

1 According to model, undo the retaining bolts and rotary fasteners and remove the battery cover and engine covers as applicable.

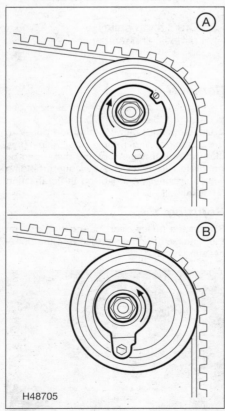

H48705

7.0 Two types of tensioner type (A) and (B)

A Roller tensions clockwise
B Roller tensions anti-clockwise

6.13 Lower cover retaining bolts (arrowed)

2 Pull the inlet manifold pressure sensor out of the air cleaner air duct, then release the retaining clip and detach the air duct from the air cleaner assembly.

3 Release the wiring harness from the top of the upper cover.

4 Prise open the three metal spring clips, then withdraw the upper cover from the engine.

5 Refitting is a reversal of removal, noting that the lower edge of the upper cover engages with the centre cover.

Centre outer cover

6 Remove the auxiliary drivebelt as described in Chapter 1, Section 27.

7 Remove the upper outer cover as described previously.

8 Remove the air duct and hoses between the intercooler and turbocharger.

9 Unscrew and remove the retaining bolts from the centre cover (see illustration). Withdraw the centre cover from the engine, noting how it fits over the lower cover. Note that if the auxiliary drivebelt tensioner is in the 'locked' position as described in the belt removal procedure, the locking drill bit/rod must be removed for access to the cover retaining bolt.

10 Refitting is a reversal of removal.

Lower outer cover

11 Remove the upper and centre covers as described previously.

12 If not already done, remove the crankshaft pulley as described in Section 5.

13 Unscrew the remaining bolts securing the lower cover, and remove it (see illustration).

7.4 Slacken the sprocket-to-hub bolts (arrowed)

14 Refitting is a reversal of removal; locate the centre cover in place before fitting the top two bolts.

Rear cover

15 Remove the timing belt, tensioner and sprockets as described in Section 7 and Section 8.

16 Slacken and withdraw the retaining bolts and lift the timing belt inner cover from the studs on the end of the engine, and remove it from the engine compartment.

17 Refitting is a reversal of removal.

7 Timing belt – removal, inspection and refitting

Note: *There are two types of tensioner fitted to this engine and they are not interchangeable (see illustration). Check to see which type is fitted before removing the timing belt. Type A tensioner requires a locking pin for installation and it tensions the belt by rotating clockwise. Type B tensioner does not require a locking pin for installation and it tensions the belt by rotating anti-clockwise. See text.*

Removal

1 The primary function of the toothed timing belt is to drive the camshaft, but it also drives the coolant pump and high-pressure fuel pump. Should the belt slip or break in service, the valve timing will be disturbed and piston-to-valve contact may occur, resulting in serious engine damage. For this reason, it is important that the timing belt is tensioned correctly, and inspected regularly for signs of wear or deterioration.

2 Disconnect the battery negative terminal (refer to *Disconnecting the battery*).

3 Set the engine to TDC on No1 cylinder as described in Section 3.

4 Slacken the three bolts securing the sprocket to the camshaft hub (see illustration).

5 Slacken the three bolts securing the sprocket to the high-pressure fuel pump (see illustration).

Type A tensioner

6 Insert a suitable Allen key into the tensioner hub, then slacken the retaining nut and rotate

7.5 Slacken the high-pressure fuel pump sprocket bolts (arrowed)

7.6 Insert an Allen key, slacken the nut, and rotate the hub anti-clockwise until a 2 mm rod/drill bit (arrowed) can be inserted to lock the hub to the pulley

7.7 Rotate the tensioner hub clockwise until it hits the stop

7.15 Rotate the high-pressure fuel pump clockwise until a 6 mm drill bit/rod can be inserted into the housing and hub (arrowed)

the tensioner hub anti-clockwise until it can be locked in place using a 2.0 mm pin/drill bit **(see illustration)**.

7 Leaving the pin in place, now rotate the tensioner hub clockwise to the stop, and hand-tighten the retaining nut **(see illustration)**.

Type B tensioner

8 Insert a suitable Allen key into the tensioner hub, then slacken the retaining nut and rotate the tensioner hub clockwise to relieve the tension on the timing belt. Hand tighten the retaining nut.

All engines

9 If the original timing belt is to be refitted, mark the running direction of the belt, to ensure correct refitting.

Caution: If the belt appears to be in good condition and can be re-used, it is essential that it is refitted the same way around, otherwise accelerated wear will result, leading to premature failure.

10 Slide the belt from the sprockets, taking care not to twist or kink the belt excessively if it is to be re-used.

Inspection

11 Examine the belt for evidence of contamination by coolant or lubricant. If this is the case, find the source of the contamination before progressing any further. Check the belt for signs of wear or damage, particularly around the leading edges of the belt teeth. Renew the belt if its condition is in doubt; the cost of belt renewal is negligible compared with potential cost of the engine repairs, should the belt fail in service. The belt must be renewed if it has covered the mileage given in Chapter 1, however, if it has covered less, it is prudent to renew it regardless of condition, as a precautionary measure.

12 If the timing belt is not going to be refitted for some time, it is a wise precaution to hang a warning label on the steering wheel, to remind yourself (and others) not to attempt to start the engine.

Refitting

13 Ensure that the crankshaft and camshaft are still set to TDC on No 1 cylinder, as described in Section 3. The camshaft sprocket

bolts should be renewed, and slackened at this point.

14 Renew the high-pressure fuel pump sprocket bolts one at a time. They should be kept loose.

15 Using a screwdriver on the bolts heads, rotate the high-pressure fuel pump clockwise until a 6.0 mm locking pin/drill bit can be inserted into the housing adjacent to the sprocket, locking the pump in place **(see illustration)**.

16 Rotate the camshaft sprocket and high-pressure fuel pump sprocket fully clockwise so that the securing bolts are at the end of the elongated holes **(see illustrations)**.

17 Loop the timing belt loosely under the crankshaft sprocket. **Note:** *Observe any direction of rotation markings on the belt.*

18 Fit the belt around the tensioner pulley,

7.16a Rotate the sprockets fully clockwise until the fuel pump sprocket...

7.19 Timing belt routing

engage the timing belt teeth with the camshaft sprockets, then manoeuvre it into position around the coolant pump sprocket and the fuel pump sprocket. Make sure that the belt teeth seat correctly on the sprockets. **Note:** *Slight adjustment to the position of the camshaft sprocket may be necessary to achieve this. Avoid bending the belt back on itself or twisting it excessively as you do this.*

19 Finally, fit the belt around the idler roller **(see illustration)**. Ensure that any slack in the belt is in the section of belt that passes over the tensioner roller.

Type A tensioner

20 Loosen the timing belt tensioner securing nut, and pull out the tensioner locking pin. Turn the tensioner clockwise with an Allen key until the pointer is just past the middle of the gap in the tensioner backplate **(see illustrations)**.

7.16b ...and camshaft sprocket bolts are at the end of the elongated holes

7.20a Rotate the tensioner clockwise...

7.20b ...until the pointer (arrowed) is just past the gap in the base plate

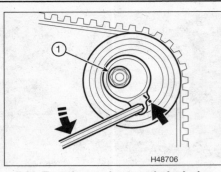

7.21 Turn the tensioner anti-clockwise until the mark on the moving segment is aligned with the mark on the fixed segment, then tighten the retaining nut (1)

7.22a Counterhold the camshaft sprocket...

7.22b ...and the pump sprocket, while the bolts are tightened

7.23a Remove the upper locking pins...

7.23b ...and crankshaft locking tool

With the tensioner held in this position, tighten the securing nut to the specified torque and angle.

Type B tensioner

21 Loosen the timing belt tensioner securing nut. Turn the tensioner anti-clockwise with an Allen key until the mark on the moving segment is aligned with the mark on the fixed segment **(see illustration)**. With the tensioner held in this position, tighten the securing nut to the specified torque and angle.

All engines

22 Counterhold the camshaft sprocket and fuel pump sprocket with a homemade tool to prevent any rotation, and then tighten the camshaft sprocket and fuel pump sprocket bolts to 20 Nm (15 lbf ft) **(see illustrations)**.

7.25 The pointer (arrowed) should be centred in, or within 5 mm to the right of, the gap in the backplate

23 Remove the sprockets locking tools and the crankshaft locking tool **(see illustrations)**.
24 Using a spanner or wrench and socket on the crankshaft pulley centre bolt, rotate the crankshaft clockwise through two complete revolutions. Reset the engine to TDC on No1 cylinder, with reference to Section 3 and refit the crankshaft locking tool.
25 On the early type tensioner, check that the tensioner roller indicator arm is centred, or within a maximum of 5 mm to the right of the gap in the backplate **(see illustration)**. If not, hold the tensioner hub stationary with an Allen key, slacken the retaining nut and position the arm in the centre of the notch. Tighten the retaining nut to the specified torque. Remove the Allen key.
26 On the later type tensioner, check that the marks on the moving segment and fixed segment are still aligned. If not, slacken the retaining nut, reposition the moving segment with an Allen key, then tighten the retaining nut to the specified torque. Remove the Allen key.
27 Check that the camshaft sprocket locking pin can still be inserted. **Note:** *It's very difficult to align the locking point of the fuel pump hub again. However, a misalignment of holes will not affect engine performance.*
28 If the camshaft sprocket locking pin cannot be inserted, pull the crankshaft locking tool slight away from the engine, and rotate the crankshaft *anti-clockwise* slightly past TDC. Now slowly rotate the crankshaft clockwise until the camshaft sprocket locking tool can be inserted.
29 If the locating pin of the crankshaft locking

tool is to the left of the corresponding hole, slacken the camshaft sprocket bolts, slowly rotate the crankshaft clockwise until the locking tool can be fully inserted. Tighten the camshaft sprocket bolts to 20 Nm (15 lbf ft).
30 If the locating pin of the crankshaft locking tool is to the right of the corresponding hole, slacken the camshaft sprocket bolts, rotate the crankshaft *anti-clockwise* slightly until the pin is to the left of the hole, then slowly rotate it clockwise until the lock tool can be fully inserted. Tighten the camshaft sprocket bolts to 20 Nm (15 lbf ft).
31 Remove the crankshaft and camshaft locking tools, then rotate the crankshaft two complete revolutions clockwise and check the locking tools can be reinserted. If necessary, repeat the adjustment procedure described previously.
32 Tighten the camshaft and fuel pump sprocket bolts to the specified torque.
33 The remainder of refitting is a reversal of removal.

---

8 Timing belt tensioner and sprockets –
removal and refitting

Timing belt tensioner

Removal

1 In order to remove the timing belt tensioner, then engine mounting bracket must first be removed. Either support the engine from above using a crossbeam or an engine hoist, or support if from underneath with a trolley jack and block of wood.

2 Remove the timing belt as described in Section 7.

3 Undo the bolts and remove the right-hand engine mounting.

4 Undo the 3 retaining bolts and remove the engine mounting bracket **(see illustration)**.

5 Unscrew the timing belt tensioner nut, and remove the tensioner from the engine.

Refitting

6 When refitting the type A tensioner to the engine, ensure that the lug on the tensioner backplate engages with the corresponding cut-out in the rear timing belt cover, then refit the tensioner nut **(see illustration)**.

7 The remainder of refitting is a reversal of removal.

Idler pulleys

Removal

8 Remove the timing belt as described in Section 7.

9 Unscrew the relevant idler pulley/roller securing bolt/nut, and then withdraw the pulley **(see illustration)**.

Refitting

10 Refit the pulley and tighten the securing bolt or nut to the specified torque. **Note:** *Renew the large roller/pulley retaining bolt (where applicable).*

11 Refit and tension the timing belt as described in Section 7.

Crankshaft sprocket

Note: *A new crankshaft sprocket securing bolt must be used on refitting.*

Removal

12 Remove the timing belt as described in Section 7.

13 The sprocket securing bolt must now be slackened, and the crankshaft must be prevented from turning as the sprocket bolt is unscrewed. To hold the sprocket, make up a suitable tool, and bolt it to the sprocket using two bolts bolted into two of the crankshaft pulley bolt holes.

14 Hold the sprocket using the tool, then slacken the sprocket securing bolt. Take care, as the bolt is very tight. Do not allow the crankshaft to turn as the bolt is slackened.

15 Unscrew the bolt, and slide the sprocket from the end of the crankshaft, noting which way round the sprocket's raised boss is fitted. If required, use a puller to withdraw the sprocket from the end of the crankshaft **(see illustration)**.

Refitting

16 Commence refitting by positioning the sprocket on the end of the crankshaft.

17 Fit a new sprocket securing bolt, then counter hold the sprocket using the method employed on removal, and tighten the bolt to the specified torque in the two stages given in the Specifications.

8.4 Engine mounting bracket bolts (arrowed)

18 Refit the timing belt as described in Section 7.

Camshaft sprocket

Removal

19 Remove the timing belt as described in Section 7, then rotate the crankshaft 90° anti-clockwise to prevent any accidental piston-to-valve contact.

20 Unscrew and remove the three retaining bolts and remove the camshaft sprocket from the camshaft hub.

Refitting

21 Refit the sprocket ensuring that it is fitted the correct way round, as noted before removal, then insert the new sprocket bolts, and tighten by hand only at this stage.

22 If the crankshaft has been turned, turn the crankshaft clockwise 90° back to TDC.

8.9 Timing belt idler pulleys

8.25 Fabricate a home-made tool to counterhold the hub. Undo the bolt...

8.6 Ensure the lug on the backplate engages with the cut-out in the timing belt cover (arrowed)

23 Refit and tension the timing belt as described in Section 7.

Camshaft hub

Note: *VW technicians use special tool T10051 to counter hold the hub, however it is possible to fabricate a suitable alternative.*

Removal

24 Remove the camshaft sprocket as described previously in this Section.

25 Engage special tool T10051 with the three locating holes in the face of the hub to prevent the hub from turning. If this tool is not available, fabricate a suitable alternative. Whilst holding the tool, undo the central hub retaining bolt about two turns **(see illustration)**.

26 Slide the hub from the camshaft. If necessary, attach VW tool T10052 (or a similar three-legged puller) to the hub, and evenly tighten the puller until the hub is free of the camshaft taper **(see illustration)**.

8.15 Using a puller to remove the crankshaft sprocket

8.26 ...and slide the hub from the camshaft

8.27 Ensure the integral key aligns with the keyway in the camshaft (arrowed)

Refitting

27 Ensure that the camshaft taper and the hub centre are clean and dry, locate the hub on the taper, noting that the built-in key in the hub taper must align with the keyway in the camshaft taper **(see illustration)**.

28 Hold the hub in this position with tool T10051 (or similar home-made tool), and tighten the central bolt to the specified torque.

29 Refit the camshaft sprocket as described previously in this Section.

Coolant pump sprocket

30 The coolant pump sprocket is integral with the coolant pump. Refer to Chapter 3 for details of coolant pump removal.

---

9 Camshaft and hydraulic tappets – removal, inspection and refitting

---

Note: *A new camshaft oil seal(s) will be required on refitting. VW removal tool T40094 (or similar tool) will be required to refit the camshafts – this is necessary to prevent damage to the retaining frame and cylinder head as the camshafts are refitted.*

Removal

1 Remove the camshaft hub as described in Section 8.

2 Remove the camshaft cover as described in Section 4.

3 Remove the brake vacuum pump as described in Chapter 9, Section 20.

4 Undo the EGR cooler upper retaining bolt at the left-hand and right-hand ends of the cooler.

5 Progressively unscrew the camshaft retaining frame bolts in the **reverse** of the sequence shown in illustration 9.20, and carefully remove the retaining frame.

6 Carefully lift the camshafts from the cylinder head, keeping them identified for location. Remove the oil seal from the end of the camshaft and discard it – a new one will be required for refitting.

7 Lift the rocker arms and hydraulic tappets from the cylinder head. Store the rockers and tappets in a container with numbered compartments to ensure they are refitted to their correct locations.

8 Thoroughly clean the retaining frame and cylinder head mating faces, ensuring all traces of old sealant are removed.

Inspection

9 With the camshafts removed, examine the retaining frame and the bearing locations in the cylinder head for signs of obvious wear or pitting. If evident, a new cylinder head will probably be required. Also check that the oil supply holes in the cylinder head are free from obstructions.

10 Visually inspect the camshafts for evidence of wear on the surfaces of the lobes and journals. Normally their surfaces should be smooth and have a dull shine; look for scoring, erosion or pitting and areas that appear highly polished, indicating excessive wear. Accelerated wear will occur once the hardened exterior of the camshaft has been damaged, so always renew worn items. **Note:**

If these symptoms are visible on the tips of the camshaft lobes, check the corresponding rocker arm, as it will probably be worn as well.

11 If the machined surfaces of the camshaft appear discoloured or blued, it is likely that it has been overheated at some point, probably due to inadequate lubrication. This may have distorted the shaft, so have the camshaft runout and endfloat checked by an automotive engine reconditioning specialist.

12 Inspect the hydraulic tappets for obvious signs of wear or damage, and renew if necessary. Check that the oil holes in the tappets are free from obstructions.

Refitting

13 Oil the rocker arms and hydraulic tappets, and then refit them to their original positions.

⚠️ *Warning: After fitting hydraulic tappets, wait a minimum of 30 minutes (or preferably, leave overnight) before starting the engine, to allow the tappets time to settle, otherwise the valve heads will strike the pistons.*

14 To set up the tool, remove the supports number 3, 4 and 5, then install the supports number 1, 2, 9 and 10 as shown **(see illustrations)**.

15 Position the inlet camshaft as shown with the cylinder head bolt indent facing outwards, then slide the support number 8 into the slot in the end of the camshaft and remove any free play with a 0.50 mm feeler gauge **(see illustration)**.

16 Position the exhaust camshaft on supports numbers 9 and 10, and fit the tool No 11 into the slot in the end of the camshaft **(see illustration)**.

17 Fit the clamping tool No T40096 to the gear on the exhaust camshaft, tightening the knurled thumb wheel until the faces of the gear teeth are in alignment. If necessary, use a 13 mm spanner **(see illustration)**.

18 Slide the exhaust camshaft towards the inlet camshaft until the gear teeth engage.

19 Ensure the gasket faces of the retaining

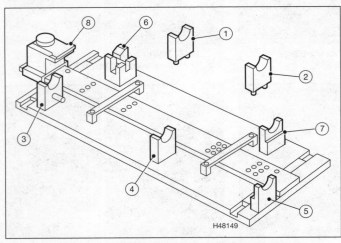

9.14a The different elements of tool No T40094

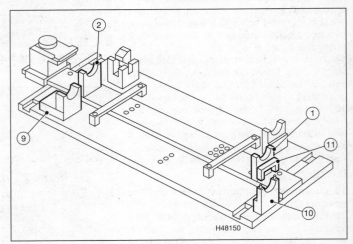

9.14b Position tools No 1, 2, 9 and 10 as shown

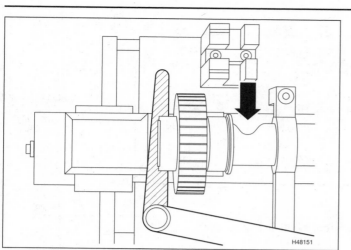

9.15 Position the inlet camshaft on the tool with the bolt indent (arrowed) facing outwards, then slide tool No 8 in to the slot in the end of the camshaft and use a 0.50 mm feeler gauge to remove any free play

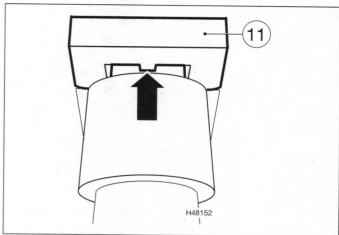

9.16 Fit tool No 11 into the slot (arrowed) in the end of the exhaust camshaft

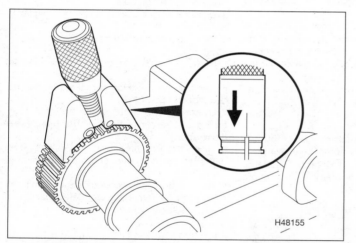

9.17 Tighten the thumb wheel to align the gear teeth. Ensure the clamping jaw with the arrow is seated on the wider gear

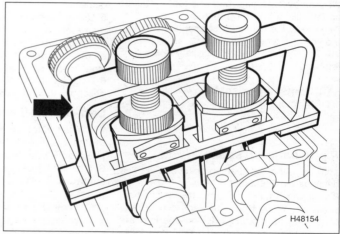

9.20 Secure the camshafts in place in the frame using tool No T40095 (arrowed)

frame are clean, then apply a smear of clean engine oil to the bearing surfaces and lower the frame into position over the camshafts. Ensure the bearing surfaces locate correctly on the camshafts.

20 Fit the clamping tool No T40095 over the camshafts and frame, and tighten the thumb wheels to hold the camshafts in position in the frame (see illustration).

21 Ensure the sealing surfaces of the cylinder head are clean, and then apply a 2.0 mm wide bead of sealant (D 176 501 A1 or equivalent) as shown. Take care not to apply too much sealant, ensuring the oil holes supply holes are not blocked (see illustration).

22 Slide out tool No's 8 and 11, then lift the camshafts, retaining frame and clamping tool from the tool No T40094. Place the camshafts, frame and tool in place on the cylinder head. Progressively and carefully, hand-tighten the frame retaining bolts in the sequence shown,

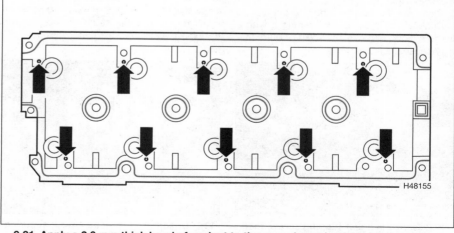

9.21 Apply a 2.0 mm thick bead of sealant to the area shown by the thick, black line. Take care not to block the oil holes (arrowed)

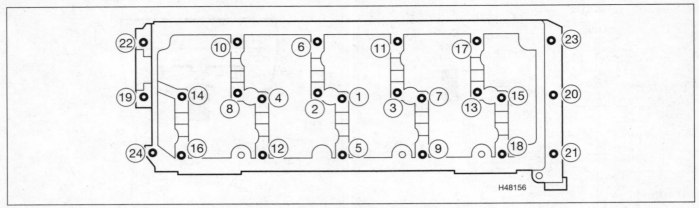

9.22 Camshaft retaining frame bolt tightening sequence

until the retaining frame makes contact with the cylinder head over the complete surface, then tighten the bolts to the specified torque, again in the correct sequence **(see illustration)**.

23 Remove the gear aligning tool (T40096) and the clamping tool (T40095).

24 Renew the camshaft oil seal (Section 10), then drive in a new sealing cap.

25 The remainder of refitting is a reversal of removal.

10 Camshaft oil seals – renewal

Right-hand oil seal

1 Remove the camshaft sprocket and hub, as described in Section 8.

2 Drill two small holes into the existing oil seal, diagonally opposite each other. Take great care to avoid drilling through into the seal housing or camshaft sealing surface. Thread two self-tapping screws into the holes, and using a pair of pliers, pull on the heads of the screws to extract the oil seal **(see illustration)**.

3 Clean out the seal housing and the sealing surface of the camshaft by wiping it with a lint-free cloth. Remove any swarf or burrs that may cause the seal to leak.

10.2 Screw in a self-tapping screw, then pull the screw to extract the seal

4 Do not lubricate the lip and outer edge of the new oil seal, push it over the camshaft until it is positioned in place above its housing. To prevent damage to the sealing lips, wrap some adhesive tape around the end of the camshaft.

5 Using a hammer and a socket of suitable diameter, drive the seal squarely into its housing. **Note:** *Select a socket that bears only on the hard outer surface of the seal, not the inner lip that can easily be damaged.*

6 Refit the camshaft sprocket and its hub, as described in Section 8.

Left-hand oil seal

7 The left-hand camshaft oil seal is formed, by the brake vacuum pump seal, which is fitted to the cylinder head. Refer to Chapter 9, Section 20 for details of brake vacuum pump removal and refitting.

11 Cylinder head – removal, inspection and refitting

Note: *The cylinder head must be removed with the engine cold. New cylinder head bolts and a new cylinder head gasket will be required on refitting, and suitable studs will be required to guide the cylinder head into position – see text.*

11.7 Unscrew the bolt (arrowed) securing the rear timing belt cover to the cylinder head

Removal

1 Disconnect the battery negative terminal (refer to *Disconnecting the battery*).

2 Drain the cooling system as described in Chapter 1, Section 30.

3 Drain the engine oil as described in Chapter 1, Section 3.

4 Remove the camshaft cover as described in Section 4.

5 Remove the timing belt as described in Section 7.

6 Remove the camshaft sprocket and hub as described in Section 8.

7 Unscrew the bolt securing the rear timing belt cover to the cylinder head **(see illustration)**.

8 Undo the retaining bolt and release the camshaft position sensor from the cylinder head.

9 Release the wiring connector and loom from the cooling system expansion tank, then undo the two bolts and move the expansion tank to one side.

10 Remove the diesel particulate filter as described in Chapter 4A, Section 15.

11 Remove the turbocharger as described in Chapter 4B, Section 15.

12 Remove the EGR cooler as described in Chapter 4C, Section 2.

13 Pull back the heat shield, then disconnect the wiring connector from the oil pressure warning light switch on the left-hand end of the cylinder head.

14 Remove the inlet manifold as described in Chapter 4B, Section 9.

15 Disconnect the vacuum hose from the vacuum pump at the left-hand end of the cylinder head.

16 Disconnect the wiring connector from the coolant temperature sensor at the left-hand end of the cylinder head.

17 Note their fitted locations, then release the clamps and disconnect the various coolant hoses from the cylinder head.

18 Make a final check to ensure all relevant wiring and vacuum hoses have been disconnected. Note the loom/hose routing to aid refitting. Using an M12 multi-splined tool (12-pointed star), undo the cylinder head bolts, working from the outside-in, evenly and gradually. Remove the bolts and recover the washers. Check that nothing remains connected, and starting at the transmission end, lift the cylinder head from the engine block, sliding the belt tensioner from the mounting stud as the cylinder head is removed. Seek assistance if possible, as it is a heavy assembly.

19 Remove the gasket from the top of the block, noting the locating dowels. If the dowels are a loose fit, remove them and store them with the head for safekeeping. Do not discard the gasket yet – it will be needed for identification purposes.

Inspection

20 Dismantling and inspection of the cylinder head is covered in Chapter 2D, Section 6.

Cylinder head gasket selection

Note: *A dial test indicator (DTI) will be required for this operation.*

21 Examine the old cylinder head gasket for manufacturer's identification markings **(see illustration)**. These will be in the form of holes, and a part number on the edge of the gasket. Unless new pistons have been fitted, the new cylinder head gasket must be of the same type as the old one.

22 If new piston assemblies have been fitted as part of an engine overhaul, or if a new short engine is to be fitted, the projection of the piston crowns above the cylinder head mating face of the cylinder block at TDC must be measured. This measurement is used to determine the thickness of the new cylinder head gasket required.

23 Anchor a dial test indicator (DTI) to the top face (cylinder head gasket mating face) of the cylinder block, and zero the gauge on the gasket mating face.

24 Rest the gauge probe on No 1 piston crown, and turn the crankshaft slowly by hand until the piston reaches TDC. Measure and record the maximum piston projection at TDC **(see illustration)**.

25 Repeat the measurement for the remaining pistons, and record the results.

26 If the measurements differ from piston-to-piston, take the highest figure, and use this to determine the thickness of the head gasket required as follows.

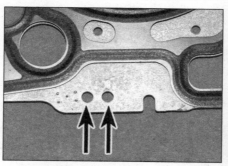

11.21 The holes (arrowed) identify the thickness of the cylinder head gasket

Piston projection	Gasket identification (number of holes)
0.91 to 1.00 mm	1
1.01 to 1.10 mm	2
1.11 to 1.20 mm	3

27 Purchase a new gasket according to the results of the measurements.

Refitting

28 The mating faces of the cylinder head and block must be perfectly clean before refitting the head. Use a scraper to remove all traces of gasket and carbon, also clean the tops of the pistons. Take particular care with the aluminium surfaces, as the soft metal is easily damaged.

29 Make sure that debris is not allowed to enter the oil and water passages – this is particularly important for the oil circuit, as carbon could block the oil supply to the camshaft and crankshaft bearings. Using adhesive tape and paper, seal the water, oil and bolt holes in the cylinder block.

30 To prevent carbon entering the gap between the pistons and bores, smear a little grease in the gap. After cleaning a piston, rotate the crankshaft to that the piston moves down the bore, and then wipe out the grease and carbon with a cloth rag. Clean the other piston crowns in the same way.

31 Check the head and block for nicks, deep scratches and other damage. If slight, they may be removed carefully with a file. More serious damage may be repaired by machining, but this is a specialist job.

32 If warpage of the cylinder head is suspected, use a straight-edge to check it

11.24 Measure the piston protrusion using a DTI guage

for distortion, as described in Chapter 2D, Section 6.

33 Ensure that the cylinder head bolt holes in the crankcase are clean and free of oil. Syringe or soak up any oil left in the bolt holes. This is most important in order that the correct bolt tightening torque can be applied, and to prevent the possibility of the block being cracked by hydraulic pressure when the bolts are tightened.

34 Turn the crankshaft anti-clockwise all the pistons at an equal height, approximately halfway down their bores from the TDC position (see Section 3). This will eliminate any risk of piston-to-valve contact as the cylinder head is refitted.

35 Ensure that the cylinder head locating dowels are in place in the cylinder block, and then fit the new cylinder head gasket over the dowels, ensuring that the part number is uppermost **(see illustration)**. Note that VW recommend that the gasket is only removed from its packaging immediately prior to fitting.

36 Lower the cylinder head into position on the gasket, ensuring that it engages correctly over the dowels. Refit the timing belt tensioner as the cylinder head is refitted.

37 Fit the washers in place then fit the new cylinder head bolts to the locations, and bolt them in as far as possible by hand. Do not oil the bolt threads.

38 Working progressively, in sequence, tighten all the cylinder head bolts to the specified Stage 1 torque **(see illustrations)**.

39 Again working progressively, in sequence, tighten all the cylinder head bolts to the specified Stage 2 torque.

11.35 Ensure the dowels are in place, then fit the new gasket with the part number uppermost (arrowed)

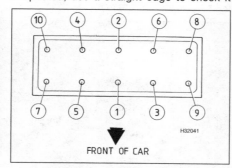

11.38a Cylinder head bolt tightening sequence

FRONT OF CAR

H32041

11.38b Tighten the cylinder head bolts to the Stage 1 torque

11.40 Use an angle-tightening gauge

12.5 Electric coolant circulation pump retaining bolt (arrowed)

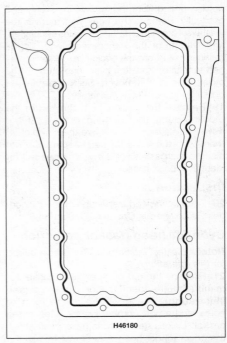

12.8 Apply a bead of sealant around the inside of the bolt holes

40 Tighten all the cylinder head bolts, in sequence, through the specified Stage 3 angle **(see illustration)**.
41 Finally, tighten all the cylinder head bolts, in sequence, through the specified Stage 4 angle.
42 The remainder of the refitting procedure is a reversal of the removal procedure, noting the following points:
  a) *Tighten all fasteners to their specified torque where given.*
  b) *Renew all seals and gaskets.*
  c) *Refill the engine oil, as described in Chapter 1, Section 3.*
  d) *Refill the cooling system, as described in Chapter 1, Section 30.*
  e) *Ensure all wiring is correctly routed.*

12 Sump –
removal and refitting

Removal

1 Firmly apply the handbrake, then jack up the front of the vehicle and support it securely on axle stands (see *Jacking and vehicle support*).
2 Where fitted, undo the retaining bolts and remove the engine undertray.
3 Drain the engine oil as described in Chapter 1, Section 3.
4 Where fitted, disconnect the wiring connector from the oil level/temperature sender in the sump.
5 Undo the retaining bolt and move the electric coolant circulation pump to one side **(see illustration)**.

6 Unscrew and remove the bolts securing the sump to the cylinder block, and the bolts securing the sump to the transmission casing, then withdraw the sump. If necessary, release the sump by tapping with a soft-faced hammer.

Refitting

7 Begin refitting by thoroughly cleaning the mating faces of the sump and cylinder block. Ensure that all traces of old sealant are removed.
8 Ensure that the cylinder block mating face of the sump is free from all traces of old sealant, oil and grease, and then apply a 2.0 to 3.0 mm thick bead of silicone sealant (VW D 176 404 A2 or equivalent) to the sump **(see illustration)**. Note that the sealant should be run around the inside of the bolt holes in the sump. The sump must be fitted within 5 minutes of applying the sealant.
9 Offer the sump up to the cylinder block, then refit the sump-to-cylinder block bolts, and lightly tighten them by hand, working progressively in a diagonal sequence. **Note:** *If the sump is being refitted with the engine and transmission separated, make sure that the sump is flush with the flywheel end of the cylinder block.*
10 Refit the sump-to-transmission casing bolts, and tighten them lightly, using a socket.
11 Again working in a diagonal sequence, lightly tighten the sump-to-cylinder block bolts, using a socket.
12 Tighten the sump-to-transmission casing bolts to the specified torque.

13 Working in a diagonal sequence, progressively tighten the sump-to-cylinder block bolts to the specified torque.
14 The remainder of refitting is a reversal of removal, noting to allow at least 30 minutes from the time of refitting the sump for the sealant to dry, then refill the engine with oil, with reference to Chapter 1, Section 3.

13 Oil pump (engines without a balance shaft) – removal, inspection and refitting

Removal

1 Remove the sump as described in Section 12.
2 Unscrew the flange bolts and remove the oil pick-up pipe/filter from the oil pump **(see illustration)**. Recover the O-ring seal and discard, as a new one will be required for refitting.
3 Unscrew the securing bolt, and remove the oil baffle from the cylinder block **(see illustration)**.
4 Unscrew and remove the mounting bolts, and release the oil pump from the dowels in the crankcase **(see illustration)**. Unhook the oil pump drive sprocket from the belt and withdraw the oil pump from the engine. Note that the bolt holding the baffle plate is also one of the pump mounting bolts.

Inspection

5 At the time of writing, it would appear that no parts are available for the oil pump. If defective, the oil pump assembly must be renewed. Consult a VW dealer or parts specialist.

13.2 Remove the oil pick-up pipe/filter from the oil pump

13.3 Unscrew the securing bolt, and remove the oil baffle from the cylinder block

Refitting

6 Prime the pump with oil by pouring oil into the pick-up pipe aperture while turning the sprocket.

7 Engage the oil pump sprocket with the toothed drive belt, then locate the oil pump on the dowels. Place the oil baffle plate in position then refit and tighten the three mounting bolts to the specified torque.

8 Refit the pick-up pipe to the oil pump, using a new O-ring seal, and tighten the securing bolts **(see illustration)**.

9 Refit the sump as described in Section 12.

13.4 Oil pump mounting bolts (arrowed)

13.8 Fit a new seal to the end of the oil pick-up pipe

14 Oil pump and balance shaft assembly – removal, inspection and refitting

Removal

1 Remove the sump as described in Section 12.

Oil pump

2 Remove the retaining circlip, then pull the oil pump shaft out using an M3 bolt **(see illustrations)**.

3 Undo the retaining bolts, and then detach the pick-up pipe from the pump **(see illustration)**.

4 Undo the bolts and detach the oil pump from the balance shaft assembly **(see illustration)**.

Balance shaft assembly

5 Lock the camshafts and crankshaft at TDC on No 1 cylinder as described in Section 3.

6 Working gradually and evenly, undo the retaining bolts and detach the balance shaft assembly from the base of the cylinder block.

Inspection

7 At the time of writing, it would appear that no parts are available for the oil pump or balance shaft assembly. If defective, the oil pump or balance shaft assembly must be renewed. Consult a VW dealer or parts specialist.

Refitting

Oil pump

8 Refit the pump to the balance shaft assembly and tighten the retaining bolts to the specified torque.

9 Refit the oil pick-up pipe using a new O-ring, then tighten the retaining bolts to the specified torque **(see illustration)**.

10 Push the driveshaft into place, and secure it with the circlip.

11 The remainder of refitting is a reversal of removal.

Balance shaft assembly

Note: *If the original balance shaft assembly is being refitted, it's essential that neither the drivegear on the crankshaft or the crankshaft itself has been renewed, or the idler gear bolt has been slackened. If they have, proceed under the heading for the installation of a new balance shaft assembly*.

Refitting the original assembly

12 Rotate the balance shaft until VW tool No T10255 can be fitted into the groove on the left-hand end of the rear shaft **(see illustrations)**.

13 Ensure the engine is still locked at TDC for

14.2a Remove the circlip...

14.2b ...and pull out the oil pump shaft using an M3 bolt

14.3 Oil pump pick-up pipe bolts (arrowed)

14.4 Oil pump mounting bolts (arrowed)

14.9 Renew the pick-up pipe O-ring seal

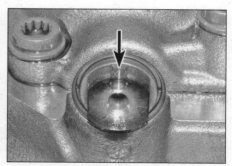

14.12a Rotate the balance shaft until the groove (arrowed) on the end of the rear shaft is vertical...

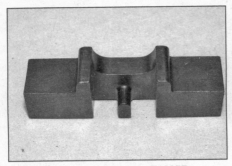

14.12b ...and tool No T10255...

14.12c ...can be fitted

No 1 cylinder, and then position the balance shaft assembly over the locating dowels on the base of the cylinder block. The idler gear must engage with the drivegear of the crankshaft, and there must be noticeable backlash.

14 Fit the new balance shaft assembly retaining bolts, and working from the centre outwards, tighten them to the specified torque. Remove the VW tool.

15 The remainder of refitting is a reversal of removal.

Fitting a new balance shaft assembly

16 New balance shaft assemblies are supplied with an idler gear with a special coating. Once fitted, the coating wears down to give the correct backlash between the gears.

17 Ensure the engine is still locked at TDC for No 1 cylinder as described in Section 3.

18 Slacken the idler gear retaining bolt 90°.

19 Position the balance shaft assembly over the locating dowels on the base of the cylinder block, ensuring the white mark on the idler gear is centrally aligned with the crankshaft drivegear. Idler gears not marked with a white mark can be installed in any position.

20 Fit the new balance shaft assembly retaining bolts, and working from the centre outwards, tighten them to the specified torque.

21 Rotate the balance shaft until VW tool No T10255 can be fitted into the groove on the left-hand end of the rear shaft **(see illustration 14.12a, 14.12b and 14.12c)**.

22 Fit the balance shaft drivegear onto the shaft so the holes in the gear align with the

holes in the shaft. Tighten the retaining bolts to the specified torque.

23 Have an assistant push the idler gear between the two gears to remove any backlash. At the same time, rotate the balance shaft anti-clockwise slightly, and tighten the idler gear retaining bolt to the specified torque. Remove the balance shaft locking tool.

24 The remainder of refitting is a reversal of removal.

---

15 Flywheel –
removal, inspection
and refitting

Removal

1 Remove the transmission as described in Chapter 7A, Section 6.

2 Remove the clutch assembly as described in Chapter 6, Section 7.

3 Rotate the outside of the dual-mass flywheel so that the bolts align with the holes (if necessary).

4 Unscrew the bolts and remove the flywheel. Use a locking tool to counterhold the flywheel **(see illustration)**. Discard the bolts, as new ones must be fitted. **Note:** *In order not to damage the flywheel, do not allow the bolt heads to make contact with the flywheel during the unscrewing procedure.*

Inspection

5 Check the flywheel for wear and damage. Examine the starter ring gear for excessive wear to the teeth. The ring gear may be

renewed separately from the flywheel, but the work should be entrusted to a VW dealer. If the clutch friction face is discoloured or scored excessively, it may be possible to regrind it, but this work should also be entrusted to a VW dealer.

6 The following are *guidelines* only, but should indicate whether professional inspection is necessary. The dual-mass flywheel should be checked as follows:

There should be no cracks in the drive surface of the flywheel. If cracks are evident, the flywheel may need renewing.

Warpage

Place a straightedge across the face of the drive surface, and check by trying to insert a feeler gauge between the straightedge and the drive surface **(see illustration)**. The flywheel will normally warp like a bowl – i.e. higher on the outer edge. If the warpage is more than 0.40 mm, the flywheel may need renewing.

Free rotational movement

This is the distance the drive surface of the flywheel can be turned independently of the flywheel primary element, using finger effort alone. Move the drive surface in one direction and make a mark where the locating pin aligns with the flywheel edge. Move the drive surface in the other direction (finger pressure only) and make another mark **(see illustration)**. The total of free movement should not exceed 20.0 mm. If it's more, the flywheel may need renewing.

Total rotational movement

This is the total distance the drive surface can be turned independently of the flywheel primary element. Insert two bolts into the clutch pressure plate/damper unit mounting holes, and with the crankshaft/flywheel held stationary, use a lever/pry bar between the bolts and use some effort to move the drive surface fully in one direction – make a mark where the locating pin aligns with the flywheel edge. Now force the drive surface fully in the opposite direction, and make another mark. The total rotational movement should not exceed 44.0 mm. If it does, have the flywheel professionally inspected.

Lateral movement

The lateral movement (up and down) of the drive surface in relation to the primary element

15.4 Use a locking tool to counterhold the flywheel

15.6a Flywheel warpage check – see text

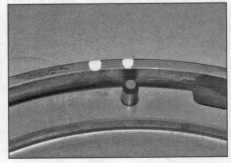

15.6b Flywheel free rotational movement check alignment marks – see text

of the flywheel should not exceed 2.0 mm. If it does, the flywheel may need renewing. This can be checked by pressing the drive surface down on one side into the flywheel (flywheel horizontal) and making an alignment mark between the drive surface and the inner edge of the primary element. Now press down on the opposite side of the drive surface, and make another mark above the original one. The difference between the two marks is the lateral movement (see illustration).

Refitting

7 Refitting is a reversal of removal. Use new bolts when refitting the flywheel and coat the threads of the bolts with locking fluid before inserting them (note that new bolts may be supplied ready-coated). Tighten them to the specified torque, then through the specified angle whilst preventing the flywheel from turning as during removal.

16 Crankshaft oil seals – renewal

Note: *The oil seals are a PTFE (Teflon) type and are fitted dry, without using any grease or oil. These have a wider sealing lip and have been introduced instead of the coil spring type oil seal.*

Timing belt end oil seal

1 Remove the timing belt as described in Section 7, and the crankshaft sprocket with reference to Section 8.
2 To remove the seal without removing the housing, drill two small holes diagonally opposite each other, insert self-tapping screws, and pull on the heads of the screws with pliers (see illustration).
3 Alternatively, to remove the oil seal complete with its housing, proceed as follows.
 a) Remove the sump as described in Section 12. This is necessary to ensure a satisfactory seal between the sump and oil seal housing on refitting.
 b) Unscrew and remove the oil seal housing.
 c) Working on the bench, lever the oil seal from the housing using a suitable screwdriver. Take care not to damage the seal seating in the housing (see illustration).

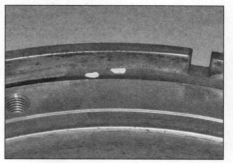

15.6c Flywheel lateral movement check marks – see text

4 Thoroughly clean the oil seal seating in the housing.
5 Wind a length of tape around the end of the crankshaft to protect the oil seal lips as the seal (and housing, where applicable) is fitted.
6 Fit a new oil seal to the housing, pressing or driving it into position using a socket or tube of suitable diameter. Ensure that the socket or tube bears only on the hard outer ring of the seal, and take care not to damage the seal lips. Press or drive the seal into position until it is seated on the shoulder in the housing. Make sure that the closed end of the seal is facing outwards.
7 If the oil seal housing has been removed, proceed as follows, otherwise proceed to paragraph 11.
8 Clean all traces of old sealant from the crankshaft oil seal housing and the cylinder block, then coat the cylinder block mating faces of the oil seal housing with a 2.0 to

16.2 Pull the screw and seal from place using pliers

3.0 mm thick bead of silicone sealant (VW D 176 404 A2, or equivalent). Note that the seal housing must be refitted within 5 minutes of applying the sealant.
Caution: DO NOT put excessive amounts of sealant onto the housing as it may get into the sump and block the oil pick-up pipe.
9 Refit the oil seal housing, and tighten the bolts progressively to the specified torque (see illustration).
10 Refit the sump as described in Section 12.
11 Refit the crankshaft sprocket with reference to Section 8, and the timing belt as described in Section 7.

Flywheel end oil seal

Note: *In these engines, the seal, sealing flange and sender wheel are a complete unit. Special tools are required to refit the sealing flange, and press the sender wheel onto the end of the crankshaft. It is not possible to accurately fit these parts without the tools, which may be available from VW (part No T10134) and are available from aftermarket automotive tool specialists.*
12 Remove the flywheel as described in Section 14, then prise the intermediate plate from the locating dowels on the cylinder block.
13 Undo the bolts securing the sealing flange to the cylinder block (see illustration).
14 Insert three 6 x 35 mm bolts into the threaded holes in the sealing flange. Tighten the bolts gradually and evenly, and press the sealing flange and sender wheel from the crankshaft/cylinder block (see illustration).

16.3 Prise the oil seal from the crankshaft oil seal housing

16.9 Slide the oil seal housing over the end of the crankshaft

16.13 Sealing flange bolts (arrowed)

16.14 Bolt in three 6 x 35 mm bolts (arrowed) and draw the sealing flange and sender wheel from place

16.16a Rotate the nut until it is level with the end of the clamping surface (arrowed)...

16.16b ...then clamp it in a vice

16.17 Rotate the nut until the inner part of the tool is flush with the housing (arrowed)

The seal, sender wheel and sealing flange are supplied as a complete unit.

15 Ensure the mating face of the cylinder block is clean and free from debris. The new sealing flange/seal/sender wheel assembly is supplied with a sealing lip support ring, which serves as a fitting sleeve, and must not be removed prior to installation. Equally, the sender wheel must not be separated from the assembly.

16 If using the VW tool, proceed as follows. If using an aftermarket tool specialist's product, follow the instructions supplied with the tool. Rotate the large spindle nut until it's level with the end of the clamping surface of the spindle, then clamp the spindle in a vice (see illustrations).

17 Press the tool housing downwards until it rests on the nut and washer. Rotate the nut until the inner part of the tool is at the same height as the housing (see illustration).

18 Remove the seal securing clip. The hole on the sender wheel must align with the marking on the sealing flange (see illustrations).

19 Place the flange outer side down on a clean, flat surface, then press the seal guide fitting sleeve (supplied ready fitted), housing, and sender wheel downwards until all the components are flat on the surface. In this position the upper edge of the sender wheel should be level with the edge of the sealing flange (see illustrations).

20 Place the sealing flange on the assembly tool, so the pin locates in the hole in the sender wheel (see illustration).

21 Push the sealing flange and guide fitting

sleeve against the tool whilst tightening the 3 knurled bolts. Ensure the pin is still located in the sender wheel (see illustration).

22 Ensure the end of the crankshaft is clean, and is locked at TDC on No 1 cylinder as described in Section 3.

23 Unscrew the large nut to the end of the spindle threads, then press the spindle inwards as far as possible (see illustration).

24 Align the flat side of the assembly with the sump flange, then secure the tool to the crankshaft using the integral Allen bolts (see illustration). Only hand-tighten the bolts.

25 Insert two M7 x 35 mm bolts to guide the sealing flange to the cylinder block (see illustration).

26 Using hand-pressure alone, push the tool assembly onto the crankshaft until the seal

16.18a Remove the securing clip...

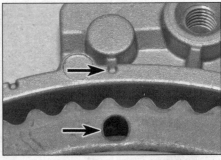

16.18b ...the hole in the sender wheel should align with the marking on the flange (arrowed)

16.19a Press the assembly downwards on a clean, flat surface...

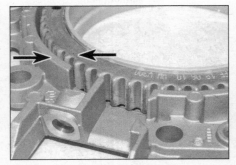

16.19b ...so the upper edge of the sender wheel is level with the edge of the flange (arrowed)

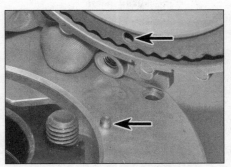

16.20 Fit the flange to the tool, ensuring the pin locates in the hole (arrowed)

16.21 With the pin engaged in the hole, tighten the 3 knurled bolts to secure the flange to the tool

16.23 Unscrew the nut to the end of the thread, and push the spindle in as far as possible

16.24 Hand-tighten the Allen bolts to secure the tool to the crankshaft (arrowed)

16.25 Use 2 M7 x 35 mm bolts (arrowed) to guide the sealing flange

16.26 Push the black knob (arrowed) into the hole in the crankshaft

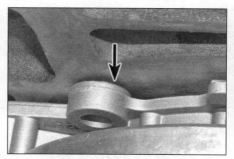

16.27 After tightening the spindle nut there should be an air gap between the sealing flange and the cylinder block (arrowed)

16.29 Measure the fitted depth of the sender wheel in relation to the end of the crankshaft

guide fitting sleeve contacts the crankshaft flange, then push the guide pin (black knob) into the hole in the crankshaft. This is to ensure the sender wheel reaches its correct installation position **(see illustration)**.

27 Rotate the large nut until it makes contact with the tool housing, then tighten it to 35 Nm (26 lbf ft). After tightening this nut, a small air gap must still be present between the sealing flange and cylinder block **(see illustration)**.

28 Unscrew the large nut; the two M7 x 35 mm bolts, the three knurled bolts and the Allen bolts securing the tool to the crankshaft. Remove the tool, and pull the seal guide fitting sleeve from place (if it didn't come out with the tool).

29 Use a vernier caliper or feeler gauge to measure the fitted depth of the sender wheel in relation to the crankshaft flange **(see illustration)**. The correct depth is 0.5 mm.

30 If the gap is correct, fit the sealing flange bolts and tighten them to the specified torque.

31 If the gap is too small, re-attach the tool to the sealing flange and crankshaft, then refit the two M7 x 35 mm guide bolts to the flange. Tighten the large spindle nut to 40 Nm (30 lbf ft), remove the tool and measure the air gap. If the gap is still too small, re-attach the tool and tighten the spindle nut to 45 Nm (33 lbf ft). Measure the gap again. When the gap is correct, refit the flange retaining bolts, and tighten them to the specified torque.

32 The remainder of refitting is a reversal of removal.

17 Engine/transmission mountings –
inspection and renewal

Refer to Chapter 2A, Section 20 for the basic procedure, but note that slight differences in the engine and transmission brackets will be noticed. Use new bolts when refitting the mountings and tighten the bolts to the torque wrench settings given in this Part of Chapter 2.

18 Engine oil cooler/ filter housing –
removal and refitting

Removal

1 The oil cooler is mounted on the lower

18.6a Undo the engine oil cooler retaining screws

part of the oil filter housing on the front of the cylinder block.

2 Where applicable, undo the retaining bolts and remove the engine undertray. According to model, undo the retaining bolts and rotary fasteners and remove the battery cover and engine covers as applicable.

3 Move the body front crossmember to the service position as described in Chapter 11, Section 25.

4 Position a container beneath the oil filter housing to catch escaping oil and coolant.

5 Clamp the oil cooler coolant hoses to minimise coolant spillage, or drain the cooling system as described in Chapter 1, Section 30.

6 Unscrew the oil cooler retaining screws and remove the oil cooler from the front of the oil filter housing **(see illustrations)**. Recover the O-rings from between the cooler and the oil filter housing, new ones will be required for refitting.

18.6b Renew the seals/gaskets

18.7a Disconnect the coolant hoses...

18.7b ...release the oil dipstick guide tube retaining clip (arrowed)...

18.7c ...and undo the filter housing retaining bolts (arrowed)

18.8 Renew the seals/gaskets

7 If required, disconnect the coolant hose, release the dipstick from the side of the housing, then undo the retaining bolts and remove the oil filter housing from the cylinder block **(see illustrations).**

Refitting

8 Refitting is a reversal of removal, bearing in mind the following points:
a) *Use new oil cooler and housing O-rings* **(see illustration).**
b) *Tighten the oil cooler and filter housing bolts to the specified torque.*
c) *Return the body front crossmember to its normal position as described in Chapter 11, Section 25.*
d) *On completion, check and if necessary top-up the oil and coolant levels.*

19 Oil pressure warning light switch – removal and refitting

Removal

1 The oil pressure warning light switch is fitted to the left-hand rear of the cylinder head, below the engine lifting eye. Access to the switch is poor and is best performed from the right-hand side behind the cylinder head. According to model, undo the retaining bolts and rotary fasteners and remove the battery cover and engine covers as applicable.
2 Pull back the heat shield in the vicinity of the switch.
3 Undo the retaining bolt and remove the

clamp plate securing the coolant pipes to the support bracket. Now undo the retaining bolt and remove the support bracket.
4 Undo the retaining bolt and remove the engine lifting eye.
5 Disconnect the wiring connector and wipe clean the area around the switch.
6 Unscrew the switch and remove it, along with its sealing washer (where fitted). If the switch is to be left removed from the engine for any length of time, plug the aperture in the cylinder head.

Refitting

7 Refitting is a reversal of removal, bearing in mind the following points:
a) *Examine the sealing washer for signs of damage or deterioration and if necessary renew.*
b) *Tighten the switch to the specified torque.*
c) *On completion, check and if necessary top-up the engine oil as described in Weekly checks.*

20 Oil level/temperature sender – removal and refitting

Removal

1 The oil level/temperature sender is fitted to bottom of the sump.
2 Drain the engine oil as described in Chapter 1, Section 3.
3 Disconnect the wiring connector from the sender.
4 Wipe clean the area around the sender, then undo the three retaining bolts and remove the sender.

Refitting

5 Examine the sealing washer for signs of damage or deterioration and if necessary renew.
6 Refit the switch and tighten the retaining bolts to the specified torque.
7 Refill the engine with oil as described in Chapter 1, Section 3.
8 On completion, check and, if necessary, top-up the engine oil as described in Weekly checks.

Chapter 2 Part C:
2.5 litre engine in-vehicle repair procedures

Contents

Degrees of difficulty

| **Easy,** suitable for novice with little experience | 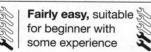 | **Fairly easy,** suitable for beginner with some experience | | **Fairly difficult,** suitable for competent DIY mechanic | | **Difficult,** suitable for experienced DIY mechanic | | **Very difficult,** suitable for expert DIY or professional | |

Specifications

General

Engine type	5-cylinder, in-line, single overhead camshaft
Engine codes:	
96 kW engines	AXD and BNZ
120 kW engines	BLJ
128 kW engines	AXE and BPC
Capacity	2461 cc
Bore	81.0 mm
Stroke	95.5 mm
Compression ratio	18.5 : 1
Compression pressures:	
Minimum compression pressure	Approximately 19.0 bar
Maximum difference between cylinders	Approximately 5.0 bar
Firing order	1 – 2 – 4 – 5 – 3 (No 1 cylinder at right-hand end of engine)
Direction of crankshaft rotation	Clockwise (seen from right-hand side of vehicle)

Camshaft

Camshaft endfloat (maximum)	0.15 mm
Camshaft bearing running clearance (maximum)	0.11 mm
Camshaft run-out (maximum)	0.01 mm

Lubrication system

Oil pump type	Gear type, driven from crankshaft
Oil pressure (oil temperature 80°C, at 2000 rpm)	2.0 bar

Torque wrench settings

	Nm	lbf ft
Alternator driveshaft hub bolt*:		
Stage 1	50	37
Stage 2	Angle-tighten a further 90°	
Big-end bearing caps bolts*:		
Stage 1	30	22
Stage 2	Angle-tighten a further 90°	
Camshaft bearing cap bolts*:		
Stage 1	8	6
Stage 2	Angle-tighten a further 90°	
Camshaft cover bolts	15	11
Camshaft drive gear bolt*:		
Stage 1	150	111
Stage 2	Angle-tighten a further 90°	
Cylinder block sealing flange bolts	10	7
Cylinder head bolts*:		
Stage 1	60	44
Stage 2	Angle-tighten a further 90°	
Stage 3	Angle-tighten a further 90°	
Stage 4	Angle-tighten a further 90°	
Stage 5	Angle-tighten a further 90°	
Stage 6	Slacken by 90°	
Eccentric pin cover plate bolts	10	7
Eccentric pin bolt*:		
Stage 1	20	15
Stage 2	Angle-tighten a further 90°	
Engine/transmission mountings*:		
Front mounting lower part-to-upper part:		
Stage 1	50	37
Stage 2	Angle-tighten a further 90°	
Front mounting through-bolt		
Stage 1	90	66
Stage 2	Angle-tighten a further 180°	
Front mounting bracket-to-cylinder block:		
Stage 1	50	37
Stage 2	Angle-tighten a further 90°	
Front mounting-to-subframe bolts:		
Stage 1	20	15
Stage 2	Angle-tighten a further 90°	
Left-hand mounting-to-body bolts:		
Stage 1	50	37
Stage 2	Angle-tighten a further 90°	
Left-hand mounting-to-transmission bolts:		
Stage 1	50	37
Stage 2	Angle-tighten a further 90°	
Right-hand mounting-to-body bolts:		
Stage 1	50	37
Stage 2	Angle-tighten a further 90°	
Right-hand mounting-to-engine bracket bolt:		
Stage 1	90	66
Stage 2	Angle-tighten a further 90°	
Right-hand engine bracket-to-cylinder block:		
Stage 1	50	37
Stage 2	Angle-tighten a further 90°	
Rear mounting through-bolt:		
Stage 1	50	37
Stage 2	Angle-tighten a further 90°	
Rear mounting-to-subframe nuts:		
Stage 1	20	15
Stage 2	Angle-tighten a further 180°	
Rear mounting engine bracket-to-cylinder block:		
Stage 1	50	37
Stage 2	Angle-tighten a further 90°	
Flywheel/driveplate bolts*:		
Stage 1	60	44
Stage 2	Angle-tighten a further 90°	
Gear train housing cover bolts	20	15
Main bearing cap tie bolts*	30	22

Torque wrench settings (continued)

	Nm	lbf ft
Oil cooler-to-oil filter housing bolts	10	7
Oil filter housing-to-cylinder block bolts	20	15
Oil filter cover	25	18
Oil level/temperature sensor-to-sump bolts	10	7
Oil pick-up pipe securing bolts	10	7
Oil pressure warning light switch	25	18
Oil pump baffle plate bolts	15	11
Oil pump securing bolts:		
Large bolts	20	15
Small bolts	10	7
Pump injector rocker shaft bolts*:		
Stage 1	20	15
Stage 2	Angle-tighten a further 90°	
Piston oil spray jet bolt	25	18
Roadwheel bolts	180	133
Sump:		
Drain plug	30	22
Sump-to-cylinder block bolts	15	11
Sump-to-transmission bolts	45	33

Note: *Use new bolts*

1 General information

Using this Chapter

Chapter 2 is divided into four Parts; A, B, C and D. Repair operations that can be carried out with the engine in the vehicle are described in Part A (1.9 litre engines), Part B (2.0 litre engines), and Part C (2.5 litre engines). Part D covers the removal of the engine/transmission as a unit, and describes the engine dismantling and overhaul procedures.

In Parts A, B and C, the assumption is made that the engine is installed in the vehicle, with all ancillaries connected. If the engine has been removed for overhaul, the preliminary dismantling information which precedes each operation may be ignored.

Engine description

The engines are water-cooled, single overhead camshaft, in-line five-cylinder units, with aluminium-alloy cylinder blocks and cylinder heads. All are mounted transversely at the front of the vehicle, with the transmission bolted to the left-hand end of the engine.

An unusual feature of these engines is that the camshaft, oil pump, coolant pump, tandem (fuel/vacuum) pump, power steering pump and alternator are all driven by a helical gear train. The gear train is located at the flywheel/driveplate end of the engine and is driven by the crankshaft. Because of this arrangement auxiliary drivebelts are not needed and a conventional crankshaft pulley is not fitted. A vibration damper is bolted to the crankshaft adjacent to the No 1 main bearing location.

The crankshaft is of six-bearing type, and thrustwashers are fitted to No 4 main bearing to control crankshaft endfloat.

The camshaft is mounted at the top of the cylinder head, and rotates in horizontally-split

bearing shells. The camshaft is secured by bearing caps.

The valves are closed by coil springs, and run in guides pressed into the cylinder head. The camshaft actuates the valves directly, via hydraulic tappets.

The duocentric oil pump is gear-driven via the crankshaft helical drive gear. Oil is drawn from the sump through a strainer, and then forced through an externally-mounted, renewable filter. From there, it is distributed to the cylinder head, where it lubricates the camshaft journals and hydraulic tappets, and also to the crankcase, where it lubricates the main bearings, connecting rod big-ends, gudgeon pins and cylinder bores. A coolant-fed oil cooler is fitted to the oil filter housing on all engines. Oil jets are fitted to the base of each cylinder – these spray oil onto the underside of the pistons, to improve cooling.

A brake servo vacuum pump, driven by the engine gear train, is attached to the transmission end of the cylinder head. The vacuum pump and the fuel injection system fuel pump are combined in one unit, termed a 'tandem pump'.

Engine coolant is circulated by a pump, driven by the engine gear train. For details of the cooling system, refer to Chapter 3.

Repairs possible with the engine installed in the vehicle

The following operations can be performed without removing the engine:
a) Compression pressure – testing.
b) Camshaft cover – removal and refitting.
c) Camshaft drive gear – removal and refitting.
d) Camshaft and hydraulic tappets – removal, inspection and refitting.
e) Pump injector rocker shaft assembly – removal and refitting.
f) Cylinder head – removal and refitting.
g) Cylinder head and pistons – decarbonising.

h) Sump – removal and refitting.
i) Oil pump – removal and refitting.
j) Oil seals – renewal.
k) Oil cooler/filter housing – removal and refitting
l) Engine/transmission mountings – inspection and renewal.
m) Flywheel/driveplate – removal, inspection and refitting.

Note: *It is possible to remove the pistons and connecting rods (after removing the cylinder head and sump) without removing the engine. However, this is not recommended. Work of this nature is more easily and thoroughly completed with the engine on the bench, as described in Chapter 2D.*

2 Compression and leakdown tests – description and interpretation

Compression test

Note: *A compression tester suitable for use with diesel engines will be required for this test.*

1 When engine performance is down, or if misfiring occurs which cannot be attributed to the ignition or fuel systems, a compression test can provide diagnostic clues as to the engine's condition. If the test is performed regularly, it can give warning of trouble before any other symptoms become apparent.

2 The engine must be fully warmed-up to normal operating temperature, the battery must be fully-charged and you will require the aid of an assistant. According to model, undo the retaining bolts and rotary fasteners and remove the battery cover and engine covers as applicable.

3 Move the body front crossmember to the service position as described in Chapter 11, Section 25.

4 Remove the inlet manifold as described in Chapter 4A, Section 9.

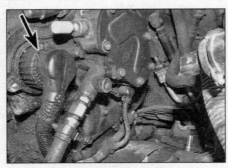

2.5 Slacken the knurled nut (arrowed) and disconnect the injector solenoids wiring connector

5 Disconnect the injector solenoids by disconnecting the wiring connector at the end of the cylinder head **(see illustration)**. To do this, pull out the red locking pin and loosen the knurled nut. **Note:** *As a result of the wiring being disconnected, faults will be stored in the ECU memory. On completion of the test it will be necessary to have the fault codes cleared by a VW dealer or suitably equipped garage, using specialist diagnostic equipment.*

6 Remove the glow plugs as described in Chapter 5, Section 13 then fit a compression tester to the No 1 cylinder glow plug hole. The type of tester which screws into the plug thread is preferred.

7 Have your assistant, crank the engine for several seconds on the starter motor. After one or two revolutions, the compression pressure should build-up to a maximum figure and then stabilise. Record the highest reading obtained.

8 Repeat the test on the remaining cylinders, recording the pressure in each.

9 The cause of poor compression is less easy to establish on a diesel engine than on a petrol engine. The effect of introducing oil into the cylinders (wet testing) is not conclusive, because there is a risk that the oil will sit in the recess on the piston crown, instead of passing to the rings. However, the following can be used as a rough guide to diagnosis.

10 All cylinders should produce very similar pressures. Any difference greater than that specified indicates the existence of

a fault. Note that the compression should build-up quickly in a healthy engine. Low compression on the first stroke, followed by gradually increasing pressure on successive strokes, indicates worn piston rings. A low compression reading on the first stroke, which does not build-up during successive strokes, indicates leaking valves or a blown head gasket (a cracked head could also be the cause).

11 A low reading from two adjacent cylinders is almost certainly due to the head gasket having blown between them and the presence of coolant in the engine oil will confirm this.

12 On completion, remove the compression tester, and refit the glow plugs, with reference to Chapter 5, Section 13.

13 Reconnect the injector solenoids wiring connector.

14 Refit the inlet manifold as described in Chapter 4A, Section 9.

15 Return the body front crossmember to its normal position as described in Chapter 11, Section 25.

Leakdown test

16 A leakdown test measures the rate at which compressed air fed into the cylinder is lost. It is an alternative to a compression test, and in many ways it is better, since the escaping air provides easy identification of where pressure loss is occurring (piston rings, valves or head gasket).

17 The equipment required for leakdown testing is unlikely to be available to the home mechanic. If poor compression is suspected, have the test performed by a suitably-equipped garage.

---

3 Engine assembly and valve timing marks – general information and usage

General information

1 TDC is the highest point in the cylinder that each piston reaches as it travels up-and-down when the crankshaft turns. Each piston reaches TDC at the end of the compression stroke and again at the end of the exhaust

stroke, but TDC generally refers to piston position on the compression stroke. No 1 piston is at the right-hand end of the engine.

2 Positioning No 1 piston at TDC is an essential part of all procedures which entail removing or altering the position of any of the gears in the helical gear train.

3 To set No 1 piston at TDC and to lock the various engine components in the TDC position, numerous VW special tools or after market alternatives are required. Note that because a crankshaft pulley is not fitted to these engines, it is not even possible to turn the engine over without the use of a special tool. The VW tools required are as follows:

a) *Crankshaft turning and setting tool –
   T10225*
b) *Crankshaft holding tool – T10226*
c) *Camshaft holding tool - T10193*

4 As an alternative to the manufacturer's tools, after market equivalents are available from a number of automotive tool specialists. These tools are usually supplied as a kit containing all the tools necessary for setting and locking the engine rotating components. A kit of this type was used in the preparation of this manual and was supplied by Auto Service Tools (www.asttools.co.uk) **(see illustrations)**.

Setting TDC on No 1 cylinder

5 Remove the air cleaner assembly as described in Chapter 4A, Section 2.

6 Firmly apply the handbrake, then jack up the front of the vehicle and support it securely on axle stands (see *Jacking and vehicle support*). Remove the right-hand roadwheel.

7 Where fitted, undo the retaining bolts and remove the engine undertray.

8 Remove the wheel arch liner on the right-hand side.

9 Release the lower coolant pipe.

10 Using a suitable hooked tool, prise out the camshaft end cap from the right-hand end of the cylinder head **(see illustration)**. Note that a new end cap will be required for refitting.

11 Undo the rearmost retaining bolt from the right-hand engine/transmission mounting engine bracket **(see illustration)**.

12 Undo the five retaining bolts and remove the sealing flange from the right-hand end of the cylinder block **(see illustration)**.

3.4a Auto Service Tools timing kit...

3.4b ...for setting TDC on No1 cylinder

3.10 Using a hooked tool, prise out the camshaft end cap from the cylinder head

3.11 Undo the rearmost retaining bolt (arrowed) from the right-hand engine/ transmission mounting engine bracket

3.12 Undo the five retaining bolts and remove the sealing flange from the right-hand end of the cylinder block

3.13a Locate the crankshaft turning and setting tool over the end of the crankshaft...

3.13b ...and secure the tool in place with the retaining bolt

3.14 Rotate the crankshaft until the line on the tool (arrowed) is horizontal and towards the rear of the vehicle

13 Locate the crankshaft turning and setting tool (T10225 or equivalent) over the end of the crankshaft and secure the tool in place with the retaining bolt **(see illustrations)**. Note that the tool will only fit on the crankshaft in one position.

14 Using a socket or spanner on the tool, rotate the crankshaft in the normal direction of rotation until the line on the tool is horizontal and towards the rear of the vehicle **(see illustration)**.

15 Remove tool T10225 and fit the crankshaft holding tool (T10226 or equivalent) and the camshaft holding tool (T10193 or equivalent) **(see illustrations)**. Note that the tools will only fit in one position. If it is not possible to fit the

tools, refit the crankshaft turning and setting tool and rotate the crankshaft one complete turn.

16 With the holding tools in place the crankshaft and camshaft are set at TDC for No 1 cylinder on compression and are locked in that position.

17 On completion, remove the special tools

3.15a Fit the crankshaft holding tool...

3.15b ...and the camshaft holding tool to lock the crankshaft and camshaft at TDC

3.20 Fit a new camshaft end cap and tap it fully into position using a hammer and block of wood

4.5a Pull the breather valve out of the camshaft cover...

4.5b ...then remove the rubber seal

and clean off all traces of sealant from the cylinder block and the sealing flange.

18 Apply a bead of silicone sealant to the joint between the cylinder block and the sump. Place the sealing flange in position then refit the retaining bolts and tighten them progressively to the specified torque.

19 Refit the retaining bolt to the right-hand engine/transmission mounting engine bracket and tighten it to the specified torque.

20 Locate a new camshaft end cap on the cylinder head and tap it fully into position using a hammer and block of wood (see illustration).

21 Secure the right-hand lower coolant pipe, then refit the wheel arch liner and engine undertray (where applicable). Refit the roadwheel, then lower the vehicle to the ground.

22 Refit the air cleaner assembly as described in Chapter 4A, Section 2.

4 Camshaft cover – removal and refitting

Removal

1 Undo the retaining bolts and rotary fasteners and remove the battery cover and engine covers as applicable.

2 Remove the air duct and hoses between the intercooler and turbocharger and between the intercooler and inlet manifold.

3 Remove the EGR valve connecting pipe as described in Chapter 4C, Section 2.

4 Disconnect the crankcase ventilation hose from the breather valve on the camshaft cover.

5 Pull the breather valve out of the camshaft cover, then remove the rubber seal (see illustrations).

6 Undo the three retaining bolts, remove the oil filler tube and collect the rubber seal (see illustrations).

7 Undo the two retaining bolts and remove the inlet manifold support bracket (see illustration).

8 Remove the sound deadening cover, then undo the retaining bolts and lift off the camshaft cover (see illustration).

9 Recover the camshaft cover gasket. Inspect the gasket carefully, and renew it if damage or deterioration is evident.

10 Clean the mating surfaces of the cylinder head and camshaft cover thoroughly, removing all traces of oil.

Refitting

11 Refitting is a reversal of the removal procedure, bearing in mind the following points:
a) Tighten the camshaft cover retaining bolts progressively to the specified torque.
b) Refit the EGR valve connecting pipe as described in Chapter 4C, Section 2.

5 Pump injector rocker shaft assembly – removal and refitting

Removal

1 The pump injector rocker shaft assembly consists of two separate shafts. The right-hand shaft contains two rockers, for cylinders 1 and 2. The left-hand shaft contains three rockers for cylinders 3, 4 and 5. Do not interchange the two assemblies.

4.6a Undo the three retaining bolts...

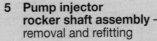

4.6b ...remove the oil filler tube...

4.6c ...and collect the rubber seal

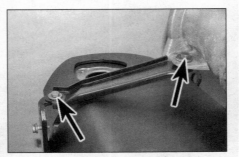

4.7 Undo the two retaining bolts (arrowed) and remove the inlet manifold support bracket

4.8 Undo the retaining bolts and lift off the camshaft cover

5.3a Undo the retaining bolts (arrowed)...

5.3b ...and lift the relevant rocker shaft off the camshaft bearing caps

2 Remove the camshaft cover as described in Section 4.

3 Starting with the outer bolts first, carefully and evenly slacken the rocker shaft retaining bolts. Discard the rocker shaft bolts, new ones must be fitted. Lift the relevant rocker shaft off the camshaft bearing caps **(see illustrations)**.

Refitting

4 Carefully check the rocker shaft, rocker arms and camshaft bearing cap seating surface for any signs of excessive wear or damage.

5 Ensure that the shaft seating surface is clean and position the relevant rocker shaft assembly in its original location in the camshaft bearing caps.

6 Insert the new rocker shaft retaining bolts, and starting with the inner bolts, gradually and evenly tighten the bolts to the specified Stage 1 torque setting.

7 Again, starting with the inner retaining bolts, tighten the bolts through the specified Stage 2 angle.

8 If a new rocker shaft assembly has been fitted, carry out the injector basic clearance setting procedure as described in Chapter 4A, Section 8.

9 Refit the camshaft cover as described in Section 4.

6 Camshaft drive gear –
general information, removal and refitting

General information

1 Removal and refitting of the camshaft drive gear entails the use of numerous VW special tools or after market alternatives. In addition to the tools listed in Section 3, the following tools will also be needed.

   a) *Camshaft drive gear clamping tool – T10199*
   b) *Camshaft drive gear setting tool – T10199/1*
   c) *Injector wiring harness conector clamp ring releasing/tightening tool – T10211*

2 As an alternative to the manufacturer's tools, after market equivalents are available from a number of automotive tool specialists. These tools are usually supplied as a kit containing all the tools necessary for setting and locking the engine rotating components.

Removal

3 Set the engine to TDC on No 1 cylinder as described in Section 3.

4 Remove the camshaft cover as described in Section 4.

5 Remove the brake system vacuum pump as described in Chapter 9, Section 20.

6 Disconnect the injector solenoids wiring connector at the end of the cylinder head **(see illustration 2.5)**. To do this, pull out the red locking pin and loosen the knurled nut. Using the releasing/tightening tool (T10211) turn the clamp ring securing the connector socket to the cylinder head and camshaft bearing cap 90° anti-clockwise.

7 Locate the camshaft drive gear clamping tool (T10199 or equivalent) over the drive gear and in contact with the cylinder head. Tighten the retaining bolts to secure the tool to the drive gear **(see illustration)**.

8 Undo the camshaft drive gear retaining bolt and remove the bolt and the vacuum pump drive shaft **(see illustration)**. Note that a new bolt will be required for refitting.

9 Remove the camshaft drive gear clamping tool.

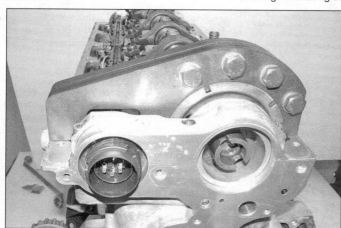

6.7 Fit the clamping tool over the camshaft drive gear and tighten the bolts to secure the tool to the gear

6.8 Undo the camshaft drive gear retaining bolt and remove the bolt and the vacuum pump drive shaft

6.10 Withdraw the drive gear from the end of the camshaft and lift it out of the gear train housing

6.11 Collect the diamond coated washer from the end of the camshaft

6.13 Undo the three bolts (arrowed) and remove the eccentric pin cover plate

6.14 Undo the retaining bolt and remove the eccentric pin

6.15 Undo the retaining bolts and remove the camshaft outer bearing cap

6.16 Lift out the camshaft intermediate drive gear, together with the balancer plate components

10 Withdraw the camshaft drive gear from the end of the camshaft and lift it up and out of the gear train housing **(see illustration)**.
11 Collect the diamond coated washer from

the end of the camshaft **(see illustration)**. Note that a new diamond coated washer **must** be obtained for refitting.
12 Disconnect the camshaft position sensor

wiring connector, then undo the retaining bolt and remove the sensor from the end of the cylinder head.
13 Undo the three bolts and remove the eccentric pin cover plate from the end of the cylinder head **(see illustration)**.
14 Undo the retaining bolt and remove the eccentric pin **(see illustration)**. Note that a new retaining bolt will be required for refitting.
15 Undo the retaining bolts and remove the camshaft outer bearing cap from the cylinder head **(see illustration)**. Note that new retaining bolts will be required for refitting.
16 Carefully lift out the camshaft intermediate drive gear, together with the balancer plate components from the gear train housing **(see illustration)**. Remove the guide sleeve, intermediate drive gear and the washer, from the balancer plate.

Refitting

17 Thoroughly lubricate the guide sleeve with clean engine oil and slide it into the intermediate drive gear **(see illustrations)**.
18 Mount the washer on the guide sleeve engaging the lugs on the washer with the grooves in the guide sleeve **(see illustrations)**.
19 Locate the intermediate drive gear together with the guide sleeve and washer on the balancer plate and align the notch on the guide sleeve with the mark on the balancer plate **(see illustration)**.
20 Carefully insert the camshaft intermediate drive gear, together with the balancer plate components into the gear train housing.

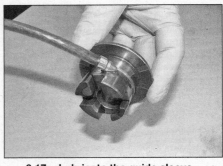

6.17a Lubricate the guide sleeve...

6.18a Mount the washer on the guide sleeve...

6.18b ...engaging the lugs on the washer with the grooves in the guide sleeve

6.17b ...and slide it into the intermediate drive gear

6.19 Align the notch (arrowed) on the guide sleeve with the mark on the balancer plate

6.21a Lubricate the eccentric pin and insert it into the guide sleeve

6.21b The notch (arrowed) on the eccentric pin must point vertically upwards...

6.21c ...and the lugs (arrowed) on the balancer plate must align with the sealing surface of the cylinder head

6.24a Turn the eccentric pin anti-clockwise using moderate force and initially tighten the retaining bolt

6.24b Tighten the eccentric pin retaining bolt to the specified torque...

21 Thoroughly lubricate the eccentric pin with clean engine oil and insert it into the guide sleeve. The notch on the eccentric pin must point vertically upwards and the lugs on the balancer plate must align with the sealing surface of the cylinder head **(see illustrations)**.

22 Refit the camshaft outer bearing cap but only tighten the retaining bolts hand-tight at this stage.

23 Fit the new eccentric pin retaining bolt and tighten it until it just contacts the eccentric pin. The eccentric pin must still be free to turn.

24 Engage angled circlip pliers or a similar tool with the two holes in the eccentric pin. Turn the eccentric pin anti-clockwise using moderate force (approximately 50 Ncm). Hold the eccentric pin in this position and tighten the retaining bolt to the specified torque, then through the specified angle **(see illustrations)**.

25 Remove the camshaft outer bearing cap once more, then thoroughly clean the mating surfaces of the bearing cap and cylinder head. Apply a thin bead of silicone sealant (Loctite 5970) to the mating surface of the bearing cap and spread the sealant evenly over the entire surface using a spatula or similar **(see illustrations)**.

26 Locate the bearing cap in position on the cylinder head and insert the new retaining bolts. Tighten the bolts to the specified torque, then through the specified angle.

27 Using the releasing/tightening tool (T10211) turn the clamp ring securing the

wiring connector socket to the cylinder head and camshaft bearing cap 90° clockwise to secure. Reconnect the injector solenoids wiring connector to the socket.

6.24c ...then through the specified angle

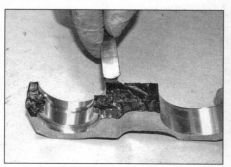

6.25b ...and spread the sealant evenly over the entire surface using a spatula

28 Renew the O-ring seal on the eccentric pin cover plate, then refit the plate and tighten the retaining bolts securely **(see illustrations)**.

29 Refit the camshaft position sensor to the

6.25a Apply a thin bead of silicone sealant to the mating surface of the bearing cap...

6.28a Renew the O-ring seal on the eccentric pin cover plate...

6.28b ...then refit the plate and tighten the retaining bolts securely

6.31a Lubricate the drive gear and refit it to the camshaft...

6.31b ...with the mark (arrowed) on the sender wheel aligned with the upper edge of the cylinder head

cylinder head and tighten the retaining bolt securely.

30 Locate a new diamond-coated washer on the end of the camshaft **(see illustration 6.11)**.

31 Thoroughly lubricate the teeth of the camshaft drive gear with clean engine oil, then refit the drive gear to the camshaft. Note that the drive gear must be positioned so that the mark on the sender wheel aligns with the upper edge of the cylinder head **(see illustrations)**.

32 Fit the new camshaft drive gear retaining bolt together with the vacuum pump drive shaft. Tighten the bolt hand-tight only at this stage. The drive gear must still be free to turn.

33 Locate the camshaft drive gear setting tool (T10199/1 or equivalent) over the drive gear and securely tighten the retaining bolts to secure the tool to the drive gear **(see illustration)**.

34 Attach a torque wrench to the tool and apply a torque of 80 Nm in a clockwise direction. Hold the drive gear in this position then, using a second torque wrench, tighten the drive gear retaining bolt to 50 Nm **(see illustration)**.

35 Remove the setting tool and refit the drive gear clamping tool (T10199 or equivalent) over the drive gear and in contact with the cylinder head. Tighten the retaining bolts to secure the tool to the drive gear.

36 Tighten the drive gear retaining bolt to the specified torque, then through the specified angle.

37 Remove the drive gear clamping tool and the tools used to secure the crankshaft and camshaft at the TDC position.

38 Refit the brake system vacuum pump as described in Chapter 9, Section 20.

39 Refit the camshaft cover as described in Section 4.

40 Rotate the crankshaft two complete turns and return it to the TDC position for No1 cylinder. Check that the crankshaft and camshaft locking tools described in Section 3 can still be fitted.

41 If all is satisfactory, proceed as described in Section 3, paragraphs 17 to 22.

7 Camshaft and hydraulic tappets – removal, inspection and refitting

Removal

1 Remove the pump injector rocker shaft assembly as described in Section 5.

2 Remove the camshaft drive gear as described in Section 6.

3 Check the camshaft bearing caps for identification markings. The bearing caps are normally stamped with their respective cylinder numbers. If no marks are present, make suitable marks using a scriber or punch. The caps should be numbered from 1 to 7, with No 1 at the right-hand end of the engine. Note on which side of the bearing caps the marks are made to ensure that they are refitted the correct way round.

4 The camshaft rotates in shell bearings. As the camshaft bearing caps are removed, recover the shell bearing halves from the camshaft. Number the back of the bearings with a felt pen to ensure that, if re-used, the bearings are fitted to their original locations. **Note:** *Fitted into the cylinder head, under each camshaft bearing cap, is a washer for each cylinder head bolt.*

5 Starting with the outer bolts first, carefully and evenly slacken the bearing cap retaining bolts, slackening the bolts for the last two caps alternately and diagonally. Note that new bearing cap retaining bolts will be required for refitting.

6 Once all the bearing cap retaining bolts have been fully slackened, remove them, then lift off the bearing caps **(see illustration)**.

7 Carefully lift the camshaft from the cylinder head, keeping it level and supported at both ends as it is removed so that the journals and lobes are not damaged **(see illustration)**.

8 Lift the hydraulic tappets from their bores in the cylinder head, and store them with the valve contact surfaces facing downwards,

6.33 Locate the camshaft drive gear setting tool over the drive gear and securely tighten the retaining bolts

6.34 Attach a torque wrench to the tool and apply a torque of 80 Nm in a clockwise direction then tighten the drive gear retaining bolt

to prevent the oil from draining out **(see illustration)**. Make a note of the position of each tappet, as they must be refitted in their original locations on reassembly – accelerated wear leading to early failure will result if the tappets are interchanged.

9 Recover the lower shell bearing halves from the cylinder head; number the back of the shells with a felt pen to ensure that, if re-used, the bearings are fitted to their original locations **(see illustration)**.

Inspection

10 With the camshaft removed, examine the bearing caps and the bearing locations in the cylinder head for signs of obvious wear or pitting. If evident, a new cylinder head will probably be required. Also check that the oil supply holes in the cylinder head are free from obstructions.

11 Visually inspect the camshaft for evidence of wear on the surfaces of the lobes and journals. Normally their surfaces should be smooth and have a dull shine; look for scoring, erosion or pitting and areas that appear highly polished, indicating excessive wear. Accelerated wear will occur once the hardened exterior of the camshaft has been damaged, so always renew worn items. **Note:** *If these symptoms are visible on the tips of the camshaft lobes, check the corresponding tappet, as it will probably be worn as well.*

12 If the machined surfaces of the camshaft appear discoloured or blued, it is likely that it has been overheated at some point, probably due to inadequate lubrication. This may have distorted the shaft, so check the run-out as follows: place the camshaft between two V-blocks and using a DTI gauge, measure the run-out at the centre journal. If it exceeds the figure quoted in the Specifications at the start of this Chapter, renew the camshaft.

13 To measure the camshaft endfloat, temporarily refit the camshaft to the cylinder head, then fit Nos 2, 4 and 6 bearing caps and tighten the retaining bolts to the specified torque setting. Anchor a DTI gauge to the right-hand end of the cylinder head. Push the camshaft to one end of the cylinder head as far as it will travel, then rest the DTI gauge probe on the end face of the camshaft, and zero the gauge. Push the camshaft as far as it will go to the other end of the cylinder head, and record the gauge reading. Verify the reading by pushing the camshaft back to its original position and checking that the gauge indicates zero again. **Note:** *The hydraulic tappets must **not** be fitted whilst this measurement is being taken.*

14 Check that the camshaft endfloat measurement is within the limit listed in the Specifications. If the measurement is outside the specified limit, wear is unlikely to be confined to any one component, so renewal of the camshaft, cylinder head and bearing caps must be considered.

15 The camshaft bearing running clearance should now be measured. This will be difficult to achieve without a range of micrometers or

7.6 Lift off the camshaft bearing caps...

7.7 ...carefully lift the camshaft from the cylinder head...

7.8 ...and lift out the hydraulic tappets

7.9 Recover the lower shell bearing halves from the cylinder head

internal/external expanding calipers, measure the outside diameters of the camshaft bearing surfaces and the internal diameters formed by the bearing caps and shell bearings, and the bearing locations in the cylinder head. The difference between these two measurements is the running clearance.

16 Compare the camshaft running clearance measurements with the figure given in Specifications; if any are outside the specified tolerance, the camshaft, cylinder head and bearing caps and shell bearings should be renewed.

17 Inspect the hydraulic tappets for obvious signs of wear or damage, and renew if necessary. Check that the oil holes in the tappets are free from obstructions.

Refitting

18 Thoroughly clean the contact surfaces of

the cylinder head and Nos 1 and 7 bearing caps ensuring that all traces of old sealant are removed.

19 Smear some clean engine oil onto the sides of the hydraulic tappets, and offer them into position in their original bores in the cylinder head **(see illustration)**. Push them down until they contact the valves, then lubricate the camshaft lobe contact surfaces.

⚠️ *Warning: After fitting hydraulic tappets, wait a minimum of 30 minutes (or preferably, leave overnight) before starting the engine, to allow the tappets time to settle, otherwise the valve heads will strike the pistons.*

20 Fit the bearing shells to their original locations in the cylinder head and bearing caps, ensuring that the tab on each shell engages in the notch in the cylinder head or bearing cap **(see illustration)**.

7.19 Lubricate the hydraulic tappets, and offer them into position in their original bores in the cylinder head

7.20 Fit the bearing shells ensuring that the tab on each shell engages in the notch in the cylinder head or bearing cap

7.22 Refit the cylinder head retaining bolt washers to their locations adjacent to the camshaft bearing journals

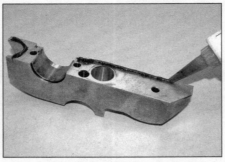

7.25a Apply a thin bead of silicone sealant to the mating surface of the bearing cap...

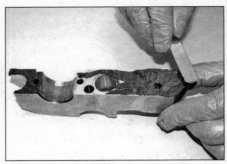

7.25b ...and spread the sealant evenly over the entire surface using a spatula

21 Lubricate the bearing shells with clean engine oil, then carefully lower the camshaft into position in the cylinder head.

22 Refit the cylinder head retaining bolt washers to their locations adjacent to the camshaft bearing journals **(see illustration)**.

23 Oil the upper surfaces of the camshaft bearing journals and bearing shells, then fit Nos 2, 3, 4, 5 and 6 bearing caps. Ensure that they are fitted the right way round and in the correct locations. Fit the new retaining bolts and tighten them progressively, in a diagonal sequence to force the camshaft down against the pressure of the valve springs. Once all the bearing caps are in contact with the cylinder head, tighten the bolts in a diagonal sequence to the specified torque, then through the specified angle.

24 Wipe clean the contact surfaces of the cylinder head and No 7 bearing cap.

25 Apply a thin bead of silicone sealant (Loctite 5970) to the contact surface of the bearing cap and spread the sealant evenly over the entire surface using a spatula or similar **(see illustrations)**.

26 Locate the bearing cap in position on the cylinder head and insert the new retaining bolts. Tighten the bolts to the specified torque, then through the specified angle. **Note:** *No 1 bearing cap is fitted as part of the camshaft drive gear refitting procedure described in Section 6.*

27 Refit the pump injector rocker shaft assembly as described in Section 5.

28 Refit the camshaft drive gear as described in Section 6.

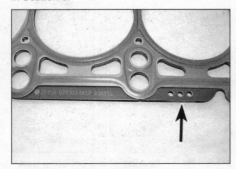

8.13 Location of cylinder head gasket identification holes (arrowed)

8 Cylinder head – removal, inspection and refitting

Note: *The cylinder head must be removed with the engine cold. New cylinder head bolts and a new cylinder head gasket will be required for refitting.*

Removal

1 Disconnect the battery negative terminal (refer to *Disconnecting the battery*).

2 Move the body front crossmember to the service position as described in Chapter 11, Section 25.

3 Drain the cooling system as described in Chapter 1, Section 30.

4 Drain the engine oil as described in Chapter 1, Section 3.

5 Remove the inlet manifold as described in Chapter 4A, Section 9.

6 Remove the exhaust manifold as described in Chapter 4A, Section 12.

7 Remove the camshaft drive gear as described in Section 6.

8 Undo the two bolts securing the gear train housing cover to the underside of the cylinder head.

9 Disconnect all necessary coolant and vacuum hoses as well as all wiring connections on the cylinder head.

10 Using a multi-splined tool, undo the cylinder head bolts, working from the outside-in, evenly and gradually. Check that nothing remains connected, and lift the cylinder head from the

8.16 Measure the piston protrusion using a DTI gauge

engine block. Seek assistance if possible, as it is an awkward assembly.

11 Remove the gasket from the top of the block, noting the locating dowels. If the dowels are a loose fit, remove them and store them with the head for safe-keeping. Do not discard the gasket yet – it will be needed for identification purposes.

Inspection

12 Dismantling of the cylinder head is covered in Chapter 2D, Section 6.

Cylinder head gasket selection

Note: *A dial test indicator (DTI) will be required for this operation.*

13 Examine the old cylinder head gasket for manufacturer's identification markings **(see illustration)**. These will be in the form of holes, and a part number on the edge of the gasket. Unless new pistons have been fitted, the new cylinder head gasket must be of the same type as the old one. In this case, purchase a new gasket, and proceed to paragraph 20.

14 If new piston assemblies have been fitted as part of an engine overhaul, or if a new short engine is to be fitted, the projection of the piston crowns above the cylinder block mating face of the cylinder block at TDC must be measured. This measurement is used to determine the thickness of the new cylinder head gasket required.

15 Anchor a dial test indicator (DTI) to the top face (cylinder head gasket mating face) of the cylinder block, and zero the gauge on the gasket mating face.

16 Rest the gauge probe on No 1 piston crown, and turn the crankshaft slowly by hand until the piston reaches TDC. Measure and record the maximum piston projection at TDC **(see illustration)**.

17 Repeat the measurement for the remaining pistons, and record the results.

18 If the measurements differ from piston-to-piston, take the highest figure, and use this to determine the thickness of the head gasket required as follows.

Gasket identification

Piston projection	(number of holes)
0.51 to 0.66 mm	1
0.66 to 0.72 mm	2
0.72 to 0.82 mm	3

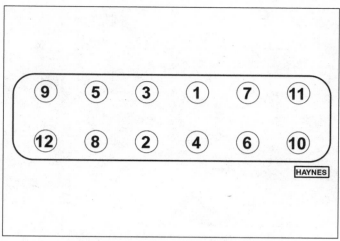

8.30 Cylinder head bolt tightening sequence

9.10 Apply a bead of sealant around the inside of the bolt holes

19 Purchase a new gasket according to the results of the measurements.

Refitting

20 The mating faces of the cylinder head and block must be perfectly clean before refitting the head. Use a scraper to remove all traces of gasket and carbon, also clean the tops of the pistons. Take particular care with the aluminium surfaces, as the soft metal is easily damaged.

21 Make sure that debris is not allowed to enter the oil and water passages – this is particularly important for the oil circuit, as carbon could block the oil supply to the camshaft and crankshaft bearings. Using adhesive tape and paper, seal the water, oil and bolt holes in the cylinder block.

22 To prevent carbon entering the gap between the pistons and bores, smear a little grease in the gap. After cleaning a piston, rotate the crankshaft so that the piston moves down the bore, then wipe out the grease and carbon with a cloth rag. Clean the other piston crowns in the same way.

23 Check the head and block for nicks, deep scratches and other damage. If slight, they may be removed carefully with a file.

24 If warpage of the cylinder head is suspected, use a straight-edge to check it for distortion, as described in Chapter 2D, Section 6.

25 Ensure that the cylinder head bolt holes in the crankcase are clean and free of oil. Syringe or soak up any oil left in the bolt holes. This is most important in order that the correct bolt tightening torque can be applied, and to prevent the possibility of the block being cracked by hydraulic pressure when the bolts are tightened.

26 Turn the crankshaft anti-clockwise until all the pistons are at an equal height, approximately halfway down their bores from the TDC position. This will eliminate any risk of piston-to-valve contact as the cylinder head is refitted.

27 Ensure that the cylinder head locating dowels are in place in the cylinder block, then fit the new cylinder head gasket over the dowels, ensuring that the part number is uppermost. Where applicable, the OBEN/TOP marking should also be uppermost. Note that VW recommend that the gasket is only removed from its packaging immediately prior to fitting.

28 Lower the cylinder head into position on the gasket, ensuring that it engages correctly over the guide studs and dowels.

29 Fit the new cylinder head bolts and screw them in as far as possible by hand.

30 Working progressively, in sequence, tighten all the cylinder head bolts to the specified Stage 1 torque **(see illustration)**.

31 Tighten all the cylinder head bolts, in sequence, through the specified Stage 2 angle, then through the Stage 3, 4 and 5 angles.

32 Finally, **slacken** all the cylinder head bolts, in sequence, through the specified Stage 6 angle.

33 After finally tightening the cylinder head bolts, set the engine back to TDC on No 1 cylinder as described in Section 3.

34 The remainder of the refitting procedure is a reversal of the removal procedure, bearing in mind the following points.

a) *Refit the camshaft drive gear as described in Section 6.*

b) *Refit the exhaust manifold as described in Chapter 4A, Section 12.*

c) *Refit the inlet manifold as described in Chapter 4A, Section 9.*

d) *Return the body front crossmember to its normal position as described in Chapter 11, Section 25.*

e) *Refill the engine with oil as described in Chapter 1, Section 3*

f) *Refill the cooling system as described in Chapter 1, Section 30.*

9 Sump – removal and refitting

Removal

1 Firmly apply the handbrake, then jack up the front of the vehicle and support it securely on axle stands (see *Jacking and vehicle support*).

2 Where fitted, undo the retaining bolts and remove the engine undertray.

3 Drain the engine oil as described in Chapter 1, Section 3.

4 Remove the sound deadening material from the sump.

5 Release the coolant pipe from the sump.

6 Where fitted, disconnect the wiring connector from the oil level/temperature sender in the sump.

7 Undo the sump retaining bolts, then loosen the sump with light blows of a rubber-headed hammer.

8 If necessary, using a wide-bladed scraper or similar tool inserted between the sump and cylinder block, carefully break the joint to release the sump, then manoeuvre the sump out from under the vehicle.

Refitting

9 Begin refitting by thoroughly cleaning the mating faces of the sump and cylinder block. Ensure that all traces of old sealant are removed.

10 Ensure that the cylinder block mating face of the sump is free from all traces of old sealant, oil and grease, and then apply a 2.0 to 3.0 mm thick bead of silicone sealant to the sump **(see illustration)**. Note that the sealant should be run around the inside of the bolt holes in the sump. The sump must be fitted within 5 minutes of applying the sealant.

11 Offer the sump up to the cylinder block, then refit the sump-to-cylinder block bolts, and lightly tighten them by hand, working progressively in a diagonal sequence. **Note:**

10.2a Undo the retaining bolts (arrowed)...

10.2b ...and remove the oil pick-up pipe

10.3 Remove the oil baffle plate

10.4a Oil pump front securing bolts (arrowed)

10.4b ...and rear securing bolt

If the sump is being refitted with the engine and transmission separated, make sure that the sump is flush with the flywheel end of the cylinder block.

12 Refit the sump-to-transmission casing bolts, and tighten them lightly, using a socket.

13 Again working in a diagonal sequence, *lightly* tighten the sump-to-cylinder block bolts, using a socket.

14 Tighten the sump-to-transmission casing bolts to the specified torque.

15 Working in a diagonal sequence, progressively tighten the sump-to-cylinder block bolts to the specified torque.

16 Secure the coolant pipe to the sump, then refit the sound deadening material.

11.2 Prevent the flywheel from turning by locking the ring gear teeth with a suitable tool

17 Refit the wiring connector to the oil level/temperature sender, then refit the engine undertray, and lower the vehicle to the ground.

18 Allow at least 30 minutes from the time of refitting the sump for the sealant to dry, then refill the engine with oil, with reference to Chapter 1, Section 3.

10 Oil pump – removal, inspection and refitting

Removal

1 Remove the sump as described in Section 9.

2 Undo the two bolts securing the oil pick-up pipe to the base of the oil pipe and the two bolts securing the pipe to the baffle plate. Remove the pick-up pipe and recover the gasket **(see illustrations)**.

3 Unscrew the securing bolts, and remove the oil baffle plate from the cylinder block **(see illustration)**.

4 Unscrew and remove the four mounting bolts, and release the oil pump from the dowels in the crankcase **(see illustrations)**.

Inspection

5 At the time of writing, it would appear that no parts are available for the oil pump. If defective, the oil pump assembly must be renewed. Consult a VW dealer or parts specialist.

Refitting

6 Prime the pump with oil by pouring oil into the pick-up pipe aperture while turning the drive gear.

7 Locate the pump in position on the dowels, then refit and tighten the mounting bolts to the specified torque.

8 Refit the baffle plate and tighten the retaining bolts to the specified torque.

9 Place a new gasket on the pick-up pipe then place the pipe in position. Fit the four retaining bolts to the specified torque.

10 Refit the sump as described in Section 9.

11 Flywheel/driveplate – removal, inspection and refitting

Removal

Note: *New flywheel/driveplate retaining bolts will be required on refitting.*

Manual transmission models

1 Remove the transmission as described in Chapter 7A, Section 6 then remove the clutch assembly as described in Chapter 6, Section 7.

2 Prevent the flywheel from turning by locking the ring gear teeth with a similar arrangement to that shown **(see illustration)**.

3 Slacken and remove the retaining bolts and remove the flywheel **(see illustration)**.
Caution: Take care, as the flywheel is heavy.

Automatic transmission models

4 Remove the transmission as described in Chapter 7B, Section 5, then remove the driveplate as described in paragraphs 2 and 3 but note the location of the shim and spacer.

Inspection

Flywheel

5 Check the flywheel for wear and damage. Examine the starter ring gear for excessive wear to the teeth. The ring gear may be renewed separately from the flywheel, but the work should be entrusted to a VW dealer. If the clutch friction face is discoloured or scored excessively, it may be possible to regrind it, but this work should also be entrusted to a VW dealer.

6 The following are *guidelines* only, but should indicate whether professional inspection is necessary. The dual-mass flywheel should be checked as follows:

There should be no cracks in the drive surface of the flywheel. If cracks are evident, the flywheel may need renewing.

Warpage

Place a straightedge across the face of the drive surface, and check by trying to insert a feeler gauge between the straightedge and the drive surface **(see illustration)**. The flywheel will normally warp like a bowl – i.e. higher on the outer edge. If the warpage is more than 0.40 mm, the flywheel may need renewing.

Free rotational movement

This is the distance the drive surface of the flywheel can be turned independently of the flywheel primary element, using finger effort alone. Move the drive surface in one direction and make a mark where the locating pin aligns with the flywheel edge. Move the drive surface in the other direction (finger pressure only) and make another mark **(see illustration)**. The total of free movement should not exceed 20.0 mm. If it's more, the flywheel may need renewing.

Total rotational movement

This is the total distance the drive surface can be turned independently of the flywheel primary element. Insert two bolts into the clutch pressure plate/damper unit mounting holes, and with the crankshaft/flywheel held stationary, use a lever/pry bar between the bolts and use some effort to move the drive surface fully in one direction – make a mark where the locating pin aligns with the flywheel edge. Now force the drive surface fully in the opposite direction, and make another mark. The total rotational movement should not exceed 44.0 mm. If it does, have the flywheel professionally inspected.

Lateral movement

The lateral movement (up and down) of the drive surface in relation to the primary

11.3 Flywheel retaining bolts

11.6a Flywheel warpage check – see text

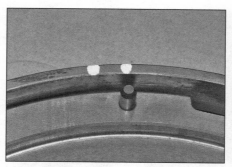

11.6b Flywheel free rotational movement check alignment marks – see text

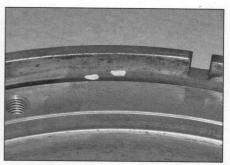

11.6c Flywheel lateral movement check marks – see text

element of the flywheel should not exceed 2.0 mm. If it does, the flywheel may need renewing. This can be checked by pressing the drive surface down on one side into the flywheel (flywheel horizontal) and making an alignment mark between the drive surface and the inner edge of the primary element. Now press down on the opposite side of the drive surface, and make another mark above the original one. The difference between the two marks is the lateral movement **(see illustration)**.

Driveplate

7 Closely examine the driveplate and ring gear teeth for signs of wear or damage and check the driveplate surface for any signs of cracks.

8 If there is any doubt about the condition of the driveplate, seek the advice of a VW dealer or engine reconditioning specialist.

Refitting

Manual transmission models

9 Clean the mating surfaces of the flywheel and crankshaft.

10 Offer up the flywheel and engage it on the crankshaft. Apply a drop of locking compound to the threads of each new flywheel retaining bolt (unless they are already precoated) and install the new bolts.

11 Lock the flywheel by the method used on removal then, working in a diagonal sequence, evenly and progressively tighten the retaining bolts to the specified Stage 1 torque, then through the specified Stage 2 angle.

12 Refit the clutch as described in Chapter 6, Section 7, then remove the locking tool and refit the transmission as described in Chapter 7A, Section 6.

Automatic transmission models

13 Clean the mating surfaces of the driveplate and crankshaft.

14 Offer up the driveplate and engage it on the crankshaft. Apply a drop of locking compound to the threads of each new driveplate retaining bolt (unless they are already precoated) and install the new bolts.

15 Lock the driveplate by the method used on removal then, working in a diagonal sequence, evenly and progressively tighten the retaining bolts to the specified Stage 1 torque, then through the specified Stage 2 angle.

16 Remove the locking tool, and refit the transmission as described in Chapter 7B, Section 5.

12 Oil seals –
renewal

Note: *The oil seals are a PTFE (Teflon) type and are fitted dry, without using any grease or oil. These have a wider sealing lip and have been introduced instead of the coil spring type oil seal.*

Crankshaft left-hand oil seal

1 Remove the flywheel/driveplate as described in Section 11.

2 Carefully prise out the old seal from its

12.2 Carefully prise out the old oil seal using a screwdriver or similar hooked tool

12.5a The new crankshaft oil seal is supplied with a fitting sleeve

12.5b Position the seal, together with the fitting sleeve over the end of the crankshaft...

12.5c ...then tap the seal into position using a suitable socket or tube, or a wooden block

12.9 Remove the alternator rubber drive coupling from the drive shaft hub

12.10 Alternator driveshaft hub retaining bolt (arrowed)

location using a screwdriver or similar hooked tool **(see illustration)**.

3 Clean the oil seal seat and the crankshaft journal with a clean cloth.

4 The new oil seal is supplied with a fitting sleeve which should be left in place until the seal is installed.

5 Position the seal, together with the fitting sleeve over the end of the crankshaft, then tap the seal into position using a suitable socket or tube, or a wooden block, until it is flush with the outer faces of the gear train housing cover **(see illustrations)**.

6 Once the seal is in position, remove the fitting sleeve.

7 Refit the flywheel/driveplate as described in Section 11.

Alternator driveshaft oil seal

8 Remove the alternator as described in Chapter 5, Section 7.

9 If still in place, remove the alternator rubber drive coupling from the drive shaft hub **(see illustration)**.

10 Prevent the alternator drive shaft hub from turning using a 27 mm AF ring spanner, then unscrew the hub retaining bolt **(see illustration)**. Note that a new bolt will be required for refitting.

11 Withdraw the hub from the alternator drive shaft.

12 Carefully prise out the old seal from its location using a screwdriver or similar hooked tool.

13 Thoroughly clean the oil seal seating in the cylinder block.

14 Fit a new oil seal to the cylinder block, pressing or driving it into position using a socket or tube of suitable diameter. Ensure that the socket or tube bears only on the hard outer ring of the seal, and take care not to damage the seal lips. Press or drive the seal into position until it is fully seated. Make sure that the closed end of the seal is facing outwards.

15 Refit the hub to the alternator drive shaft, then fit the new retaining bolt. Hold the hub using the ring spanner and tighten the retaining bolt to the specified torque, then through the specified angle.

16 Refit the alternator rubber drive coupling

13.8a Undo the three air conditioning compressor mounting bolts (arrowed)...

to the drive shaft hub, then refit the alternator as described in Chapter 5, Section 7.

13 Engine oil cooler/ filter housing – removal and refitting

Removal

1 The oil cooler is mounted on top of the oil filter housing on the front of the cylinder block.

2 Disconnect the battery negative terminal (refer to *Disconnecting the battery*).

3 Firmly apply the handbrake, then jack up the front of the vehicle and support it securely on axle stands (see *Jacking and vehicle support*).

4 Where fitted, undo the six retaining bolts and remove the engine undertray.

5 Move the body front crossmember to the service position as described in Chapter 11, Section 25.

6 Drain the cooling system as described in Chapter 1, Section 30.

7 Drain the engine oil as described in Chapter 1, Section 3.

8 On models with air conditioning, undo the three compressor mounting bolts. Disengage the compressor from the rubber drive coupling, move it to one side and support it using cable ties **(see illustrations)**. Do not disconnect the refrigerant hoses.

9 On models with air conditioning, undo the two bolts and remove the compressor mounting bracket (see illustration).

10 Undo the retaining bolt and remove the coolant hose support bracket from the front of the oil filter housing.

11 Disconnect the wiring connector from the oil pressure switch on the oil filter housing base.

12 Release the retaining clip and disconnect the coolant hose from the oil filter housing.

13 Undo the five retaining bolts, remove the oil filter housing from the cylinder block and collect the gasket (see illustrations).

14 Unscrew the oil cooler retaining screws and remove the oil cooler from the top of the oil filter housing. Recover the O-rings from between the cooler and the oil filter housing, new ones will be required for refitting.

Refitting

15 Refitting is a reversal of removal, bearing in mind the following points:
  a) Use new oil cooler O-rings and a new filter housing gasket.
  b) Tighten the oil filter housing bolts to the specified torque.
  c) Return the body front crossmember to its normal position as described in Chapter 11, Section 25.
  d) Refill the engine with oil, with reference to Chapter 1, Section 3.
  e) Refill the cooling system with reference to Chapter 1, Section 30.

14 Oil pressure warning light switch – removal and refitting

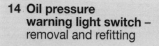

Removal

1 The oil pressure warning light switch is fitted to the base of the oil filter housing. Undo the retaining bolts and rotary fasteners and remove the battery cover and engine covers as applicable.

2 Disconnect the wiring connector and wipe clean the area around the switch.

3 Unscrew the switch from the filter housing and remove it, along with its sealing washer (see illustration). If the switch is to be left removed from the engine for any length of time, plug the oil filter housing aperture.

Refitting

4 Examine the sealing washer for signs of damage or deterioration and if necessary renew.

5 Refit the switch, complete with washer, and tighten it to the specified torque.

6 Securely reconnect the wiring connector then check and, if necessary, top-up the engine oil as described in *Weekly checks*. On completion, refit the battery cover and engine covers.

13.8b ...then disengage the compressor from the drive coupling and move it to one side

13.13a Undo the five retaining bolts (arrowed)...

15 Oil level/temperature sender – removal and refitting

Removal

1 The oil level/temperature sender is fitted to bottom of the sump.

2 Drain the engine oil as described in Chapter 1 Section 3.

3 Disconnect the wiring connector from the sender.

4 Wipe clean the area around the sender, then undo the three retaining bolts and remove the sender.

Refitting

5 Examine the sealing washer for signs of

13.13c ...and collect the gasket

13.9 Undo the two bolts (arrowed) and remove the compressor mounting bracket

13.13b ...remove the oil filter housing from the cylinder block...

damage or deterioration and if necessary renew.

6 Refit the switch and tighten the retaining bolts to the specified torque.

7 Refill the engine with oil as described in Chapter 1, Section 3.

16 Engine/transmission mountings – inspection and renewal

Refer to Chapter 2A, Section 20 for the basic procedure, but note that slight differences in the engine and transmission brackets will be noticed. Use new bolts when refitting the mountings and tighten the bolts to the torque wrench settings given in this Part of Chapter 2.

14.3 Oil pressure warning light switch (arrowed)

Chapter 2 Part D:
Engine removal and overhaul procedures

Contents

Degrees of difficulty

Easy, suitable for novice with little experience 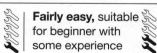	**Fairly easy,** suitable for beginner with some experience 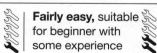	**Fairly difficult,** suitable for competent DIY mechanic 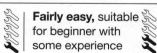	**Difficult,** suitable for experienced DIY mechanic 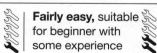	**Very difficult,** suitable for expert DIY or professional

Specifications

Engine identification

Engine type	Manufacturer's engine code
1.9 litre engines:	
77 kW engines	AXB
63 kW engines	AXC
62 kW engines	BRR
75 kW engines	BRS
2.0 litre engines:	
62 kW engines	CAAA
75 kW engines	CAAB
84 kW engines	CAAD
100 kW engines	CAAE and CCHB
103 kW engines	CAAC and CCHA
132 kW engines	CFCA
2.5 litre engines:	
96 kW engines	AXD and BNZ
120 kW engines	BLJ
128 kW engines	AXE and BPC

1.9 litre engines

Cylinder head

Cylinder head gasket surface, maximum distortion	0.1 mm

Valves

Valve stem diameter:	
Inlet	6.98 mm
Exhaust	6.95 mm
Valve length	89.95 mm
Valve head diameter:	
Inlet	35.95 mm
Exhaust	31.45 mm
Maximum valve head deflection (end of valve stem flush with top of guide)	1.30 mm

Cylinder block

Bore diameter:	
Standard	79.51 mm
1st oversize	79.76 mm
2nd oversize	80.01 mm
Maximum bore wear	0.08 mm

Pistons and piston rings

Piston diameter:	
Standard	79.47 mm
1st oversize	79.72 mm
2nd oversize	79.97 mm
Piston ring-to-groove clearance:	
Top compression ring:	
Standard	0.06 to 0.09 mm
Service limit	0.25 mm
2nd compression ring:	
Standard	0.05 to 0.08 mm
Service limit	0.25 mm
Oil scraper ring:	
Standard	0.03 to 0.06 mm
Service limit	0.15 mm
Piston ring end gaps:*	
Compression rings:	
Standard	0.20 to 0.40 mm
Service limit	1.0 mm
Oil scraper ring:	
Standard	0.25 to 0.50 mm
Service limit	1.0 mm

*Note: Piston ring end gaps should be offset at 120° to each other when fitted

Crankshaft

Endfloat:	
Standard	0.07 to 0.17 mm
Service limit	0.37 mm
Main bearing journal diameter	54.00 mm (nominal)
Main bearing running clearances:	
Standard	0.03 to 0.08 mm
Service limit	0.17 mm
Crankpin journal diameter	47.80 mm (nominal)
Big-end bearing running clearance:	
Standard	N/A
Service limit	0.08 mm

Torque wrench settings

Refer to Chapter 2A Specifications

2.0 litre engines

Cylinder head

Cylinder head gasket surface, maximum distortion. . . . . 0.1 mm
Cylinder head gasket identification:
  Piston protrusion:
    0.91 to 1.00 mm . . . . 1 notch/hole
    1.01 to 1.10 mm . . . . 2 notches/holes
    1.11 to 1.20 mm . . . . 3 notches/holes

Valves

Valve stem diameter:
  Inlet. . . . . 5.94 mm
  Exhaust. . . . . 5.94 mm
Valve length:
  Inlet. . . . . 99.30 mm
  Exhaust. . . . . 99.10 mm
Valve head diameter:
  Inlet. . . . . 26.6 mm
  Exhaust. . . . . 26.00 mm
Maximum valve head deflection
  (end of valve stem flush with top of guide). . . . . 1.30 mm

Cylinder block

Bore diameter. . . . . 81.01 mm

Pistons and piston rings

Piston diameter . . . . 80.96 mm
Piston ring-to-groove clearance:
  Top compression ring:
    Standard. . . . . 0.06 to 0.09 mm
    Service limit . . . . 0.25 mm
  2nd compression ring:
    Standard. . . . . 0.05 to 0.08 mm
    Service limit . . . . 0.25 mm
  Oil scraper ring:
    Standard. . . . . 0.05 to 0.08 mm
    Service limit . . . . 0.15 mm
Piston ring end gaps:*
  Compression rings:
    Standard. . . . . 0.20 to 0.40 mm
    Service limit . . . . 1.0 mm
  Oil scraper ring:
    Standard. . . . . 0.25 to 0.50 mm
    Service limit . . . . 1.0 mm
*Note: Piston ring end gaps should be offset at 120° to each other when fitted

Crankshaft

Endfloat:
  Standard. . . . . 0.07 to 0.17 mm
  Service limit . . . . 0.37 mm
Main bearing journal diameter . . . . 54.00 mm (nominal)
Main bearing running clearances:
  Standard. . . . . 0.03 to 0.08 mm
  Service limit . . . . 0.17 mm
Crankpin journal diameter . . . . 50.90 (nominal)
Big-end bearing running clearance:
  Standard. . . . . N/A
  Service limit . . . . 0.08 mm

Torque wrench settings

Refer to Chapter 2B Specifications

2.5 litre engines

Cylinder head

Cylinder head gasket surface, maximum distortion................	0.1 mm
Cylinder head gasket identification:	
Piston protrusion:	
0.51 to 0.66 mm	1 hole
0.66 to 0.72 mm	2 holes
0.72 to 0.82 mm	3 holes

Valves

Valve stem diameter:	
Inlet..	6.98 mm
Exhaust..	6.95 mm
Valve length	89.95 mm
Valve head diameter:	
Inlet..	35.95 mm
Exhaust..	31.45 mm
Maximum valve head deflection	
(end of valve stem flush with top of guide).................	1.3 mm

Cylinder block

Bore diameter...	81.00 mm

Pistons and piston rings

Piston diameter	80.97 mm
Piston ring-to-groove clearance:	
Top compression ring:	
Standard...	0.09 to 0.13 mm
Service limit	0.25 mm
2nd compression ring:	
Standard...	0.04 to 0.08 mm
Service limit	0.25 mm
Oil scraper ring:	
Standard...	0.03 to 0.07 mm
Service limit	0.15 mm
Piston ring end gaps:*	
Top compression ring:	
Standard...	0.25 to 0.40 mm
Service limit	1.0 mm
2nd compression ring:	
Standard...	0.30 to 0.50 mm
Service limit	1.0 mm
Oil scraper ring:	
Standard...	0.25 to 0.50 mm
Service limit	1.0 mm

*Note: Piston ring end gaps should be offset at 120° to each other when fitted

Crankshaft

Endfloat:	
Standard...	0.07 to 0.23 mm
Service limit	0.25 mm
Main bearing journal diameters	58.00 mm (nominal)
Main bearing running clearances:	
Standard...	0.026 to 0.040 mm
Service limit	0.16 mm
Crankpin journal diameters	50.90 mm (nominal)
Big-end bearing running clearance:	
Standard...	N/A
Service limit	0.08 mm

Torque wrench settings

Refer to Chapter 2C Specifications

1 General information

This Part of Chapter 2 is devoted to engine/transmission removal and refitting, to those repair procedures requiring the removal of the engine/transmission from the vehicle, and to the overhaul of engine components. It includes only the Specifications relevant to those procedures. Refer to Part A, B or C (depending on engine type) for additional Specifications and for all torque wrench settings.

The information ranges from advice concerning preparation for an overhaul and the purchase of new parts, to detailed step-by-step procedures covering removal and installation of internal engine components and the inspection of parts.

The following Sections have been written based on the assumption that the engine has been removed from the vehicle. For information concerning in-vehicle engine repair, as well as removal and installation of the external components necessary for the overhaul, see Part A, B or C of this Chapter.

2 Engine overhaul –
general information

It's not always easy to determine when, or if, an engine should be completely overhauled, as a number of factors must be considered.

High mileage is not necessarily an indication that an overhaul is needed, while low mileage doesn't preclude the need for an overhaul. Frequency of servicing is probably the most important consideration. An engine that has had regular and frequent oil and filter changes, as well as other required maintenance, will most likely give many thousands of miles of reliable service. Conversely, a neglected engine may require an overhaul very early in its life.

Excessive oil consumption is an indication that piston rings, valve seals and/or valve guides are in need of attention. Make sure that oil leaks are not responsible before deciding that the rings and/or guides are worn. Perform a cylinder compression test (refer to Part A, B or C of this Chapter) to determine the likely cause of the problem.

Check the oil pressure with a gauge fitted in place of the oil pressure switch, and compare it with that specified in Chapter 2A, 2B or 2C as applicable. If it is extremely low, the main and big-end bearings, and/or the oil pump, are probably worn out.

Loss of power, rough running, knocking or metallic engine noises, excessive valve gear noise, and high fuel consumption may also point to the need for an overhaul, especially if they are all present at the same time. If a complete service does not cure the situation, major mechanical work is the only solution.

A full engine overhaul involves restoring all internal parts to the specification of a new engine. During a complete overhaul, the pistons and the piston rings are renewed, and the cylinder bores are reconditioned. New main and big-end bearings are generally fitted. If necessary, the crankshaft may be reground (where possible), to compensate for wear in the journals. The valves are also serviced as well, since they are usually in less-than-perfect condition at this point. Always pay careful attention to the condition of the oil pump when overhauling the engine, and renew it if there is any doubt as to its serviceability. The end result should be an as-new engine that will give many trouble-free miles.

Critical cooling system components such as the hoses, thermostat and coolant pump should be renewed when an engine is overhauled. The radiator should also be checked carefully, to ensure that it is not clogged or leaking.

Before beginning the engine overhaul, read the entire procedure, to familiarise yourself with the scope and requirements of the job. Check on the availability of parts and make sure that any necessary special tools and equipment are obtained in advance. Most work can be done with typical hand tools, although a number of precision measuring tools are required for inspecting parts to determine if they must be renewed.

The services provided by an engineering machine shop or engine reconditioning specialist will almost certainly be required, particularly if major repairs such as crankshaft regrinding or cylinder reboring are necessary. Apart from carrying out machining operations, these establishments will normally handle the inspection of parts, offer advice concerning reconditioning or renewal and supply new components such as pistons, piston rings and bearing shells. It is recommended that the establishment used is a member of the Federation of Engine Re-Manufacturers, or a similar society.

Always wait until the engine has been completely dismantled, and until all components (especially the cylinder block/crankcase and the crankshaft) have been inspected before deciding what service and repair operations must be performed by an engineering works. The condition of these components will be the major factor to consider when determining whether to overhaul the original engine, or to buy a reconditioned unit. Do not, therefore, purchase parts or have overhaul work done on other components until they have been thoroughly inspected. As a general rule, time is the primary cost of an overhaul, so it does not pay to fit worn or sub-standard parts.

As a final note, to ensure maximum life and minimum trouble from a reconditioned engine, everything must be assembled with care, in a spotlessly clean environment.

3 Engine/transmission removal
– methods and precautions

If you have decided that the engine must be removed for overhaul or major repair work, several preliminary steps should be taken.

Locating a suitable place to work is extremely important. Adequate work space, along with storage space for the vehicle, will be needed. If a workshop or garage is not available, at the very least a solid, level, clean work surface is required.

If possible, clear some shelving close to the work area and use it to store the engine components and ancillaries as they are removed and dismantled. In this manner, the components stand a better chance of staying clean and undamaged during the overhaul. Laying out components in groups together with their fixings bolts, screws, etc will save time and avoid confusion when the engine is refitted.

Cleaning the engine compartment and engine/transmission before beginning the removal procedure will help keep tools clean and organised.

An engine hoist will also be necessary. Make sure the equipment is rated in excess of the combined weight of the engine and transmission. Safety is of primary importance, considering the potential hazards involved in removing the engine/transmission from the vehicle.

The help of an assistant is essential. Apart from the safety aspects involved, there are many instances when one person cannot simultaneously perform all of the operations required during engine/transmission removal.

Plan the operation ahead of time. Before starting work, arrange for the hire of or obtain all of the tools and equipment you will need. Some of the equipment necessary to perform engine/transmission removal and installation safely (in addition to an engine hoist) is as follows: a heavy duty trolley jack, complete sets of spanners and sockets as described in the rear of this manual, wooden blocks, and plenty of rags and cleaning solvent for mopping up spilled oil, coolant and fuel. If the hoist must be hired, make sure that you arrange for it in advance, and perform all of the operations possible without it beforehand. This will save you money and time.

Plan for the vehicle to be out of use for quite a while. An engineering machine shop or engine reconditioning specialist will be required to perform some of the work which cannot be accomplished without special equipment. These places often have a busy schedule, so it would be a good idea to consult them before removing the engine, in order to accurately estimate the amount of time required to rebuild or repair components that may need work.

4.13 Rotate the two turnbuckles (arrowed) and open the cover of the electrics box

4.14 Undo the retaining screws, release the fuse carrier, then lift off the upper part of the electrics box

During the engine/transmission removal procedure, it is advisable to make notes of the locations of all brackets, cable ties, earthing points, etc, as well as how the wiring harnesses, hoses and electrical connections are attached and routed around the engine and engine compartment. An effective way of doing this is to take a series of photographs of the various components before they are disconnected or removed; the resulting photographs will prove invaluable when the engine/transmission is refitted.

Always be extremely careful when removing and refitting the engine/transmission. Serious injury can result from careless actions. Plan ahead and take your time, and a job of this nature, although major, can be accomplished successfully.

On all models, the engine must be removed complete with the transmission as an assembly. There is insufficient clearance in the engine compartment to remove the engine leaving the transmission in the vehicle. The assembly is removed by raising the front of the vehicle, and lowering the assembly from the engine compartment.

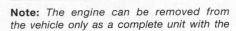

4   Engine/transmission –
   removal, separation
   and refitting

Note: *The engine can be removed from the vehicle only as a complete unit with the*

transmission; the two are then separated for overhaul. The engine/transmission unit is lowered out of position, and withdrawn from under the vehicle. Bearing this in mind, and also bearing in mind the information contained in Section 3, ensure the vehicle is raised sufficiently so that there is enough clearance between the front of the vehicle and the floor to allow the engine/transmission unit to be slid out once it has been lowered out of position.
Note: *Such is the complexity of the power unit arrangement on these vehicles, and the variations that may be encountered according to model and optional equipment fitted, that the following should be regarded as a guide to the work involved, rather than a step-by-step procedure. Where differences are encountered, or additional component disconnection or removal is necessary, make notes of the work involved as an aid to refitting.*

Removal

1 On models with air conditioning, have the system fully discharged by an air conditioning specialist.
2 Firmly apply the handbrake, then jack up the front of the vehicle and support it securely on axle stands (see *Jacking and vehicle support*). Remove the front roadwheels.
3 Remove the body front crossmember as described in Chapter 11, Section 25.
4 Remove the air cleaner assembly and air ducts as described in Chapter 4A, Section 2, or Chapter 4B, Section 2.

5 If the engine is going to be dismantled, drain the engine oil as described in Chapter 1, Section 3.
6 On 1.9 and 2.0 litre engines, remove the auxiliary drivebelts as described in Chapter 1, Section 27.
7 Release the retaining clips and disconnect the coolant hoses at the expansion tank. Disconnect the wiring connector, undo the retaining bolts and remove the expansion tank.
8 Release the retaining clips and disconnect the coolant hoses at the thermostat housing, coolant pump, cylinder head and heater matrix inlet and outlet ports at the bulkhead.
9 Disconnect the brake servo vacuum hose from the vacuum pump on the cylinder block.
10 Disconnect the fuel supply and return hoses from the fuel filter or fuel injection pump.
11 Remove the exhaust system front pipe as described in Chapter 4A, Section 15, or diesel particulate filter as described in Chapter 4B, Section 16.
12 Remove the battery and battery tray as described in Chapter 5, Section 4.
13 Rotate the two turnbuckles and open the cover of the electrics box (see illustration). Push the locking mechanism on the fuse insert in the direction of the housing and pull the fuse insert upwards out of the electrics box.
14 Undo the nine screws securing the upper part of the electrics box to the centre part. Slide the fuse carrier out of its location and push it downwards, then lift off the upper part of the electrics box (see illustration).
15 Undo the retaining nut and disconnect the left-hand cable from the wiring carrier terminal stud (see illustration).
16 Release the locking catch and lift the relay carrier from its location in the electrics box (see illustration).
17 Undo the eight retaining screws on the inside and outside of the electrics box and lift off the centre part of the box (see illustration).
18 Pull out the locking bars and disconnect the wiring connectors from the engine management ECU. Release the locking

4.15 Undo the retaining nut and disconnect the left-hand cable (arrowed) from the wiring carrier terminal stud

4.16 Release the locking catch and lift the relay carrier from its location

4.17 Undo the eight retaining screws and lift off the centre part of the electrics box

catch and lift the ECU from its location in the electrics box. **(see illustrations)**.

19 Disconnect the relevant wiring connectors in the electrics box to enable the wiring harness to be removed with the engine. Release the wiring harness from its attachments and place it over the engine.

20 On manual transmission models, carry out the following:

a) *On models, with the 5-speed transmissions, undo the two bolts and withdraw the clutch slave cylinder from the transmission. Tie the cylinder to one side.* **Note:** *The hydraulic pipe remains connected.*

b) *On models with 6-speed transmissions, clamp the clutch hydraulic hose with a suitable hose clamp. Pull out the retaining clip to its stop and disconnect the bleed screw housing from the end of the slave cylinder* **(see illustrations)**. *Suitably cover the disconnected unions to prevent dirt entry.*

c) *Disconnect the wiring connector from the reversing light switch.*

d) *Disconnect the gear selection mechanism from the transmission by pushing in the retaining clips and disconnecting the inner cable end fittings from the transmission selector lever ballpins. Push the retaining catch forward and detach the outer cables support bracket from the mounting bracket on the transmission* **(see illustrations)**.

21 On automatic transmission models, carry out the following:

a) *Press together the retaining catches and pull the selector cable upwards out of the transmission support bracket. Using a large screwdriver or similar tool, prise the selector inner cable end fitting off the ballpin on the transmission selector lever.*

b) *Clamp the coolant hoses leading to the transmission fluid cooler, then release the*

4.18a Disconnect the wiring connectors from the ECU...

4.20a Pull out the retaining clip to its stop...

4.18b ...then release the locking catch and lift the ECU from its location

4.20b ...and disconnect the bleed screw housing from the end of the slave cylinder

clips and disconnect the hoses from the cooler ports.

c) *Unplug the wiring harness from the transmission at the connectors; label each connector to aid refitting later.*

22 On vehicles with air conditioning, unbolt the compressor and suitably support it clear of the engine.

23 Working around the engine and transmission, disconnect all remaining electrical wiring, vacuum hoses and fuel connections, labelling each connector carefully to ensure correct refitting.

24 Refer to Chapter 8, Section 2 and remove the driveshafts.

25 Remove the front subframe as described in Chapter 10, Section 9.

26 Attach a suitable hoist and lifting tackle to the engine lifting brackets on the cylinder head, and support the weight of the engine/transmission.

27 Make a final check to ensure that all relevant pipes, hoses, wires, etc, have been disconnected, and that they are positioned clear of the engine and transmission.

28 Remove the left-hand and right-hand

4.20c Push in the retaining clip (arrowed) and disconnect each selector inner cable end fitting from the transmission selector lever

4.20d Push the retaining catch (arrowed) forward and detach the outer cables support bracket from the transmission

4.34 Undo the retaining bolts and remove the sealing flange from the right-hand end of the cylinder block

4.35a Locate the crankshaft turning and setting tool over the end of the crankshaft...

4.35b ...and secure the tool in place with the retaining bolt

engine/transmission mountings as described in Chapter 2A, Section 20.

29 With the help of an assistant, carefully lower the engine/transmission assembly to the ground. Make sure that the surrounding components in the engine compartment are not damaged. Ideally, the assembly should be lowered onto a trolley jack or low platform with castors, so that it can easily be withdrawn from under the vehicle.

30 Ensure that the assembly is adequately supported, then disconnect the engine hoist and lifting tackle, and withdraw the engine/transmission assembly from under the front of the vehicle.

Separation

31 Rest the engine and transmission assembly on a firm, flat surface, and use wooden blocks as wedges to keep the unit steady.

Manual transmission

32 The transmission is secured to the engine by a combination of bolts and studs with nuts, threaded into the cylinder block and bellhousing – the total number of fixings depends on the type of transmission and vehicle specification.

33 Starting at the bottom, remove all the bolts and nuts then carefully draw the transmission away from the engine, resting it securely on wooden blocks. Collect the locating dowels if they are loose enough to be extracted.

Caution: Take care to prevent the transmission from tilting, until the input shaft is fully disengaged from the clutch friction plate.

Automatic transmission

Note: *VW special tool T10225 (crankshaft turning and setting tool) or a suitable alternative will be required for this procedure.*

34 Undo the five retaining bolts and remove the sealing flange from the right-hand end of the cylinder block **(see illustration)**.

35 To enable the crankshaft to be turned, locate the crankshaft turning and setting tool (T10225 or equivalent) over the end of the crankshaft and secure the tool in place with the retaining bolt **(see illustrations)**. Note that the tool will only fit on the crankshaft in one position.

36 Working at the rear of the torque converter housing, remove the sealing grommet for access to the torque converter retaining nuts.

37 Using a socket or spanner on the special tool, turn the crankshaft until one of the six torque converter retaining nuts becomes accessible through the opening in the bellhousing.

38 Undo the first torque converter retaining nut, then turn the crankshaft one sixth of a turn until the next nut becomes accessible. Unscrew the nut then continue this procedure until all six nuts have been removed. Note that new nuts will be required for refitting.

39 The transmission is secured to the engine by a combination of bolts and studs with nuts, threaded into the cylinder block and bellhousing – the total number of fixings depends on the type of transmission and vehicle specification.

40 Starting at the bottom, remove all the screws and nuts then carefully draw the transmission away from the engine, resting it securely on wooden blocks. Collect locating dowels if they are loose enough to be extracted.

Caution: Take care to prevent the torque converter from sliding off the transmission input shaft – hold it in place as the transmission is withdrawn.

41 Place a length of batten across the open face of the bellhousing, fastening it with cable ties, to keep the torque converter in place in its housing.

Refitting

42 If the engine and transmission have not been separated, proceed to paragraph 49.

Manual transmission

43 Smear a little high-melting-point grease on the splines of the transmission input shaft. Do not use an excessive amount as there is the risk of contaminating the clutch friction plate. Carefully offer up the transmission to the cylinder block, guiding the dowels into the mounting holes in cylinder block.

44 Refit the bellhousing bolts and nuts, hand tightening them to secure the transmission in position. **Note:** *Do not tighten them to force the engine and transmission together.* Ensure that the bellhousing and cylinder block

mating faces will butt together evenly without obstruction, before tightening the bolts and nuts to their specified torque.

Automatic transmission

45 Remove the torque converter restraint from the face of the bellhousing. Check that the drive lugs on the torque converter hub are correctly engaged with the recesses in the inner wheel of the automatic transmission fluid pump.

46 Carefully offer up the transmission to the cylinder block, guiding the dowels into the mounting holes in cylinder block.

47 Refit the bellhousing bolts and nuts, hand-tightening them to secure the transmission in position. **Note:** *Do not tighten them to force the engine and transmission together.* Ensure that the bellhousing and cylinder block mating faces will butt together evenly without obstruction, before tightening the bolts and nuts to their specified torque.

48 Fit the new torque converter-to-driveplate nuts and tighten them lightly only to start, then go around and tighten them to the specified torque (see Chapter 7B).

All models

49 Manoeuvre the engine or engine/transmission back into position under the front of the vehicle and reconnect the engine hoist and lifting tackle.

50 With the help of an assistant, carefully raise the engine/transmission assembly into position making sure that the surrounding components in the engine compartment are not damaged.

51 Refit the left-hand and right-hand engine/transmission mountings as described in Chapter 2A, Section 20.

52 Disconnect and remove the hoist and lifting tackle from the engine.

53 The remainder of the refitting sequence is the direct reverse of the removal procedure, noting the following points:

a) *Ensure that all sections of the wiring harness follow their original routing; use new cable-ties to secure the harness in position, keeping it away from sources of heat and abrasion.*

b) *On vehicles with a 6-speed manual transmission, bleed the clutch hydraulic* system as described in Chapter 6, Section 2.

c) Ensure that all hoses are correctly routed and are secured with the correct hose clips, where applicable.

d) Refill the engine with appropriate grade and quantities of oil as described in Chapter 1, Section 3.

e) Refill the cooling system as described in Chapter 1, Section 30.

f) When the engine is started for the first time, check for air, coolant, lubricant and fuel leaks from manifolds, hoses etc. If the engine has been overhauled, read the notes in Section 15 before attempting to start it.

g) Have the air conditioning system evacuated, charged and leak-tested by the specialist who discharged it.

5 Engine overhaul – dismantling sequence

1 It is much easier to dismantle and work on the engine if it is mounted on a portable engine stand. These stands can often be hired from a tool hire shop. Before the engine is mounted on a stand, the flywheel should be removed so that the stand bolts can be tightened into the end of the cylinder block/crankcase.

2 If a stand is not available it is possible to dismantle the engine with it mounted on blocks, on a sturdy workbench or on the floor. Be extra careful not to tip or drop the engine when working without a stand.

3 If you are going to obtain a reconditioned engine, all external components must be removed first to be transferred to the new engine (just as they will if you are doing a complete engine overhaul yourself). **Note:** When removing the external components from the engine, pay close attention to details that may be helpful or important during refitting. Note the fitted position of gaskets, seals, spacers, pins, washers, bolts and other small items. These external components include the following:

a) Alternator (including mounting brackets) and starter motor.

b) The glow plug/pre-heating system components.

c) All fuel system components, including the fuel injection pump, all sensors and actuators.

d) Cooling system/thermostat housings.

e) The vacuum pump.

f) All electrical switches, actuators and sensors, and the engine wiring harness.

g) Inlet and exhaust manifolds and turbocharger.

h) The engine oil level dipstick and its tube.

i) Engine mountings.

j) Flywheel/driveplate.

k) Clutch components – manual transmission models.

4 If you are obtaining a short engine (the engine cylinder block/crankcase, crankshaft,

pistons and connecting rods, all fully assembled), then the cylinder head, sump, oil pump, timing belt (together with its tensioner and covers), auxiliary belt (together with its tensioner), coolant pump, thermostat housing, coolant outlet elbows, oil filter housing and where applicable oil cooler will also have to be removed, according to engine type.

5 If you are planning a full overhaul, the engine can be dismantled in the order given below:

a) Inlet and exhaust manifolds (see the relevant part of Chapter 4).

b) Timing belt, sprockets and tensioner (4-cylinder engines – see the relevant part of Chapter 2).

c) Cylinder head (see the relevant part of Chapter 2).

d) Flywheel/driveplate (see the relevant part of Chapter 2).

e) Sump (see the relevant part of Chapter 2).

f) Oil pump (see the relevant part of Chapter 2).

g) Piston/connecting rod assemblies (Section 7).

h) Crankshaft (Section 8).

6 Cylinder head – dismantling, cleaning, inspection and reassembly

Note: New and reconditioned cylinder heads are available from VW, and from engine reconditioning specialists. Specialist tools are required for the dismantling and inspection procedures, and new components may not be readily available. It may, therefore, be more practical for the home mechanic to buy a reconditioned head, rather than to dismantle, inspect and recondition the original head.

Dismantling

1 Remove the cylinder head as described in Chapter 2A, Section 13 (1.9 litre engines), Chapter 2B, Section 11 (2.0 litre engines) or Chapter 2C, Section 8 (2.5 litre engines).

2 If not already done, remove the inlet manifold as described in Chapter 4A, Section 9, or Chapter 4B, Section 9.

3 If not already done, remove the exhaust manifold as described in Chapter 4A, Section 12, or Chapter 4B, Section 13.

4 Remove the camshaft and hydraulic tappets

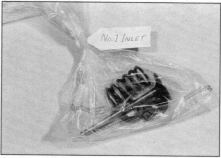

6.10 Keep groups of components together in labelled bags or boxes

as described in Chapter 2A, Section 10, Chapter 2B, Section 9 or Chapter 2C, Section 7.

5 Remove the fuel injectors as described in Chapter 4A, Section 8 or Chapter 4B, Section 8.

6 Remove the glow plugs as described in Chapter 5, Section 13.

7 Where applicable, unscrew the nut and remove the timing belt tensioner pulley from the stud on the timing belt end of the cylinder head.

8 Undo the retaining bolts and remove the relevant coolant outlet elbows together with their gaskets/O-rings.

9 Unbolt any remaining components (auxiliary brackets, engine lifting brackets etc.) as necessary, noting their locations to aid refitting.

10 It is important that groups of components are kept together when they are removed and, if still serviceable, refitted in the same groups. If they are refitted randomly, accelerated wear leading to early failure will occur. Stowing groups of components in plastic bags or storage bins will help to keep everything in the right order – label them according to their fitted location, eg 'No 1 exhaust', 'No 2 inlet', etc **(see illustration)**.

11 Turn the cylinder head over, and rest it on one side. Using a valve spring compressor, compress each valve spring in turn, extracting the split collets when the upper valve spring seat has been pushed far enough down the valve stem to free them **(see illustration)**. If the spring seat sticks, tap the upper jaw of the compressor with a hammer to free it.

12 Release the valve spring compressor and remove the upper spring seat, valve spring(s) and lower spring seat **(see illustrations)**. **Note:** Depending on specification, engines

6.11 Compress the valve springs with a compressor tool

6.12a Remove the upper spring seat...

6.12b ...and valve spring

6.13a Use a removal tool...

6.13b ...to extract the valve stem oil seal

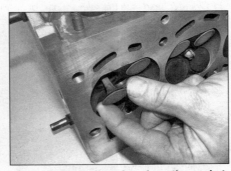

6.13c Remove the valves from the gasket side of the cylinder head

may have concentric double valve springs, or single valve springs with no lower spring seat.

13 Use a pair of pliers or a special removal tool to extract the valve stem oil seal, then remove the lower spring seat from the valve guide. Withdraw the valve itself from the head gasket side of the cylinder head. Repeat this process for the remaining valves (see illustrations).

Cleaning

14 Using a suitable degreasing agent, remove all traces of oil deposits from the cylinder head, paying particular attention to the journal bearings, hydraulic tappet bores, valve guides and oilways. Scrape off any traces of old gasket from the mating surfaces, taking care not to score or gouge them. If using emery paper, do not use a grade of less than 100. Turn the head over and using a blunt blade, scrape any carbon deposits from the combustion chambers and ports.

Caution: Do not erode the sealing surface of the valve seat. Finally, wash the entire head casting with a suitable solvent to remove the remaining debris.

15 Clean the valve heads and stems using a fine wire brush. If the valve is heavily coked, scrape off the majority of the deposits with a blunt blade first, then use the wire brush.
Caution: Do not erode the sealing surface of the valve face.

16 Thoroughly clean the remainder of the components using solvent and allow them to dry completely. Discard the oil seals, as new items must be fitted when the cylinder head is reassembled.

Inspection

Cylinder head casting

Note: The cylinder heads and valves cannot be reworked (although valves may be

lapped in); new or exchange units must be obtained.

17 Examine the head casting closely to identify any damage sustained or cracks that may have developed. Pay particular attention to the areas around the mounting holes and valve seats. If cracking is discovered between the valve seats, Volkswagen state that the cylinder head may be re-used, provided the cracks are no larger than 0.5 mm wide. More serious damage will mean the renewal of the cylinder head casting.

18 Moderately pitted and scorched valve seats can be repaired by lapping the valves in during reassembly, as described later in this Section. Badly worn or damaged valve seats may be restored by recutting; this is a highly specialised operation involving precision machining and accurate angle measurement and as such should be entrusted to an engine reconditioning specialist.

19 Measure any distortion of the gasket surfaces using a straight edge and a set of feeler blades. Take one measurement longitudinally on both the inlet and exhaust manifold mating surfaces. Take several measurements across the head gasket surface, to assess the level of distortion in all planes (see illustration). Compare the measurements with the figures in the Specifications. If there is any doubt about the condition of the cylinder head, seek the advice of an engine reconditioning specialist.

Camshaft

20 Inspection of the camshaft is covered in Chapter 2A, Section 10, Chapter 2B, Section 9 or Chapter 2C, Section 7, as applicable.

Valves and associated components

Note: On all engines, the valve heads cannot be re-cut (although they may be lapped in); new or exchange units must be obtained.

21 Examine each valve closely for signs of wear. Inspect the valve stems for wear ridges, scoring or variations in diameter; measure their diameters at several points along their lengths with a micrometer.

22 The valve heads should not be cracked, badly pitted or charred. Note that light pitting of the valve head can be rectified by grinding-in the valves during reassembly, as described later in this Section.

23 Check that the valve stem end face is free from excessive pitting or indentation; this would be caused by defective hydraulic tappets.

24 Place the valves in a V-block and using a DTI gauge, measure the runout at the valve head. A maximum figure is not quoted by the manufacturer, but the valve should be renewed if the runout appears excessive.

25 Insert each valve into its respective guide in the cylinder head and set up a DTI gauge against the edge of the valve head. With the valve end face flush with the top of the valve guide, measure the maximum side to side deflection of the valve in its guide (see illustration).

6.19 Measure the gasket surface distortion with a straight-edge and feeler gauges

6.25 Measure the maximum deflection of the valve in its guide using a DTI

26 If the measurement is out of tolerance, the valve and valve guide should be renewed as a pair. **Note:** *Valve guides are an interference fit in the cylinder head and their removal requires access to a hydraulic press. For this reason, it would be wise to entrust the job to an engine reconditioning specialist.*

27 Using vernier callipers, measure the free length of each of the valve springs. As a manufacturer's figure is not quoted, the only way to check the length of the springs is by comparison with a new component. Note that valve springs are usually renewed during a major engine overhaul **(see illustration)**.

28 Stand each spring on its end on a flat surface, against an engineer's square **(see illustration)**.Check the squareness of the spring visually; if it appears distorted, renew the spring.

Reassembly

Caution: Unless all new components are to be used, maintain groups when refitting valve train components – do not mix components between cylinders and ensure that components are refitted in their original positions.

29 To achieve a gas-tight seal between the valves and their seats, it will be necessary to grind, or 'lap', the valves in. To complete this process you will need a quantity of fine/coarse grinding paste and a grinding tool – this can either be of the dowel and rubber sucker type, or the automatic type which are driven by a rotary power tool.

30 Smear a small quantity of *fine* grinding paste on the sealing face of the valve head. Turn the cylinder head over so that the combustion chambers are facing upwards and insert the valve into the correct guide. Attach the grinding tool to the valve head and using a backward/forward rotary action, grind the valve head into its seat. Periodically lift the valve and rotate it to redistribute the grinding paste **(see illustration)**.

31 Continue this process until the contact between valve and seat produces an unbroken, matt grey ring of uniform width, on both faces. Repeat the operation for the remaining valves.

32 If the valves and seats are so badly pitted that coarse grinding paste must be used,

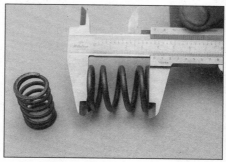
6.27 Measure the free length of each valve spring

6.28 Check the squareness of the valve springs

check first that there is enough material left on both components to make this operation worthwhile – if too little material is left remaining, the valve stems may protrude too far above their guides, impeding the correct operation of the hydraulic tappets. Refer to an engine reconditioning specialist for advice.

33 Assuming the repair is feasible, work as described in the previous paragraphs but use the coarse grinding paste initially, to achieve a dull finish on the valve face and seat. Then, wash off coarse paste with solvent and repeat the process using fine grinding paste to obtain the correct finish.

34 When all the valves have been ground in, remove all traces of grinding paste from the cylinder head and valves with solvent, and allow them to dry completely.

35 Working on one valve at a time, lubricate the valve stem with clean engine oil, and

insert it into the guide. Fit one of the protective plastic sleeves supplied with the new valve stem oil seals over the valve end face – this will protect the oil seal whilst it is being fitted **(see illustrations)**.

36 Dip a new valve stem seal in clean engine oil, and carefully push it over the valve and onto the top of the valve guide – take care not to damage the stem seal as it passes over the valve end face. Use a suitable long reach socket to press it firmly into position **(see illustrations)**.

37 Locate the valve spring(s) over the valve stem **(see illustration)**. Where a lower spring seat is fitted, ensure that the springs locate squarely on the stepped surface of the seat. **Note:** *Depending on specification, engines may have either concentric double valve springs, or single valve springs with no lower spring seat.*

6.30 Grind in the valves with a reciprocating rotary motion

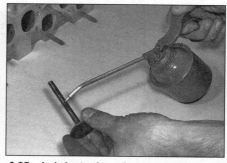
6.35a Lubricate the valve stem with clean engine oil

6.35b Fit a protective sleeve over the valve stem before fitting the oil seal

6.36a Fit a new stem seal over the valve

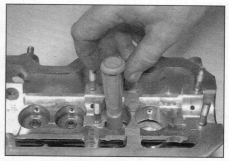
6.36b Use a special installer or long reach socket to fit the valve stem oil seals

6.37 Fit the valve spring(s)

6.38a Fit the upper seat over the top of the valve spring

6.38b Use grease to hold the two halves of the spring collets in the groove

38 Fit the upper seat over the top of the spring(s), then using a valve spring compressor, compress the springs until the upper seat is pushed beyond the collet grooves in the valve stem. Refit the split collet, using a dab of grease to hold the two halves in the grooves **(see illustrations)**. Gradually release the spring compressor, checking that the collet remains correctly seated as the spring extends. When correctly seated, the upper seat should force the two halves of the collet together, and hold them securely in the grooves in the end of the valve.

39 Repeat this process for the remaining sets of valve components. To settle the components after installation, strike the end of each valve stem with a mallet, using a block of wood to protect the stem from damage. Check before progressing any further that the split collets remain firmly held in the end of the valve stem by the upper spring seat.

40 The remainder of refitting is a reversal of removal.

7 Piston/connecting rod assemblies – removal and inspection

Removal

1 Remove the cylinder head, sump, and oil pump/balance shaft assembly, as applicable, as described in Chapter 2A, 2B or 2C.
2 Inspect the tops of the cylinder bores for ridges at the point where the pistons reach top dead centre. These must be removed otherwise the pistons may be damaged when they are pushed out of their bores. Use a scraper or ridge reamer to remove the ridges.
3 Rotate the crankshaft until piston No 1 is at bottom dead centre. On 4-cylinder engines, piston No 4 will also be at bottom dead centre.

Unless they are already identified, mark the big-end bearing caps and connecting rods with their respective piston numbers, using a centre-punch or a scribe **(see illustration)**. Note the orientation of the bearing caps in relation to the connecting rod; it may be difficult to see the manufacturer's markings at this stage, so scribe alignment arrows on them both to ensure correct reassembly.
4 Unscrew the bearing cap bolts half a turn at a time, until they can be removed and the cap withdrawn **(see illustrations)**. Recover the bottom shell bearing, and tape it to the cap for safe keeping. Note that if the shell bearings are to be re-used, they must be refitted to the same connecting rod.
5 Drive the piston out of the top of the bore using a piece of dowel or a hammer handle. As the piston and connecting rod emerge, recover the top shell bearing and tape it to the connecting rod for safekeeping. Take care not to allow the connecting rod to damage the piston cooling jet as the piston is being removed.
6 On 4-cylinder engines remove No 4 piston and connecting rod in the same manner, then turn the crankshaft through half a turn and remove No 2 and 3 pistons and connecting rods. On 5-cylinder engines turn the crankshaft to bring piston No 2 to bottom dead centre, then remove No 2 piston. Similarly remove pistons 4, 5 and 3. Remember to maintain the components in their cylinder groups, whilst they are in a dismantled state.
7 Undo the retaining bolts and withdraw the piston cooling jets from the bottom of the cylinder **(see illustrations)**.

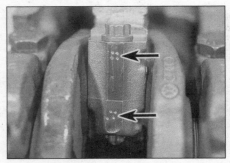

7.3 Mark the big-end caps and connecting rods with their cylinder numbers

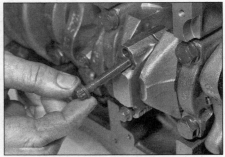

7.4a Unscrew the big-end cap bolts...

7.4b ...and remove the cap

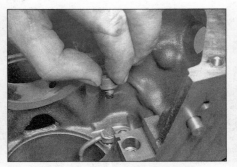

7.7a Remove the piston cooling jet retaining bolts...

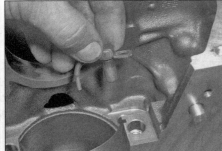

7.7b ...and withdraw the jets from their mounting holes

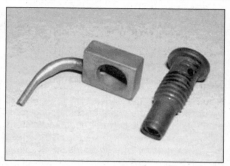

7.7c Piston cooling jet and retaining bolt

7.8a Insert a small screwdriver into the slot and prise out the circlips

7.8b Push out the gudgeon pin to separate the piston and connecting rod

Inspection

8 Insert a small flat-bladed screwdriver into the removal slot and prise the gudgeon pin circlips from each piston. Push out the gudgeon pin, and separate the piston and connecting rod **(see illustrations)**. Discard the circlips as new items must be fitted on reassembly. If the pin proves difficult to remove, heat the piston to 60°C with hot water – the resulting expansion will then allow the two components to be separated.

9 Before an inspection of the pistons can be carried out, the existing piston rings must be removed, using a removal/installation tool, or an old feeler blade if such a tool is not available **(see illustration)**. Always remove the upper piston rings first, expanding them to clear the piston crown. The rings are very brittle and will snap if they are stretched too much – sharp edges are produced when this happens, so protect your eyes and hands. Discard the rings on removal, as new items must be fitted when the engine is reassembled.

10 Use a section of old piston ring to scrape the carbon deposits out of the ring grooves, taking care not to score or gouge the edges of the groove.

11 Carefully scrape away all traces of carbon from the tops of the pistons. A hand-held wire brush (or a piece of fine emery cloth) can be used, once the majority of the deposits have been scraped away. Be careful not to remove any metal from the piston, as it is relatively soft. **Note:** *Make sure each piston is kept identified for position during cleaning.*

12 Once the deposits have been removed, clean the pistons and connecting rods with paraffin or a suitable solvent, and dry thoroughly. Make sure that the oil return holes in the ring grooves are clear.

13 Examine the pistons for signs of excessive wear or damage. Some normal wear will be apparent, in the form of a vertical 'grain' on the piston thrust surfaces and a slight looseness of the top compression ring in its groove. Abnormal wear should be carefully examined, to assess whether the component is still serviceable and what the cause of the wear might be.

14 Scuffing or scoring of the piston skirt may indicate that the engine has been overheating, through inadequate cooling or lubrication.

7.9 Piston rings can be removed using an old feeler gauge

Scorch marks on the skirt indicate that blow-by has occurred, perhaps caused by worn bores or piston rings. Burnt areas on the piston crown are usually an indication of pre-ignition, pinking or detonation. In extreme cases, the piston crown may be melted by operating under these conditions. Corrosion pit marks in the piston crown indicate that coolant has seeped into the combustion chamber. The faults causing these symptoms must be corrected before the engine is brought back into service, or the same damage will recur.

15 Check the pistons, connecting rods, gudgeon pins and bearing caps for cracks. Lay the connecting rods on a flat surface, and look along the length to see if it appears bent or twisted. If you have doubts about their condition, have them measured by an engine reconditioning specialist. Inspect the small-end bush bearing in the connecting rod for signs of wear or cracking.

16 Have the diameter of the pistons checked by an engine reconditioning specialist at the same time as the cylinder block is inspected.

17 Locate a new piston ring in the appropriate groove and measure the ring-to-groove clearance using a feeler blade **(see illustration)**. Note that the rings are of different widths, so use the correct ring for the groove. Compare the measurements with those listed; if the clearances are outside the tolerance band, then the piston must be renewed. Confirm this by checking the width of the piston ring with a micrometer.

18 Examine the small-end bearing and gudgeon pin for wear and damage. If

7.17 Measure the piston ring-to-groove clearance using a feeler gauge

excessive, the gudgeon pin will have to be renewed and a new bush fitted to the connecting rod. This work must be entrusted to an engine reconditioning specialist.

19 The orientation of the piston with respect to the connecting rod must be correct when the two are reassembled. The piston crown is marked with an arrow (which may be obscured by carbon deposits) **(see illustrations)**; this must point towards the timing belt end of the engine (or right-hand end of the engine on 5-cylinder engines) when the piston is installed. The connecting rod and its bearing cap both have recesses machined into them, close to their mating surfaces - these recesses must both face the same way as the arrow on the piston crown (ie towards the timing belt end or right-hand end of the engine) when correctly installed. Reassemble the two components to satisfy this requirement.

7.19a The piston crown is marked with an arrow which must point towards the timing belt (or right-hand) end of the engine

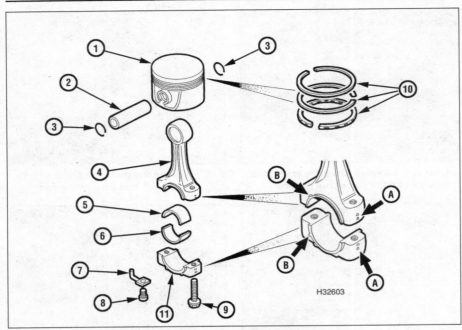

7.19b Piston assembly

1 Piston
2 Gudgeon pin
3 Circlips
4 Connecting rod
5 Bearing shell
6 Bearing shell
7 Oil jet for piston cooling
8 Oil jet retaining bolt
9 Big-end bearing cap bolts
10 Piston rings
11 Bearing cap
A Connecting rod/bearing cap identification marks
B Connecting rod/bearing cap orientation marks

20 Lubricate the gudgeon pin and small-end bush with clean engine oil. Slide the pin into the piston, engaging the connecting rod small-end. Fit two new circlips to the piston at either end of the gudgeon pin. Repeat this operation for the remaining pistons.

8.2 On 5-cylinder engines, remove the gear train housing cover

8.4 Measure the crankshaft endfloat using a DTI gauge...

8.5 ...or feeler gauges

8.6 Manufacturers identification markings on the main bearing caps (arrowed)

8 Crankshaft – removal and inspection

Removal

Note: *On 4-cylinder engines, if no work is to be done on the pistons and connecting rods, then removal of the cylinder head and pistons will not be necessary. Instead, the pistons need only be pushed far enough up the bores so that the connecting rods are positioned clear of the crankpins. On 5-cylinder engines, the cylinder head must be removed before undoing the main bearing cap tie-bolts, irrespective of whether work is to be done on the pistons and connecting rods or not. The use of an engine stand is strongly recommended.*

1 On 4-cylinder engines, with reference to Chapter 2A or 2B as applicable, carry out the following:
a) *Remove the timing belt and crankshaft sprocket.*
b) *Remove the clutch components and flywheel.*
c) *Remove the sump, baffle plate, oil pump/ balance shaft assembly and pickup tube.*
d) *Remove the crankshaft oil seal housings.*

2 On 5-cylinder engines, with reference to Chapter 2C, carry out the following:
a) *Remove the cylinder head.*
b) *Remove the clutch components and flywheel or driveplate (as applicable).*
c) *Remove the sump, pick-up tube, baffle plate and oil pump.*
d) *Remove the gear train housing cover (see illustration).*

3 Remove the pistons and connecting rods or disconnect them from the crankshaft as described in Section 7 (see Note above).
4 With the cylinder block upside down on the bench, carry out a check of the crankshaft endfloat as follows. **Note:** *This can only be accomplished when the crankshaft is still installed in the cylinder block/crankcase, but is free to move.* Set up a DTI gauge so that the probe is in line with the crankshaft axis and is in contact with a fixed point on the end of the crankshaft. Push the crankshaft along its axis to the end of its travel, and then zero the gauge. Push the crankshaft fully the other way, and record the endfloat indicated on the dial **(see illustration)**. Compare the result with the figure given in the Specifications and establish whether new thrustwashers are required.
5 If a dial gauge is not available, feeler blades can be used. First push the crankshaft fully towards the flywheel end of the engine, then use a feeler blade to measure the gap between cylinder No 3 crankpin web (4-cylinder engines) or No 4 crankpin web (5-cylinder engines) and the main bearing thrustwasher **(see illustration)**. Compare the results with the Specifications.
6 Observe the manufacturer's identification marks on the main bearing caps. The number indicates the cap position in the crankcase, as

counted from the timing belt or right-hand end of the engine (see illustration).

7 Loosen the main bearing cap bolts half a turn at a time, until they can be removed. Using a soft-faced mallet, strike the caps lightly to free them from the crankcase. Recover the lower main bearing shells, taping them to the cap for safekeeping. Mark them to aid identification, but do not score or scratch them in any way. Remove the two lower thrustwasher bearings from either side of No 3 bearing saddle (4-cylinder engines) or No 4 bearing saddle (5-cylinder engines).

8 Carefully lift the crankshaft out, taking care not to dislodge the upper main bearing shells (see illustration).

9 Extract the upper main bearing shells from the crankcase, and tape them to their respective bearing caps. Remove the two upper thrustwasher bearings from either side of No 3 bearing saddle (4-cylinder engines) or No 4 bearing saddle (5-cylinder engines).

Inspection

10 Wash the crankshaft in a suitable solvent and allow it to dry. Flush the oil holes thoroughly, to ensure they are not blocked – use a pipe cleaner or a needle brush if necessary.

11 Inspect the main bearing and crankpin journals carefully. If uneven wear, cracking, scoring or pitting are evident then the advice of an engine reconditioning specialist should be sought.

12 Use a micrometer to measure the diameter of each main bearing journal. Taking a number of measurements on the surface of each journal will reveal if it is worn unevenly. Differences in diameter measured at 90° intervals indicate that the journal is out of round. Differences in diameter measured along the length of the journal, indicate that the journal is tapered. Again, if wear is detected, the advice of an engine reconditioning specialist should be sought.

13 Check the oil seal journals at either end of the crankshaft. If they appear excessively scored or damaged, they may cause the new seals to leak when the engine is reassembled. It may be possible to repair the journal; seek the advice of an engine reconditioning specialist.

14 Measure the crankshaft runout by setting up a DTI gauge on the centre main bearing (4-cylinder engines) or 3rd and 4th main bearings (5-cylinder engines) and rotating the shaft in V-blocks. The maximum deflection of the gauge will indicate the runout. Take precautions to protect the bearing journals and oil seal mating surfaces from damage during this procedure. A maximum runout figure is not quoted by the manufacturer, but use the figure of 0.03 mm as a rough guide. If the runout exceeds this figure, crankshaft renewal should be considered – consult an engine reconditioning specialist for advice.

15 Refer to Section 10 for details of main and big-end bearing inspection.

9 Cylinder block/crankcase – cleaning and inspection

Note: On 5-cylinder engines, the unusual arrangement of the gear train components limits the extent to which the following procedures can be carried out. The gear train components should not be disturbed as none of the gears are available as replacement parts. Cleaning should be carried out carefully and steam cleaning is not advisable.

Cleaning

1 Remove all external components as applicable including lifting eyes, mounting brackets, the coolant pump, oil filter mounting housing, fuel injection pump mounting bracket and electrical switches/sensors from the block. For complete cleaning, the core plugs should ideally be removed. Drill a small hole in the plugs, then insert a self-tapping screw into the hole. Extract the plugs by pulling on the screw with a pair of grips, or by using a slide hammer.

2 Scrape all traces of gasket and sealant from the cylinder block/crankcase, taking care not to damage the sealing surfaces.

3 Remove all oil gallery plugs (where fitted). The plugs are usually very tight – they may have to be drilled out, and the holes re-tapped. Use new plugs when the engine is reassembled.

4 If the casting is extremely dirty, it should be steam-cleaned. After this, clean all oil holes and galleries one more time. Flush all internal passages with warm water until the water runs clear. Dry thoroughly, and apply a light film of oil to all mating surfaces and cylinder bores, to prevent rusting. If you have access to compressed air, use it to speed up the drying process, and to blow out all the oil holes and galleries.

⚠️ **Warning: Wear eye protection when using compressed air!**

5 If the castings are not very dirty, you can do an adequate cleaning job with hot, soapy water and a stiff brush. Take plenty of time, and do a thorough job. Regardless of the cleaning method used, be sure to clean all oil holes and galleries very thoroughly, and to dry all components well. Protect the cylinder bores as described above, to prevent rusting.

6 All threaded holes must be clean, to ensure accurate torque readings during reassembly. To clean the threads, run the correct-size tap into each of the holes to remove rust, corrosion, thread sealant or sludge, and to restore damaged threads (see illustration). If possible, use compressed air to clear the holes of debris produced by this operation. Note: Take extra care to exclude all cleaning liquid from blind tapped holes, as the casting may be cracked by hydraulic action if a bolt is threaded into a hole containing liquid.

7 Apply suitable sealant to the new oil gallery plugs, and insert them into the holes in the block. Tighten them securely.

8.8 Lift the crankshaft from the crankcase

8 If the engine is not going to be reassembled immediately, cover it with a large plastic bag to keep it clean; protect all mating surfaces and the cylinder bores as described above, to prevent rusting.

Inspection

9 Visually check the castings for cracks and corrosion. Look for stripped threads in the threaded holes. If there has been any history of internal coolant leakage, it may be worthwhile having an engine overhaul specialist check the cylinder block/crankcase for cracks with special equipment. If defects are found, have them repaired, if possible, or renew the assembly.

10 Check each cylinder bore for scuffing and scoring.

11 If in any doubt as the condition of the cylinder block have the block/bores inspected and measured by an engine reconditioning specialist. They will be able to advise on whether the block is serviceable, and supply the appropriate pistons and rings.

12 If the bores are in reasonably good condition and not excessively worn, then it may only be necessary to renew the piston rings.

13 If this is the case, the bores should be honed, to allow the new rings to bed-in correctly and provide the best possible seal. Consult an engine reconditioning specialist

14 The cylinder block/crankcase should now be completely clean and dry, with all components checked for wear or damage, and repaired or overhauled as necessary.

15 Apply a light coating of engine oil to the

9.6 Use a correct-sized tap to clean the cylinder block threads

mating surfaces and cylinder bores to prevent rust forming.

16 Refit as many ancillary components as possible, for safekeeping. If reassembly is not to start immediately, cover the block with a large plastic bag to keep it clean, and protect the machined surfaces as described above to prevent rusting.

10 Main and big-end bearings – inspection and selection

Inspection

1 Even though the main and big-end bearings should be renewed during the engine overhaul, the old bearings should be retained for close examination, as they may reveal valuable information about the condition of the engine (see illustration).

2 Bearing failure can occur due to lack of lubrication, the presence of dirt or other foreign particles, overloading the engine, or corrosion. Regardless of the cause of bearing failure, the cause must be corrected before the engine is reassembled, to prevent it from happening again.

3 When examining the bearing shells, remove them from the cylinder block/crankcase, the main bearing caps, the connecting rods and the connecting rod big-end bearing caps. Lay them out on a clean surface in the same general position as their location in the engine. This will enable you to match any bearing problems with the corresponding crankshaft journal. *Do not* touch any shell's internal bearing surface with your fingers while checking it, or the delicate surface may be scratched.

4 Dirt and other foreign matter gets into the engine in a variety of ways. It may be left in the engine during assembly, or it may pass

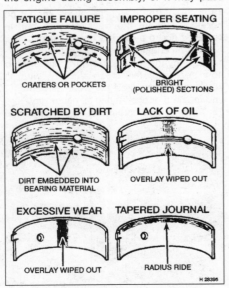

10.1 Typical bearing failures

FATIGUE FAILURE — CRATERS OR POCKETS

IMPROPER SEATING — BRIGHT (POLISHED) SECTIONS

SCRATCHED BY DIRT — DIRT EMBEDDED INTO BEARING MATERIAL

LACK OF OIL — OVERLAY WIPED OUT

EXCESSIVE WEAR — OVERLAY WIPED OUT

TAPERED JOURNAL — RADIUS RIDE

H 28395

through filters or the crankcase ventilation system. It may get into the oil, and from there into the bearings. Metal chips from machining operations and normal engine wear are often present. Abrasives are sometimes left in engine components after reconditioning, especially when parts are not thoroughly cleaned using the proper cleaning methods. Whatever the source, these foreign objects often end up embedded in the soft bearing material, and are easily recognised. Large particles will not embed in the bearing, but will score or gouge the bearing and journal. The best prevention for this cause of bearing failure is to clean all parts thoroughly, and keep everything spotlessly-clean during engine assembly. Frequent and regular engine oil and filter changes are also recommended.

5 Lack of lubrication (or lubrication breakdown) has a number of interrelated causes. Excessive heat (which thins the oil), overloading (which squeezes the oil from the bearing face) and oil leakage (from excessive bearing clearances, worn oil pump or high engine speeds) all contribute to lubrication breakdown. Blocked oil passages, which usually are the result of misaligned oil holes in a bearing shell, will also oil-starve a bearing, and destroy it. When lack of lubrication is the cause of bearing failure, the bearing material is wiped or extruded from the steel backing of the bearing. Temperatures may increase to the point where the steel backing turns blue from overheating.

6 Driving habits can have a definite effect on bearing life. Full-throttle, low-speed operation (labouring the engine) puts very high loads on bearings, tending to squeeze out the oil film. These loads cause the bearings to flex, which produces fine cracks in the bearing face (fatigue failure). Eventually, the bearing material will loosen in pieces, and tear away from the steel backing.

7 Short-distance driving leads to corrosion of bearings, because insufficient engine heat is produced to drive off the condensed water and corrosive gases. These products collect in the engine oil, forming acid and sludge. As the oil is carried to the engine bearings, the acid attacks and corrodes the bearing material.

8 Incorrect bearing installation during engine assembly will lead to bearing failure as well. Tight-fitting bearings leave insufficient bearing running clearance, and will result in oil starvation. Dirt or foreign particles trapped behind a bearing shell result in high spots on the bearing, which lead to failure.

9 *Do not* touch any shell's internal bearing surface with your fingers during reassembly as there is a risk of scratching the delicate surface, or of depositing particles of dirt on it.

10 As mentioned at the beginning of this Section, the bearing shells should be renewed as a matter of course during engine overhaul. To do otherwise is false economy.

Selection – main and big-end bearings

11 Main and big-end bearings for the engines

described in this Chapter are only available in standard sizes.

12 Have the crankshaft measured by an engine reconditioning specialist. They will be able to supply the correctly sized bearings.

11 Engine overhaul – reassembly sequence

1 Before reassembly begins, ensure that all new parts have been obtained, and that all necessary tools are available. Read through the entire procedure to familiarise yourself with the work involved, and to ensure that all items necessary for reassembly of the engine are at hand. In addition to all normal tools and materials, thread-locking compound will be needed. A suitable tube of silicone sealant will also be required for the joint faces that are without gaskets. It is recommended that the manufacturer's own products are used, which are specially formulated for this purpose.

2 In order to save time and avoid problems, engine reassembly should ideally be carried out in the following order:

 a) *Crankshaft (see Section 12).*
 b) *Piston/connecting rod assemblies (see Section 14).*
 c) *Oil pump.*
 d) *Sump.*
 e) *Flywheel/driveplate.*
 f) *Cylinder head.*
 g) *Timing belt, sprockets and tensioner (4-cylinder engines).*
 h) *Inlet and exhaust manifolds.*
 i) *Engine external components and ancillaries.*
 j) *Auxiliary drivebelts, pulleys and tensioners (4-cylinder engines).*

3 At this stage, all engine components should be absolutely clean and dry, with all faults repaired. The components should be laid out (or in individual containers) on a completely clean work surface.

12 Crankshaft – refitting

1 Crankshaft refitting is the first stage of engine reassembly following overhaul. At this point, it is assumed that the crankshaft, cylinder block/crankcase and bearings have been cleaned, inspected and reconditioned or renewed. Where removed, the oil jets must be refitted at this stage and their mounting bolts tightened securely.

2 Place the cylinder block on a clean, level worksurface, with the crankcase facing upwards. Wipe out the inner surfaces of the main bearing caps and crankcase with a clean cloth – they must be kept spotlessly clean.

3 Clean the rear surface of the new bearing shells with a cloth and lay them on the bearing saddles in the crankcase. Ensure that the

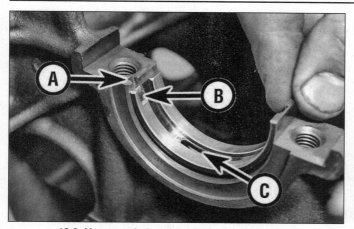

12.3 Upper main bearing shells correctly fitted

A Recess in the bearing
   saddle
B Lug on the bearing shell
C Oil hole

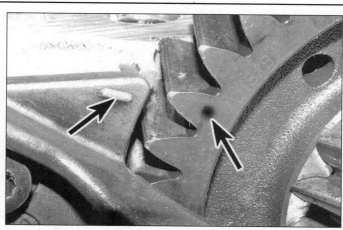

12.6 On 5-cylinder engines, turn the gear train until the mark on the upper intermediate gear is aligned with the projection on the housing (arrowed)

orientation lugs on the shells engage with the recesses in the saddles, and that the oil holes are correctly aligned **(see illustration)**. Do not hammer or otherwise force the bearing shells into place. It is critically important that the surfaces of the bearings are kept free from damage and contamination.

4 Fit the thrustwashers either side of the No 3 bearing saddle (4-cylinder engines) or No 4 bearing saddle (5-cylinder engines). Use a small quantity of grease to hold them in place. Ensure that they are seated correctly in the machined recesses, with the oil grooves facing outwards.

5 Give the newly-fitted main bearing shells and the crankshaft journals a final clean with a cloth. Check that the oil holes in the crankshaft are free from dirt, as any left here will become embedded in the new bearings when the engine is first started.

6 On 5-cylinder engines, the gear train must be set in the assembly position before refitting the crankshaft. To do this, turn the gear train until the mark on the upper intermediate gear is aligned with the projection on the adjacent housing **(see illustration)**.

7 Liberally coat the bearing shells in the crankcase with clean engine oil **(see illustration)**.

8 On 4-cylinder engines, lower the crankshaft into position so that No 1 cylinder crankpin is at BDC, ready for fitting No 1 piston.

9 On 5-cylinder engines, refer to Chapter 2C, Section 3 and attach the crankshaft turning and setting tool (T10225 or equivalent) to the end of the crankshaft. Lower the crankshaft into position so that it will be in the TDC position for No 1 cylinder when the drive gear engages with the gear train. With the gear train set in the assembly position as described in paragraph 6 and the crankshaft in position, the line on the turning and setting tool should be horizontal and towards the rear facing side of the engine. Now turn the crankshaft so that No 1 cylinder crankpin is at BDC, ready for fitting No 1 piston.

10 Lubricate the lower bearing shells in the main bearing caps with clean engine oil, then

fit the thrustwashers to each side of bearing cap No 3 or No 4 (as applicable), noting that the lugs protruding from the washers engage the recesses in the side of the bearing cap **(see illustrations)**. Make sure that the locating lugs on the shells are still engaged with the corresponding recesses in the caps.

11 Fit the main bearing caps in the correct order and orientation – No 1 bearing cap must be at the timing belt end or right-hand end of the engine and the bearing shell locating recesses in the bearing saddles and caps must be adjacent to each other **(see illustrations)**. Insert the bearing cap bolts and hand tighten them only.

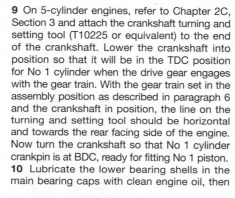

12.7 Liberally coat the upper bearing shells...

12.10a ...and lower bearing shells with clean engine oil...

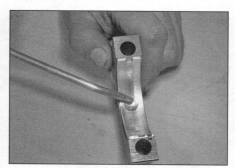

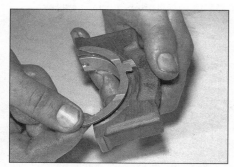

12.10b ...then fit the thrustwashers each side of the bearing cap

12.11a Fit the No 3 main bearing cap

12.11b Fit the No 1 main bearing cap

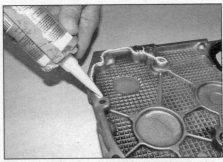

12.17 Apply a 2 to 3 mm diameter bead of sealant to the gear train housing cover

12 Working from the centre bearing cap outwards, tighten the retaining bolts to their specified torque.

13 Check that the crankshaft rotates freely by turning it manually.

14 Carry out a check of the crankshaft endfloat as described at the beginning of Section 8. If the thrust surfaces of the crankshaft have been checked and new thrust bearings have been fitted, then the endfloat should be within specification.

15 Refit the pistons and connecting rods or reconnect them to the crankshaft as described in Section 14.

16 On 4-cylinder engines, with reference to Chapter 2A or 2B as applicable, carry out the following:

a) *Refit the crankshaft oil seal housings, together with new oil seals.*

b) *Refit the oil pump/balance shaft assembly and pick-up tube, baffle plate and sump.*

13.5 Check the piston ring end gap using feeler gauges

14.3a Lubricate the pistons...

c) *Refit the flywheel and clutch components.*

d) *Refit the crankshaft sprocket and timing belt.*

17 On 5-cylinder engines, with reference to Chapter 2C where applicable, carry out the following:

a) *Thoroughly clean the mating faces of the cylinder block and gear train housing cover. Apply a 2 to 3 mm diameter bead of sealant to the housing cover, ensuring the bead passes around the inside of the bolt holes* **(see illustration)**. *Refit the cover and progressively tighten the retaining bolts to the specified torque.*

b) *Refit the oil pump, baffle plate, pick-up tube and sump.*

c) *Refit the flywheel/driveplate and clutch components (as applicable).*

d) *Refit the cylinder head*

13 Pistons and piston rings – assembly

1 At this point it is assumed that the pistons have been correctly assembled to their respective connecting rods and that the piston ring-to-groove clearances have been checked. If not, refer to the end of Section 7.

2 Before the rings can be fitted to the pistons, the end gaps must be checked with the rings fitted into the cylinder bores.

3 Lay out the piston assemblies and the new ring sets on a clean work surface so that the components are kept together in their groups during and after end gap checking. Place the

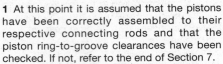

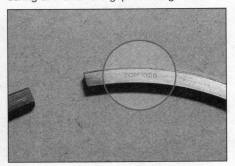

13.7 Piston ring top marking

14.3b ...and the big-end upper bearing shells

crankcase on the work surface on its side, allowing access to the top and bottom of the bores.

4 Take the No 1 piston top ring and insert it into the top of the bore. Using the No 1 piston, push the ring close to the bottom of the bore, at the lowest point of the piston travel. Ensure that it is perfectly square in the bore by pushing firmly against the piston crown.

5 Use a set of feeler blades to measure the gap between the ends of the piston ring. The correct blade will just pass through the gap with a minimal amount of resistance **(see illustration)**. Compare this measurement with that listed in Specifications. Check that you have the correct ring before deciding that a gap is incorrect. Repeat the operation for the remaining rings.

6 If new rings are being fitted, it is unlikely that the end gaps will be too small. If a measurement is found to be undersize, it must be corrected or there is the risk that the ends of the ring may contact each other during operation, possibly resulting in engine damage. This is achieved by gradually filing down the ends of the ring, using a file clamped in a vice. Fit the ring over the file such that both its ends contact opposite faces of the file. Move the ring along the file, removing small amounts of material at a time. Take great care as the rings are brittle and form sharp edges if they fracture. Remember to keep the rings and piston assemblies in the correct order.

7 When all the piston ring end gaps have been verified, they can be fitted to the pistons. Work from the lowest ring groove (oil control ring) upwards. Note that the oil control ring comprises two side rails separated by an expander ring. Note also that the two compression rings are different in cross-section, and so must be fitted in the correct groove and the right way up, using a piston ring fitting tool. Both of the compression rings have marks stamped on one side to indicate the top facing surface. Ensure that these marks face up when the rings are fitted **(see illustration)**.

8 Distribute the end gaps around the piston, spaced at 120° intervals to the each other. **Note:** *If the piston ring manufacturer supplies specific fitting instructions with the rings, follow these exclusively.*

14 Piston/connecting rod assemblies – refitting

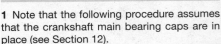

1 Note that the following procedure assumes that the crankshaft main bearing caps are in place (see Section 12).

2 Ensure that the bearing shells are correctly fitted. If new shells are being fitted, ensure that all traces of the protective grease are cleaned off using paraffin. Wipe dry the shells and connecting rods with a lint-free cloth.

3 Lubricate the cylinder bores, the pistons, piston rings and upper bearing shells with clean engine oil **(see illustrations)**. Lay out each piston/connecting rod assembly in order on a worksurface.

4 Start with piston/connecting rod assembly No 1. Make sure that the piston rings are still spaced as described in Section 13, then clamp them in position with a piston ring compressor.

5 Insert the piston/connecting rod assembly into the top of cylinder No 1. Lower the big-end in first, guiding it to protect the cylinder bores. Where oil jets are located at the bottoms of the bores, take particular care not to break them off when guiding the connecting rods onto the crankpins.

6 Ensure that the orientation of the piston in its cylinder is correct – the piston crown, connecting rods and big-end bearing caps have markings, which must point towards the timing belt end, or right-hand end of the engine when the piston is installed in the bore – refer to Section 7 for details.

7 On engines with the combustion chamber in the piston, the piston crowns are specially shaped to improve the engine's combustion characteristics. Because of this, pistons 1 and 2 are different to the remaining pistons. When correctly fitted, the larger inlet valve chambers on pistons 1 and 2 must face the flywheel/driveplate end of the engine, and the larger inlet valve chambers on the remaining pistons must face the timing belt end, or right-hand end of the engine. New pistons have number markings on their crowns to indicate their type – 1/2 denotes piston 1 or 2, 3/4 indicates piston 3 or 4, and 3/4/5 indicated pistons 3, 4 or 5 **(see illustration)**.

8 Using a block of wood or hammer handle against the piston crown, tap the assembly into the cylinder until the piston crown is flush with the top of the cylinder **(see illustration)**.

9 Ensure that the bearing shell is still correctly installed. Liberally lubricate the crankpin and both bearing shells with clean engine oil. Taking care not to mark the cylinder bores, tap the piston/connecting rod assembly down the bore and onto the crankpin. Fit the big-end bearing cap, tightening its retaining bolts finger-tight at first. Note that the orientation of the bearing cap with respect to the connecting rod must be correct when the two components

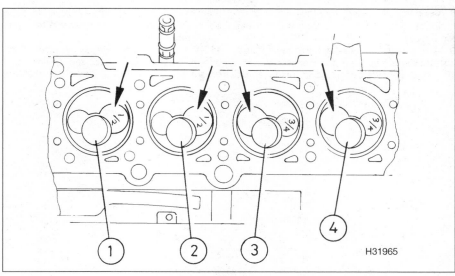

14.7 Piston orientation and coding

are reassembled. The connecting rod and its corresponding bearing cap both have recesses machined into them, close to their mating surfaces – these recesses must both face in the same direction as the arrow on the piston crown (ie towards the timing belt end or right-hand end of the engine) when correctly installed.

10 Tighten the retaining bolts to the specified Stage 1 torque **(see illustration)**.

11 Angle-tighten the retaining bolts to the specified Stage 2 angle **(see illustration)**.

12 Refit the remaining three piston/connecting rod assemblies in the same way.

13 Rotate the crankshaft by hand. Check that it turns freely; some stiffness is to be expected if new parts have been fitted, but there should be no binding or tight spots.

15 Engine –
initial start-up after overhaul and reassembly

1 Refit the remainder of the engine components in the order listed in Section 11 of this Chapter, referring to Parts A, B and C where necessary. Refit the engine to the

vehicle as described in Section 4 of this Chapter. Double-check the engine oil and coolant levels and make a final check that everything has been reconnected. Make sure that there are no tools or rags left in the engine compartment.

2 Disconnect the injector harness wiring plug.

3 Turn the engine using the starter motor until the oil pressure warning lamp goes out.

4 If the lamp fails to extinguish after several seconds of cranking, check the engine oil level and oil filter security. Assuming these are correct, check the security of the oil pressure switch cabling – do not progress any further until you are satisfied that oil is being pumped around the engine at sufficient pressure.

5 Reconnect the injector harness wiring plug.

6 Start the engine, but be aware that as fuel system components have been disturbed, the cranking time may be a little longer than usual.

7 While the engine is idling, check for fuel, water and oil leaks. Don't be alarmed if there are some odd smells and the occasional plume of smoke as components heat up and burn off oil deposits.

14.8 Use a hammer handle to tap the piston into its bore

14.10 Tighten the big-end bearing cap bolts to the Stage 1 setting...

14.11 ...and then angle-tighten them to the Stage 2 setting

8 Assuming all is well, keep the engine idling until hot water is felt circulating through the top hose.

9 After a few minutes, recheck the oil and coolant levels, and top-up as necessary.

10 On all engines described in this Chapter, there is no need to re-tighten the cylinder head bolts once the engine has been run following reassembly.

11 If new pistons, rings or crankshaft bearings have been fitted, the engine must be treated as new, and run-in for the first 600 miles (1000 km). *Do not* operate the engine at full-throttle, or allow it to labour at low engine speeds in any gear. It is recommended that the engine oil and filter are changed at the end of this period.

Chapter 3
Cooling, heating and ventilation systems

Contents

Degrees of difficulty

Easy, suitable for novice with little experience	Fairly easy, suitable for beginner with some experience	Fairly difficult, suitable for competent DIY mechanic	Difficult, suitable for experienced DIY mechanic	Very difficult, suitable for expert DIY or professional

Specifications

General
Maximum system pressure .... 1.4 to 1.6 bar

Thermostat
Starts to open:
  1.9 and 2.0 litre engines.................................. 85° C
  2.5 litre engines .... 80° C
Fully open.. 105°C
Minimum valve lift....................................... 7 mm

Air conditioning
Refrigerant:
  Type R134a
  Capacity:
    Up to model year 2010:
      Models with a single evaporator........................ 650 ± 50g
      Models with a second evaporator .... 950 ± 50g
    Model year 2010 onward:
      Models with a single evaporator........................ 525 ± 25g
      Models with a second evaporator .... 825 ± 25g
Compressor make/type:
  Denso .... 6SEU14C, 7SEU16C or 7SEU17C
  Sanden SD7V16
Refrigerant oil type:
  Denso .... G 052 300 A2
  Sanden .... G 052 154 A2

Torque wrench settings

	Nm	lbf ft
1.9 and 2.0 litre engines		
Air conditioning compressor bolts	45	33
Air conditioning refrigerant pipe union bolts:		
To compressor	20	15
To condenser	12	9
To expansion valve	10	7
Coolant pump bolts	15	12
Thermostat cover/connection flange bolts	15	12
2.5 litre engines		
Air conditioning compressor bolts	45	33
Air conditioning refrigerant pipe union bolts:		
To compressor	20	15
To condenser	12	9
To expansion valve	10	7
Coolant pump bolts:*		
Stage 1	20	15
Stage 2	Angle-tighten through a further 90°	
Coolant pump cover bolts	25	18
Coolant pump drain plug	20	15
Coolant pump drive gear nut	84	62
Coolant pump overflow plug	20	15
Cylinder block sealing flange bolts	10	7
Thermostat housing:		
M6 bolts	10	7
M8 bolts	20	15

*Use new bolts

1 General information and precautions

General information

The cooling system is of pressurised type, comprising a coolant pump, an aluminium crossflow radiator, electric cooling fan(s), a thermostat, heater matrix, and all associated hoses and switches. On 1.9 and 2.0 litre engines the coolant pump is driven by the timing belt, whereas on 2.5 litre engines it is gear-driven from the engine geartrain at the flywheel/driveplate end of the engine. On 2.0 litre engines an additional electrically operated coolant pump is also fitted.

When the engine is cold, the coolant in the engine is pumped around the cylinder block and head passages, and through the oil cooler. After cooling the cylinder bores, combustion surfaces and valve seats, the coolant passes through the heater, and is returned via the cylinder block to the coolant pump. The thermostat is initially closed, preventing the cold coolant from the radiator entering the engine.

When the coolant in the engine reaches a predetermined temperature, the thermostat opens. The cold coolant from the radiator is then allowed to enter the engine through the bottom hose and the hot coolant from the engine flows through the top hose to the radiator. As the coolant circulates through the radiator, it is cooled by the inrush of air when the vehicle is in forward motion. The airflow is supplemented by the action of the cooling fan(s) when necessary. Upon reaching the bottom of the radiator, the coolant has now cooled, and the cycle is repeated.

The operation of the cooling fans is controlled by a thermostatic switch. At a predetermined coolant temperature, the switch/sensor actuates the fans.

An expansion tank is fitted at the front of the engine compartment to accommodate expansion of the coolant when hot.

Refer to Section 10 for information on the air conditioning system.

Precautions

⚠ **Warning: Do not attempt to remove the expansion tank filler cap, or to disturb any part of the cooling system, while the engine is hot, as there is a high risk of scalding. If the expansion tank filler cap must be removed before the engine and radiator have fully cooled (even though this is not recommended), the pressure in the cooling system must first be relieved. Cover the cap with a thick layer of cloth to avoid scalding, and slowly unscrew the filler cap until a hissing sound is heard. When the hissing has stopped, indicating that the pressure has reduced, slowly unscrew the filler cap until it can be removed; if more hissing sounds are heard, wait until they have stopped before unscrewing the cap completely. At all times, keep well away from the filler cap opening, and protect your hands.**

⚠ **Warning: Do not allow antifreeze to come into contact with your skin, or with the painted surfaces of the vehicle. Rinse off spills immediately, with plenty of water. Never leave antifreeze lying around in an open container, or in a puddle in the driveway or on the garage floor. Children and pets are attracted by its sweet smell, but antifreeze can be fatal if ingested.**

⚠ **Warning: If the engine is hot, the electric cooling fans may start rotating even if the engine is not running. Be careful to keep your hands, hair, and any loose clothing well clear when working in the engine compartment.**

⚠ **Warning: Refer to Section 10 for precautions to be observed when working on models equipped with air conditioning.**

2 Cooling system hoses – disconnection and renewal

Note: *Refer to the warnings given in Section 1 of this Chapter before proceeding. Hoses should only be disconnected once the engine has cooled sufficiently to avoid scalding.*

1 If the checks described in Chapter 1, Section 7 reveal a faulty hose, it must be renewed as follows.

2 First drain the cooling system (see Chapter 1, Section 30). If the coolant is not due for renewal, it may be re-used, providing it is collected in a clean container.

3 Before disconnecting a hose, first note its routing in the engine compartment, and whether it is secured by any additional retaining clips or cable ties. Use a pair of pliers to release the clamp-type clips, or a screwdriver to slacken the screw-type clips, then move the clips along the hose, clear of the relevant inlet/outlet union. Carefully work the hose free.

4 Note that the radiator inlet and outlet unions are fragile; do not use excessive force when attempting to remove the hoses. If a hose proves to be difficult to remove, try to release it by rotating the hose ends before attempting to free it. It may be beneficial to spray an penetrating aerosol lubricant (WD-40 or equivalent) onto the end of the hose to aid its release.

5 When fitting a hose, first slide the clips onto the hose, then work the hose into position. On some hose connections alignment marks are provided on the hose and union; if marks are present, ensure they are correctly aligned.

6 Ensure the hose is correctly routed, then slide each clip back along the hose until it passes over the flared end of the relevant inlet/outlet, before tightening the clip securely.

7 Refill the cooling system as described in to Chapter 1, Section 30.

8 Check thoroughly for leaks as soon as possible after disturbing any part of the cooling system.

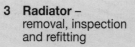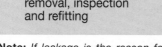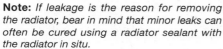

3 Radiator –
removal, inspection
and refitting

Note: *If leakage is the reason for removing the radiator, bear in mind that minor leaks can often be cured using a radiator sealant with the radiator in situ.*

Removal

Up to model year 2010

1 Disconnect the battery negative terminal (refer to *Disconnecting the battery*).

2 Firmly apply the handbrake, then jack up the front of the vehicle and support it securely on axle stands (see *Jacking and vehicle support*).

3 Remove the engine undertray as described in Chapter 11, Section 25.

4 Drain the cooling system as described in Chapter 1, Section 30.

5 Move the body front crossmember to the service position as described in Chapter 11, Section 25.

6 Remove the intercooler as described in Chapter 4A, Section 11.

7 Undo the retaining screw at the left-hand end of the power steering fluid cooler. Unclip

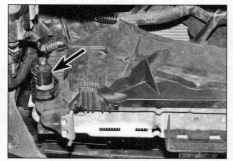

3.11 Disconnect the wiring connector (arrowed) from the thermostatic switch

3.7 Unclip the power steering fluid cooler from the top of the radiator

3.9a Undo the retaining screw (arrowed) on each side of the condenser...

the fluid cooler from the top of the radiator and move it to one side **(see illustration)**.

8 On models equipped with air conditioning, undo the two screws securing the refrigerant pipe connecting block to the radiator **(see illustration)**.

9 Undo the retaining screw on each side of the condenser, then lift the condenser out of its mounting brackets and position it to one side. **Do not** disconnect the refrigerant pipes **(see illustrations)**.

10 Release the retaining clips and disconnect the top and bottom coolant hoses and the expansion tank hose from the radiator.

11 Disconnect the wiring connector from the thermostatic switch on the left-hand side of the radiator **(see illustration)**.

12 Disconnect the electric cooling fan wiring at the connectors at the cooling fan control unit.

3.13a Undo the radiator upper retaining screw (arrowed) on each side...

3.8 Undo the two screws (arrowed) securing the refrigerant pipe connecting block to the radiator

3.9b ...then lift the condenser out of its mounting brackets

13 Undo the radiator upper retaining screw on each side. Insert a screwdriver into the retaining screw slot and push the rubber mounting down into the radiator **(see illustrations)**.

14 Tip the radiator forward at the top, then lift the radiator and cooling fan assembly from its location.

Model year 2010 onwards

15 Carry out the operations described previously in paragraphs 1 to 5.

16 Remove the intercooler as described in Chapter 4B, Section 12.

17 Using a screwdriver, prise out all the catches securing the radiator air duct. Detach the coolant hose from the holder on the air duct, then remove the air duct.

18 Undo the retaining screw from the radiator lower mounting on each side.

3.13b ...then insert a screwdriver into the retaining screw slot and push the rubber mounting down

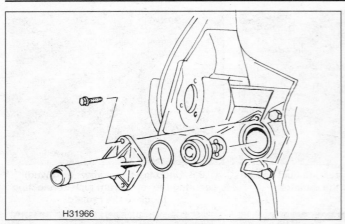

4.5 Thermostat components – 1.9 litre engines

4.23 Remove the thermostat housing from the cylinder block, then remove the gasket from the housing – 2.5 litre engines

19 Disconnect the electric cooling fan wiring connector.
20 Release the retaining clips and disconnect the top and bottom coolant hoses and the expansion tank hose from the radiator.
21 Unclip the power steering fluid cooler from the top of the radiator and move it to one side.
22 On models equipped with air conditioning, undo the two screws securing the refrigerant pipe connecting block to the radiator. Depress the retaining catches on each side and move the condenser away from the radiator slightly at the top. Lift the condenser out of its mounting brackets and position it to one side. **Do not** disconnect the refrigerant pipes
23 Undo the radiator upper retaining screw on each side. Press the catches together, then insert a screwdriver into the retaining screw slot. Push the rubber mounting down into the radiator.
24 With the help of an assistant, lift up the left-hand side of the condenser (where fitted). Carefully slide the radiator to the left, then lift it up and out of its location. Take care not to strain the refrigerant pipes during this operation.

Inspection

25 If the radiator has been removed due to suspected blockage, reverse-flush it as described in Chapter 1, Section 30. Clean dirt and debris from the radiator fins, using an air line (in which case, wear eye protection) or a soft brush. Be careful, as the fins are sharp, and easily damaged.
26 If necessary, a radiator specialist can perform a flow test on the radiator, to establish whether an internal blockage exists.
27 A leaking radiator must be referred to a specialist for permanent repair. Do not attempt to weld or solder a leaking radiator, as damage to the plastic components may result.
28 If the radiator is to be sent for repair or renewed, remove the cooling fan, thermostatic switch and all remaining attachments.
29 Inspect the condition of the radiator mounting rubbers, and renew them if necessary.

Refitting

30 Refitting is a reversal of removal, bearing in mind the following points.
 a) *Make sure all coolant hoses are correctly reconnected and securely retained by their clips.*
 b) *Refill the cooling system as described in Chapter 1, Section 30.*

4 Thermostat – removal, testing and refitting

Removal

1.9 litre engines

1 The thermostat is located behind a connection flange on the front facing side of the cylinder block, at the timing belt end.
2 According to model, undo the retaining bolts and rotary fasteners and remove the battery cover and engine covers as applicable.
3 Drain the cooling system as described in Chapter 1, Section 30.
4 Release the securing clip and disconnect the coolant hose from the thermostat cover/connection flange.
5 Unscrew the two securing bolts, and remove the thermostat cover/connection flange complete with the thermostat. Note the locations of any brackets secured by the bolts. Recover the O-ring if it is loose **(see illustration)**.
6 To remove the thermostat from the cover, twist the thermostat 90° clockwise, and pull it from the cover.

2.0 litre engines

7 The thermostat is located behind the alternator on the front facing side of the cylinder block, at the timing belt end.
8 According to model, undo the retaining bolts and rotary fasteners and remove the battery cover and engine covers as applicable.
9 Drain the cooling system as described in Chapter 1, Section 30.
10 Remove the coolant electric circulation pump as described in Section 7.

11 Undo the two bolts securing the front engine/transmission mounting to the subframe and the three bolts securing the mounting bracket to the cylinder block. Note that new bolts will be required for refitting. Remove the mounting and mounting bracket from the engine.
12 Remove the alternator as described in Chapter 5, Section 7.
13 Remove the engine oil filter housing as described in Chapter 2B, Section 18.
14 Slacken the coolant pipe retaining bolts and pull the pipe slightly backwards.
15 Remove the adjacent wiring harness connector from the support bracket, then undo the retaining bolt and remove the support bracket.
16 Release the retaining clips and disconnect the coolant hoses from the thermostat.
17 Unscrew the two securing bolts, and remove the thermostat housing assembly complete with the thermostat. Recover the housing O-ring. The thermostat is integral with the housing and can only be renewed as a complete assembly.

2.5 litre engines

18 The thermostat is located behind the turbocharger air duct elbow on the rear facing side of the cylinder block, at the right-hand end.
19 According to model, undo the retaining bolts and rotary fasteners and remove the battery cover and engine covers as applicable.
20 Drain the cooling system as described in Chapter 1, Section 30.
21 Undo the two bolts and disconnect the air duct elbow from the turbocharger. Move the elbow to one side for access to the thermostat
22 Release the securing clip and disconnect the coolant hose from the thermostat housing.
23 Undo the two bolts and remove the thermostat housing from the cylinder block. Remove the gasket from the thermostat housing noting its fitted position **(see illustration)**.
24 Remove the thermostat from the housing noting its fitted position.

Testing

Note: *If there is any question about the operation of the thermostat, it's best to renew it – they are not usually expensive items. Testing involves heating in, or over, an open pan of boiling water, which carries with it the risk of scalding. A thermostat that has seen more than five years' service may well be past its best already.*

25 A rough test of the thermostat, may be made by suspending it with a piece of string in a container full of water, but not touching the container. Heat the water to bring it to the boil – the thermostat must open by the time the water boils. If not, renew it.

26 If a thermometer is available, the precise opening temperature of the thermostat may be determined, and compared with the figures given in the Specifications. The opening temperature is also marked on the thermostat. On engines where the thermostat is integral with the housing accurate testing will be difficult, but some indication may be obtained by testing with the thermostat assembled inside the housing.

27 A thermostat which fails to close as the water cools must also be renewed.

Refitting

28 Refitting is a reversal of removal, bearing in mind the following points.
  a) *Refit the thermostat using a new gasket or O-ring.*
  b) *On 1.9 litre engines, insert the thermostat into the cover and twist 90° anti-clockwise. The thermostat should be fitted with the brace almost vertical.*
  c) *Ensure that any brackets are in place on the thermostat cover/housing bolts as noted before removal.*
  d) *Refit the engine oil filter housing (where applicable) as described in Chapter 2B, Section 18.*
  e) *Refit the alternator (where applicable) with reference to Chapter 5, Section 7.*
  f) *Use new bolts when refitting the front engine mounting components (where applicable) and tighten the bolts to the specified torque settings given in Chapter 2B.*
  g) *Refill the cooling system with the correct type and quantity of coolant as described in Chapter 1, Section 30.*

---

5 Electric cooling fans – removal and refitting

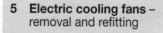

Removal

1 Remove the radiator as described in Section 3.

2 Undo the two bolts each side and remove the fan shroud from the radiator **(see illustration)**.

3 Undo the three bolts and remove the fan motor from the shroud **(see illustration)**.

5.2 Cooling fan shroud left-hand retaining bolts (arrowed)

Refitting

4 Refitting is a reversal of removal, but ensure that the fan shroud engages with the lower edge of the radiator.

---

6 Cooling system electrical switches and sensors – removal and refitting

Electric cooling fan thermostatic switch

Removal

1 The switch is located at the lower left-hand side of the radiator **(see illustration 3.11)**. The engine and radiator should be cold before removing the switch.

2 Firmly apply the handbrake, then jack up the front of the vehicle and support it securely on axle stands (see *Jacking and vehicle support*).

3 Remove the engine undertray as described in Chapter 11, Section 25.

4 Drain the cooling system as described in Chapter 1, Section 30.

5 Disconnect the wiring connector from the switch.

6 Pull out the clip and remove the switch from the radiator. Recover the O-ring seal.

Refitting

7 Refitting is a reversal of removal, making sure that the switch is located securely in the radiator, using a new O-ring seal. On completion, refill the cooling system with the correct type and quantity of coolant as described in Chapter 1, Section 30).

6.10 Coolant temperature sensor location (arrowed) – 1.9 litre engines

5.3 Fan motor retaining bolts (arrowed)

8 Start the engine and run it until it reaches normal operating temperature, then continue to run the engine and check that the cooling fan cuts in and functions correctly. Check for any leaks around the hose and thermal switch.

Coolant temperature sensor

Removal – 1.9 litre engines

9 According to model, undo the retaining bolts and rotary fasteners and remove the battery cover and engine covers as applicable.

10 The coolant temperature sensor is clipped into the rear of the hose connector bolted to the left-hand end of the cylinder head **(see illustration)**.

11 Disconnect the battery negative terminal (refer to *Disconnecting the battery*).

12 Drain the cooling system to just below the level of the switch as described in Chapter 1, Section 30.

13 Disconnect the wiring connector from the sensor.

14 Carefully withdraw the retaining clip and pull the sensor from the housing. Recover the O-ring.

Removal – 2.0 litre engines

15 The coolant temperature sensor is clipped into the coolant housing at the left-hand end of the cylinder head **(see illustration)**

16 Remove the intercooler air ducts as necessary for access to the sensor then proceed as described in paragraphs 11 to 14.

Removal – 2.5 litre engines

17 According to model, undo the retaining

6.15 Coolant temperature sensor location (arrowed) – 2.0 litre engines

6.18 Coolant temperature sensor location (arrowed) – 2.5 litre engines

bolts and rotary fasteners and remove the battery cover and engine covers as applicable.
18 The coolant temperature sensor bolted to the front facing side of the cylinder block, above the engine oil cooler/filter housing **(see illustration)**.
19 Disconnect the battery negative terminal (refer to *Disconnecting the battery*).
20 Move the body front crossmember to the service position as described in Chapter 11, Section 25.
21 Drain the cooling system to just below the level of the switch as described in Chapter 1, Section 30.
22 Disconnect the wiring connector from the sensor.
23 Undo the bolt and remove the sensor retaining plate.
24 Pull the sensor out of the cylinder block then remove the O-ring from the sensor location.

Refitting – all engines
25 Refitting is a reversal of removal, bearing in mind the following points.
a) Fit a new O-ring to the sensor or to the sensor location, as applicable.
b) Refill the cooling system with the correct type and quantity of coolant as described in Chapter 1, Section 30.
c) Where applicable, return the body front crossmember to its normal position as described in Chapter 11, Section 25.

7 Coolant pump – removal and refitting

1.9 litre engines
1 According to model, undo the retaining bolts and rotary fasteners and remove the battery cover and engine covers as applicable.
2 Disconnect the battery negative terminal (refer to *Disconnecting the battery*).
3 Remove the engine undertray as described in Chapter 11, Section 25.
4 Drain the cooling system as described in Chapter 1, Section 30
5 Remove the timing belt as described in Chapter 2A, Section 7.
6 Unscrew the coolant pump retaining bolts, and remove the pump from the cylinder block. Recover the O-ring seal from the pump groove **(see illustrations)**.
7 Refitting is a reversal of removal, bearing in mind the following points.

a) Fit the coolant pump with a new O-ring.
b) Lubricate the O-ring with coolant.
c) Install the pump with the cast lug facing down.
d) Refit the timing belt as described in Chapter 2A, Section 7.
d) Refill the cooling system as described in Chapter 1, Section 30.

2.0 litre engines
Belt driven pump
8 Proceed as described for 1.9 litre engines in paragraphs 1 to 7, but remove and refit the timing belt as described in Chapter 2B, Section 7.

Electric circulation pump
9 According to model, undo the retaining bolts and rotary fasteners and remove the battery cover and engine covers as applicable.
10 Disconnect the battery negative terminal (refer to *Disconnecting the battery*).
11 Remove the engine undertray as described in Chapter 11, Section 25.
12 Disconnect the wiring connector to the pump **(see illustration)**.
13 Fit hose clamps to the coolant hoses connected to the pump, and release the clips and disconnect the hoses from the pump **(see illustration)**. Be prepared for some loss of coolant.
14 Undo the retaining bolt and remove the pump **(see illustration)**.
15 Refitting is a reversal of removal. Top up the coolant, as described in *Weekly checks*.

7.6a Undo the coolant pump bolts...

7.6b ...remove it from the cylinder block...

7.6c ...and renew the O-ring seal – 1.9 and 2.0 litre engines

7.12 Disconnect the wiring connector (arrowed)...

7.13 ...disconnect the coolant hoses (arrowed)...

7.14 ...and undo the pump bracket retaining bolt (arrowed)

2.5 litre engines

Note: *This is a complicated and involved operation. Read through the entire procedure and ensure you have access to the special tools or their equivalents, before proceeding.*

16 To remove and refit the coolant pump, numerous VW special tools or after market alternatives are required. Note that because a crankshaft pulley is not fitted to these engines, it is not even possible to turn the engine over without the use of a special tool. The VW tools required are as follows:

a) *Crankshaft turning and setting tool – T10225*
b) *Gear puller – T10221*
c) *Pump removal tool - T10222*

17 According to model, undo the retaining bolts and rotary fasteners and remove the battery cover and engine covers as applicable.

18 Disconnect the battery negative terminal (refer to *Disconnecting the battery*).

19 Remove the engine undertray as described in Chapter 11, Section 25.

20 Drain the cooling system as described in Chapter 1, Section 30.

21 Where fitted, remove the diesel particulate filter as described in Chapter 4A, Section 15.

22 Undo the two bolts and move the cooling system expansion tank to one side **(see illustration)**.

23 Working at the rear facing side of the cylinder block in the coolant pump area, unscrew and remove the coolant pump drain plug and overflow plug.

24 Undo the three bolts and remove the coolant pump cover from the gear train housing cover.

25 On manual transmission models, note the fitted locations of the selector cables at their transmission attachments.

26 Push in the retaining clips and disconnect the inner cable end fittings from the transmission selector lever ballpins **(see illustration)**.

7.22 Undo the two bolts (arrowed) and move the expansion tank to one side

7.27 Push the retaining catch (arrowed) forward and detach the outer cables support bracket from the transmission

27 Push the retaining catch forward and detach the outer cables support bracket from the mounting bracket on the transmission **(see illustration)**. Move the transmission selector lever into the 5th or 6th gear position.

28 On automatic transmission models, press together the retaining catches and pull the selector cable upwards out of the support bracket.

29 Using a large screwdriver or similar tool, prise the selector inner cable end fitting off the ballpin on the transmission selector lever.

7.26 Push in the retaining clip (arrowed) and disconnect each selector inner cable end fitting from the transmission selector lever

7.30 Undo the five retaining bolts and remove the sealing flange from the right-hand end of the cylinder block

30 Again, on automatic transmission models, undo the five retaining bolts and remove the sealing flange from the right-hand end of the cylinder block **(see illustration)**.

31 Locate the crankshaft turning and setting tool (VW special tool T10225 or equivalent) over the end of the crankshaft and secure the tool in place with the retaining bolt **(see illustrations)**. Note that the tool will only fit on the crankshaft in one position.

32 Using a socket or spanner on the tool, rotate the crankshaft in the normal direction of

7.31a Locate the crankshaft turning and setting tool over the end of the crankshaft...

7.31b ...and secure the tool in place with the retaining bolt

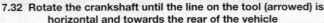

7.32 Rotate the crankshaft until the line on the tool (arrowed) is horizontal and towards the rear of the vehicle

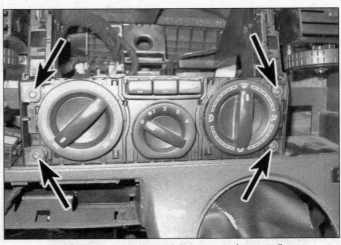

9.3a Undo the four retaining screws(arrowed)...

rotation until the line on the tool is horizontal and towards the rear of the vehicle (see illustration). The crankshaft is now positioned at TDC for No1 cylinder. Rotate the crankshaft a quarter of a turn in the normal direction of rotation. The crankshaft must not be positioned at TDC for removal of the coolant pump.

33 On all engines, slacken the coolant pump drive gear retaining nut two or three turns. Attach the gear puller (VW special tool T10221) to the coolant pump drive gear and tighten the centre bolt to release the taper of the pump drive gear. Once the taper has released, remove the puller, unscrew the retaining nut and remove the drive gear.

34 Undo the two coolant pump retaining bolts. Note that new bolts will be required for refitting.

35 Place the pump removal tool (VW special tool T10222) against the gear train housing cover and screw in the centre bolt. Tighten the centre bolt to draw the coolant pump from its location.

36 Once the pump is released, remove the special tool and remove the coolant pump from the cylinder block. Remove the two O-rings from the pump.

37 Refitting is a reversal of removal, bearing in mind the following points.

a) Fit two new O-rings to the coolant pump and lubricate the O-rings with coolant.
b) Tighten the pump drive gear retaining nut to the specified torque.
c) Lightly lubricate the sealing lip of the coolant pump cover.
d) Where applicable, refit the diesel particulate filter as described in Chapter 4A, Section 15.
e) Refill the cooling system as described in Chapter 1, Section 30.

8 Heating and ventilation system – general information

The heating/ventilation system consists of a four-speed blower motor (housed in the passenger compartment), face-level vents in the centre and at each end of the facia, and air ducts to the footwells.

The control unit is located in the facia, and the controls operate flap valves to deflect and mix the air flowing through the various parts of the heating/ventilation system. The flap valves are contained in the air distribution housing, which acts as a central distribution unit, passing air to the various ducts and vents.

Cold air enters the system through the grille at the rear of the engine compartment. A pollen filter is fitted to the ventilation inlet to filter out dust, soot, pollen and spores from the air entering the vehicle.

The airflow, which can be boosted by the blower, then flows through the various ducts, according to the settings of the controls. Stale air is expelled through ducts at the rear of the vehicle. If warm air is required, the cold air is passed through the heater matrix, which is heated by the engine coolant.

If necessary, the outside air supply can be closed off, allowing the air inside the vehicle to be recirculated. This can be useful to prevent unpleasant odours entering from outside the vehicle, but should only be used briefly, as the recirculated air inside the vehicle will soon deteriorate.

9 Heater/ventilation components – removal and refitting

Heater/ventilation control unit

Removal

1 Disconnect the battery negative terminal (refer to *Disconnecting the battery*).

2 Remove the facia centre trim panel as described in Chapter 11, Section 29.

3 Undo the four retaining screws, pull the control unit from its location and disconnect the wiring connector (see illustrations).

4 Unclip the control cables and release each cable from the control unit, noting each cable's correct fitted location and routing; to avoid confusion on refitting, label each cable as it is disconnected (see illustration).

Refitting

5 Refitting is reversal of removal, bearing in mind the following points.

a) Connect the temperature flap cable (red) first, followed by the footwell flap cable (yellow), then the defroster flap cable (blue).

9.3b ...then pull the control unit from its location and disconnect the wiring connector

9.4 Unclip the control cables and release each cable from the control unit

b) *Ensure that the control cables are correctly routed and reconnected to the control panel, as noted before removal.*

c) *Clip the outer cables in position and check the operation of each knob before refitting the trim panel.*

d) *On completion, refit the facia centre trim panel as described in Chapter 11, Section 29.*

Blower motor

Removal

6 Disconnect the battery negative terminal (refer to *Disconnecting the battery*).

7 Remove the facia left-hand lower trim panel as described in Chapter 11, Section 29.

8 Disconnect the blower motor wiring connector.

9 Undo the seven screws securing the blower motor to the air distribution housing.

10 Withdraw the blower motor from the air distribution housing and remove it from under the facia.

Refitting

11 Refitting is reversal of removal.

Blower motor resistor

Removal

12 Disconnect the battery negative terminal (refer to *Disconnecting the battery*).

13 Remove the facia left-hand lower trim panel as described in Chapter 11, Section 29.

14 Disconnect the blower motor resistor wiring connector.

15 Undo the two retaining screws and withdraw the resistor from the air distribution housing.

Refitting

16 Refitting is reversal of removal.

Air distribution housing

Removal

Note: *On models with air conditioning, it is not possible to remove the air distribution housing without opening the refrigerant circuit (see Sections 10 and 11). Have the refrigerant discharged at a dealer service department or an automotive air conditioning repair facility before proceeding.*

Note: *This is an involved and complex operation and it is suggested that the contents of this Section, and Chapter 11, Section 29 and 30 are studied carefully to gain an understanding of the work involved, before proceeding.*

17 Disconnect the battery negative terminal (refer to *Disconnecting the battery*).

18 Remove the facia as described in Chapter 11, Section 29.

19 Remove the facia crossmember as described in Chapter 11, Section 30.

20 Using hose clamps, clamp the heater matrix inlet and return hoses located on the bulkhead at the rear of the engine compartment. Place a container beneath the

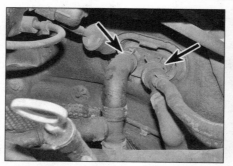

9.20 Heater matrix hose connections (arrowed) at the engine compartment bulkhead

hoses, then release the retaining clips and disconnect them **(see illustration)**. Note the location of the hoses for correct refitting.

21 With the hoses disconnected, remove the coolant from the matrix by blowing air into the upper tube, preferably using an airline, then the coolant can be caught coming out of the lower tube using a container.

Caution: Always use eye protection when using an airline.

22 On models with air conditioning, unscrew the bolts securing the refrigerant lines to the expansion valve on the bulkhead at the rear of the engine compartment, and detach them **(see illustration)**. Recover the seals and plug the lines to prevent entry of foreign matter and water vapour. Discard the seals, as new ones must be used on refitting.

23 Disconnect the blower motor and blower motor resistor wiring connectors.

24 Release the retaining clips and remove any remaining air ducts from the air distribution housing.

25 Where applicable, disconnect the vacuum hose from the recirculating air flap actuator.

26 Ease the air distribution housing away from the bulkhead, detaching the water drain tube when sufficient clearance exists, then remove the housing from the vehicle.

Refitting

27 Refitting is reversal of removal. On completion check, and if necessary top-up, the cooling system as described in *Weekly checks*. On models with air conditioning,

9.35 Removing a facia centre air vent

have the system evacuated, charged and leak-tested by the specialist who discharged it.

Heater matrix

Removal

28 Remove the air distribution housing as described previously in this Section.

29 Release the pipe clamps and pull the coolant pipes from the matrix. Take care not to damage the pipes as they are removed. Discard the seals, as new ones must be used on refitting.

30 Undo the retaining screws and remove the three retaining clips securing the upper half of the air distribution housing to the lower half. Lift off the upper half.

31 Recover the seal which is fitted between the matrix pipe unions and the bulkhead; the seal should be renewed if it shows signs of damage or deterioration.

32 Withdraw the matrix from the air distribution housing.

Refitting

33 Refitting is reversal of removal, bearing in mind the following points:

a) *Apply silicone adhesive sealant to the matrix-to-housing gasket and ensure it is fitted free of gaps all around.*

b) *Use new seals on all disturbed pipe fittings.*

c) *Refit the air distribution housing as described previously in this Section.*

Facia centre air vents

Removal

34 Remove the facia centre trim panel as described in Chapter 11, Section 29.

35 Withdraw the air vent from its location in the facia **(see illustration)**.

Refitting

36 Refitting is reversal of removal.

Facia side air vents

Removal

37 Using a plastic spatula or similar tool, carefully prise off the relevant facia side cover **(see illustration)**.

9.22 Unscrew the bolts (arrowed) securing the refrigerant lines to the expansion valve on the bulkhead

9.37 Carefully prise off the relevant facia side cover

9.38a Push in the centre pins...

9.38b ...withdraw the two expanding rivets...

9.38c ...and remove the air duct from the facia crossmember

9.39 Undo the screw (arrowed) securing the air vent to the facia (shown with facia removed)

38 Push in the centre pins then withdraw the two expanding rivets securing the air duct to the facia crossmember. Withdraw the air duct from the side of the facia **(see illustrations)**.
39 Reach in through air duct aperture and undo the screw securing the air vent to the facia **(see illustration)**.
40 Using a plastic spatula or similar tool, carefully prise the air vent from the facia.

Refitting

41 Refitting is reversal of removal.

10 Air conditioning system – general information and precautions

General information

1 An air conditioning system is available on

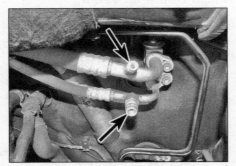

10.6 Air conditioning service ports (arrowed)

certain models. It enables the temperature of incoming air to be lowered, and also dehumidifies the air, which makes for rapid demisting and increased comfort.
2 The cooling side of the system works in the same way as a domestic refrigerator. Refrigerant gas is drawn into a belt-driven compressor, and passes into a condenser mounted on the front of the radiator, where it loses heat and becomes liquid. The liquid passes through an expansion valve to an evaporator, where it changes from liquid under high pressure to gas under low pressure. This change is accompanied by a drop in temperature, which cools the evaporator. The refrigerant returns to the compressor, and the cycle begins again.
3 Air blown through the evaporator passes to the air distribution housing, where it is mixed with hot air blown through the heater matrix to achieve the desired temperature in the passenger compartment.
4 The heating side of the system works in the same way as on models without air conditioning (see Section 9).
5 There are two different types of air conditioning system available, a manually-controlled system which has a traditional panel with control knobs, and an automatic system which has a push-button control panel with an LCD display. On either system, any problems should be referred to a VW dealer or air conditioning system specialist.

Air conditioning service ports

6 The air conditioning service ports are

located in the refrigerant lines connected to the expansion valve on the bulkhead at the rear of the engine compartment **(see illustration)**.

Precautions

7 When an air conditioning system is fitted, it is necessary to observe special precautions whenever dealing with any part of the system, or its associated components. If for any reason the system must be disconnected, entrust this task to a VW dealer or air conditioning system specialist.

⚠ *Warning: The refrigeration circuit contains a liquid refrigerant. This refrigerant is potentially dangerous, and should only be handled by qualified persons. If it is splashed onto the skin, it can cause frostbite. It is not itself poisonous, but in the presence of a naked flame it forms a poisonous gas; inhalation of the vapour through a lighted cigarette could prove fatal. Uncontrolled discharging of the refrigerant is dangerous, and potentially damaging to the environment. Do not disconnect any part of the system unless it has been discharged by a VW dealer or an air conditioning specialist. Caution: Do not operate the air conditioning system if it is known to be short of refrigerant, as this may damage the compressor.*

11 Air conditioning system components – removal and refitting

⚠ *Warning: The air conditioning system is under high pressure. Do not loosen any fittings or remove any components until after the system has been discharged. Air conditioning refrigerant should be properly discharged into an approved type of container at a dealer service department or an automotive air conditioning repair facility capable of handling R134a refrigerant. Cap or plug the pipe lines as soon as they are disconnected, to prevent the entry of moisture. Always wear eye protection when disconnecting air conditioning system fittings.*

Note: *This Section refers to the components of the air conditioning system itself – refer to Sections 8 and 9 for details of components common to the heating/ventilation system.*

Compressor

Removal – 1.9 and 2.0 litre models

1 Have the refrigerant discharged at a dealer service department or an automotive air conditioning repair facility.

2 Disconnect the battery negative terminal (refer to *Disconnecting the battery*).

3 Firmly apply the handbrake, then jack up the front of the vehicle and support it securely on axle stands (see *Jacking and vehicle support*).

4 Remove the engine undertray as described in Chapter 11, Section 25.

5 Remove the auxiliary drivebelt as described in Chapter 1, Section 27.

6 With the system discharged, undo the two retaining bolts and disconnect the refrigerant pipes from the compressor. Discard the O-ring seals – new ones must be used when refitting. Suitably cap the open fittings immediately to keep moisture and contamination out of the system.

7 Disconnect the compressor wiring connector.

8 Undo the two retaining bolts, and withdraw the compressor from the mounting bracket.

Refitting – 1.9 and 2.0 litre models

9 Refitting is reversal of removal, bearing in mind the following points
   a) *Fit new seals to all disturbed unions.*
   b) *Have the system evacuated, charged and leak-tested by the specialist that discharged it.*

Removal – 2.5 litre models

10 Have the refrigerant discharged at a dealer service department or an automotive air conditioning repair facility.

11 Disconnect the battery negative terminal (refer to *Disconnecting the battery*).

12 Firmly apply the handbrake, then jack up the front of the vehicle and support it securely on axle stands (see *Jacking and vehicle support*).

13 Remove the engine undertray as described in Chapter 11, Section 25.

14 Move the body front crossmember to the service position as described in Chapter 11, Section 25.

15 With the system discharged, undo the two retaining bolts and disconnect the refrigerant pipes from the compressor. Discard the O-ring seals – new ones must be used when refitting. Suitably cap the open fittings immediately to keep moisture and contamination out of the system.

16 Disconnect the compressor wiring connector.

17 Undo the three compressor mounting bolts, disengage the compressor from the rubber drive coupling and lift it out of the engine compartment **(see illustration)**.

18 Check the condition of the rubber drive coupling and renew it if there is any sign of wear, damage or deterioration.

Refitting – 2.5 litre models

19 Refitting is reversal of removal, bearing in mind the following points
   a) *Tighten the compressor mounting bolts to the specified torque.*
   b) *Fit new seals to all disturbed unions.*
   c) *Return the body front crossmember to its normal position as described in Chapter 11, Section 25.*
   d) *Have the system evacuated, charged and leak-tested by the specialist that discharged it.*

Condenser

Removal

20 Have the refrigerant discharged at a dealer service department or an automotive air conditioning repair facility.

21 Disconnect the battery negative terminal (refer to *Disconnecting the battery*).

22 Remove the front bumper as described in Chapter 11, Section 22.

23 Remove the intercooler as described in Chapter 4A, Section 11.

24 Undo the retaining bolts and disconnect the two refrigerant pipes from the condenser connecting block. Discard the seals – new ones must be used when refitting. Suitably cap the open fittings immediately to keep moisture and contamination out of the system.

25 Undo the two screws securing the

11.17 Undo the mounting bolts and disengage the compressor from the rubber drive coupling

refrigerant pipe connecting block to the radiator **(see illustration 4.8)**.

26 Undo the retaining screw on each side of the condenser, then lift the condenser out of its mounting brackets and remove it from the engine compartment **(see illustrations 4.9a and 4.9b)**.

Refitting

27 Refitting is reversal of removal, bearing in mind the following points
   a) *Refit the intercooler as described in Chapter 4A, Section 11.*
   b) *Fit new seals to all disturbed unions.*
   c) *Refit the front bumper as described in Chapter 11, Section 22.*
   d) *Have the system evacuated, charged and leak-tested by the specialist that discharged it.*

Receiver/dryer

Removal – up to model year 2010

28 Have the refrigerant discharged at a dealer service department or an automotive air conditioning repair facility.

29 Disconnect the battery negative terminal (refer to *Disconnecting the battery*).

30 Remove the radiator grille as described in Chapter 11, Section 25.

31 Using a T55 Torx bit, unscrew the cap from the receiver/drier **(see illustration)**.

32 Insert a 5 mm bolt into the receiver/drier sealing cover. Push the cover downwards slightly, extract the retaining circlip, then pull out the cover **(see illustrations)**.

11.31 Using a Torx bit, unscrew the cap from the receiver/drier

11.32a Insert a 5 mm bolt, push down and extract the circlip (arrowed)...

11.32b ...then pull out the cover

11.33 Pull the receiver/dryer element out of the condenser

33 Pull the receiver/drier element out of the condenser **(see illustration)**.

Removal – model year 2010 onward

34 Have the refrigerant discharged at a dealer service department or an automotive air conditioning repair facility.

35 Disconnect the battery negative terminal (refer to *Disconnecting the battery*).
36 Remove the radiator grille as described in Chapter 11, Section 25.
37 Remove the receiver/dryer cap from the condenser.
38 Pull the receiver/dryer out of the condenser using long-nose pliers.

Refitting – all models

39 Refitting is reversal of removal, bearing in mind the following points
   a) Fit new seals to the receiver/dryer cover.
   b) Refit the radiator grille as described in Chapter 11, Section 25.
   c) Have the system evacuated, charged and leak-tested by the specialist that discharged it.

Evaporator

Removal

40 Remove the air distribution housing as described in Section 9.

41 Undo the two bolts and remove the expansion valve. Discard the seals, as new ones must be used on refitting.
42 Undo the retaining screws and remove the three retaining clips securing the upper half of the air distribution housing to the lower half. Lift off the upper half.
43 Withdraw the evaporator from the air distribution housing.

Refitting

44 Refitting is reversal of removal, bearing in mind the following points:
   a) Apply silicone adhesive sealant to the matrix-to-housing gasket and ensure it is fitted free of gaps all around.
   b) Use new seals on all disturbed fittings.
   c) Refit the air distribution housing as described in Section 9.

Chapter 4 Part A:
Fuel and exhaust systems – 1.9 and 2.5 litre engines

Contents

Degrees of difficulty

Easy, suitable for novice with little experience 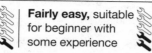	Fairly easy, suitable for beginner with some experience 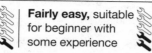	Fairly difficult, suitable for competent DIY mechanic 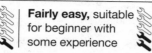	Difficult, suitable for experienced DIY mechanic 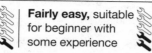	Very difficult, suitable for expert DIY or professional

Specifications

General

System type	Electronic direct injection via unit injectors, turbocharger, catalytic converter and exhaust gas recirculation
Firing order:	
1.9 litre engines	1-3-4-2
2.5 litre engines	1-2-4-5-3
Idle speed.	Non-adjustable, electronically controlled
Fast idle speed.	Non-adjustable, electronically controlled

Torque wrench settings

	Nm	lbf ft
EGR pipe/cooler bolts/nuts	25	18
Exhaust front section mounting bracket-to-subframe bolts	25	18
Exhaust manifold bolts (1.9 litre engines).	25	18
Exhaust manifold nuts (2.5 litre engines)	25	18
Fuel cooler retaining bolts	20	15
Fuel tank support strap bolts.	20	15
Inlet manifold bolts.	22	16
Inlet manifold flap housing bolts	10	7
Injector clamping block bolt*:		
Stage 1	12	9
Stage 2	Angle-tighten a further 270°	
Injector rocker shaft bolts*:		
Stage 1	20	15
Stage 2	Angle-tighten a further 90°	
Particulate filter mounting bolts	60	44
Particulate filter support bracket bolts.	60	44
Tandem pump retaining bolts:		
Upper	25	18
Lower	10	7
Turbocharger support bracket bolts (1.9 litre engines).	25	18
Turbocharger support bracket bolts (2.5 litre engines).	40	30
Turbocharger-to-cylinder block (2.5 litre engines)	40	30
Turbocharger-to-exhaust manifold bolts (2.5 litre engines)	25	18

*Use new bolts

2.2 Disconnect the airflow meter wiring connector

1 General information and precautions

General information

The fuel system comprises a fuel tank, a fuel supply pump, a fuel filter with an integral water separator, fuel supply and return lines and four (1.9 litre engines) or five (2.5 litre engines) fuel injectors.

Fuel is delivered by a camshaft driven 'tandem pump' at low pressure to the injectors (known as 'Unit injectors'). A 'roller rocker' assembly, mounted above the camshaft bearing caps, uses an extra set of camshaft lobes to compress the top of each injector once per firing cycle. This arrangement creates far higher injection pressures. The precise timing of the pre-injection and main injection is controlled by the engine management ECU and a solenoid on each injector. The resultant effect of this system is improved engine torque and power output, greater combustion efficiency, and lower exhaust emissions. All engines are fitted with a turbocharger.

The direct-injection fuelling system is controlled electronically by a diesel engine management system, comprising an Electronic Control Unit (ECU) and its associated sensors, actuators and wiring.

In addition, the ECU manages the operation of the exhaust gas recirculation (EGR) emission control system, the turbocharger boost pressure control system and the glow plug control system.

2.3 Release the hose clip (arrowed) and disconnect the air outlet duct

The flap valve fitted to the inlet manifold is closed by the ECU for 3 seconds as the engine is switched off, to minimise the air intake as the engine shuts down. This minimises the vibration felt as the pistons come up against the volume of highly compressed air present in the combustion chambers. A vacuum reservoir provides the vacuum supply to a vacuum capsule which operates the flap.

It should be noted that fault diagnosis of the diesel engine management system is only possible with dedicated electronic test equipment. Problems with the system's operation should therefore be referred to a VW dealer or suitably-equipped specialist for assessment. Once the fault has been identified, the removal/refitting sequences detailed in the following Sections will then allow the appropriate component(s) to be renewed as required.

Precautions

Many of the operations described in this Chapter involve the disconnection of fuel lines, which may cause an amount of fuel spillage. Before commencing work, refer to the warnings below and the information in 'Safety first!' at the beginning of this manual.

⚠ *Warning: When working on any part of the fuel system, avoid direct contact skin contact with diesel fuel – wear protective clothing and gloves when handling fuel system components. Ensure that the work area is well ventilated to prevent the build up of diesel fuel vapour.*

Fuel injectors operate at extremely high pressures and the jet of fuel produced at

the nozzle is capable of piercing skin, with potentially fatal results. When working on pressurised injectors, take great to avoid exposing any part of the body to the fuel spray. It is recommended that any pressure testing of the fuel system components should be carried out by a diesel fuel systems specialist.

Under no circumstances should diesel fuel be allowed to come into contact with coolant hoses – wipe off accidental spillage immediately. Hoses that have been contaminated with fuel for an extended period should be renewed. Diesel fuel systems are particularly sensitive to contamination from dirt, air and water. Pay particular attention to cleanliness when working on any part of the fuel system, to prevent the ingress of dirt. Thoroughly clean the area around fuel unions before disconnecting them. Store dismantled components in sealed containers to prevent contamination and the formation of condensation. Only use lint-free cloths and clean fuel for component cleansing. Avoid using compressed air when cleaning components in situ.

2 Air cleaner assembly – removal and refitting

Removal

1 The air cleaner housing is situated on the right-hand side of the engine compartment. According to model, undo the retaining bolts and rotary fasteners and remove the battery cover and engine cover as applicable.

2 Disconnect the wiring connector from the airflow meter located on the air cleaner cover **(see illustration)**.

3 Release the hose clip and disconnect the air outlet duct from the airflow meter **(see illustration)**.

4 Release the two catches securing the air cleaner cover to the housing. Lift the cover up, disengage it from the housing and manipulate it out from the engine compartment **(see illustrations)**.

5 Lift out the element, noting its direction of fitting, and wipe out the housing **(see illustration)**.

2.4a Release the catch (arrowed) on each side of the air cleaner housing...

2.4b ...then lift the cover up and disengage it from the housing

2.5 Lift out the air cleaner element and wipe out the housing

6 Undo the bolt securing the air cleaner housing to the inner wing panel **(see illustration)**.
7 Lift the housing up, disengage the mounting lug and manipulate the housing out of the engine compartment **(see illustration)**.

Refitting

8 Refitting is a reverse of the removal procedure.

3 Accelerator pedal/ position sensor – removal and refitting

Removal

1 Remove the right-hand footwell trim panel as described in Chapter 11, Section 29.
2 Disconnect the wiring connector from the top of the accelerator pedal position sensor.
3 Undo the two upper retaining bolts and one lower retaining bolt and remove the pedal/ position sensor.

Refitting

4 Refitting is the reverse of the removal procedure. On completion, check the action of the pedal with the engine running.

4 Fuel system – priming and bleeding

1 After disconnecting part of the fuel supply system or running out of fuel, it is necessary to prime the fuel system and bleed off any air which may have entered the system components, as follows.
2 According to model, undo the retaining bolts and rotary fasteners and remove the battery cover and engine cover as applicable.
3 Undo the two bolts and move the cooling system expansion tank to one side, clear of the fuel filter.
4 Clean around the fuel pipes on the top of the filter housing to prevent any dirt entering the fuel system. Place some cloth around the filter housing to catch any fuel spillage.
5 Depress the tab on the fuel pipe union and disconnect the fuel return pipe from the filter. The pipe union is coloured blue and is connected to the pipe stub marked RT.
6 Obtain a suitable length of rubber or plastic hose that is a snug fit on the filter pipe stub. Connect one end of the hose to the pipe stub marked RT and insert the other end of the hose into a jar or container.
7 Turn the ignition on for a few seconds, then switch it off again. This will energize the in-tank fuel supply pump and deliver fuel to the filter, then to the tandem pump and back to the filter. The supply pump only runs for a few seconds when the ignition is switched on so it will be necessary to repeat this procedure quite a few times. When fuel emerges from the end of the hose, the system has been primed.
8 Disconnect the priming hose and reconnect the fuel pipe to the filter.

2.6 Undo the bolt (arrowed) securing the air cleaner housing to the inner wing panel

9 Place the cooling system expansion tank back in position and secure with the two retaining bolts.
10 Start and run the engine at idle, then check around the fuel filter for fuel leaks. **Note:** *It may take a few seconds of cranking before the engine starts.*
11 On completion, refit the engine cover and battery cover where applicable.

5 Fuel tank – removal and refitting

Note: *Refer to the precautions contained in Section 1 before proceeding.*

Removal

1 Before removing the fuel tank, all fuel must be drained from the tank. Since a fuel

5.3 Unscrew the filler cap strap retaining screw (arrowed) and remove the filler cap

5.5 Undo the filler neck retaining screw (arrowed) at the top of the filler neck aperture

2.7 Lift the housing up, disengage the mounting lug and manipulate the housing out of the engine compartment

tank drain plug is not provided, it is therefore preferable to carry out the removal operation when the tank is nearly empty. The remaining fuel can then be syphoned or hand-pumped from the tank.
2 Disconnect the battery negative terminal (refer to *Disconnecting the battery*).
3 Unscrew the fuel tank filler cap strap retaining screw and remove the filler cap **(see illustration)**.
4 Remove the rubber boot from the filler neck and body panel **(see illustration)**.
5 Undo the filler neck retaining screw at the top of the filler neck aperture **(see illustration)**.
6 Firmly apply the handbrake, then jack up the front of the vehicle and support it securely on axle stands (see *Jacking and vehicle support*).
7 Undo the retaining bolts and remove the underbody cover and heat shield **(see illustration)**.

5.4 Remove the rubber boot from the filler neck and body panel

5.7 Undo the retaining bolts and remove the underbody cover and heat shield (arrowed)

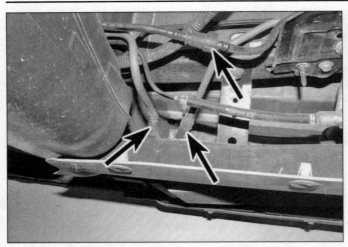

5.8 Disconnect the fuel supply pipe and the two fuel return pipes (arrowed)

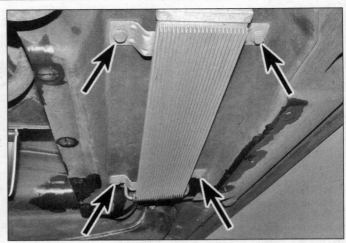

5.9 Undo the four bolts (arrowed) and remove the fuel cooler

5.14a Release the fuel pump/fuel gauge sender unit wiring from the clips on the tank...

5.14b ...then disconnect the wiring connector

8 Depress the tab on the fuel pipe unions and disconnect the fuel supply pipe and the two fuel return pipes at the fuel cooler (see illustration).

9 Undo the four bolts and remove the fuel cooler (see illustration).

10 Undo the retaining bolts and remove the underbody panel for access to the fuel tank retaining strap bolts.

11 Support the weight of the fuel tank on a jack with interposed block of wood.

12 Undo the retaining bolts and remove the fuel tank support straps.

13 Taking care not to strain the fuel lines and wiring, partially lower the tank until access can be gained to the connections on the top of the tank.

14 Release the fuel pump/fuel gauge sender unit wiring from the clips on the tank, then disconnect the wiring connector (see illustrations).

15 Lower the tank to the ground and remove it from under the vehicle.

16 If the tank contains sediment or water, it may cleaned out with two or three rinses of clean fuel. Remove the fuel pump/fuel gauge sender unit as described in Section 6. Shake the tank vigorously, and change the fuel as necessary to remove all contamination from the tank.

17 Any repairs to the fuel tank should be carried out by a professional. Do not under any circumstances attempt any form of DIY repair to a fuel tank.

Refitting

18 Refitting is the reverse of the removal procedure, noting the following points:
a) *When raising the tank back into position, take care to ensure that none of the fuel lines become trapped between the tank and vehicle body. Refit the retaining straps and tighten the bolts to the specified torque.*
b) *Ensure all pipes and hoses are correctly*

6.3 Arrows on the fuel pump/fuel gauge sender unit indicate the direction of fuel flow

routed and all hose unions are securely joined.
c) *On completion, refill the tank with a small amount of fuel, and check for signs of leakage prior to taking the vehicle out on the road.*

6 Fuel pump/ fuel gauge sender unit – removal and refitting

Note: *Refer to the precautions contained in Section 1 before proceeding. VW specify the use of their service tool 3217 to remove and refit the fuel pump/fuel gauge sender unit locking ring. Suitable alternatives to this tool are readily available from accessory stores and motor factor outlets.*

Removal

1 A combined fuel supply pump and fuel gauge sender unit is located in the top face of the fuel tank. The combined unit can only be detached and withdrawn from the tank after the tank is released and lowered from under the car. Refer to Section 5 and remove the fuel tank, then proceed as follows.

2 Release the fuel pipes from the clips on the side of the fuel tank.

3 Note the locations of the fuel pipe attachments at the fuel pump/fuel gauge sender unit. The supply pipe to the tandem pump (and auxiliary heater, where fitted) is/are coloured black and there is an arrow on the pump/gauge sender unit pointing away from the tank. The return pipe is coloured blue and there is an arrow on the pump/gauge sender unit pointing towards the tank (see illustration).

4 Depress the tab on the quick-release fittings and disconnect the fuel pipes from the fuel pump/fuel gauge sender unit (see illustration). Suitably plug the disconnected pipes and unions.

5 Using a suitable removal tool, unscrew the plastic securing ring and lift it out. Lift

the pump/sender unit from the tank, holding it above the level of the fuel in the tank until the excess fuel has drained out. Recover the rubber seal and obtain a new seal for refitting **(see illustrations)**.

6 Place the pump/sender unit on an absorbent card or rag. Inspect the float at the end of the swinging arm for punctures and fuel ingress – renew the sender unit if it appears damaged.

7 The fuel pick-up incorporated in the pump is spring loaded to ensure that it always draws fuel from the lowest part of the tank. Check that the pick-up is free to move under spring tension with respect to the sender unit body.

8 Inspect the sender unit wiper and track; clean off any dirt and debris that may have accumulated and look for breaks in the track. An electrical specification for the sender unit is not quoted by VW, but the integrity of the wiper and track may be verified by connecting a multimeter, set to the resistance function, across the sender unit connector terminals. The resistance should vary as the float arm is moved up and down, and an open circuit reading indicates that the sender is faulty and should be renewed.

9 To remove the sender unit wiper and track, depress the tabs on the wiring connectors and disconnect them from the wiper and track contacts **(see illustration)**.

10 Lift the retaining tabs with a small screwdriver and slide the wiper and track from its location **(see illustrations)**.

Refitting

11 Refitting is a reversal of removal, noting the following points:
- a) The arrow markings on the pump/sender unit body and the fuel tank must be aligned **(see illustration)**.
- b) Smear the tank aperture rubber seal with clean fuel before fitting it in position.

---

7 Diesel engine management system – component removal and refitting

Note: *According to model, to gain access to the engine management system components, undo the retaining bolts and rotary fasteners and remove the battery cover and engine cover as applicable.*

Note: *Observe the precautions in Section 1 before working on fuel system components.*

Accelerator pedal position sensor

1 Proceed as described in Section 3.

Coolant temperature sensor

2 Proceed as described in Chapter 3, Section 6.

Fuel temperature sensor

Removal

3 The fuel temperature sensor is located in the fuel return line from the tandem pump to the fuel filter.

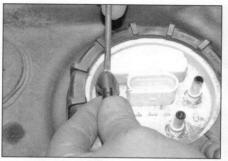

6.4 Depress the tab on the quick-release fittings and disconnect the fuel pipes

6.5a Using a suitable removal tool, unscrew the plastic securing ring and lift it out

6.5b Lift the pump/sender unit from the tank...

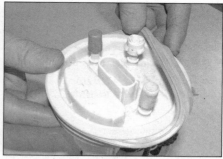

6.5c ...then recover the rubber seal and obtain a new seal for refitting

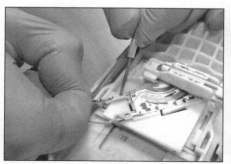

6.9 Depress the tabs on the wiring connectors and disconnect them from the wiper and track contacts

6.10a Lift the retaining tabs with a small screwdriver...

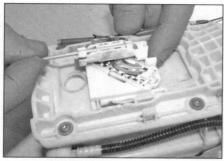

6.10b ...and slide the wiper and track from its location

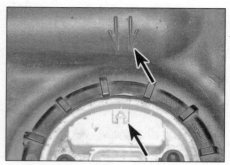

6.11 The arrow markings on the pump/sender unit body and the fuel tank must be aligned when refitting

7.6 Inlet air temperature/charge pressure sensor (arrowed) located in the intercooler air duct

4 Disconnect the wiring from the sensor, then pull out the retaining clip and remove the sensor.

Refitting

5 Refitting is a reversal of removal.

Inlet air temperature/ charge pressure sensor

Removal

6 An inlet air temperature sensor is built into the airflow meter. This sensor is an integral part of the airflow meter, and cannot be renewed separately. An additional inlet air temperature/charge pressure sensor is fitted, located in the air duct between the intercooler and inlet manifold **(see illustration)**.

7 To remove the sensor, disconnect the wiring connector, then undo the two retaining screws and withdraw the sensor. Recover the O-ring seal.

Refitting

8 Refitting is a reversal of removal.

Engine speed sensor

Removal – 1.9 litre engines

9 The engine speed sensor is mounted on the front cylinder block, adjacent to the mating surface of the block and transmission bellhousing.

10 On engine codes BRR and BRS, remove the engine oil cooler/filter housing as described in Chapter 2A, Section 19.

7.17 Engine speed sensor retaining bolt (arrowed)

11 Trace the wiring back from the sensor, and disconnect it at the plug behind the oil filter housing.

12 Undo the retaining bolt and withdraw the sensor from the cylinder block.

Refitting – 1.9 litre engines

13 Refitting is a reversal of removal.

Removal – 2.5 litre engines

14 The engine speed sensor is mounted on the front cylinder block, adjacent to the mating surface of the block and transmission bellhousing.

15 Working as described in Chapter 10, Section 22, Unbolt the power steering pump and move to one side. Do not disconnect the fluid pipes.

16 Trace the wiring back from the sensor, and disconnect it at the connector.

17 Undo the retaining bolt and withdraw the sensor from the cylinder block **(see illustration)**.

Refitting – 2.5 litre engines

18 Refitting is a reversal of removal.

Airflow meter

Removal

19 Disconnect the airflow meter wiring connector **(see illustration 2.2)**.

20 Release the hose clip and disconnect the air outlet duct from the airflow meter **(see illustration 2.3)**.

21 Undo the two bolts and pull the airflow meter from the guide on the air cleaner housing. Handle the airflow meter carefully, as it is a delicate component.

Refitting

22 Refitting is a reversal of removal.

Inlet manifold flap housing

Removal

23 As diesel engines have a very high compression ratio, when the engine is turned off, the pistons still compress a large quantity of air for a few revolutions and cause the engine unit to shudder. The inlet manifold change-over flap is located in the inlet flange housing bolted to the inlet manifold. When the ignition switch is turned to the 'off' position, the engine management ECU-controlled valve actuates the flap, which shuts off the air supply to the cylinders. This allows the pistons to compress very little air, and the engine runs softly to a halt. The flap must open again approximately 3 seconds after switching off the ignition.

24 Release the retaining clip, and disconnect the air duct from the inlet manifold flap housing.

25 Disconnect the wiring connector from the inlet manifold flap motor. Where applicable, undo the nuts/bolts and disconnect the EGR pipe from the housing.

26 Disconnect the vacuum hoses from the EGR valve and the vacuum actuator **(see illustration)**.

27 Undo the retaining bolts, and remove the manifold flap housing from the manifold. Discard the O-ring seal, a new one must be fitted **(see illustrations)**.

Refitting

28 Refitting is a reversal of removal. Tighten the inlet manifold flap housing bolts to the specified torque.

Clutch and brake pedal switches

Removal

29 The clutch and brake pedal switches are located on the clutch and brake pedal mounting brackets in the driver's footwell **(see illustrations)**.

30 Remove the facia right-hand footwell trim panel as described in Chapter 11, Section 29.

7.26 Disconnect the vacuum hoses (arrowed) from the EGR valve and the vacuum actuator

7.27a Undo the retaining bolts (arrowed) and remove the inlet manifold flap housing...

7.27b ...then remove and discard the O-ring seal

31 Disconnect the wiring connector from the relevant switch.

32 Turn the switch 45° anti-clockwise and remove it from the mounting bracket.

33 The brake pedal switches were modified in January 2007 and the manufacturers advise that whenever an early type switch is removed, it should always be replaced with a later type switch. The later type switches can be identified by the bright tip of the plunger.

Refitting

34 Without moving the relevant pedal, insert the switch into the mounting bracket and turn it 45° clockwise to lock it in position.

35 Reconnect the switch wiring connector.

36 On completion, refit the facia right-hand footwell trim panel as described in Chapter 11, Section 29.

Electronic control unit (ECU)

Caution: The ECU is programmed and identified specifically for the vehicle it is fitted to, and the identity coding must be transferred to any new module. This process requires the use of dedicated VW diagnostic equipment. For this reason, it is recommended that ECU renewal is carried out by a VW dealer or suitably-equipped specialist, however removal and refitting of the original ECU is possible by the home mechanic. Note also that if the ECU is renewed, the identification of the new ECU must be transferred to the immobiliser control module by a VW dealer or specialist.
Caution: Always wait at least 30 seconds after switching off the ignition before disconnecting the wiring from the ECU. When the wiring is disconnected, all the learned values may be erased, although any contents of the fault memory are retained. After reconnecting the wiring, the vehicle must be driven for several miles so that the ECU can learn its basic settings. If the engine still runs erratically, the basic settings may be reinstated by a VW dealer or specialist using a special test instrument.

Removal

37 The ECU is located in the engine compartment electrics box, below the battery.

7.29a Clutch pedal switch (arrowed)...

38 Remove the battery and battery tray as described in Chapter 5, Section 4.

39 Rotate the two turnbuckles and open the cover of the electrics box **(see illustration)**. Push the locking mechanism on the fuse insert in the direction of the housing and pull the fuse insert upwards out of the electrics box.

40 Undo the nine screws securing the upper part of the electrics box to the centre part. Slide the fuse carrier out of its location and push it downwards, then lift off the upper part of the electrics box **(see illustration)**.

41 Pull out the locking bars and disconnect the wiring connectors from the ECU. Release the locking catch and lift the ECU from its location in the electrics box **(see illustrations)**.

Refitting

42 Refitting is a reversal of removal.

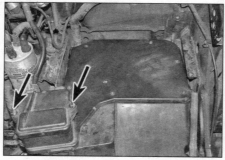

7.39 Rotate the two turnbuckles (arrowed) and open the cover of the electrics box

7.29b ...and brake pedal switch (arrowed) located on the pedal mounting brackets

Camshaft position sensor

Removal – 1.9 litre engines

43 Remove the timing belt upper cover as described in Chapter 2A, Section 6.

44 Undo the retaining bolt, and remove the sensor from the cylinder head. Trace the sensor wiring back to the connector and unplug it.

45 Prise out the grommet in the timing belt rear cover and manoeuvre the sensor out through the hole.

Refitting – 1.9 litre engines

46 Refitting is a reversal of removal.

Removal – 2.5 litre engines

47 Disconnect the wiring connector from the camshaft sensor, located below the fuel/vacuum tandem pump **(see illustration)**.

7.40 Undo the retaining screws, release the fuse carrier, then lift off the upper part of the electrics box

7.41a Disconnect the wiring connectors from the ECU...

7.41b ...then release the locking catch and lift the ECU from its location

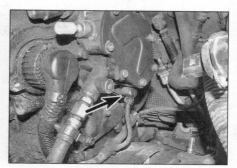

7.47 Disconnect the wiring connector (arrowed) from the camshaft sensor – 2.5 litre engines

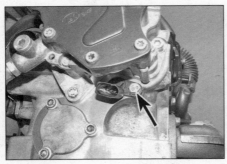

7.48 Undo the retaining bolt (arrowed) and remove the sensor from the cylinder head – 2.5 litre engines

48 Undo the retaining bolt, and remove the sensor from the cylinder head (see illustration). Check the condition of the O-ring and renew it if necessary.

Refitting – 2.5 litre engines

49 Refitting is a reversal of removal.

8 Injectors –
general information, removal and refitting

Warning: Exercise extreme caution when working on the fuel injectors. Never expose the hands or any

8.7 Undo the adjustment bolt until the rocker arm lies against the plunger pin of the injector

part of the body to injector spray, as the high working pressure can cause the fuel to penetrate the skin, with possibly fatal results. You are strongly advised to have any work which involves testing the injectors under pressure carried out by a dealer or fuel injection specialist. Refer to the precautions in Section 1 of this Chapter before proceeding.

General information

1 Injectors deteriorate with prolonged use, and it is reasonable to expect them to need reconditioning or renewal after 60 000 miles or so. Accurate testing, overhaul and calibration of the injectors must be left to a specialist.

1.9 litre engines

Removal

Note: *Take care not to allow dirt into the injectors or fuel pipes during this procedure. Do not drop the injectors or allow the needles at their tips to become damaged. The injectors are precision-made to fine limits, and must not be handled roughly. Keep the injectors identified for position to ensure correct refitting.*

2 According to model, undo the retaining bolts and rotary fasteners and remove the battery cover and engine cover as applicable.

3 Disconnect the battery negative terminal (refer to *Disconnecting the battery*).

4 Remove the timing belt upper cover as described in Chapter 2A, Section 6.

5 Remove the camshaft cover as described in Chapter 2A, Section 4.

6 Using a spanner or socket, turn the crankshaft pulley until the rocker arm for the injector which is to be removed, is at its highest, ie, the injector plunger spring is under the least amount of tension.

7 Slacken the locknut of the adjustment bolt on the end of the rocker arm above the injector, and undo the adjustment bolt until the rocker arm lies against the plunger pin of the injector (see illustration).

8 Starting with the outer bolts first, carefully and evenly slacken and remove the rocker shaft retaining bolts and lift off the rocker shaft. Discard the rocker shaft bolts, new ones must be fitted (see illustration). Check the contact face of each adjustment bolt, and renew any that show signs of wear.

9 Undo the clamping block securing bolt and remove the block from the side of the injector (see illustration).

10 Using a small screwdriver, carefully prise the wiring connector from the injector.

11 VW technicians use a slide hammer (tool T10055) to pull the injector from the cylinder head. This is a slide hammer which engages in the side of the injector. If this tool is not available, it is possible to fabricate an equivalent using a short section of angle-iron, a length of threaded rod, a cylindrical weight, and two locknuts. Weld/braze the rod to the angle-iron, slide the weight over the rod, and lock the two nuts together at the end of the rod to provide the stop for the weight (see illustration). Seat

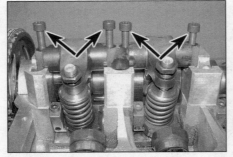

8.8 Start with the outer bolts first, carefully and evenly slacken the rocker shaft retaining bolts (arrowed)

8.9 Undo the clamping block securing bolt (arrowed) and remove the block from the side of the injector

8.11b Seat the slide hammer/tool in the slot on the side of the injector, and pull the injector out

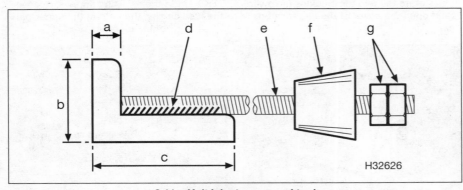

8.11a Unit injector removal tool

a = 5 mm   d Weld/braze the rod to   f Cylindrical weight
b = 15 mm   the angle iron   g Locknuts
c = 25 mm   e Threaded rod

H32626

the slide hammer/tool in the slot on the side on the injector, and pull the injector out using a few gently taps. Recover the circlip, heat shield and O-rings and discard. New ones must be used for refitting **(see illustration)**.

12 If required, the injector wiring loom/rail can be removed from the cylinder head as follows. Disconnect the wiring from the unit injectors and glow plugs. To disconnect the wiring connector from the left-hand end of the cylinder head, use a screwdriver to pull out the plastic red lock, then unscrew the collar and pull the connector from the pins. To remove the wiring conduit, first undo the bolts retaining it to the cylinder head, then release the multipin plug by raising the clip and unscrewing the outer threaded collar, ideally using the special VW tool T10310 which engages the three slots **(see illustrations)**.

13 To prevent the wiring connectors fouling the cylinder head casting as the assembly is withdrawn, insert the connectors into the storage slots in the plastic wiring rail. Carefully push the assembly to the rear, and out of the casting **(see illustrations)**.

Refitting

14 Prior to refitting the injectors, the three O-rings, heat insulation washer and clip must be renewed. Due to the high injection pressures, it is essential that the O-rings are fitted without being twisted. VW recommend the use of three special assembly sleeves to install the O-rings squarely, although suitably-equivalent tools are available from automotive tool manufacturers. It may be prudent to entrust O-ring renewal to a VW dealer or suitably-equipped injection specialist, rather than risk subsequent leaks **(see illustration)**.

15 After renewing the O-rings, fit the heat shield and secure it in place with the circlip **(see illustration)**.

16 Smear clean engine oil onto the O-rings, and push the injector evenly down into the cylinder head onto its stop.

17 Fit the clamping block alongside the injector, but only hand-tighten the new retaining bolt at this stage.

18 It is essential that the injectors are fitted at right-angles to the clamping block. In order to achieve this, measure the distance from

8.14 Great care must be used to ensure that the injector O-rings are fitted without being twisted

8.12a Wiring loom connector showing the three pins (arrowed) in the outer collar

8.12b Retaining clip (arrowed) on the inside of the wiring loom connector

8.13a Undo the two nuts at the left-hand end of the head and slide the injector loom/rail out

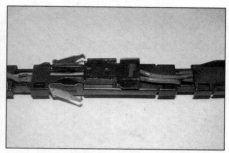

8.13b The injector connectors will slide into the loom/rail to prevent them from being damaged as the assembly is withdrawn/inserted into the cylinder head

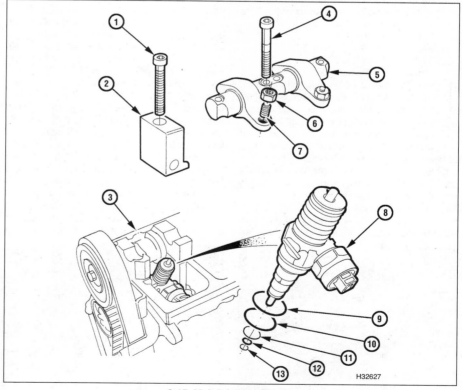

8.15 Unit injector details

1 Bolt	3 Cylinder head	5 Rocker arm	8 Unit injector	11 O-ring
2 Clamping block	4 Bolt	6 Nut	9 O-ring	12 Heat shield
		7 Adjuster	10 O-ring	13 Circlip

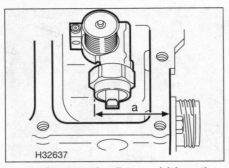

8.18a Measure the distance (a) from the end of the cylinder head to the rounded section of the injector

8.18b Use a set square against the rounded edge of the injector...

8.18c ...and measure the distance to the end of the cylinder head

8.21 Attach a DTI (Dial Test Indicator) gauge to the cylinder head upper surface

the end of the cylinder head to the rounded section of the injector **(see illustrations)**. The dimensions (a) are as follows:

    Cylinder 1 = 333.0 ± 0.8 mm
    Cylinder 2 = 245.0 ± 0.8 mm
    Cylinder 3 = 153.6 ± 0.8 mm
    Cylinder 4 = 65.6 ± 0.8 mm

19 Once the injector(s) are aligned correctly, tighten the clamping bolt to the specified Stage 1 torque setting, and the Stage 2 angle tightening setting. **Note:** *If an injector has been renewed, it is essential that the adjustment bolt, locknut of the corresponding rocker and ball-pin are renewed at the same time. The ball-pins simply pull out of the injector spring cap. There is an O-ring in each spring cap to stop the ball-pins from falling out.*

20 Smear some grease (VW No G000 100) onto the contact face of each rocker arm adjustment bolt, and refit the rocker shaft

assembly to the camshaft bearing caps, tightening the retaining bolts as follows. Starting from the inside out, hand-tighten the bolts. Again, from the inside out, tighten the bolts to the Stage 1 torque setting. Finally, from the inside out, tighten the bolts to the Stage 2 angle tightening setting.

21 The following procedure is only necessary if an injector has been removed. Attach a DTI (Dial Test Indicator) gauge to the cylinder head upper surface, and position the DTI probe against the top of the adjustment bolt **(see illustration)**. Turn the crankshaft until the rocker arm roller is on the highest point of its corresponding camshaft lobe, and the adjustment bolt is at its lowest. Once this position has been established, remove the DTI gauge, screw the adjustment bolt in until firm resistance is felt, and the injector spring cannot be compressed further. Turn

the adjustment bolt **anti-clockwise** 180°, and tighten the locknut securely. Repeat this procedure for any other injectors that have been removed.

22 Reconnect the wiring plug to the injector.
23 Refit the camshaft cover as described in Chapter 2A, Section 4.
24 Refit the timing belt upper cover as described in Chapter 2A, Section 6.
25 Reconnect the battery negative terminal.
26 Start the engine and check that it runs correctly.
27 Where applicable, refit the engine cover and battery cover.

2.5 litre engines

Removal

Note: *Take care not to allow dirt into the injectors or fuel pipes during this procedure. Do not drop the injectors or allow the needles at their tips to become damaged. The injectors are precision-made to fine limits, and must not be handled roughly. Keep the injectors identified for position to ensure correct refitting.*

Note: *To enable the crankshaft to be turned, VW special tool T10225 (Crankshaft turning and setting tool) or equivalent, will be required.*

28 According to model, undo the retaining bolts and rotary fasteners and remove the battery cover and engine cover as applicable.
29 Disconnect the battery negative terminal (refer to *Disconnecting the battery*).
30 Remove the camshaft cover as described in Chapter 2C, Section 4.
31 Remove the inlet manifold as described in Section 9.
32 Undo the five retaining bolts and remove the sealing flange from the right-hand end of the cylinder block **(see illustration)**.
33 Locate the crankshaft turning and setting tool (VW special tool T10225 or equivalent) over the end of the crankshaft and secure the tool in place with the retaining bolt **(see illustrations)**. Note that the tool will only fit on the crankshaft in one position.
34 Using a socket or spanner on the tool, rotate the crankshaft in the normal direction of rotation until the rocker arm for the injector which is to be removed, is at its highest, ie,

8.32 Undo the five retaining bolts and remove the sealing flange from the right-hand end of the cylinder block

8.33a Locate the crankshaft turning and setting tool over the end of the crankshaft...

8.33b ...and secure the tool in place with the retaining bolt

8.35 Undo the adjustment bolt until the rocker arm lies against the plunger pin of the injector

8.36a Undo the retaining bolts (arrowed)...

8.36b ...and lift the relevant rocker shaft off the camshaft bearing caps

8.37 Undo the clamping block securing bolt and remove the block from the side of the injector

8.38 Carefully prise the wiring connector from the injector

the injector plunger spring is under the least amount of tension.

35 Slacken the locknut of the adjustment bolt on the end of the rocker arm above the injector, and undo the adjustment bolt until the rocker arm lies against the plunger pin of the injector **(see illustration)**.

36 Starting with the outer bolts first, carefully and evenly slacken the rocker shaft retaining bolts. Discard the rocker shaft bolts, new ones must be fitted. Lift the relevant rocker shaft off the camshaft bearing caps **(see illustrations)**. Check the contact face of

each adjustment bolt, and renew any that show signs of wear.

37 Undo the clamping block securing bolt and remove the block from the side of the injector **(see illustration)**.

38 Using a small screwdriver, carefully prise the wiring connector from the injector **(see illustration)**.

39 VW technicians use a slide hammer (tool T10055) to pull the injector from the cylinder head. This is a slide hammer which engages in the side of the injector. If this tool is not available, it is possible to fabricate an

equivalent using a short section of angle-iron, a length of threaded rod, a cylindrical weight, and two locknuts. Weld/braze the rod to the angle-iron, slide the weight over the rod, and lock the two nuts together at the end of the rod to provide the stop for the weight **(see illustration 8.11a)**. Seat the slide hammer/ tool in the slot on the side on the injector, and pull the injector out using a few gently taps **(see illustration 8.11b)**. Recover circlip, the heat shield and O-rings and discard **(see illustrations)**. New ones must be used for refitting.

8.39a Remove the circlip and heat shield (arrowed)...

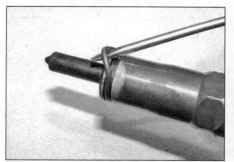

8.39b ...the lower O-ring...

8.39c ...and upper O-rings from the injector

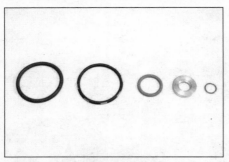

8.42 Prior to refitting the injectors, the three O-rings, heat shield and circlip must be renewed

40 If required, the injector wiring loom/rail can be removed from the cylinder head as follows. Disconnect the wiring from the unit injectors and glow plugs. To disconnect the wiring connector from the left-hand end of the cylinder head, use a screwdriver to pull out the plastic red lock, then unscrew the collar and pull the connector from the pins. To remove the wiring conduit, first undo the bolts retaining it to the cylinder head, then release the multipin plug by unscrewing the outer threaded collar, ideally using the special VW tool T10310 which engages the three slots **(see illustrations 8.12a and 8.12b)**.

41 To prevent the wiring connectors fouling the cylinder head casting as the assembly is withdrawn, insert the connectors into the storage slots in the plastic wiring rail. Carefully push the assembly to the rear, and out of the casting **(see illustrations 8.13a and 8.13b)**.

8.46a Using a 7 mm diameter bar (arrowed) to align the injector

8.46c ...then through the Stage 2 angle

Refitting

42 Prior to refitting the injectors, the three O-rings, heat shield washer and circlip must be renewed **(see illustration)**. Due to the high injection pressures, it is essential that the O-rings are fitted without being twisted. VW recommend the use of three special assembly sleeves to install the O-rings squarely, although suitably-equivalent tools are available from automotive tool manufacturers. It may be prudent to entrust O-ring renewal to a VW dealer or suitably-equipped injection specialist, rather than risk subsequent leaks.

43 After renewing the O-rings, fit the heat shield and secure it in place with the circlip.

44 Smear clean engine oil onto the O-rings, and push the injector evenly down into the cylinder head onto its stop.

45 Fit the clamping block alongside the injector, but only hand-tighten the new retaining bolt at this stage.

46 It is essential that the injectors are fitted at a specific angle to allow correct location of the clamping block. Insert a 7 mm diameter bar (metal rod, drill bit etc.) between the side of the injector body and the cylinder head casting adjacent to the injector **(see illustration)**. Push the injector against the bar and tighten the clamping bolt to the specified Stage 1 torque setting, then through the Stage 2 angle **(see illustrations)**. **Note:** *If an injector has been renewed, it is essential that the adjustment bolt, locknut of the corresponding rocker and ball-pin are renewed at the same time. The ball-pins simply pull out of the injector spring*

8.46b Push the injector against the bar and tighten the clamping bolt to the specified Stage 1 torque setting...

8.48 Attach a DTI (Dial Test Indicator) gauge to the cylinder head upper surface

cap. There is an O-ring in each spring cap to stop the ball-pins from falling out.

47 Smear some grease (VW No G000 100) onto the contact face of each rocker arm adjustment bolt, and refit the rocker shaft assembly to the camshaft bearing caps, tightening the retaining bolts as follows. Starting from the inside out, hand-tighten the bolts. Again, from the inside out, tighten the bolts to the Stage 1 torque setting. Finally, from the inside out, tighten the bolts to the Stage 2 angle tightening setting.

48 The following procedure is only necessary if an injector has been removed. Attach a DTI (Dial Test Indicator) gauge to the cylinder head upper surface, and position the DTI probe against the top of the adjustment bolt **(see illustration)**. Turn the crankshaft until the rocker arm roller is on the highest point of its corresponding camshaft lobe, and the adjustment bolt is at its lowest. Once this position has been established, remove the DTI gauge, screw the adjustment bolt in until firm resistance is felt, and the injector spring cannot be compressed further. Turn the adjustment bolt **anti-clockwise** 180°, and tighten the locknut securely. Repeat this procedure for any other injectors that have been removed.

49 Reconnect the wiring plug to the injector.

50 Remove the special tool and clean off all traces of sealant from the cylinder block and the sealing flange.

51 Apply a bead of silicone sealant to the joint between the cylinder block and the sump. Place the sealing flange in position then refit the retaining bolts and tighten them progressively to the specified torque.

52 Refit the camshaft cover as described in Chapter 2C, Section 4.

53 Reconnect the battery negative terminal.

54 Start the engine and check that it runs correctly.

55 Where applicable, refit the engine cover and battery cover.

9 Inlet manifold – removal and refitting

Note: *Observe the precautions in Section 1 before working on fuel system components.*

1.9 litre engines

Removal

1 According to model, undo the retaining bolts and rotary fasteners and remove the battery cover and engine cover as applicable.

2 Disconnect the battery negative terminal (refer to *Disconnecting the battery*).

3 Remove the inlet manifold flap housing as described in Section 7.

4 On engine codes BRR and BRS unbolt the EGR pipe from the EGR valve.

5 Remove the heat shield from the manifold, then unscrew the mounting nuts/bolts and remove the inlet manifold from the cylinder head. Recover the gaskets from the inlet manifold.

9.11 Undo the two retaining bolts (arrowed) and remove the inlet manifold support bracket

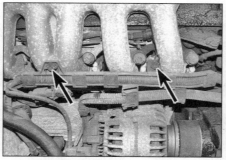

9.12 Extract the expanding plastic rivets (arrowed) securing the wiring harness to the inlet manifold

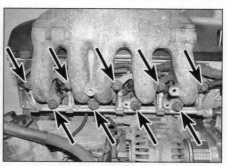

9.13a Undo the nine retaining bolts (arrowed)...

Refitting

6 Refitting is a reversal of removal, using new manifold, EGR pipe and manifold flap assembly gaskets.

2.5 litre engines

Removal

7 According to model, undo the retaining bolts and rotary fasteners and remove the battery cover and engine cover as applicable.
8 Disconnect the battery negative terminal (refer to *Disconnecting the battery*).
9 Move the body front crossmember to the service position as described in Chapter 11, Section 25.
10 Remove the inlet manifold flap housing as described in Section 7.
11 Undo the two retaining bolts and remove the inlet manifold support bracket **(see illustration)**.
12 Pull out the centre pin and extract the expanding plastic rivets securing the wiring harness to the inlet manifold **(see illustration)**.
13 Undo the nine retaining bolts and remove the inlet manifold from the cylinder head. Recover the gaskets from the inlet manifold **(see illustrations)**.

Refitting

14 Refitting is a reversal of removal, using new manifold, EGR pipe and manifold flap assembly gaskets. Return the body front crossmember to the normal position as described in Chapter 11, Section 25.

---

10 Tandem fuel pump – removal and refitting

1.9 litre engines

Note: *The fuel pump and the braking system vacuum pump are combined in one unit, termed a 'tandem pump'.*

Removal

1 According to model, undo the retaining bolts and rotary fasteners and remove the battery cover and engine cover as applicable.
2 Disconnect the battery negative terminal (refer to *Disconnecting the battery*).
3 Leaving the coolant hoses connected, undo

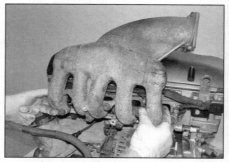

9.13b ...remove the inlet manifold from the cylinder head...

the two bolts and move the cooling system expansion tank to one side.
4 Remove the air duct between the inlet manifold and the intercooler.
5 Release the retaining clip (where fitted) and disconnect the brake servo vacuum pipe from the tandem pump **(see illustration)**.
6 Disconnect the fuel supply hose (marked white) from the tandem pump **(see illustration 10.5)**. Be prepared for fuel spillage.
7 Unscrew the four retaining bolts and move the tandem pump away from the cylinder head **(see illustration 10.5)**. As the pump is lifted up, disconnect the fuel return hose (marked blue). Be prepared for fuel spillage. There are no serviceable parts within the tandem pump. If the pump is faulty, it must be renewed.

9.13c ...and recover the gaskets

Refitting

8 Reconnect the fuel return hose to the pump and refit the pump to the cylinder head, using new rubber seals, and ensuring that the pump pinion engages correctly with the drive slot in the camshaft **(see illustration)**.
9 Refit the pump retaining bolts, and tighten them to the specified torque.
10 Re-attach the fuel supply hose and brake servo hose to the pump.
11 Refit the air duct between the inlet manifold and the intercooler.
12 Place the cooling system expansion tank back in position and secure with the two retaining bolts.
13 Reconnect the battery negative terminal, then refit the engine covers.

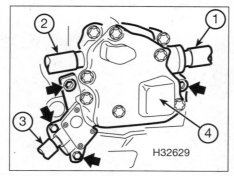

10.5 Tandem fuel pump securing bolts (arrowed) – 1.9 litre engines

1 Brake servo hose　　3 Fuel return hose
2 Fuel supply hose　　4 Tandem pump

10.8 Ensure that the tandem pump pinion engages correctly with the drive slot in the camshaft – 1.9 litre engines

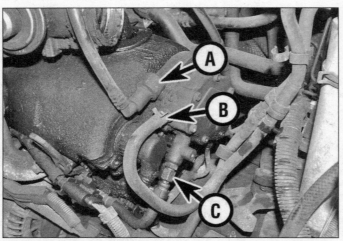

10.18 Brake servo vacuum pipe (A), upper fuel hose (B) and lower fuel hose (C) at the tandem pump – 2.5 litre engines

10.22 Place a new gasket on the pump, then locate the pump on the cylinder head – 2.5 litre engines

2.5 litre engines

Note: *The fuel pump and the braking system vacuum pump are combined in one unit, termed a 'tandem pump'.*

Removal

14 According to model, undo the retaining bolts and rotary fasteners and remove the battery cover and engine cover as applicable.

15 Disconnect the battery negative terminal (refer to *Disconnecting the battery*).

16 Leaving the coolant hoses connected, undo the two bolts and move the cooling system expansion tank to one side.

17 Remove the air duct between the inlet manifold and the intercooler.

18 Release the quick-release fitting and disconnect the brake servo vacuum pipe from the tandem pump (**see illustration**).

19 Release the retaining clip and disconnect the upper fuel hose from the pump (**see illustration 10.18**). Be prepared for fuel spillage.

20 Release the quick-release fitting and disconnect the lower fuel hose from the pump (**see illustration 10.18**).

21 Unscrew the three retaining bolts and remove the tandem pump from the cylinder head. There are no serviceable parts within the tandem pump. If the pump is faulty, it must be renewed.

Refitting

22 Place a new gasket on the pump, then locate the pump on the cylinder head (**see illustration**). Ensure that the pump pinion engages correctly with the drive slot in the camshaft

23 Refit the pump retaining bolts, and tighten them to the specified torque.

24 Re-attach the two fuel hoses and brake servo vacuum pipe to the pump.

25 Refit the air duct between the inlet manifold and the intercooler.

26 Place the cooling system expansion tank back in position and secure with the two retaining bolts.

27 Reconnect the battery negative terminal, then refit the engine covers.

11.2 Extract the retaining clips slightly and disconnect the air ducts from the intercooler

11.3 Undo the bolt each side (arrowed) securing the intercooler to the radiator

11.4 Lift the intercooler off the lower mountings on the radiator (arrowed) and remove it from the engine compartment

11.5 Check the condition of the sealing rings in the intercooler air ducts

| 11 Intercooler – removal and refitting | |

Removal

1 Remove the front bumper as described in Chapter 11, Section 22.

2 Extract the retaining clips slightly and disconnect the air ducts from the intercooler (**see illustration**).

3 Undo the bolt each side securing the intercooler to the radiator (**see illustration**).

4 Lift the intercooler off the lower mountings on the radiator and remove it from the engine compartment (**see illustration**).

Refitting

5 Refitting is a reversal of removal, bearing in mind the following points:

a) Check the condition of the sealing rings in the intercooler air ducts and renew if necessary (**see illustration**).

b) *Lubricate the sealing rings with clean engine oil before refitting to the intercooler.*
c) *Ensure that the air duct retaining clips are correctly refitted – attempt to pull the air duct off and check that is securely retained by the clip.*

12 Exhaust manifold – removal and refitting

1.9 litre engines

Removal

1 Firmly apply the handbrake, then jack up the front of the vehicle and support it securely on axle stands (see *Jacking and vehicle support*).
2 Remove the engine undertray as described in Chapter 11, Section 25.
3 Release the fasteners and detach the air ducts from the turbocharger.
4 Undo the nuts/bolts and remove the heat shields form the turbocharger (as applicable).
5 Remove the particulate filter/catalytic converter (as applicable) as described in Section 15.
6 Unscrew the union nut and disconnect the oil supply pipe from the turbocharger **(see illustration)**. Release the oil supply pipe supporting bracket from its mounting point.
7 Undo the bolts/nuts, and remove the support bracket from the underside of the turbocharger.
8 Note their fitted positions, then disconnect the vacuum hose/wiring plug from the turbocharger wastegate control.
9 Undo the union nut and disconnect the oil return pipe from the cylinder block.
10 Undo the nuts and remove the EGR pipe from the inlet manifold flap housing and exhaust manifold.
11 Undo the bolts securing the exhaust manifold to the cylinder head, then lower the manifold and turbocharger assembly and remove them from under the vehicle.
12 The turbocharger is integral with the exhaust manifold. If defective, the complete assembly must be renewed.

Refitting

13 Refitting is a reversal of removal, bearing in mind the following points:
a) *Use new gaskets and seals at all disturbed connections.*
b) *Tighten all fastenings to the specified torque (where given).*
c) *Before reconnecting the oil supply pipe, fill the turbocharger with clean engine oil via the oil supply pipe connection.*
d) *When the engine is started after refitting, allow it idle for approximately one minute to give the oil time to circulate around the turbine shaft bearings.*

12.6 Turbocharger oil supply pipe union (arrowed) – 1.9 litre engines

2.5 litre engines

Removal

14 Firmly apply the handbrake, then jack up the front of the vehicle and support it securely on axle stands (see *Jacking and vehicle support*).
15 Remove the engine undertray as described in Chapter 11, Section 25.
16 Remove the turbocharger as described in Section 14.
17 Where applicable, undo the two nuts and separate the EGR cooler from the exhaust manifold.
18 Progressively unscrew the mounting nuts and remove the washers, then withdraw the exhaust manifold from the studs on the cylinder head. Recover the gasket.

Refitting

19 Refitting is a reversal of removal, but fit new gaskets and tighten the mounting nuts to the specified torque. On completion, refit the turbocharger as described in Section 14.

13 Turbocharger – general information and precautions

General information

A turbocharger is fitted to all engines covered in this Manual, and on 1.9 litre engines it is integral with the exhaust manifold.

The turbocharger increases engine efficiency by raising the pressure in the inlet manifold above atmospheric pressure. Instead of the air simply being sucked into the cylinders, it is forced in. Additional fuel is supplied by the injectors, in proportion to the increased amount of air.

Energy for the operation of the turbocharger comes from the exhaust gas. The gas flows through a specially-shaped housing (the turbine housing) and in so doing, spins the turbine wheel. The turbine wheel is attached to a shaft, at the end of which is another vaned wheel, known as the compressor wheel. The compressor wheel spins in its own housing, and compresses the inducted air on the way to the inlet manifold.

Between the turbocharger and the inlet manifold, the compressed air passes through an intercooler. The purpose of the intercooler is to remove from the inducted air some of the heat gained in being compressed. Because cooler air is denser, removal of this heat further increases engine efficiency.

The turbo shaft is pressure-lubricated by its own dedicated oil feed pipe. The shaft 'floats' on a cushion of oil. Oil is returned to the sump via a return pipe that connects to the sump.

The turbocharger unit has an integral wastegate valve and vacuum actuator diaphragm, which is used to control the boost pressure applied to the inlet manifold.

Precautions

Caution: Do not operate the engine if any of air intake ducts are disconnected or the filter element is removed. Any debris entering the engine will cause severe damage to the turbocharger.
Caution: To prevent damage to the turbocharger, do not race the engine immediately after start-up, especially if it is cold. Allow it to idle smoothly to give the oil a few seconds to circulate around the turbocharger bearings. Always allow the engine to return to idle speed before switching it off – do not blip the throttle and switch off, as this will leave the turbo spinning without lubrication.
Caution: Observe the recommended intervals for oil and filter changing, and use a reputable oil of the specified quality. Neglect of oil changing, or use of inferior oil, can cause carbon formation on the turbo shaft, leading to subsequent failure.

14 Turbocharger – removal and refitting

Note: *The turbocharger should only be removed with the engine completely cool.*

1.9 litre engines

1 The turbocharger is integral with the exhaust manifold. Removal and refitting details are contained in Section 12.

2.5 litre engines

Removal

2 Firmly apply the handbrake, then jack up the front of the vehicle and support it securely on axle stands (see *Jacking and vehicle support*).
3 Remove the engine undertray as described in Chapter 11, Section 25.
4 Release the fasteners and detach the air ducts from the turbocharger.
5 Remove the particulate filter/catalytic converter (as applicable) as described in Section 15.
6 Remove the rear engine/transmission

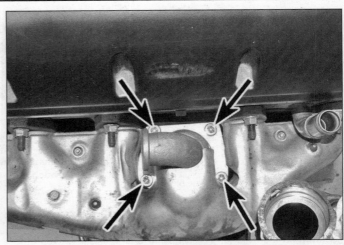

14.7 Release the retaining clamp (arrowed) and disconnect the EGR pipe from the exhaust manifold – 2.5 litre engines

14.9 Turbocharger-to-exhaust manifold retaining bolts (arrowed) – 2.5 litre engines

mounting as described in Chapter 2C, Section 16.

7 Release the retaining clamp and disconnect the EGR pipe from the exhaust manifold (see illustration).

8 Note their fitted positions, then disconnect the vacuum hose/wiring plug from the turbocharger wastegate control.

9 Undo the four bolts securing the turbocharger to the exhaust manifold (see illustration).

10 Undo the two bolts and remove the turbocharger lower support bracket (see illustration).

11 Undo the three bolts securing the turbocharger to the cylinder block. Withdraw the turbocharger from its location and recover the gaskets (see illustrations).

Refitting

12 Refitting is a reversal of removal, bearing in mind the following points:
  a) Use new gaskets and seals at all disturbed connections.
  b) Tighten all fastenings to the specified torque (where given).
  c) When the engine is started after refitting, allow it idle for approximately one minute to give the oil time to circulate around the turbine shaft bearings.

15 Exhaust system – general information and component renewal

⚠️ *Warning: Inspection and repair of exhaust system components should be done only after the system has cooled completely. This applies particularly to the catalytic converter, which runs at very high temperatures.*

General information

1 On vehicles without a particulate filter, the exhaust system consists of the front section, containing the catalytic converter, and the rear section which contains the two silencers. A semi-flexible coupling is used in the front section attachment at the turbocharger elbow.

2 On vehicles with a particulate filter, the exhaust system consists of the diesel particulate filter, the front section and the rear section which contains the two silencers. A semi-flexible coupling is used in the front section attachment to the particulate filter.

3 On all vehicles, the exhaust rear section is initially manufactured as one unit, but the two silencers are available separately as service items.

4 The system is suspended throughout its entire length by rubber mountings, which are secured to the underside of the vehicle by metal brackets.

Removal

5 Each exhaust section can be removed individually or, alternatively, the complete system can be removed as a unit.

6 To remove the system or part of the system, first jack up the front or rear of the vehicle and support it on axle stands (see *Jacking and Vehicle Support*). Alternatively position the vehicle over an inspection pit or on car ramps.

Particulate filter

7 Trace the exhaust gas temperature, pressure and oxygen sensor wiring looms back to their connectors in the engine compartment, releasing them from any retaining clips. Note their fitted positions, then unplug the connectors.

8 Unscrew the exhaust gas pressure sensor retaining bolt and release the hoses from their clips and supports. The hoses remain attached to the sensor and are removed with the particulate filter.

9 Remove the clamp securing the exhaust system front section to the particulate

14.10 Undo the two bolts (arrowed) and remove the turbocharger lower support bracket – 2.5 litre engines

14.11a Undo the three bolts securing the turbocharger to the cylinder block...

14.11b ...then withdraw the turbocharger from its location and recover the gaskets

filter. Undo the two bolts securing the front section mounting bracket to the subframe and disconnect the front section from the particulate filter.

10 Undo the two bolts and remove the particulate filter support bracket.

11 Slacken the clamp securing the particulate filter to the turbocharger.

12 Undo the two particulate filter mounting bolts and remove the filter from under the vehicle. Collect the two seals.

Front section and catalytic converter

13 Slacken the clamp bolts and slide the connecting sleeve between the exhaust front section and rear section rearwards and separate the two sections.

14 Slacken the clamp securing the front section to the turbocharger/particulate filter.

15 Undo the two bolts securing the front section mounting bracket to the subframe and remove the front section from under the vehicle.

Rear section and silencers

16 Working under the vehicle, support the front pipe on an axle stand or trolley jack.

17 If the original rear section is fitted, it will be necessary to cut through it to allow removal over the rear suspension components. The cutting point is 144 mm to the rear of the edge of the front silencer. Make a mark on the pipe at this point, then using a hacksaw, cut through the pipe at right-angles.

18 Slacken the clamp bolts and slide the connecting sleeve between the exhaust front section and rear section rearwards and separate the two sections.

19 Disconnect the rubber mountings and withdraw the pipe(s) and silencer(s) from under the vehicle.

Refitting

20 Each section is refitted by a reverse of the removal sequence, noting the following points:

a) Ensure that all traces of corrosion have been removed from the flanges or pipe ends and renew all necessary gaskets/ seals.

b) Inspect the rubber mountings for signs of damage or deterioration and renew as necessary.

c) Prior to tightening the exhaust system mounting, ensure that all rubber mountings are correctly located and that there is adequate clearance between the exhaust system and vehicle underbody.

d) Renew all self-locking nuts.

e) Apply high-temperature grease to all mounting studs.

f) If the particulate filter or temperature sensors have been renewed, the values stored in the engine management ECM must be adapted using VW diagnostic equipment. Entrust this task to a VW dealer or suitably-equipped specialist.

Chapter 4 Part B:
Fuel and exhaust systems – 2.0 litre engines

Contents

Degrees of difficulty

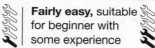

Easy, suitable for novice with little experience	**Fairly easy,** suitable for beginner with some experience	**Fairly difficult,** suitable for competent DIY mechanic	**Difficult,** suitable for experienced DIY mechanic	**Very difficult,** suitable for expert DIY or professional

Specifications

General

System type	Electronic direct common rail injection, turbocharger, catalytic converter and exhaust gas recirculation
Firing order	1-3-4-2
Maximum engine speed.	N/A (ECU controlled)
Engine fast idle speed	N/A (ECU controlled)

Torque wrench settings

	Nm	lbf ft
Camshaft position sensor	10	7
EGR pipe/cooler bolts	8	6
EGR pipe/cooler nuts.	25	18
Exhaust manifold bolts.	25	18
Fuel pressure regulating valve (left-hand end of fuel rail).	80	59
Fuel pressure sender (right-hand end of fuel rail).	100	74
Fuel pump bolts*:		
Two lower bolts (long):		
Stage 1	20	15
Stage 2	Angle-tighten a further 180°	
One upper bolt (short):		
Stage 1	20	15
Stage 2	Angle-tighten a further 45°	
Fuel rail bolts	22	16
High-pressure fuel pipe unions	28	20
Injector clamp bolts*:		
Stage 1	8	6
Stage 2	Angle-tighten a further 180°	
Inlet manifold to cylinder head.	8	6
Toothed belt pulley on high-pressure pump bolts*	20	15

*Use new bolts

7.5 Disconnect the airflow meter wiring connector

1 General information and precautions

General information

The fuel system comprises a fuel tank, a fuel supply pump, a fuel filter with an integral water separator, fuel supply and return lines and four fuel injectors.

The system is the familiar Common Rail system, where fuel is supplied from a timing belt-driven high-pressure pump to a common fuel rail (or reservoir). The four injectors are fitted into the cylinder head and are connected to the fuel rail by rigid metal pipes. The precise timing of the pre-, main, and post-injections are controlled by the engine management ECU and an electrically operated Piezo crystal incorporated into the injector design. All engines are fitted with a turbocharger.

The direct-injection fuelling system is controlled electronically by a diesel engine management system, comprising an Electronic Control Unit (ECU) and its associated sensors, actuators and wiring. In addition, the ECU manages the operation of the Exhaust Gas Recirculation (EGR) emission control system (Chapter 4C), the turbocharger boost pressure control system and the glow plug control system (Chapter 5).

A flap valve/throttle valve module fitted to the inlet manifold is closed by the ECU for 3 seconds as the engine is switched off, to minimise the air intake as the engine shuts down. This minimises the vibration felt as the pistons come up against the volume of highly compressed air present in the combustion chambers.

It should be noted that fault diagnosis of the diesel engine management system is only possible with dedicated electronic test equipment. Problems with the system's operation should therefore be referred to a VW dealer or suitably equipped specialist for assessment. Once the fault has been identified, the removal/refitting sequences detailed in the following Sections will then allow the appropriate component(s) to be renewed as required.

Precautions

Many of the operations described in this Chapter involve the disconnection of fuel lines, which may cause an amount of fuel spillage. Before commencing work, refer to the warnings below and the information in *Safety first!* at the beginning of this manual.

⚠ *Warning: When working on any part of the fuel system, avoid direct contact skin contact with diesel fuel – wear protective clothing and gloves when handling fuel system components. Ensure that the work area is well ventilated to prevent the build-up of diesel fuel vapour.*

• *Fuel injectors operate at extremely high pressures and the jet of fuel produced at the nozzle is capable of piercing skin, with potentially fatal results. When working with pressurised injectors, take care to avoid exposing any part of the body to the fuel spray. It is recommended that a diesel fuel systems specialist should carry out any pressure testing of the fuel system components.*

• *Under no circumstances should diesel fuel be allowed to come into contact with coolant hoses – wipe off accidental spillage immediately. Hoses that have been contaminated with fuel for an extended period should be renewed.*

• *Diesel fuel systems are particularly sensitive to contamination from dirt, air and water. Pay particular attention to cleanliness when working on any part of the fuel system, to prevent the ingress of dirt. Thoroughly clean the area around fuel unions before disconnecting them. Only use lint-free cloths and clean fuel for component cleansing.*

• *Store dismantled components in sealed containers to prevent contamination and the formation of condensation.*

2 Air cleaner assembly – removal and refitting

Refer to the procedures contained in Chapter 4A, Section 2.

3 Accelerator pedal/ position sensor – removal and refitting

Refer to the procedures contained in Chapter 4A, Section 3.

4 Fuel system – priming and bleeding

1 Prime the high pressure fuel pump by filling it with clean diesel through the fuel supply aperture **(see illustration 10.11)**, then operate the starter for shorts bursts (no more than 10 seconds at a time) until the engine starts. Operate the engine at a fast idle (approx 2000 rpm) for several minutes before allowing it to return to its normal idle speed.

2 If the engine fails to start, it must be filled/ bled using VW diagnostic equipment. Using this equipment operates the electric fuel pumps for 3 minutes.

3 Once the engine has been started, test drive the vehicle over a distance of at least 15 miles with at least one period of full acceleration. If there is any air left in the fuel system, the engine management ECU may switch to 'limp home' mode, and store a fault code. Have the fault code cleared and road test the vehicle again.

5 Fuel tank – removal and refitting

Refer to the procedures contained in Chapter 4A, Section 5.

6 Fuel pump/ fuel gauge sender unit – removal and refitting

Refer to the procedures contained in Chapter 4A, Section 6.

7 Diesel engine management system – component removal and refitting

Note: *According to model, to gain access to the engine management system components, undo the retaining bolts and rotary fasteners and remove the battery cover and engine cover as applicable.*

Note: *Observe the precautions in Section 1 before working on fuel system components.*

Throttle valve housing/module

1 Slacken the retaining clip and remove the air duct from the throttle housing.

2 Disconnect the wiring connector, from the throttle housing/module.

3 Unscrew and remove the retaining bolts, then lift the throttle housing/module away from the inlet manifold. Recover the O-ring seal; a new one will be required for refitting.

4 Refitting is a reversal of removal, noting the following:

a) Use a new throttle housing-to-inlet manifold seal.

b) Tighten the throttle housing bolts evenly to the specified torque.

c) Ensure that all hoses and electrical connectors are refitted securely.

Airflow meter

5 Disconnect the airflow meter wiring connector **(see illustration)**.

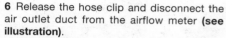

7.6 Release the hose clip (arrowed) and disconnect the air outlet duct

7.9 Inlet air temperature/charge pressure sensor (arrowed) located in the intercooler air duct

7.14 Pressure regulator valve fitted to the left-hand end of the fuel rail

6 Release the hose clip and disconnect the air outlet duct from the airflow meter **(see illustration)**.

7 Undo the two bolts and pull the airflow meter from the guide on the air cleaner housing. Handle the airflow meter carefully, as it is a delicate component.

8 Refitting is a reversal of removal.

Inlet air temperature/charge pressure sensor

9 An inlet air temperature sensor is built into the airflow meter. This sensor is an integral part of the airflow meter, and cannot be renewed separately. An additional inlet air temperature/charge pressure sensor is fitted, located in the air duct between the intercooler and inlet manifold **(see illustration)**.

10 To remove the sensor, disconnect the wiring connector, then undo the two retaining screws and withdraw the sensor. Recover the O-ring seal.

11 Refitting is a reversal of removal.

Fuel pressure regulating valve

12 The fuel pressure regulating valve is fitted to the left-hand end of the fuel rail. If the valve is removed from the fuel rail, then it will need to be renewed, as it has a deformable sealing lip as part of the valve.

13 To renew the valve, remove the fuel rail as described in Section 11.

14 Clean around the valve, then slacken the valve from the end of the fuel rail **(see illustration)**; counterhold the fuel rail using the flats on the housing. Plug the end of the rail to prevent dirt from entering.

15 Fit the new valve by reversing the removal procedure, making sure that the threads are all clean before fitting. Check the deformable seal on the new valve, before fitting, to check it is not damaged. Apply a small amount of Molybdenum grease to seal and threads.

Fuel pressure sender

16 The fuel pressure sender is fitted to the right-hand end of the fuel rail. If the engine will not start, disconnect the fuel pressure sender wiring connector and see if the engine will start. If the engine starts, the fuel pressure sender is faulty. With the connector

7.17 Disconnect the wiring connector from the fuel pressure sender

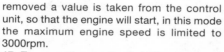

removed a value is taken from the control unit, so that the engine will start, in this mode the maximum engine speed is limited to 3000rpm.

17 To renew the sender, first disconnect the wiring plug connector **(see illustration)**.

18 Clean around the sender, then slacken it from the end of the fuel rail **(see illustration)**; plug the end of the rail to prevent dirt from entering.

19 Refit the pressure sender by reversing the removal procedure, making sure that the threads are all clean before refitting. The sender has a deformable seal, check for damage. Keep the threads free of oil and grease.

Coolant temperature sensors

20 Refer to Chapter 3, Section 6.

7.21 Camshaft position sensor (arrowed)

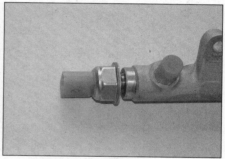

7.18 The fuel pressure sender is fitted to the right-hand end of the fuel rail

Camshaft position sensor

21 The camshaft position sensor is located behind the timing belt cover, below the camshaft sprocket **(see illustration)**.

22 Remove the timing belt, as described in Chapter 2B, Section 7.

23 Disconnect the sensor wiring connector.

24 To make access easier undo the retaining bolt and remove the timing belt idler pulley **(see illustration)**.

25 Using a screwdriver prise out the aperture cover in the rear plastic cover, then withdraw the wiring plug through the cover, unhooking it from the rear cover **(see illustration)**.

26 Undo the retaining bolt and remove the camshaft sensor from the cylinder head.

27 Refitting is a reversal of removal, but

7.24 Unbolt the Idler pulley

7.25 Prise up the aperture cover (arrowed)

7.28 Engine speed sensor (arrowed)

7.30a Undo the retaining bolt...

7.30b ...and withdraw the sensor

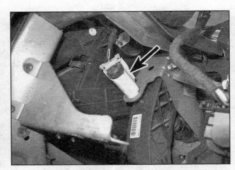

7.32a Clutch pedal switch (arrowed)...

7.32b ...and brake pedal switch (arrowed) located on the pedal mounting brackets

tighten the bolt to the specified torque setting and fit rubber plugs to the aperture for the wiring in the rear plastic cover.

Engine speed sensor

28 The engine speed sensor is mounted on the front facing side of the cylinder block, adjacent to the mating surface of the block and transmission bellhousing **(see illustration)**.

29 Access is from beneath the engine compartment. Apply the handbrake, and then jack up the front of the vehicle and support it on axle stands (see *Jacking and vehicle support*). Remove the engine undertray.

30 Remove the retaining screw and withdraw the sensor from the cylinder block **(see illustrations)**.

31 Refit the sensor by reversing the removal procedure.

Clutch and brake pedal switches

32 The clutch and brake pedal switches are located on the clutch and brake pedal mounting brackets in the driver's footwell **(see illustrations)**.

33 Remove the facia right-hand footwell trim panel as described in Chapter 11, Section 29.

34 Disconnect the wiring connector from the relevant switch.

35 Turn the switch 45° anti-clockwise and remove it from the mounting bracket.

36 The brake pedal switches were modified in January 2007 and the manufacturers advise that whenever an early type switch is removed, it should always be replaced with

a later type switch. The later type switches can be identified by the bright tip of the plunger.

37 Without moving the relevant pedal, insert the switch into the mounting bracket and turn it 45° clockwise to lock it in position.

38 Reconnect the switch wiring connector.

39 On completion, refit the facia right-hand footwell trim panel as described in Chapter 11, Section 29.

Electronic control unit (ECU)

Caution: The ECU is programmed and identified specifically for the vehicle it is fitted to, and the identity coding must be transferred to any new module. This process requires the use of dedicated VW diagnostic equipment. For this reason, it is recommended that ECU renewal is carried out by a VW dealer or suitably-

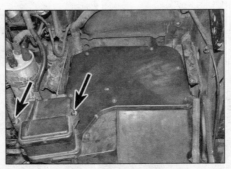

7.42 Rotate the two turnbuckles (arrowed) and open the cover of the electrics box

equipped specialist, however removal and refitting of the original ECU is possible by the home mechanic. Note also that if the ECU is renewed, the identification of the new ECU must be transferred to the immobiliser control module by a VW dealer or specialist.

Caution: Always wait at least 30 seconds after switching off the ignition before disconnecting the wiring from the ECU. When the wiring is disconnected, all the learned values may be erased, although any contents of the fault memory are retained. After reconnecting the wiring, the vehicle must be driven for several miles so that the ECU can learn its basic settings. If the engine still runs erratically, the basic settings may be reinstated by a VW dealer or specialist using a special test instrument.

40 The ECU is located in the engine compartment electrics box, below the battery.

41 Remove the battery and battery tray as described in Chapter 5, Section 4.

42 Rotate the two turnbuckles and open the cover of the electrics box **(see illustration)**. Push the locking mechanism on the fuse insert in the direction of the housing and pull the fuse insert upwards out of the electrics box.

43 Undo the nine screws securing the upper part of the electrics box to the centre part. Slide the fuse carrier out of its location and push it downwards, then lift off the upper part of the electrics box **(see illustration)**.

7.43 Undo the retaining screws, release the fuse carrier, then lift off the upper part of the electrics box

7.44a Disconnect the wiring connectors from the ECU...

7.44b ...then release the locking catch and lift the ECU from its location

44 Pull out the locking bars and disconnect the wiring connectors from the ECU. Release the locking catch and lift the ECU from its location in the electrics box **(see illustrations)**.
45 Refitting is a reversal of removal.

8 Injectors – general information, removal and refitting

⚠️ *Warning: Exercise extreme caution when working on the fuel injectors. Never expose the hands or any part of the body to injector spray, as the high pressure can cause the fuel to penetrate the skin, with possibly fatal results. You are strongly advised to have any work which involves testing the injectors under pressure carried out by a dealer or fuel injection specialist. Refer to the precautions given in Section 1 of this Chapter before proceeding.*

General information

1 Injectors do deteriorate with prolonged use, and it is reasonable to expect them to need reconditioning or renewal after 60,000 miles (100,000 km) or so. Accurate testing, overhaul and calibration of the injectors must be left to a specialist.

Removal

Note: *Take care not to allow dirt into the injectors or fuel pipes during this procedure. Do not drop the injectors or allow the needles at their tips to become damaged. The injectors are precision-made to fine limits, and must not be handled roughly. Keep the injectors identified for position to ensure correct refitting.*
2 According to model, undo the retaining bolts and rotary fasteners and remove the battery cover and engine cover as applicable.
3 Ensure the area around the injectors and the pipes/return hoses is clean and free from debris. The use of a vacuum cleaner is recommended. Plug all fuel lines when they have been disconnected to prevent any dirt ingress **(see illustration)**.
4 Disconnect the injector wiring plug connectors.

5 Push the return hose connector downwards at its outer tabs, then pull up the centre piece and disconnect them from the top of the injectors. Plug the openings to prevent contamination.
6 Undo the unions and remove the high-pressure pipes from between the fuel rail and the injectors. Counterhold the injector with an open-ended spanner when releasing the pipe union **(see illustrations)**. Plug the openings to prevent contamination.
7 Undo the bolt securing the injector clamp between the two injectors, note that one clamp secures two injectors in place.
8 VW technicians use a slide hammer (tool T10055) and adapter (T10415) to pull the injector from the cylinder head. If this tool is not available, it may be possible to fabricate an equivalent tool to pull the injector out of the cylinder head.

9 Two injectors will need to be removed together, as the clamping piece is slotted into both injectors. Recover the copper seal and O-rings and discard. New ones must be used for refitting. **Note:** *The injectors can only be refitted to their original positions. Mark the injectors to avoid confusion if refitting the original injectors.*

Refitting

10 If required, renew the injector seals in the top of the camshaft cover. Using a screwdriver, prise the seal out from the cover; the new seal can then be pressed firmly into the cover **(see illustrations)**. There are different size seals depending on engine code, make sure the correct seals are supplied. Also make sure the spring on the inside lip of the seal does not drop into the camshaft cover.
11 Ensure the area around the injector

8.3 Fit sealing caps to prevent dirt ingress

8.6a Hold down the outer tabs, and prise up the centre piece (arrowed)...

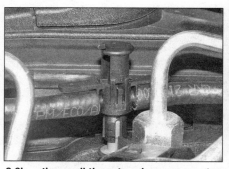

8.6b ...then pull the return hose connector upwards from the injector

8.10a Carefully prise out the seal...

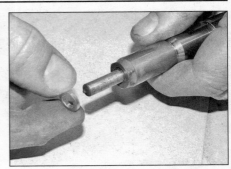

8.10b ...making sure the spring does not fall into the cover

8.12a Clean off the carbon around the end of the injector...

8.12b ...and fit a new sealing washer

locations in the cylinder head are clean and free from debris. Use a vacuum cleaner if available. Clean any carbon deposits from the injector and sealing surfaces with a cloth soaked in clean engine oil or rust-releasing spray.

12 To remove the copper sealing washer, spray rust-releasing spray around the injector nozzle, then clamp the seal in a vice, and use a twisting motion to pull the injector from the seal. Push the new copper seal into place **(see illustrations)**. Do not touch the very end of the injector, or you could block up the nozzle.

13 Apply a little clean engine oil to the return pipe connection on the injector, and fit the new O-ring **(see illustration)**.

14 To renew the main injector O-ring seal, VW specify the use of tool no. T10377. This tool allows the O-ring to slide over the end

of the injector without twisting. With care, the seals can be fitted without the tool **(see illustration)**.

15 Apply a smear of clean engine oil to the main O-ring seal, and insert the injector into place in the cylinder head **(see illustrations)**. Note that if the original injectors are being refitted, they must go into their original positions. Tighten the injector clamping bolt/nut to the specified torque.

16 Refit the high-pressure fuel pipes and tighten the unions to the specified torque. Note that the pipes may be re-used providing the tapered seats are undamaged and the pipes are not deformed, constricted or corroded. Counterhold the injector with an open-ended spanner when tightening the pipe union.

17 The remainder of refitting is a reversal of removal, noting the following:

a) *If one or more injectors have been renewed, the 'injector delivery calibration values' and 'injector voltage calibration values' must be entered into the ECU using VW diagnostic equipment. Entrust this task to a VW dealer or suitably equipped specialist.*

b) *After completion of the work, the fuel system must be bled as described in Section 4.*

9 Inlet manifold – removal and refitting

Removal

1 Remove the throttle housing, as described in Section 7.

2 Remove the fuel rail from the top of the inlet manifold, as described in Section 11.

3 Undo the two retaining screws and move the coolant return pipe to one side.

4 Release the retaining clips and disconnect the fuel feed and return hoses from the fuel pipes. Be prepared for fuel spillage and suitably plug the disconnected hoses and pipes.

5 Disconnect the fuel injector wiring connectors.

6 Unbolt/release all coolant and vacuum pipes connected to the inlet manifold, then disconnect and move aside the various wiring harnesses.

7 Undo the bolts and remove the EGR cooler pipe from the manifold.

8 Unbolt the oil dipstick guide tube.

9 Undo the manifold retaining bolts, starting from the outside and working inwards in a diagonal sequence. Lift the manifold from the cylinder head and retrieve the gasket seals; discard, as new ones will be required for refitting.

Refitting

10 Refitting is a reversal of removal, using new seals and gaskets. Remember to renew any self-locking nuts. Tighten the manifold retaining bolts to the specified torque setting, starting from the inside and working outwards in a diagonal sequence.

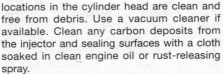

8.13 Fit the new return pipe O-ring (arrowed) to the top of the injector

8.14 Fit a new main O-ring seal without twisting it

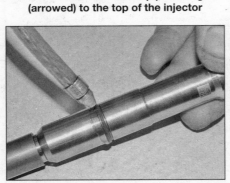

8.15a Lubricate the seal with some clean oil...

8.15b ...then slide the injectors down into the cylinder head

10 High-pressure fuel pump – removal and refitting

Removal

1 Remove the timing belt and fuel pump sprocket as described in Chapter 2B, Section 7.
2 Disconnect the fuel supply hose from the pump **(see illustration)**. Plug all openings to prevent contamination.
3 Disconnect the wiring connector from the sensor on the pump.
4 Slacken the unions and disconnect the high-pressure fuel pipe between the pump and common fuel rail. Undo the retaining screws to release the fuel pipe from the support brackets.
5 On some models it may be necessary to disconnect he wiring connectors from the glow plugs. Pulling only under the ridge at the top of the connectors, disconnect the wiring connectors. **Note:** *Take care not to damage the connectors or wiring, as the glow plug wiring loom/connectors are only available as a complete assembly.*
6 Undo the bolts securing the coolant pipe to the inlet manifold, and position the pipe to one side.

7 Disconnect the fuel return pipes from the pump and the common fuel rail **(see illustration)**.
8 Counterhold the pump hub using VW tool No. T10051, and undo the pump hub nut. In the absence of this special tool, counterhold the hub using a suitable C-spanner **(see illustration)**.
9 Using a suitable two-legged puller and two 8 mm bolts, remove the hub from the pump shaft **(see illustrations)**.
10 Undo the 3 retaining bolts and remove the pump.

Refitting

11 Refitting is a reversal of removal, noting the following points:

a) Ensure all fuel pipes/hose connections are clean and free from debris.
b) The high-pressure fuel pipe from the pump to the common rail maybe re-used providing it's not been damaged.
c) Tighten all fasteners to their specified torque where given.
d) Fill the pump with clean fuel through the fuel supply pipe aperture prior to starting **(see illustration)**.
e) Bleed the fuel system as described in Section 4.

10.2 Release the clip (arrowed) and disconnect the fuel supply hose

11 Fuel rail – removal and refitting

Note: *Observe the precautions in Section 1 before working on any component in the fuel system.*

Removal

1 According to model, undo the retaining bolts and rotary fasteners and remove the battery cover and engine cover as applicable.
2 Disconnect the wiring connectors from the fuel injectors.

10.7 Fuel pump return hose (arrowed)

10.8 Counterhold the pump hub with a C-spanner, and undo the nut

10.9a Use a two-legged puller and 8 mm bolts to pull the hub from the pump shaft

10.9b Note the locating peg (arrowed) in the pump shaft

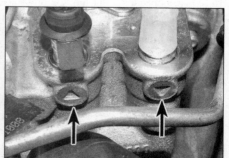

10.11 The triangles adjacent to the pump apertures indicate fuel flow (arrowed)

11.4a Disconnect the hose from the return pipe...

11.4b ...and the return pipe from the fuel rail

3 Counterhold the injector with an open-ended spanner when releasing the pipe union. Undo the unions and remove the high-pressure pipes from between the fuel rail and the injectors (see illustrations). Plug the openings to prevent contamination.
4 Release the retaining clips and disconnect the fuel return hose from the fuel rail (see illustrations)
5 Undo the retaining bolts, disconnect the coolant return hose from the expansion tank, and move the coolant pipe/hose to one side.
6 Slacken the fuel pipe unions and remove the high-pressure pipe from the pump to the fuel rail.
7 Disconnect the wiring plugs from the glow plugs, fuel pressure regulating valve, and the fuel pressure sensor at each end of the fuel rail. Unclip the wiring loom retaining bracket from the top of the fuel rail and move it to one side.
8 Undo the multi-spline retaining bolts and remove the fuel rail.
9 If required, note their fitted positions, then unscrew the fuel pressure sensor and pressure regulating valve from the fuel rail, as described in Section 3. **Note:** *VW insist that once removed, the pressure regulating valve cannot be re-used.*

Refitting

10 Where applicable, refit the fuel pressure sensor and the new regulating valve to the fuel rail, and tighten them to the specified torque. Note that the threads of the sensors must be clean and free from oil and grease.
11 The remainder of refitting is a reversal of removal, noting the following points:
a) *Refit the high-pressure fuel pipes and tighten the unions to the specified torque. Note that the high-pressure fuel pipes may be re-used providing the tapered seats are undamaged and the pipes are not deformed, constricted or corroded.*
b) *After completion of the work, the fuel system must be bled as described in Section 4.*

12 Intercooler – removal and refitting

Refer to the procedures contained in Chapter 4A, Section 11.

13 Exhaust manifold – removal and refitting

Removal

1 Firmly apply the handbrake, then jack up the front of the vehicle and support it securely on axle stands (see *Jacking and vehicle support*). Undo the retaining bolts and remove the engine undertray.
2 According to model, undo the retaining bolts and rotary fasteners and remove the battery cover and engine cover as applicable.
3 Remove the air cleaner assembly and ducting as described in Section 2.
4 Remove the particulate filter as described in Chapter 4A, Section 15.
5 Undo the retaining bolt, unclip the breather pipe and disconnect the air intake hose from the turbocharger.
6 Disconnect the wiring connector and vacuum pipe from the vacuum unit on top of the turbocharger.
7 Located at the engine compartment bulkhead, disconnect the exhaust gas temperature sensor wiring plugs, and detach the connector from the bulkhead bracket. Note that there is one wiring connector behind the mounting plate on the bulkhead, trace the wiring back from the relevant sensor, noting its routing and releasing it from any retaining clips.
8 Undo the retaining screws and remove the EGR metal connecting pipes.
9 Undo the two upper securing bolts and the lower banjo bolts for the oil supply and return for the turbocharger. Then remove the

oil return pipe/support from the rear of the engine.
10 Undo the two retaining screws and remove the heat shield from the manifold.
11 Check around the turbocharger/exhaust manifold and unclip any wiring or hoses still connected, noting their fitted position and the routing of all cables.
12 Undo the retaining nuts and manoeuvre the exhaust manifold/turbocharger assembly out from the engine compartment.

Refitting

13 Refit the turbocharger by following the removal procedure in reverse, noting the following points:
a) *Renew exhaust maniflold gaskets, sealing washers and O-rings.*
b) *Fit a new gasket to the oil return pipe upper flange.*
c) *Fit a new banjo bolt to the oil return pipe.*
d) *Fit new sealing washers to the oil supply pipe.*
e) *Before reconnecting the oil supply pipe, fill the turbocharger with fresh oil using an oil can.*
f) *Tighten all nuts and bolts to the specified torque, where given.*
g) *Ensure that the air hose clips are securely tightened, to prevent air leaks.*
h) *When the engine is started after refitting, allow it to idle for approximately one minute to give the oil time to circulate around the turbine shaft bearings. Check for signs of oil or coolant leakage from the relevant unions.*

14 Turbocharger – general information and precautions

General information

A turbocharger is fitted to all engines covered in this Manual, and on 2.0 litre engines it is integral with the exhaust manifold.

The turbocharger increases engine

efficiency by raising the pressure in the inlet manifold above atmospheric pressure. Instead of the air simply being sucked into the cylinders, it is forced in. Additional fuel is supplied by the injectors, in proportion to the increased amount of air.

Energy for the operation of the turbocharger comes from the exhaust gas. The gas flows through a specially-shaped housing (the turbine housing) and in so doing, spins the turbine wheel. The turbine wheel is attached to a shaft, at the end of which is another vaned wheel, known as the compressor wheel. The compressor wheel spins in its own housing, and compresses the inducted air on the way to the inlet manifold.

Between the turbocharger and the inlet manifold, the compressed air passes through an intercooler. The purpose of the intercooler is to remove from the inducted air some of the heat gained in being compressed. Because cooler air is denser, removal of this heat further increases engine efficiency.

The turbo shaft is pressure-lubricated by its own dedicated oil feed pipe. The shaft 'floats' on a cushion of oil. Oil is returned to the sump via a return pipe that connects to the sump.

The turbocharger unit has an integral wastegate valve and vacuum actuator diaphragm, which is used to control the boost pressure applied to the inlet manifold.

Precautions

Caution: Do not operate the engine if any of air intake ducts are disconnected or the filter element is removed. Any debris entering the engine will cause severe damage to the turbocharger.

Caution: To prevent damage to the turbocharger, do not race the engine immediately after start-up, especially if it is cold. Allow it to idle smoothly to give the oil a few seconds to circulate around the turbocharger bearings. Always allow the engine to return to idle speed before switching it off – do not blip the throttle and switch off, as this will leave the turbo spinning without lubrication.

Caution: Observe the recommended intervals for oil and filter changing, and use a reputable oil of the specified quality. Neglect of oil changing, or use of inferior oil, can cause carbon formation on the turbo shaft, leading to subsequent failure.

15 Turbocharger – removal and refitting

The turbocharger is integral with the exhaust manifold. Removal and refitting details are contained in Section 13.

16 Exhaust system – general information and component renewal

Refer to the procedures contained in Chapter 4A, Section 15.

Notes

Chapter 4 Part C:
Emission control systems

Contents

Degrees of difficulty

Easy, suitable for novice with little experience	Fairly easy, suitable for beginner with some experience	Fairly difficult, suitable for competent DIY mechanic	Difficult, suitable for experienced DIY mechanic	Very difficult, suitable for expert DIY or professional

Specifications

Torque wrench settings	Nm	lbf ft
EGR pipe/cooler bolts/nuts (1.9 litre engines)	25	18
EGR pipe/cooler bolts/nuts (2.0 and 2.5 litre engines)		
Bolts	8	6
Nuts	25	18
Oxygen sensor	52	38

1 General information

Emission control systems

All models have a crankcase emission control system, and in addition are fitted with a catalytic converter, and an Exhaust Gas Recirculation (EGR) system to reduce exhaust emissions. Some models are also fitted with a particulate filter in the exhaust system to further reduce harmful emissions from the exhaust.

Crankcase emission control

To reduce the emission of unburned hydrocarbons from the crankcase into the atmosphere, the engine is sealed and the blow-by gases and oil vapour are drawn from inside the crankcase, through a wire mesh oil separator, into the inlet manifold to be burned by the engine during normal combustion.

A pressure regulating valve (on the camshaft cover) controls the flow of gases from the crankcase.

If the engine is worn, the raised crankcase pressure (due to increased blow-by) will cause some of the flow to return through the inlet manifold under all operating conditions.

Exhaust emission control

An oxidation catalyst is fitted in the exhaust system on most models. This has the effect of removing a large proportion of the gaseous hydrocarbons, carbon monoxide and particulates present in the exhaust gas.

The Exhaust Gas Recirculation (EGR) system reduces the level of nitrogen oxides produced during combustion by introducing a proportion of the exhaust gas back into the inlet manifold, under certain engine operating conditions, via a plunger valve. The system is controlled electronically by the diesel engine management ECU.

2 Emission control systems – general information and component renewal

Crankcase emission control

1 The crankcase emission control system consists of a series of hoses that connect the crankcase vent to the camshaft cover vent and the air inlet, a pressure regulating valve (where applicable) and an oil separator unit.
2 The system requires no attention other than to check at regular intervals that the hose(s) are free of blockages and undamaged.

Exhaust emission control

Catalytic converter/ diesel particulate filter renewal

3 Refer to Chapter 4A, Section 15 (1.9 and 2.5 litre engines) or Chapter 4B, Section 16 (2.0 litre engines).

Oxygen sensor renewal

4 Warm the engine up to normal operating temperature then stop the engine and disconnect the battery negative terminal (refer to *Disconnecting the battery*).

5 Firmly apply the handbrake, then jack up the front of the vehicle and support it securely on axle stands (see *Jacking and vehicle support*).
6 From under the car, trace the oxygen sensor wiring back to the connector and disconnect it. Release the wiring harness from the retaining clips.
7 Unscrew the oxygen sensor and remove it from the particulate filter.
8 Refitting is a reverse of the removal procedure. Prior to installing the sensor, apply a smear of high temperature grease to the sensor threads (VW recommend the use of a special grease available from your dealer). Tighten the sensor to the specified torque and ensure that the wiring is correctly routed and in no danger of contacting either the exhaust system or engine.

Exhaust Gas Recirculation (EGR) system

9 The EGR system consists of the EGR valve, the modulator (solenoid) valve and a series of connecting vacuum hoses.
10 On 1.9 and 2.5 litre engines, the EGR valve is part of the inlet manifold flap housing, and is joined to the exhaust manifold by a flanged pipe. On 2.0 litre engines, the EGR valve is integral with the EGR cooler.

EGR solenoid renewal

11 The EGR solenoid valve/modulator valve is mounted on the bulkhead at the rear of the engine compartment.
12 According to model, undo the retaining bolts and rotary fasteners and remove the battery cover and engine cover as applicable.

13 Disconnect the wiring connector from the solenoid valve.

14 Disconnect the vacuum hose which leads to the EGR valve, and the other vacuum hose on the base of the solenoid valve.

15 Unscrew the solenoid valve mounting bolt, and remove the valve from the engine.

16 Refitting is a reversal of removal. Ensure that the hoses and wiring plug are reconnected securely and correctly.

EGR valve renewal – 1.9 and 2.5 litre engines

17 According to model, undo the retaining bolts and rotary fasteners and remove the battery cover and engine cover as applicable.

18 The EGR valve is part of the inlet manifold flap housing, and cannot be removed separately. Removal and refitting procedures for the inlet manifold flap housing are given in Chapter 4A, Section 7.

19 If required, the pipe from the housing to the exhaust manifold can be removed, after unscrewing the flange nuts and bolts. Recover the gasket from each end of the pipe.

20 Refitting the pipe is a reversal of removal. Use new gaskets, and tighten the flange nuts and bolts to the specified torque.

EGR valve renewal – 2.0 litre engines

21 According to model, undo the retaining bolts and rotary fasteners and remove the battery cover and engine cover as applicable.

22 Slacken the retaining clip and remove the air duct from the throttle housing.

23 Using suitable hose clamps, clamp the two coolant hoses leading to the EGR cooler.

24 Release the retaining clips and disconnect the two coolant hoses.

25 Disconnect the vacuum hose and the EGR valve wiring connector.

26 Undo the two nuts securing the EGR pipe to the exhaust manifold. Undo the two bolts securing the EGR pipe to the EGR valve and remove the pipe.

27 Undo the four retaining bolts and remove the cooler and EGR valve upwards and to the right.

28 Refitting the pipe is a reversal of removal. Use new gaskets, and tighten the flange nuts and bolts to the specified torque.

3 Catalytic converter – general information and precautions

General information

1 The catalytic converter reduces harmful exhaust emissions by chemically converting the more poisonous gases to ones which (in theory at least) are less harmful. The chemical reaction is known as an 'oxidising' reaction, or one where oxygen is 'added'.

2 Inside the converter is a honeycomb structure, made of ceramic material and coated with the precious metals palladium, platinum and rhodium (the 'catalyst' which promotes the chemical reaction). The chemical reaction generates heat, which itself promotes the reaction – therefore, once the vehicle has been driven several miles, the body of the converter will be very hot.

3 The ceramic structure contained within the converter is understandably fragile, and will not withstand rough treatment. Since the converter runs at a high temperature, driving through deep standing water (in flood conditions, for example) is to be avoided, since the thermal stresses imposed when plunging the hot converter into cold water may well cause the ceramic internals to fracture, resulting in a 'blocked' converter – a common cause of failure. A converter which has been damaged in this way can be checked by shaking it (do not strike it) – if a rattling noise is heard, this indicates probable failure. **Note:** *Checking the operation of a catalytic converter requires expensive and sophisticated diagnostic equipment, starting with a high-quality exhaust gas analyser. If the level of CO in the exhaust gases is too high, a full check of the engine management system must be carried out to eliminate all other possibilities before the converter is suspected of being faulty. The vehicle should be taken to a VW dealer for this work to be carried out using the correct diagnostic equipment. Do not waste time trying to test the system without such facilities.*

Precautions

4 The catalytic converter is a reliable and simple device which needs no maintenance in itself, but there are some facts of which an owner should be aware if the converter is to function properly for its full service life.

a) *DO NOT use fuel or engine oil additives – these may contain substances harmful to the catalytic converter.*

b) *DO NOT continue to use the vehicle if the engine burns oil to the extent of leaving a visible trail of blue smoke.*

c) *Remember that the catalytic converter operates at very high temperatures. DO NOT, therefore, park the vehicle in dry undergrowth, over long grass or piles of dead leaves after a long run.*

d) *Remember that the catalytic converter is FRAGILE – do not strike it with tools during servicing work.*

e) *The catalytic converter, used on a well-maintained and well-driven vehicle, should last for between 50 000 and 100 000 miles – if the converter is no longer effective it must be renewed. Renewal procedures are contained in Chapter 4A, Section 15 (1.9 and 2.5 litre engines) or Chapter 4B, Section 16 (2.0 litre engines).*

Chapter 5
Starting and charging systems

Contents

Degrees of difficulty

Easy, suitable for novice with little experience 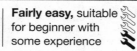	**Fairly easy,** suitable for beginner with some experience 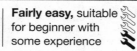	**Fairly difficult,** suitable for competent DIY mechanic 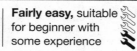	**Difficult,** suitable for experienced DIY mechanic 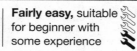	**Very difficult,** suitable for expert DIY or professional

Specifications

General
Electrical system type .... 12 volt, negative-earth

Starter motor
Type .... Pre-engaged

Glow plugs
Current consumption .... 10 amps per glow plug

Torque wrench settings

	Nm	lbf ft
Alternator mounting bolts (1.9 and 2.0 litre engines)	20	15
Alternator mounting bracket bolts (2.5 litre engines)	20	15
Front engine mounting-to-subframe bolts (2.5 litre engines):*		
Stage 1	20	15
Stage 2	Angle-tighten a further 90°	
Front engine mounting bracket bolts (2.5 litre engines):*		
Stage 1	50	37
Stage 2	Angle-tighten a further 90°	
Glow plugs:		
1.9 litre engines	15	11
2.0 litre engines	17	13
2.5 litre engines:		
8 mm glow plugs	12	9
10 mm glow plugs	15	11
Starter motor retaining bolts:		
M10 bolts	40	30
M12 bolts	75	55

*Use new bolts.

1 General information, precautions and battery disconnection

General information

The engine electrical system consists mainly of the charging and starting systems, and the engine pre/post-heating system. Because of their engine-related functions, these components are covered separately from the body electrical devices such as the lights, instruments, etc (which are covered in Chapter 12).

The electrical system is of 12-volt negative earth type.

The battery is of the maintenance-free (sealed for life) type, and is charged by the alternator. On 1.9 and 2.0 litre engines, the alternator is belt-driven from the crankshaft pulley. On 2.5 litre engines, the alternator is gear-driven via a rubber coupling from the engine geartrain at the flywheel/driveplate end of the engine.

The starter motor is of pre-engaged type incorporating an integral solenoid. On starting, the solenoid moves the drive pinion into engagement with the flywheel/driveplate ring gear before the starter motor is energised. Once the engine has started, a one-way clutch prevents the motor armature being driven by the engine until the pinion disengages.

Further details of the various systems are given in the relevant Sections of this Chapter. While some repair procedures are given, the usual course of action is to renew the component concerned.

Precautions

It is necessary to take extra care when working on the electrical system to avoid damage to semi-conductor devices (diodes and transistors), and to avoid the risk of personal injury. In addition to the precautions given in *Safety first!* at the beginning of this manual, observe the following when working on the system:

• *Always remove rings, watches, etc before working on the electrical system. Even with the battery disconnected, capacitive discharge could occur if a component's live terminal is earthed through a metal object. This could cause a shock or nasty burn.*

3.1 Battery charge condition indicator (arrowed)

• *Do not reverse the battery connections. Components such as the alternator, electronic control units, or any other components having semi-conductor circuitry could be irreparably damaged.*
• *If the engine is being started using jump leads and a slave battery, connect the batteries positive-to-positive and negative-to-negative (see 'Jump starting'). This also applies when connecting a battery charger but in this case both of the battery terminals should first be disconnected.*
• *Never disconnect the battery terminals, the alternator, any electrical wiring or any test instruments when the engine is running.*
• *Do not allow the engine to turn the alternator when the alternator is not connected.*
• *Never test for alternator output by flashing the output lead to earth.*
• *Never use an ohmmeter of the type incorporating a hand-cranked generator for circuit or continuity testing.*
• *Always ensure that the battery negative lead is disconnected when working on the electrical system.*
• *Before using electric arc welding equipment on the vehicle, disconnect the battery, alternator and components such as the engine management electronic control unit to protect them from the risk of damage.*

Battery disconnection

Refer to the precautions listed in *Disconnecting the battery* at the end of this manual.

2 Electrical fault finding – general information

Refer to Chapter 12, Section 2.

3 Battery – testing and charging

Testing

1 All models are factory fitted with a maintenance-free battery with a built-in 'magic-eye' charge condition indicator. The indicator is located in the top of the battery casing, and indicates the condition of the battery from its colour **(see illustration)**. Tap the indicator inspection window lightly and carefully using the handle of a screwdriver. The air bubbles, which can influence the display, will dissipate when doing this. This will make the colour indicator reading more accurate. If the indicator shows green, then the battery is in a good state of charge. If the indicator turns darker, eventually to black, then the battery requires charging, as described later in this Section. If the indicator shows clear/

yellow, then the electrolyte level in the battery is too low to allow further use, and the battery should be renewed. **Do not** attempt to charge, load or jump start a battery when the indicator shows clear/yellow.
2 An alternative (and more accurate) way to test a battery is with a voltmeter (or multimeter set to voltage testing) – connect the voltmeter across the battery terminals, observing the correct polarity. The test is only accurate if the battery has not been subjected to any kind of charge for the previous six hours. If this is not the case, switch on the headlights for 30 seconds, then wait four to five minutes before testing the battery after switching off the headlights. All other electrical circuits must be switched off, so check that the doors and, where applicable, the tailgate are fully shut when making the test.
3 If the voltage reading is less than 12.0 volts, then the battery is less than healthy. Under 11.5 volts and the battery needs charging. However, as little as 11.0 volts will still usually be enough to start the engine, though a battery in this condition could not be relied on. A reading of around 10.0 volts suggests that one of the six battery cells has died – a common way for modern batteries to fail.
4 If the battery is to be charged, remove it from the vehicle (see Section 4) and charge it as described in the next sub-Section.

Charging

Note: *The following is intended as a guide only. Always refer to the manufacturer's recommendations (often printed on a label attached to the battery), and always disconnect both terminal leads (or preferably remove the battery) before charging.*

5 Maintenance-free type batteries take considerably longer to fully recharge than the traditional low-maintenance type, the time taken being dependent on the extent of discharge, but it will take anything up to three days.
6 A constant voltage type charger is required, to be set, when connected, to 13.9 to 14.9 volts with a charger current below 25 amps. Using this method, the battery should be usable within three hours, giving a voltage reading of 12.5 volts, but this is for a partially-discharged battery and, as mentioned, full charging can take considerably longer.
7 If the battery is to be charged from a fully discharged state, have it recharged by your dealer or local automotive electrician, as the charge rate is higher and constant supervision during charging is necessary.

4 Battery and battery tray – removal and refitting

Note: *Refer to 'Disconnecting the battery' before proceeding.*

Battery

Removal

1 Where fitted, turn the three plastic retainers

half a turn and lift off the cover over the battery **(see illustrations)**.

2 Disconnect the lead at the negative (–) terminal by unscrewing the retaining nut and removing the terminal clamp. Note that the battery negative (–) and positive (+) terminal connections are stamped on the battery case **(see illustration)**.

3 Disconnect the lead at the positive (+) terminal by unscrewing the retaining nut and removing the terminal clamp.

4 If fitted, pull the hose for the central venting off the battery.

5 Unscrew the retaining bolt and remove the battery retaining clamp **(see illustration)**.

6 Lift up the handles and carefully lift the battery from its location and remove it from the vehicle **(see illustration)**. Make sure the battery is kept upright at all times.

Refitting

Note: *As a precaution, before refitting the battery check that all doors are unlocked.*

7 Refitting is a reversal of removal, but smear petroleum jelly on the terminals after reconnecting the leads to reduce corrosion, and always reconnect the positive lead(s) first, followed by the negative lead(s).

Battery tray

Removal

8 Remove the battery as described previously.

9 Undo the retaining bolt and remove the cover from the side of the battery tray **(see illustration)**.

10 Undo the four retaining bolts and lift the battery tray from its location **(see illustrations)**.

Refitting

11 Refitting is a reversal of removal.

---

5 Charging system – testing

Note: *Refer to the precautions given in 'Safety first!' and in Section 1 of this Chapter before starting work.*

1 If a malfunction occurs in the charging circuit, don't automatically assume that the alternator is causing the problem. First check the following items:

a) *On 1.9 and 2.0 litre engines, check the tension and condition of the auxiliary drivebelt (see Chapter 1, Section 9) – renew it if it is worn or deteriorated.*
b) *Ensure the alternator mounting bolts are tight.*
c) *Inspect the alternator wiring harness and the electrical connections at the alternator; they must be in good condition and tight.*
d) *Start the engine and check the alternator for abnormal noises – for example, a shrieking or squealing sound may indicate a badly-worn bearing or bush.*

4.1a Turn the three plastic retainers (arrowed) half a turn...

4.1b ...and lift the cover off the battery

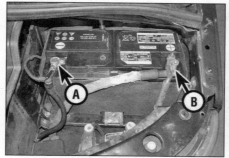

4.2 Battery negative (–) terminal (A) and positive (+) terminal (B)

4.5 Unscrew the retaining bolt (arrowed) and remove the battery retaining clamp

e) *Make sure the battery is fully-charged – one bad cell in a battery can cause overcharging by the alternator.*
f) *Disconnect the battery leads (negative first, then positive). Inspect the battery*

posts and the lead clamps for corrosion. Clean them thoroughly if necessary (see Weekly checks). Reconnect the lead to the positive terminal.
g) *With the ignition and all accessories*

4.6 Using the handles, carefully lift the battery from the battery tray

4.9 Undo the retaining bolt and remove the cover from the side of the battery tray

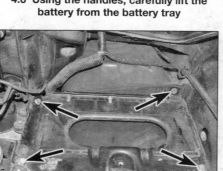

4.10a Undo the four retaining bolts (arrowed)...

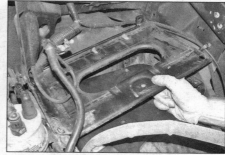

4.10b ...and lift the battery tray from its location

7.4 Disconnect the charge warning light wiring connector from the alternator – 1.9 litre engines

switched off, insert a test light between the battery negative post and the disconnected negative lead clamp:

1) If the test light does not come on, re-attach the clamp and proceed to the next step.

2) If the test light comes on, there is a short in the electrical system of the vehicle. The short must be repaired before the charging system can be checked.

3) To find the short, disconnect the alternator wiring harness. If the light goes out, the alternator is at fault. If the light stays on, remove each fuse until it goes out – this will tell you which component is short-circuited.

2 Using a voltmeter, check the battery voltage with the engine off. It should be approximately 12.0 volts.

3 Start the engine and check the battery voltage again. Increase the engine speed until the voltmeter remains steady; it should now be approximately 13.5 to 14.6 volts.

4 Switch on as many electrical accessories (eg, the headlights and heater blower) as possible, and check that the alternator maintains the regulated voltage at around

13.0 to 14.0 volts. The voltage may drop and then come back up; it may also be necessary to increase engine speed slightly, even if the charging system is working properly.

5 If the regulated voltage is not as stated, the fault may be due to worn brushes, weak brush springs, a faulty voltage regulator, a faulty diode, a severed phase winding, or worn or damaged slip rings. The alternator should be renewed or taken to a dealer or auto electrician for testing and repair.

6 Auxiliary drivebelt – removal and refitting

Note: *An auxiliary drivebelt is only fitted to 1.9 and 2.0 litre engines. On 2.5 litre engines, the engine ancillary components are gear-driven from the engine geartrain at the flywheel/driveplate end of the engine.*

Refer to Chapter 1, Section 27.

7 Alternator – removal and refitting

1.9 litre engines
Removal

1 Disconnect the battery negative terminal (refer to *Disconnecting the battery*).

2 Remove the auxiliary drivebelt as described in Chapter 1, Section 27.

3 On engine codes BRR and BRS with air conditioning, carry out the following operations:

a) *Remove the air duct from the top of the engine.*

b) *Undo the retaining bolt and move the power steering hydraulic fluid reservoir to one side.*

c) *Prise out the cover cap, undo the*

retaining bolt and remove the vibration damper from the front subframe.

d) *Unbolt and remove the auxiliary drivebelt tensioner.*

4 On all engines, disconnect the charge warning light wiring from the alternator at the connector **(see illustration)**.

5 Remove the protective cap and unscrew the nut, then disconnect the positive cable from the alternator at the screw terminal. Where applicable, unbolt and remove the cable guide **(see illustration)**.

6 Unscrew and remove the lower then upper mounting bolts, then lift the alternator upwards away from its bracket **(see illustration)**.

Refitting

7 Refitting is a reversal of removal, bearing in mind the following points:

a) *Prior to refitting the alternator, drive the threaded sleeves approximately 4 mm out of the alternator housing toward the rear of the alternator.*

b) *Tighten the alternator mounting bolts to the specified torque.*

c) *On engine codes BRR and BRS, refit the components listed in paragraph 3.*

d) *Refit the auxiliary drivebelt as described in Chapter 1, Section 27.*

2.0 litre engines
Removal

8 Disconnect the battery negative terminal (refer to *Disconnecting the battery*).

9 Firmly apply the handbrake, then jack up the front of the vehicle and support it securely on axle stands (see *Jacking and vehicle support*).

10 Where fitted, undo the six retaining bolts and remove the engine undertray.

11 Move the body front crossmember to the service position as described in Chapter 11, Section 25.

12 Remove the auxiliary drivebelt as described in Chapter 1, Section 27.

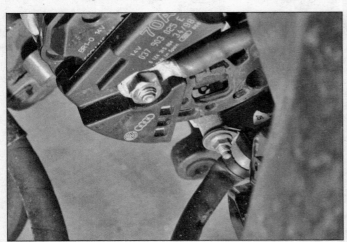

7.5 Disconnect the positive cable from the alternator at the screw terminal – 1.9 litre engines

7.6 Unscrew and remove the lower then upper alternator mounting bolts (arrowed) – 1.9 litre engines

13 On models with air conditioning, unbolt the air conditioning compressor and support it to one side. Do not disconnect the refrigerant hoses.

14 Unbolt the power steering pump and support it to one side.

15 Disconnect the charge warning light wiring from the alternator at the connector.

16 Remove the protective cap and unscrew the nut, then disconnect the positive cable from the alternator at the screw terminal. Where applicable, unbolt and remove the cable guide.

17 Remove the air duct running in front of the alternator.

18 Unscrew and remove the lower then upper mounting bolts, then lower the alternator downwards away from its bracket.

Refitting

19 Refitting is a reversal of removal, bearing in mind the following points:

a) *Prior to refitting the alternator, drive the threaded sleeves approximately 4 mm out of the alternator housing toward the rear of the alternator.*

b) *Tighten the alternator mounting bolts to the specified torque.*

c) *Refit the auxiliary drivebelt as described in Chapter 1, Section 27.*

d) *Return the body front crossmember to its normal position as described in Chapter 11, Section 25.*

2.5 litre engines

Removal

20 Disconnect the battery negative terminal (refer to *Disconnecting the battery*).

21 Firmly apply the handbrake, then jack up the front of the vehicle and support it securely on axle stands (see *Jacking and vehicle support*).

22 Where fitted, undo the six retaining bolts and remove the engine undertray.

23 Move the body front crossmember to the service position as described in Chapter 11, Section 25.

24 Prise out the cover cap, undo the retaining bolt and remove the vibration damper from the front subframe.

25 Undo the two bolts securing the front engine mounting to the subframe. Note that new bolts will be required for refitting.

26 Undo the five bolts securing the front engine mounting lower bracket to the upper bracket and to the cylinder block, then remove the lower bracket. Note that new bolts will be required for refitting.

27 Undo the two bolts securing the front engine mounting upper bracket to the cylinder block and remove the upper bracket. Note that new bolts will be required for refitting.

28 On models with air conditioning, undo the three compressor mounting bolts. Disengage the compressor from the rubber drive coupling, move it to one side and support it clear of the alternator using cable ties **(see illustrations)**. Do not disconnect the refrigerant hoses.

29 Disconnect the charge warning light wiring from the alternator at the connector.

30 Remove the protective cap and unscrew the nut, then disconnect the positive cable from the alternator at the screw terminal. Where applicable, unbolt and remove the cable guide.

31 Mark the direction of rotation of the alternator rubber drive coupling.

32 Undo the three bolts securing the alternator mounting bracket to the cylinder block. Disengage the alternator rubber drive coupling from the drive shaft hub, then lower the alternator and remove it from under the vehicle **(see illustration)**. Note that the alternator must not be separated from its mounting bracket.

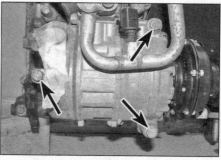

7.28a Undo the three compressor mounting bolts (arrowed)...

Refitting

33 Refitting is a reversal of removal, bearing in mind the following points:

a) *Prior to refitting the alternator, check the condition of the rubber drive coupling and renew it if there is any sign of wear, damage or deterioration.*

b) *Tighten the alternator mounting bracket retaining bolts to the specified torque.*

c) *Renew the front engine mounting and mounting bracket retaining bolts and tighten the bolts to the specified torque.*

d) *Return the body front crossmember to its normal position as described in Chapter 11, Section 25.*

8 Alternator – testing and overhaul

If the alternator is thought to be suspect, it should be removed from the vehicle and taken to an auto electrician for testing. Most auto electricians will be able to supply and fit brushes at a reasonable cost. However, check on the cost of repairs before proceeding as it may prove more economical to obtain a new or exchange alternator.

7.28b ...then disengage the compressor from the rubber drive coupling – 2.5 litre engines

7.32 Undo the three alternator retaining bolts then disengage the alternator rubber drive coupling from the drive shaft hub – 2.5 litre engines

9 Starting system – testing

Note: *Refer to the precautions given in 'Safety first!' and in Section 1 of this Chapter before starting work.*

1 If the starter motor fails to operate during the normal starting procedure, the possible causes are as follows:
  a) *The engine immobiliser is faulty.*
  b) *The battery is faulty.*
  c) *The electrical connections between the switch, solenoid, battery and starter motor are somewhere failing to pass the necessary current from the battery through the starter to earth.*
  d) *The solenoid is faulty.*
  e) *The starter motor is mechanically or electrically defective.*

2 To check the battery, switch on the headlights. If they dim after a few seconds, this indicates that the battery is discharged – recharge (see Section 3) or renew the battery. If the headlights glow brightly, operate the starter switch while watching the headlights. If they dim, then this indicates that current is reaching the starter motor, therefore the fault must lie in the starter motor. If the lights continue to glow brightly (and no clicking sound can be heard from the starter motor solenoid), this indicates that there is a fault in the circuit or solenoid – see the following paragraphs. If the starter motor turns slowly when operated, but the battery is in good condition, then this indicates either that the starter motor is faulty, or there is considerable resistance somewhere in the circuit.

3 If a fault in the circuit is suspected, disconnect the battery leads (including the earth connection to the body), the starter/solenoid wiring and the engine/transmission earth strap. Thoroughly clean the connections, and reconnect the leads and wiring. Use a voltmeter or test light to check that full battery voltage is available at the battery positive lead connection to the solenoid. Smear petroleum jelly around the battery terminals to prevent corrosion – corroded connections are among the most frequent causes of electrical system faults.

4 If the battery and all connections are in good condition, check the circuit by disconnecting the ignition switch supply wire from the solenoid terminal. Connect a voltmeter or test lamp between the wire end and a good earth (such as the battery negative terminal), and check that the wire is live when the ignition switch is turned to the 'start' position. If it is, then the circuit is sound – if not the circuit wiring can be checked as described in Chapter 12, Section 2.

5 The solenoid contacts can be checked by connecting a voltmeter or test light between the battery positive feed connection on the starter side of the solenoid and earth. When the ignition switch is turned to the 'start' position, there should be a reading or lighted bulb, as applicable. If there is no reading or lighted bulb, the solenoid is faulty.

6 If the circuit and solenoid are proved sound, the fault must lie in the starter motor. In this event, it may be possible to have the starter motor overhauled by a specialist, but check on the cost of spares before proceeding, as it may prove more economical to obtain a new or exchange motor.

10 Starter motor – removal and refitting

Removal

1 Disconnect the battery negative terminal (refer to *Disconnecting the battery*).
2 Firmly apply the handbrake, then jack up the front of the vehicle and support it securely on axle stands (see *Jacking and vehicle support*).
3 Where fitted, undo the six retaining bolts and remove the engine undertray.
4 Undo the two bolts and move the cooling system expansion tank to one side.
5 Where applicable, remove the intercooler air duct for improved access to the starter motor.
6 Note the location of the two wires on the starter motor. Disconnect the wire from the solenoid, then unscrew the nut and disconnect the battery cable from the main terminal.
7 Unscrew the nut on the starter motor upper retaining stud bolt, withdraw the wiring guide and move the wiring harness to one side.
8 Undo the starter motor upper retaining stud bolt.
9 Unscrew the nut on the starter motor lower retaining stud bolt and disconnect the earth lead.
10 Undo the starter motor lower retaining stud bolt and remove the motor from the engine compartment.

Refitting

11 Refitting is a reversal of removal, but tighten the retaining stud bolts to the specified torque.

11 Starter motor – testing and overhaul

If the starter motor is thought to be suspect, it should be removed from the vehicle and taken to an auto electrician for testing. Most auto electricians will be able to supply and fit brushes at a reasonable cost. However, check on the cost of repairs before proceeding as it may prove more economical to obtain a new or exchange motor.

12 Pre/post-heating system – general information

To assist cold starting, a pre-heating system is fitted, which comprises a glow plug for each cylinder, a glow plug relay, glow period control unit or engine management ECU (depending on engine), a facia mounted warning lamp and the associated electrical wiring.

The glow plugs are miniature electric heating elements, encapsulated in a metal case with a probe at one end and electrical connection at the other. Each swirl chamber/inlet tract has a glow plug threaded into it, the glow plug probe is positioned directly in line with incoming spray of fuel. When the glow plug is energised, the fuel passing over it is heated, allowing its optimum combustion temperature to be achieved more readily when it reaches the cylinder.

The duration of the pre-heating period is governed by the engine management ECU or glow period control unit, which monitors the temperature of the engine via the coolant temperature sensor and alters the pre-heating time to suit the conditions.

A facia mounted warning lamp informs the driver that pre-heating is taking place. The lamp extinguishes when sufficient pre-heating has taken place to allow the engine to be started, but power will still be supplied to the glow plugs for a further period until the engine is started. If no attempt is made to start the engine, the power supply to the glow plugs is switched off to prevent battery drain and glow plug burn-out.

After the engine has been started, the glow plugs continue to operate for a further period of time. This helps to improve fuel combustion whilst the engine is warming up, resulting in quieter, smoother running and reduced exhaust emissions.

13 Glow plugs – testing, removal and refitting

Testing

1 If the system malfunctions, testing is ultimately by substitution of known good units, but some preliminary checks may be made as described in the following paragraphs.
2 Connect a voltmeter or 12 volt test lamp between the glow plug supply cable and a good earth point on the engine.
Caution: Make sure that the live connection is kept well clear of the engine and bodywork.
3 Have an assistant activate the pre-heating system with the ignition key and check that battery voltage is applied to the glow plug electrical connection. Note that the voltage

will drop to zero when the pre-heating period ends.

4 If no supply voltage can be detected at the glow plug, then either the glow plug relay or the supply cabling must be faulty.

5 To locate a faulty glow plug, first disconnect the battery negative terminal (refer to *Disconnecting the battery*).

6 Remove the supply cabling from the glow plug terminal. Measure the electrical resistance between the glow plug terminal and the engine earth. A reading of anything more than an Ohm indicates that the plug is defective.

7 If a suitable ammeter is available, connect it between the glow plug and its supply cable and measure the steady state current consumption (ignore the initial current surge which will be about 50% higher). Compare the result with the Specifications – high current consumption (or no current draw at all) indicates a faulty glow plug.

8 As a final check, remove the glow plugs and inspect them visually, as described in the following paragraphs.

Removal

9 If not already done, disconnect the battery negative terminal (refer to *Disconnecting the battery*).

10 Move the body front crossmember to the service position as described in Chapter 11, Section 25.

11 On 2.0 litre engines, to improve access to the glow plugs, disconnect the wiring connectors from the fuel injectors and any other adjacent components as necessary.

12 On 2.5 litre engines it will be necessary to remove the inlet manifold as described in Chapter 4A, Section 9, unless only No 1 or No 5 cylinder glow plugs are to be removed.

13 Pull the glow plug wiring connector off the end of the relevant glow plug.

14 Slacken and withdraw the glow plug **(see illustration)**.

15 Inspect the glow plug probe for signs of damage. A badly burned or charred probe is usually an indication of a faulty fuel injector.

13.14 Removing a glow plug from the cylinder head

Refitting

16 Refitting is a reversal of removal, noting the following points:
  a) *Apply a little anti-seize compound (or copper brake grease) to the glow plug threads.*
  b) *Tighten the glow plugs to the specified torque.*
  c) *Make sure when remaking the glow plug wiring connections that the contact surfaces are clean.*

Notes

Chapter 6
Clutch

Contents

Degrees of difficulty

Easy, suitable for novice with little experience		Fairly easy, suitable for beginner with some experience	Fairly difficult, suitable for competent DIY mechanic	Difficult, suitable for experienced DIY mechanic	Very difficult, suitable for expert DIY or professional	

Specifications

General

Type . . . . Single dry plate, hydraulically-operated with automatic adjustment

Torque wrench settings	Nm	lbf ft
Clutch pressure plate-to-flywheel:		
5-speed transmissions:		
With solid (single-mass) flywheel	22	16
With dual-mass flywheel:		
M6 bolts	13	10
M7 bolts	22	16
6-speed transmissions	22	16
Clutch master cylinder mounting nuts	25	18
Clutch pedal mounting bracket retaining bolt/nuts	25	18
Clutch pedal pivot bolt nut	25	18
Clutch slave cylinder retaining bolts:		
5-speed transmissions	25	18
6-speed transmissions	20	15

1 General information

The clutch consists of a friction disc, a pressure plate assembly, and the release mechanism; all of these components are contained in the large cast-aluminium alloy bellhousing, sandwiched between the engine and the transmission.

The friction disc is fitted between the engine flywheel and the clutch pressure plate, and is allowed to slide on the transmission input shaft splines.

The pressure plate assembly is bolted to the engine flywheel. When the engine is running, drive is transmitted from the crankshaft, via the flywheel, to the friction disc (these components being clamped securely together by the pressure plate assembly) and from the friction disc to the transmission input shaft.

To interrupt the drive, the pressure plate spring pressure must be relaxed. This is achieved using a hydraulic release mechanism which consists of a master cylinder, and a slave cylinder and release bearing. On vehicles equipped with 5-speed transmissions, the clutch release bearing is fitted concentrically around the transmission

input shaft and the slave cylinder is mounted externally on the bellhousing. The bearing is pushed onto the pressure plate assembly by means of a release lever actuated by the slave cylinder. On vehicles equipped with 6-speed transmissions, the release bearing is integral with the slave cylinder to form a single release assembly fitted concentrically around the transmission input shaft.

The clutch pedal is connected to the clutch master cylinder by a short pushrod. The master cylinder is mounted behind the clutch pedal and receives its hydraulic fluid supply from a separate chamber in the brake master cylinder reservoir. Depressing the clutch

2.4 Clutch slave cylinder bleed screw (arrowed) – 6-speed transmissions

pedal moves the piston in the master cylinder forwards, so forcing hydraulic fluid through the clutch hydraulic pipe to the slave cylinder. On vehicles with an externally mounted slave cylinder, the piston in the slave cylinder moves forward on the entry of the fluid and actuates the clutch release lever by means of a short pushrod. The release lever pivots on its mounting stud and presses the release bearing against the pressure plate spring fingers. This causes the springs to deform and releases the clamping force on the pressure plate. On vehicles with an integral release bearing and slave cylinder assembly, the piston in the slave cylinder moves forward on the entry of the fluid and presses the integral release bearing directly against the pressure plate spring fingers.

On all models, the clutch operating mechanism is self-adjusting and no manual adjustment is required.

2 Hydraulic system – bleeding

⚠️ **Warning: Hydraulic fluid is poisonous; thoroughly wash off spills from bare skin without delay. Seek immediate medical advice if any fluid is swallowed or gets into the eyes. Certain types of hydraulic fluid are inflammable and may ignite when brought into contact with hot components. Hydraulic fluid is also an effective paint stripper. If spillage**

occurs onto painted bodywork or fittings, it should be washed off immediately, using copious quantities of cold water. It is also hygroscopic (i.e. it can absorb moisture from the air) which then renders it useless. Old fluid may have suffered contamination, and should never be re-used.

1 If any part of the hydraulic system is dismantled, or if air has accidentally entered the system, the system will need to be bled. The presence of air is characterised by the pedal having a spongy feel and it results in difficulty in changing gear.

2 The design of the clutch hydraulic system does not allow bleeding to be carried out using the conventional method of pumping the clutch pedal. In order to remove all air present in the system, it is necessary to use pressure bleeding equipment. This is available from auto accessory shops at relatively low cost and is usually operated by a reservoir of pressurised air contained in the vehicle spare tyre.

3 Connect the pressure bleeding equipment to the brake/clutch hydraulic fluid reservoir in accordance with the manufacturer's instructions.

4 Open the clutch slave cylinder bleed screw, located near the top of the transmission, approximately half a turn **(see illustration)**. With the bleed screw open, quickly depress and release the clutch pedal by hand approximately fifteen to twenty times.

5 Close the bleed screw, then disconnect and remove the bleeding equipment.

6 Check the operation of the clutch to see that it is satisfactory. If air still remains in the system, repeat the bleeding operation.

7 Discard any fluid which is bled from the system, even if it looks clean. Hydraulic fluid absorbs water and its re-use can cause internal corrosion of the master and slave cylinders, leading to excessive wear and failure of the seals.

3 Clutch master cylinder – removal and refitting

Note: Refer to the warning in Section 2

concerning the dangers of hydraulic fluid before proceeding.

Removal

1 The clutch master cylinder is located inside the car, attached to the clutch and brake pedal mounting bracket. Hydraulic fluid for the unit is supplied from the brake master cylinder reservoir.

2 Remove the facia right-hand footwell trim panel as described in Chapter 11, Section 29.

3 Where fitted, remove the clutch pedal switch as described in Chapter 4A, Section 7 (1.9 and 2.5 litre models) or Chapter 4B, Section 7 (2.0 litre models).

4 Cover the floor beneath the pedals to protect against hydraulic fluid spillage.

5 Clamp off the flexible hydraulic fluid hose leading from the fluid reservoir to the master cylinder using a brake hose clamp.

6 Carefully pull the hydraulic fluid supply hose from the master cylinder **(see illustration)**. If necessary, plug the end of the hose with a suitable bolt.

7 Pull out the retaining clip to its stop and disconnect the hydraulic pipe union from the base of the master cylinder **(see illustration)**.

8 To separate the master cylinder pushrod from the clutch pedal, insert one flat bladed screwdriver in each of the two holes on either side of the clutch pedal. Press in the tangs on each side of the clip securing the master cylinder pushrod to the pedal, while at the same time pulling the clutch pedal rearwards to release it from the pushrod clip.

9 Unscrew the two mounting nuts and withdraw the master cylinder from inside the vehicle **(see illustration)**.

Refitting

10 Refitting is a reversal of removal, bearing in mind the following points:
a) Tighten the master cylinder mounting nuts to the specified torque.
b) Where applicable, refit the clutch pedal switch as described in Chapter 4A, Section 7, or Chapter 4B, Section 7.
c) Refit the facia right-hand footwell trim panel as described in Chapter 11, Section 29.
d) Bleed the clutch hydraulic system as described in Section 2.

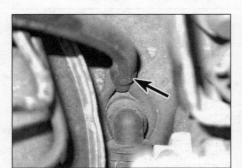

3.6 Carefully pull the hydraulic fluid supply hose (arrowed) from the master cylinder

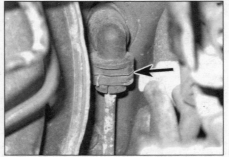

3.7 Pull out the retaining clip (arrowed) to its stop and disconnect the hydraulic pipe union from the base of the master cylinder

3.9 Master cylinder right-hand mounting nut (arrowed)

4.6 Pull out the retaining clip to its stop and disconnect the bleed screw housing – 6-speed transmissions

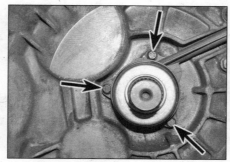

4.7a Undo the three retaining bolts (arrowed)...

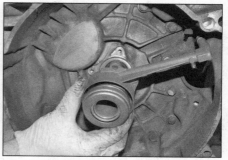

4.7b ...and remove the slave cylinder and release bearing assembly – 6-speed transmissions

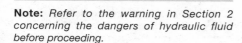

4 Clutch slave cylinder – removal and refitting

Note: *Refer to the warning in Section 2 concerning the dangers of hydraulic fluid before proceeding.*

5-speed transmissions

Removal

1 Clamp off the slave cylinder hydraulic hose using a brake hose clamp.
2 Unscrew the hydraulic pipe union from the slave cylinder, and carefully ease out the pipe.
3 Unscrew the two mounting bolts and withdraw the slave cylinder from the transmission.

Refitting

4 Refitting is a reversal of the removal procedure, noting the following points:
 a) *Ensure that the slave cylinder pushrod correctly engages with the clutch release lever.*
 b) *Tighten all nuts and bolts to the specified torque.*
 c) *On completion, bleed the clutch hydraulic system as described in Section 2.*

6-speed transmissions

Removal

5 Unless the complete engine/transmission

unit is to be removed from the vehicle and separated for major overhaul (see Chapter 2D, Section 4), the clutch release mechanism can be reached by removing the transmission only, as described in Chapter 7A, Section 6.
6 Pull out the retaining clip to its stop and disconnect the bleed screw housing from the end of the slave cylinder **(see illustration)**.
7 Undo the three retaining bolts and remove the slave cylinder and release bearing assembly from the transmission bellhousing **(see illustrations)**.
8 Spin the release bearing by hand, and check it for smooth running. Any tendency to seize or run rough will necessitate renewal of the complete assembly. If it is to be re-used, wipe it clean with a dry cloth; on no account should the bearing be washed in a liquid solvent, otherwise the internal grease will be removed.

Refitting

9 Refitting is a reversal of the removal procedure, noting the following points:
 a) *Renew the slave cylinder O-ring prior to refitting.*
 b) *Refit the engine/transmission unit as described in Chapter 2D, Section 4, or refit the transmission as described in Chapter 7A, Section 6.*
 c) *Tighten all nuts and bolts to the specified torque.*
 d) *On completion, bleed the clutch hydraulic system as described in Section 2.*

5 Clutch pedal – removal and refitting

Removal

1 Remove the clutch master cylinder as described in Section 3.
2 Remove the instrument panel as described in Chapter 12, Section 9.
3 Remove the plenum chamber cover as described in Chapter 11, Section 25.
4 Working through the instrument panel aperture in the facia, unscrew the clutch pedal mounting bracket upper retaining nut **(see illustration)**.
5 From within the plenum chamber, release the wiring harness retaining clip from the pedal mounting bracket retaining bolt, then unscrew the bolt.
6 Where fitted, remove the clutch pedal switch as described in Chapter 4A, Section 7 (1.9 and 2.5 litre models) or Chapter 4B, Section 7 (2.0 litre models).
7 Unscrew the clutch pedal mounting bracket lower retaining nut **(see illustration)**.
8 Unscrew the two nuts and remove the connecting plate between the clutch and brake pedal mounting brackets **(see illustration)**.
9 Withdraw the pedal mounting bracket from the retaining studs and manipulate it out from underneath the facia.

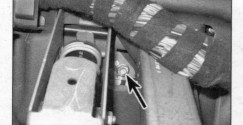

5.4 Clutch pedal mounting bracket upper retaining nut (arrowed)

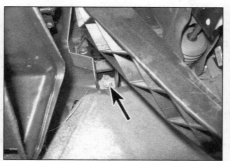

5.7 Clutch pedal mounting bracket lower retaining nut (arrowed)

5.8 Unscrew the two nuts and remove the mounting bracket connecting plate (arrowed)

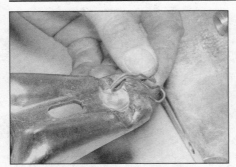

6.5a Locate the spring clip over the end of the release lever...

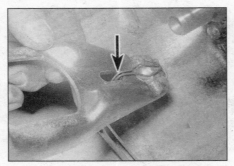

6.5b ...and press the spring into the hole – 5-speed transmissions

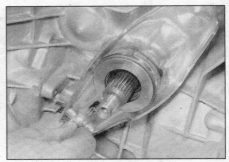

6.5c Press the release lever onto the ball stud until the spring clip holds it in position – 5-speed transmissions

10 Carefully clamp the lower section of the pedal mounting bracket in a vice.

11 Fully depress the clutch pedal to compress the over centre spring. Using a large pair if grips, compress the over centre spring further, and disengage it from the bar of the pedal mounting bracket. Guide the spring off the clutch pedal pin and carefully release the spring tension.

12 Unscrew the nut, remove the pedal pivot bolt and separate the clutch pedal from the mounting bracket.

Refitting

13 Refitting is a reversal of removal.

6 Clutch release bearing and lever – removal, inspection and refitting

Note: *The following procedure is only applicable to the 5-speed transmission. On the 6-speed transmission, the release bearing is integral with the slave cylinder.*

Removal

1 Unless the complete engine/transmission unit is to be removed from the vehicle and separated for major overhaul (see Chapter 2D, Section 4), the clutch release mechanism can be reached by removing the transmission only, as described in Chapter 7A, Section 6.

2 Use a screwdriver to prise the release lever

from the ball stud inside the transmission bellhousing. If this proves difficult, push the spring clip from the pivot end of the release lever by pushing it through the hole. This will release the pivot end of the lever from the ball stud. Now withdraw the lever together with the release bearing from the guide sleeve.

Inspection

3 Spin the release bearing by hand, and check it for smooth running. Any tendency to seize or run rough will necessitate renewal of the bearing. If it is to be re-used, wipe it clean with a dry cloth; on no account should the bearing be washed in a liquid solvent, otherwise the internal grease will be removed.

Refitting

4 Commence refitting by lubricating the ball stud with a little molybdenum disulphide grease. Smear a little grease on the release bearing surface which contacts the diaphragm spring fingers and the release lever, and also on the guide sleeve.

5 Fit the spring clip onto the release lever. Refit the lever together with the bearing and press the release lever onto the ball stud until the spring holds it in position **(see illustrations)**.

6 Refit the engine/transmission unit as described in Chapter 2D, Section 4, or refit the transmission as described in Chapter 7A, Section 6.

7 Clutch assembly – removal, inspection and refitting

⚠️ *Warning: Dust created by clutch wear and deposited on the clutch components may contain asbestos, which is a health hazard. DO NOT blow it out with compressed air, and do not inhale any of it. DO NOT use petrol or petroleum-based solvents to clean off the dust. Brake system cleaner or methylated spirit should be used to flush the dust into a suitable receptacle. After the clutch components are wiped clean with rags, dispose of the contaminated rags and cleaner in a sealed, marked container.*

Removal

1 Unless the complete engine/transmission unit is to be removed from the vehicle and separated for major overhaul (see Chapter 2D, Section 4), the clutch can be reached by removing the transmission as described in Chapter 7A, Section 6.

2 Before disturbing the clutch, use a marker pen to mark the relationship of the pressure plate assembly to the flywheel.

3 Unscrew and remove the clutch pressure plate retaining bolts, working in a diagonal sequence, and slackening the bolts only a turn at a time. If necessary, the flywheel may be held stationary using a home-made locking tool or a wide-bladed screwdriver, inserted in the teeth of the starter ring gear and resting against part of the cylinder block **(see illustration)**.

4 Ease the pressure plate off its locating dowels **(see illustration)**. Be prepared to catch the friction disc, which will drop out as the plate is removed. Note which way round the disc is fitted.

Inspection

5 The most common problem which occurs in the clutch is wear of the friction disc. However, all the clutch components should be inspected at this time, particularly if the engine has covered a high mileage. Unless the clutch components are known to be

7.3 Using a home-made locking tool to hold the flywheel

7.4 Ease the pressure plate off its locating dowels

virtually new, it is worth renewing them all as a set (disc, pressure plate and release bearing). Renewing a worn friction disc by itself is not always satisfactory, especially if the old disc was slipping and causing the pressure plate to overheat.

6 Examine the linings of the friction disc for wear, and the disc hub and rim for distortion, cracks, broken torsion springs, and worn splines. The surface of the friction linings may be highly glazed, but as long as the friction material pattern can be clearly seen, this is satisfactory. The disc must be renewed if the lining thickness has worn down to, or near, the rivets.

7 If there is any sign of oil contamination, indicated by shiny black discoloration, the disc must be renewed, and the source of the contamination traced and rectified. This will be a leaking crankshaft oil seal or transmission input shaft oil seal.

8 Check the machined faces of the flywheel and pressure plate. If either is grooved, or heavily scored, renewal is necessary. The pressure plate must also be renewed if any cracks are apparent, or if the diaphragm spring is damaged or its pressure suspect. Pay particular attention to the tips of the spring fingers, where the release bearing acts upon them.

9 With the transmission removed, it is also advisable to check the condition of the release bearing, as described in Section 6. Having got

this far, it is almost certainly worth renewing it.

Refitting

10 It is important that no oil or grease is allowed to come into contact with the friction material of the clutch disc or the pressure plate and flywheel faces. To ensure this, it is advisable to refit the clutch assembly with clean hands, and to wipe down the pressure plate and flywheel faces with a clean dry rag before assembly begins.

11 Place the friction disc against the flywheel, ensuring that it is the right way round **(see illustration)**. It should be marked GETRIEBESEITE (which means transmission side) but if not, position it as follows:

  a) *On engines with a solid (single-mass) flywheel, position the disc with the raised, torsion spring side of the hub facing away from the flywheel.*

  b) *On engines with a dual-mass flywheel, position the disc with the short end of the hub facing away from the flywheel.*

12 Place the clutch pressure plate over the dowels. Refit the retaining bolts, and tighten them finger-tight so that the friction disc is gripped lightly, but can still be moved.

13 The friction disc must now be centralised so that when the engine and transmission are mated, the splines of the transmission input shaft will pass through the splines in the centre of the disc hub. To do this, a

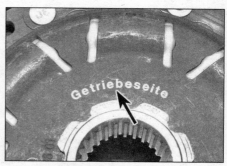

7.11 GETRIEBESEITE (transmission side) marking on the clutch friction disc (arrowed)

proprietary tool may be used, or alternatively, pass a screwdriver or other long bar through the friction disc and into the hole in the crankshaft; the friction disc can then be moved around until it is centred on the crankshaft hole.

14 Once the clutch is centralised, progressively tighten the cover bolts in a diagonal sequence to the torque setting given in the Specifications.

15 Ensure that the input shaft splines, clutch disc splines and release bearing guide sleeve are clean. Apply a thin smear of high-melting-point grease to the input shaft splines.

16 Refit the transmission to the engine as described in Chapter 7A, Section 6.

Chapter 7 Part A:
Manual transmission

Contents

Degrees of difficulty

Easy, suitable for novice with little experience	Fairly easy, suitable for beginner with some experience	Fairly difficult, suitable for competent DIY mechanic 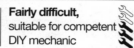	Difficult, suitable for experienced DIY mechanic	Very difficult, suitable for expert DIY or professional

Specifications

General

Type	5 or 6 forward speeds and reverse. Synchromesh on all forward speeds
Identification code:	
1.9 litre engines	02Z (5-speed)
2.0 litre engines	02Z (5-speed) or 0A5 (6-speed)
2.5 litre engines	0A5 (6-speed)

Lubrication

Lubricant type	See *Lubricants and fluids* on page 0•18
Lubricant capacity	See Chapter 1

Torque wrench settings

	Nm	lbf ft
Front engine/transmission mounting through bolt:*		
Stage 1	90	66
Stage 2	Angle-tighten a further 180°	
Gear lever housing retaining bolts	23	17
Left-hand engine/transmission mounting-to-body bolts:*		
Stage 1	50	37
Stage 2	Angle-tighten a further 90°	
Left-hand engine/transmission mounting-to-transmission bolts:*		
Stage 1	50	37
Stage 2	Angle-tighten a further 90°	
Selector cables bulkhead closure plate bolts	23	17
Transmission bellhousing to engine:		
M10 bolts	40	30
M12 bolts	80	59

* Use new bolts

1 General information

The transmission is contained in a cast-aluminium alloy casing bolted to the engine's left-hand end, and consists of the gearbox and final drive differential.

Drive is transmitted from the crankshaft via the clutch to the input shaft, which has a splined extension to accept the clutch friction disc and rotates in roller bearings at each end. From the input shaft, drive is transmitted to the output shaft (two output shafts on 6-speed transmissions) which also rotates in roller bearings at each end. From the output shaft, the drive is transmitted to the differential crown-wheel, which rotates with the differential case and planetary gears, thus driving the sun gears and driveshafts. The rotation of the planetary gears on their shaft allows the inner roadwheel to rotate at a slower speed than the outer roadwheel when the vehicle is cornering.

The input and output shafts are arranged parallel to the crankshaft and driveshafts, so that their gear pinion teeth are in constant mesh. In the neutral position, the output shaft gear pinions rotate freely, so that drive cannot be transmitted to the crownwheel.

Gear selection is via a facia-mounted lever and cable-operated selector linkage.

2.3 Carefully prise up the gear lever gaiter frame and release it from the facia

2.5 Push down the locking mechanism on the selector cable end pieces

2.7a Insert the special tool...

The selector linkage causes the appropriate selector fork to move its respective synchro-sleeve along the shaft, to lock the gear pinion to the synchro-hub. Since the synchro-hubs are splined to the output shaft(s), this locks the pinion to the shaft, so that drive can be transmitted. To ensure that gearchanging can be made quickly and quietly, a synchromesh system is fitted to all forward gears, consisting of baulk rings and spring-loaded fingers, as well as the gear pinions and synchro-hubs. The synchromesh cones are formed on the mating faces of the baulk rings and gear pinions.

Because of the complexity, possible unavailability of parts and special tools necessary, internal repair procedures for the transmission are not recommended for the home mechanic. The bulk of the information in this Chapter is therefore devoted to removal and refitting procedures.

The two different transmissions fitted to the models described in this manual can be identified as follows:
a) 02Z type 5-speed transmission – the three-digit type code is marked on the top of the transmission behind the selector shaft housing.
b) 0A5 type 6-speed transmission – the three-digit type code is marked on the

left-hand side of the differential casing, directly below the driveshaft inner CV joint.
Note: On all models, the transmission code letters also appear on the vehicle data sticker located on the facia right-hand footwell trim panel (see 'Vehicle Identification').

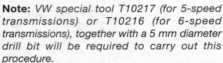

2 Selector cables – adjustment

Note: VW special tool T10217 (for 5-speed transmissions) or T10216 (for 6-speed transmissions), together with a 5 mm diameter drill bit will be required to carry out this procedure.
1 Position the gear lever in the 'neutral' position.
2 For improved access to the transmission selector lever, remove the intercooler air ducts as necessary.
3 Using a plastic spatula or similar tool, carefully prise up the gear lever gaiter frame and release it from the facia (see illustration).
4 Remove the facia centre footwell trim panel as described in Chapter 11, Section 29.
5 Push down the locking mechanism on the gear selector cable end piece to the stop.

Similarly, push down the locking mechanism on the gate selector cable end piece to the stop (see illustration).

5-speed transmissions
6 Working at the transmission, insert the special tool T10217 between the selector lever and the selector mechanism cover. Push the selector down and into contact with the special tool, then push the selector lever rearwards to engage 2nd gear. Remove the special tool.

6-speed transmissions
7 Working at the transmission, pull the gear selector lever upwards, and insert the special tool T10216, between the selector lever and the selector mechanism cover. Allow the selector lever to rest on the tool, then push the selector lever rearwards to engage 2nd gear (see illustrations).

All transmissions
8 Working inside the vehicle, move the gear lever into the second gear position, align the hole in the lever base with the hole in the gear lever housing and insert the drill bit (see illustration).
9 Press the lug on the gear selector cable end piece. This will allow the locking mechanism to return to its original position and lock the

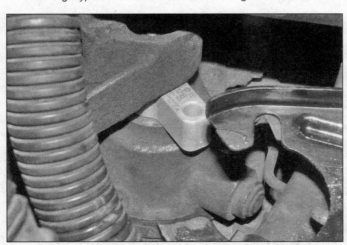

2.7b ...between the selector lever and the selector mechanism cover

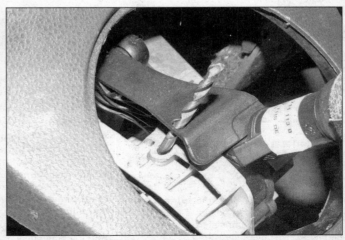

2.8 Align the hole in the gear lever base with the hole in the gear lever housing and insert a 5 mm diameter drill bit

2.9 Press the lug (arrowed) on the selector cable end pieces to return the locking mechanism to its original position

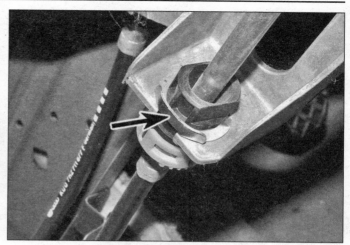

3.6 Extract the circlip (arrowed) securing each selector cable to the gear lever housing

cable **(see illustration)**. Similarly, press the lug on the gate selector cable end piece to allow the locking mechanism to return to its original position.

10 Remove the drill bit securing the gear lever in the second gear position.

11 Working at the transmission, pull the transmission selector lever forwards to shift the transmission into neutral. On 6-speed transmissions, remove the special tool.

12 Check that the gear lever can be moved smoothly through all gear positions and that all gears can be selected. If this is not the case repeat the adjustment procedure.

13 When all is satisfactory, refit the facia centre footwell trim panel as described in Chapter 11, Section 29.

14 Refit the gear lever gaiter frame to the facia.

15 Refit the intercooler air ducts removed for access.

3 Selector cables – removal and refitting

Removal

Note: *The gear selector cable and the gate*

selector cable are removed together as an assembly.

1 Position the gear lever in the 'neutral' position.

2 For improved access to the transmission selector lever, remove the intercooler air ducts as necessary.

3 Using a plastic spatula or similar tool, carefully prise up the gear lever gaiter frame and release it from the facia **(see illustration 2.3)**.

4 Remove the facia centre footwell trim panel as described in Chapter 11, Section 29.

5 Push down the locking mechanism on the gear selector cable end piece to the stop. Similarly, push down the locking mechanism on the gate selector cable end piece to the stop **(see illustration 2.4)**.

6 Extract the circlips securing the two selector cables to the gear lever housing **(see illustration)**. Note that new circlips will be required for refitting.

7 Withdraw the two selector cables down and out of their respective end pieces on the gear lever housing.

8 Working in the engine compartment, note the fitted locations of the cables at their transmission attachments.

9 Push in the retaining clips and disconnect the inner cable end fittings from the

transmission selector lever ballpins **(see illustration)**.

10 Push the retaining catch forward and detach the outer cables support bracket from the mounting bracket on the transmission **(see illustration)**.

11 From inside the car, fold back the floor covering then undo the two bolts to release the closure plate at the cable entry point on the engine compartment bulkhead **(see illustration)**.

12 Pull the two cables (complete with closure plate) out of the bulkhead and remove them from inside the vehicle.

Refitting

13 Push the selector cables through the bulkhead and locate the closure plate back into position. Refit the two retaining bolts and tighten them to the specified torque.

14 Refit the outer cables to the mounting bracket on the transmission, then engage the inner cable end fittings with the transmission selector lever ballpins.

15 Engage the selector cables with their respective end pieces on the gear lever housing, then secure the outer cables to the housing using new circlips.

16 Adjust the selector cables as described in Section 2.

3.9 Push in the retaining clip (arrowed) and disconnect each selector inner cable end fitting from the transmission selector lever

3.10 Push the retaining catch (arrowed) forward and detach the outer cables support bracket from the transmission

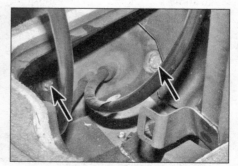

3.11 Undo the two bolts (arrowed) to release the closure plate from the bulkhead

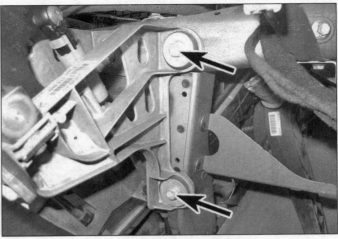

4.7a Gear lever housing left-hand retaining bolts (arrowed)...   **4.7b ...and right-hand retaining bolts**

4 Gear lever housing – removal and refitting

Removal

1 Position the gear lever in the 'neutral' position.
2 Using a plastic spatula or similar tool, carefully prise up the gear lever gaiter frame and release it from the facia **(see illustration 2.3)**.
3 Remove the facia centre footwell trim panel as described in Chapter 11, Section 29.
4 Push down the locking mechanism on the gear selector cable end piece to the stop. Similarly, push down the locking mechanism on the gate selector cable end piece to the stop **(see illustration 2.4)**.
5 Extract the circlips securing the two selector cables to the gear lever housing **(see illustration 3.6)**. Note that new circlips will be required for refitting.
6 Withdraw the two selector cables down and out of their respective end pieces on the gear lever housing.
7 Undo the four bolts securing the gear lever housing to the facia crossmember **(see illustrations)**. Withdraw the housing from the crossmember and remove it from the vehicle.
8 To remove the gear lever knob, carefully prise off the shift gate emblem from the top of the knob. Undo the retaining screw and lift off the knob, compression spring and gaiter. Note that the knob and gaiter will fit onto the gear lever in one position only.

Refitting

9 If removed, refit the gaiter, compression spring and gear lever knob. Secure the knob with the retaining screw and refit the shift gate emblem.
10 Locate the gear lever housing in position on the facia crossmember. Refit the retaining bolts and tighten them to the specified torque.
11 Engage the selector cables with their respective end pieces on the gear lever housing, then secure the outer cables to the housing using new circlips.
12 Refit the gear lever gaiter frame to the facia.
13 Adjust the selector cables as described in Section 2.

5 Reversing light switch – testing, removal and refitting

Testing

1 Ensure that the ignition switch is turned to the 'OFF' position.
2 Unplug the wiring harness from the reversing light switch at the connector. The switch is located on the gear selector housing on top of the transmission casing.
3 Connect the probes of a continuity tester, or multimeter set to the resistance measurement function, across the terminals of the reverse light switch.
4 The switch contacts are normally open, so

6.5 Undo the two bolts (arrowed) and move the cooling system expansion tank to one side

with any gear other than reverse selected, the tester/meter should indicate an open circuit. When reverse gear is then selected, the switch contacts should close, causing the tester/meter to indicate a short circuit.
5 If the switch appears to be constantly open or short circuit, or is intermittent in its operation, it should be renewed.

Removal

6 Ensure that the ignition switch is turned to the 'OFF' position.
7 Unplug the wiring harness from the reversing light switch at the connector.
8 Slacken the switch body using a ring spanner and withdraw it from the transmission casing. Recover the sealing ring.

Refitting

9 Refitting is a reversal of removal.

6 Transmission – removal and refitting

Removal

1 Disconnect the battery negative terminal (refer to *Disconnecting the battery*).
2 Firmly apply the handbrake, then jack up the front of the vehicle and support it securely on axle stands (see *Jacking and vehicle support*). There must be sufficient clearance below the vehicle for the transmission to be lowered and removed.
3 Where fitted, undo the retaining bolts and remove the engine undertray.
4 Remove the air duct between the intercooler and inlet manifold.
5 Undo the two bolts and move the cooling system expansion tank to one side **(see illustration)**.
6 Disconnect the EGR modulator valve wiring at the connector on the vacuum reservoir mounting bracket **(see illustration)**.
7 Disconnect the wiring connector from the

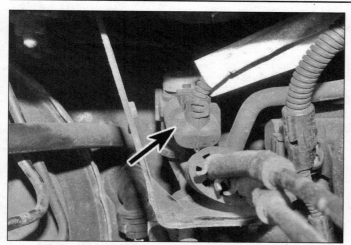

6.6 Disconnect the EGR modulator valve wiring at the connector (arrowed) on the vacuum reservoir mounting bracket

6.7 Disconnect the wiring connector (arrowed) from the temperature sensor in the fuel supply hose

fuel temperature sensor in the fuel supply hose **(see illustration)**.

8 Push in the retaining clips and disconnect the selector inner cable end fittings from the transmission selector lever ballpins **(see illustration 3.9)**.

9 Push the retaining catch forward and detach the selector outer cables support bracket from the mounting bracket on the transmission **(see illustration 3.10)**.

10 Where fitted, remove the diesel particulate filter as described in Chapter 4A, Section 15 (1.9 and 2.5 litre engines) or Chapter 4B, Section 16 (2.0 litre engines).

11 On vehicles without a diesel particulate filter, disconnect the exhaust system front pipe from the turbocharger as described in Chapter 4A, Section 15 (1.9 and 2.5 litre engines) or Chapter 4B, Section 16 (2.0 litre engines).

12 Remove both driveshafts as described in Chapter 8, Section 2.

13 Remove the front subframe as described in Chapter 10, Section 9.

14 Remove the starter motor as described in Chapter 5, Section 10.

15 Where fitted, remove the sound deadening insulation from the transmission.

16 Clamp the clutch hydraulic hose with a suitable hose clamp. Extract the retaining clip and disconnect the hydraulic pipe from the connecting piece above the starter motor location. Suitably cover the disconnected unions to prevent dirt entry.

17 Disconnect the wiring connector from the reversing light switch.

18 The engine must now be supported, as the left-hand engine/transmission mounting must be disconnected. Ideally this should be done with an engine hoist connected to the left-hand side of the engine. With an engine hoist, the engine/transmission can be manoeuvred more easily and safely; balancing the engine on a jack is not recommended.

19 Undo the front engine/transmission

mounting through bolt. Note that a new bolt will be required for refitting.

20 Support the transmission with a trolley jack from below, then undo the two bolts securing the left-hand mounting to the underbody. Note that new bolts will be required for refitting.

21 Lower the engine/transmission assembly approximately 120 mm on the left-hand side to provide sufficient clearance for removal of the transmission.

22 Working your way around the transmission casing, slacken and remove the transmission-to-engine securing bolts. Disconnect any wiring loom brackets, where applicable.

23 With the help of an assistant, withdraw the transmission squarely from the engine, taking care not to allow its weight to hang on the clutch friction disc. Once the transmission is free, lower the transmission on the jack and manoeuvre the unit out from under the vehicle.

Refitting

24 Apply a smear of high-melting-point grease to the transmission input shaft splines.

25 With the transmission secured on the trolley jack as on removal, raise it into position, and then carefully slide it onto the engine, at the same time engaging the input shaft with the clutch friction disc splines. Do not use excessive force to refit the transmission – if the input shaft does not slide into place easily, readjust the angle of the transmission so that it is level, and/or turn the input shaft so that the splines engage properly with the disc. If problems are still experienced, check that the clutch friction disc is correctly centred (see Chapter 6, Section 7).

26 The remainder of refitting is a reversal of the removal procedure, bearing in mind the following points:

a) *Use new bolts when refitting the engine/transmission mountings.*

b) *Tighten all nuts and bolts to the specified torque (where given).*

c) *Refit the front subframe as described in Chapter 10, Section 9.*

d) *Refit the driveshafts as described in Chapter 8, Section 2.*

e) *Reconnect the gear selection mechanism to the transmission as described in Section 3.*

f) *Refit the starter motor as described in Chapter 5, Section 10.*

g) *Refit the exhaust system components as described in Chapter 4A, Section 15 or Chapter 4B, Section 16.*

h) *Bleed the clutch hydraulic system as described in Chapter 6, Section 2.*

i) *Where applicable, refit the engine undertray.*

27 Make a final check that all connections have been made, and all bolts tightened fully. Road test the vehicle to check for proper transmission operation, then check the transmission visually for leakage of oil.

7 Transmission overhaul – general information

Overhauling a manual transmission unit is a difficult and involved job for the DIY home mechanic. In addition to dismantling and reassembling many small parts, clearances must be precisely measured and, if necessary, changed by selecting shims and spacers. Internal transmission components are also often difficult to obtain, and in many instances, extremely expensive. Because of this, if the transmission develops a fault or becomes noisy, the best course of action is to have the unit overhauled by a specialist repairer, or to obtain an exchange reconditioned unit.

Nevertheless, it is not impossible for the more experienced mechanic to overhaul the transmission, provided the special tools are available, and the job is done in a deliberate step-by-step manner, so that nothing is overlooked.

The tools necessary for an overhaul include internal and external circlip pliers, bearing pullers, a slide hammer, a set of pin punches, a dial test indicator, and possibly a hydraulic press. In addition, a large, sturdy workbench and a vice will be required.

During dismantling of the transmission, make careful notes of how each component is fitted, to make reassembly easier and more accurate.

Before dismantling the transmission, it will help if you have some idea what area is malfunctioning. Certain problems can be closely related to specific areas in the transmission, which can make component examination and replacement easier. Refer to the *Fault finding* Section of this manual for more information.

Chapter 7 Part B:
Automatic transmission

Contents

Degrees of difficulty

Easy, suitable for novice with little experience	**Fairly easy,** suitable for beginner with some experience	**Fairly difficult,** suitable for competent DIY mechanic	**Difficult,** suitable for experienced DIY mechanic	**Very difficult,** suitable for expert DIY or professional

Specifications

General

Type	Electro-hydraulically controlled adaptive automatic, six forward speeds and reverse, with 'Tiptronic' sequential manual gear selection capability
Identification code	09K

Lubrication

Lubricant type	See *Lubricants and fluids* on page 0•18
Lubricant capacity	See Chapter 1

Torque wrench settings

	Nm	lbf ft
Left-hand engine/transmission mounting-to-body bolts:*		
Stage 1	50	37
Stage 2	Angle-tighten a further 90°	
Left-hand engine/transmission mounting-to-transmission bolts:*		
Stage 1	50	37
Stage 2	Angle-tighten a further 90°	
Selector cable bulkhead closure plate bolts	20	15
Selector housing retaining bolts:*		
Stage 1	20	15
Stage 2	Angle-tighten a further 90°	
Torque converter retaining nuts	57	42
Transmission bellhousing to engine:		
M10 bolts	45	33
M12 bolts	80	59

Use new bolts

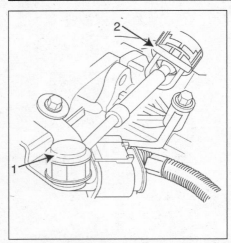

2.10 Selector cable attachments at the transmission

1 Selector inner cable end fitting
2 Selector cable support bracket

1 General information

2.5 litre models were optionally available with a six-speed, electronically-controlled automatic transmission. The transmission consists of a torque converter, an epicyclic geartrain, and hydraulically-operated clutches and brakes. The unit is controlled by the electronic control unit (ECU) via electrically-operated solenoid valves. In addition to the fully automatic operation, the transmission can also be operated manually with a six-speed sequential gear selection.

The torque converter provides a fluid coupling between engine and transmission, which acts as an automatic clutch, and also

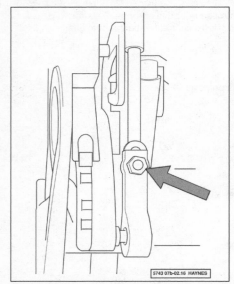

2.16 Selector inner cable-to-end fitting retaining bolt (arrowed)

provides a degree of torque multiplication when accelerating. The torque converter incorporates a lock-up function whereby the engine and transmission can be directly coupled by means of a clutch unit inside the torque converter. The lock-up function is controlled by the ECU according to operating conditions.

The epicyclic geartrain provides either of the six forward or one reverse gear ratios, according to which of its component parts are held stationary or allowed to turn. The components of the geartrain are held or released by hydraulically actuated brakes and clutches. A fluid pump within the transmission provides the necessary hydraulic pressure to operate the brakes and clutches.

In automatic mode, the transmission is fully adaptive, whereby the shift points are dependant on driver input, road speed, engine speed and vehicle operating conditions. The ECU receives inputs from various engine and drive train related sensors, and determines the appropriate shift point for each gear.

Driver control of the transmission is by a five-position selector lever. The drive 'D' position, allows automatic changing throughout the range of forward gear ratios. The sport 'S' position also allows automatic gear changing but the transmission changes to a higher gear at higher engine revs, thus fully utilising engine power. An automatic kickdown facility shifts the transmission down a gear if the accelerator pedal is fully depressed. If the selector lever is moved to the right from the 'D' position, the transmission enters manual mode. In manual mode the gear selector lever can be used to shift the transmission up or down each gear sequentially.

Due to the complexity of the automatic transmission, any repair or overhaul work must be left to a VW dealer or transmission specialist with the necessary special equipment for fault diagnosis and repair. The contents of the following Sections are therefore confined to supplying general information, and any service information and instructions that can be used by the owner.

2 Selector cable – removal, refitting and adjustment

Removal

1 Disconnect the battery negative terminal (refer to *Disconnecting the battery*).
2 Position the selector lever in the 'P' position.
3 Remove the engine compartment covers.
4 Undo the two bolts and move the cooling system expansion tank to one side.
5 For improved access to the transmission selector lever, remove the intercooler air ducts as necessary.
6 Remove the facia centre footwell trim panel as described in Chapter 11, Section 29.

7 Using a large screwdriver or similar tool, prise the selector inner cable end fitting off the ballpin on the selector housing lever.
8 Using pointed-nose pliers, carefully press together the catches on the selector cable support bracket and pull the selector cable out of the selector housing.
9 Fold back the floor covering then undo the two bolts to release the closure plate at the cable entry point on the engine compartment bulkhead.
10 Working in the engine compartment, press together the retaining catches and pull the selector cable upwards out of the support bracket **(see illustration)**.
11 Using a large screwdriver or similar tool, prise the selector inner cable end fitting off the ballpin on the transmission selector lever.
12 Pull the selector cable (complete with closure plate) out of the bulkhead and remove it from inside the vehicle.

Refitting and adjustment

13 Push the selector cable through the bulkhead and locate the closure plate back into position. Refit the two retaining bolts and tighten them to the specified torque.
14 Engage the selector cable with the support bracket on the selector housing, then press the inner cable end fitting onto the selector housing lever ballpin.
15 Check that the selector lever is still in the 'P' position. Also check that the transmission selector lever is in the 'P' position.
16 Slacken the bolt securing the selector inner cable to the end fitting at the selector housing **(see illustration)**.
17 Refit the outer cable to the support bracket on the transmission, then engage the inner cable end fitting with the transmission selector lever ballpin. Push the end fitting fully onto the ballpin.
18 Tighten the bolt securing the selector inner cable to the end fitting at the selector housing.
19 Check the operation of the selector lever and, if necessary, repeat the adjustment procedure.
20 Refit the facia centre footwell trim panel as described in Chapter 11, Section 29.
21 Move the cooling system expansion tank back into position and secure with the two retaining bolts.
22 Refit the intercooler air ducts and engine compartment covers.
23 On completion, reconnect the battery negative terminal.

3 Selector housing – removal and refitting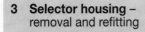

Removal

1 Disconnect the battery negative terminal (refer to *Disconnecting the battery*).
2 Position the selector lever in the 'P' position.

3 Carefully pull the selector lever lock button out of the lever knob until a slight resistance is felt and the button engages in the handle. Secure the button in this position using a cable tie.

4 Starting at the right-hand side, release the selector lever gaiter frame from the facia using a plastic spatula or similar tool. Fold the gaiter up over the top of the gear lever knob.

5 Identify the wiring connectors on the underside of the printed circuit board to aid refitting, then disconnect both connectors.

6 Remove the selector lever gaiter clamp then pull the knob and gaiter up and off the selector lever. Note that a new clamp will be required for refitting.

7 Remove the facia centre footwell trim panel as described in Chapter 11, Section 29.

8 Using a large screwdriver or similar tool, prise the selector inner cable end fitting off the ballpin on the selector housing lever.

9 Using pointed-nose pliers, carefully press together the catches on the selector cable support bracket and pull the selector cable out of the selector housing.

10 Press together the ends of the retaining clip and pull the Park Lock system locking cable out of the selector housing. Disconnect the remaining wiring connector(s) from the components on the selector housing.

11 Undo the four bolts securing the selector housing to the facia crossmember. Note that new bolts will be required for refitting. Withdraw the housing from the crossmember and remove it from the vehicle.

Refitting

12 Refitting is a reversal of the removal procedure, but note the following points:
a) *Locate the selector housing in position on the facia crossmember. Fit the new retaining bolts and tighten them to the specified torque and through the specified angle.*
b) *Refit the facia centre footwell trim panel as described in Chapter 11, Section 29.*
c) *Use a new clamp when refitting the selector lever gaiter and crimp it securely into place.*

4 Ignition key Park Lock system – description and cable renewal

Description

1 This system is a security/safety device, intended to prevent the vehicle from being left with the transmission in any position other than P. The ignition key cannot be removed from the lock unless P is selected, and once the key has been removed, no other position than P can be selected.

2 This function is provided by means of a cable fitted to the selector linkage at the selector lever, and to the ignition switch assembly.

Lock cable

Removal

3 Disconnect the battery negative terminal (refer to *Disconnecting the battery*).

4 Remove the steering wheel as described in Chapter 10, Section 16.

5 Remove the steering column shrouds as described in Chapter 11, Section 29.

6 Remove the steering column combination switch as described in Chapter 12, Section 4.

7 Remove the facia centre footwell trim panel as described in Chapter 11, Section 29.

8 Move the selector lever to the 'P' position and turn the ignition switch to the On position.

9 Press together the ends of the lock cable retaining clip and pull the cable out of the selector housing.

10 Prise the cable retaining clip from the ignition switch, and pull the cable from the switch housing.

11 Noting its routing, withdraw the cable from under the facia.

Refitting

12 Refitting is a reversal of the removal procedure, but note the following points:
a) *Fit the cable retaining clip at the ignition switch with the angled ends of the clip towards the switch.*
b) *Refit the facia centre footwell trim panel as described in Chapter 11, Section 29.*
c) *Refit the steering column combination switch as described in Chapter 12, Section 4.*
d) *Refit the steering column shrouds as described in Chapter 11, Section 29.*
e) *Refit the steering wheel as described in Chapter 10, Section 16.*

5 Automatic transmission – removal and refitting

Removal

Note: *VW special tool T10225 (crankshaft positioning tool) or a suitable alternative will be required for this procedure.*

1 Disconnect the battery negative terminal (refer to *Disconnecting the battery*).

2 Firmly apply the handbrake, then jack up the front of the vehicle and support it securely on axle stands (see *Jacking and vehicle support*). There must be sufficient clearance below the vehicle for the transmission to be lowered and removed.

3 Remove the engine compartment covers then, where fitted, undo the retaining bolts and remove the engine undertray.

4 Remove the air duct between the intercooler and inlet manifold.

5 Undo the two bolts and move the cooling system expansion tank to one side **(see illustration)**.

6 Disconnect the EGR modulator valve wiring at the connector on the vacuum reservoir mounting bracket.

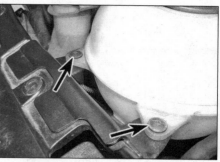

5.5 Cooling system expansion tank retaining bolts (arrowed)

7 Disconnect the wiring connector from the fuel temperature sensor in the fuel supply hose **(see illustration)**.

8 Remove the EGR valve as described in Chapter 4C, Section 2.

9 Using a large screwdriver or similar tool, prise the selector inner cable end fitting off the ballpin on the selector housing lever.

10 Using pointed-nose pliers, carefully press together the catches on the selector cable support bracket and pull the selector cable out of the selector housing.

11 Where fitted, remove the diesel particulate filter as described in Chapter 4A, Section 15.

12 On vehicles without a diesel particulate filter, disconnect the exhaust system front pipe from the turbocharger as described in Chapter 4A, Section 15.

13 Remove both driveshafts as described in Chapter 8, Section 2.

14 Remove the front subframe as described in Chapter 10, Section 9.

15 Remove the starter motor as described in Chapter 5, Section 10.

16 Disconnect the two wiring connectors from the transmission.

17 Where fitted, remove the sound deadening insulation from the transmission.

18 Using suitable hose clamps, clamp the two coolant hoses at the automatic transmission fluid cooler. Release the hose clips and disconnect the two coolant hoses from the cooler. Be prepared for coolant spillage.

19 Undo the retaining nut and disconnect the two automatic transmission fluid pipes front the front facing side of the transmission. Suitably plug or cover the open unions.

5.7 Fuel temperature sensor wiring connector (arrowed)

5.20 Remove the sealing cover from the right-hand end of the engine

5.21 Crankshaft positioning tool (arrowed) bolted to the end of the crankshaft

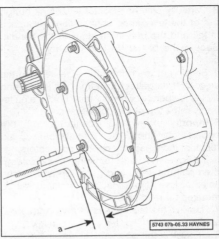

5.33 Checking the correct fitted position of the torque converter

a = 19.5 mm

20 Using a suitable hooked tool, remove the sealing cover from the right-hand end of the engine (in the area normally occupied by the crankshaft pulley) **(see illustration)**. Note that a new sealing cover will be required for refitting.

21 Bolt the special tool T10225 (or a suitable alternative) to the end of the crankshaft to enable the crankshaft to be turned **(see illustration)**. Note that the tool will only fit in one position.

22 Working at the rear of the torque converter housing, remove the sealing grommet for access to the torque converter retaining nuts.

23 Using a socket or spanner on the special tool, turn the crankshaft until one of the six torque converter retaining nuts becomes accessible through the opening in the bellhousing.

24 Undo the first torque converter retaining nut, then turn the crankshaft one sixth of a turn until the next nut becomes accessible. Unscrew the nut then continue this procedure until all six nuts have been removed. Note that new nuts will be required for refitting.

25 The engine must now be supported, as the left-hand engine/transmission mounting must be disconnected. Ideally this should be done with an engine hoist connected to the left-hand side of the engine. With an engine hoist, the engine/transmission can be manoeuvred more easily and safely; balancing the engine on a jack is not recommended.

26 Support the transmission with a trolley jack from below, then undo the two bolts securing the left-hand mounting to the underbody. Note that new bolts will be required for refitting.

27 Lower the engine/transmission assembly approximately 120 mm on the left-hand side to provide sufficient clearance for removal of the transmission.

28 Unscrew the three retaining bolts and remove the left-hand engine/transmission mounting from the transmission. Note that new bolts will be required for refitting.

29 Unhook the power steering fluid lines from the retainer on the transmission.

30 Make a final check that nothing remains attached to the transmission likely to interfere with removal.

31 Working your way around the transmission

casing, slacken and remove the transmission-to-engine securing bolts. Disconnect any wiring loom brackets, where applicable.

32 With all the bolts removed, move the trolley jack and transmission, to free it from its locating dowels. Once the transmission is free, lower the jack and manoeuvre the unit out from under the car, taking care to ensure that the torque converter does not fall off. Remove the locating dowels from the transmission or engine if they are loose, and keep them in a safe place. Retain the torque converter while the transmission is removed by bolting a strip of metal across the transmission bellhousing end face.

Refitting

33 The transmission is refitted by a reversal of the removal procedure, bearing in mind the following points.

a) *Ensure the engine/transmission locating dowels are correctly positioned and apply a smear of molybdenum disulphide grease to the torque converter locating pin and its centering bush in the crankshaft end.*

b) *Check that the torque converter is fully entered inside the transmission by measuring the distance from the transmission-to-engine mating face to the contact surface of the torque converter, using a straight-edge and vernier calipers* **(see illustration)**. *The distance must measure approximately 19.5 mm.*

c) *Once the transmission and engine are correctly joined, refit the securing bolts, tightening them to the specified torque setting.*

d) *Fit the new torque converter-to-driveplate nuts and tighten them lightly only to start, then go around and tighten them to the specified torque.*

e) *Tighten all nuts and bolts to the specified torque (where given).*

f) *Refit the starter motor as described in Chapter 5, Section 10.*

g) *Refit the front subframe assembly as described in Chapter 10, Section 9.*

h) *Refit the driveshafts as described in Chapter 8, Section 2.*

i) *Refit the exhaust system front pipe or*

diesel particulate filter as described in Chapter 4A, Section 15.

j) *Remove the EGR valve as described in Chapter 4C, Section 2.*

k) *Where applicable, refit the engine undertray.*

l) *On completion check, and if necessary top-up, the cooling system as described in 'Weekly checks'.*

6 Automatic transmission overhaul – general information

1 In the event of a fault occurring with the transmission, it is first necessary to determine whether it is of a mechanical, electrical or hydraulic nature, and to do this, special test equipment is required. It is therefore essential to have the work carried out by a VW dealer or suitably equipped specialist if a transmission fault is suspected.

2 Do not remove the transmission from the vehicle for possible repair before professional fault diagnosis has been carried out, since most tests require the transmission to be in the vehicle.

7 Transmission fluid – level checking

An accurate fluid level check can only be made with the transmission fluid at a temperature of between 35°C and 45°C. It is strongly recommended that the check be made by a VW dealer who will have the instrumentation to check the temperature and to check the transmission electronics for fault codes. Overfilling or underfilling adversely affects the function of the transmission.

Chapter 8
Driveshafts

Contents

Degrees of difficulty

Easy, suitable for novice with little experience

Fairly easy, suitable for beginner with some experience

Fairly difficult, suitable for competent DIY mechanic

Difficult, suitable for experienced DIY mechanic

Very difficult, suitable for expert DIY or professional

Specifications

General
Driveshaft type . . . . Solid steel shafts with ball-and-cage type outer constant velocity joints and ball-and-cage type or tripod type inner constant velocity joints

Lubrication (overhaul only – see text)
Lubricant type/specification. . . . . Use only special grease supplied in sachets with gaiter kits – joints are otherwise pre-packed with grease and sealed

Torque wrench settings

	Nm	lbf ft
Driveshaft retaining nut:*		
Stage 1	200	148
Stage 2	Slacken by 180°	
Stage 3	200	148
Driveshaft support bearing retaining bolts:*		
Stage 1	20	15
Stage 2	Angle-tighten through a further 90°	
Inner constant velocity joint retaining bolts:*		
Stage 1	50	37
Stage 2	Angle-tighten through a further 90°	
Roadwheel bolts	180	133
Swivel hub balljoint-to-lower arm:*		
Stage 1	60	44
Stage 2	Angle-tighten a further 90°	

Use new nuts/bolts.

TOOL TiP

A tool to hold the wheel hub stationary whilst the driveshaft retaining nut is slackened can be fabricated from two lengths of steel strip (one long, one short) and a nut and bolt; the nut and bolt forming the pivot of a forked tool.

1 General information

Drive is transmitted from the differential to the front wheels by means of two, solid steel driveshafts.

Both driveshafts are splined at their outer ends to accept the wheel hubs, and are threaded so that each hub can be fastened by a large nut. The inner end of each driveshaft is either bolted to a transmission drive flange or splined directly onto the differential splined shaft.

The outer ends of each driveshaft are fitted with ball-and-cage type constant velocity (CV) joints, to ensure the smooth and efficient transmission of drive at all the angles possible, as the roadwheels move up-and-down with the suspension, and as they turn from side to side under steering.

The inner ends of each driveshaft are fitted with either ball-and-cage type constant velocity joints or triple roller type (tripod) joints, depending on transmission type.

2 Driveshaft – removal and refitting

Removal

Note: *The driveshaft outer joint splines may be a tight fit in the hub and it is possible that a puller/extractor will be required to draw the hub assembly off the driveshaft during removal.*

1 Firmly apply the handbrake, then jack up the front of the vehicle and support it securely on axle stands (see *Jacking and vehicle support*). Remove the relevant front roadwheel.

2 Where fitted, undo the retaining bolts and remove the engine undertray.

3 To prevent rotation of the wheel hub as the driveshaft retaining nut is slackened, make up a holding tool and attach the tool to the wheel hub using two wheel bolts **(see Tool Tip and illustration)**.

4 With the holding tool in place, slacken and remove the driveshaft retaining nut using a socket and long bar **(see illustration)**. Where necessary, support the socket on an axle stand to prevent it slipping off the nut. This nut is very tight; make sure that there is no risk of pulling the vehicle off the axle stands as the nut is slackened. Note that a new nut will be required for refitting.

Left-hand driveshaft

5 If the driveshaft inner CV joint is bolted to the transmission drive flange, undo and remove the bolts securing the CV joint to the flange and recover the retaining plates from underneath the bolts. Note that new bolts will be required for refitting. Support the driveshaft by suspending it with wire or string – do not allow it to hang under its weight, or the joint may be damaged **(see illustrations)**.

6 If the driveshaft inner CV joint is splined directly onto the differential splined shaft, use a stout bar to release the CV joint from the differential. Lever between the CV joint and differential housing to release the driveshaft retaining circlip.

Right-hand driveshaft

7 Undo the two bolts securing the driveshaft support bearing to the cylinder block **(see illustration)**. Note that new bolts will be required for refitting.

All driveshafts

8 Disconnect the wiring connector at the ABS wheel speed sensor and, where applicable, at the brake pad wear sensor wiring connector. Release the wiring from the retainers on the suspension strut **(see illustrations)**.

2.3 Attach the holding tool to the wheel hub using two wheel bolts

2.4 Slacken and remove the driveshaft retaining nut

2.5a Slacken the inner driveshaft joint retaining bolts...

2.5b ...and remove them along with their retaining plates

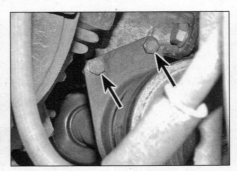

2.7 Undo the two bolts (arrowed) securing the driveshaft support bearing to the cylinder block

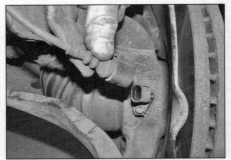

2.8a Disconnect the wiring connector at the ABS wheel speed sensor...

9 Undo the nut securing the swivel hub balljoint to the front suspension lower arm **(see illustration)**. Note that a new nut will be required for refitting. Release the balljoint from the lower arm using a universal balljoint separator.

10 Using a suitable lever, push down on the suspension lower arm and disengage the balljoint shank from the arm **(see illustration)**. Move the swivel hub to one side taking care not to damage the balljoint rubber boot. It is advisable to place a protective cover over the rubber boot such as the plastic cap from an aerosol can, suitably cut to fit.

11 Carefully pull the swivel hub assembly outwards, and withdraw the driveshaft outer constant velocity joint from the hub assembly **(see illustration)**. The outer joint may be very tight, if so tap the joint out of the hub using a soft-faced mallet. If this fails to free it from the hub, the joint will have to be pressed out using a suitable tool which is bolted to the hub.

12 Disengage the inner end of the driveshaft from the differential and manoeuvre the driveshaft out from underneath the vehicle.

13 Do not allow the vehicle to rest on its wheels with one or both driveshaft(s) removed, as damage to the wheel bearing(s) may result. If moving the vehicle is unavoidable, temporarily insert the outer end of the driveshaft(s) in the hub(s), and tighten the driveshaft retaining bolt(s); in this case, the inner end(s) of the driveshaft(s) must be supported, for example by suspending with string from the vehicle underbody. Do not allow the driveshaft to hang down under its weight, or the joint may be damaged.

Refitting

14 Check the condition of the circlip on the differential splined shaft and if necessary renew it. Apply a little grease to the splines of the differential left-hand (and where applicable) right-hand splined shafts.

Left-hand driveshaft

15 If the driveshaft inner CV joint is bolted to the transmission drive flange, align the inner joint with the transmission flange, and refit the new retaining bolts and retaining plates. Tighten the retaining bolts to the specified torque, then through the specified angle.

16 If the driveshaft inner CV joint is splined directly onto the differential splined shaft, locate the inner joint in position on the shaft – turn the driveshaft as necessary to engage the splines. With a forceful jolt, push in the driveshaft until the internal circlip engages the groove. Check that the circlip is engaged by attempting to pull out the driveshaft with only moderate force.

Right-hand driveshaft

17 Locate the inner joint in position on the differential splined shaft – turn the driveshaft as necessary to engage the splines. Refit the driveshaft support bearing to the cylinder block and tighten the two new retaining bolts to the specified torque, then through the specified angle.

2.8b ...and release the wiring from the retainers on the suspension strut

2.10 Push down on the suspension lower arm and disengage the balljoint shank from the arm

All driveshafts

18 Ensure that the outer joint and hub splines are clean and dry. Manoeuvre the driveshaft into position, and engage the outer joint with the hub. Ensure that the threads are clean, and apply a smear of oil to the contact face of the new driveshaft retaining nut. Fit the nut and use it to draw the joint fully into position.

19 Lever the suspension lower arm downwards and engage the balljoint shank with the arm. Fit the new retaining nut to the balljoint and tighten it to the specified torque, then through the specified angle.

20 Reconnect the wiring connector at the ABS wheel speed sensor and, where applicable, at the brake pad wear sensor. Engage the wiring with the retainers on the suspension strut.

21 Using the method employed on removal to prevent the hub from rotating, tighten the

3.2a Release the rubber gaiter outer retaining clip...

2.9 Undo the nut securing the swivel hub balljoint to the suspension lower arm

2.11 Pull the swivel hub outwards and withdraw the driveshaft outer constant velocity joint from the hub assembly

driveshaft retaining bolt to the specified torque. Check that the hub rotates freely.

22 Where applicable, refit the engine undertray.

23 Refit the roadwheel, lower the vehicle to the ground, and tighten the wheel bolts to the specified torque.

3 Driveshaft joint gaiters – renewal

Outer CV joint gaiter

1 Remove the driveshaft as described in Section 2.

2 Release the rubber gaiter retaining clips by cutting off the crimped portion using side cutters **(see illustrations)**. Alternatively cut through them using a junior hacksaw. Spread the clips and remove them from the gaiter.

3.2b ...by cutting off the crimped portion using side cutters

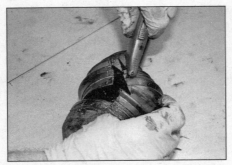

3.3 Cut the gaiter open and remove it from the driveshaft

3.5 Sharply strike the edge of the outer joint to drive it off the end of the shaft

3.6 Removing the circlip from the groove in the driveshaft splines

3 Cut the gaiter open using a suitable knife and remove it from the driveshaft **(see illustration)**.

4 Using old rags, clean away as much of the old grease as possible from the CV joint. It is advisable to wear disposable rubber gloves during this operation.

5 The CV joints are retained on the driveshaft by an internal circlip. Using a mallet, sharply strike the edge of the outer joint to compress the circlip and drive the joint off the end of the shaft **(see illustration)**.

6 Once the joint has been removed, extract the circlip from the groove in the driveshaft splines **(see illustration)**. A new circlip must be fitted on reassembly.

7 With the CV joint removed from the driveshaft, wipe away the remaining grease (do not use any solvent) to allow the joint components to be inspected.

8 Move the inner splined driving member from side to side to expose each ball in turn at the top of its track. Examine the balls for cracks, flat spots or signs of surface pitting.

9 Inspect the ball tracks on the inner and outer members. If the tracks have widened, the balls will no longer be a tight fit. At the same time, check the ball cage windows for wear or cracking between the windows.

10 If on inspection any of the constant velocity joint components are found to be worn or damaged, it will be necessary to renew the complete joint assembly. If the joint is in satisfactory condition, obtain a new gaiter and retaining clips, a constant velocity joint circlip and the correct type and quantity of grease. Grease is often supplied with the joint repair kit.

11 Slide the small retaining clip and new rubber gaiter onto the driveshaft **(see illustrations)**.

12 Fit a new circlip to the groove in the driveshaft **(see illustration)**.

13 Pack the joint with half the quantity of the specified type of grease. Work the grease well into the bearing tracks whilst twisting the joint, and fill the rubber gaiter with the remaining half **(see illustrations)**.

14 Engage the joint with the driveshaft splines. Tap the joint onto the driveshaft until the circlip engages in its groove **(see illustration)**. Make sure that the joint is securely retained, by pulling on the joint, not the shaft.

15 Ease the gaiter over the joint, and ensure that the gaiter lips are correctly located on both the driveshaft and constant velocity joint **(see illustration)**. Lift the outer sealing lip of the gaiter to equalise air pressure within the gaiter.

16 Fit the large metal retaining clip to the

3.11a Slide the small retaining clip...

3.11b ...and new rubber gaiter onto the driveshaft

3.12 Fit a new circlip to the groove in the driveshaft

3.13a Pack half of the grease in the joint...

3.13b ...and the remaining half in the gaiter

3.14 Tap the joint onto the driveshaft until the circlip engages

gaiter. Pull the clip as tight as possible, and locate the hooks on the clip in their slots. Remove any slack in the gaiter retaining clip by carefully compressing the raised section of the clip. In the absence of the special tool, a pair of side cutters may be used, taking care not to cut the clip. Secure the small retaining clip using the same procedure **(see illustrations)**.

17 Check the constant velocity joint moves freely in all directions, then refit the driveshaft to the vehicle, as described in Section 2.

Inner CV joint gaiter – ball and cage type joints

Left-hand driveshaft – 5-speed transmission

18 Remove the driveshaft as described in Section 2.

19 Clamp the driveshaft in a vice with protective jaws. Using a hammer and a small drift, drive off the protective cover from the end of the CV joint inner member. Note that a new protective cover will be required for reassembly.

20 Release the gaiter small securing clip by cutting off the crimped portion using side cutters. Alternatively cut through it using a junior hacksaw. Spread the clip and remove it from the gaiter.

21 Using a hammer and a small drift, carefully drive the gaiter metal ring from the joint outer member **(see illustration)**. Slide the gaiter down the driveshaft.

22 Using old rags, clean away as much of the old grease as possible from the CV joint. It is advisable to wear disposable rubber gloves during this operation.

23 Remove the circlip from the end of the driveshaft using circlip pliers **(see illustration)**.

24 Press or drive the driveshaft from the joint, taking great care not to damage the joint **(see illustration)**.

25 Slide the gaiter from the end of the driveshaft **(see illustration)**.

26 With the CV joint removed from the driveshaft, wipe away the remaining grease (do not use any solvent), then carry out a visual inspection of the joint as described in paragraphs 8 to 10.

27 Slide the new rubber gaiter onto the driveshaft.

28 Fit the joint to the end of the driveshaft, noting that the chamfered edge of the internal splines on the joint should face towards the driveshaft. Drive or press the joint into position until it contacts the shoulder on the driveshaft.

29 Fit a new circlip to retain the joint on the end of the driveshaft.

30 Pack the joint with half the quantity of the specified type of grease. Work the grease well into the bearing tracks whilst twisting the joint, and fill the rubber gaiter with the remaining half **(see illustrations)**.

31 Wipe away any surplus grease from the

3.15 Ease the gaiter over the joint, and ensure that the gaiter lips are correctly located

3.16a Fit the large retaining clip, pull it as tight as possible, and locate the hooks on the clip in their slots

3.16b Remove any slack in the gaiter retaining clip by carefully compressing the raised section of the clip

3.16c Secure the small retaining clip using the same procedure

3.21 Using a hammer and a small drift, drive the gaiter metal ring from the joint outer member

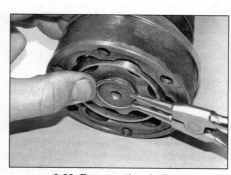

3.23 Remove the circlip...

3.24 ...followed by the joint...

3.25 ...and gaiter

3.30a Pack the inner joint with half of the grease...

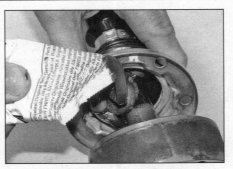

3.30b ...then pack the gaiter with the remaining half

3.32a Temporarily fit the flange bolts to ensure the bolt holes are correctly aligned...

3.32b ...then drive the metal ring onto the joint outer member

rubber gaiter contact area on the joint outer member. Apply a 2 to 3 mm diameter bead of suitable sealant to the joint contact area of the gaiter metal ring, ensuring that the bead runs around the inside of the bolt holes.

32 Slide the gaiter up the driveshaft, and press or drive the gaiter metal ring onto the joint outer member. To ensure the bolt holes are correctly positioned, temporarily fit a couple of flange bolts (see illustrations).

33 Wipe away any surplus grease from the protective cover contact area on the joint outer member. Apply a 2 to 3 mm diameter bead of suitable sealant to the joint contact area of the new protective cover, ensuring that the bead runs around the inside of the bolt holes.

34 Locate the protective cover onto the joint outer member. To ensure the bolt holes are correctly positioned, temporarily fit a couple of flange bolts. Using a plastic or copper mallet, tap the cover fully home.

35 Slide the outboard end of the gaiter into position then fit the small retaining clip as described in paragraph 16.

36 Check the driveshaft joint moves freely in all directions, then refit the driveshaft to the vehicle, as described in Section 2.

Left-hand driveshaft – 6-speed transmission

37 Remove the driveshaft as described in Section 2.

38 Release the rubber gaiter retaining clips by cutting off the crimped portion using side cutters. Alternatively cut through them using a junior hacksaw. Spread the clips and remove them from the gaiter.

39 Cut the gaiter open using a suitable knife and remove it from the driveshaft.

40 Using old rags, clean away as much of the old grease as possible from the CV joint. It is advisable to wear disposable rubber gloves during this operation.

41 The inner CV joint is retained on the driveshaft by an external snap-ring (see illustration). Use circlip pliers to expand the snap-ring as the CV joint is removed.

42 Using a mallet, strike the edge of the joint outer member to drive it off the end of the shaft.

43 Once the joint has been removed, extract the snap-ring from the joint, noting that a new snap-ring must be fitted on reassembly.

44 If still in place, withdraw the rubber gaiter from the driveshaft.

45 With the CV joint removed from the driveshaft, wipe away the remaining grease (do not use any solvent), then carry out a visual inspection of the joint as described in paragraphs 8 to 10.

46 Slide the small retaining clip and new rubber gaiter onto the driveshaft.

47 Fit a new snap-ring to the constant velocity joint (see illustration).

48 Pack the joint with half the quantity of the specified type of grease. Work the grease well into the bearing tracks whilst twisting the joint, and fill the rubber gaiter with the remaining half (see illustrations 3.13a and 3.13b).

49 Engage the joint with the driveshaft splines. Tap the joint onto the driveshaft until the snap-ring engages in its groove. Make sure that the joint is securely retained, by pulling on the joint, not the shaft.

50 Ease the gaiter over the joint, and ensure that the gaiter lips are correctly located on both the driveshaft and constant velocity joint. Lift the outer sealing lip of the gaiter to equalise air pressure within the gaiter.

51 Fit the large metal retaining clip to the gaiter. Pull the clip as tight as possible, and locate the hooks on the clip in their slots. Remove any slack in the gaiter retaining clip by carefully compressing the raised section of the clip. In the absence of the special tool, a pair of side cutters may be used, taking care not to cut the clip. Secure the small retaining clip using the same procedure.

52 Check the constant velocity joint moves freely in all directions, then refit the driveshaft to the vehicle, as described in Section 2.

Right-hand driveshaft

53 The rubber gaiter renewal procedures for the inner CV joint on the right-hand side are the same as described previously for the outer joint gaiter. Proceed as described in paragraphs 1 to 17.

Inner CV joint gaiter – tripod type joints

54 Remove the driveshaft as described in Section 2.

55 Using quick drying paint (such as correction fluid) mark the driveshaft in relation to the joint housing, to ensure correct refitting.

56 Using a screwdriver, release and remove the gaiter inner and outer retaining clips (see illustrations).

57 Withdraw the inner joint housing from the tripod (see illustration).

58 Scoop out as much grease as possible

3.41 Outer CV joint snap-ring (arrowed)

3.47 Fit a new snap-ring to the constant velocity joint

3.56a Using a screwdriver, release the gaiter inner retaining clip...

3.56b ...and outer retaining clip

3.57 Withdraw the inner joint housing from the tripod

3.60 Slide the gaiter off the driveshaft

3.63 Slide the new gaiter onto the shaft and locate the inner end in the first driveshaft groove

3.64 Ensure that the retaining clip is correctly positioned, then compress the raised section using a special pair of pincers

from the joint and gaiter, then extract the circlip retaining the tripod on the driveshaft.

59 Make alignment marks on the driveshaft and the edge of the tripod, to ensure correct refitting.

60 Using a puller, remove the tripod from the end of the driveshaft, then slide the gaiter off the driveshaft (see illustration).

61 Clean the grease from the driveshaft, tripod, bearing rollers and housing, then carefully inspect the components for signs of wear or deterioration.

62 If on inspection any of the constant velocity joint components are found to be worn or damaged, it will be necessary to renew the complete joint assembly. If the joint is in satisfactory condition, obtain a new gaiter and retaining clips, a circlip to secure the tripod and the correct type and quantity of grease. Grease is often supplied with the joint repair kit.

63 Position the retaining clips on the new gaiter, then slide the gaiter onto the shaft. Engage the inner end of the gaiter in the first groove in the driveshaft; the second groove (nearer to the outer end of the driveshaft) should still be visible (see illustration).

64 Check that the inner end retaining clip is correctly seated on the gaiter, then remove any slack in the clip by carefully compressing the raised section using a special pair of pincers (see illustration).

65 Place the tripod in position on the driveshaft splines, ensuring that the previously made marks are aligned. Note that the chamfered edge of the internal splines on the tripod should face towards the driveshaft.

66 Tap the tripod onto the driveshaft using a

soft-faced mallet and a suitable drift, until the new circlip can be installed. Ensure that the circlip is fully engaged in its groove.

67 Pack the joint housing with half the quantity of the grease supplied, then insert the tripod and driveshaft into the housing (see illustrations).

3.67a Pack the joint housing with half the specified amount of the grease supplied...

3.68a Fill the gaiter with the remainder of the grease...

Ensure that the previously made marks on the driveshaft and housing are aligned.

68 Fill the gaiter with the remainder of the grease, then locate the outer lip of the gaiter in the groove on the joint housing (see illustrations).

3.67b ...then insert the tripod and driveshaft into the housing

3.68b ...then locate the outer lip of the gaiter in the groove on the joint housing

3.69 Ensure that the retaining clip is correctly positioned, then compress the raised section using a special pair of pincers

69 Check that the outer end retaining clip is correctly seated on the gaiter, then remove any slack in the clip by carefully compressing the raised section using a special pair of pincers **(see illustration)**.

70 Check the constant velocity joint moves freely in all directions, then refit the driveshaft to the vehicle, as described in Section 2.

4 Driveshaft overhaul – general information

1 If any of the checks described in Chapter 1, Sections 16 and 24 reveal possible wear in any driveshaft joint, carry out the following procedures to identify the source of the problem.

2 Firmly apply the handbrake, then jack up the front of the vehicle and support it securely on axle stands (see *Jacking and vehicle support*).

3 Referring to the information contained in Section 2, make up a tool to hold the wheel hub, and attach the tool to the hub using two wheel bolts. Use a torque wrench to check that the driveshaft retaining nut is securely fastened, then repeat this check on the remaining driveshaft nut.

4 Road test the vehicle, and listen for a metallic clicking from the front as the vehicle is driven slowly in a circle on full-lock. If a clicking noise is heard, this indicates wear in the outer constant velocity joint.

5 If vibration, consistent with road speed, is felt through the vehicle when accelerating, there is a possibility of wear in the inner constant velocity joints.

6 To check the joints for wear, remove the driveshafts, then dismantle them as described in Section 3; if any wear or free play is found, the affected joint must be renewed.

Chapter 9
Braking system

Contents

Degrees of difficulty

Easy, suitable for novice with little experience	Fairly easy, suitable for beginner with some experience	Fairly difficult, suitable for competent DIY mechanic	Difficult, suitable for experienced DIY mechanic	Very difficult, suitable for expert DIY or professional
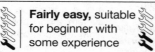

Specifications

Front brakes

Type	Ventilated disc, with single- or twin-piston calipers
Caliper type:	
With 16 inch wheels	VW FN3 floating caliper
With 17 inch wheels	VW FN3 floating caliper or VW 2FNR 44 floating caliper
Disc diameter:	
With 16 inch wheels	308.0 mm
With 17 inch wheels	333.0 mm
Disc thickness:	
New:	
With 16 inch wheels	29.5 mm
With 17 inch wheels	32.5 mm
Minimum:	
With 16 inch wheels	26.5 mm
With 17 inch wheels	29.5 mm
Maximum disc thickness variation	0.02 mm
Maximum disc run-out	0.08 mm
Minimum brake pad friction material thickness	2.0 mm

Rear brakes

Type	Ventilated disc, with single-piston sliding calipers
Disc diameter	294.0 or 314.0 mm
Disc thickness:	
New	22.0 mm
Minimum	19.5 mm
Maximum disc thickness variation	0.02 mm
Maximum disc run-out	0.08 mm
Minimum brake pad friction material thickness	2.0 mm

Handbrake

Type	Cable-operated, acting on rear brakes
Minimum handbrake shoe friction material thickness	1.0 mm

Torque wrench settings

	Nm	lbf ft
ABS wheel speed sensor retaining bolts	8	6
Brake pedal pivot bolt nut	25	18
Front brake calipers:		
Caliper mounting bracket-to-swivel hub:*		
Stage 1	180	133
Stage 2	Angle-tighten through a further 45°	
Guide pins (VW FN3 caliper)	30	22
Guide pins (VW 2FNR 44 caliper)	60	44
Handbrake lever retaining nuts	20	15
Master cylinder retaining nuts	25	18
Rear brake calipers:		
Caliper mounting bracket-to-trailing arm (standard brake caliper)	165	122
Caliper mounting bracket-to-trailing arm (VW FN 44 caliper)	180	133
Guide pin bolts (standard brake caliper)*	35	26
Guide pins (VW FN 44 caliper)	30	22
Roadwheel bolts	180	133
Vacuum pump retaining bolts:		
1.9 and 2.5 litre engines:		
Upper	25	18
Lower	10	7
2.0 litre engines	10	7
Vacuum servo unit retaining nuts	25	18

*Use new fasteners

1 General information

The braking system is of servo-assisted, dual-circuit hydraulic type split diagonally. The arrangement of the hydraulic system is such that each circuit operates one front and one rear brake from a tandem master cylinder. Under normal circumstances, both circuits operate in unison. However, in the event of hydraulic failure in one circuit, full braking force will still be available at two wheels.

All models are fitted with front and rear disc brakes. An Anti-lock Braking System (ABS) is fitted as standard equipment on all vehicles covered in this manual. Refer to Section 21 for further information on ABS operation.

The front brake discs are of the ventilated type and are fitted with single- or twin-piston sliding type brake calipers.

The rear brake discs are also of the ventilated type and are fitted with single-piston sliding type brake calipers.

The cable-operated handbrake provides an independent mechanical means of rear brake application. On vehicles equipped with the standard rear brake calipers, the handbrake comprises a mechanical mechanism in the brake calipers which act directly on the brake pads. On vehicles equipped with the VW FN 44 type rear brake calipers, the handbrake comprises two separate handbrake shoes operating within a drum-in-disc arrangement.

A vacuum servo unit is fitted between the master cylinder and the bulkhead, its function being to reduce the amount of pedal pressure required to operate the brakes. Since there is no throttling as such of the inlet manifold on diesel engines, the manifold is not a suitable source of vacuum to operate the vacuum servo unit. The servo unit is therefore connected to a separate engine-mounted vacuum pump.

⚠️ *Warning: When servicing any part of the system, work carefully and methodically; also observe scrupulous cleanliness when overhauling any part of the hydraulic system. Always renew components (in axle sets, where applicable) if in doubt about their condition, and use only genuine VW replacement parts, or at least those of known good quality. Note the warnings given in 'Safety first!' and at relevant points in this Chapter concerning the dangers of asbestos dust and hydraulic fluid.*

2 Hydraulic system – bleeding

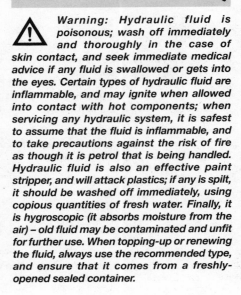

⚠️ *Warning: Hydraulic fluid is poisonous; wash off immediately and thoroughly in the case of skin contact, and seek immediate medical advice if any fluid is swallowed or gets into the eyes. Certain types of hydraulic fluid are inflammable, and may ignite when allowed into contact with hot components; when servicing any hydraulic system, it is safest to assume that the fluid is inflammable, and to take precautions against the risk of fire as though it is petrol that is being handled. Hydraulic fluid is also an effective paint stripper, and will attack plastics; if any is spilt, it should be washed off immediately, using copious quantities of fresh water. Finally, it is hygroscopic (it absorbs moisture from the air) – old fluid may be contaminated and unfit for further use. When topping-up or renewing the fluid, always use the recommended type, and ensure that it comes from a freshly-opened sealed container.*

General

1 The correct operation of any hydraulic system is only possible after removing all air from the components and circuit; this is achieved by bleeding the system. Since the clutch hydraulic system also uses fluid from the brake system reservoir, it should also be bled at the same time by referring to Chapter 6, Section 2.

2 During the bleeding procedure, add only clean, unused hydraulic fluid of the recommended type; never re-use fluid that has already been bled from the system. Ensure that sufficient fluid is available before starting work.

3 If there is any possibility of incorrect fluid being already in the system, the brake components and circuit must be flushed completely with uncontaminated, correct fluid, and new seals should be fitted to the various components.

4 If hydraulic fluid has been lost from the system, or air has entered because of a leak, ensure that the fault is cured before proceeding further.

5 Park the vehicle over an inspection pit or on car ramps. Alternatively, apply the handbrake then jack up the front and rear of the vehicle and support it on axle stands (see *Jacking and vehicle support*). For improved access with the vehicle jacked up, remove the roadwheels.

6 Check that all pipes and hoses are secure, unions tight and bleed screws closed. Clean any dirt from around the bleed screws.

7 Unscrew the master cylinder reservoir cap, and top the master cylinder reservoir up to the MAX level line; refit the cap loosely, and remember to maintain the fluid level at least above the MIN level line throughout the procedure, otherwise there is a risk of further air entering the system.

8 There are a number of one-man, do-it-yourself brake bleeding kits currently available from motor accessory shops. It is recommended that one of these kits is used whenever possible, as they greatly simplify the bleeding operation, and also reduce the risk of expelled air and fluid being drawn back into the system. If such a kit is not available, the basic (two-person) method must be used, which is described in detail below.

9 If a kit is to be used, prepare the vehicle as described previously, and follow the kit manufacturer's instructions, as the procedure may vary slightly according to the type being used; generally, they are as outlined below in the relevant sub-section.

10 Whichever method is used, the same sequence should be followed (paragraphs 11 and 12) to ensure the removal of all air from the system.

Bleeding sequence

11 If the system has been only partially disconnected, and suitable precautions were taken to minimise fluid loss, it should only be necessary to bleed that part of the system (ie, the primary or secondary circuit). If the master cylinder or main brake lines have been disconnected, then the complete system must be bled.

12 If the complete system is to be bled, then it should be done working in the following sequence:

a) *Right-hand front brake.*
b) *Left-hand front brake.*
c) *Right-hand rear brake.*
d) *Left-hand rear brake.*

If the hydraulic fluid has run dry in either chamber of the reservoir, the system must be pre-bled as follows, before carrying out the bleeding sequence described above:

a) *Bleed the front left and right brakes simultaneously.*
b) *Bleed the rear left and right brakes simultaneously.*

Bleeding

Basic (two-person) method

13 Collect together a clean glass jar or similar container, a suitable length of plastic or rubber tubing which is a tight fit over the bleed screw, and a ring spanner to fit the screw. The help of an assistant will also be required.

14 Remove the dust cap from the first bleed screw in the sequence **(see illustration)**. Fit the spanner and tube to the screw, place the other end of the tube in the jar, and pour in sufficient fluid to cover the end of the tube.

15 Ensure that the master cylinder reservoir fluid level is maintained at least above the MIN level line throughout the procedure.

16 Have the assistant fully depress the brake pedal several times to build-up pressure, then maintain it on the final downstroke.

17 While pedal pressure is maintained, unscrew the bleed screw (approximately one turn) and allow the compressed fluid and

2.14 Remove the dust cap (arrowed) from the brake caliper bleed screw

air to flow into the jar. The assistant should maintain pedal pressure, following it down to the floor if necessary, and should not release it until instructed to do so. When the flow stops, tighten the bleed screw again, have the assistant release the pedal slowly, and recheck the reservoir fluid level.

18 Repeat the steps given in paragraphs 16 and 17 until the fluid emerging from the bleed screw is free from air bubbles. If the master cylinder has been drained and refilled, and air is being bled from the first screw in the sequence, allow approximately five seconds between cycles for the master cylinder passages to refill.

19 When no more air bubbles appear, securely tighten the bleed screw, remove the tube and spanner, and refit the dust cap. Do not overtighten the bleed screw.

20 Repeat the procedure on the remaining screws in the sequence, until all air is removed from the system and the brake pedal feels firm again.

Using a one-way valve kit

21 As the name implies, these kits consist of a length of tubing with a one-way valve fitted, to prevent expelled air and fluid being drawn back into the system; some kits include a translucent container, which can be positioned so that the air bubbles can be more easily seen flowing from the end of the tube.

22 The kit is connected to the bleed screw, which is then opened **(see illustration)**. The user returns to the driver's seat, depresses the brake pedal with a smooth, steady stroke, and slowly releases it; this is repeated until the expelled fluid is clear of air bubbles.

23 Note that these kits simplify work so much that it is easy to forget the master cylinder reservoir fluid level; ensure that this is maintained at least above the MIN level line at all times.

Using a pressure-bleeding kit

24 These kits are usually operated by a reservoir of pressurised air contained in the spare tyre. However, note that it will probably be necessary to reduce the pressure to a lower level than normal (maximum of 1 bar); refer to the instructions supplied with the kit.

25 By connecting a pressurised, fluid-filled container to the master cylinder reservoir,

2.22 Bleeding a front brake using a one-way valve kit

bleeding can be carried out simply by opening each screw in turn (in the specified sequence), and allowing the fluid to flow out until no more air bubbles can be seen in the expelled fluid.

26 This method has the advantage that the large reservoir of fluid provides an additional safeguard against air being drawn into the system during bleeding.

27 Pressure-bleeding is particularly effective when bleeding 'difficult' systems, or when bleeding the complete system at the time of routine fluid renewal.

All methods

28 When bleeding is complete, and firm pedal feel is restored, wash off any spilt fluid, securely tighten the bleed screws, and refit the dust caps.

29 Check the hydraulic fluid level in the master cylinder reservoir, and top-up if necessary.

30 Discard any hydraulic fluid that has been bled from the system; it will not be fit for re-use.

31 Check the feel of the brake pedal. If it feels at all spongy, air must still be present in the system, and further bleeding is required. Failure to bleed satisfactorily after a reasonable repetition of the bleeding procedure may be due to worn master cylinder seals.

3 Hydraulic pipes and hoses – renewal

Note: *Before starting work, refer to the note at the beginning of Section 2 concerning the dangers of hydraulic fluid.*

1 If any pipe or hose is to be renewed, minimise fluid loss by first removing the master cylinder reservoir cap and screwing it down onto a piece of polythene. Alternatively, flexible hoses can be sealed, if required, using a proprietary brake hose clamp. Metal brake pipe unions can be plugged (if care is taken not to allow dirt into the system) or capped immediately they are disconnected. Place a wad of rag under any union that is to be disconnected, to catch any spilt fluid.

2 If a flexible hose is to be disconnected, unscrew the brake pipe union nut before removing the spring clip which secures the hose to its mounting bracket.

4.3a Push the brake pad retaining spring toward the front of the caliper...

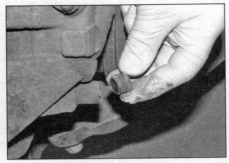

4.3b ...then disconnect the spring legs and remove the spring

4 Front brake pads – renewal

⚠️ **Warning:** *Renew BOTH sets of front brake pads at the same time – NEVER renew the pads on only one wheel, as uneven braking may result. Note that the dust created by wear of the pads may contain asbestos, which is a health hazard. Never blow it out with compressed air, and do not inhale any of it. An approved filtering mask should be worn when working on the brakes. DO NOT use petroleum-based solvents to clean brake parts – use brake cleaner or methylated spirit only.*

Note: *Two different types of front brake calipers have been fitted to Transporter vehicles, depending primarily on model year and wheel size. The following procedure describes brake pad renewal on the VW FN3 brake caliper. The pad renewal procedures for the VW 2FNR 44 caliper are essentially the same; the main difference between the two caliper types is that the FN3 unit has a single piston and the 2FNR 44 unit has two pistons.*

Remove the upper protective cap...

 4.4a Remove the upper protective cap...

4.4b ...and lower protective cap over the caliper guide pins

3 To unscrew union nuts, it is preferable to obtain a brake pipe spanner of the correct size; these are available from most motor accessory shops. Failing this, a close-fitting open-ended spanner will be required, though if the nuts are tight or corroded, their flats may be rounded-off if the spanner slips. In such a case, a self-locking wrench is often the only way to unscrew a stubborn union, but it follows that the pipe and the damaged nuts must be renewed on reassembly. Always clean a union and surrounding area before disconnecting it. If disconnecting a component with more than one union, make a careful note of the connections before disturbing any of them.

4 If a brake pipe is to be renewed, it can be obtained, cut to length and with the union nuts and end flares in place, from VW dealers. All that is then necessary is to bend it to

shape, following the line of the original, before fitting it to the vehicle. Alternatively, most motor accessory shops can make up brake pipes from kits, but this requires very careful measurement of the original, to ensure that the replacement is of the correct length. The safest answer is usually to take the original to the shop as a pattern.

5 On refitting, do not overtighten the union nuts.

6 When refitting, make sure that the hoses are positioned so that they will not touch surrounding bodywork or the roadwheels.

7 Ensure that the pipes and hoses are correctly routed, with no kinks, and that they are secured in the clips or brackets provided. After fitting, remove the polythene from the reservoir, and bleed the hydraulic system as described in Section 2. Wash off any spilt fluid, and check carefully for fluid leaks.

1 Apply the handbrake, then jack up the front of the vehicle and support it on axle stands (see *Jacking and vehicle support*). Remove the front roadwheels.

2 If the inner brake pad is equipped with a pad wear sensor, disconnect the wiring at the connector on the caliper, then remove the wiring connector from the caliper bracket.

3 Using a screwdriver, push the brake pad retaining spring toward the front of the caliper, then disconnect the spring legs and remove the spring **(see illustrations)**.

4 Remove the upper and lower protective caps over the caliper guide pins **(see illustrations)**.

5 Using a suitable hexagon key unscrew and remove the upper and lower caliper guide pins **(see illustrations)**.

6 Lift the caliper away from the brake pads and disc, and tie it to the suspension strut using a suitable piece of wire **(see illustration)**. Do not allow the caliper to hang unsupported on the flexible brake hose.

7 Remove the inner brake pad from the caliper

4.5a Using a suitable hexagon key unscrew the upper guide pin...

4.5b ...and remove it from the caliper...

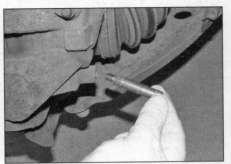

4.5c ...then remove the lower guide pin in the same way

4.6 Lift the caliper away from the brake pads and disc, and tie it to the suspension strut

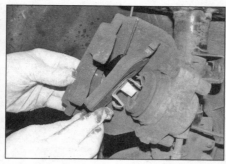

4.7a Remove the inner brake pad from the caliper piston...

4.7b ...and remove the outer pad from the caliper mounting bracket

4.8 Measure the thickness of friction material on each brake pad

4.9 Using brake cleaner, clean the dust and dirt from the caliper and piston

4.10 Using a piston retractor tool to push back the caliper piston

piston and remove the outer pad from the caliper mounting bracket **(see illustrations)**.

8 Measure the thickness of friction material on each brake pad **(see illustration)**. If either pad is worn at any point to the specified minimum thickness or less, all four pads must be renewed. Also, the pads should be renewed if any are fouled with oil or grease; there is no satisfactory way of degreasing friction material, once contaminated. If any of the brake pads are worn unevenly, or are fouled with oil or grease, trace and rectify the cause before reassembly.

9 Prior to fitting the pads, check that the guide pins are a snug fit in the caliper mounting bracket. Using brake cleaner, clean the dust and dirt from the caliper and piston, but do not inhale it, as it is injurious to health **(see illustration)**. Inspect the dust seal around the piston for damage, and the piston for evidence

of fluid leaks, corrosion or damage. If attention to any of these components is necessary, refer to Section 6.

10 If new brake pads are to be fitted, the caliper piston must be pushed back into the cylinder to allow for the extra pad thickness. Either use a G-clamp or similar tool, or use suitable pieces of wood as levers **(see illustration)**. Clamp off the flexible brake hose leading to the caliper then connect a brake bleeding kit to the caliper bleed screw. Open the bleed screw as the piston is retracted, the surplus brake fluid will then be collected in the bleed kit vessel. Close the bleed screw just before the caliper piston is pushed fully into the caliper. This should ensure no air enters the hydraulic system.

Note: *The ABS hydraulic unit contains hydraulic components that are very sensitive to impurities in the brake fluid. Even the smallest particles*

can cause the system to fail through blockage. The pad retraction method described here prevents any debris in the brake fluid expelled from the caliper from being passed back to the ABS hydraulic unit, as well as preventing any chance of damage to the master cylinder seals.

11 Apply a smear of high-temperature silicone lubricant to the contact areas of the caliper mounting bracket and the brake pad backing plate **(see illustration)**.

12 Place the inner brake pad in the caliper, engaging its spring retainer with the caliper piston **(see illustration)**. Where fitted, feed the pad wear sensor wiring connector through the opening in the caliper.

13 If the outer brake pad contains an anti-squeal pad on the metal backing plate, peel off the protective foil from the pad. Place the outer pad in position in the caliper mounting bracket **(see illustration)**.

4.11 Apply a high-temperature silicone lubricant to the contact areas of the brake pad backing plate

4.12 Place the inner brake pad in the caliper, engaging its spring retainer with the caliper piston

4.13 Place the outer pad in position in the caliper mounting bracket

4.14 Lower the caliper back down and in position on the mounting bracket

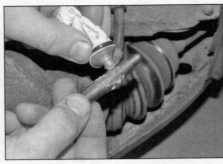

4.15a Lubricate the guide pins with high-temperature silicone lubricant...

4.15b ...and insert them back into the caliper bracket

4.16a Tighten both guide pins to the specified torque...

4.16b ...then refit the upper and lower protective caps

4.17 Refit the brake pad retaining spring ensuring that the spring legs fully engage with their locations

14 Lower the caliper back down and in position on the mounting bracket **(see illustration)**.

15 Liberally lubricate the guide pins with high-temperature silicone lubricant and insert them back into the caliper bracket **(see illustrations)**.

16 Tighten both guide pins to the specified torque, then refit the upper and lower protective caps **(see illustrations)**.

17 Refit the brake pad retaining spring ensuring that the spring legs fully engage with their locations **(see illustration)**.

18 Where fitted, locate the wear sensor wiring connector in the caliper bracket and reconnect the wiring

19 With the brake pads installed, depress the brake pedal repeatedly, until normal (non-assisted) pedal pressure is restored, and the pads are pressed into firm contact with the brake disc.

20 Repeat the above procedure on the remaining front brake caliper.

21 Refit the roadwheels, then lower the vehicle to the ground and tighten the roadwheel bolts to the specified torque setting.

22 Check the hydraulic fluid level as described in *Weekly checks*.

Caution: New pads will not give full braking efficiency until they have bedded-in. Be prepared for this, and avoid hard braking as far as possible for the first hundred miles or so after pad renewal.

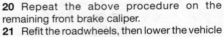

5 Front brake disc – inspection, removal and refitting

Note: *Before starting work, refer to the warning at the beginning of Section 4 concerning the dangers of asbestos dust.*

5.3 Measuring brake disc thickness using a micrometer

5.4 Checking brake disc run-out using a dial gauge

Inspection

Note: *If either disc requires renewal, BOTH should be renewed at the same time, to ensure even and consistent braking.*

1 Firmly apply the handbrake, then jack up the front of the vehicle and support it securely on axle stands (see *Jacking and vehicle support*). Remove the appropriate front roadwheel.

2 Slowly rotate the brake disc so that the full area of both sides can be checked; remove the brake pads if better access is required to the inner surface. Light scoring is normal in the area swept by the brake pads, but if heavy scoring is found, the disc must be renewed.

3 It is normal to find a lip of rust and brake dust around the disc's perimeter; this can be scraped off if required. If, however, a lip has formed due to excessive wear of the brake pad swept area, then the disc's thickness must be measured using a micrometer. Take measurements at several places around the disc, at the inside and outside of the pad swept area; if the disc has worn at any point to the specified minimum thickness or less, the disc must be renewed **(see illustration)**.

4 If the disc is thought to be warped, it can be checked for run-out either using a dial gauge mounted on any convenient fixed point, while the disc is slowly rotated, or by using feeler gauges to measure (at several points all around the disc) the clearance between the disc and a fixed point such as the caliper mounting bracket **(see illustration)**. To ensure that the disc is squarely seated on the hub, fit two wheel bolts, complete with spacers approximately 10 mm thick, and tighten them securely. If the measurements obtained are at the specified maximum or beyond, the disc is excessively warped and must be renewed; however, it is worth checking first that the hub bearing is in good condition as described in Chapter 1, Section 17.

5 Check the disc for cracks, especially around the wheel bolt holes, and for any other wear or damage, and renew if necessary.

Removal

6 Where applicable, remove the roadwheel bolts and spacers used when checking the disc.

7 Unbolt and remove the front brake caliper complete with disc pads and mounting bracket and support it on an axle stand (see illustrations). Do not allow the caliper to hang unsupported from the flexible brake hose.

8 Remove the securing screw and withdraw the disc from the hub (see illustration).

Refitting

9 Refitting is the reverse of the removal procedure, noting the following points:
 a) Ensure that the mating surfaces of the disc and hub are clean and flat.
 b) If a new disc has been fitted, use a suitable solvent to wipe any preservative coating from the disc before refitting the caliper.
 c) Tighten the caliper mounting bracket retaining bolts to the specified torque.
 d) Refit the roadwheel, then lower the vehicle to the ground and tighten the roadwheel bolts to the specified torque. On completion, repeatedly depress the brake pedal until normal (non-assisted) pedal pressure returns.

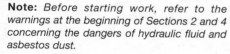

6 Front brake caliper – removal, overhaul and refitting

Note: Before starting work, refer to the warnings at the beginning of Sections 2 and 4 concerning the dangers of hydraulic fluid and asbestos dust.

Removal

1 Apply the handbrake, then jack up the front of the vehicle and support it on axle stands (see Jacking and vehicle support). Remove the roadwheel.

2 Minimise fluid loss by first removing the master cylinder reservoir cap and screwing it down onto a piece of polythene. Alternatively, use a brake hose clamp to clamp the flexible hose leading to the brake caliper.

3 Loosen the union on the caliper end of the flexible brake hose. Once loosened, do not try to unscrew the hose at this stage.

4 Remove the brake pads as described in Section 4.

5 Support the caliper in one hand, and prevent the hydraulic hose from turning with

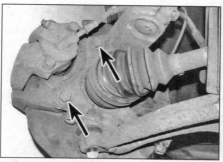

5.7a Undo the two retaining bolts (arrowed)...

5.7c ...and support it on an axle stand

the other hand. Unscrew the caliper from the hose, making sure that the hose is not twisted unduly or strained. Once the caliper is detached, plug the open hydraulic unions in the caliper and hose, to keep out dust and dirt.

6 If required, the caliper mounting bracket can be unbolted from the swivel hub.

Overhaul

Note: Before starting work, check on the availability of parts (caliper overhaul kit/seals).

7 With the caliper on the bench, brush away all traces of dust and dirt, but take care not to inhale any dust, as it may be harmful to your health.

8 Pull the dust cover rubber seal from the end of the piston.

9 Apply low air pressure to the fluid inlet union, to eject the piston. Only low air pressure is required for this, such as is produced by a foot-operated tyre pump.

Caution: The piston may be ejected with some force. Position a thin piece of wood between the piston and the caliper body, to prevent damage to the end face of the piston, in the event of it being ejected suddenly.

10 Using a suitable blunt instrument, prise the piston seal from the groove in the cylinder bore (see illustration). Take care not to scratch the surface of the bore.

11 If working on the twin-piston caliper, repeat paragraphs 8, 9 and 10 on the second piston.

12 Clean the piston(s) and caliper body with

5.7b ...remove the front brake caliper complete with disc pads and mounting bracket...

5.8 Remove the securing screw and withdraw the disc from the hub

methylated spirit, and allow to dry. Examine the surfaces of the piston and cylinder bore for wear, damage and corrosion. If the cylinder bore and piston are unserviceable, the complete caliper must be renewed. The seals must be renewed, regardless of the condition of the other components.

13 Coat the piston and seals with clean brake fluid, then manipulate the piston seal into the groove in the cylinder bore.

14 Push the piston squarely into its bore, taking care not to damage the seal.

15 Fit the dust cover rubber seal onto the piston and caliper, then depress the piston fully.

16 If working on the twin-piston caliper, repeat paragraphs 13, 14 and 15 on the second piston.

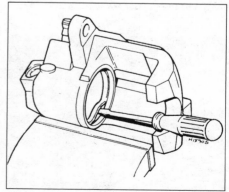

6.10 Use a small screwdriver to extract the caliper piston hydraulic seal

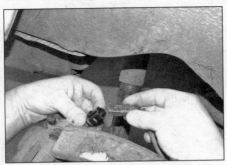

7.2 Where applicable, disconnect the brake pad wear sensor wiring connector

Refitting

17 Refit the caliper by reversing the removal operations. Make sure that the flexible brake hose is not twisted. Tighten the mounting

7.3 Lever down the handbrake operating lever on the brake caliper and disengage the handbrake cable end fitting

7.5 Lift the caliper away from the brake pads

7.6b ...followed by the inner brake pad...

bolts and wheel bolts to the specified torque.

18 Bleed the brake circuit according to the procedure given in Section 2, remembering to remove the brake hose clamp (where applicable) from the flexible hose. Make sure there are no leaks from the hose connections. Test the brakes carefully before returning the vehicle to normal service.

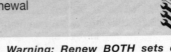

7 Rear brake pads – renewal

⚠️ *Warning: Renew BOTH sets of rear brake pads at the same time – NEVER renew the pads on only one wheel, as uneven braking may result. Note that the dust created by wear of the pads*

7.4 Slacken and remove the caliper upper and lower guide pin bolts

7.6a Withdraw the outer brake pad...

7.6c ...then recover the pad retainers from the caliper mounting bracket

may contain asbestos, which is a health hazard. Never blow it out with compressed air, and do not inhale any of it. An approved filtering mask should be worn when working on the brakes. DO NOT use petroleum-based solvents to clean brake parts – use brake cleaner or methylated spirit only.

Standard brake caliper

1 Chock the front wheels, then jack up the rear of the vehicle, and support it securely on axle stands (see *Jacking and vehicle support*). Remove the rear roadwheels.

2 Where applicable, disconnect the brake pad wear sensor wiring connector and release the wiring from the retainer on the brake caliper (see illustration).

3 Using an adjustable spanner and pointed-nose pliers, lever down the handbrake operating lever on the brake caliper and disengage the handbrake cable end fitting from the lever (see illustration). Release the handbrake outer cable from the caliper bracket.

4 Slacken and remove the caliper upper and lower guide pin bolts, using a slim open-ended spanner to prevent the guide pins from rotating (see illustration). Discard the guide pin bolts – new bolts must be used on refitting.

5 Lift the caliper away from the brake pads, and suspend it from a suitable place under the wheel arch using cable ties or similar (see illustration). Do not allow the caliper to hang unsupported on the flexible brake hose.

6 Withdraw the two brake pads from the caliper mounting bracket. If the old pads are to be refitted, ensure that they are identified so that they can be returned to their original positions. Recover the pad retainers from the mounting bracket, noting their correct fitted locations (see illustrations).

7 Measure the thickness of friction material on each brake pad. If either pad is worn at any point to the specified minimum thickness or less, all four pads must be renewed. Also, the pads should be renewed if any are fouled with oil or grease; there is no satisfactory way of degreasing friction material, once contaminated. If any of the brake pads are worn unevenly, or are fouled with oil or grease, trace and rectify the cause before reassembly.

8 If the brake pads are still serviceable, carefully clean them using a clean, fine wire brush or similar, paying particular attention to the sides and back of the metal backing. Clean out the grooves in the friction material (where applicable), and pick out any large embedded particles of dirt or debris. Carefully clean the pad locations in the caliper body/mounting bracket.

9 Prior to fitting the pads, check that the guide pins are free to slide easily in the caliper bracket, and check that the rubber guide pin gaiters are undamaged. Brush the dust and dirt from the caliper and piston, but **do not** inhale it, as it is injurious to health. Inspect the dust seal around the piston for damage, and the piston for evidence of fluid leaks, corrosion or damage.

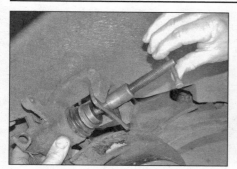

7.10 Using a piston retractor tool to push back the caliper piston

7.11 Fit the upper and lower pad retainers (arrowed) to the caliper mounting bracket

7.12 Place the brake pads in position in the caliper mounting bracket

10 If new brake pads are to be fitted, it will be necessary to retract the piston fully into the caliper bore by rotating it in a clockwise direction. Special tools are readily available at moderate cost to achieve this (see illustration). While the caliper is being retracted, clamp off the flexible brake hose leading to the caliper then connect a brake bleeding kit to the caliper bleed screw. Open the bleed screw as the piston is retracted, the surplus brake fluid will then be collected in the bleed kit vessel. Close the bleed screw just before the caliper piston is pushed fully into the caliper. This should ensure no air enters the hydraulic system.

Note: *The ABS hydraulic unit contains hydraulic components that are very sensitive to impurities in the brake fluid. Even the smallest particles can cause the system to fail through blockage. The pad retraction method described here prevents any debris in the brake fluid expelled from the caliper from being passed back to the ABS hydraulic unit, as well as preventing any chance of damage to the master cylinder seals.*

11 Fit the upper and lower pad retainers to the caliper mounting bracket, ensuring that they are correctly located (see illustration).

12 Apply a smear of high-temperature silicone lubricant to the contact areas of the caliper mounting bracket and the brake pad backing plate, then place the pads in position in the caliper bracket (see illustration).

13 If the threads of the new guide pin bolts are not already pre-coated with locking compound, apply a suitable thread-locking compound to them. Press the caliper into position, then install the bolts, tightening them to the specified torque setting while retaining the guide pin with an open-ended spanner (see illustrations).

14 Where applicable, reconnect the brake pad wear sensor wiring connector and secure the wiring to the retainer on the brake caliper.

15 Depress the brake pedal repeatedly, until the pads are pressed into firm contact with the brake disc, and normal (non-assisted) pedal pressure is restored.

16 Repeat the above procedure on the remaining rear brake caliper.

17 Reconnect the handbrake cables to

7.13a Press the caliper into position...

the calipers, and adjust the handbrake as described in Section 12.

18 Refit the roadwheels, then lower the vehicle to the ground and tighten the roadwheel bolts to the specified torque setting.

19 Check the hydraulic fluid level as described in *Weekly Checks*.

Caution: New pads will not give full braking efficiency until they have bedded-in. Be prepared for this, and avoid hard braking as far as possible for the first hundred miles or so after pad renewal.

VW FN 44 brake caliper

20 Chock the front wheels, then jack up the rear of the vehicle, and support it securely on axle stands (see *Jacking and vehicle support*). Remove the rear roadwheels.

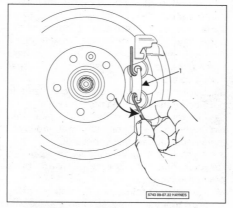

7.22 Disconnect the spring legs and remove the pad retaining spring (1)

7.13b ...then install the guide pin bolts, tightening them to the specified torque

21 If the inner brake pad is equipped with a pad wear sensor, disconnect the wiring at the connector on the caliper, then remove the wiring connector from the caliper bracket.

22 Using a screwdriver, push the brake pad retaining spring toward the front of the caliper, then disconnect the spring legs and remove the spring (see illustration).

23 Remove the upper and lower protective caps over the caliper guide pins.

24 Using a suitable hexagon key unscrew and remove the upper and lower caliper guide pins (see illustration).

25 Lift the caliper away from the brake pads, and suspend it from a suitable place under the wheel arch using cable ties or similar. Do not allow the caliper to hang unsupported on the flexible brake hose.

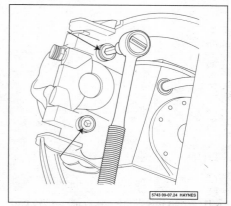

7.24 Using a hexagon key unscrew and remove the caliper guide pins (arrowed)

7.26 Remove the inner brake pad from the caliper piston and the outer pad from the caliper mounting bracket

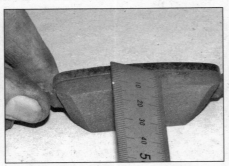

7.27 Measure the thickness of friction material on each brake pad

7.29 Using a piston retractor tool to push back the caliper piston

26 Remove the inner brake pad from the caliper piston and remove the outer pad from the caliper mounting bracket (see illustration).

27 Measure the thickness of friction material on each brake pad (see illustration). If either pad is worn at any point to the specified minimum thickness or less, all four pads must be renewed. Also, the pads should be renewed if any are fouled with oil or grease; there is no satisfactory way of degreasing friction material, once contaminated. If any of the brake pads are worn unevenly, or are fouled with oil or grease, trace and rectify the cause before reassembly.

28 Prior to fitting the pads, check that the guide pins are a snug fit in the caliper mounting bracket. Using brake cleaner, clean the dust and dirt from the caliper and piston, but do not inhale it, as it is injurious to health. Inspect the dust seal around the piston for damage, and the piston for evidence of fluid leaks, corrosion or damage.

29 If new brake pads are to be fitted, the caliper piston must be pushed back into the cylinder to allow for the extra pad thickness. Either use a G-clamp or similar tool, or use suitable pieces of wood as

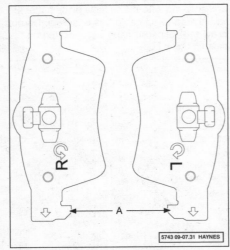

7.31 When fitted, the arrow (A) on the pad backing plate must point in the direction of rotation of the disc

levers (see illustration). Clamp off the flexible brake hose leading to the caliper then connect a brake bleeding kit to the caliper bleed screw. Open the bleed screw as the piston is retracted, the surplus brake fluid will then be collected in the bleed kit vessel. Close the bleed screw just before the caliper piston is pushed fully into the caliper. This should ensure no air enters the hydraulic system.

Note: *The ABS hydraulic unit contains hydraulic components that are very sensitive to impurities in the brake fluid. Even the smallest particles can cause the system to fail through blockage. The pad retraction method described here prevents any debris in the brake fluid expelled from the caliper from being passed back to the ABS hydraulic unit, as well as preventing any chance of damage to the master cylinder seals.*

30 Apply a smear of high-temperature silicone lubricant to the contact areas of the caliper mounting bracket and the brake pad backing plate.

31 Place the inner brake pad in the caliper, engaging its spring retainer with the caliper piston. Where fitted, feed the pad wear sensor wiring connector through the opening in the caliper. Note that the brake pads are directional. When fitted, the arrow on the pad backing plate must point in the direction of rotation of the disc (see illustration).

32 If the outer brake pad contains an anti-squeal pad on the metal backing plate, peel off the protective foil from the pad. Place the outer pad in position in the caliper mounting bracket.

33 Lower the caliper back down and in position on the mounting bracket.

34 Liberally lubricate the guide pins with high-temperature silicone lubricant and insert them back into the caliper bracket.

35 Tighten both guide pins to the specified torque, then refit the upper and lower protective caps.

36 Refit the brake pad retaining spring ensuring that the spring legs fully engage with their locations.

37 Where fitted, locate the wear sensor

wiring connector in the caliper bracket and reconnect the wiring

38 With the brake pads installed, depress the brake pedal repeatedly, until normal (non-assisted) pedal pressure is restored, and the pads are pressed into firm contact with the brake disc.

39 Repeat the above procedure on the remaining rear brake caliper.

40 Refit the roadwheels, then lower the vehicle to the ground and tighten the roadwheel bolts to the specified torque setting.

41 Check the hydraulic fluid level as described in *Weekly checks*.

Caution: *New pads will not give full braking efficiency until they have bedded-in. Be prepared for this, and avoid hard braking as far as possible for the first hundred miles or so after pad renewal.*

8 Rear brake disc – inspection, removal and refitting

Note: *Before starting work, refer to the warning at the beginning of Section 7 concerning the dangers of asbestos dust.*

Inspection

Note: *If either disc requires renewal, BOTH should be renewed at the same time, to ensure even and consistent braking.*

1 Chock the front wheels, then jack up the rear of the vehicle, and support it securely on axle stands (see *Jacking and vehicle support*). Remove the appropriate rear roadwheel.

2 Inspect the disc as described in Section 5.

Removal

3 Where applicable, remove the roadwheel bolts and spacers used when checking the disc.

4 Unbolt and remove the rear brake caliper complete with disc pads and mounting bracket and suspend it from a convenient place under the wheel arch using cable ties (see illustration). Do not allow the caliper to hang unsupported from the flexible brake hose.

5 Remove the securing screw and withdraw the disc from the hub **(see illustrations)**.

6 If removing a disc on a vehicle equipped with the VW FN 44 rear brake caliper, it may be difficult to remove the disc due to the handbrake shoes binding on the inner circumference of the drum-in-disc. If the handbrake shoes are binding, first check that the handbrake is fully released, then proceed as follows.

7 Turn the disc until the handbrake shoe adjustment nut is visible through the wheel bolt hole.

8 Insert a screwdriver into the wheel bolt hole and turn the adjustment nut until the disc is no longer binding **(see illustration 12.14)**. It should now be possible to withdraw the disc from the hub.

Refitting

9 Refitting is the reverse of the removal procedure, noting the following points:
   a) Remove all traces of rust and corrosion from the hub face and ensure that the mating surfaces of the disc and hub are clean and flat **(see illustration)**.
   b) If a new disc has been fitted, use a suitable solvent to wipe any preservative coating from the disc before refitting the caliper.
   c) Tighten the caliper mounting bracket retaining bolts to the specified torque.
   d) If working on a vehicle equipped with the VW FN 44 brake caliper, adjust the handbrake as described in Section 12.
   e) Refit the roadwheel, then lower the vehicle to the ground and tighten the roadwheel bolts to the specified torque. On completion, repeatedly depress the brake pedal until normal (non-assisted) pedal pressure returns.

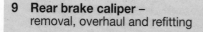

9 Rear brake caliper – removal, overhaul and refitting

Note: Before starting work, refer to the note at the beginning of Section 2 concerning the dangers of hydraulic fluid, and to the warning at the beginning of Section 7 concerning the dangers of asbestos dust.

Standard brake caliper

Removal

1 Chock the front wheels, then jack up the rear of the vehicle and support on axle stands (see *Jacking and vehicle support*). Remove the relevant rear roadwheel, then make sure that the handbrake is fully released.

2 Where applicable, disconnect the brake pad wear sensor wiring connector and release the wiring from the retainer on the brake caliper.

3 Using an adjustable spanner and pointed-nose pliers, lever down the handbrake operating lever on the brake caliper and disengage the handbrake cable end fitting from the lever **(see illustration 7.3)**. Release

8.4 Undo the two bolts (arrowed) and remove the rear brake caliper complete with disc pads and mounting bracket

8.5b ...and withdraw the disc from the hub

the handbrake outer cable from the caliper bracket.

4 Minimise fluid loss by first removing the master cylinder reservoir cap and screwing it down onto a piece of polythene. Alternatively, use a brake hose clamp to clamp the flexible hose leading to the brake caliper.

5 Clean the area around the caliper brake hose union. Slacken (but do not completely unscrew) the union on the caliper end of the flexible hose.

6 Slacken and remove the caliper upper and lower guide pin bolts, using a slim open-ended spanner to prevent the guide pins from rotating **(see illustration 7.4)**. Discard the guide pin bolts – new bolts must be used on refitting.

7 Lift the caliper off the brake pads. Support the caliper in one hand, and prevent the flexible hose from turning with the other hand. Unscrew the caliper from the hose, making

9.8a Undo the two retaining bolts...

8.5a Remove the securing screw...

8.9 Remove all traces of rust and corrosion from the mating surfaces of the hub and disc

sure that the hose is not twisted unduly or strained. Once the caliper is detached, plug the open hydraulic unions in the caliper and hose, to keep out dust and dirt.

8 If necessary, remove the brake pads with reference to Section 7, then undo the two retaining bolts and remove the caliper mounting bracket **(see illustrations)**.

Overhaul

9 No overhaul procedures, or parts, were available at the time of writing. Check the availability of spares before dismantling the caliper. Do not attempt to dismantle the handbrake mechanism inside the caliper; if the mechanism is faulty, the complete caliper assembly must be renewed.

Refitting

10 Refit the caliper by reversing the removal operations. Make sure that the flexible brake

9.8b ...and remove the caliper mounting bracket

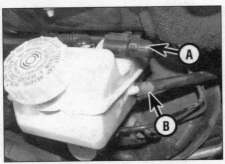

10.2 Brake fluid level sensor wiring connector (A) and clutch hydraulic hose connection (B)

hose is not twisted. Tighten the mounting bracket bolts, guide pin bolts and roadwheel bolts to the specified torque.
11 Bleed the brake circuit according to the procedure given in Section 2, remembering to remove the brake hose clamp (where applicable) from the flexible hose. Make sure there are no leaks from the hose connections. Test the brakes carefully before returning the vehicle to normal service.

VW FN 44 brake caliper

Removal

12 Chock the front wheels, then jack up the rear of the vehicle, and support it securely on axle stands (see *Jacking and vehicle support*). Remove the rear roadwheels.
13 If the inner brake pad is equipped with a pad wear sensor, disconnect the wiring at the connector on the caliper, then remove the wiring connector from the caliper bracket.
14 Minimise fluid loss by first removing the master cylinder reservoir cap and screwing it down onto a piece of polythene. Alternatively, use a brake hose clamp to clamp the flexible hose leading to the brake caliper.
15 Clean the area around the caliper brake hose union. Slacken (but do not completely unscrew) the union on the caliper end of the flexible hose.
16 Using a screwdriver, push the brake pad retaining spring toward the front of the caliper, then disconnect the spring legs and remove the spring **(see illustration 7.22)**.
17 Remove the upper and lower protective caps over the caliper guide pins.

10.5 Unscrew the union nuts (arrowed) and move the brake pipes to one side

18 Using a suitable hexagon key unscrew and remove the upper and lower caliper guide pins **(see illustration 7.24)**.
19 Lift the caliper off the brake pads. Support the caliper in one hand, and prevent the flexible hose from turning with the other hand. Unscrew the caliper from the hose, making sure that the hose is not twisted unduly or strained. Once the caliper is detached, plug the open hydraulic unions in the caliper and hose, to keep out dust and dirt.
20 If necessary, remove the brake pads with reference to Section 7, then undo the two retaining bolts and remove the caliper mounting bracket.

Overhaul

21 No overhaul procedures, or parts, were available at the time of writing. Check the availability of spares before dismantling the caliper.

Refitting

22 Refit the caliper by reversing the removal operations. Make sure that the flexible brake hose is not twisted. Tighten the mounting bracket bolts, guide pins and roadwheel bolts to the specified torque.
23 Bleed the brake circuit according to the procedure given in Section 2, remembering to remove the brake hose clamp (where applicable) from the flexible hose. Make sure there are no leaks from the hose connections. Test the brakes carefully before returning the vehicle to normal service.

10 Master cylinder – removal, overhaul and refitting

Note: Before starting work, refer to the warning at the beginning of Section 2 concerning the dangers of hydraulic fluid.

Removal

1 Remove the master cylinder reservoir cap, and syphon the hydraulic fluid from the reservoir. **Note:** *Do not syphon the fluid by mouth, as it is poisonous therefore use a syringe or an old hydrometer.* Alternatively, open the front brake caliper bleed screws, one at a time, and gently pump the brake pedal to expel the fluid through a plastic tube connected to the screw (see Section 2).
2 Disconnect the wiring connector from the brake fluid level sensor on the reservoir **(see illustration)**.
3 Disconnect the clutch hydraulic hose from the fluid reservoir. Tape over or plug the outlet.
4 Where applicable, disconnect the wiring connectors from the brake pressure sensor on the underside of the master cylinder and, on later models, from the brake stop-light switch on the side of the master cylinder.
5 Place cloth rags beneath the master cylinder to collect escaping brake fluid. Identify the brake pipes for position, then unscrew the union nuts and move the pipes to one side

(see illustration). Plug or tape over the pipe ends to prevent dirt entry.
6 Unscrew the two mounting nuts and withdraw the master cylinder from the vacuum servo unit. Take care not to spill fluid on the vehicle paintwork. Recover the master cylinder-to-servo unit seal.
7 If required, the fluid reservoir can be removed from the master cylinder by extracting the retainer pin (where fitted) then pulling the reservoir up and off the mounting seals.

Overhaul

8 If the master cylinder is faulty, it must be renewed. Repair kits are not available from VW dealers, so the cylinder must be treated as a sealed unit.
9 The only items which can be renewed are the mounting seals for the fluid reservoir; if these show signs of deterioration, pull off the reservoir and remove the old seals. Lubricate the new seals with clean brake fluid, and press them into the master cylinder ports. Ease the fluid reservoir into position, and push it fully home.

Refitting

10 Place the master cylinder-to-servo unit seal in position, then fit the master cylinder to the servo unit. Ensure that the servo unit pushrod enters the master cylinder piston centrally. Fit the retaining nuts and tighten them to the specified torque.
11 Refit the brake pipes and tighten the union nuts securely.
12 Reconnect the clutch hydraulic hose to the fluid reservoir.
13 Reconnect the wiring connector to the brake fluid level sensor and, where applicable, to the brake stop-light switch and brake pressure sensor.
14 Remove the reservoir filler cap and polythene, then top-up the reservoir with fresh hydraulic fluid to the MAX mark (see *Weekly checks*).
15 Bleed the brake and clutch hydraulic systems as described in Section 2 and Chapter 6, Section 2 then refit the filler cap. Thoroughly check the operation of the brakes and clutch before using the vehicle on the road.

11 Brake pedal – removal and refitting

Removal

1 Remove the facia right-hand footwell trim panel as described in Chapter 11, Section 29.
2 If the stop-light switch is located on the brake pedal mounting bracket, remove the switch as described in Section 17.
3 It is now necessary to release the brake pedal from the ball on the vacuum servo unit pushrod. To do this, a VW special tool is available, but a suitable alternative can be improvised **(see illustration)**. Note that the plastic lugs in the pedal are very stiff, and it will not be possible to release them by hand.

Hold the brake pedal, then, using the tool, release the securing lugs, and pull the pedal from the servo pushrod (see illustrations).

4 Undo the four nuts securing the vacuum servo unit to the bulkhead.

5 Working in the engine compartment pull the vacuum servo unit away from the bulkhead by approximately 10.0 mm, taking care not to strain the brake pipes. If necessary, engage the help of an assistant to hold the servo unit in this position.

6 Undo and remove the pedal pivot bolt nut.

7 Slide the pivot bolt out, until the pedal is free, then remove the pedal.

Refitting

8 Prior to refitting, apply a smear of multi-purpose grease to the pivot bolt and pedal bearing surfaces.

9 Manoeuvre the pedal into position, ensuring that the pivot bush is correctly located.

10 Insert the pedal pivot bolt and tighten the retaining nut to the specified torque.

11 Hold the servo unit pushrod, and push the pedal back onto the pushrod ball until it audibly engages. Make sure the pedal is securely fastened to the pushrod.

12 Refit the four nuts to the vacuum servo unit and tighten them to the specified torque.

13 If the stop-light switch is located on the brake pedal mounting bracket, refit the switch as described in Section 17.

14 Refit the facia right-hand footwell trim panel as described in Chapter 11, Section 29.

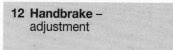

12 Handbrake – adjustment

Note: Two different handbrake mechanisms may be fitted depending on rear brake caliper type. On the standard brake caliper, the handbrake operating mechanism is incorporated in the caliper and acts on the rear brake pads. On the VW FN 44 type caliper the handbrake comprises two separate handbrake shoes operating within a drum-in-disc arrangement. Identify the type being worked on and proceed as described in the applicable sub-Section below.

Standard brake caliper

1 Apply the footbrake firmly several times to establish correct pad-to-disc clearance, then apply and release the handbrake several times.

2 Applying normal moderate pressure, pull the handbrake lever to the fully applied position, counting the number of clicks from the handbrake ratchet mechanism. If adjustment is correct, there should be approximately 5 to 7 clicks before the handbrake is fully applied. If this is not the case, adjust as follows.

3 Chock the front wheels, then jack up the rear of the vehicle, and support it securely on axle stands (see Jacking and vehicle support).

4 Make sure that the handbrake is in the released position.

5 From underneath the vehicle, locate the

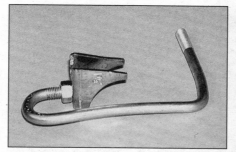

11.3a Improvised special tool made from a modified exhaust clamp, used to release the brake pedal from the servo pushrod

11.3c Rear view of the brake pedal showing plastic lugs (arrowed) securing pedal to servo pushrod

handbrake adjusting nut on the end of the front handbrake cable (see illustration).

6 Tighten the handbrake adjusting nut until the handbrake operating levers on the rear brake calipers lift off their stops by a maximum of 1.0 mm (see illustration).

7 Apply and release the handbrake several times. With the handbrake released, check that the wheels are free to rotate without binding.

8 On completion, lower the vehicle to the ground.

VW FN 44 brake caliper

9 Applying normal moderate pressure, pull the handbrake lever to the fully applied position, counting the number of clicks from the handbrake ratchet mechanism. If adjustment

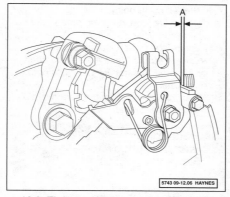

12.6 Tighten the handbrake adjusting nut until a gap of 1.0 mm (A) exists at the handbrake operating levers

11.3b Using the tool to release the brake pedal from the servo pushrod

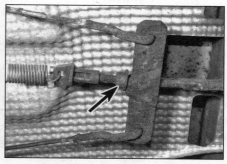

12.5 Handbrake adjusting nut (arrowed)

is correct, there should be approximately 5 to 7 clicks before the handbrake is fully applied. If this is not the case, adjust as follows.

10 Chock the front wheels, then jack up the rear of the vehicle, and support it securely on axle stands (see Jacking and vehicle support).

11 Remove one rear roadwheel retaining bolt on each side.

12 Make sure that the handbrake is in the released position.

13 Turn one of the roadwheels until the brake shoe adjustment nut is visible through the wheel bolt hole.

14 Insert a screwdriver into the wheel bolt hole and turn the adjustment nut until the roadwheel can no longer be turned (see illustration). Now back off the adjustment nut

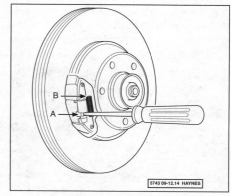

12.14 Using a screwdriver, turn the handbrake adjusting nut (A) against the resistance of the spring (B)

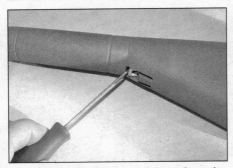

13.1a Carefully lift the retaining tab on the underside of the handbrake lever upper trim...

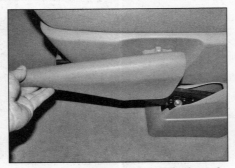

13.1b ...and pull the trim off the lever

13.2 Lift the handbrake lever lower trim off the lever base

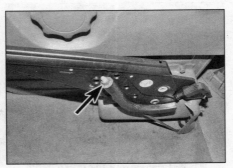

13.3 Front handbrake cable retaining nut (arrowed)

2 Disconnect the wiring connector from the warning light switch on the side of the handbrake lever.
3 Extract the plastic rivet and remove the switch from the handbrake lever bracket.

Refitting

4 Refitting is a reversal of removal.

15 Handbrake cables – removal and refitting

1 The handbrake cable assembly consists of a front cable linking the handbrake lever with the cable compensator, and two rear cables linking the compensator with the relevant rear brake. Each of the handbrake cable components can be removed and refitted individually as described in the following sub-Sections.

Front cable

Removal

2 Carry out the operations described in Section 13, paragraphs 1 to 3.
3 Chock the front wheels, then jack up the rear of the vehicle, and support it securely on axle stands (see *Jacking and vehicle support*).
4 Detach the handbrake cable return spring from the spring holder on the end of the front cable, then unscrew the spring holder from the cable (see illustration).
5 Unscrew the handbrake adjusting nut and remove it from the end of the front cable. Withdraw the inner cable from the compensator.
6 Pull the cable forward and disengage it from the support bracket on the underbody. Pull the cable out from the vehicle interior and remove it from below.

Refitting

7 Refitting is a reversal of removal, but adjust the handbrake as described in Section 12 before lowering the vehicle to the ground.

Rear cables – standard brake caliper

Removal

8 Chock the front wheels, then jack up the rear of the vehicle, and support it securely on axle stands (see *Jacking and vehicle support*).
9 Detach the handbrake cable return spring from the spring holder on the end of the front cable, then unscrew the spring holder from the cable (see illustration 15.4).
10 Unscrew the handbrake adjusting nut and remove it from the end of the front cable.
11 Using an adjustable spanner and pointed-nose pliers, lever down the handbrake operating lever on the brake caliper and disengage the handbrake cable end fitting from the lever (see illustration 7.3). Release the handbrake outer cable from the caliper bracket.
12 Disengage the forward end of the inner cable from the compensator.

by 6 teeth and check that the roadwheel is free to turn.
15 Repeat paragraphs 13 and 14 on the remaining rear brake.
16 Apply and release the handbrake several times. With the handbrake released, check that the wheels are free to rotate without binding.
17 On completion, lower the vehicle to the ground. Refit the two wheel bolts and tighten them to the specified torque.

13 Handbrake lever – removal and refitting

Removal

1 Pull the handbrake lever fully up. Carefully lift the retaining tab on the underside of the

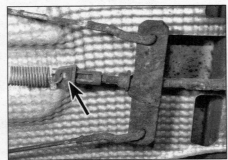

15.4 Detach the handbrake cable return spring from the spring holder (arrowed) on the end of the front cable

handbrake lever upper trim and pull the trim off the lever **(see illustrations)**.
2 Lift the handbrake lever lower trim off the lever base **(see illustration)**.
3 Measure and record the number of exposed threads visible on the end of the front handbrake cable. Undo the front handbrake cable retaining nut and disengage the cable from the handbrake lever **(see illustration)**.
4 Disconnect the wiring connector at the handbrake warning light switch.
5 Undo the two nuts securing the handbrake lever to the floor. Lift the handbrake lever off the mounting studs and remove it from inside the vehicle.

Refitting

6 Refitting is a reversal of removal, bearing in mind the following points:
a) Tighten the lever retaining nuts to the specified torque.
b) Position the front handbrake cable retaining nut so that the same number of exposed threads are visible as noted during removal.
c) On completion, adjust the handbrake as described in Section 12.

14 Handbrake warning light switch – removal and refitting

Removal

1 Remove the handbrake lever upper trim and lower trim as described in Section 13.

13 Disengage the outer cable from the two support brackets on the trailing arm **(see illustration)**.

14 Depress the tabs on the outer cable end fitting and pull the outer cable out of the support bracket on the underbody **(see illustration)**. Remove the cable from under the vehicle.

Refitting

15 Refitting is a reversal of removal, but adjust the handbrake as described in Section 12 before lowering the vehicle to the ground.

Rear cables – VW FN 44 brake caliper

Removal

16 Chock the front wheels, then jack up the rear of the vehicle, and support it securely on axle stands (see *Jacking and vehicle support*).

17 Detach the handbrake cable return spring from the spring holder on the end of the front cable, then unscrew the spring holder from the cable **(see illustration 15.4)**.

18 Unscrew the handbrake adjusting nut and remove it from the end of the front cable.

19 Disengage the forward end of the inner cable from the compensator.

20 Insert a screwdriver through the wheel bolt hole and press the handbrake cable nipple against the retaining spring in the expander until the cable can be pulled out.

21 Disengage the outer cable from the two support brackets on the trailing arm **(see illustration 15.13)**.

22 Depress the tabs on the outer cable end fitting and pull the outer cable out of the support bracket on the underbody **(see illustration 15.14)**. Remove the cable from under the vehicle.

Refitting

23 Refitting is a reversal of removal, but adjust the handbrake as described in Section 12 before lowering the vehicle to the ground.

16 Handbrake shoes – renewal

1 Remove the rear brake disc as described in Section 8.

2 Working carefully and taking the necessary precautions, remove all traces of brake dust from the brake disc, backplate and handbrake shoes.

3 Measure the thickness of friction material on each handbrake shoe at several points. If either shoe is worn at any point to the specified minimum thickness or less, all four shoes must be renewed. Also, the shoes should be renewed if any are fouled with oil or grease; there is no satisfactory way of degreasing friction material, once contaminated. If any of the handbrake shoes are worn unevenly, or are fouled with oil or grease, trace and rectify the cause before reassembly.

15.13 Disengage the handbrake cable from the two support brackets (arrowed) on the trailing arm

4 Note the location and orientation of all components before dismantling as an aid to reassembly.

5 Unhook the return springs and remove them from the handbrake shoes.

6 Remove the hold-down pins along with the springs, then remove the handbrake shoes from the backplate.

7 Examine the return springs. If they are distorted, or if they have seen extensive service, renewal is advisable. Weak springs may cause the handbrake to bind.

8 Prior to installation, clean the brake backplate thoroughly. Apply a thin smear of high-temperature copper-based brake grease or anti-seize compound to all those surfaces of the backplate which bear on the shoes, particularly the pivot points. Do not allow the lubricant to foul the friction material.

9 Place the handbrake shoes in position on the backplate and refit the hold-down springs and pins.

10 Reconnect the return springs to the handbrake shoes noting that the spring with the larger number of coils is fitted next to the adjustment nut.

11 Refit the rear brake disc as described in Section 8.

12 On completion, adjust the handbrake as described in Section 12.

17 Stop-light switch – removal and refitting

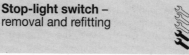

Up to model year 2010

Removal

1 The stop-light switch is located on the brake pedal mounting bracket in the driver's footwell.

2 Remove the facia right-hand footwell trim panel as described in Chapter 11, Section 29.

3 Disconnect the wiring connector from the stop-light switch **(see illustration)**.

4 Turn the switch 45° anti-clockwise and remove it from the mounting bracket.

5 The stop-light switches were modified in January 2007 and the manufacturers advise that whenever an early type switch is removed, it should always be replaced with a

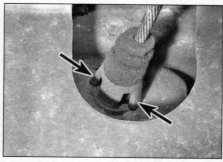

15.14 Depress the tabs (arrowed) and pull the outer handbrake cable out of the support bracket on the underbody

later type switch. The later type switches can be identified by the bright tip of the plunger.

Refitting

6 Without moving the brake pedal, insert the switch into the mounting bracket and turn it 45° clockwise to lock it in position.

7 Reconnect the wiring connector and check the operation of the stop-lights.

8 On completion, refit the facia right-hand footwell trim panel as described in Chapter 11, Section 29.

Model year 2010 onwards

Removal

9 The stop-light switch is located in the side of the brake master cylinder.

10 Where applicable, remove the engine compartment covers.

11 Disconnect the wiring connector from the stop-light switch.

12 Undo the switch retaining bolt, disengage the switch from the upper locating clip and remove it from the master cylinder.

Refitting

13 Refitting is a reversal of removal.

18 Vacuum servo unit – testing, removal and refitting

Testing

1 To test the operation of the servo unit, with the engine switched off, depress the footbrake

17.3 Disconnect the wiring connector (arrowed) from the stop-light switch

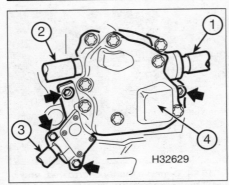

20.5 Tandem pump retaining bolts (arrowed) – 1.9 litre engines

1 *Brake servo vacuum pipe*
2 *Fuel hose*
3 *Fuel hose*
4 *Tandem pump*

pedal several times to exhaust the vacuum. Now start the engine, keeping the pedal firmly depressed. As the engine starts, there should be a noticeable 'give' in the brake pedal as the vacuum builds-up. Allow the engine to run for at least two minutes, then switch it off. The brake pedal should now feel normal, but further applications should result in the pedal feeling firmer, the pedal stroke decreasing with each application.

2 If the servo does not operate as described, first inspect the servo unit check valve as described in Section 19.

3 If the servo unit still fails to operate satisfactorily, the fault lies within the unit itself. Repairs to the unit are not possible; if faulty, the servo unit must be renewed.

Removal

4 Remove the brake master cylinder as described in Section 10.

5 For improved access remove the air cleaner assembly and air ducts as described in Chapter 4A, Section 2 (1.9 and 2.5 litre engines) or Chapter 4B, Section 2 (2.0 litre engines).

6 Carefully ease the vacuum hose out of the servo unit, taking care not to displace the sealing grommet.

7 Where fitted, disconnect the wiring connectors at the servo unit potentiometer and brake hydraulic pressure sensor.

20.8 Ensure that the tandem pump pinion engages correctly with the drive slot in the camshaft – 1.9 litre engines

8 Release the wiring harness from the support bracket on the servo.

9 Release the servo unit pushrod from the brake pedal as described in Section 11, paragraphs 1 to 3.

10 Undo the four nuts securing the vacuum servo unit to the bulkhead.

11 Return to the engine compartment, and lift the servo unit out of position. Recover the servo unit-to-bulkhead gasket.

Refitting

12 Refit the gasket, then locate the vacuum servo unit in position on the bulkhead, ensuring that the pushrod is aligned with the brake pedal.

13 Hold the servo unit pushrod, and push the pedal back onto the pushrod ball until it audibly engages. Make sure the pedal is securely fastened to the pushrod.

14 Refit the four nuts to the vacuum servo unit and tighten them to the specified torque.

15 If the stop-light switch is located on the brake pedal mounting bracket, refit the switch as described in Section 17.

16 Refit the facia right-hand footwell trim panel as described in Chapter 11, Section 29.

17 Attach the wiring harness to the support bracket on the servo.

18 Where fitted, reconnect the wiring connectors to the servo unit potentiometer and brake hydraulic pressure sensor.

19 Refit the vacuum hose to the servo grommet, ensuring that the hose is correctly seated.

20 Refit the air cleaner assembly and air ducts as described in Chapter 4A, Section 2 (1.9 and 2.5 litre engines) or Chapter 4B, Section 2 (2.0 litre engines).

21 Refit the brake master cylinder as described in Section 10.

---

19 Vacuum servo unit check valve and hose – removal, testing and refitting

1 The check valve is in the vacuum hose from the vacuum pump to the brake servo. If the valve is to be renewed, the complete hose/valve assembly should be replaced.

Removal

2 Ease the vacuum hose out of the servo unit, taking care not to displace the grommet.

3 Where applicable, disconnect the secondary vacuum hoses from the main vacuum hose.

4 Note the routing of the hose, then disconnect the opposite end of the hose assembly from the vacuum pump and remove it from the engine compartment.

Testing

5 Examine the check valve and vacuum hose for signs of damage, and renew if necessary.

6 The valve may be tested by blowing through it in both directions, air should flow through the valve in one direction only;

when blown through from the servo unit end of the valve. Renew the valve if this is not the case.

7 Examine the servo unit rubber sealing grommet for signs of damage or deterioration, and renew as necessary.

Refitting

8 Ensure that the sealing grommet is correctly fitted to the servo unit.

9 Ease the hose union into position in the servo, taking great care not to displace or damage the grommet.

10 Ensure that the hose is correctly routed, and connect it to the vacuum pump.

11 Where applicable, reconnect the secondary vacuum hoses from the main vacuum hose.

12 On completion, start the engine and check the check valve to servo unit connection for signs of air leaks.

---

20 Vacuum pump – removal and refitting

1.9 litre engines

Note: *The vacuum pump and the fuel injection system fuel pump are combined in one unit, termed a 'tandem pump'.*

Removal

1 Unclip and remove the engine top cover.

2 Disconnect the battery negative terminal (refer to *Disconnecting the battery*).

3 Leaving the coolant hoses connected, undo the two bolts and move the cooling system expansion tank to one side.

4 Remove the air duct between the inlet manifold and the intercooler.

5 Release the retaining clip (where fitted) and disconnect the brake servo vacuum pipe from the tandem pump **(see illustration)**.

6 Disconnect the fuel supply hose (marked white) from the tandem pump **(see illustration 20.5)**. Be prepared for fuel spillage.

7 Unscrew the four retaining bolts and move the tandem pump away from the cylinder head **(see illustration 20.5)**. As the pump is lifted up, disconnect the fuel return hose (marked blue). Be prepared for fuel spillage. There are no serviceable parts within the tandem pump. If the pump is faulty, it must be renewed.

Refitting

8 Reconnect the fuel return hose to the pump and refit the pump to the cylinder head, using new rubber seals, and ensuring that the pump pinion engages correctly with the drive slot in the camshaft **(see illustration)**.

9 Refit the pump retaining bolts, and tighten them to the specified torque.

10 Re-attach the fuel supply hose and brake servo hose to the pump.

11 Refit the air duct between the inlet manifold and the intercooler.

12 Place the cooling system expansion tank

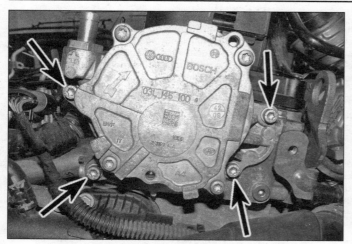

**20.21 Vacuum pump retaining bolts (arrowed) –
2.0 litre engines**

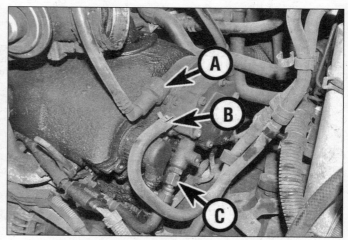

**20.33 Pipe and hose connections at the tandem pump –
2.5 litre engines**

A *Brake servo vacuum pipe*	B *Upper fuel hose*
	C *Lower fuel hose*

back in position and secure with the two retaining bolts.

13 Reconnect the battery negative terminal, then refit the engine top cover.

2.0 litre engines

Removal

14 Unclip and remove the engine top cover.
15 Disconnect the battery negative terminal (refer to *Disconnecting the battery*).
16 Leaving the coolant hoses connected, undo the two bolts and move the cooling system expansion tank to one side.
17 Remove the air duct between the inlet manifold and the intercooler.
18 Release the clip, undo the retaining bolt and pull the exhaust pressure sensor out of the mounting bracket.
19 Undo the retaining bolts as necessary and move the pipes and support brackets in the vicinity of the vacuum pump to one side for access.
20 Disconnect the vacuum hose from the top of the pump.
21 Unscrew the four mounting bolts and withdraw the vacuum pump from the cylinder head **(see illustration)**. Recover the O-ring seal and discard, as a new one will be required for refitting.

Refitting

22 Fit the new O-ring seal to the vacuum pump, and apply a smear of oil to aid installation.
23 Manoeuvre the vacuum pump into position, making sure that the slot in the pump drive gear aligns with the slot on the pump driveshaft.
24 Refit the pump retaining bolts, and tighten to the specified torque.
25 Refit the exhaust pressure sensor to the mounting bracket.
26 Refit the air duct between the inlet manifold and the intercooler.

27 Place the cooling system expansion tank back in position and secure with the two retaining bolts.
28 Reconnect the battery negative terminal, then refit the engine top cover.

2.5 litre engines

Note: *The vacuum pump and the fuel injection system fuel pump are combined in one unit, termed a 'tandem pump'.*

Removal

29 Unclip and remove the engine top cover.
30 Disconnect the battery negative terminal (refer to *Disconnecting the battery*).
31 Leaving the coolant hoses connected, undo the two bolts and move the cooling system expansion tank to one side.
32 Remove the air duct between the inlet manifold and the intercooler.
33 Release the quick-release fitting and disconnect the brake servo vacuum pipe from the tandem pump **(see illustration)**.
34 Release the retaining clip and disconnect the upper fuel hose from the pump **(see illustration 20.33)**. Be prepared for fuel spillage.
35 Release the quick-release fitting and disconnect the lower fuel hose from the pump **(see illustration 20.33)**.
36 Unscrew the three retaining bolts and remove the tandem pump from the cylinder head. There are no serviceable parts within the tandem pump. If the pump is faulty, it must be renewed.

Refitting

37 Place a new gasket on the pump, then locate the pump on the cylinder head **(see illustration)**. Ensure that the pump pinion engages correctly with the drive slot in the camshaft
38 Refit the pump retaining bolts, and tighten them to the specified torque.
39 Re-attach the two fuel hoses and brake servo vacuum pipe to the pump.

40 Refit the air duct between the inlet manifold and the intercooler.
41 Place the cooling system expansion tank back in position and secure with the two retaining bolts.
42 Reconnect the battery negative terminal, then refit the engine top cover.

21 Anti-lock braking system (ABS) –
general information

Note: *On models equipped with traction control, the ABS unit is a dual function unit, controlling both the anti-lock braking system (ABS) and the electronic differential locking (EDL) and/or electronic stability program (ESP) system functions.*

ABS is fitted as standard equipment on all models covered in this manual. The system comprises a hydraulic modulator and electronic control unit together with four wheel speed sensors. The hydraulic modulator contains the electronic control unit (ECU), the hydraulic solenoid valves (one set for each brake) and the electrically-driven pump. The purpose of the system is to prevent the wheel(s) locking during heavy braking. This is

20.37 Place a new gasket on the tandem pump – 2.5 litre engines

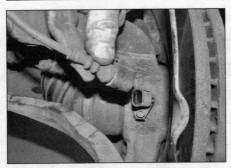

22.4 Disconnect the wheel speed sensor wiring connector

achieved by automatic release of the brake on the relevant wheel, followed by re-application of the brake.

The solenoid valves are controlled by the ECU, which itself receives signals from the four wheel speed sensors which monitor the speed of rotation of each wheel. By comparing these signals, the ECU can determine the speed at which the vehicle is travelling. It can then use this speed to determine when a wheel is decelerating at an abnormal rate, compared to the speed of the vehicle, and therefore predicts when a wheel is about to lock. During normal operation, the system functions in the same way as a conventional braking system.

If the ECU senses that a wheel is about to lock, it operates the relevant solenoid valve(s) in the hydraulic unit, which then isolates from the master cylinder the relevant brake(s) on the wheel(s) which is/are about to lock, effectively sealing-in the hydraulic pressure.

If the speed of rotation of the wheel continues to decrease at an abnormal rate, the ECU operates the electrically-driven pump which pumps the hydraulic fluid back into the master cylinder, releasing the brake. Once the speed of rotation of the wheel returns to an acceptable rate, the pump stops, and the solenoid valves switch again, allowing the hydraulic master cylinder pressure to return to the caliper, which then re-applies the brake. This cycle can be carried out many times a second.

The action of the solenoid valves and return pump creates pulses in the hydraulic circuit. When the ABS system is functioning, these pulses can be felt through the brake pedal.

On models with traction control, the ABS hydraulic modulator incorporates an additional set of solenoid valves which operate the traction control system. The system operates using the signals supplied by the wheel speed sensors. If the ECU senses that a driving wheel is about to lose traction, the ECU communicates with the engine management ECU which will reduce engine power. In severe cases of traction loss the ABS ECU will momentarily apply the relevant front brake to assist with traction recovery.

The electronic stability program (ESP) is a further development of ABS and traction control. Using additional sensors to monitor steering wheel position, vehicle yaw rate, acceleration and deceleration, in conjunction with the ABS sensors, the ECU can intervene under conditions of vehicle instability. Using the signals from the various sensors, the ECU can determine driver intent (steering wheel position, throttle position, vehicle speed and engine speed). From the sensor inputs from the wheel speed sensors, yaw rate sensors and acceleration sensors the ECU can calculate whether the vehicle is responding to driver input, or whether an unstable driving situation is occurring. If instability is detected, the ECU will intervene by applying or releasing the relevant front or rear brake, in conjunction with a power reduction, until vehicle stability returns.

The operation of the ABS system is entirely dependent on electrical signals. To prevent the system responding to any inaccurate signals, a built-in safety circuit monitors all signals received by the ECU. If an inaccurate signal or low battery voltage is detected, the ABS system is automatically shut down, and the warning light on the instrument panel is illuminated, to inform the driver that the ABS system is not operational. Normal braking should still be available, however.

If a fault does develop in the ABS system, the vehicle must be taken to a VW dealer or diagnostic specialist for fault diagnosis and repair.

22 Anti-lock braking system (ABS) components – removal and refitting

Hydraulic modulator unit

1 Removal and refitting of the hydraulic modulator unit is best entrusted to a VW dealer. It is positioned in the left-hand rear corner of the engine compartment, behind the battery. If the fluid is lost from the hydraulic unit, there is no guarantee that the unit can be sufficiently filled or the fluid bled through the unit. Also a fault diagnosis check must be performed on completion using specialist equipment.

Electronic control unit (ECU)

2 The ECU is mounted on the hydraulic modulator unit, secured by Torx screws. Although it can be separated from the hydraulic unit, due to the delicacy of the components and the need for absolute cleanliness, it is recommended that the work be entrusted to a VW dealer. See hydraulic modulator unit information in paragraph 1.

Front wheel speed sensor

Removal

3 Firmly apply the handbrake, then jack up the front of the vehicle and support it securely on axle stands (see *Jacking and vehicle support*). Remove the relevant front roadwheel.
4 Disconnect the wiring connector at the wheel speed sensor **(see illustration)**.
5 Slacken and remove the bolt securing the sensor to the swivel hub, and remove the sensor from the vehicle.

Refitting

6 Prior to refitting, apply a thin coat of multi-purpose grease to the sensor body (VW recommend the use of polycarbamide grease – available from VW dealers).
7 Ensure that the sensor and swivel hub sealing faces are clean, then fit the sensor to the hub. Refit the retaining bolt and tighten it to the specified torque. Reconnect the sensor wiring connector.
8 Refit the roadwheel, then lower the vehicle to the ground and tighten the roadwheel bolts to the specified torque.

Rear wheel speed sensor

Removal

9 Chock the front wheels, then jack up the rear of the vehicle, and support it securely on axle stands (see *Jacking and vehicle support*). Remove the relevant rear roadwheel.
10 Remove the sensor as described above in paragraphs 4 and 5.

Refitting

11 Refit the sensor as described above in paragraphs 6 to 8.

Chapter 10
Suspension and steering

Contents

Degrees of difficulty

Easy, suitable for novice with little experience | **Fairly easy,** suitable for beginner with some experience | **Fairly difficult,** suitable for competent DIY mechanic | **Difficult,** suitable for experienced DIY mechanic | **Very difficult,** suitable for expert DIY or professional

Specifications

Front suspension
Type . . . . Independent, with MacPherson struts incorporating coil springs and telescopic shock absorbers. Anti-roll bar fitted to all models

Rear suspension
Type . . . . Independent with trailing arms, coil springs and telescopic shock absorbers. Anti-roll bar fitted to all models.

Steering
Type . . . . Hydraulic power-assisted rack and pinion
Power steering fluid type . . . . See *Lubricants and fluids* on page 0•18

Torque wrench settings

	Nm	lbf ft
Front suspension		
Anti-roll bar clamp bolts.	110	81
Anti-roll bar connecting link nuts:*		
Stage 1	60	44
Stage 2	Angle-tighten through a further 45°	
Brake caliper mounting bracket bolts:		
Stage 1	180	133
Stage 2	Angle-tighten through a further 45°	
Driveshaft retaining nut:*		
Stage 1	200	148
Stage 2	Slacken by 180°	
Stage 3	200	148
Front engine/transmission mounting-to-subframe bolts:*		
Stage 1	20	15
Stage 2	Angle-tighten a further 90°	
Front engine/transmission mounting bracket bolts:*		
Stage 1	50	37
Stage 2	Angle-tighten a further 90°	
Front engine/transmission mounting through-bolt:*		
Stage 1	90	66
Stage 2	Angle-tighten a further 180°	
Lower arm mounting bolts:*		
Stage 1	110	81
Stage 2	Angle-tighten a further 120°	
Rear engine/transmission mounting bracket to mounting:*		
Stage 1	50	37
Stage 2	Angle-tighten a further 180°	
Subframe mounting bolts:*		
Stage 1	150	111
Stage 2	Angle-tighten a further 180°	
Suspension strut piston nut	80	59
Suspension strut upper mounting nut	80	59
Suspension strut-to-swivel hub clamp bolt nuts:*		
Vehicles up to 3000 kg gross weight:		
Stage 1	75	55
Stage 2	Angle-tighten a further 180°	
Vehicles over to 3000 kg gross weight:		
Stage 1	150	111
Stage 2	Angle-tighten a further 90°	
Swivel hub balljoint-to-suspension lower arm:*		
Stage 1	60	44
Stage 2	Angle-tighten a further 90°	
Swivel hub balljoint-to-swivel hub:*		
Stage 1	90	66
Stage 2	Angle-tighten a further 45°	
Rear suspension		
Anti-roll bar-to-trailing arm clamp bolts	30	22
Anti-roll bar to underbody bracket clamp bolts	60	44
Shock absorber lower mounting bolt nut:*		
Stage 1	120	89
Stage 2	Angle-tighten a further 180°	
Shock absorber upper mounting bolt:*		
Stage 1	80	59
Stage 2	Angle-tighten a further 90°	
Trailing arm inner mounting bolt nut:*		
Stage 1	100	74
Stage 2	Angle-tighten a further 180°	
Trailing arm outer mounting bolt nut:*		
Stage 1	120	89
Stage 2	Angle-tighten a further 180°	
Steering		
Air conditioning compressor mounting bolts	45	33
Intermediate shaft-to-steering gear pinion clamp bolt nut:*		
Stage 1	20	15
Stage 2	Angle-tighten a further 90°	

Torque wrench settings (continued)

	Nm	lbf ft
Steering (continued)		
Power steering pump mounting bolts:		
1.9 and 2.0 litre engines	25	18
2.5 litre engines:*		
Stage 1	40	30
Stage 2	Angle-tighten a further 45°	
Stage 3	Angle-tighten a further 45°	
Power steering pump pulley bolts	25	18
Power steering pump hydraulic banjo union bolts	35	26
Power steering pump pressure pipe flange union bolts	10	7
Steering column shaft-to-intermediate shaft clamp bolt nut:*		
Stage 1	20	15
Stage 2	Angle-tighten a further 90°	
Steering column mounting bolts	20	15
Steering gear hydraulic pipe union nuts	33	24
Steering gear-to-front subframe:*		
Stage 1	33	24
Stage 2	Angle-tighten a further 90°	
Steering wheel retaining bolt	50	37
Track rod end balljoint nut:*		
Stage 1	60	44
Stage 2	Angle-tighten a further 90°	
Roadwheels		
Roadwheel bolts	180	133

Use new nuts/bolts

1 General information

The independent front suspension is of the MacPherson strut type, incorporating coil springs and integral telescopic shock absorbers. The struts are located by transverse lower arms, which are attached to the front subframe via rubber bushes at their inner ends, and incorporate a balljoint at their outer ends. The swivel hubs, which carry the hub bearings, brake calipers and the hub/disc assemblies, are attached to the MacPherson struts by clamp bolts, and connected to the lower arms through the balljoints. A front anti-roll bar is fitted to all models,

TOOL TIP

A tool to hold the wheel hub stationary whilst the driveshaft retaining bolt is slackened can be fabricated from two lengths of steel strip (one long, one short) and a nut and bolt; the nut and bolt forming the pivot of a forked tool.

and is attached to the subframe and to the MacPherson struts via connecting links.

The rear suspension is also independent by means of two trailing arms attached to the underbody via rubber pivot bushes. The trailing arms contain the rear brake assemblies and rear hub bearings. Springing and damping is by means of coil springs and telescopic shock absorbers. An anti-roll bar is fitted to all models.

The steering column incorporates an upper steering shaft containing a universal joint at its lower end. An intermediate shaft is connected to the steering column shaft universal joint and to the steering gear pinion shaft by means of a further universal joint. The steering column is adjustable for height and reach.

Hydraulic power steering is fitted to all models. On 1.9 and 2.0 litre engines, the power steering pump is belt-driven from the crankshaft pulley. On 2.5 litre engines, the power steering pump is gear-driven from the engine geartrain at the flywheel/driveplate end of the engine.

2.3 Attach the holding tool to the wheel hub using two wheel bolts

2 Front swivel hub – removal and refitting

Removal

1 Firmly apply the handbrake, then jack up the front of the vehicle and support it securely on axle stands (see *Jacking and vehicle support*). Remove the relevant front roadwheel.

2 Where fitted, undo the retaining bolts and remove the engine undertray.

3 To prevent rotation of the wheel hub as the driveshaft retaining nut is slackened, make up a holding tool and attach the tool to the wheel hub using two wheel bolts **(see Tool Tip and illustration)**.

4 With the holding tool in place, slacken and remove the driveshaft retaining nut using a socket and long bar **(see illustration)**. Where necessary, support the socket on an axle stand to prevent it slipping off the nut. This

2.4 Removing the driveshaft retaining nut

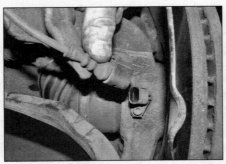

2.5a Disconnect the wiring connector at the ABS wheel speed sensor...

2.5b ...then release the wiring from the retainers on the suspension strut

2.6 Release the brake hydraulic hose grommet from the retainer on the suspension strut

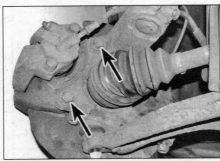

2.7a Undo the two brake caliper mounting bracket retaining bolts (arrowed)...

2.7b ...then remove the brake caliper complete with disc pads and mounting bracket...

2.7c ...and support it on an axle stand

2.8a Undo the retaining nut...

2.8b ...then disconnect the steering track rod end from the swivel hub using a universal balljoint separator tool

nut is very tight; make sure that there is no risk of pulling the vehicle off the axle stands as the nut is slackened. Note that a new nut will be required for refitting.

5 Disconnect the wiring connector at the ABS wheel speed sensor and, where applicable, at the brake pad wear sensor wiring connector. Release the wiring from the retainers on the suspension strut **(see illustrations)**.

6 Release the brake hydraulic hose grommet from the retainer on the suspension strut **(see illustration)**.

7 Unbolt and remove the front brake caliper complete with disc pads and mounting bracket and support it on an axle stand **(see illustrations)**. Do not allow the caliper to hang unsupported from the flexible brake hose.

8 Undo the retaining nut then disconnect the steering track rod end balljoint from the swivel hub using a universal balljoint separator tool **(see illustrations)**.

9 Undo the nut securing the swivel hub balljoint to the front suspension lower arm **(see illustration)**. Note that a new nut will be required for refitting. Release the balljoint from the lower arm using a universal balljoint separator tool.

10 Using a suitable lever, push down on the suspension lower arm and disengage the balljoint shank from the arm **(see illustration)**. Move the swivel hub to one side taking care not to damage the balljoint

2.9 Undo the nut securing the swivel hub balljoint to the front suspension lower arm

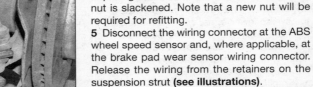

2.10 Push down on the lower arm and disengage the balljoint shank from the arm

rubber boot. It is advisable to place a protective cover over the rubber boot such as the plastic cap from an aerosol can, suitably cut to fit.

11 Carefully pull the swivel hub assembly outwards, and withdraw the driveshaft outer constant velocity joint from the hub assembly **(see illustration)**. The outer joint may be very tight, if so tap the joint out of the hub using a soft-faced mallet. If this fails to free it from the hub, the joint will have to be pressed out using a suitable tool which is bolted to the hub.

12 Remove the securing screw and withdraw the disc from the hub **(see illustration)**.

13 Undo the three retaining bolts and remove the brake backplate from the swivel hub.

14 Undo the two nuts and remove the two clamp bolts securing the swivel hub to the suspension strut **(see illustration)**. Note that new nuts and bolts will be required for refitting.

15 The swivel hub must now be released from the strut. To do this, VW technicians insert a special tool into the split in the swivel hub, and turn it through 90° to open up the clamp. A similar tool can be made out of an old screwdriver, or alternatively a suitable cold chisel can be driven into the split as a wedge. Slightly press inwards the top of the swivel hub, and then push it downwards from the bottom of the strut **(see illustration)**.

Refitting

16 Engage the swivel hub with the bottom of the suspension strut; making sure that the hole in the side plate aligns with the holes in the split housing. Remove the tool used to open the split.

17 Insert the new swivel hub-to-suspension strut clamp bolts with their bolt heads toward the rear of the vehicle. Fit the two new nuts and tighten them to the specified torque, then through the specified angle.

18 Ensure that the driveshaft outer joint and hub splines are clean and dry. Manoeuvre the driveshaft into position, and engage the outer joint with the hub. Ensure that the threads are clean, and apply a smear of oil to the contact face of the new driveshaft retaining nut. Fit the nut and use it to draw the joint fully into position.

19 Lever the suspension lower arm downwards and engage the balljoint shank with the arm. Fit the new retaining nut to the balljoint and tighten it to the specified torque, then through the specified angle.

20 Locate the track rod end balljoint on the steering arm. Screw on a new nut and tighten it to the specified torque. If the balljoint shank is hollow, a 5 mm Allen key can be used to prevent the balljoint from rotating as the nut is tightened. If the shank is solid, use a stout bar to lever down on the top of the track rod end. This will lock the balljoint shank taper in the steering arm and prevent rotation as the nut is tightened.

2.11 Pull the swivel hub outwards, and withdraw the driveshaft constant velocity joint from the hub assembly

2.14 Undo the nuts and remove the two clamp bolts (arrowed) securing the swivel hub to the suspension strut

21 Using the method employed on removal to prevent the hub from rotating, and tighten the driveshaft retaining nut to the specified torque setting. Check that the hub rotates freely.

22 Refit the brake backplate and tighten the retaining bolts securely.

23 Thoroughly clean the mating surfaces of the brake disc and hub flange ensuring that all traces of dirt and corrosion are removed.

24 Place the disc in position on the hub flange, then refit the retaining screw and tighten it securely.

25 Slide the brake caliper assembly over the disc and into position on the swivel hub. Refit the two mounting bracket retaining bolts and tighten them to the specified torque, then through the specified angle.

26 Refit the brake hydraulic hose grommet to the retainer on the suspension strut.

27 Reconnect the wiring connector at the ABS wheel speed sensor and, where applicable, at the brake pad wear sensor wiring connector. Refit the wiring to the retainers on the suspension strut.

28 Where applicable, refit the engine undertray.

29 Refit the roadwheel, lower the vehicle to the ground, and tighten the wheel bolts to the specified torque.

30 It is advisable to have the front wheel alignment checked and, if necessary, adjusted at the earliest opportunity (see Section 24).

2.12 Remove the securing screw and withdraw the disc from the hub

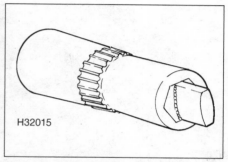

H32015

2.15 Tool used by VW technicians to open up the split in the swivel hub

3 Front hub bearing renewal – general information

The front hub bearings incorporate the wheel hub flanges as a sealed assembly and are an interference fit in the swivel hubs. Once the bearings are removed from the swivel hub they must be renewed as the removal process renders the bearing unserviceable.

Hub bearing renewal entails the use of VW special tools or commercially available alternatives. The design of the hub and bearing assembly is such that conventional bearing pullers or a hydraulic press are not suitable. Any attempt to renew the hub bearing assembly without special tools specifically designed for this purpose is likely to damage the new (and very expensive) bearing.

The cost of purchasing the special tools necessary for bearing renewal makes this an uneconomic option although it may be possible to borrow or hire them. If the special tools can be obtained the actual renewal procedure is relatively straightforward bearing in mind the problems likely to be encountered due to age and corrosion. Follow the tool manufacturer's instructions for the actual bearing renewal procedure.

If the special tools are not available it will be necessary to entrust the work to a VW dealer or suitably equipped independent garage. Financially, this may ultimately prove to be the best option anyway.

4.2 Undo the two retaining bolts and remove the plenum chamber side cover

4.3 Unscrew the nut and disconnect the anti-roll bar connecting link from the suspension strut

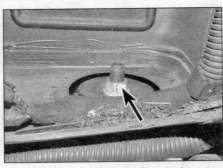

4.5 Unscrew the suspension strut upper mounting nut (arrowed)

4.6 Lower the suspension strut and withdraw it from under the front wing

4.9 Fit a spring compressor tool, and compress the coil spring to relieve the pressure on the spring seats

4 Front suspension strut – removal, overhaul and refitting

Removal

1 Remove the plenum chamber cover as described in Chapter 11, Section 25.

2 Undo the two retaining bolts and remove the plenum chamber side cover on the side being worked on (see illustration).

3 Unscrew the nut and disconnect the anti-roll bar connecting link from the strut. Use a suitable Torx key inserted into the link to hold the link while the nut is being loosened (see illustration).

4 Carry out the operations described in paragraphs 1 to 11 in Section 2.

5 Engage the help of an assistant to support the strut beneath the front wing. From within the engine compartment, lift off the plastic cap (if fitted) and unscrew the strut upper mounting nut (see illustration). Note that a new nut will be required for refitting.

6 Lift off the upper mounting plate, then lower the strut and withdraw it from under the front wing (see illustration).

7 To separate the strut from the swivel

hub, undo the two nuts and remove the two clamp bolts securing the swivel hub to the suspension strut. Note that new nuts and bolts will be required for refitting.

8 The swivel hub must now be released from the strut. To do this, VW technicians insert a special tool into the split in the swivel hub, and turn it through 90° to open up the clamp. A similar tool can be made out of an old screwdriver, or alternatively a suitable cold chisel can be driven into the split as a wedge. Slightly press inwards the top of the swivel hub, and then push it downwards from the bottom of the strut (see illustration 2.15).

4.10 With the coil spring compressed, unscrew the strut piston nut

Overhaul

Note: *A spring compressor tool will be required for this operation. Before overhaul, mark the position of each component in relationship with each other for reassembly.*

9 With the suspension strut resting on a bench, or clamped in a vice, fit a spring compressor tool, and compress the coil spring to relieve the pressure on the spring seats (see illustration). Ensure that the compressor tool is securely located on the spring, in accordance with the tool manufacturer's instructions.

10 Mark the position of the spring relative to the top and bottom mountings, then counter-hold the strut piston rod with a Torx key or suitable bit, and unscrew the strut piston nut (see illustration).

11 Remove the strut upper mounting, upper spring seat together with the bump stop and support ring, thrust bearing with rubber gaiter and the spring (see illustrations).

12 With the strut assembly now completely dismantled, examine all the components for wear, damage or deformation. Renew any of the components as necessary.

13 Examine the strut for signs of fluid leakage. Check the strut piston for signs of pitting along its entire length, and check the

strut body for signs of damage. While holding it in an upright position, test the operation of the strut by moving the piston through a full stroke, and then through short strokes of 50 to 100 mm. In both cases, the resistance felt should be smooth and continuous. If the resistance is jerky or uneven or if there is any visible sign of wear or damage to the strut, renewal is necessary.

14 If any doubt exists as to the condition of the coil spring, carefully remove the spring compressors and check the spring for distortion and signs of cracking. Renew the spring if it is damaged or distorted, or if there is any doubt as to its condition.

15 Inspect all other components for damage or deterioration, and renew any that are suspect.

16 Begin reassembly by placing the spring in position on the strut, ensuring that the end of the spring locates against the stop on the spring seat with the side of the lower coil against the raised projection on the spring seat (see illustrations).

17 Engage the upper edge of the rubber gaiter with the thrust bearing, then fit the gaiter and thrust bearing to the strut (see illustration).

18 Fit the bump stop to the support ring, then fit the support ring to the upper spring seat (see illustrations). Locate this assembly over the strut piston and against the thrust bearing.

19 Screw on the piston nut and tighten the nut to the specified torque while counterholding the strut piston (see illustration).

4.11a Remove the strut upper mounting...

4.11b ...upper spring seat together with the bump stop and support ring...

4.11c ...thrust bearing with rubber gaiter...

4.11d ...and the spring

20 Slowly slacken the spring compressor tool to relieve the tension in the spring. Check that the end of the spring locates correctly against the stop on the lower spring seat. If necessary,

turn the spring so that it locates correctly before the compressor tool is completely slackened. Remove the compressor tool when the spring is fully seated.

4.16a Place the spring in position ensuring that the end of the spring locates against the stop (arrowed) on the spring seat...

4.16b ...with the side of the lower coil against the raised projection (arrowed) on the spring seat

4.17 Engage the upper edge of the gaiter with the thrust bearing, then fit the gaiter and thrust bearing to the strut

4.18a Fit the bump stop to the support ring...

4.18b ...then fit the support ring to the upper spring seat

4.19 Tighten the piston nut to the specified torque while counterholding the strut piston

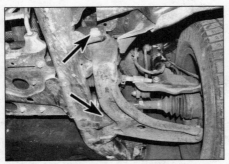

5.6 Lower arm front and rear mounting bolts (arrowed)

21 Engage the swivel hub with the bottom of the suspension strut; making sure that the hole in the side plate aligns with the holes in the split housing. Remove the tool used to open the split.

22 Insert the new swivel hub-to-suspension strut clamp bolts with their bolt heads toward the rear of the vehicle. Fit the two new nuts and tighten them to the specified torque, then through the specified angle.

Refitting

23 Locate the strut in position under the front wing and place the upper mounting plate in position. Fit the new upper mounting nut and tighten it to the specified torque. Where applicable, refit the plastic cap.

24 Ensure that the driveshaft outer joint and hub splines are clean and dry. Manoeuvre the driveshaft into position, and engage the outer joint with the hub. Ensure that the threads are clean, and apply a smear of oil to the contact face of the new driveshaft retaining nut. Fit the nut and use it to draw the joint fully into position.

25 Lever the suspension lower arm downwards and engage the balljoint shank with the arm. Fit the new retaining nut to the balljoint and tighten it to the specified torque, then through the specified angle.

26 Locate the track rod end balljoint on the steering arm. Screw on a new nut and tighten it to the specified torque. If the balljoint shank is hollow, a 5 mm Allen key can be used to prevent the balljoint from rotating as the nut is tightened. If the shank is solid, use a stout bar to lever down on the top of the track rod end.

6.2 Cut off the bush shoulder from the front facing side of the bush

This will lock the balljoint shank taper in the steering arm and prevent rotation as the nut is tightened.

27 Using the method employed on removal to prevent the hub from rotating, and tighten the driveshaft retaining nut to the specified torque setting. Check that the hub rotates freely.

28 Refit the anti-roll bar connecting link to the strut and use a Torx key to hold the link while tightening the nut to the specified torque.

29 Slide the brake caliper assembly over the disc and into position on the swivel hub. Refit the two mounting bracket retaining bolts and tighten them to the specified torque.

30 Refit the brake hydraulic hose grommet to the retainer on the suspension strut.

31 Reconnect the wiring connector at the ABS wheel speed sensor and, where applicable, at the brake pad wear sensor wiring connector. Refit the wiring to the retainers on the suspension strut.

32 Where applicable, refit the engine undertray.

33 Refit the roadwheel, lower the vehicle to the ground, and tighten the wheel bolts to the specified torque.

34 Refit the plenum chamber side cover and secure with the two retaining bolts.

35 Refit the plenum chamber cover as described in Chapter 11, Section 25.

36 It is advisable to have the front wheel alignment checked and, if necessary, adjusted at the earliest opportunity (see Section 24).

5 Front lower arm – removal and refitting

Removal

1 Before starting work, measure and record the distance from the centre of the front hub to the upper edge of the wheel arch. When refitting the lower arm, this dimension will be used to position the arm prior to tightening the mounting bolt nuts.

2 Firmly apply the handbrake, then jack up the front of the vehicle and support it securely on axle stands (see *Jacking and vehicle support*). Remove the relevant front roadwheel.

3 Where fitted, undo the retaining bolts and remove the engine undertray.

4 Undo the nut securing the swivel hub balljoint to the front lower arm **(see illustration 2.9)**. Release the balljoint from the lower arm using a universal balljoint separator tool.

5 Using a suitable lever, push down on the lower arm and disengage the balljoint shank from the arm **(see illustration 2.10)**. Move the swivel hub to one side taking care not to damage the balljoint rubber boot. It is advisable to place a protective cover over the rubber boot such as the plastic cap from an aerosol can, suitably cut to fit.

6 Undo the retaining nuts and remove the lower arm front and rear mounting bolts **(see**

illustration). Note that new nuts and new bolts will be required for refitting.

7 Disengage the lower arm mounting bushes from their locations in the subframe and remove the arm from the vehicle.

8 Thoroughly clean the lower arm and the area around the mounting locations on the subframe, removing all traces of dirt and underseal. Check carefully for cracks, distortion or any other signs of wear or damage, paying particular attention to the mounting bushes. If required, the bushes can be renewed as described in Section 6.

Refitting

9 Place the lower arm in position in the subframe and insert the new front and rear mounting bolts with their bolt heads toward the rear of the vehicle. Fit the new retaining nuts to the bolts, but only tighten the nuts finger tight at this stage.

10 Lever the lower arm downwards and engage the balljoint shank with the arm. Fit the new retaining nut to the balljoint and tighten it to the specified torque, then through the specified angle.

11 Before finally tightening the lower arm mounting bolt nuts, the arm must be raised to the normal ride height position, which is the dimension measured prior to removal. Using a trolley jack positioned beneath the lower balljoint, raise the arm until it is in the normal ride height position.

12 With the lower arm correctly positioned, tighten the front and rear mounting bolt nuts to the specified torque, then through the specified angle. Remove the jack from beneath the lower balljoint.

13 Where applicable, refit the engine undertray.

14 Refit the roadwheel, lower the vehicle to the ground, and tighten the wheel bolts to the specified torque.

15 It is advisable to have the front wheel alignment checked and, if necessary, adjusted at the earliest opportunity (see Section 24).

6 Front lower arm mounting bushes – renewal

Note: *A press will be required to renew the front and rear mounting bushes.*

Front mounting bush

1 Remove the front lower arm as described in Section 5 and securely mount it in a vice.

2 Using a hacksaw, cut off the bush shoulder from the front facing side of the bush **(see illustration)**.

3 Using a hammer and chisel, bend up the metal lip on the rear facing side of the bush **(see illustration)**. It won't be possible to bend the lip up all the way round as the body of the lower arm is in the way, but bend up as much as is accessible.

6.3 Using a hammer and chisel, bend up the metal lip on the rear facing side of the bush

6.6 Press the wishbone down onto the new front mounting bush

6.10 Support the wishbone on the press bed and press the rear mounting bush out of the wishbone

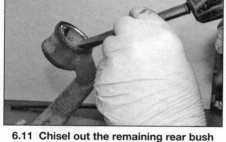

6.11 Chisel out the remaining rear bush metal casing from the wishbone

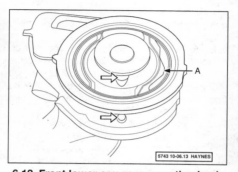

6.13 Front lower arm rear mounting bush fitting details – right-hand side shown

A = Larger kidney shaped recess
Arrows indicate markings on the bush and lower arm which must be aligned

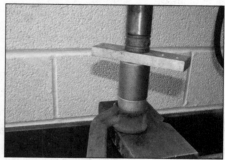

6.14 Align the positioning marks and press the bush into the wishbone using suitable mandrels

4 Support the rear facing side of the bush location in the lower arm on the press bed. Using suitable mandrels, press the mounting bush out of the arm.

5 Thoroughly clean the bush location in the lower arm, removing all traces of dirt and grease. Polish away any burrs or raised edges which might hinder fitment of the new bush.

6 Lubricate the new bush with liquid soap then place it in position on the pressbed with the metal casing downward. Using a hollow tube or mandrel in contact with the lower arm, press the arm down onto the bush up to the metal collar (see illustration).

7 Lift up the lower arm and place a small nut under the metal centre sleeve of the bush, then position this arrangement back on the pressbed. Again using the hollow tube or mandrel, continue pressing the lower arm onto the bush until the shoulder on the bush pops out of the arm.

8 On completion, refit the lower arm as described in Section 5.

Rear mounting bush

9 Remove the front lower arm as described in Section 5.

10 Support the front facing side of the bush location in the lower arm on the press bed. Using suitable mandrels, press the mounting bush out of the arm (see illustration).

11 It is quite likely that the centre rubber portion of the bush will press out leaving

the metal casing still in the lower arm. If this happens, chisel out the remaining metal casing, taking care not to damage the bush location in the arm (see illustration).

12 Thoroughly clean the bush location in the lower arm, removing all traces of dirt and grease. Polish away any burrs or raised edges which might hinder fitment of the new bush.

13 In the lower arm's fitted position, the larger kidney shaped recess in the rubber must be toward the centre of the vehicle and the markings on the bush and lower arm must align (see illustration).

14 Support the front facing side of the bush location in the lower arm on the press bed. Place the new bush in position as described in paragraph 13 and press the bush into the arm using suitable mandrels (see illustration).

15 On completion, refit the lower arm as described in Section 5.

7 Swivel hub balljoint – renewal

1 Firmly apply the handbrake, then jack up the front of the vehicle and support it securely on axle stands (see *Jacking and vehicle support*). Remove the relevant front roadwheel.

2 Undo the two bolts securing the balljoint to the swivel hub (see illustration). Note that new bolts will be required for refitting.

Disengage the balljoint from the base of the swivel hub then move the swivel hub slightly to one side.

3 Undo the nut securing the balljoint to the front suspension lower arm. Note that a new nut will be required for refitting. Release the balljoint from the lower arm using a universal balljoint separator tool.

4 Clean the balljoint locating area in the swivel hub and lower arm and remove any burrs that might hinder refitting.

5 Fit the balljoint to the lower arm and fit the new retaining nut. Tighten the nut to the specified torque then tighten it further through the specified angle. If necessary use an Allen key inserted in the joint shank to prevent rotation as the nut is tightened.

7.2 Swivel hub balljoint retaining bolts (arrowed)

6 Engage the balljoint with the swivel hub, fit the new retaining bolts, and tighten them to the specified torque, then through the specified angle.

7 Refit the roadwheel, lower the vehicle to the ground, and tighten the wheel bolts to the specified torque.

8 Front anti-roll bar – removal and refitting

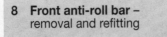

Removal

1 Firmly apply the handbrake, then jack up the front of the vehicle and support it securely on axle stands (see *Jacking and vehicle support*). Remove the front roadwheels.

2 Where fitted, undo the retaining bolts and remove the engine undertray.

3 Where fitted, undo the nut and two bolts and remove the wheel arch liner lower trim on each side.

4 Unscrew the nut and disconnect the connecting link from the anti-roll bar. Use a suitable Torx key inserted into the link to hold the link while the nut is being loosened. Note that a new nut will be required for refitting.

5 Unscrew the bolts securing the anti-roll bar clamps to the subframe. Mark the anti-roll bar to indicate which way round it is fitted, and the position of the rubber mounting bushes; this will aid refitting.

6 Manipulate the anti-roll bar sideways and remove it from under the wheel arch.

7 Carefully examine the anti-roll bar components for signs of wear, damage or deterioration, paying particular attention to the rubber mounting bushes. Renew worn components as necessary.

Refitting

8 Refitting is a reversal of removal, but tighten all nuts and bolts to the specified torque.

9 Front subframe – removal and refitting

Removal

1 Firmly apply the handbrake, then jack up the front of the vehicle and support it securely on axle stands (see *Jacking and vehicle support*). Remove the front roadwheels.

2 Where fitted, undo the retaining bolts and remove the engine undertray.

3 Undo the front engine/transmission mounting through-bolt. Undo the two bolts securing the mounting to the subframe and remove the mounting. Note that new bolts will be required for refitting.

4 Undo the nut and remove the bolt securing the rear engine/transmission mounting bracket to the mounting.

5 Undo the retaining nuts and remove the two bolts securing the steering gear assembly to

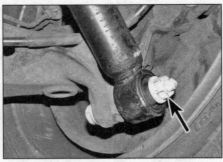

11.4 Rear shock absorber lower mounting bolt nut (arrowed)

the subframe. Suitably secure the steering gear assembly to the underbody on both sides.

6 Undo the nuts securing the swivel hub balljoints to the front suspension lower arms on each side. Note that new nuts will be required for refitting. Release the balljoints from the lower arms using a universal balljoint separator tool.

7 Undo the bolts securing the exhaust system support bracket to the subframe.

8 According to engine type and equipment fitted, release all remaining pipes, hoses, wiring and brackets from their subframe attachments.

9 Support the subframe with a cradle across a trolley jack. Alternatively, two trolley jacks and the help of an assistant will be required.

10 Accurately mark the fitted position of the subframe and underbody or alternatively (and preferably) use the VW locating pins (special tool T10227) to accurately align the subframe when refitting.

11 Undo the two bolts each side securing the subframe to the underbody, then slowly and carefully lower the subframe to the ground. Note that new bolts will be required for refitting. As the subframe is lowered, make sure there are no cables or wiring still attached.

12 If necessary remove the components attached to the subframe with reference to the relevant Sections of this Chapter.

Refitting

13 Refitting is a reversal of removal, but tighten all nuts and bolts to the specified torque and, where applicable, through the specified angle.

10 Rear hub bearing renewal – general information

The rear hub bearings incorporate the wheel hub flanges as a sealed assembly and are identical to the front hub bearings. Refer to the front hub bearing renewal information contained in Section 3 which is equally applicable to the rear bearings.

11 Rear shock absorber – removal and refitting

Note: *Always renew shock absorbers in pairs to maintain good road handling.*

Removal

1 Chock the front wheels then jack up the rear of the vehicle and securely support it on axle stands (see *Jacking and vehicle support*). Remove the rear roadwheel.

2 Using a trolley jack, slightly raise the trailing arm on the relevant side.

3 Unscrew and remove the shock absorber upper mounting bolt. Note that a new bolt will be required for refitting.

4 Unscrew the shock absorber lower mounting bolt nut **(see illustration)**. Withdraw the mounting bolt from the trailing arm and remove the shock absorber from under the wheel arch. Not that a new lower mounting bolt and nut will be required for refitting.

5 To test the shock absorber for efficiency, grip the lower mounting eye in a vice, and then pump the piston repeatedly through its full stroke. If the resistance is weak or is felt to be uneven, the shock absorber is defective and must be renewed. It must also be renewed if it is leaking fluid. It is advisable to renew both front shock absorbers at the same time, or the handling characteristics of the vehicle could be adversely affected.

Refitting

6 Refitting is a reversal of removal, but tighten the new mounting bolts and nut to the specified torque then through the specified angle.

12 Rear coil spring – removal and refitting

Note: *Always renew coil springs in pairs to maintain good handling.*

Removal

1 Chock the front wheels, then jack up the rear of the vehicle, and support it securely on axle stands (see *Jacking and vehicle support*). Remove the relevant rear roadwheel.

2 Remove the rear anti-roll bar as described in Section 15.

3 Position a trolley jack under the trailing arm and raise the arm slightly.

4 Unscrew and remove the shock absorber upper mounting bolt. Note that a new bolt will be required for refitting.

5 Carefully lower the trailing arm until all tension is removed from the coil spring.

6 Remove the coil spring from the underbody and trailing arm, and withdraw it from under the vehicle.

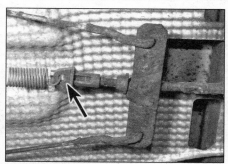

13.3 Detach the handbrake cable return spring from the spring holder (arrowed) on the end of the front cable

Refitting

7 Refitting is a reversal of removal, but note the following points.
  a) *Ensure that the spring locates correctly on the upper and lower seats.*
  b) *Tighten the new shock absorber upper mounting bolt to the specified torque and through the specified angle.*
  c) *Refit the anti-roll bar as described in Section 15.*

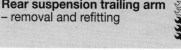

13 Rear suspension trailing arm – removal and refitting

Removal

1 Before starting work, measure and record the distance from the centre of the rear hub to the upper edge of the wheel arch. When refitting the trailing arm, this dimension will be used to position the arm prior to tightening the mounting bolt nuts.
2 Chock the front wheels, then jack up the rear of the vehicle, and support it securely on axle stands (see *Jacking and vehicle support*). Remove the relevant rear roadwheel.
3 Detach the handbrake cable return spring from the spring holder on the end of the front cable, then unscrew the spring holder from the cable **(see illustration)**.
4 Unscrew the handbrake adjusting nut and remove it from the end of the front cable.
5 Disengage the relevant handbrake inner cable from the compensator.
6 Depress the tabs on the handbrake outer cable end fitting and pull the outer cable out of the support bracket on the underbody **(see illustration)**.
7 Disconnect the wiring connector from the ABS rear wheel speed sensor and release the wiring from the trailing arm.
8 Where applicable, disconnect the brake pad wear sensor wiring at the connector on the underbody.
9 Using a brake hose clamp, clamp the flexible hydraulic hose leading to the trailing arm.
10 Unscrew the union nut and disconnect the rear brake hydraulic pipe from the flexible hose at the support bracket on the trailing

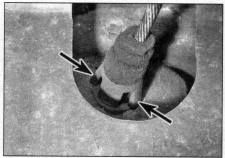

13.6 Depress the tabs (arrowed) and pull the outer handbrake cable out of the support bracket on the underbody

arm. Be prepared for some loss of brake fluid, and plug or tape over the ends of the pipe and hose to prevent the entry of dust and dirt.
11 Extract the retaining clip and release the brake flexible hose from the support bracket on the trailing arm.
12 Remove the rear coil spring as described in Section 12.
13 Mark the fitted position of the eccentric washer fitted to the trailing arm inner mounting bolt, in relation to the mounting bracket **(see illustration)**. The position of the eccentric washer determines the rear wheel toe-setting and it must be refitted in the same position to preserve the setting. The inner mounting bolt itself has an eccentric portion behind the bolt head and this should also be marked in relation to the mounting bracket. A new mounting bolt and nut must be obtained for refitting. The position of the alignment mark on the old bolt can be transferred to the new bolt when refitting.
14 Undo the nuts from the trailing arm inner and outer mounting bolts and collect the eccentric washer from the inner bolt **(see illustrations)**. Suitably support the trailing arm on a trolley jack, then remove the two mounting bolts. Lower the jack and remove the trailing arm from under the vehicle.
15 If necessary, remove the components remaining on the trailing arm with reference to the relevant Chapters of this manual.

Refitting

16 Refitting is a reversal of removal, but note the following points:

13.14a Trailing arm inner mounting bolt nut (arrowed)...

13.13 Mark the fitted position of the trailing arm inner mounting bolt eccentric washer, in relation to the mounting bracket

  a) *Make an alignment mark on the new inner mounting bolt corresponding to the position of the mark on the old bolt.*
  b) *Ensure that the inner mounting bolt and eccentric washer are fitted in the positions marked during removal.*
  c) *Before finally tightening the mounting bolt nuts, the arm must be raised to the normal ride height position, which is the dimension measured prior to removal.*
  d) *Tighten the new mounting bolt nuts to the specified torque, then through the specified angle.*
  e) *Refit the rear coil spring as described in Section 12.*
  f) *Bleed the brake hydraulic system as described in Chapter 9, Section 2.*
  g) *Adjust the handbrake as described in Chapter 9, Section 12.*
  h) *It is advisable to have the rear wheel alignment checked, and if necessary adjusted, at the earliest opportunity.*

14 Rear suspension trailing arm bushes – renewal

Note: *A commercially available bush renewal tool will be required for this operation. The renewal procedure is the same for both the inner and outer bushes.*

1 Remove the relevant trailing arm as described in Section 13.
2 To aid removal of the old bush, cut off the

13.14b ...and outer mounting bolt nut (arrowed)

14.2 Cut off the shoulder from one end of the trailing arm bush

bush shoulder from outer end of the bush **(see illustration)**.

3 Assemble the bush renewal tool over the trailing arm and old bush, then use a suitable socket to drive the bush out of the trailing arm **(see illustration)**.

4 Thoroughly clean the bush location area in the trailing arm and polish away any burrs or raised edges which might hinder fitment of the new bush.

5 Liberally lubricate the trailing arm and the new bush with liquid soap, then locate the bush in the trailing arm. Position the bush so that the mark on the side of the bush casing aligns with the projection on the trailing arm.

6 Assemble the bush renewal tool and push the bush into the arm until the bush shoulder contacts the arm. Using a smaller diameter mandrel or socket in contact with the centre of the bush, push the bush in further until the shoulder on the other end of the bush pops out of the arm.

7 On completion, refit the trailing arm as described in Section 13.

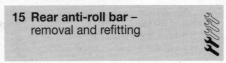

15 Rear anti-roll bar –
removal and refitting

Removal

1 Chock the front wheels, then jack up the rear of the vehicle, and support it securely on axle stands (see *Jacking and vehicle support*).

2 Undo the two bolts each side securing the

15.2 Undo the two bolts (arrowed) each side securing the anti-roll bar clamps to the trailing arms

14.3 Using a bush renewal tool to remove a trailing arm bush

anti-roll bar clamps to the trailing arms and lift off the clamps **(see illustration)**.

3 Suitably support the anti-roll bar and undo the two bolts each side securing the anti-roll bar clamps to the underbody brackets. Lift off the clamps and remove the anti-roll bar from under the vehicle.

4 Carefully examine the anti-roll bar components for signs of wear, damage or deterioration, paying particular attention to the rubber mounting bushes. Renew worn components as necessary.

Refitting

5 Refitting is a reversal of removal, but tighten the clamp bolts to the specified torque.

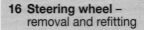

16 Steering wheel –
removal and refitting

 Warning: Make sure that the airbag safety recommendations given in Chapter 12, Section 18 are followed, to prevent personal injury.

Removal

1 Remove the airbag as described in Chapter 12, Section 19.

2 Set the front wheels in the straight-ahead position, then lock the column in position after removing the ignition key.

3 Undo and remove the steering wheel retaining bolt **(see illustration)**.

4 Mark the steering wheel and steering column shaft in relation to each other then

16.3 Undo and remove the steering wheel retaining bolt

lift the steering wheel off the column splines, taking care not to damage the contact unit wiring **(see illustration)**.

Refitting

5 Refitting is a reversal of removal. Align the marks made on removal and tighten the retaining bolt to the specified torque.

17 Ignition switch/
steering column lock –
removal and refitting

Ignition switch

Removal

1 Disconnect the battery negative terminal (refer to *Disconnecting the battery*).

2 Remove the steering wheel as described in Section 16.

3 Remove the steering column shrouds as described in Chapter 11, Section 29.

4 Disconnect the ignition switch wiring connector

5 Remove the locking paint from the switch retaining screw heads, then loosen them slightly and pull out the switch from the steering lock housing.

Refitting

6 Insert the ignition key and turn it to the 'On' position. Also turn the switch to the same position.

7 Carefully insert the switch into the housing, then insert the screws and tighten securely. Lock the screws by applying some paint over their heads and onto the housing.

8 Reconnect the ignition switch wiring connector.

9 Refit the steering column shrouds as described in Chapter 11, Section 29.

10 Refit the steering wheel as described in Section 16.

11 On completion, reconnect the battery negative terminal.

Lock cylinder

Removal

12 Disconnect the battery negative terminal (refer to *Disconnecting the battery*).

16.4 Mark the steering wheel and steering column shaft in relation to each other

13 Remove the steering wheel as described in Section 16.

14 Remove the steering column shrouds as described in Chapter 11, Section 29.

15 Disconnect the wiring connector from the transponder around the ignition switch **(see illustration)**.

16 Insert the ignition key and turn the lock cylinder to the Drive position (which is 90° from the off position).

17 Insert a piece of wire 1.2 mm in diameter in the drilling next to the ignition key, slide it in to release the locking lever, then withdraw the lock cylinder from the housing **(see illustrations)**. To make the piece of wire locate in the locking lever easier, file an angle on the end of the wire.

Refitting

18 Refit the lock cylinder with the ignition key in the Drive position, then remove the wire.

19 Reconnect the wiring connector to the transponder.

20 Refit the steering column shrouds as described in Chapter 11, Section 29.

21 Refit the steering wheel as described in Section 16.

22 On completion, reconnect the battery negative terminal.

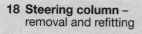

18 Steering column – removal and refitting

Removal

1 Disconnect the battery negative terminal (refer to *Disconnecting the battery*).

2 Set the roadwheels in the straight-ahead position.

3 Release the locking lever and move the steering column fully down and fully out.

4 Remove the steering wheel as described in Section 16.

5 Remove the steering column shrouds and the facia right-hand lower trim panel as described in Chapter 11, Section 29.

6 Remove the steering column switch module as described in Chapter 12, Section 4.

7 Fold up the rubber boot (if fitted) then unscrew the nut and remove the eccentric clamp bolt securing the steering column shaft to the intermediate shaft **(see illustration)**.

8 Undo the two lower steering column mounting bolts **(see illustration)**.

9 Undo the domed nut and disconnect the earth lead from the top of the steering column.

10 Release the cable ties and detach the wiring harness from the steering column.

11 On models with automatic transmission, prise the park lock system cable retaining clip from the ignition switch, and pull the cable from the switch housing.

12 Undo the steering column upper mounting bolts and manipulate the column assembly out from its location **(see illustration)**.

17.15 Disconnect the wiring connector from the transponder around the ignition switch

17.17b Insert a thin rod through the hole...

Refitting

13 Refitting is a reversal of removal, bearing in mind the following points:

a) *Tighten the steering column mounting bolts to the specified torque.*

b) *Connect the steering column shaft to the intermediate shaft using a new retaining nut tightened to the specified torque, then through the specified angle.*

c) *Refit the steering column switch module as described in Chapter 12, Section 4.*

d) *Refit the facia trim panel and steering column shrouds as described in Chapter 11, Section 29.*

e) *Refit the steering wheel as described in Section 16.*

17.17a Hole (arrowed) provided in the ignition switch

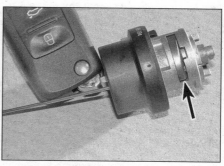

17.17c ...to release the locking lever (arrowed)

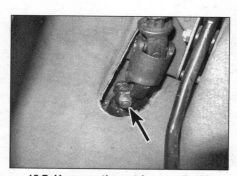

18.7 Unscrew the nut (arrowed) and remove the eccentric clamp bolt securing the steering column shaft to the intermediate shaft

18.8 Steering column lower right-hand retaining bolt (arrowed)

18.12 Steering column upper right-hand retaining bolt (arrowed)

19 Steering gear assembly – removal and refitting

Removal

1 Firmly apply the handbrake, then jack up the front of the vehicle and support it securely on axle stands (see *Jacking and vehicle support*). Remove both front roadwheels.
2 Where fitted, undo the retaining bolts and remove the engine undertray.
3 Undo the retaining nuts then disconnect the steering track rod end balljoints from the swivel hubs using a universal balljoint separator tool **(see illustrations 2.8a and 2.8b)**.
4 Cut off the metal clip securing the intermediate shaft protective rubber boot to the steering gear housing. Note that a new metal clip will be required for refitting.
5 Push the lower end of the protective rubber boot up the intermediate shaft to expose the intermediate shaft universal joint. Retain the rubber boot in this position by sliding a suitable Allen key through the universal joint so that the boot rests on the Allen key.
6 Unscrew the nut and remove the eccentric clamp bolt securing the intermediate shaft universal joint to the steering gear pinion.
7 Remove the front anti-roll bar as described in Section 8.
8 Fit a hose clamp to the fluid return hose leading from the steering gear to the power steering fluid reservoir. Also fit a hose clamp to the power steering pump fluid inlet hose.
9 Mark the unions to ensure that they are correctly positioned on reassembly, then unscrew the feed and return pipe union nuts from the steering gear assembly; be prepared for fluid spillage, and position a suitable container beneath the pipes whilst unscrewing the union nuts. Disconnect both pipes, and recover their sealing rings. Plug the pipe ends and steering gear orifices, to prevent fluid leakage and to keep dirt out of the hydraulic system. Release the pipes from the retaining brackets on the steering gear.
10 Undo the two nuts and remove the bolts securing the steering gear to the front subframe. Note that new nuts and bolts will be required for refitting.
11 Move the steering gear sideways to disengage the steering gear pinion from the intermediate shaft universal joint, then manipulate the steering gear out from its location.

Refitting

12 Refitting is a reversal of removal, but note the following points.
 a) *Tighten all nuts and bolts to the specified torque and, where applicable, through the specified angle.*

 b) *Use new retaining bolts and nuts when attaching the steering gear to the subframe.*
 c) *Use a new retaining nut when connecting the intermediate shaft universal joint to the steering gear pinion.*
 d) *When refitting the intermediate shaft protective rubber boot to the steering gear housing, ensure that the triangular marks on the boot and housing align.*
 e) *Secure the intermediate shaft protective rubber boot using a new metal clip. Remove any slack in the clip by carefully compressing the raised section using a pair of side cutters. Take care not to cut the clip.*
 f) *On completion, bleed the power steering system as described in Section 21.*

20 Steering gear rubber gaiters – renewal

1 Remove the relevant track rod end as described in Section 23.
2 Mark the position of the track rod end lock nut on the track rod and count the number of exposed threads from the nut to the end of the track rod. Unscrew and remove the lock nut.
3 Mark the correct fitted position of the gaiter on the track rod, then release the retaining clip(s) and slide the gaiter off the steering gear housing and track rod.
4 Thoroughly clean the track rod and the steering gear housing, using fine abrasive paper to polish off any corrosion, burrs or sharp edges, which might damage the new gaiter's sealing lips on installation. Scrape off all the grease from the old gaiter, and apply it to the track rod inner balljoint. (This assumes that grease has not been lost or contaminated as a result of damage to the old gaiter. Use fresh grease if in doubt).
5 Carefully slide the new gaiter onto the track rod, and locate it on the steering gear housing. Align the outer edge of the gaiter with the mark made on the track rod prior to removal. Make sure the gaiter is not twisted, then lift the outer sealing lip of the gaiter to equalise air pressure within the gaiter.
6 Secure it in position with new retaining clip(s). Where crimped-type clips are used, pull the clip as tight as possible, and locate the hooks on the clip in their slots. Remove any slack in the gaiter retaining clip by carefully compressing the raised section of the clip. In the absence of the special tool, a pair of side cutters may be used, taking care not to actually cut the clip.
7 Refit the track rod end lock nut to the track rod, and screw it on to the exact position noted during removal.
8 Refit the track rod end as described in Section 23.

21 Power steering hydraulic system – bleeding

1 This procedure will only be necessary when any part of the hydraulic system has been disconnected.
2 Referring to *Weekly checks*, remove the fluid reservoir filler cap, and top-up with the specified fluid to the MAX level mark on the dipstick.
3 Firmly apply the handbrake, then jack up the front of the vehicle and support it securely on axle stands (see *Jacking and vehicle support*).
4 With the engine stopped, quickly move the steering from lock-to-lock ten times to purge out the trapped air.
5 Lower the vehicle to the ground and top-up the fluid level to the MAX level mark.
6 Start the engine and allow it to idle. With the engine idling, move the steering from lock-to-lock ten times to purge out any remaining trapped air, then switch the engine off.
7 Check that fluid level is up to the MAX mark on the reservoir dipstick, topping-up if necessary, then securely refit the reservoir cap.

22 Power steering pump – removal and refitting

1.9 litre engines

Removal

1 Firmly apply the handbrake, then jack up the front of the vehicle and support it securely on axle stands (see *Jacking and vehicle support*).
2 Where fitted, undo the retaining bolts and remove the engine undertray.
3 Remove the auxiliary drivebelt as described in Chapter 1, Section 27.
4 Unscrew and remove the bolts and remove the pulley from the power steering pump.
5 Fit a hose clamp to the hose leading from the fluid reservoir to the power steering pump.
6 Position a suitable container beneath the pump to catch spilt fluid, then release the clip and disconnect the supply hose. Note that the hose and pump stub have alignment marks to ensure correct refitting.
7 Unscrew the banjo union bolt and disconnect the pressure hose union from the pump. Recover the copper sealing washers. Tape over or plug the ends of the hoses and the apertures in the pump to prevent entry of dust and dirt into the hydraulic system. The end of the pressure line can be wrapped in a plastic bag if preferred.
8 Unscrew and remove the three mounting bolts from the pulley end of the pump, and the single mounting bolt from the engine side of the pump. Withdraw the power steering pump from the engine.

Refitting

9 Before refitting the pump (and especially if fitting a new pump), prime it with fresh fluid as follows. Place the pump in a container with the supply hose stub uppermost. Pour hydraulic fluid into the supply hose stub and turn the pulley drive flange clockwise by hand until fluid emerges from the pressure hose aperture.

10 Tilt the pump to retain the fluid, then locate it in the engine compartment and fit the supply hose and clip. Make sure that the alignment mark on the hose is in line with the seam on the pump supply stub.

11 Locate the pump in its mounting bracket and secure with the mounting bolts, tightened to the specified torque.

12 Reconnect the pressure hose union, together with new copper sealing washers, and tighten to the specified torque.

13 Remove the hose clamp from the supply hose.

14 Locate the pulley on the pump, insert the bolts, and tighten them securely while holding the drive flange with an Allen key.

15 Refit the auxiliary drivebelt with reference to Chapter 1, Section 27.

16 Where applicable, refit the engine undertray, lower the vehicle to the ground.

17 Bleed the power steering hydraulic system as described in Section 21.

2.0 litre engines

Removal

18 Firmly apply the handbrake, then jack up the front of the vehicle and support it securely on axle stands (see *Jacking and vehicle support*).

19 Where fitted, undo the retaining bolts and remove the engine undertray.

20 Remove the auxiliary drivebelt as described in Chapter 1, Section 27.

21 Unscrew and remove the bolts and remove the pulley from the power steering pump. Use a forked tool inserted in the holes of the pulley to prevent rotation as the bolts are unscrewed.

22 Fit a hose clamp to the hose leading from the fluid reservoir to the power steering pump.

23 Position a suitable container beneath the pump to catch spilt fluid, then release the clip and disconnect the supply hose. Note that the hose and pump stub have alignment marks to ensure correct refitting.

24 Undo the two bolts securing the pressure pipe flange union and disconnect the pressure pipe from the pump. Recover the seal from the end of the pipe. Tape over or plug the ends of the hose and pipe and also the apertures in the pump to prevent entry of dust and dirt into the hydraulic system. The end of the pressure pipe can be wrapped in a plastic bag if preferred.

25 Unscrew and remove the three mounting bolts from the pulley end of the pump, and the single mounting bolt from the engine side of the pump.

22.43a Undo the air conditioning compressor mounting bolts (arrowed)...

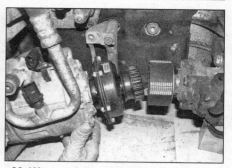

22.43b ...and disengage the compressor from the rubber drive coupling – 2.5 litre engines

26 Release the adjacent coolant hose from its plastic support bracket. Withdraw the power steering pump from the engine and manipulate it down and out from under the vehicle. For additional clearance it may be necessary to undo the bumper lower retaining bolt and ease the bumper forward slightly.

Refitting

27 Before refitting the pump (and especially if fitting a new pump), prime it with fresh fluid as follows. Place the pump in a container with the supply hose stub uppermost. Pour hydraulic fluid into the supply stub and turn the pulley drive flange clockwise by hand until fluid emerges from the pressure hose aperture.

28 Tilt the pump to retain the fluid, then locate it in the engine compartment and fit the supply hose and clip. Make sure that the alignment mark on the hose is in line with the seam on the pump supply stub.

29 Locate the pump in its mounting bracket and secure with the mounting bolts, tightened to the specified torque. Refit any components disturbed to provide additional clearance.

30 Fit a new seal to the pressure pipe then refit the pipe to the pump. Tighten the two retaining bolts to the specified torque.

31 Remove the hose clamp from the supply hose.

32 Locate the pulley on the pump, insert the bolts, and tighten them securely while holding the pulley as done during removal.

33 Refit the auxiliary drivebelt with reference to Chapter 1, Section 27.

34 Where applicable, refit the engine undertray, lower the vehicle to the ground.

35 Bleed the power steering hydraulic system as described in Section 21.

2.5 litre engines

Removal

36 Firmly apply the handbrake, then jack up the front of the vehicle and support it securely on axle stands (see *Jacking and vehicle support*).

37 Where fitted, undo the retaining bolts and remove the engine undertray.

38 Move the body front crossmember to the service position as described in Chapter 11, Section 25.

39 Prise out the cover cap, undo the retaining

bolt and remove the vibration damper from the front subframe.

40 Undo the two bolts securing the front engine mounting to the subframe. Note that new bolts will be required for refitting.

41 Undo the five bolts securing the front engine mounting lower bracket to the upper bracket and to the cylinder block, then remove the lower bracket. Note that new bolts will be required for refitting.

42 Undo the two bolts securing the front engine mounting upper bracket to the cylinder block and remove the upper bracket. Note that new bolts will be required for refitting.

43 On models with air conditioning, undo the three compressor mounting bolts. Disengage the compressor from the rubber drive coupling, move it to one side and support it clear of the alternator using cable ties **(see illustrations)**. Do not disconnect the refrigerant hoses.

44 On models with air conditioning remove the compressor rubber drive coupling from the power steering pump **(see illustration)**.

45 Fit a hose clamp to the hose leading from the fluid reservoir to the power steering pump.

46 Position a suitable container beneath the pump to catch spilt fluid, then release the clip and disconnect the supply hose. Note that the hose and pump stub have alignment marks to ensure correct refitting.

47 Unscrew the banjo union bolt and disconnect the pressure hose union from the pump. Recover the copper sealing washers. Tape over or plug the ends of the hoses and

22.44 Remove the compressor rubber drive coupling from the power steering pump – 2.5 litre engines

22.48a Undo the two mounting bolts (arrowed)...

22.48b ...remove the power steering pump...

22.48c ...and collect the O-ring seal from the driven end of the pump – 2.5 litre engines

the apertures in the pump to prevent entry of dust and dirt into the hydraulic system. The end of the pressure line can be wrapped in a plastic bag if preferred.

48 Undo the two mounting bolts and remove the power steering pump from the engine. Collect the O-ring seal from the driven end of the pump and obtain a new seal for refitting **(see illustrations)**.

49 On models with air conditioning, check the condition of the compressor rubber drive coupling and renew it if there is any sign of wear, damage or deterioration.

Refitting

50 Lubricate the new O-ring seal with clean engine oil and place it in position on the pump.

51 Before refitting the pump (and especially if fitting a new pump), prime it with fresh fluid as follows. Place the pump in a container with the supply hose stub uppermost. Pour hydraulic fluid into the supply stub and turn the pulley drive flange clockwise by hand until fluid emerges from the pressure hose aperture.

52 Tilt the pump to retain the fluid, then locate it in the engine compartment and fit the supply hose and clip.

53 Locate the pump on the engine and secure with the two mounting bolts, tightened to the specified torque, then through the specified angles.

54 Reconnect the pressure hose banjo union, together with new copper sealing washers, and tighten to the specified torque.

55 Remove the hose clamp from the supply hose.

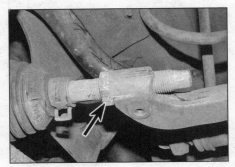

23.2 Track rod end lock nut (arrowed)

56 On models with air conditioning refit the compressor rubber drive coupling to the power steering pump. Engage the compressor with the drive coupling, then position it in the mounting bracket. Refit the three mounting bolts and tighten them to the specified torque.

57 Locate the front engine mounting upper bracket in position on the cylinder block. Fit the two new retaining bolts and tighten them to the specified torque, then through the specified angle. Similarly refit the front engine mounting lower bracket to the upper bracket and tighten the five new retaining bolts to the specified torque, then through the specified angle.

58 Fit the two new bolts securing the front engine mounting to the subframe and tighten them to the specified torque, then through the specified angle.

59 Refit the vibration damper to the subframe, refit the retaining bolt and tighten it securely. Refit the cover cap.

60 Return the body front crossmember to its normal position as described in Chapter 11, Section 25.

61 Where applicable, refit the engine undertray, lower the vehicle to the ground.

62 Bleed the power steering hydraulic system as described in Section 21.

23 Track rod end –
removal and refitting

Removal

1 Firmly apply the handbrake, then jack up the front of the vehicle and support it securely on axle stands (see *Jacking and vehicle support*). Remove the relevant front roadwheel.

2 Hold the track rod, and unscrew the track rod end locknut by a quarter of a turn **(see illustration)**. Do not move the locknut from this position, as it will serve as a handy reference mark on refitting.

3 Slacken and remove the nut securing the track rod end balljoint to the swivel hub, and release the balljoint tapered shank using a universal balljoint separator **(see illustrations 2.8a and 2.8b)**.

4 Counting the *exact* number of turns necessary to do so, unscrew the track rod end from the track rod.

5 Carefully clean the track rod end and the threads. Renew the end if its movement is sloppy or too stiff, if excessively worn, or if damaged in any way; carefully check the stud taper and threads. If the gaiter is damaged, the complete track rod end must be renewed; it is not possible to obtain the gaiter separately.

Refitting

6 Screw the track rod end onto the track rod by the number of turns noted on removal. This should bring the track rod end to within a quarter of a turn from the locknut.

7 Bring the locknut back into contact with the track rod end and tighten it securely.

8 Refit the track rod end balljoint shank to the swivel hub, then fit a new retaining nut and tighten it to the specified torque, then through the specified angle.

9 Refit the roadwheel, lower the vehicle to the ground, and tighten the wheel bolts to the specified torque.

10 It is advisable to have the front wheel alignment checked and, if necessary, adjusted at the earliest opportunity (see Section 24).

24 Wheel alignment
and steering angles –
general information

Definitions

1 A vehicle's steering and suspension geometry is defined in three basic settings – all angles are expressed in degrees (toe settings are also expressed as a measurement); the steering axis is defined as an imaginary line drawn through the axis of the wishbone balljoints, extended where necessary to contact the ground **(see illustration)**.

2 Camber is the angle between each roadwheel and a vertical line drawn through its centre and tyre contact patch, when viewed from the front or rear of the vehicle. Positive camber is when the roadwheels are tilted outwards from the vertical at the top; negative camber is when they are tilted inwards.

3 The front and rear wheel camber angle is not adjustable.

4 Castor is the angle between the steering axis and a vertical line drawn through each roadwheel's centre and tyre contact patch, when viewed from the side of the vehicle. Positive castor is when the steering axis is tilted so that it contacts the ground ahead of the vertical; negative castor is when it contacts the ground behind the vertical.

5 The front wheel castor angle is not adjustable.

6 Toe is the difference, viewed from above, between lines drawn through the roadwheel centres and the vehicle's centre-line. 'Toe-in' is when the roadwheels point inwards, towards each other at the front, while 'toe-out' is when they splay outwards from each other at the front.

7 The front wheel toe setting is adjusted by screwing the track rod in or out of its track rod ends, to alter the effective length of the track rod assembly.

8 Rear wheel toe setting is adjusted by slackening the rear trailing arm inner mounting bolt retaining nut and altering the position of the eccentric washer at the inner mounting.

Checking and adjustment

9 Due to the special measuring equipment necessary to check the wheel alignment and steering angles, and the skill required to use it properly, the checking and adjustment of these settings is best left to a VW dealer or similar expert. Note that most tyre-fitting shops now possess sophisticated checking equipment.

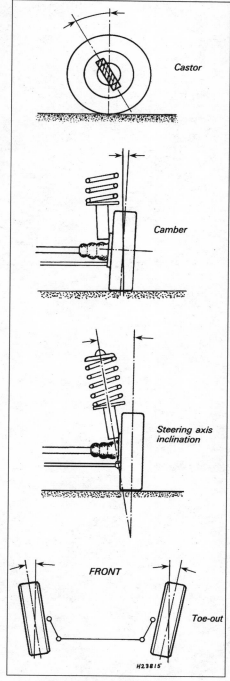

24.1 Front wheel geometry

Chapter 11
Bodywork and fittings

Contents

Degrees of difficulty

Easy, suitable for novice with little experience | **Fairly easy,** suitable for beginner with some experience | **Fairly difficult,** suitable for competent DIY mechanic | **Difficult,** suitable for experienced DIY mechanic | **Very difficult,** suitable for expert DIY or professional

Specifications

Torque wrench settings

	Nm	lbf ft
Body front crossmember retaining bolts:		
Lower bolts	20	15
Upper bolts	8	6
Facia crossmember mounting nuts	20	15
Front door hinge bolts:		
Stage 1	20	15
Stage 2	Angle-tighten a further 90°	
Front seat retaining bolts (single seats)	20	15
Front seat retaining nuts (double bench seats)	40	30
Rear door hinge bolts	20	15
Seat belt mounting bolts	40	30

1 General information

The bodyshell is conventional welded steel unitary construction available in a number of versions according to vehicle application and territory of export. In addition, an extensive list of optional body, interior and exterior is available to suit each version.

Due to the large number of specialist applications of this vehicle range, information contained in this Chapter is given on parts found to be common on the popular factory-produced versions. No information is provided on special body versions.

2 Maintenance – bodywork and underframe

The general condition of a vehicle's bodywork is the one thing that significantly affects its value. Maintenance is easy, but needs to be regular. Neglect, particularly after minor damage, can lead quickly to further deterioration and costly repair bills. It is important also to keep watch on those parts of the vehicle not immediately visible, for instance the underside, inside all the wheel arches, and the lower part of the engine compartment.

The basic maintenance routine for the bodywork is washing – preferably with a lot of water, from a hose. This will remove all the loose solids which may have stuck to the vehicle. It is important to flush these off in such a way as to prevent grit from scratching the finish. The wheel arches and underframe need washing in the same way, to remove any accumulated mud, which will retain moisture and tend to encourage rust. Paradoxically enough, the best time to clean the underframe and wheel arches is in wet weather, when the mud is thoroughly wet and soft. In very wet weather, the underframe is usually cleaned of large accumulations automatically, and this is a good time for inspection.

Periodically, except on vehicles with a wax-based underbody protective coating, it is a good idea to have the whole of the underframe of the vehicle steam-cleaned, engine compartment included, so that a thorough inspection can be carried out to see what minor repairs and renovations are necessary. Steam-cleaning is available at many garages, and is necessary for the removal of the accumulation of oily grime, which sometimes is allowed to become thick in certain areas. If steam-cleaning facilities are not available, there are some excellent grease solvents available which can be brush-applied; the dirt can then be simply hosed off. Note that these methods should not be used on vehicles with wax-based underbody protective coating, or the coating will be removed. Such vehicles should be inspected annually, preferably just prior to Winter, when the underbody should be washed down, and any damage to the wax coating repaired. Ideally, a completely fresh coat should be applied. It would also be worth considering the use of such wax-based protection for injection into door panels, sills, box sections, etc, as an additional safeguard against rust damage, where such protection is not provided by the vehicle manufacturer.

After washing paintwork, wipe off with a chamois leather to give an unspotted clear finish. A coat of clear protective wax polish will give added protection against chemical pollutants in the air. If the paintwork sheen has dulled or oxidised, use a cleaner/polisher combination to restore the brilliance of the shine. This requires a little effort, but such dulling is usually caused because regular washing has been neglected. Care needs to be taken with metallic paintwork, as special non-abrasive cleaner/polisher is required to avoid damage to the finish. Always check that the door and ventilator opening drain holes and pipes are completely clear, so that water can be drained out. Brightwork should be treated in the same way as paintwork. Windscreens and windows can be kept clear of the smeary film which often appears, by the use of proprietary glass cleaner. Never use any form of wax or other body or chromium polish on glass.

3 Maintenance – upholstery and carpets

Mats and carpets should be brushed or vacuum-cleaned regularly, to keep them free of grit. If they are badly stained, remove them from the vehicle for scrubbing or sponging, and make quite sure they are dry before refitting. Seats and interior trim panels can be kept clean by wiping with a damp cloth. If they do become stained (which can be more apparent on light-coloured upholstery), use a little liquid detergent and a soft nail brush to scour the grime out of the grain of the material. Do not forget to keep the headlining clean in the same way as the upholstery. When using liquid cleaners inside the vehicle, do not over-wet the surfaces being cleaned. Excessive damp could get into the seams and padded interior, causing stains, offensive odours or even rot.

4 Minor body damage – repair

Minor scratches

If the scratch is very superficial, and does not penetrate to the metal of the bodywork, repair is very simple. Lightly rub the area of the scratch with a paintwork renovator, or a very fine cutting paste, to remove loose paint from the scratch, and to clear the surrounding bodywork of wax polish. Rinse the area with clean water.

Apply touch-up paint to the scratch using a fine paint brush; continue to apply fine layers of paint until the surface of the paint in the scratch is level with the surrounding paintwork. Allow the new paint at least two weeks to harden, then blend it into the surrounding paintwork by rubbing the scratch area with a paintwork renovator or a very fine cutting paste. Finally, apply wax polish.

Where the scratch has penetrated right through to the metal of the bodywork, causing the metal to rust, a different repair technique is required. Remove any loose rust from the bottom of the scratch with a penknife, then apply rust-inhibiting paint to prevent the formation of rust in the future. Using a rubber or nylon applicator, fill the scratch with bodystopper paste. If required, this paste can be mixed with cellulose thinners to provide a very thin paste which is ideal for filling narrow scratches. Before the stopper-paste in the scratch hardens, wrap a piece of smooth cotton rag around the top of a finger. Dip the finger in cellulose thinners, and quickly sweep it across the surface of the stopper-paste in the scratch; this will ensure that the surface of the stopper-paste is slightly hollowed. The scratch can now be painted over as described earlier in this Section.

Dents

When deep denting of the vehicle's bodywork has taken place, the first task is to pull the dent out, until the affected bodywork almost attains its original shape. There is little point in trying to restore the original shape completely, as the metal in the damaged area will have stretched on impact, and cannot be reshaped fully to its original contour. It is better to bring the level of the dent up to a point which is about 3 mm below the level of the surrounding bodywork. In cases where the dent is very shallow anyway, it is not worth trying to pull it out at all. If the underside of the dent is accessible, it can be hammered out gently from behind, using a mallet with a wooden or plastic head. Whilst doing this, hold a suitable block of wood firmly against the outside of the panel, to absorb the impact from the hammer blows and thus prevent a large area of the bodywork from being 'belled-out'.

Should the dent be in a section of the bodywork which has a double skin, or some other factor making it inaccessible from behind, a different technique is called for. Drill several small holes through the metal inside the area – particularly in the deeper section. Then screw long self-tapping screws into the holes, just sufficiently for them to gain a good purchase in the metal. Now the dent can be pulled out by pulling on the protruding heads of the screws with a pair of pliers.

The next stage of the repair is the removal of the paint from the damaged area, and from an inch or so of the surrounding 'sound' bodywork. This is accomplished most easily by using a wire brush or abrasive pad on a power drill, although it can be done just as effectively by hand, using sheets of abrasive paper. To complete the preparation for filling, score the surface of the bare metal with a screwdriver or the tang of a file, or alternatively, drill small holes in the affected area. This will provide a really good 'key' for the filler paste.

To complete the repair, see the Section on filling and respraying.

Rust holes or gashes

Remove all paint from the affected area, and from an inch or so of the surrounding 'sound' bodywork, using an abrasive pad or a wire brush on a power drill. If these are not available, a few sheets of abrasive paper will do the job most effectively. With the paint removed, you will be able to judge the severity of the corrosion, and therefore decide whether to renew the whole panel (if this is possible) or to repair the affected area. New body panels are not as expensive as most people think, and it is often quicker and more satisfactory to fit a new panel than to attempt to repair large areas of corrosion.

Remove all fittings from the affected area, except those which will act as a guide to the original shape of the damaged bodywork (eg headlight shells etc). Then, using tin snips or a hacksaw blade, remove all loose metal and any other metal badly affected by corrosion. Hammer the edges of the hole inwards, in order to create a slight depression for the filler paste.

Wire-brush the affected area to remove the powdery rust from the surface of the remaining metal. Paint the affected area with rust-inhibiting paint, if the back of the rusted area is accessible, treat this also.

Before filling can take place, it will be necessary to block the hole in some way. This can be achieved by the use of aluminium or plastic mesh, or aluminium tape.

Aluminium or plastic mesh, or glass-fibre matting, is probably the best material to use for a large hole. Cut a piece to the approximate size and shape of the hole to be filled, then position it in the hole so that its edges are below the level of the surrounding bodywork. It can be retained in position by several blobs of filler paste around its periphery.

Aluminium tape should be used for small or very narrow holes. Pull a piece off the roll, trim it to the approximate size and shape required, then pull off the backing paper (if used) and stick the tape over the hole; it can be overlapped if the thickness of one piece is insufficient. Burnish down the edges of the tape with the handle of a screwdriver or similar, to ensure that the tape is securely attached to the metal underneath.

Filling and respraying

Before using this Section, see the Sections on dent, deep scratch, rust holes and gash repairs.

Many types of bodyfiller are available, but generally speaking, those proprietary kits which contain a tin of filler paste and a tube of resin hardener are best for this type of repair. A wide, flexible plastic or nylon applicator will be found invaluable for imparting a smooth and well-contoured finish to the surface of the filler.

Mix up a little filler on a clean piece of card or board – measure the hardener carefully (follow the maker's instructions on the pack), otherwise the filler will set too rapidly or too slowly. Using the applicator, apply the filler paste to the prepared area; draw the applicator across the surface of the filler to achieve the correct contour and to level the surface. As soon as a contour that approximates to the correct one is achieved, stop working the paste – if you carry on too long, the paste will become sticky and begin to 'pick-up' on the applicator. Continue to add thin layers of filler paste at 20-minute intervals, until the level of the filler is just proud of the surrounding bodywork.

Once the filler has hardened, the excess can be removed using a metal plane or file. From then on, progressively-finer grades of abrasive paper should be used, starting with a 40-grade production paper, and finishing with a 400-grade wet-and-dry paper. Always wrap the abrasive paper around a flat rubber, cork, or wooden block – otherwise the surface of the filler will not be completely flat. During the smoothing of the filler surface, the wet-and-dry paper should be periodically rinsed in water. This will ensure that a very smooth finish is imparted to the filler at the final stage.

At this stage, the 'dent' should be surrounded by a ring of bare metal, which in turn should be encircled by the finely 'feathered' edge of the good paintwork. Rinse the repair area with clean water, until all of the dust produced by the rubbing-down operation has gone.

Spray the whole area with a light coat of primer – this will show up any imperfections in the surface of the filler. Repair these imperfections with fresh filler paste or bodystopper, and once more smooth the surface with abrasive paper. Repeat this spray-and-repair procedure until you are satisfied that the surface of the filler, and the feathered edge of the paintwork, are perfect. Clean the repair area with clean water, and allow to dry fully.

The repair area is now ready for final spraying. Paint spraying must be carried out in a warm, dry, windless and dust-free atmosphere. This condition can be created artificially if you have access to a large indoor working area, but if you are forced to work in the open, you will have to pick your day very carefully. If you are working indoors,

dousing the floor in the work area with water will help to settle the dust which would otherwise be in the atmosphere. If the repair area is confined to one body panel, mask off the surrounding panels; this will help to minimise the effects of a slight mis-match in paint colours. Bodywork fittings (eg chrome strips, door handles etc) will also need to be masked off. Use genuine masking tape, and several thicknesses of newspaper, for the masking operations.

Before commencing to spray, agitate the aerosol can thoroughly, then spray a test area (an old tin, or similar) until the technique is mastered. Cover the repair area with a thick coat of primer; the thickness should be built up using several thin layers of paint, rather than one thick one. Using 400-grade wet-and-dry paper, rub down the surface of the primer until it is really smooth. While doing this, the work area should be thoroughly doused with water, and the wet-and-dry paper periodically rinsed in water. Allow to dry before spraying on more paint.

Spray on the top coat, again building up the thickness by using several thin layers of paint. Start spraying at one edge of the repair area, and then, using a side-to-side motion, work until the whole repair area and about 2 inches of the surrounding original paintwork is covered. Remove all masking material 10 to 15 minutes after spraying on the final coat of paint.

Allow the new paint at least two weeks to harden, then, using a paintwork renovator, or a very fine cutting paste, blend the edges of the paint into the existing paintwork. Finally, apply wax polish.

Plastic components

With the use of more and more plastic body components by the vehicle manufacturers (eg bumpers. spoilers, and in some cases major body panels), rectification of more serious damage to such items has become a matter of either entrusting repair work to a specialist in this field, or renewing complete components. Repair of such damage by the DIY owner is not really feasible, owing to the cost of the equipment and materials required for effecting such repairs. The basic technique involves making a groove along the line of the crack in the plastic, using a rotary burr in a power drill. The damaged part is then welded back together, using a hot-air gun to heat up and fuse a plastic filler rod into the groove. Any excess plastic is then removed, and the area rubbed down to a smooth finish. It is important that a filler rod of the correct plastic is used, as body components can be made of a variety of different types (eg polycarbonate, ABS, polypropylene).

Damage of a less serious nature (abrasions, minor cracks etc) can be repaired by the DIY owner using a two-part epoxy filler repair material. Once mixed in equal proportions, this is used in similar fashion to the bodywork filler used on metal panels. The filler is usually cured in twenty to thirty minutes, ready for sanding and painting.

If the owner is renewing a complete component himself, or if he has repaired it with epoxy filler, he will be left with the problem of finding a suitable paint for finishing which is compatible with the type of plastic used. At one time, the use of a universal paint was not possible, owing to the complex range of plastics encountered in body component applications. Standard paints, generally speaking, will not bond to plastic or rubber satisfactorily. However, it is now possible to obtain a plastic body parts finishing kit which consists of a pre-primer treatment, a primer and coloured top coat. Full instructions are normally supplied with a kit, but basically, the method of use is to first apply the pre-primer to the component concerned, and allow it to dry for up to 30 minutes. Then the primer is applied, and left to dry for about an hour before finally applying the special-coloured top coat. The result is a correctly-coloured component, where the paint will flex with the plastic or rubber, a property that standard paint does not normally possess.

5 Major body damage – repair

With the exception of Chassis Cab versions, the chassis members are spot-welded to the underbody, and in this respect can be termed of being monocoque or unit construction. Major damage repairs to this type of body combination must of necessity be carried out by body shops with welding and hydraulic straightening facilities.

Extensive damage to the body may distort the chassis, and result in unstable and dangerous handling, as well as excessive wear to tyres and suspension or steering components. It is recommended that checking of the chassis alignment be entrusted to a VW agent or accident repair specialist with special checking jigs.

6 Bonnet – removal, refitting and adjustment

Removal

1 Open the bonnet and, where applicable, support it with its stay rod.
2 Grip the windscreen washer jets and push them toward the rear while at the same time pulling them out of the bonnet. Disconnect the washer hose and, where applicable, the wiring connectors, and remove the jets.
3 Pull the washer hose out of the bonnet. If the vehicle is equipped with heated washer jets, also pull the wiring harness out of the bonnet.
4 Mark around the bonnet hinges, to show

the outline of their fitted positions for correct realignment on assembly.
5 Engage the help of an assistant to support the bonnet. If the bonnet is held open with a stay rod, disengage the rod from the bonnet. If the bonnet is held open by a gas support strut, use a small screwdriver to release the retaining clip, then disconnect the support strut from the bonnet.
6 Unscrew and remove the two bonnet-to-hinge retaining bolts each side, then lift the bonnet clear.

Refitting

7 Refitting is a reversal of removal. Tighten the hinge bolts fully when bonnet alignment is satisfactory.

Adjustment

8 Adjustment of the bonnet fit is carried out by slackening the bonnet-to-hinge retaining bolts and the hinge-to-body retaining bolts and repositioning the bonnet as necessary. Adjust the front bump stops so that the bonnet aligns with the front wings on each side.

7 Bonnet lock – removal and refitting

Removal

1 Open the bonnet and, where applicable, support it with its stay rod.
2 Disconnect the wiring for the contact micro switch at the connector located by the left-hand headlight.
3 Note the location of the three bonnet lock mounting bolts in their slots to ease refitting, then unscrew and remove them **(see illustration)**.
4 Withdraw the lock from its location, then depress the tab at the cable end fitting and disconnect the bonnet release cable from the lock.

Refitting

5 Refitting is a reversal of removal. Check that the bonnet fastens and releases satisfactorily. If adjustment is necessary, loosen the bonnet lock retaining bolts, and adjust the position of the lock to suit. Finally, tighten the bolts.

7.3 Bonnet lock mounting bolts (arrowed)

8 Bonnet release cable – removal and refitting

Removal

1 Open the bonnet and, where applicable, support it with its stay rod.
2 Depress the tab at the cable end fitting and disconnect the bonnet release cable from the bonnet lock.
3 Release the cable from the retaining clips on the body front crossmember and inner wing.
4 Working inside the vehicle, locate the release lever and pull it out slightly, then insert a small screwdriver into the gap between the release lever and its securing clip. Let the lever return to its original position, then release the clip with a screwdriver.
5 Undo the three retaining screws and withdraw the bonnet release lever from the bottom of the A-pillar.
6 Release the outer cable from the mounting bracket, and then detach the inner cable from the lever.
7 Tie a length of string to the end of the cable inside the vehicle, and then withdraw the cable through into the engine compartment.
8 Once the cable is free, untie the string and leave it in position in the vehicle; the string can then be used to draw the new cable back into position.

Refitting

9 Refitting is a reversal of removal bearing in mind the following points:
a) *Before refitting the bonnet release lever, fit the securing clip back into the lever first, and then push the lever back into place.*
b) *Ensure that the cable is correctly routed and secured to all the relevant retaining clips.*
c) *Before closing the bonnet, check the operation of the release lever and cable.*

9 Door/tailgate trim panels – removal and refitting

Front doors

Note: *The following procedure describes removal and refitting of the high specification trim panel. Slight differences may be encountered on low specification trim panels.*

Removal

1 On models with manual window regulators, slide the spacer ring located between the handle and the trim panel away from the handle arm and pull the handle off the regulator shaft.
2 Using a plastic spatula or similar tool, carefully prise free the trim panel from the top edge of the door trim panel. Where applicable, disconnect the wiring connectors from

9.2a Carefully prise free the trim panel from the top edge of the door trim panel...

9.2b ...then disconnect the wiring connectors from the switch panel and remove the trim

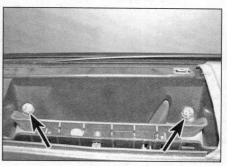

9.3 Undo the two bolts (arrowed) located in the trim panel aperture

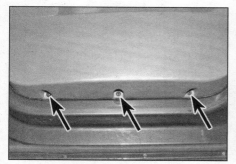

9.4 Undo the three screws (arrowed) securing the lower edge of the trim panel to the door

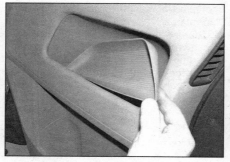

9.5a Remove the insert for the storage compartment...

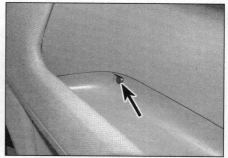

9.5b ...and undo the screw (arrowed) now exposed

the switch panel and remove the trim **(see illustrations)**.

3 Undo the two bolts located in the trim panel aperture **(see illustration)**.

4 Undo the three screws securing the lower edge of the trim panel to the door **(see illustration)**.

5 Remove the insert for the storage compartment and undo the screw now exposed **(see illustrations)**.

6 Using a plastic spatula or similar tool, carefully prise the sides of the panel away from door to release the internal clips. Lift the panel upward to release it from the window aperture.

7 Once the panel is free, reach behind and disconnect the wiring connectors, then release the wiring from the trim panel. Lift the front edge of the door lock operating cable end fitting, slide the outer cable out of the trim panel retainer then disengage the inner cable end from the interior handle **(see illustrations)**.

Refitting

8 Before refitting, check whether any of the trim panel retaining studs where broken on removal, and renew them as necessary. If the retaining clip part of the stud has been pressed down onto the stud, then it will need to be withdrawn back into position to the end of the centre stud **(see illustration)**. The refitting of the trim panel is then a reversal of removal. Check the operation of the door electrical equipment.

9.7a Disconnect the wiring connectors, then release the wiring from the trim panel

9.7b Lift the door lock operating cable end fitting (arrowed) and slide the outer cable out of the panel retainer...

9.7c ...then disengage the inner cable end from the interior handle

9.8 Clip on the left shows how it should be before refitting the trim panel

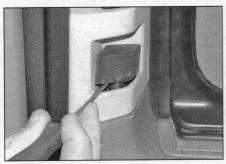

9.9 Lift up the sliding side door locking knob, then using a small screwdriver, prise it up and off the lock operating rod

9.10a Carefully prise off the trim cap...

9.10b ...then undo the retaining screw now exposed

Sliding side door

Note: *The following procedure describes removal and refitting of the high specification trim panels. The low specification trim panels are secured by plastic expanding rivets which are removed by unscrewing the centre portion using an Allen key, then pulling the rivet out of the panel.*

Removal

9 Lift up the door locking knob, then using a small screwdriver, prise it up and off the lock operating rod **(see illustration)**.
10 Carefully prise off the trim cap, then undo the retaining screw now exposed **(see illustrations)**.
11 Using a plastic spatula or similar tool, carefully prise free the door handle trim and remove the trim from the door **(see illustrations)**.
12 Starting at the sides, pull off the upper trim to release it from the internal clips and remove the trim from the door **(see illustration)**.
13 Again using a plastic spatula, prise free the lower trim panel and remove the panel from the door **(see illustrations)**.

Refitting

14 Before refitting, check whether any of the trim panel retaining studs where broken on removal, and renew them as necessary. If the retaining clip part of the stud has been pressed down onto the stud, then it will need to be withdrawn back into position to the end of the centre stud **(see illustration 9.8)**. The

refitting of the trim panel is then a reversal of removal. Check the operation of the door electrical equipment.

Rear doors

Removal

15 If working on the left-hand door, carefully push the inner lock trim upwards and remove it from the panel.
16 Using an Allen key, unscrew the centre portion, then pull out the expanding plastic rivets securing the trim panel to the door. Remove the panel from the door.

Refitting

17 Refitting is a reversal of removal. Check the condition of the expanding plastic rivets and renew any that were damaged during removal.

Tailgate

Removal

18 Starting at the sides, pull the upper trim away from the top of the tailgate and remove the trim.
19 Undo the retaining screws and remove the pull strap from the tailgate.
20 Using a plastic spatula, release the sides of the trim panel from the tailgate, then pull the panel away to release the internal clips **(see illustration)**.

Refitting

21 Before refitting, check whether any of

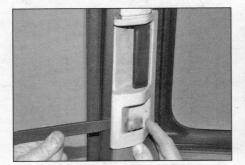

9.11a Carefully prise free the door handle trim...

9.11b ...and remove the trim from the door

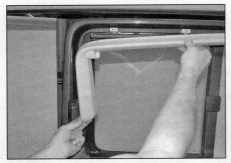

9.12 Starting at the sides, pull off the upper trim to release it from the internal clips

9.13a Prise free the lower trim panel...

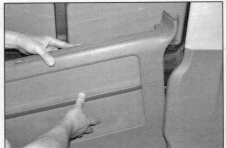

9.13b ...and remove the panel from the door

9.20 Release the sides of the tailgate trim panel, then pull the panel away to release the internal clips

10.1 Carefully prise out the blanking cap from the rear edge of the front door

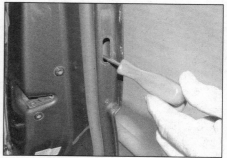

10.2 With the exterior door handle held open, turn the handle locking screw anti-clockwise a few turns

10.3 Withdraw the fixed part of the handle from the door

10.4 Using a small screwdriver, detach the operating link from the handle

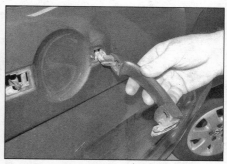

10.5 Pivot the handle away from the door, disengage the front location from the handle frame and remove the handle

the trim panel retaining studs where broken on removal, and renew them as necessary. If the retaining clip part of the stud has been pressed down onto the stud, then it will need to be withdrawn back into position to the end of the centre stud **(see illustration 9.8)**. The refitting of the trim panel is then a reversal of removal. Check the operation of the door electrical equipment.

10 Front door fittings –
removal and refitting

Exterior handle

Removal

1 Open the door and carefully prise out the blanking cap from the rear edge of the door to gain access to the handle locking screw **(see illustration)**.
2 Pull the exterior door handle outwards and hold it in that position. With the exterior door handle held in the open position, turn the handle locking screw anti-clockwise a few turns but do not completely unscrew it **(see illustration)**.
3 Withdraw the fixed part of the handle, (containing the lock cylinder on the driver's side), from the door **(see illustration)**.
4 Using a small screwdriver, detach the operating link from the handle **(see illustration)**.

5 Pivot the handle away from the door, disengage the front location from the handle frame and remove the handle from the door **(see illustration)**.

Refitting

6 Refitting is a reversal of removal.

Door lock

Removal

7 Remove the front door trim panel as described in Section 9.
8 Remove the exterior handle as described previously.
9 Lever out the two sealing plugs from the assembly carrier **(see illustration)**.

10 On models with electric front windows, temporarily reconnect the electric window switch. On models with manually operated windows, temporarily refit the regulator handle.
11 Lower the window until the clamping bolts for the window glass are accessible through the openings in the assembly carrier **(see illustration)**.
12 Slacken (but do not remove) the two window glass clamping bolts and free the glass from the regulator.
13 Slide the window glass to the fully closed position. Retain the window glass in the closed position using adhesive tape over the top of the door frame.
14 Lever out the interior lock rod grommet

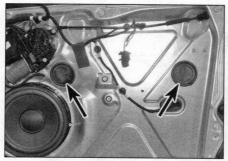

10.9 Lever out the two sealing plugs (arrowed) from the assembly carrier

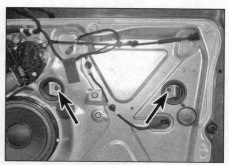

10.11 Position the window so the clamping bolts for the glass are accessible through the assembly carrier openings (arrowed)

10.14 Lever out the interior lock rod grommet from the assembly carrier and push it into the door

10.15 Disconnect the wiring connectors at the control unit on the window regulator motor

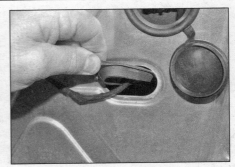

10.16 Lever out the wiring harness grommets from the assembly carrier

10.17 Release the wiring harness retaining clips from the assembly carrier

10.18 Disconnect the wiring connector from the door loudspeaker

10.19 Undo the two bolts (arrowed) securing the door lock to the edge of the door

from the assembly carrier and push it into the door **(see illustration)**.

15 Disconnect the wiring connectors at the control unit on the window regulator motor **(see illustration)**.

16 Lever out the wiring harness grommets from the assembly carrier **(see illustration)**.

17 Using a forked tool, release the wiring harness retaining clips from the assembly carrier **(see illustration)**.

18 Disconnect the wiring connector from the door loudspeaker **(see illustration)**.

19 Undo the two bolts securing the door lock to the edge of the door **(see illustration)**.

20 Undo the eight bolts securing the assembly carrier to the door **(see illustration)**.

21 Withdraw the assembly carrier from the door, guiding the door lock assembly out from behind the door frame **(see illustration)**.

22 Disconnect the wiring connector from the door lock, then withdraw the wiring harness from the assembly carrier **(see illustrations)**.

23 Drill off the heads of the two pop rivets

securing the door lock mounting bracket to the assembly carrier **(see illustration)**.

24 Release the lock operating cable from the lock frame, then rotate the inner cable through 90° and disconnect the inner cable from the lock lever **(see illustration)**.

25 If a new lock assembly is to be fitted, it will not be supplied with the mounting bracket. It will therefore be necessary to drill out the remaining pop rivet, remove the mounting bracket from the old lock and secure it to the new lock using a new pop rivet.

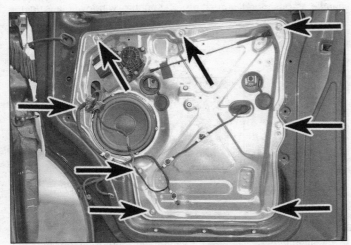

10.20 Undo the eight bolts (arrowed) securing the assembly carrier to the door

10.21 Withdraw the assembly carrier from the door, guiding the door lock assembly out from behind the door frame

Refitting

26 Refitting is a reversal of removal, using new pop rivets to secure the lock mounting bracket to the assembly carrier.

11 Front door –
removal, refitting and adjustment

Removal

1 Using a plastic spatula or similar tool, carefully prise off the triangular plastic trim from the outside of the A-pillar, just forward of the exterior mirror.
2 Remove the facia right-hand trim panel or left-hand trim panel as applicable, with reference to Section 29.
3 Release the rubber bellows by pressing the catch on the side and pulling the bellows off the A-pillar **(see illustration)**.
4 Trace the door wiring harness back to the connectors under the facia and disconnect them. Fold back the floor covering in the footwell and disconnect the earth lead from the earthing point. Pull the wiring harness out of the A-pillar.
5 Remove the protective caps from the upper and lower door hinge bolts, then unscrew the two socket-head hinge bolts **(see illustration)**.
6 Engage the help of an assistant and lift the door up and off the hinges.

Refitting and adjustment

7 Refitting is a reversal of removal, tightening the door hinge bolts to the specified torque. Don't refit the facia trim panel until the door adjustment is completed.
8 Close the door and check the door alignment with surrounding body panels. Adjustment of the door position can be made by slackening the door-to-hinge and hinge-to-A-pillar retaining bolts and repositioning the door as necessary. Note that any slackened bolts must be renewed. Tighten the new hinge retaining bolts to the specified torque and through the specified angle.
9 If necessary, adjust the position of the door striker plate so that the lock engages the striker plate centrally without having to lift or push down the door **(see illustration)**. The door must not have any play when it is closed. On completion, refit the facia trim panel as described in Section 29.

12 Sliding side door fittings –
removal and refitting

Interior release handle

Removal

1 Remove the door inner trim panel as described in Section 9.
2 Undo the two retaining screws and remove the interior release handle from the door **(see illustration)**.

10.22a Disconnect the wiring connector from the door lock...

10.22b ...then withdraw the wiring harness from the assembly carrier

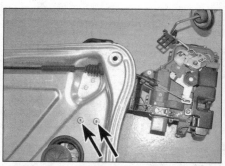
10.23 Drill off the heads of the two pop rivets (arrowed) securing the door lock mounting bracket to the assembly carrier

10.24 Release the operating cable from the lock frame (arrowed) then disconnect the inner cable from the lock lever

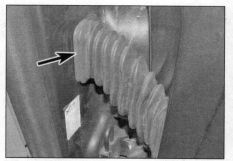
11.3 Release the rubber bellows (arrowed) by pressing the catch on the side and pulling the bellows off the A-pillar

11.5 Remove the protective caps (arrowed) from the door hinge bolts, then unscrew the two socket-head hinge bolts

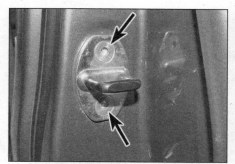
11.9 Door striker plate retaining bolts (arrowed)

12.2 Undo the two screws (arrowed) and remove the sliding side door interior release handle

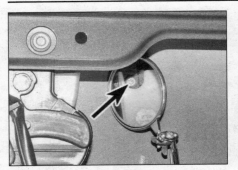

12.5a Look behind the remote door release mechanism and locate the exterior handle locking screw (arrowed)...

12.5b ...then turn the screw anti-clockwise a few turns

Refitting

3 Refitting is a reversal of removal.

Exterior handle

Removal

4 Remove the door inner trim panel as described in Section 9.

5 From inside the door, and working behind the remote door release mechanism, turn the handle locking screw anti-clockwise a few turns but do not completely unscrew it (see illustrations).

6 Withdraw the fixed part of the handle, from the door (see illustration).

7 Pivot the handle away from the door, disengage the front location from the handle frame and remove the handle from the door (see illustration).

Refitting

8 Refitting is a reversal of removal.

Door lock unit

Removal

9 Remove the door inner trim panel as described in Section 9.

10 Undo the two screws securing the lock unit to the edge of the door (see illustration).

11 Withdraw the lock into the door and disconnect the lock wiring connector (see illustration).

12 Disconnect the remote door release outer cable from the lock by depressing the two retaining tabs on the end fitting. Disengage the inner cable from the door lock operating lever and remove the lock (see illustrations).

Refitting

13 Refitting is a reversal of removal.

Remote door release mechanism

Removal

14 Remove the exterior release handle and the door lock unit as described previously.

15 Undo the two retaining screws and withdraw the electrical contact module from the door. Disconnect the wiring connector and remove the module (see illustrations).

12.6 Withdraw the fixed part of the handle, from the door

12.7 Pivot the handle away from the door, disengage the front location from the handle frame and remove the handle

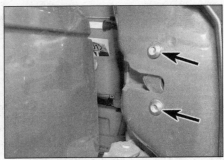

12.10 Undo the two screws (arrowed) securing the lock unit to the edge of the door

12.11 Withdraw the lock into the door and disconnect the lock wiring connector

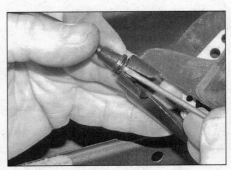

12.12a Depress the two tabs on the end fitting...

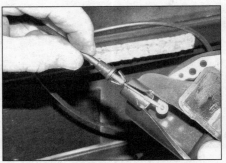

12.12b ...disconnect the remote door release outer cable from the lock...

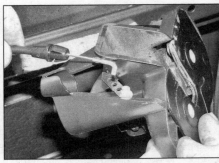

12.12c ...then disengage the inner cable from the door lock operating lever

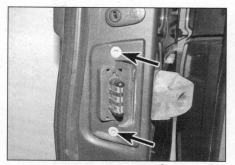

12.15a Undo the two retaining screws (arrowed) and withdraw the electrical contact module from the door

12.15b Depress the retaining tab...

12.15c ... and disconnect the module wiring connector

16 Using a screwdriver, carefully prise out the childproof lock from the edge of the door **(see illustration)**.
17 Disconnect the remote door release mechanism wiring connector **(see illustration)**.
18 Undo the three bolts securing the release mechanism to the door and swivel the unit out from its location **(see illustrations)**.
19 Disconnect the Bowden cable from the release mechanism. Disengage the inner cable from the operating lever and remove the release mechanism **(see illustrations)**.

Refitting

20 Refitting is a reversal of removal. When refitting the electrical contact module, initially tighten the retaining screws finger tight only. Close the sliding door to centralise the contact module, then open the door and tighten the screws securely.

12.16 Carefully prise out the childproof lock from the edge of the door

Middle guide rail

Removal

21 Remove the rear light cluster on the side

12.17 Disconnect the remote door release mechanism wiring connector

being worked on as described in Chapter 12, Section 7.
22 Undo the retaining screw at each end of the middle rail cover **(see illustrations)**.

12.18a Undo the three bolts (arrowed) securing the release mechanism to the door...

12.18b ...and swivel the unit out from its location

12.19a Disconnect the Bowden cable from the release mechanism...

12.19b ...then disengage the inner cable from the operating lever

12.22a Undo the retaining screw (arrowed) at the front...

12.22b ...and at the rear (arrowed) of the middle rail cover

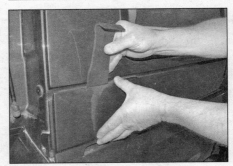

12.23a Carefully prise free the middle rail cover...

12.23b ...to release the seven retaining clips

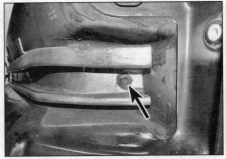

12.24a Undo the retaining bolt (arrowed) at the front edge of the guide rail...

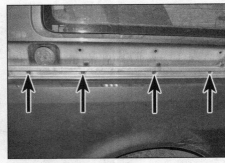

12.24b ...then undo the remaining four retaining bolts (arrowed)

23 Using a plastic spatula or similar tool, carefully prise free the middle rail cover to release the seven retaining clips, then remove the cover from the body panel **(see illustrations)**.
24 Undo the retaining bolt at the front edge

of the guide rail, then undo the remaining four retaining bolts **(see illustrations)**.
25 Slide the guide rail out of the roller on the sliding door and remove the rail from the vehicle.

Refitting
26 Refitting is a reversal of removal.

13 Sliding side door – removal, refitting and adjustment

Removal

Note: *Before slackening any retaining bolts, make alignment marks on the guide supports to aid alignment when refitting.*

1 Remove the door inner trim panel as described in Section 9.
2 Undo the two retaining bolts (three on later models) and remove the door arrestor **(see illustration)**.
3 Engage the help of an assistant to support the door, then undo the two bolts securing the hinge to the door **(see illustration)**.
4 Open the sliding door and pull the hinge fitting out of the door.
5 Pull the lower roller guide out of the lower guide rail.
6 Lower the sliding door at the front until the upper roller guide can be removed from the upper guide rail, then remove the door from the vehicle.

Refitting
7 Refitting is a reversal of removal.

Adjustment

8 Check the door for satisfactory flush-fitting adjustment. Adjust if necessary by slackening the bolts securing the door bracket to the door and to the lower guide roller. Reposition the door as required, then tighten them and recheck the fitting. Further adjustment can be obtained by slackening the upper guide roller retaining bolts and repositioning the guide roller on its bracket and by repositioning the centre rail hinge link **(see illustrations)**.
9 When fitted, and in the closed position, the door should be aligned flush to the surrounding body, and should close securely. If required, adjust the striker plate position to suit.

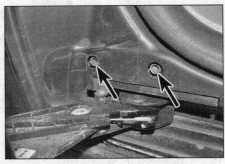

13.2 Undo the retaining bolts (arrowed) and remove the door arrestor

13.3 Undo the two bolts (arrowed) securing the hinge to the door

13.8a Door bracket-to-door retaining bolts (arrowed)

13.8b Door bracket-to-lower guide roller retaining bolts (arrowed)

13.8c Upper guide roller-to-bracket retaining bolts (arrowed)

14 Rear door fittings – removal and refitting

Assembly carrier

Removal

1 Remove the door inner trim panel as described in Section 9.
2 Disconnect the two wiring connectors and release the wiring from the retaining clips on the assembly carrier.
3 Unclip the lower latch pull rod and the door lock cylinder relay lever pull rod from the lock carrier.
4 Unclip the upper latch operating cable from the lock carrier.
5 Undo the two nuts and two bolts securing the assembly carrier to the door.
6 Guide the assembly carrier down and pull the pull rod for the exterior handle out of the lock carrier. Remove the assembly carrier from the door.

Refitting

7 Refitting is a reversal of removal.

Exterior handle

Removal

8 Remove the assembly carrier as described previously.
9 Undo the two retaining bolts and remove the exterior handle from the door.

Refitting

10 Refitting is a reversal of removal.

Door lock cylinder

Removal

11 Remove the exterior handle as described previously.
12 Fold the protective plate, on the top of the door handle upwards.
13 Using a screwdriver inserted through the opening beneath the protective plate, lift up the lock cylinder retaining clip.
14 Again using a screwdriver, carefully prise the lock cylinder relay lever off the exterior handle.
15 Press the lock cylinder out of the exterior handle.

Refitting

16 Carefully press the lock cylinder relay lever onto the exterior handle.
17 Push the lock cylinder into the exterior handle until it audibly engages with the handle.
18 Push the retaining clip down, then close the protective plate.
19 Refit the exterior handle as described previously.

Interior release mechanism

Removal

20 Remove the assembly carrier as described previously.
21 Unclip the interior release mechanism pull rod and the door lock cylinder relay lever pull rod from the lock carrier.
22 Using a screwdriver, disengage the two interior release mechanism locking hooks from the catches on the assembly carrier.
23 Pull the interior release mechanism together with the two pull rods out of the assembly carrier.

Refitting

24 Refitting is a reversal of removal.

Lock carrier

Removal

25 Remove the door inner trim panel as described in Section 9.
26 Disconnect the upper of the two wiring connectors and release the wiring from the retaining clip on the assembly carrier.
27 Unclip the interior locking mechanism pull rod and locking rod from the lock carrier.
28 Unclip the lower latch pull rod and the door lock cylinder relay lever pull rod from the lock carrier.
29 Unclip the upper latch operating cable from the lock carrier.
30 Undo the three bolts securing the lock carrier to the assembly carrier.
31 Unclip the pull rod for the exterior handle from the lock carrier, then remove the lock carrier from the door.

Refitting

32 Refitting is a reversal of removal.

Release lever (right-hand door)

Removal

33 Remove the door inner trim panel as described in Section 9.
34 Unclip the lower latch pull rod and the upper latch operating cable from the release lever.
35 Undo the two bolts securing the lever mechanism to the release lever.
36 Withdraw the release handle from the outside of the door, then remove the lever mechanism from the inside.

Refitting

37 Refitting is a reversal of removal.

Lock upper latch

Removal

38 Remove the door inner trim panel as described in Section 9.
39 Pull the trim cover off the upper latch.
40 Unclip the lower end of the upper latch operating cable from the lock carrier (left-hand door) or from the release lever (right-hand door).
41 Undo the two bolts securing the upper latch to the door.
42 Withdraw the latch upward, together with the operating cable and remove it from the door.

Refitting

43 Refitting is a reversal of removal.

Lock lower latch

Removal

44 Remove the door inner trim panel as described in Section 9.
45 Unclip the upper end of the lower latch pull rod from the lock carrier (left-hand door) or from the release lever (right-hand door).
46 Undo the two bolts securing the lower latch to the door.
47 Withdraw the latch from the door and disconnect the wiring connector. Remove the latch, together with the pull rod from the base of the door.

Refitting

48 Refitting is a reversal of removal.

15 Rear doors – removal, refitting and adjustment

Removal

1 Remove the door inner trim panel as described in Section 9.
2 Disconnect the wiring connectors for all the electrical components inside the door, and also disconnect the rear door washer hose (where applicable). Release the grommet from the door and withdraw the wiring harness.
3 Undo the two bolts securing the check strap to the door.
4 Position a suitable padded jack or support blocks underneath the door; don't lift the door, just take its weight.
5 Using a small screwdriver, carefully prise out the two upper and single lower plastic covers over the hinge retaining bolts.
6 Have an assistant support the door, then undo the bolts securing the upper and lower hinges to the door and carefully lift away the door.

Refitting and adjustment

7 Refitting is a reversal of removal, tightening the door hinge bolts to the specified torque.
8 Close the door and check the door alignment with surrounding body panels and with the other door. Initial adjustment of the door position can be made by slackening the three bolts securing each hinge to the body and repositioning the door as necessary. Note that adjustment should always be carried out on the right-hand door first, then on the left-hand door.
9 If necessary, adjust the position of the door upper and lower striker plates so that the latch engages the striker plate centrally without having to lift or push down the door. The door must not have any play when it is closed.

16 Tailgate fittings –
removal and refitting

Lock latch

Removal

1 Remove the tailgate inner trim panel as described in Section 9.
2 Unclip the lock latch pull rod from the lock carrier **(see illustration)**.
3 Undo the two bolts securing the latch to the tailgate **(see illustration)**.
4 Withdraw the latch slightly and disconnect the wiring connector **(see illustration)**.
5 Remove the latch together with the pull rod from the tailgate **(see illustration)**.

Refitting

6 Refitting is a reversal of removal.

16.2 Unclip the tailgate lock latch pull rod from the lock carrier

Lock carrier

Removal

7 Remove the lock latch as described previously.

8 Insert the key into the tailgate lock cylinder and turn the cylinder to the locked position.
9 Disconnect the two lock carrier wiring connectors **(see illustration)**.
10 Open the end fittings and disconnect the two pull rods from the lock carrier **(see illustration)**. To maintain the adjustment when refitting, either count the number of exposed threads visible on each rod or attach a cable tie, in contact with the end fittings.
11 Open the lock carrier guide over the right-hand pull rod **(see illustration)**.
12 Undo the three bolts securing the lock carrier to the tailgate and collect the anti-theft protection plate **(see illustrations)**.
13 Using a screwdriver, move the lock cylinder retaining clip to a position which will allow removal, then remove the retaining clip **(see illustration)**.
14 Again using a screwdriver, push in the locking lugs on the left-hand and right-hand

16.3 Undo the two bolts (arrowed) securing the latch to the tailgate

16.4 Withdraw the latch slightly and disconnect the wiring connector

16.5 Remove the latch together with the pull rod from the tailgate

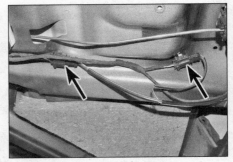
16.9 Disconnect the two lock carrier wiring connectors (arrowed)

16.10 Open the end fittings and disconnect the two pull rods from the lock carrier

16.11 Open the lock carrier guide over the right-hand pull rod

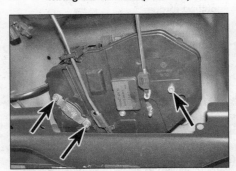
16.12a Undo the three bolts (arrowed) securing the lock carrier to the tailgate...

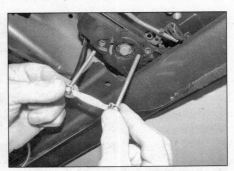
16.12b ...and collect the anti-theft protection plate from the lower bolts

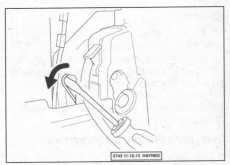
16.13 Move the lock cylinder retaining clip to a position which will allow removal, then remove the retaining clip

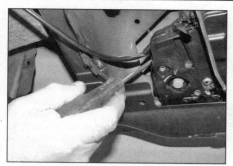

16.14a Push in the locking lugs on the left-hand side...

16.14b ...and right-hand side of the lock carrier and pull the lock carrier a few millimetres out of the tailgate

16.15 Pull the exterior handle to the open position then remove the handle body from the tailgate

16.16a Depress the central retaining tab at the top of the lock carrier...

16.16b ...move the carrier downward...

16.16c ...and manipulate it out of the tailgate

side of the lock carrier and pull the lock carrier a few millimetres out of the tailgate **(see illustrations)**. Make sure the lock cylinder remains engaged in the lock carrier.

15 Pull the exterior handle to the open position then remove the handle body from the tailgate **(see illustration)**. The lock cylinder must remain engaged in the lock carrier.

16 Depress the central retaining tab at the top of the lock carrier, move the carrier downward and manipulate it out of the tailgate **(see illustrations)**.

Refitting

17 Refitting is a reversal of removal, bearing in mind the following points:
a) *Refit the lock cylinder retaining clip to the exterior handle before refitting the handle.*

b) *Ensure that the lock cylinder is in the locked position before refitting.*

Exterior handle

18 Removal and refitting of the exterior handle is part of the lock carrier removal and refitting procedures described previously.

Tailgate lock cylinder

Removal

19 Remove the lock carrier as described previously.

20 Insert the key into the lock cylinder and turn the cylinder to the unlocked position.

21 Push the lock cylinder out of the lock carrier **(see illustration)**.

Refitting

22 Refitting is a reversal of removal.

Interior release mechanism

Removal

23 Remove the tailgate inner trim panel as described in Section 9.

24 Disconnect the two pull rods from the lock carrier as described in paragraphs 10 and 11.

25 Using a screwdriver, lever up the two retaining catches and remove the release mechanism, together with the pull rods, from the tailgate **(see illustrations)**.

Refitting

26 Refitting is a reversal of removal.

16.21 Push the lock cylinder to remove it from the lock carrier

16.25a Lever up the two retaining catches...

16.25b ...and remove the interior release mechanism, together with the pull rods, from the tailgate

17.5 Tailgate hinge retaining bolts (arrowed)

17 Tailgate –
removal, refitting and adjustment

Removal

1 The aid of two assistants will be required to support the tailgate as it is removed.

2 Remove the tailgate inner trim panel as described in Section 9.

3 Disconnect the wiring connectors for all the electrical components inside the tailgate, and also disconnect the tailgate washer hose (where applicable). Release the grommet from the tailgate and withdraw the wiring harness.

4 Have the two assistants support the weight of the tailgate. Prise up the retaining clips securing the tailgate strut balljoints, and detach the balljoint from the stud each side. Take care not to lift the clips by more than 4 mm.

5 Undo the two bolts each side securing the tailgate to the hinges and lift away the tailgate (see illustration).

Refitting

6 Refit the tailgate in the reverse order of removal. Press the strut balljoints onto their studs, using hand pressure only. Note that the struts are gas-filled, and therefore cannot be repaired. If renewing them, be sure to obtain the correct replacements.

Adjustment

7 When the tailgate is refitted, check its adjustment and if necessary re-adjust as follows.

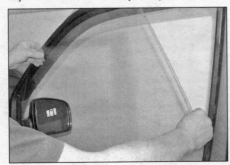

18.7 Lift the window glass upwards at the rear, and remove it from the inside of the door

18.2 Prise up the window inner waist seal from the door aperture

8 Close the tailgate and check the alignment with the surrounding body panels. If adjustment is necessary, first slacken the retaining bolts on each side until the centring lugs can move freely. The guide wedges must be able to move in the centring lugs without resistance. Tailgate adjustment is carried out by altering the position of the hinges at their attachments to the vehicle roof. To gain access to the hinge retaining nuts it will be necessary to remove the tailgate aperture upper trim (see Section 24).

9 When fitted, and in the closed position, the tailgate should be aligned flush to the surrounding body, and should close securely. If required, adjust the striker plate position to suit.

10 Ensure all nuts and bolts are securely tightened on completion.

18 Front door window glass –
removal and refitting

Removal

1 Remove the front door trim panel as described in Section 9.

2 Using a plastic wedge or similar tool, prise up the window inner waist seal from the door aperture. Lift the seal up and remove it from the door (see illustration).

3 Lever out the two sealing plugs from the assembly carrier (see illustration 10.9).

4 On models with electric front windows, temporarily reconnect the electric window

19.5 Disconnect the wiring connectors at the control unit on the window regulator motor

switch. On models with manually operated windows, temporarily refit the regulator handle.

5 Lower the window until the clamping bolts for the window glass are accessible through the openings in the assembly carrier (see illustration 10.11).

6 Slacken (but do not remove) the two window glass clamping bolts and free the glass from the regulator.

7 Carefully lift the window glass upwards at the rear, and remove it from the inside of the door (see illustration).

Refitting

8 Refitting is a reversal of removal. Push the glass to the rear, fully into the guide rail before tightening the clamping bolts.

19 Front door window regulator
– general information

1 The door window regulator is an integral part of the front door assembly carrier and is not available as a separate component. If the regulator is in need of renewal, it will be necessary to obtain the complete assembly carrier. Details of assembly carrier removal and refitting are given in the door lock removal and refitting procedures contained in Section 10.

2 On models with electric windows the window regulator motor can be removed and refitted as follows.

3 Close the window fully and retain the window glass in the closed position using adhesive tape over the top of the door frame.

4 Remove the front door trim panel as described in Section 9.

5 Disconnect the wiring connectors at the control unit on the window regulator motor (see illustration).

6 Undo the three retaining bolts and remove the motor from the assembly carrier.

7 Refitting is a reversal of removal.

20 Windscreen/tailgate/door
and fixed/sliding windows –
removal and refitting

The windscreen, tailgate and fixed/sliding side window assemblies are direct-glazed to the body, using special adhesive. Purpose-made tools are required to remove the old glass and fit the new glass, and therefore this work is best entrusted to a specialist.

21 Exterior mirrors –
removal and refitting

Exterior mirror

Removal

1 Remove the front door trim panel as described in Section 9.

2 Disconnect the mirror wiring connector at the control unit on the window regulator motor and release the wiring harness grommet from the door panel **(see illustration)**.

3 Support the mirror from the outside, then undo the three screws securing the mirror to the door **(see illustration)**.

4 Withdraw the mirror from the door and feed the wiring harness through the door aperture.

Refitting

5 Refitting is a reversal of removal.

Mirror glass

Removal

6 If the mirror glass is broken it is advisable to cover it with masking tape prior to removal.

7 Push the bottom of the mirror glass inward so that the upper edge pivots outward.

8 Using a plastic wedge, prise the upper edge of the glass outwards to release the internal retaining clips, then remove the glass.

Refitting

9 Refitting is a reversal of removal. Carefully press the mirror glass into the housing until the centre retainer clips are engaged.

---

22 Front bumper – removal and refitting

Removal

1 Firmly apply the handbrake, then jack up the front of the vehicle and support it securely on axle stands (see *Jacking and vehicle support*).

2 Where fitted, undo the retaining bolts and remove the engine undertray.

3 Remove the radiator grille as described in Section 25.

4 Using a plastic spatula or similar tool, carefully prise free and remove the bumper trim strips on both sides **(see illustrations)**.

5 Similarly, prise free and remove the foglight trim surrounds on both sides **(see illustrations)**.

6 Undo the two screws (3 screws on certain models) each side securing the edge of the wheel arch liner to the bumper **(see illustration)**.

21.2 Disconnect the mirror wiring connector and release the wiring harness grommet from the door panel

7 Pull the wheel arch liner back slightly and undo the screw each side securing the bumper to the front wing **(see illustration)**.

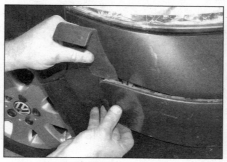

22.4a Carefully prise free...

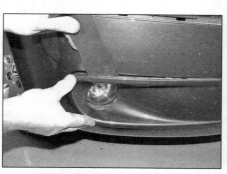

22.5a Similarly, prise free...

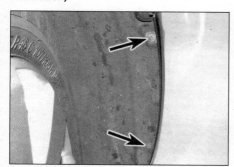

22.6 Undo the two screws (arrowed) each side securing the edge of the wheel arch liner to the bumper

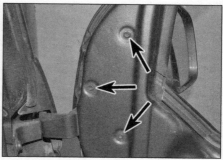

21.3 Support the mirror from the outside, then undo the three screws (arrowed) securing the mirror to the door

8 Working under the wheel arch, undo the two nuts each side securing the bumper to the body front crossmember **(see illustration)**.

22.4b ...and remove the bumper trim strips on both sides

22.5b ...and remove the foglight trim surrounds on both sides

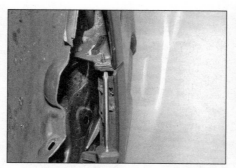

22.7 Undo the screw each side securing the bumper to the front wing

22.8 Undo the two nuts each side (arrowed) securing the bumper to the body front crossmember

22.9 Undo the retaining bolt (arrowed) and move the power steering fluid reservoir to one side

22.10 Undo the screw (arrowed) securing the washer reservoir filler neck to the body front crossmember

22.11 Undo the four bolts securing the upper part of the bumper to the body front crossmember

22.12 Undo the three screws each side (arrowed) securing the front edge of the wheel arch liner to the bumper

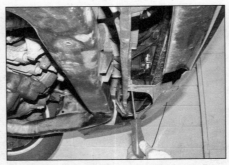

22.13 Undo the three bolts securing the bumper lower supports to the underbody

22.14 Undo the bolt each side (arrowed) securing the front of the bumper to the body front crossmember

9 Undo the retaining bolt and move the power steering fluid reservoir to one side **(see illustration)**.

10 Undo the screw securing the washer reservoir filler neck to the body front crossmember **(see illustration)**.

11 Undo the four bolts securing the upper part of the bumper to the body front crossmember **(see illustration)**.

12 Undo the three screws each side securing the front edge of the wheel arch liner to the bumper **(see illustration)**.

13 Undo the three bolts securing the bumper lower supports to the underbody **(see illustration)**.

14 Undo the bolt(s) each side securing the front of the bumper to the body front crossmember **(see illustration)**.

15 With the help of an assistant, withdraw the bumper from its location. When sufficient clearance exists, disconnect the wiring connectors for the headlights and front foglights and pull the wiring harness out from behind the body front crossmember **(see illustrations)**. Disconnect the headlight washer hose (where applicable) and the wiring connectors for any additional electrical equipment fitted, according to mode. When everything has been disconnected, remove the bumper from the vehicle.

Refitting

16 Refitting is a reversal of removal.

23 Rear bumper –
removal and refitting

Removal

1 Remove the rear light clusters on each side as described in Chapter 12, Section 7.

2 Using an Allen key, unscrew the centre portion, then pull out the two expanding plastic rivets securing the end pieces to the

22.15a Withdraw the bumper from its location...

22.15b ... disconnect the wiring connectors...

22.15c ... and pull the wiring harness out from behind the body front crossmember

bumper on each side **(see illustration)**. Pull the end pieces upward off the bumper.

3 Using an Allen key, unscrew the centre portion, then pull out the four expanding plastic rivets securing the end piece brackets to the rear wings on each side. Pull the brackets upward off the bumper.

4 Using an Allen key, unscrew the centre portion, then pull out the two expanding plastic rivets securing the upper edge of the bumper to the bumper carrier on each side.

5 Working on one side at a time, undo the retaining screws as necessary and pull the base of the wheel arch liner forward for access to the front edge of the bumper. From under the wheel arch, undo the screw securing the front edge of the bumper to the underbody.

6 Using an Allen key, unscrew the centre portion, then pull out the three expanding plastic rivets securing the lower edge of the bumper to the bumper carrier.

7 With the help of an assistant, withdraw the bumper from its location, disconnect any relevant wiring connectors depending on equipment fitted, then remove the bumper from the vehicle.

Refitting

8 Refitting is a reversal of removal.

---

24 Interior trim –
removal and refitting

Door/tailgate trim panels

1 Refer to the procedures contained in Section 9.

A-pillar trim

Removal

2 Where applicable, carefully lever off the grab handle outer trim using a screwdriver, then undo the two screws and remove the handle from the A-pillar **(see illustration)**.

3 Using a plastic spatula or similar tool, lever up the rear edge of the loudspeaker grille, then disengage the lugs at the front and remove the grille **(see illustrations)**:

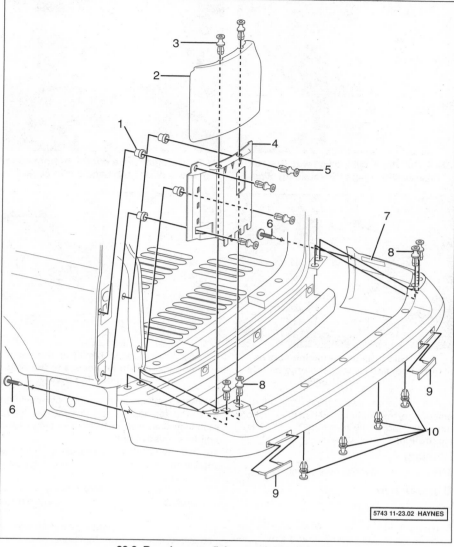

23.2 Rear bumper fixings and attachments

1 Grommet	4 End piece bracket	7 Bumper
2 End piece	5 Expanding plastic rivet	8 Expanding plastic rivet
3 Expanding plastic rivet	6 Screw	9 Reflector
		10 Expanding plastic rivet

24.2 Carefully lever off the A-pillar grab handle outer trim

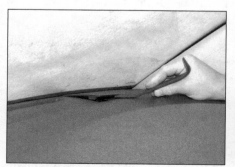

24.3a Carefully lever up the rear edge of the loudspeaker grille...

24.3b ...then disengage the lugs at the front and remove the grille

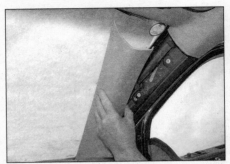

24.4 Pull the A-pillar trim away from the pillar to disengage the retaining clips

24.7a Carefully prise out the bottom edge of the B-pillar grab handle trim cover...

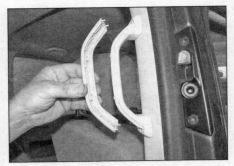

24.7b ...then remove the trim cover from the handle

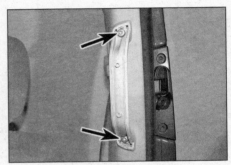

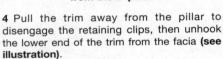

24.8 Undo the two retaining screws (arrowed) and remove the grab handle from the B-pillar

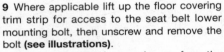

24.9a Where applicable lift up the floor covering trim strip for access to the seat belt lower mounting bolt...

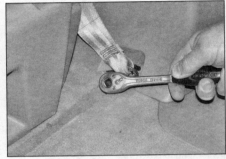

24.9b ...then unscrew and remove the bolt

4 Pull the trim away from the pillar to disengage the retaining clips, then unhook the lower end of the trim from the facia **(see illustration)**.

Refitting

5 Refitting is a reversal of removal.

B-pillar trim

Removal

6 Where fitted, carefully prise off the trim cover, undo the retaining bolt and remove the coat hook from the top of the B-pillar.

7 Carefully prise out the bottom edge of the grab handle trim cover then remove the trim cover from the handle **(see illustrations)**.

8 Undo the two retaining screws and remove the grab handle from the B-pillar **(see illustration)**.

9 Where applicable lift up the floor covering trim strip for access to the seat belt lower mounting bolt, then unscrew and remove the bolt **(see illustrations)**.

10 Pull the upper trim panel away from the B-pillar to release the internal retaining clips **(see illustration)**.

11 Feed the seat belt through the aperture in the panel, then remove the panel from the vehicle.

12 Using a plastic spatula or similar tool, if necessary, pull the lower trim panel away from the B-pillar to release the internal retaining clips. Where applicable, disconnect the switch wiring connector, then remove the panel from the vehicle **(see illustrations)**.

Refitting

13 Refitting is a reversal of removal.

Side and rear trim panels

14 Numerous variations of interior trim panels are fitted as standard according to vehicle specification and model type. Additionally, there is an extensive assortment of non-standard trim panels fitted to specialist conversions. As it is impossible to provide removal and refitting procedures for all the panels available, the following information can be used as a general guide.

a) *The interior trim panels are secured either by screws or by various types of trim fasteners, usually studs or clips.*

b) *Check that there are no other panels overlapping the one to be removed. Usually there is a sequence that has to be followed that will become obvious on close inspection.*

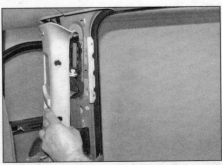

24.10 Pull the upper trim panel away from the B-pillar to release the internal retaining clips

24.12a Pull the lower trim panel away from the B-pillar to release the internal retaining clips...

24.12b ...then, where applicable, disconnect the switch wiring connector

25.1a Undo the retaining bolts and rotary fasteners and remove the battery cover...

25.1b ...and engine covers as applicable

25.2 Detach the grille from the body front crossmember at the top and pull it forwards out of the lower guide

c) *Remove all obvious fasteners, such as screws. If the panel will not come free then it is held by hidden clips or fasteners. These are usually situated around the edge of the panel and can be prised up to release them. Note, however, that they can break quite easily, so care should be exercised. The best way of releasing such clips is to use a plastic spatula or large flat-bladed screwdriver. Pad the screwdriver blade by wrapping insulating tape around it, to avoid scratching paintwork. Note that in many cases, rubber sealing strips (such as those fitted to door or tailgate apertures) may need to be prised back when releasing a panel.*

d) *When removing a panel, never use excessive force or the panel may be damaged. Always check carefully that all fasteners have been removed or released before attempting to withdraw a panel.*

e) *When refitting a panel, secure the fasteners by pressing them firmly into place and ensure that all disturbed components are correctly secured to prevent rattles.*

25 Body exterior fittings – removal and refitting

Radiator grille

Removal – up to model year 2010

1 According to model, undo the retaining bolts and rotary fasteners and remove the battery cover and engine covers as applicable **(see illustrations)**.

2 Detach the radiator grille from the body front crossmember at the top and pull the grille forwards out of the lower guide **(see illustration)**.

Removal – model year 2010 onwards

3 Undo the retaining bolt and remove the battery cover.

4 Undo the centre piece and remove the three expanding rivets securing the radiator grille to the body front crossmember.

5 Carefully pull the radiator grille towards the front and out of the catches in the bumper, keeping it parallel to the bumper.

Refitting – all model years

6 Refitting is a reversal of removal.

Engine undertray

Removal

7 Firmly apply the handbrake, then jack up the front of the vehicle and support it securely on axle stands (see *Jacking and vehicle support*).

8 Undo the six bolts securing the undertray to the front subframe.

9 On later models, release the clip at the rear of the undertray.

10 Pull the undertray rearwards and remove it from under the vehicle.

Refitting

11 Refitting is a reversal of removal.

Plenum chamber cover

Removal

12 Remove the windscreen wiper arms as described in Chapter 12, Section 11.

13 Pull the bonnet weatherstrip off the plenum chamber and bulkhead flange **(see illustration)**.

14 Starting from the edge of the windscreen, pull the plenum chamber cover upwards and out of the windscreen seal on the bottom edge of the windscreen **(see illustration)**. Do not use any tools when doing this as there is a risk of damaging the windscreen.

Refitting

15 Refitting is a reversal of removal.

25.13 Pull the bonnet weatherstrip off the plenum chamber and bulkhead flange

Wheel arch liners and body under-panels

16 The various covers and panels fitted to the underside of the vehicle are secured in position by a mixture of screws, nuts and retaining clips and removal will be fairly obvious on inspection. Work methodically around the panel removing its retaining screws and releasing its retaining clips until the panel is free and can be removed from the underside of the vehicle. Most clips used on the vehicle are simply prised out of position. Remove the wheels to ease the removal of the wheel arch liners.

17 On refitting, renew any retaining clips that may have been broken on removal, and ensure that the panel is securely retained by all the relevant clips and screws.

Body front crossmember

Moving to the service position

18 Where additional working clearance is required around the front facing side of the engine, the body front crossmember can be moved to what is described as the 'service position'. This will provide approximately 150 mm additional working clearance between the radiator and engine. To support the crossmember in the service position VW special guide pins (T10228) or commercially available alternatives will be required.

19 Begin by removing the front bumper as described in Section 22.

20 If the bonnet is held open by a gas

25.14 Pull the plenum chamber cover upwards and out of the windscreen seal

25.21 Undo the two bolts (arrowed) and move the cooling system expansion tank to one side

25.22a Undo the two body front crossmember retaining bolts (arrowed) each side...

25.22b ...and screw the guide pins into the retaining bolt holes

25.23 Undo the two body front crossmember inner retaining bolts (arrowed) on each side

25.24 Undo the two bolts each side (arrowed) securing the upper part of the body front crossmember to the inner wing panel

support strut, suitably support it in the open position. Use a small screwdriver to release the retaining clip, then disconnect the support strut from the body front crossmember.

21 Undo the two bolts and move the cooling system expansion tank to one side (see illustration).

22 Working through the holes in the bumper carrier, undo the two body front crossmember outer retaining bolts each side. Screw the VW guide pins, or commercially available alternatives, into the retaining bolt holes (see illustrations).

25.25 Undo the bolt (arrowed) each side securing the lower part of the body front crossmember to the inner wing panel

23 Undo the two body front crossmember inner retaining bolts on each side (see illustration).

24 Undo the two bolts each side securing the upper part of the body front crossmember to the inner wing panel (see illustration).

25 Undo the lower bolt each side securing the lower part of the body front crossmember to the inner wing panel (see illustration).

26 Disconnect the air ducts from the intercooler as described in Chapter 4A, Section 11 (1.9 and 2.5 litre models) or Chapter 4B, Section 12 (2.0 litre models).

27 Carefully slide the body front crossmember forward on the guide pins as far as possible. While doing this, guide the hoses, wiring and other attachments in the same direction at the same time.

28 Return the body front crossmember to its normal position using the reverse of this procedure. Align the crossmember with the surrounding panels then tighten the retaining bolts to the specified torque.

Removal

29 On models with air conditioning, have the refrigerant discharged at a dealer service department or an automotive air conditioning repair facility.

30 Disconnect the battery negative terminal (refer to *Disconnecting the battery*).

31 Where fitted, remove the engine undertray as described previously.

32 Drain the cooling system as described in Chapter 1, Section 30.

33 Remove the intercooler as described in Chapter 4A, Section 11 (1.9 and 2.5 litre models) or Chapter 4B, Section 12 (2.0 litre models).

34 On models with air conditioning, remove the condenser as described in Chapter 3, Section 11.

35 Remove the radiator as described in Chapter 3, Section 3.

36 Undo the retaining bolt and move the power steering fluid reservoir to one side.

37 Depress the tab at the bonnet release cable end fitting and disconnect the cable from the bonnet lock.

38 Release the cable from the retaining clips on the body front crossmember.

39 Disconnect the wiring connectors from the headlights and any other associated components, then free the wiring harness from the body front crossmember.

40 With the help of an assistant, suitably support the body front crossmember. Remove the two guide pins from each side, then lift the crossmember off the vehicle.

Refitting

41 Refitting is a reversal of removal, bearing in mind the following points:

a) *Tighten the retaining bolts to the specified torque.*

b) *Refit the radiator as described in Chapter 3, Section 3.*

c) *On models with air conditioning, refit the condenser as described in Chapter 3, Section 11.*

d) *Refit the intercooler as described in Chapter 4A, Section 11 or Chapter 4B, Section 12.*

e) *Refill the cooling system as described in Chapter 1, Section 30.*

f) *On models with air conditioning, have the system evacuated, charged and leak-tested by the specialist that discharged it.*

26 Seats –
removal and refitting

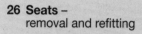

Front single seats

⚠ **Warning: The front seats may be equipped with side airbags incorporated into the outer sides of the seats. Where side airbags are fitted, refer to Chapter 12, Section 18 for the precautions which should be observed when dealing with an airbag system.**

Removal

Note: *The amount of wiring connectors under the seat may vary depending on the vehicle specification.*

1 Disconnect the battery negative terminal (refer to *Disconnecting the battery*).

2 On vehicles equipped with side airbags, also disconnect the negative terminal of the second battery (where fitted). Remove fuse S171 from the relay carrier beneath the seat.

3 Move the seat fully forward then undo the two rear bolts securing the seat rails to the seat frame **(see illustration)**.

4 Move the seat fully rearward then undo the two front bolts (or nuts) securing the seat rails to the seat frame **(see illustration)**.

⚠ **Warning: As a precaution against unintentional electrostatic discharge into the airbag, briefly touch part of the vehicle body before disconnecting the wiring.**

5 Tilt the seat back slightly and disconnect the seat wiring connectors. VW technicians fit an adapter to the airbag wiring connector as a safety precaution; however, wrap the wiring connectors with insulation tape or similar, to prevent any contact of the wiring.

6 When removing the seat from the vehicle, do not lift the seat by the seat belt stalk or by the seat adjustment levers. If necessary, have an assistant help to remove the seat, as it is heavy, and surrounding trim panels may be otherwise damaged. Make sure that the seat rails; do not damage the paintwork as the seat is withdrawn.

26.3 Front seat rear retaining bolts (arrowed)

Refitting

7 Refitting is a reversal of removal, tightening the seat mounting bolts securely.

Front passenger's double bench seat

Removal

8 Disconnect the battery negative terminal (refer to *Disconnecting the battery*).

9 Fold open the double bench seat.

10 If fitted, remove the second vehicle battery from under the seat.

11 Undo the eight nuts securing the seat to the floor and, where applicable lift out the tray for the second battery.

12 With the help of an assistant, remove the seat from the vehicle.

Refitting

13 Refitting is a reversal of removal, tightening the seat mounting nuts securely.

Second row rear seats

Removal

14 Fold the backrest forward onto the cushion, then move the seat to the rearmost position.

15 Remove the seat rail plastic end caps by inserting a flat bladed screwdriver into the rail and in contact with the end cap lug. Press the lug in and lift out the end caps.

16 Remove the aluminium covers from the seat rails by pulling them upwards out of the rails.

17 Reposition the seat so that the feet of the seat are over the openings in the seat rails.

18 With the help of an assistant, remove the seat from the vehicle.

Refitting

19 Refitting is a reversal of removal.

Third row rear seats

Removal

20 Remove the second row rear seats as described previously.

21 Fold the backrest forward onto the cushion, then move the seat so that the feet of the seat are over the openings in the seat rails.

22 With the help of an assistant, remove the seat from the vehicle.

26.4 Front seat left-hand retaining nut (arrowed)

Refitting

23 Refitting is a reversal of removal.

27 Seat belt components –
removal and refitting

Note: *Various combinations of seat belts may be fitted, according to vehicle type and specification. The following removal and refitting procedures can be used as a guide for most seat belt installations.*

Front seat belt – single seats

Removal

1 Disconnect the battery negative terminal (refer to *Disconnecting the battery*).

⚠ **Warning: Seat belt tensioners are incorporated in the inertia reel of the seat belts. Before proceeding, wait a minimum of 3 minutes, as a precaution against accidental firing of the seat belt tensioners. This period ensures that any residual electrical energy is dissipated.**

2 Remove the B-pillar trim as described in Section 24. On models without a sliding side door, also remove the body side trim panel.

3 Where fitted, remove the plastic cover from the seat belt upper mounting.

4 Unscrew the mounting bolt, and lift seat belt inertia reel unit to remove it from the base of the B-pillar **(see illustration)**.

5 Disconnect the seat belt tensioner wiring connector.

27.4 Front seat belt inertia reel retaining bolt (arrowed)

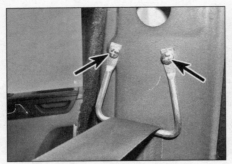

27.6 Seat belt guide retaining bolts (arrowed)

27.7 Seat belt upper mounting bolt (arrowed)

⚠️ *Warning: As a precaution against unintentional electrostatic discharge into the seat belt tensioner, briefly touch part of the vehicle body before disconnecting the wiring.*

6 Undo the two bolts and remove the seat belt guide from the B-pillar (see illustration).
7 Undo the seat belt upper mounting bolt and remove the seat belt from the vehicle (see illustration).

Refitting

8 Refitting is a reversal of removal, tightening the retaining bolts to the specified torque.

Front seat belt – double bench seat

9 The inertia reel for the double bench seat belt is located internally within the seat backrest. To gain access, the backrest must be completely dismantled. This is a complex operation and considerable expertise is needed to remove and refit the seat upholstery and internal components without damage. Therefore, any problems with the double bench seat belt and reel should be referred to a VW dealer.

Rear seat belt

Removal and refitting

10 If the seat belt inertia reel is not located inside the seat, the general procedures for removal and refitting of the rear seat belts are similar to those given for the front seat belts earlier in this Section, but it may be necessary in some instances to remove certain interior trim panels for access.
11 If the seat belt inertia reel is located inside the seat, the seat trim must be removed and the backrest must be completely dismantled. This is a complex operation and considerable expertise is needed to remove and refit the seat upholstery and internal components without damage. Therefore, any problems with the seat belt and reel should be referred to a VW dealer.

Seat belt stalks

12 Various combinations of seat belt stalks may be fitted, according to vehicle type and specification. The removal and refitting procedures are essentially self-explanatory, but it may be necessary in some instances to remove certain interior trim panels for access. Ensure that all attachment bolts are tightened to the specified torque when refitting.

28 Sunroof – general information

Due to the complexity of the sunroof mechanism, considerable expertise is needed to repair, renew or adjust the sunroof components successfully. Removal of the roof first requires the headlining to be removed, which is a complex and tedious operation, and not a task to be undertaken lightly. Therefore, any problems with the sunroof should be referred to a VW dealer. If the sunroof motor fails to operate, first check the relevant fuse. If the fault cannot be traced and rectified, the sunroof can be opened and closed manually using an Allen key to turn the motor spindle (a suitable key is supplied with the vehicle, and is located in the tool kit).

29 Facia panel components – removal and refitting

Glovebox

Removal

1 Open the glovebox lid and carefully remove the trim caps over the two side retaining screws and three lower retaining screws (see illustration).
2 Undo the screws securing the glovebox to the facia and lift the glovebox from its location (see illustrations).
3 Where applicable, disconnect the glovebox light wiring connector. On vehicles equipped with passenger air bag deactivation, disconnect the wiring connector from the switch, then remove the glovebox from the vehicle (see illustration).

Refitting

4 Refitting is a reversal of removal.

Right-hand footwell trim panel

Removal

5 Undo the seven screws securing the

29.1 Carefully remove the trim caps over the glovebox retaining screws

29.2a Undo the outer retaining screws (arrowed)...

29.2b ...and the inner retaining screw...

29.2c ...and lift the glovebox from its location

29.3 Where applicable, disconnect the wiring connector from the passenger air bag deactivation switch

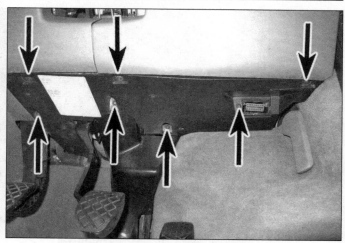

29.5a Undo the retaining screws (arrowed)...

29.5b ...and remove the right-hand footwell trim panel

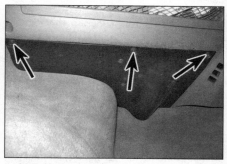

29.7 Undo the three screws (arrowed) securing the top edge of the left-hand footwell trim panel

29.8 Lower the panel down and pull it away from the facia to disengage the lower retaining hook

footwell trim panel to the right-hand lower trim panel and centre trim panel, then remove the footwell trim (see illustration).

Refitting

6 Refitting is a reversal of removal.

Left-hand footwell trim panel

Removal

7 Undo the three screws securing the top edge of the panel to the facia (see illustration).

8 Lower the panel down, pull it away from the facia to disengage the lower retaining hook, then remove the footwell trim (see illustration).

Refitting

9 Refitting is a reversal of removal.

Centre footwell trim panel

Removal

10 Remove the right-hand footwell trim panel as described previously.

11 Using a screwdriver, turn the retaining catch and open the fusebox cover. Lift the cover up and remove it from the facia (see illustrations).

12 Open the drink holder in the centre of the facia.

13 Undo the two trim panel retaining screws located in the right-hand footwell trim panel aperture (see illustration).

14 Undo the panel retaining screw on the lower left-hand side and in the drink holder aperture (see illustrations).

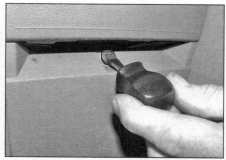

29.11a Turn the retaining catch and open the fusebox cover...

29.11b ...then lift the cover up and remove it from the facia

29.13 Undo the two centre footwell retaining screws (arrowed) located in the right-hand footwell trim panel aperture

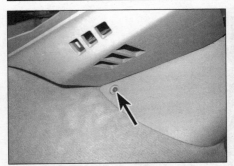

29.14a Undo the retaining screw on the lower left-hand side (arrowed)...

29.14b ...and in the drink holder aperture (arrowed)

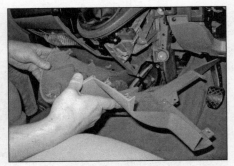

29.15 Pull the panel to the rear to disengage the retaining clips, then remove the panel from the facia

15 Pull the panel to the rear to disengage the internal retaining clips, then remove the panel from the facia **(see illustration)**.

Refitting

16 Refitting is a reversal of removal.

Lower steering column cover

Removal

17 Remove the right-hand footwell trim panel as described previously.

18 Unhook the upper part of the cover from the steering column.

19 Disengage the steering column cover from the floor covering and remove it from the vehicle.

Refitting

20 Refitting is a reversal of removal.

Right-hand lower trim panel

Removal

21 Using a plastic spatula or similar tool, carefully prise off the facia right-hand side cover **(see illustration)**.

22 Undo the screw securing the exterior light switch trim surround to the facia **(see illustration)**.

23 Again, using a plastic spatula or similar tool, carefully prise off the light-switch trim surround **(see illustration)**. Disconnect the wiring connector from the headlight range control and instrument illumination switch, then remove the trim surround.

24 Remove the centre footwell trim panel as described previously.

25 Undo the two lower trim panel retaining

screws on the right-hand side and the single screw on the left-hand side, then withdraw the panel from the facia **(see illustrations)**.

Refitting

26 Refitting is a reversal of removal.

Left-hand lower trim panel

Removal

27 Using a plastic spatula or similar tool, carefully prise off the facia left-hand side cover.

28 Remove the left-hand footwell trim panel as described previously.

29 Undo the screw securing the left-hand trim strip to the side of the facia. Using a plastic spatula or similar tool, carefully prise free the trim strip and remove it from the facia **(see illustrations)**.

29.21 Carefully prise off the facia right-hand side cover

29.22 Undo the screw securing the exterior light switch trim surround to the facia...

29.23 ...then carefully prise off the trim surround

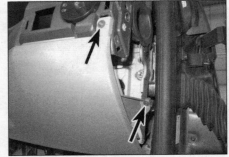

29.25a Undo the two lower trim panel retaining screws on the right-hand side (arrowed)...

29.25b ...and the single retaining screw on the left-hand side (arrowed)...

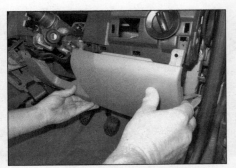

29.25c ...then withdraw the right-hand lower trim panel from the facia

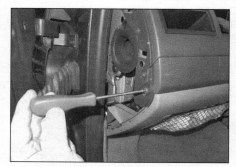

29.29a Undo the screw securing the left-hand trim strip to the side of the facia...

29.29b ...then carefully prise free the trim strip

29.31 Undo the three screws (arrowed) securing the left-hand side of the lower trim panel to the facia

30 Using a screwdriver, turn the retaining catch and open the fusebox cover. Lift the cover up and remove it from the facia **(see illustrations 29.11a and 29.11b).**
31 Undo the three screws securing the left-hand side of the lower trim panel to the facia **(see illustration).**
32 Undo the three screws securing the lower trim panel in the vicinity of the fusebox **(see illustration).**
33 Undo the screw securing the base of the centre footwell trim panel, and the left-hand lower trim panel, to the facia **(see illustration 29.14a).**
34 Using a plastic spatula or similar tool carefully prise free the upper edge of the trim panel. Press down the trim and release it from the facia in the transition area to the fusebox.
35 Unhook the lower mountings, pull the edge of the trim panel out from behind the centre footwell trim panel and remove the lower trim panel from the vehicle **(see illustration).**

Refitting

36 Refitting is a reversal of removal.

Centre drink holder

Removal

37 Remove the centre footwell trim panel and the left-hand lower trim panel as described previously.
38 Undo the screw each side securing the drink holder to the facia **(see illustration).**
39 Withdraw the drink holder from the facia, disconnect the wiring connector and remove the drink holder.

Refitting

40 Refitting is a reversal of removal.

Centre trim panel

Removal

41 Where fitted, remove the tachograph – the procedure is similar to audio unit removal as described in Chapter 12, Section 15.
42 If the audio unit is of the type incorporating slots for the insertion of removal tools, then remove the audio unit as described in Chapter 12, Section 15.
43 On vehicles without a tachograph, lift out the centre storage compartment from the audio unit aperture **(see illustration).**

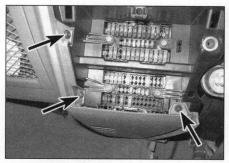

29.32 Undo the three screws (arrowed) securing the lower trim panel in the vicinity of the fusebox

44 Undo the two screws securing the upper edge of the centre trim panel to the facia.
45 Using a plastic spatula or similar tool carefully prise free the upper edge of the trim

29.38 Undo the screw (arrowed) each side securing the drink holder to the facia

29.45a Carefully prise free the upper edge of the trim panel, followed by the lower edge...

29.35 Unhook the lower mountings and remove the left-hand lower trim panel

panel, followed by the lower edge. Disconnect the wiring connectors from the rear of the switches and remove the trim panel **(see illustrations).**

29.43 Lift out the centre storage compartment from the audio unit aperture

29.45b ...then disconnect the switch wiring connectors and remove the trim panel

29.48 Undo the retaining screw (arrowed) located at the left-hand side of the heater/ventilation control unit

Refitting

46 Refitting is a reversal of removal.

Centre storage compartment

Removal

47 Remove the centre trim panel as described previously.

48 Undo the storage compartment retaining screw located at the left-hand side of the heater/ventilation control unit (see illustration).

49 Withdraw the storage compartment from the facia and disconnect the hazard warning light switch wiring connector (see illustration).

Refitting

50 Refitting is a reversal of removal.

29.49 Withdraw the storage compartment from the facia and disconnect the hazard warning light switch wiring connector

Upper storage compartment

Removal

51 Remove the centre trim panel as described previously.

52 Using a plastic spatula or similar tool carefully prise up the front area of the storage compartment, then lift the compartment off the facia (see illustration).

Refitting

53 Refitting is a reversal of removal.

Steering column shrouds

Removal

54 Remove the steering wheel as described in Chapter 10, Section 16

55 Unclip the upper shroud from the lower

29.52 Carefully prise up the front area of the storage compartment, then lift the compartment off the facia

shroud and pivot it up against the instrument panel (see illustration).

56 Release the four locking catches on the gap cover and unclip the gap cover from the upper shroud (see illustrations).

57 Undo the two screws securing the lower shroud to the steering column switch module (see illustration).

58 Release the steering column locking lever, undo the retaining screw in the locking lever aperture, and remove the lower shroud from the steering column (see illustrations).

Refitting

59 Refitting is a reversal of removal.

Complete facia assembly

Note: *This is an involved operation entailing the removal of numerous components and*

29.55 Unclip the steering column upper shroud from the lower shroud

29.56a Release the four locking catches (arrowed) on the gap cover...

29.56b ...and unclip the gap cover from the upper shroud

29.57 Undo the two screws securing the lower shroud to the steering column switch module

29.58a Undo the retaining screw in the column locking lever aperture...

29.58b ...and remove the lower shroud from the steering column

29.66a Undo the two screws (arrowed)...

29.66b ...and remove the audio unit support strip

29.68 Undo the four screws (arrowed) securing the fusebox to the facia

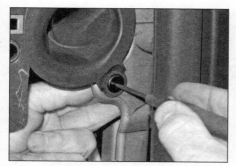

29.70a Push in the centre pins...

29.70b ...withdraw the two expanding rivets...

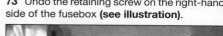

29.70c ...and remove the air ducts from each side of the facia

assemblies, and the disconnection of a multitude of wiring connectors. Make notes on the location of all disconnected wiring, or attach labels to the connectors, to avoid confusion when refitting. Taking a series of photographs throughout the removal procedure will prove invaluable when refitting, particularly as an aid to the routing and location of the various wiring looms.

Removal

60 Disconnect the battery negative terminal (refer to *Disconnecting the battery*).
61 Remove the A-pillar trim panels on both sides as described in Section 24.
62 Remove all the facia panel components as described previously in this Section.
63 Remove the steering column switch module as described in Chapter 12, Section 4.
64 Remove the instrument panel as described in Chapter 12, Section 9.
65 Remove the exterior light switch as described in Chapter 12, Section 4.
66 Undo the two screws and remove the audio unit support strip located above the heater/ ventilation control unit **(see illustrations)**.
67 Remove the heater/ventilation control unit as described in Chapter 3, Section 9.
68 Undo the four screws securing the fusebox to the facia **(see illustration)**. Push the fusebox forward to release it from the facia.
69 Unclip the gear/selector lever gaiter upwards from the facia, then pass it down through the facia opening.
70 Push in the centre pins then withdraw the two expanding rivets each side securing the air ducts to the facia crossmember. Withdraw

the air ducts from each side of the facia **(see illustrations)**.
71 Undo the three screws each side securing the facia to the facia crossmember **(see illustration)**.

29.71 Undo the three screws each side (arrowed) securing the facia to the crossmember

29.72b ...and on the left-hand side of the steering column (arrowed)

72 Undo the two retaining screws below the instrument panel on either side of the steering column **(see illustrations)**.
73 Undo the retaining screw on the right-hand side of the fusebox **(see illustration)**.

29.72a Undo the retaining screw (arrowed) on the right-hand side of the steering column...

29.73 Undo the retaining screw (arrowed) at the right-hand side of the fusebox

29.74 Undo the retaining screw above the air distribution housing

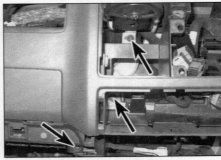

29.75 Undo the three retaining screws (arrowed) in the centre of the facia

29.76 Undo the retaining bolt (arrowed) in the heater/ventilation control unit aperture

29.77 Pull the facia rearward to release it from its side mountings

30.4a Undo the left-hand retaining bolts (arrowed)...

30.4b ...and right-hand retaining bolts (arrowed) then move the gear lever/selector housing to one side

30.5 Undo the two screws (arrowed) securing the wiring harness connector blocks to the left-hand side of the facia crossmember

30.9 Undo the bolt (arrowed) securing the heater blower motor to the front facing side of the facia crossmember

74 Undo the retaining screw above the air distribution housing **(see illustration)**.

75 Undo the three retaining screws in the centre of the facia **(see illustration)**.

76 Undo the retaining bolt in the heater/ventilation control unit aperture **(see illustration)**.

77 With the help of an assistant, pull the facia rearward sufficiently to release it from its side mountings **(see illustration)**.

78 Reach up underneath the facia on each side and disconnect the wiring connectors from the loudspeakers.

79 Disconnect any remaining wiring connectors from the facia depending on equipment level.

80 Check that nothing remains connected to the facia likely to impede removal, then remove the facia from the vehicle.

Refitting

81 Refitting is a reversal of removal ensuring that all wiring and components are correctly reconnected and all mountings securely tightened.

30 Facia crossmember – removal and refitting

Removal

1 Remove the facia assembly as described in Section 29.

2 Remove the passenger's airbag as described in Chapter 12, Section 19.

3 Remove the steering column as described in Chapter 10, Section 18.

4 Undo the four bolts securing the gear lever/selector housing to the facia crossmember and move the housing to one side **(see illustrations)**.

5 Undo the two screws securing the wiring harness connector blocks to the left-hand side of the facia crossmember **(see illustration)**.

6 Undo the two bolts securing the wiring harness connector blocks to the right-hand side of the facia crossmember.

7 Pull off the isolator relay bracket for the second vehicle battery rearwards from the facia crossmember brace.

8 Depending on equipment level, release the mobile telephone electronic control unit from the facia crossmember.

9 Undo the bolt securing the heater blower motor to the front facing side of the facia crossmember **(see illustration)**.

10 Undo the two bolts securing the air distribution housing support brackets to the facia crossmember **(see illustration)**.

11 Undo the bolt securing the brake pedal mounting bracket support to the underside of the facia crossmember **(see illustration)**.

12 Release the wiring harness from the facia crossmember.

13 As an aid to refitting, mark the position of the two crossmember brace-to-floor retaining bolts, by drawing around the bolt head flanges using a suitable pen, then undo the two bolts **(see illustration)**.

14 Similarly mark the position of the two facia crossmember mounting nuts on the left-hand and right-hand sides, then undo the nuts **(see illustration)**.

15 With the help of an assistant, carefully withdraw the facia crossmember from the bulkhead and air distribution housing. Check that all wiring has been disconnected, then remove the facia crossmember from the car.

Refitting

16 Refitting is a reversal of removal, bearing in mind the following points:

a) *Use the marks made during removal on the mounting nuts and bolts to align the facia crossmember.*

b) *Tighten the facia crossmember mounting nuts to the specified torque.*

c) *Ensure that all wiring is correctly routed and connected.*

30.10 Undo the two bolts (arrowed) securing the support brackets to the facia crossmember

30.11 Undo the bolt (arrowed) securing the brake pedal mounting bracket support to the underside of the facia crossmember

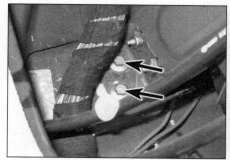

30.13 Undo the two crossmember brace-to-floor retaining bolts (arrowed)

30.14 Undo the two facia crossmember mounting nuts (arrowed) on the left-hand and right-hand sides

Chapter 12
Body electrical systems

Contents

Degrees of difficulty

Easy, suitable for novice with little experience 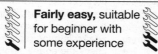	**Fairly easy,** suitable for beginner with some experience 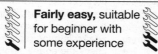	**Fairly difficult,** suitable for competent DIY mechanic 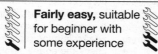	**Difficult,** suitable for experienced DIY mechanic 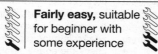	**Very difficult,** suitable for expert DIY or professional

Specifications

System type	12-volt negative earth
Fuses	Refer to the printed cards attached to the inside of the fusebox cover

Torque wrench settings	Nm	lbf ft
Tailgate/rear window wiper arm nut	12	9
Windscreen wiper arm nuts	20	15

1 General information and precautions

⚠️ *Warning: Before carrying out any work on the electrical system, read through the precautions given in 'Safety first!' at the beginning of this manual, and in Chapter 5, Section 1.*

1 The electrical system is of the 12 volt negative earth type. Power for the lights and all electrical accessories is supplied by a lead-acid type battery, which is charged by the engine-driven alternator.

2 This Chapter covers repair and service procedures for the various electrical components not associated with the engine. Information on the battery, alternator and starter motor can be found in Chapter 5.

3 It should be noted that, prior to working on any component in the electrical system, the battery negative terminal should first be disconnected, to prevent the possibility of electrical short-circuits and/or fires.

Caution: Before proceeding, refer to 'Disconnecting the battery'.

2 Electrical fault finding – general information

Note: *Refer to the precautions given in 'Safety first!' at the beginning of this manual and in Chapter 5, Section 1 before starting work. The following tests relate to testing of the main electrical circuits, and should not be used to test delicate electronic circuits, particularly where an electronic control unit is used.*

General

1 A typical electrical circuit consists of an electrical component, any switches, relays, motors, fuses, fusible links or circuit breakers related to that component, and the wiring and connectors which link the component to both the battery and the chassis. To help to pinpoint a problem in an electrical circuit, wiring diagrams are included at the end of this Chapter.

2 Before attempting to diagnose an electrical fault, first study the appropriate wiring diagram, to obtain a complete understanding of the components included in the particular circuit concerned. The possible sources of a fault can be narrowed down by noting if other components related to the circuit are operating properly. If several components or circuits fail at one time, the problem is likely to be related to a shared fuse or earth connection.

3 Electrical problems usually stem from simple causes, such as loose or corroded connections, a faulty earth connection, a blown fuse, a melted fusible link, or a faulty relay (refer to Section 3 for details of testing relays). Visually inspect the condition of all fuses, wires and connections in a problem

circuit before testing the components. Use the wiring diagrams to determine which terminal connections will need to be checked in order to pinpoint the trouble-spot.

4 The basic tools required for electrical fault-finding include a circuit tester or voltmeter (a 12-volt bulb with a set of test leads can also be used for certain tests); an ohmmeter (to measure resistance and check for continuity); a battery and set of test leads; and a jumper wire, preferably with a circuit breaker or fuse incorporated, which can be used to bypass suspect wires or electrical components. Before attempting to locate a problem with test instruments, use the wiring diagram to determine where to make the connections.

5 To find the source of an intermittent wiring fault (usually due to a poor or dirty connection, or damaged wiring insulation), a 'wiggle' test can be performed on the wiring. This involves wiggling the wiring by hand to see if the fault occurs as the wiring is moved. It should be possible to narrow down the source of the fault to a particular section of wiring. This method of testing can be used in conjunction with any of the tests described in the following sub-Sections.

6 Apart from problems due to poor connections, two basic types of fault can occur in an electrical circuit – open-circuit, or short-circuit.

7 Open-circuit faults are caused by a break somewhere in the circuit, which prevents current from flowing. An open-circuit fault will prevent a component from working.

8 Short-circuit faults are caused by a 'short' somewhere in the circuit, which allows the current flowing in the circuit to 'escape' along an alternative route, usually to earth. Short-circuit faults are normally caused by a breakdown in wiring insulation, which allows a feed wire to touch either another wire, or an earthed component such as the bodyshell. A short-circuit fault will normally cause the relevant circuit fuse to blow.

Finding an open-circuit

9 To check for an open-circuit, connect one lead of a circuit tester or the negative lead of a voltmeter either to the battery negative terminal or to a known good earth.

10 Connect the other lead to a connector in the circuit being tested, preferably nearest to the battery or fuse. At this point, battery voltage should be present, unless the lead from the battery or the fuse itself is faulty (bearing in mind that some circuits are live only when the ignition switch is moved to a particular position).

11 Switch on the circuit, then connect the tester lead to the connector nearest the circuit switch on the component side.

12 If voltage is present (indicated either by the tester bulb lighting or a voltmeter reading, as applicable), this means that the section of the circuit between the relevant connector and the switch is problem-free.

13 Continue to check the remainder of the circuit in the same fashion.

14 When a point is reached at which no voltage is present, the problem must lie between that point and the previous test point with voltage. Most problems can be traced to a broken, corroded or loose connection.

Finding a short-circuit

15 To check for a short-circuit, first disconnect the load(s) from the circuit (loads are the components which draw current from a circuit, such as bulbs, motors, heating elements, etc).

16 Remove the relevant fuse from the circuit, and connect a circuit tester or voltmeter to the fuse connections.

17 Switch on the circuit, bearing in mind that some circuits are live only when the ignition switch is moved to a particular position.

18 If voltage is present (indicated either by the tester bulb lighting or a voltmeter reading, as applicable), this means that there is a short-circuit.

19 If no voltage is present during this test, but the fuse still blows with the load(s) reconnected, this indicates an internal fault in the load(s).

Finding an earth fault

20 The battery negative terminal is connected to 'earth' – the metal of the engine/transmission and the vehicle body – and many systems are wired so that they only receive a positive feed, the current returning via the metal of the vehicle body. This means that the component mounting and the body form part of that circuit. Loose or corroded mountings can therefore cause a range of electrical faults, ranging from total failure of a circuit, to a puzzling partial failure. In particular, lights may shine dimly (especially when another circuit sharing the same earth point is in operation), motors (eg wiper motors or the heater blower motor) may run slowly, and the operation of one circuit may have an apparently-unrelated effect on another. Note that on many vehicles, earth straps are used between certain components, such as the engine/transmission and the body, usually where there is no metal-to-metal contact between components, due to flexible rubber mountings, etc.

21 To check whether a component is properly earthed, disconnect the battery and connect one lead of an ohmmeter to a known good earth point. Connect the other lead to the wire or earth connection being tested. The resistance reading should be zero; if not, check the connection as follows.

22 If an earth connection is thought to be faulty, dismantle the connection, and clean both the bodyshell and the wire terminal (or the component earth connection mating surface) back to bare metal. Be careful to remove all traces of dirt and corrosion, then use a knife to trim away any paint, so that a clean metal-to-metal joint is made. On reassembly, tighten the joint fasteners securely; if a wire terminal is being refitted, use serrated washers between the terminal and the bodyshell, to ensure a clean and secure connection. When the connection is remade, prevent the onset of corrosion in the future by applying a coat of petroleum jelly or silicone-based grease, or by spraying on (at regular intervals) a proprietary water-dispersant lubricant.

3 Fuses and relays – general information

Fuses

1 Fuses are designed to break a circuit when a predetermined current is reached, in order to protect the components and wiring, which could be damaged by excessive current flow. Any excessive current flow will be due to a fault in the circuit, usually a short-circuit (see Section 2).

2 The main fusebox is located under the centre of the facia. To gain access on Multivan models, open the bottle holder, press the two levers together and remove the bottle holder from the facia. Open the transparent cover over the fuses. To gain access on Transporter models, use a screwdriver to turn the retaining catch and open the fusebox cover. Lift the cover up and remove it from the facia. A list of the circuits each fuse protects are given on printed cards attached to the inside of the cover (see illustrations).

3 Additional fuses are located in a separate fusebox in the engine compartment in front of the battery. On some models (depending on specification), some additional fuses are located under the left-hand front seat.

4 To remove a fuse, pull it out of its location in the holder. The wire within the fuse is clearly visible, and it will be broken if the fuse is blown (see illustration).

5 Always renew a fuse with one of an identical rating; never use a fuse with a different rating from the original, nor substitute anything else. Never renew a fuse more than once without tracing the source of the trouble. The fuse rating is stamped on top of the fuse; note that the fuses are also colour-coded for easy recognition.

6 If a new fuse blows immediately, find the cause before renewing it again; a short to earth as a result of faulty insulation is most likely. Where a fuse protects more than one circuit, try to isolate the defect by switching on each circuit in turn (if possible) until the fuse blows again. Always carry a supply of spare fuses of each relevant rating on the vehicle.

Relays

7 A relay is an electrically operated switch, which is used for the following reasons:
a) *A relay can switch a heavy current remotely from the circuit in which the current is flowing, allowing the use of lighter-gauge wiring and switch contacts.*
b) *A relay can receive more than one control input, unlike a mechanical switch.*
c) *A relay can have a timer function – for example, the intermittent wiper relay.*

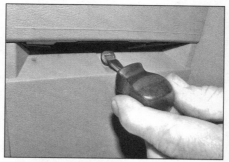

3.2a Turn the retaining catch and open the fusebox cover...

3.2c A list of the circuits each fuse protects are given on printed cards attached to the inside of the cover

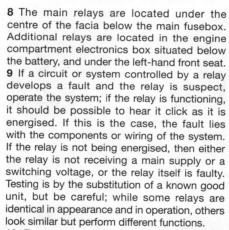

4.5 Slacken the steering column switch module clamp retaining screw

8 The main relays are located under the centre of the facia below the main fusebox. Additional relays are located in the engine compartment electronics box situated below the battery, and under the left-hand front seat.

9 If a circuit or system controlled by a relay develops a fault and the relay is suspect, operate the system; if the relay is functioning, it should be possible to hear it click as it is energised. If this is the case, the fault lies with the components or wiring of the system. If the relay is not being energised, then either the relay is not receiving a main supply or a switching voltage, or the relay itself is faulty. Testing is by the substitution of a known good unit, but be careful; while some relays are identical in appearance and in operation, others look similar but perform different functions.

10 To renew a relay, first ensure that the ignition switch is off. The relay can then simply

3.2b ...then lift the cover up and remove it from the facia

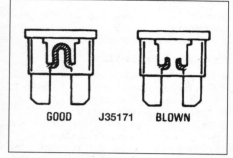

3.4 The fuses can be checked visually to determine if they are blown

be pulled out from the socket and the new relay pressed in.

4 Switches – removal and refitting

Note: *Disconnect the battery negative terminal (refer to Disconnecting the battery) before removing any switch, and reconnect the terminal after refitting.*

Ignition switch/ steering column lock

1 Refer to Chapter 10, Section 17.

Steering column switch module

2 The steering column switch module consists of the headlight dip/flasher switch, direction indicator switch, wiper/washer switch, multi-function display control switches and, where fitted, cruise control switches. The airbag wiring contact unit is also clipped onto the top of the switch module.

3 Remove the steering wheel as described in Chapter 10, Section 16.

4 Remove the steering column shrouds as described in Chapter 11, Section 29. It is not necessary to remove the upper shroud completely, just fold it back and lay it against the instrument panel.

5 Using a screwdriver, slacken the switch module clamp retaining screw (see illustration).

6 Pull up the locking lever of the contact connector housing, then slide the switch

4.6 Pull up the locking lever of the contact connector housing, then slide the switch module off the steering column

4.8 Press the light switch centre inwards, turn it slightly to the right, then pull the switch from the facia

4.9 Disconnect the wiring connector and remove the light switch

module off the steering column **(see illustration)**.

7 Refitting is a reversal of removal.

Exterior light switch

8 With the light switch in position O, press the switch centre inwards and turn it slightly to the right. Hold this position and pull the switch from the facia **(see illustration)**.

9 Disconnect the wiring connector and remove the light switch **(see illustration)**.

10 To refit the switch, first reconnect the wiring connector, then hold the switch and press the rotary part inwards and slightly to the right. Insert the switch into the facia, turn the rotary part to position O

and release. Check the switch for correct operation.

Headlight range control and instrument illumination switch

11 Using a plastic spatula or similar tool, carefully prise off the facia right-hand side cover **(see illustration)**.

12 Undo the screw securing the light switch trim surround to the facia **(see illustration)**.

13 Again, using a plastic spatula or similar tool, carefully prise off the light-switch trim surround **(see illustration)**. Disconnect the wiring connector from the headlight range control and instrument illumination switch, then remove the trim surround.

14 Squeeze together the retaining tabs and withdraw the switch from the trim surround **(see illustration)**.

15 Refitting is a reversal of removal.

Facia centre trim panel switches

16 Remove the facia centre trim panel as described in Chapter 11, Section 29.

17 Push the relevant switch out of the trim panel **(see illustration)**.

18 Refitting is a reversal of removal.

Hazard warning light switch

19 Remove the facia centre storage compartment as described in Chapter 11, Section 29.

4.11 Carefully prise off the facia right-hand side cover

4.12 Undo the screw securing the light switch trim surround to the facia...

4.13 ...then carefully prise off the trim surround

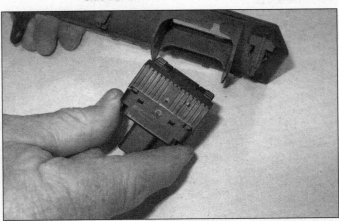

4.14 Squeeze together the tabs and withdraw the headlight range control and instrument illumination switch from the trim surround

4.17 Push the relevant switch out of the facia centre trim panel

20 Depress the retaining tabs and pull the hazard warning light switch out from the rear of the storage compartment **(see illustrations)**.
21 Refitting is a reversal of removal.

Glovebox light switch

22 Remove the glovebox as described in Chapter 11, Section 29.
23 Release the retaining lugs and remove the switch from the glovebox.
24 Refitting is a reversal of removal.

Passenger air bag deactivation switch

25 Remove the glovebox as described in Chapter 11, Section 29.
26 Depress the retaining tabs and push the switch out of the glovebox.
27 Refitting is a reversal of removal.

Stop-light switch

28 Refer to Chapter 9, Section 17.

Handbrake warning light switch

29 Refer to Chapter 9, Section 14.

Front door trim panel switches

30 Using a plastic spatula or similar tool, carefully prise free the switch panel from the top of the door trim panel. Disconnect the switch wiring connectors and remove the switch panel **(see illustrations)**.
31 The individual switches can be removed from the switch panel by depressing the retaining lugs on the underside of the relevant switch then pulling the switch from the panel.
32 Refitting is a reversal of removal.

Heating/ventilation/air conditioning system switches

33 The switches are all an integral part of the heating/ventilation control unit, and cannot be individually removed. Should a switch become faulty, the complete control unit assembly must be renewed (see Chapter 3, Section 9).

5 Bulbs (exterior lights) – renewal

General

1 Whenever a bulb is renewed, note the following points:
a) Switch off the ignition and all electrical consumers before commencing work.
b) Remember that if the light has just been in use the bulb may be extremely hot.
c) Always check the bulb contacts and holder, ensuring that there is clean metal-to-metal contact. Clean off any corrosion or dirt before fitting a new bulb.
d) Wherever bayonet-type bulbs are fitted ensure that the spring-tensioned arms bear firmly against the bulb contacts.
e) Always ensure that the new bulb is of the correct rating and that it is thoroughly clean before fitting it.

4.20a Depress the retaining tabs (arrowed)...

4.30a Carefully prise free the switch panel from the top of the door trim panel...

f) According to model, undo the retaining bolts and rotary fasteners and remove the battery cover and engine covers as applicable, for access to the headlights.

Twin filament halogen headlight

Up to model year 2010

2 Release the locking lug and remove the cover at the rear of the headlight unit.
3 Disconnect the headlight bulb wiring connector.
4 Release the legs of the retaining spring clip from their locations in the light unit. Pivot the clip off the bulb, then lift the bulb out of the light unit. When handling the new bulb, use a tissue or clean cloth to avoid touching the glass with the fingers; moisture and grease from the skin can cause blackening and rapid failure of this type of bulb. If the glass is accidentally touched, wipe it clean using methylated spirit.
5 Fit the new bulb to the headlight unit and secure with the spring clip.
6 Reconnect the wiring connector, then refit the cover to the rear of the headlight unit.
7 Check for satisfactory operation on completion.

Model year 2010 onward

8 Remove the headlight bulb cover at the rear of the headlight unit.
9 Release the legs of the retaining spring clip from their locations in the light unit. Pivot the clip off the bulb, then lift the bulb out of the light unit.
10 Hold the bulb by its base and disconnect the wiring connector. When handling the

4.20b ...and pull the hazard warning light switch out from the rear of the storage compartment

4.30b ...then disconnect the switch wiring connectors and remove the switch panel

new bulb, use a tissue or clean cloth to avoid touching the glass with the fingers; moisture and grease from the skin can cause blackening and rapid failure of this type of bulb. If the glass is accidentally touched, wipe it clean using methylated spirit.
11 Reconnect the wiring connector to the new bulb. Fit the new bulb to the headlight unit and secure with the spring clip.
12 Refit the headlight bulb cover to the rear of the headlight unit.
13 Check for satisfactory operation on completion.

Halogen headlight main beam

Up to model year 2010

14 Pull the retaining clamp upwards and remove the cover at the rear of the headlight unit **(see illustrations)**.

5.14a Pull the retaining clamp upwards...

5.14b ...and remove the cover at the rear of the headlight unit

5.15 Disconnect the headlight main beam bulb wiring connector (arrowed)

17 Lift the bulb out of the light unit (see illustration). When handling the new bulb, use a tissue or clean cloth to avoid touching the glass with the fingers; moisture and grease from the skin can cause blackening and rapid failure of this type of bulb. If the glass is accidentally touched, wipe it clean using methylated spirit.
18 Fit the new bulb to the headlight unit and secure with the spring clip.
19 Reconnect the wiring connector, then refit the cover to the rear of the headlight unit.
20 Check for satisfactory operation on completion.

Model year 2010 onward

Note: The main beam bulb also serves as the daytime running light.
21 Remove the rubber cover from the rear of the headlight (see illustration).
22 Turn the bulbholder anti-clockwise a quarter of a turn and remove it from the rear of the headlight unit (see illustration). Note: The bulb is integral with the bulbholder.
23 When handling the new bulb, use a tissue or clean cloth to avoid touching the glass with the fingers; moisture and grease from the skin can cause blackening and rapid failure of this type of bulb. If the glass is accidentally touched, wipe it clean using methylated spirit.
24 Fit the new bulb; ensuring that it is located correctly in the headlight unit, turn it clockwise to secure it in position with the electrical terminals (see illustration).
25 Refit the cover to the rear of the headlight unit.
26 Check for satisfactory operation on completion.

5.16 Disengage the bulb retaining clip (arrowed) from the hooks in the light unit, then pivot the clip off the bulb

5.17 Lift the bulb out of the light unit

15 Disconnect the headlight main beam bulb wiring connector (see illustration).
16 Push the bulb retaining spring clip in, move it sideways to disengage it from the hooks in the light unit, then pivot the clip off the bulb (see illustration).

Halogen headlight dipped beam

Up to model year 2010

27 Pull the retaining clamp upwards and remove the cover at the rear of the headlight unit (see illustrations 5.14a and 5.14b).
28 Disconnect the headlight dipped beam bulb wiring connector (see illustration).
29 Push the bulb retaining spring clip in, move it sideways to disengage it from the hooks in the light unit, then pivot the clip up off the bulb (see illustration).

5.21 Remove the rubber cover from the rear of the headlight

5.22 Turn the bulbholder anti-clockwise to remove

5.24 Make sure of good connections (arrowed)

5.28 Disconnect the headlight dipped beam bulb wiring connector

5.29 Disengage the bulb retaining clip from the hooks in the light unit, then pivot the clip up off the bulb

5.30 Lift the bulb out of the light unit

5.34 Remove the outermost rubber cover

5.35a Turn the bulb anti-clockwise to remove...

30 Lift the bulb out of the light unit **(see illustration)**. When handling the new bulb, use a tissue or clean cloth to avoid touching the glass with the fingers; moisture and grease from the skin can cause blackening and rapid failure of this type of bulb. If the glass is accidentally touched, wipe it clean using methylated spirit.

31 Fit the new bulb to the headlight unit and secure with the spring clip.

32 Reconnect the wiring connector, then refit the cover to the rear of the headlight unit.

33 Check for satisfactory operation on completion.

Model year 2010 onward

34 Remove the outermost rubber cover from the rear of the headlight unit **(see illustration)**.

35 Turn the bulbholder anti-clockwise and remove it from the rear of the headlight unit. The bulb can then be pulled out from the bulb holder **(see illustrations)**.

36 When handling the new bulb, use a tissue or clean cloth to avoid touching the glass with the fingers; moisture and grease from the skin can cause blackening and rapid failure of this type of bulb. If the glass is accidentally touched, wipe it clean using methylated spirit.

37 Fit the new bulb to the bulbholder, ensuring that the location lugs are aligned, then fit the bulbholder to the headlight and turn clockwise to secure **(see illustration)**.

38 Refit the cover to the rear of the headlight unit.

39 Check for satisfactory operation on completion.

Gas discharge headlight dipped beam

⚠ **Warning: The headlight bulb contains gas at very high pressure, and it is recommended that gloves and eye protection be worn to prevent potential personal injury.**

Up to April 2011

40 Pull the retaining clamp upwards and remove the cover at the rear of the headlight unit **(see illustrations 5.14a and 5.14b)**.

41 Disconnect the wiring connector from the gas discharge starter unit by releasing the

5.35b ...then pull the bulb from the holder

securing clip and pulling the wiring connector from the starter unit.

42 Turn the starter unit anti-clockwise and remove it from the bulb.

43 Disengage the bulb retaining spring clip from the hooks in the light unit, then pivot the clip up off the bulb.

44 Lift the bulb out of the light unit. When handling the new bulb, use a tissue or clean cloth to avoid touching the glass with the fingers; moisture and grease from the skin can cause blackening and rapid failure of this type of bulb. If the glass is accidentally touched, wipe it clean using methylated spirit.

45 Fit the new bulb to the headlight unit and secure with the spring clip.

46 Refit the gas discharge starter unit to the bulb and turn it clockwise to secure. Reconnect the wiring connector.

47 Refit the cover to the rear of the headlight unit.

48 Check for satisfactory operation on completion.

May 2011 onwards

49 Remove the outermost rubber cover from the rear of the headlight unit.

50 Turn the gas discharge bulb and holder anti-clockwise and carefully withdraw it from the headlight. **Note:** *The gas discharge bulb is integral with the bulbholder.*

51 When handling the new bulb, use a tissue or clean cloth to avoid touching the glass with the fingers; moisture and grease from the skin can cause blackening and rapid failure of this type of bulb. If the glass is accidentally touched, wipe it clean using methylated spirit.

5.37 The bulb holder can only be fitted in one position

52 Fit the new gas discharge bulb and holder to the headlight and turn clockwise to secure. Reconnect the wiring connector to the lower part of the bulb.

53 Refit the cover to the rear of the headlight unit.

54 Check for satisfactory operation on completion.

Front sidelight

55 Depending on the type of headlight unit fitted, it may be necessary to remove the cover from the rear of the headlight unit.

56 If the sidelight bulbholder is located within the headlight unit, pull the bulbholder from its location. If the sidelight bulbholder is mounted on the rear of the headlight unit, turn the bulbholder anti-clockwise and withdraw it from the light unit **(see illustration)**.

57 Pull the push-fit bulb out of the bulbholder

5.56 Turn the sidelight bulbholder anti-clockwise and withdraw it from the light unit

5.57 Pull the push-fit bulb out of the bulbholder

5.60 Turn the direction indicator bulbholder anti-clockwise, and remove it from the light unit

5.61 Twist the bayonet type bulb to remove

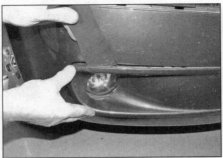

5.63a Carefully prise free the foglight trim surround...

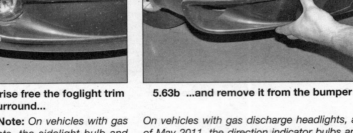

5.63b ...and remove it from the bumper

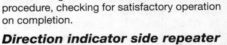

5.64 Undo the three retaining screws (arrowed) and withdraw the foglight unit from the bumper

(see illustration). **Note:** *On vehicles with gas discharge headlights, the sidelight bulb and bulbholder on early models are a single unit and cannot be separated. On later models, the daytime running light LED's also perform the function of the sidelight. The LED's are incorporated in the headlight unit and cannot be renewed separately.*

58 Fit the new bulb using a reversal of the removal procedure. Check for satisfactory operation on completion.

Front direction indicator

59 Depending on the type of headlight unit fitted, it may be necessary to remove the cover from the rear of the headlight unit.

60 Turn the indicator bulbholder anti-clockwise, and remove it from the light unit (see illustration).

61 The bulb is a bayonet fit in the holder, and can be removed by pressing it and twisting in an anti-clockwise direction (see illustration). **Note:**

On vehicles with gas discharge headlights, as of May 2011, the direction indicator bulbs and bulbholders are a single unit and cannot be separated.

62 Fit the new bulb and the light unit using a reversal of the removal procedure. Check for satisfactory operation on completion.

Front foglight

63 Using a plastic spatula or similar tool, carefully prise free and remove the foglight trim surround (see illustrations).

64 Undo the three retaining screws and withdraw the foglight unit from the front bumper (see illustration).

65 Disconnect the wiring connector from the bulbholder and remove the foglight unit.

66 Twist the foglight bulbholder anti-clockwise, and remove it from the rear of the light unit. The bulb and bulbholder are a single unit and cannot be separated. When handling the new bulb, use a tissue or clean cloth to

avoid touching the glass with the fingers; moisture and grease from the skin can cause blackening and rapid failure of this type of bulb. If the glass is accidentally touched, wipe it clean using methylated spirit.

67 Refitting is a reverse of the removal procedure, checking for satisfactory operation on completion.

Direction indicator side repeater

Note: *It is only possible to remove the side repeater in one direction and care must be taken to avoid damaging the light unit or the vehicle paintwork. When seen from the outside in the installed condition it is not possible to tell on which side of the light unit the retaining lug is located and on which side of the light unit the spring clip is located. Therefore locate the spring clip by pushing the light unit sideways.*

68 Using a plastic spatula or similar tool, carefully push the light unit sideways against spring pressure to release the retaining lug and withdraw the unit from the front wing.

69 Pull the bulbholder out of the light unit. The bulb is of the capless (push-fit) type, and can be removed by simply pulling it out of the bulbholder.

70 Refitting is a reverse of the removal procedure, aligning the lug on the bulbholder with the corresponding lug on the light unit. Check for satisfactory operation on completion.

Rear light cluster

Van models

71 Undo the two retaining screws and withdraw the light unit from the rear wing (see illustrations).

5.71a Undo the two retaining screws (arrowed)...

5.71b ...and withdraw the light unit from the rear wing

5.72a Depress the retaining tab...

5.72b ...and disconnect the wiring
connector from the bulbholder

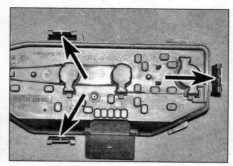

5.73a Release the three retaining catches
(arrowed)...

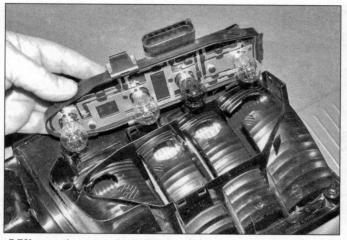

5.73b ...and remove the bulbholder from the rear of the light unit

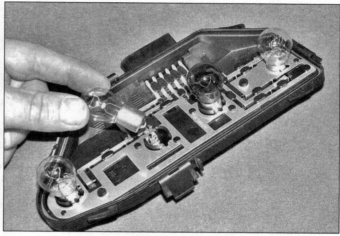

5.74 Twist the bayonet type bulb to remove

72 Using a small screwdriver, depress the retaining tab and disconnect the wiring connector from the bulbholder **(see illustrations)**.

73 On pre-2010 model year vehicles, release the three retaining catches and remove the bulbholder from the rear of the light unit **(see illustrations)**. On later vehicles, undo the four retaining screws and remove the bulbholder from the light unit.

74 The bulbs are a bayonet fit in the bulbholder, and can be removed by pressing in and twisting in an anti-clockwise direction **(see illustration)**.

75 Fit the new bulb(s), then refit the light unit using a reversal of the removal procedure. Check for satisfactory operation on completion.

Chassis Cab models

76 Undo the four retaining screws and lift the lens off the light unit.

77 The bulbs are a bayonet fit in the light unit, and can be removed by pressing in and twisting in an anti-clockwise direction.

78 Fit the new bulb(s) using a reversal of the removal procedure. Check for satisfactory operation on completion.

Rear number plate light

Van models

79 Undo the two screws and remove the light unit **(see illustrations)**.

80 Remove the festoon bulb from its holder by pulling it free.

81 Fit the new bulb using a reversal of the removal procedure. Check for satisfactory operation on completion.

Chassis Cab models

82 Undo the retaining screw and lift off the number plate light cover and lens.

83 The bulb is a bayonet fit in the light unit, and can be removed by pressing in and twisting in an anti-clockwise direction.

84 Fit the new bulb using a reversal of the removal procedure. Check for satisfactory operation on completion.

5.79a Undo the two screws (arrowed)...

High-level stop-light

85 The high-level stop-light bulbs are of the LED (light emitting diode) type and cannot be individually renewed. Remove the complete light unit as described in Section 7.

6 Bulbs (interior lights) – renewal

Note: *Various types of interior light units may be fitted depending on vehicle type, model year and trim level. In general the procedure for bulb renewal is similar for all types. Typical installations are described here.*

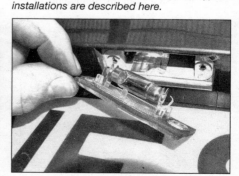

5.79b ...and remove the number plate light unit

6.2 Carefully unclip the lens from the interior light unit

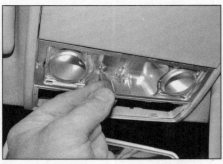

6.3 Pull the festoon type bulb from the contacts

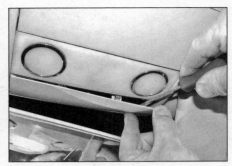

6.5 Carefully unclip the trim plate below the reading light unit lens

d) Wherever bayonet-type bulbs are fitted ensure that the spring-tensioned arms bear firmly against the bulb contacts.

e) Always ensure that the new bulb is of the correct rating and that it is thoroughly clean before fitting it.

Front interior light

2 Using a small screwdriver, carefully unclip the light unit lens **(see illustration)**.
3 The light has a festoon-type bulb, and this type is simply pulled from its contacts **(see illustration)**.
4 Fit the new bulb using a reversal of the removal procedure. Check for satisfactory operation on completion.

Front reading light

5 Using a small screwdriver, carefully unclip the trim plate below the light unit lens **(see illustration)**.
6 Similarly, carefully unclip the light unit lens **(see illustration 6.2)**.
7 Reach in through the aperture below the light unit and push the light unit out from the console **(see illustration)**.
8 To remove the bulb, turn the bulbholder anti-clockwise and remove it from the rear of the light unit, then remove the push-fit bulb from the holder **(see illustration)**.
9 Fit the new bulb using a reversal of the removal procedure. Check for satisfactory operation on completion.

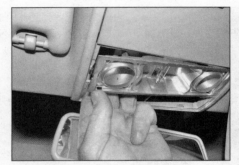

6.7 Reach in through the aperture and push the light unit out from the console

General

1 Whenever a bulb is renewed, note the following points:

a) Switch off the ignition and all electrical consumers before commencing work.

6.8 Turn the bulbholder anti-clockwise and remove it from the rear of the light unit

b) Remember that if the light has just been in use the bulb may be extremely hot.
c) Always check the bulb contacts and holder, ensuring that there is clean metal-to-metal contact. Clean off any corrosion or dirt before fitting a new bulb.

Vanity mirror light

10 Fold down the sunvisor for access to the light unit.
11 Insert a small screwdriver in the recess in the light unit and carefully release the light unit from the headlining **(see illustration)**.
12 The light has a festoon-type bulb, and this type is simply pulled from its contacts **(see illustration)**.
13 Fit the new bulb using a reversal of the removal procedure. Check for satisfactory operation on completion.

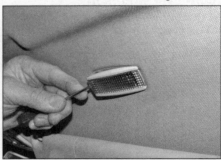

6.11 Carefully release the vanity mirror light unit from the headlining

6.12 Pull the festoon type bulb from the contacts

Centre/rear interior light

14 Using a thin spatula or similar tool, carefully lever out the light unit. Disconnect the wiring connector and remove the light unit **(see illustrations)**.

6.14a Carefully lever out the centre interior light unit...

6.14b ...then disconnect the wiring connector and remove the light unit

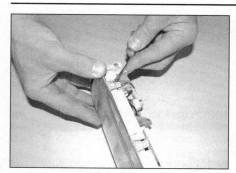

6.15a Release the six retaining tabs...

6.15b ...and remove the lens from the light unit

6.16 Pull the festoon type bulb from the contacts

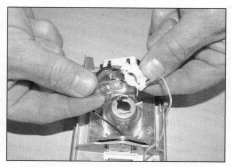

6.19 Remove the centre reading light push-fit bulb from the holder

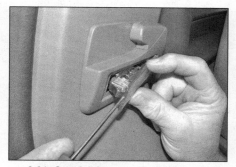

6.21 Carefully lever out the luggage compartment light unit

6.22 Pull the festoon type bulb from the contacts

15 Using a small screwdriver, release the six retaining tabs and remove the lens from the light unit **(see illustrations)**.
16 The light has a festoon-type bulb, and this type is simply pulled from its contacts **(see illustration)**.
17 Fit the new bulb using a reversal of the removal procedure. Check for satisfactory operation on completion.

Centre/rear reading light

18 Using a thin spatula or similar tool, carefully lever out the light unit. Disconnect the wiring connector and remove the light unit **(see illustrations 6.14a and 6.14b)**.
19 To remove the bulb, turn the bulbholder anti-clockwise and remove it from the rear of the light unit, then remove the push-fit bulb from the holder **(see illustration)**.
20 Fit the new bulb using a reversal of the removal procedure. Check for satisfactory operation on completion.

Luggage compartment light

21 Using a small screwdriver, carefully lever out the light unit **(see illustration)**.
22 The light has a festoon-type bulb, and this type is simply pulled from its contacts **(see illustration)**.
23 Fit the new bulb using a reversal of the removal procedure. Check for satisfactory operation on completion.

Footwell light

24 Using a small screwdriver, carefully unclip the light unit lens **(see illustration)**.

25 Remove the relevant push-fit bulb from the light unit **(see illustration)**.
26 Fit the new bulb using a reversal of the removal procedure. Check for satisfactory operation on completion.

Glovebox illumination light

27 Open the glovebox, then use a screwdriver to prise out the lens. Disconnect the wiring connector.
28 Unclip the lens from the metal heat shield, and remove the push-fit bulb.
29 Fit the new bulb using a reversal of the removal procedure. Check for satisfactory operation on completion.

Instrument panel illumination/warning lights

30 The instrument panel illumination/warning lights are non-renewable LEDs.

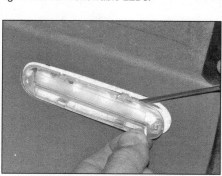

6.24 Carefully unclip the footwell light unit lens

Heater/ventilation control panel illumination

31 The control panel is illuminated by LEDs built into the panel. Consequently, if a fault develops, renewal of the panel is necessary.

Switch illumination

32 The switch illumination bulbs are integral with the switches. If a bulb fails, the complete switch must be renewed.

---

7 Exterior light units – removal and refitting

Note: *Disconnect the battery negative terminal (refer to 'Disconnecting the battery') before removing any light unit. Reconnect the terminal after refitting.*

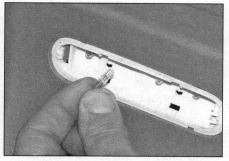

6.25 Remove the relevant push-fit bulb from the light unit

7.3 Undo the two bolts (arrowed) securing the lower part of the headlight unit to the body front crossmember

7.4a Undo the two bolts (arrowed) securing the upper part of the headlight unit to the body front crossmember...

7.4b ...then withdraw the headlight unit from its location...

7.4c ...and disconnect the wiring connector

Headlight unit

1 According to model, undo the retaining bolts and rotary fasteners and remove the battery cover and engine covers as applicable.
2 Remove the front bumper as described in Chapter 11, Section 22.
3 On pre-2010 model year vehicles, undo the two bolts securing the lower part of the headlight unit to the body front crossmember (**see illustration**). On later models undo the lower mounting bolt and the side mounting bolt.
4 Undo the two bolts securing the upper part of the headlight unit to the body front crossmember. Withdraw the headlight unit from its location, disconnect the wiring connector and remove the headlight (**see illustrations**).
5 Refit in the reverse order of removal. Refer to Section 8 for details on headlight beam

alignment. Check the headlights, sidelights and indicators for satisfactory operation on completion.

Caution: After refitting a gas discharge headlamp, the basic setting of the Automatic Range Control system should be checked. Because of the requirement for specialised equipment, this can only be carried out by a VW dealer or suitably equipped specialist. The headlight bulb contains gas at very high pressure, and it is recommended that gloves and eye protection be worn to prevent potential personal injury.

Front foglight

6 Removal and refitting of the light unit is part of the bulb renewal procedure. Refer to the procedures contained in Section 5.

Rear light cluster

Van models

7 Removal and refitting of the light unit is part of the bulb renewal procedure. Refer to the procedures contained in Section 5.

Chassis Cab models

8 Undo the four retaining screws and lift the lens off the light unit.
9 Withdraw the bulbholder and disconnect the wiring connectors.
10 Undo the two nuts and remove the cover from the rear of the light unit.
11 Undo the two nuts and remove the unit.
12 Refit in the reverse order of removal. Check for satisfactory operation on completion.

Rear number plate light

Van models

13 Removal and refitting of the light unit is part of the bulb renewal procedure. Refer to the procedures contained in Section 5.

Chassis Cab models

14 Undo the retaining screw and lift off the number plate light cover and lens.
15 Disconnect the wiring connectors, then undo the two bolts and remove the light unit.
16 Refit in the reverse order of removal. Check for satisfactory operation on completion.

High-level stop-light

Models with a tailgate

17 Remove the tailgate upper trim as described in Chapter 11, Section 9.
18 Undo the three screws securing the light unit to the tailgate (**see illustration**).
19 Withdraw the light unit from the tailgate, disconnect the wiring connector and remove the unit (**see illustrations**).
20 Refit in the reverse order of removal. Check for satisfactory operation on completion.

Models with rear doors

21 Undo the two screws securing the light unit to the rear door.
22 Withdraw the light unit from the door, disconnect the wiring connector and remove the unit.
23 Refit in the reverse order of removal. Check for satisfactory operation on completion.

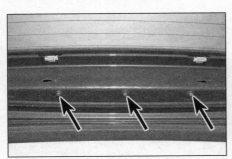

7.18 Undo the three screws (arrowed) securing the high-level stop-light to the tailgate

7.19a Withdraw the light unit from the tailgate...

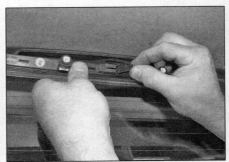

7.19b ...and disconnect the wiring connector

8 Headlight beam alignment – general information

1 Accurate adjustment of the headlight/ foglight beam is only possible using optical beam-setting equipment, and this work should therefore be carried out by a VW dealer or suitably-equipped workshop.

2 Most models have an electrically-operated headlight beam adjustment system, controlled via a switch in the facia. With the vehicle unladen, the switch should be set in position '0'. With the vehicle partially or fully loaded, set the switch position to provide adequate illumination without dazzling oncoming drivers.

9 Instrument panel – removal and refitting

Removal

Note: *The steering wheel and the steering column shrouds do not need to be removed to remove and refit the instrument panel but are shown removed for photographic clarity. The two instrument panel retaining screws are accessible from below using a long Torx screwdriver inserted through the gap between the steering column and surrounding trim.*

1 Disconnect the battery negative terminal (refer to *Disconnecting the battery*).

2 Release the locking lever and move the steering column fully down and fully out.

9.3 Undo the two screws securing the instrument panel to the facia

3 Working from below, undo the two screws securing the instrument panel to the facia **(see illustration)**.

4 Withdraw the instrument panel from the facia, disconnect the two wiring connectors and remove the panel **(see illustrations)**.

Refitting

5 Refitting is a reversal of removal.

10 Horn – removal and refitting

Removal

1 The horn is located behind the front bumper on the right-hand side.

2 Firmly apply the handbrake, then jack up the front of the vehicle and support it securely on axle stands (see *Jacking and vehicle support*).

Remove the right-hand roadwheel.

3 Release the fasteners and remove the front wheel arch liner on the right-hand side.

4 Disconnect the wiring connector from the horn, then unscrew the retaining nut and remove the horn from the mounting bracket. The horn cannot be adjusted or repaired, and therefore if defective, it must be renewed.

Refitting

5 Refit in the reverse order of removal. Check for satisfactory operation on completion.

11 Wiper arms – removal and refitting

Removal

1 With the wipers 'parked' (ie, in the normal at-rest position), check that there are lines on the glass indicating the parked position of the blades. If no lines are visible, mark the position of the blades on the windscreen/rear window, using a wax crayon or strips of masking tape **(see illustration)**.

2 On front wiper arms, prise off the wiper arm spindle nut cover, then undo the spindle nut. Lift the blade off the glass and carefully rock the wiper arm from side to side, until it releases from the spindle **(see illustrations)**. **Note:** *If both windscreen wiper arms are to be removed at the same time mark them for identification; the arms are not interchangeable.*

3 On rear wiper arms, unclip the spindle nut cover, then undo the spindle nut **(see illustration)**.

9.4a Withdraw the instrument panel from the facia...

9.4b ...and disconnect the two wiring connectors

11.1 Using masking tape (arrowed) to mark the wiper blade position on the windscreen

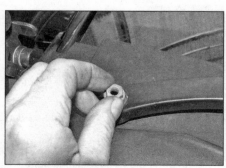

11.2a Undo the windscreen wiper arm spindle nut...

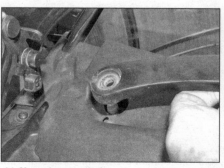

11.2b ...then rock the wiper arm from side to side, until it releases from the spindle

11.3 On rear wiper arms, unclip the spindle nut cover, then undo the spindle nut

Lift the blade off the glass and carefully rock the wiper arm from side to side, until it releases from the spindle.

4 If the arm is a tight fit on the spindle, the arm can be removed from the spindle using a small puller **(see illustration)**.

Refitting

5 Ensure that the wiper arm and spindle splines are clean and dry, and then refit the arm to the spindle, aligning the wiper blade with the line on the glass or the tape fitted on removal. Refit the spindle nut, tightening it securely, and clip the nut cover back in position.

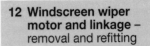

12 Windscreen wiper motor and linkage – removal and refitting

Removal

1 Disconnect the battery negative terminal (refer to *Disconnecting the battery*).
2 Remove the wiper arms as described in Section 11.
3 Remove the plenum chamber cover as described in Chapter 11, Section 25.
4 Undo the retaining bolt each side securing the ends of the wiper linkage frame to the scuttle **(see illustrations)**.
5 Undo the retaining bolt securing the centre of the wiper linkage frame to the bulkhead.
6 Disconnect the wiring connector from

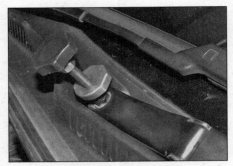

11.4 If a wiper arm is a tight fit on the spindle, it can be removed using a small puller

the wiper motor, then manoeuvre the wiper linkage frame and motor out from the scuttle **(see illustration)**.
7 To remove the motor from the linkage, prise the linkage balljoints off the motor crank arm ballpin, using a large screwdriver.
8 Undo the four retaining bolts and remove the motor from the linkage frame.

Refitting

9 Refitting is a reversal of removal, noting the following points:
a) *Switch the wiper motor on then switch it off so that it stops in the 'parked' position before refitting the wiper arms.*
b) *Refit the wiper arms as described in Section 11.*
c) *On completion, check the wipers for satisfactory operation.*

13 Tailgate/rear door wiper motor – removal and refitting

Tailgate wiper motor

Removal

1 Disconnect the battery negative terminal (refer to *Disconnecting the battery*).
2 Remove the wiper arm (see Section 11).
3 Remove the tailgate trim panel as described in Chapter 11, Section 9
4 Disconnect the washer hose at the connector on the wiper motor **(see illustration)**.
5 Disconnect the wiring connector from the wiper motor **(see illustration)**.
6 Undo the three retaining bolts and remove the wiper motor from the tailgate **(see illustration)**. Recover the wiper spindle rubber seal from the tailgate window.

Refitting

7 Refitting is a reversal of removal, aligning the mark on the spindle rubber seal with the mark on the tailgate window. If no mark is visible on the window, position the seal with the mark in the 12 o' clock position. Check for satisfactory operation on completion.

Rear door wiper motor

Removal

8 Disconnect the battery negative terminal (refer to *Disconnecting the battery*).

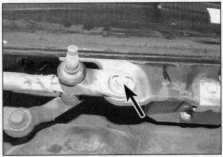

12.4a Undo the left-hand retaining bolt (arrowed)...

12.4b ...and right-hand retaining bolt securing the wiper linkage frame to the scuttle

12.6 Disconnect the wiring connector (arrowed) from the wiper motor

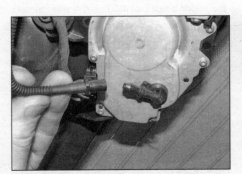

13.4 Disconnect the washer hose at the connector on the tailgate wiper motor

13.5 Disconnect the wiring connector from the tailgate wiper motor

13.6 Undo the three retaining bolts (arrowed) and remove the wiper motor from the tailgate

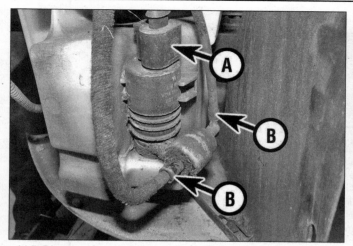
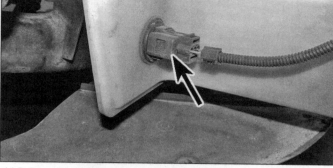

14.5 Disconnect the wiring connector (A) and washer hoses (B) from the washer pump

14.6 Disconnect the wiring connector (arrowed) from the washer fluid level sensor

9 Remove the wiper arm as described in Section 11.
10 Remove the rear door trim panel as described in Chapter 11, Section 9.
11 If working on the left-hand door, remove the assembly carrier as described in Chapter 11, Section 14.
12 Disconnect the washer hose at the connector on the wiper motor.
13 Disconnect the wiring connector from the wiper motor.
14 Undo the two bolts (left-hand door) or three bolts (right-hand door) securing the wiper motor mounting bracket to the door and remove the wiper motor and mounting bracket. Recover the wiper spindle rubber seal from the window glass.
15 If necessary, undo the three retaining bolts and remove the wiper motor from the mounting bracket.

Refitting

16 Refitting is a reversal of removal, aligning the mark on the spindle rubber seal with the mark on the window glass. If no mark is visible on the window, position the seal with the mark in the 12 o' clock position. Check for satisfactory operation on completion.

14 Windscreen/tailgate/rear door washer system components – removal and refitting

Washer reservoir

Removal

1 The washer reservoir is located behind the front bumper on the left-hand side.
2 Firmly apply the handbrake, then jack up the front of the vehicle and support it securely on axle stands (see *Jacking and vehicle support*). Remove the left-hand roadwheel.
3 Remove the front bumper as described in Chapter 11, Section 22.
4 Release the fasteners and remove the front wheel arch liner on the left-hand side.

5 Disconnect the wiring connector and washer hoses from the washer pump **(see illustration)**.
6 Disconnect the wiring connector from the washer fluid level sensor **(see illustration)**.
7 Undo the reservoir front retaining bolt, located above the fluid level sender.
8 Undo the reservoir upper retaining bolt and side retaining bolt **(see illustrations)**.
9 Pull the reservoir off the filler pipe and remove it from under the wheel arch.

Refitting

10 Refitting is a reversal of removal.
11 On completion, top-up the reservoir with the required water/washer solution mix, and check for leaks and satisfactory operation.

Washer pump

Removal

12 Firmly apply the handbrake, then jack up the front of the vehicle and support it securely on axle stands (see *Jacking and vehicle support*). Remove the left-hand roadwheel.
13 Remove the front bumper as described in Chapter 11, Section 22.
14 Release the fasteners and remove the front wheel arch liner on the left-hand side.
15 Disconnect the wiring connector and washer hoses from the washer pump **(see illustration 14.5)**.

14.8a Washer reservoir upper retaining bolt (arrowed)...

16 Carefully prise the pump upwards out of the seal in the reservoir.

Refitting

17 Refitting is a reversal of removal. Lubricate the pump seal with a little washing-up liquid, to ease fitting of the pump.
18 On completion, top-up the reservoir with the required water/washer solution mix, and check for leaks and satisfactory operation.

Windscreen washer jets

Removal

19 Open the bonnet and, where applicable, support it with its stay rod.
20 Grip the windscreen washer jet and push it toward the rear while at the same time pulling it out of the bonnet. Disconnect the washer hose and, where applicable, the wiring connector, and remove the jet.

Refitting

21 Refitting is a reversal of removal. On completion, check that each nozzle provides a strong jet of washer fluid. The jets should be aimed to spray at a point slightly above the centre of the windscreen. If necessary, adjust the jets upward or downward only (not sideways) using the adjuster on the jet.

14.8b ...and side retaining bolt (arrowed)

15.4a Insert the special tools into the slots on each side of the audio unit...

15.4b ...then pull the audio unit from the facia

15.6 Disconnect the wiring and aerial connections at the rear of the audio unit

Tailgate/rear door washer jets

Removal

22 Unclip the wiper arm spindle nut cover, then using pliers, carefully pull the washer jet out of the centre of the wiper motor spindle.

Refitting

23 Refitting is a reversal of removal. On completion, check that the nozzle provides a strong jet of washer fluid. The jet should be aimed to spray at the centre of the wiped area of the glass. If necessary, adjust the jet using a pin.

15 Audio unit –
removal and refitting

Removal

Note: *This Section applies only to VW*

standard-fit audio equipment. The range of VW audio systems available is extensive and the removal and refitting procedures vary considerably. The contents of this Section therefore describes the procedures for the most common systems available.

1 Removal of the 'ALPHA', 'BETA' and 'GAMMA' audio units require the use of two VW special tools 3316. Removal of the 'DELTA' audio unit requires the use of four VW special tools T10057. Equivalent tools are available from car audio specialists.

2 Higher specification audio units may not require the use of the special tools for removal as they are bolted to the facia. If there are no slots for insertion of the special tools visible on the face of the unit, then it is likely to be a 'bolted-in' type.

3 Remove any CDs which may be in the unit. Switch off the ignition and all electrical consumers, and remove the ignition key.

4 If the unit incorporates slots on the face of the unit, insert the special tools into the slots on each side of the audio unit. Using the tools, pull the audio unit from the facia **(see illustrations)**.

5 If no slots are visible and the unit appears to be a 'bolted-in' type, then first remove the facia centre trim panel as described in Chapter 11, Section 29. Undo the four retaining bolts and pull the audio unit from the facia.

6 Disconnect the wiring and aerial connections at the rear of the unit, and remove the unit from the vehicle **(see illustration)**.

7 Remove the special tools.

Refitting

8 Refitting is a reversal of removal. When the leads are reconnected to the rear of the unit, press it into position to the point where the retaining clips are felt to engage, or alternatively, refit and tighten the retaining bolts.

16 Loudspeakers –
removal and refitting

Facia mounted loudspeakers

Removal

1 Using a plastic spatula or similar tool, carefully lever up the rear facing edge of the speaker grille. Disengage the tabs at the front and remove the grille **(see illustrations)**.

2 Undo the two screws (three screws on some speakers), then withdraw the speaker from the facia until the wiring connector becomes accessible **(see illustration)**. Disconnect the wiring connector and remove the speaker.

Refitting

3 Refitting is a reversal of removal.

Front door mounted loudspeakers

Removal

4 Remove the front door trim panel as described in Chapter 11, Section 9.

5 Disconnect the wiring connector from the loudspeaker **(see illustration)**.

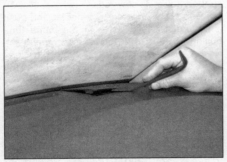

16.1a Carefully lever up the rear facing edge of the speaker grille...

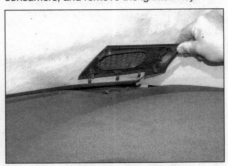

16.1b ...then disengage the tabs at the front and remove the grille

16.2 Facia mounted loudspeaker retaining screws (arrowed)

16.5 Disconnect the wiring connector from the loudspeaker

6 Drill out the retaining rivets, and withdraw the speaker from the door.

Refitting

7 Refitting is a reversal of removal. The special-sized rivets should be available from VW dealers and in-car entertainment specialists.

Side mounted loudspeakers

Removal

8 Remove the relevant side trim panel as described in Chapter 11, Section 24.
9 Disconnect the wiring connector from the loudspeaker.
10 Undo the retaining screws and remove the remove the speaker.

Refitting

11 Refitting is a reversal of removal.

17 Anti-theft alarm system and engine immobiliser – general information

An anti-theft alarm and immobiliser system is fitted as standard equipment. Should the system become faulty, the vehicle should be taken to a VW dealer or specialist for examination. They will have access to a special diagnostic tester which will quickly trace any fault present in the system.

18 Airbag system – general information and precautions

General information

A driver's airbag, located in the steering wheel centre pad is fitted as standard equipment on all models. Additionally, a passenger's airbag located in the facia, side airbags incorporated in the front seats and curtain airbags located in the roof headlining are also optionally available.

The system is armed only when the ignition is switched on however, a reserve power source maintains a power supply to the system in the event of a break in the main electrical supply. The system is activated by a 'g' sensor (deceleration sensor), incorporated in the airbag control unit and by crash sensors on both sides of the passenger compartment.

The airbags are inflated by gas generators, which force the bags out from their locations. Although these are safety items, their deployment is violently rapid, and this may cause injury if they are triggered unintentionally.

Precautions

 Warning: The following precautions must be observed when working on vehicles equipped with an airbag system, to prevent the possibility of personal injury.

General precautions

The following precautions must be observed when carrying out work on a vehicle equipped with an airbag:

a) *Do not disconnect the battery with the engine running.*
b) *Before carrying out any work in the vicinity of the airbag, removal of any of the airbag components, or any welding work on the vehicle, de-activate the system as described later in this Section.*
c) *Do not attempt to test any of the airbag system circuits using test meters or any other test equipment.*
d) *If the airbag warning light comes on, or any fault in the system is suspected, consult a VW dealer without delay.* **Do not** *attempt to carry out fault diagnosis, or any dismantling of the components.*

Precautions when handling an airbag

a) *Transport the airbag by itself, bag upward.*
b) *Do not put your arms around the airbag.*
c) *Carry the airbag close to the body, bag outward.*
d) *Do not drop the airbag or expose it to impacts.*
e) *Do not attempt to dismantle the airbag unit.*
f) *Do not connect any form of electrical equipment to any part of the airbag circuit.*

Precautions when storing an airbag

a) *Store the unit in a cupboard with the airbag upward.*
b) *Do not expose the airbag to temperatures above 80ºC.*
c) *Do not expose the airbag to flames.*
d) *Do not attempt to dispose of the airbag – consult a VW dealer.*
e) *Never refit an airbag which is known to be faulty or damaged.*

De-activation of airbag system

The system must be de-activated before carrying out any work on the airbag components or surrounding area:

a) *Switch on the ignition and check the operation of the airbag warning light on the instrument panel. The light should illuminate when the ignition is switched on, then extinguish.*
b) *Switch off the ignition.*
c) *Remove the ignition key.*
d) *Switch off all electrical equipment.*
e) *Disconnect the battery negative terminal (refer to 'Disconnecting the battery').*
f) *Insulate the battery negative terminal and the end of the battery negative lead to prevent any possibility of contact.*
g) *Wait for at least two minutes before carrying out any further work. Wait at least ten minutes if the airbag warning light did not operate correctly.*

Activation of airbag system

To activate the system on completion of any work, proceed as follows:

a) *Ensure that there are no occupants in the vehicle, and that there are no loose objects around the vicinity of the steering wheel.*
b) *Ensure that the ignition is switched off then reconnect the battery negative terminal.*
c) *Open the driver's door and switch on the ignition, without reaching in front of the steering wheel. Check that the airbag warning light illuminates briefly then extinguishes.*
d) *Switch off the ignition.*
e) *If the airbag warning light does not operate as described in paragraph c), consult a VW dealer before driving the vehicle.*

19 Airbag system components – removal and refitting

 Warning: Refer to the precautions given in Section 18 before attempting to carry out work on any of the airbag components.
Caution: To prevent any discharge of static electricity into the airbag circuit, temporarily touch the vehicle bodywork before disconnecting the wiring from any airbag unit.

Driver's airbag

Removal

1 De-activate the airbag system as described in Section 18. The airbag unit is an integral part of the steering wheel centre pad.
2 Turn the steering wheel 90º to the left so the spokes are uppermost.
3 Insert a screwdriver into the access hole in the back of the steering wheel, with the screwdriver engaged over the airbag retaining wire spring. Move the end of the screwdriver upward to release the wire spring from the lug on the airbag, while at the same time pulling the side of the airbag away from the steering wheel **(see illustration)**.
4 Turn the steering wheel 180º to the right so

19.3 Engage a screwdriver over the airbag retaining wire spring and move the end of the screwdriver upward to release the spring from the lug on the airbag

19.5a Withdraw the airbag from the steering wheel...

19.5b ...and disconnect the wiring connector

19.10 Disconnect the passenger airbag wiring at the connector (arrowed) on the airbag mounting bracket

19.11a Passenger airbag left-hand retaining bolt (arrowed)...

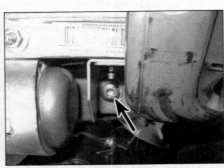

19.11b ...and right-hand retaining bolt (arrowed)

the other spokes are uppermost, then repeat the procedure described in paragraph 3.

5 Once the airbag retaining wire springs have been released, withdraw the airbag from the steering wheel and disconnect the wiring connector **(see illustrations)**. Remove the airbag and store it in a safe place, with reference to the precautions in Section 18.

Refitting

6 Refitting is a reversal of removal, noting the following points:
a) *The battery must still be disconnected when reconnecting the airbag wiring.*
b) *Ensure that the airbag wiring connector is securely reconnected.*
c) *The airbag must be firmly pressed into place to secure the retaining wire spring.*

19.20 Release the locking lever and disconnect the wiring from the airbag control unit

Passenger's airbag

Removal

7 De-activate the airbag system as described in Section 18.
8 Remove the facia left-hand lower trim panel as described in Chapter 11, Section 29.
9 Remove the heater/ventilation blower motor as described in Chapter 3, Section 9.
10 Disconnect the airbag wiring at the connector on the airbag mounting bracket **(see illustration)**.
11 Undo the two bolts securing the airbag frame to the facia crossmember **(see illustrations)**. Slide the assembly forward approximately 5.0 mm, lower it slightly and remove it from below. Store the airbag in a safe place, with reference to the precautions in Section 18.

19.21 Unscrew the three retaining nuts (arrowed) and remove the control unit

Refitting

12 Refitting is a reversal of removal, bearing in mind the following points:
a) *The battery must still be disconnected when reconnecting the airbag wiring.*
b) *Make sure that the wiring connector is securely reconnected.*
c) *Tighten the mounting bolts securely.*

Front seat side impact airbags

13 The side impact airbags are integral with the seats. As seat upholstery removal requires considerable skill and experience, if it is to be carried out without damage, it is best entrusted to an expert.

Roof curtain airbags

14 This work involves removing the headlining and major dismantling of interior trim panels, and is best entrusted to a VW dealer.

Airbag control unit

15 The airbag control unit is located beneath the centre of the facia.
16 De-activate the airbag system as described in Section 18.
17 Undo the retaining screw, slide the footrest upwards and remove it from inside the driver's footwell.
18 Remove the facia lower trim panels as necessary, as described in Chapter 11, Section 29 to enable the carpet under the facia to be folded back onto the front seats.
19 Pull the control unit cover off the retaining pins.
20 Release the locking lever and disconnect the wiring from the control unit **(see illustration)**.
21 Unscrew the three retaining nuts and remove the control unit from the vehicle **(see illustration)**.
22 Refitting is a reversal of removal making sure the wiring connector is securely reconnected.

Airbag wiring contact unit

Removal

23 The airbag wiring contact unit is clipped to the face of the steering column switch module.

24 De-activate the airbag system as described in Section 18.
25 Remove the steering wheel as described in Chapter 10, Section 16. Ensure that the roadwheels remain in the straight-ahead position.
26 Remove the steering column shrouds as described in Chapter 11, Section 29.

27 Insert a small screwdriver between the upper left-hand corner of the airbag wiring contact unit, and the steering column switch module.
28 Press the housing of the contact unit upwards slightly until the catch of the electrical connector releases (if necessary use a second small screwdriver).
29 Release the lower retaining clips and

keep the contact unit slightly under tension to prevent the clips re-engaging.
30 Release the upper clips then remove the contact unit from the switch module. Do not allow the contact unit to move out of its central position whilst removed.
Refitting
31 Refitting is a reversal of removal.

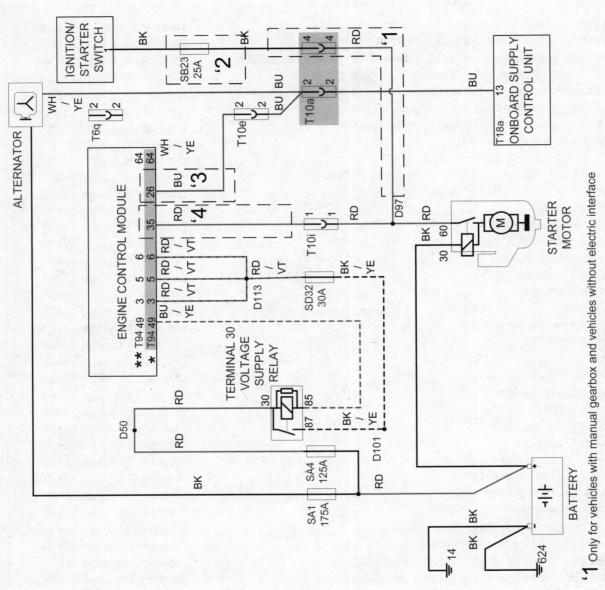

Diagram 1 – Starting and charging systems 1.9 and 2.5 diesel from 2003

'1 Only for vehicles with manual gearbox and vehicles without electric interface

'2 Only for vehicles with make year from February 2004

'3 Only for vehicles with make year from June 2006 except AXB, AXC, AXD and AXE

'4 Only for vehicles with engine codes AXB and AXC

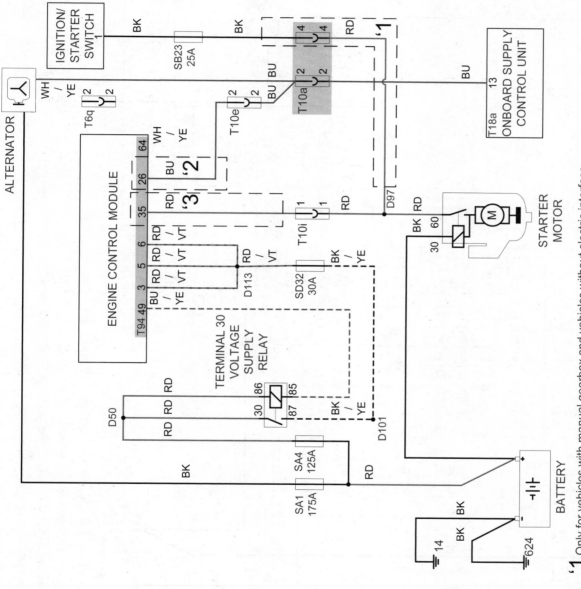

Diagram 2 – Starting and charging systems 1.9 and 2.5 diesel from November 2007

'1 Only for vehicles with manual gearbox and vehicles without electric interface

'2 Only for vehicles without engine codes AXB, AXC, AXD, AXE and BLJ

'3 Only for vehicles with engine codes AXB and AXC

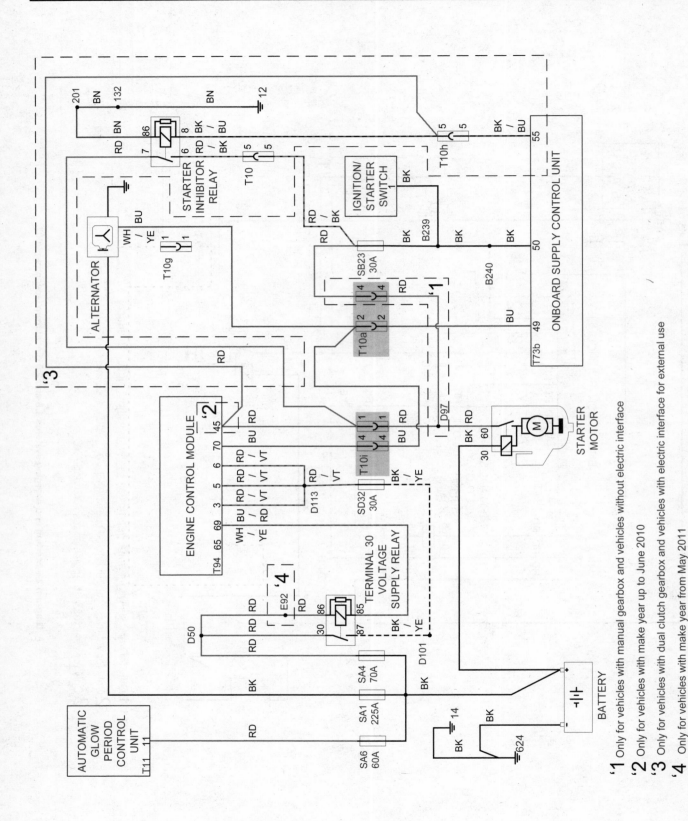

Diagram 3 – Starting and charging systems 2.0 diesel from August 2009

'1 Only for vehicles with manual gearbox and vehicles without electric interface
'2 Only for vehicles with make year up to June 2010
'3 Only for vehicles with dual clutch gearbox and vehicles with electric interface for external use
'4 Only for vehicles with make year from May 2011

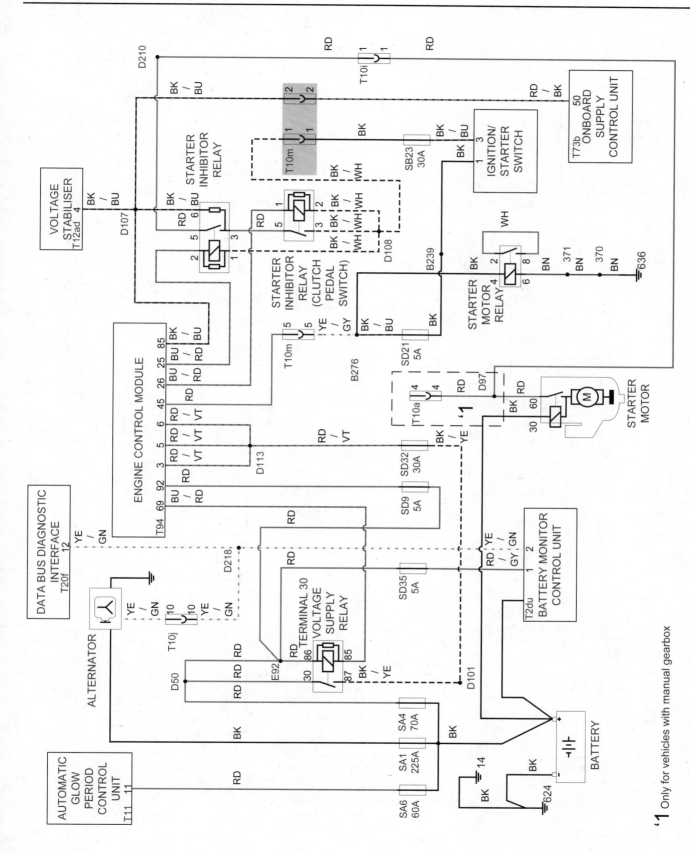

Diagram 4 – Starting and charging systems 2.0 diesel from May 2011

'1 Only for vehicles with manual gearbox

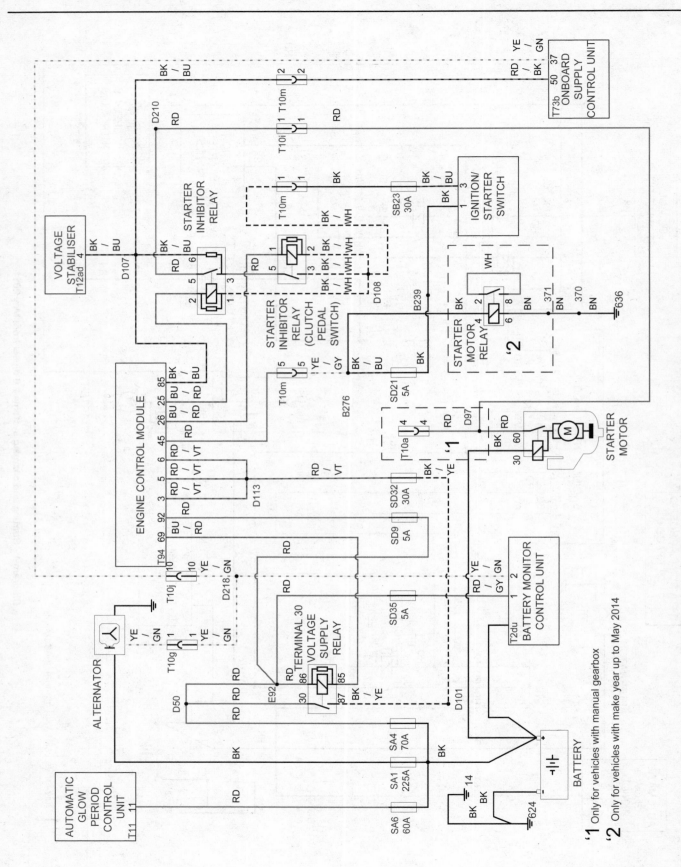

Diagram 5 – Starting and charging systems 2.0 diesel from November 2012

'1 Only for vehicles with manual gearbox

'2 Only for vehicles with make year up to May 2014

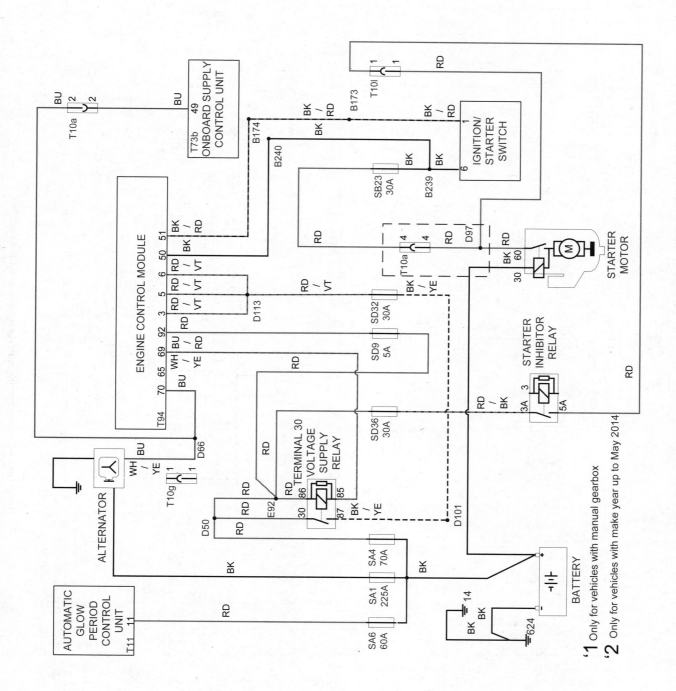

Diagram 6 – Starting and charging systems 2.0 diesel from May 2014

'1 Only for vehicles with manual gearbox
'2 Only for vehicles with make year up to May 2014

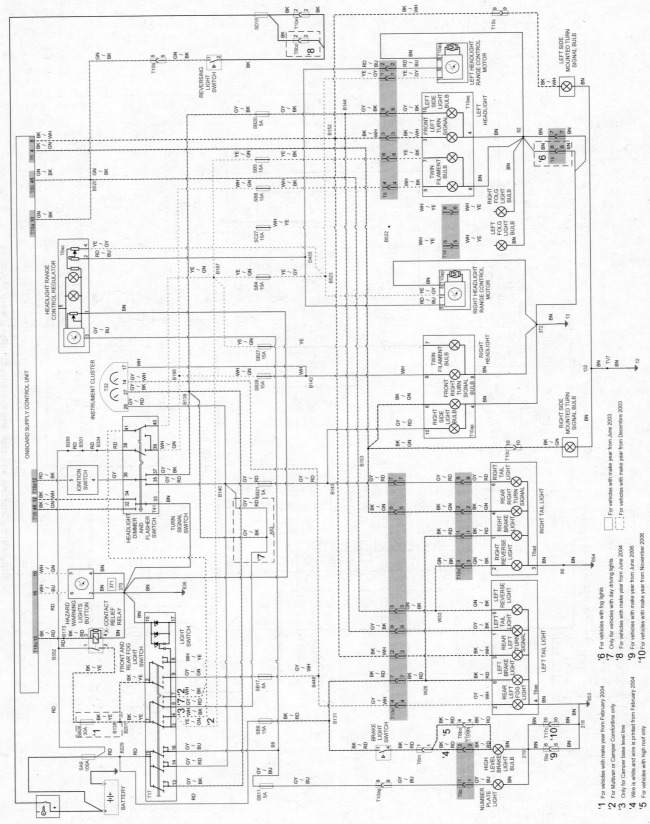

Diagram 7 – Exterior lighting with Halogen headlights from 2003

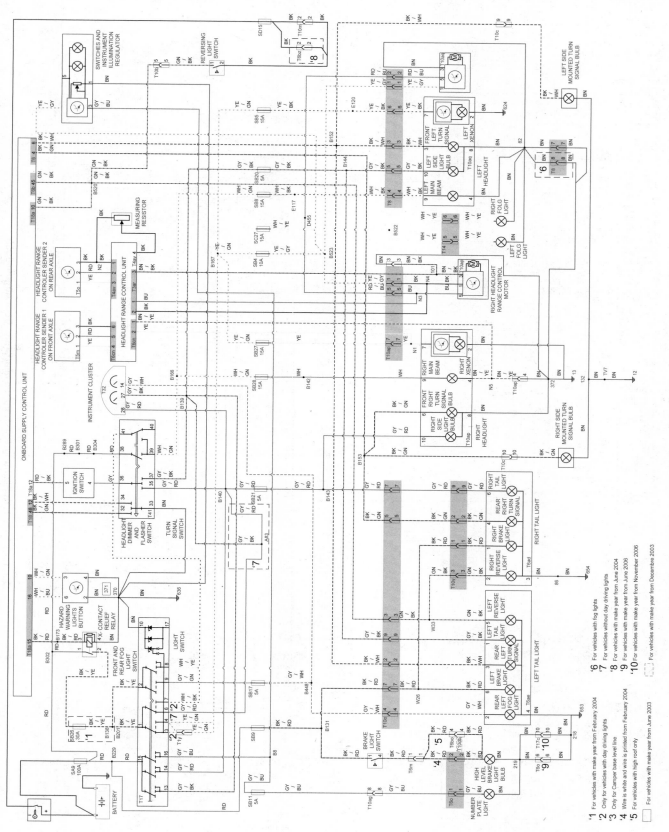

Diagram 8 – Exterior lighting with Xenon headlights from 2003

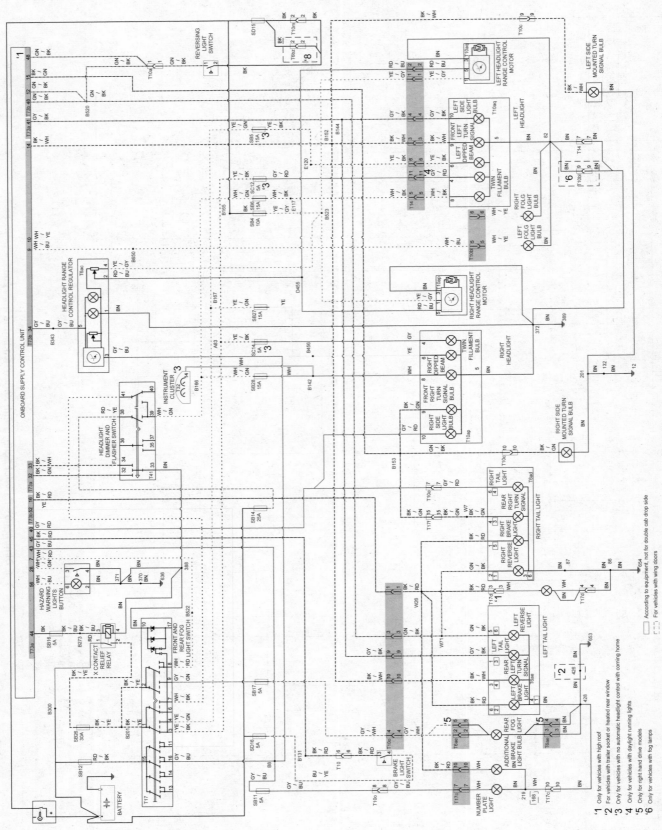

Diagram 9 – Exterior lighting with Halogen headlights from August 2009

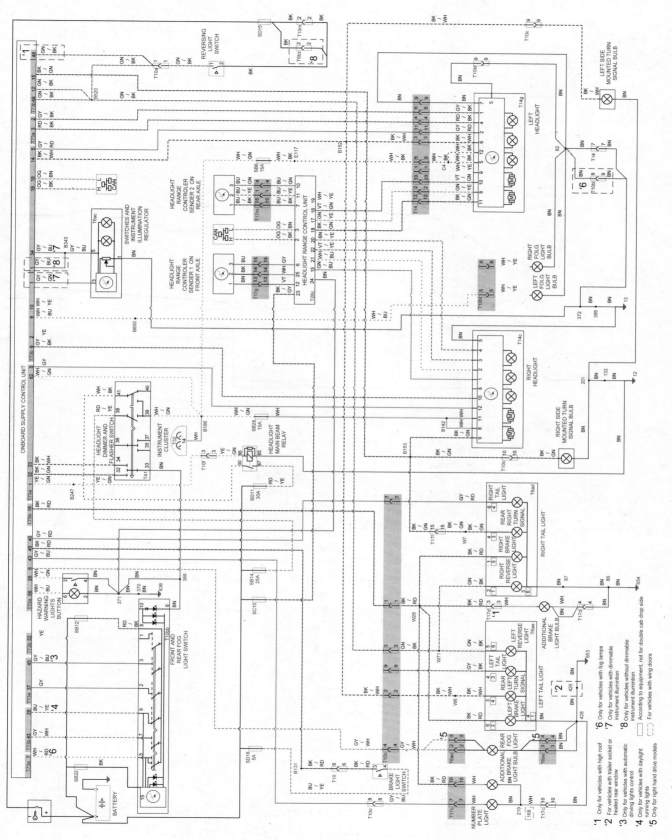

Diagram 10 – Exterior lighting with Xenon headlights from May 2011

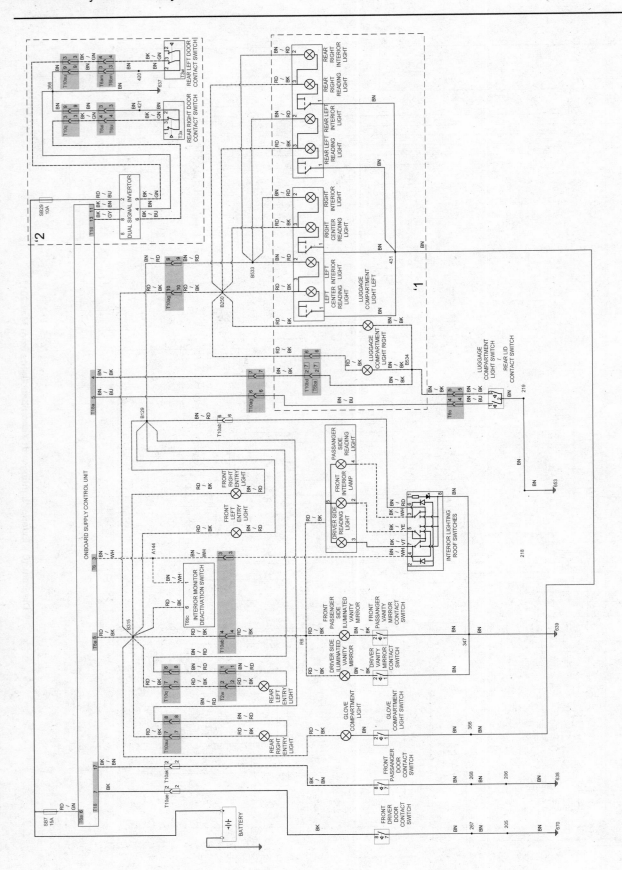

Diagram 11 – Interior lights from 2003

'1 For Multivan only

'2 For vehicles without electric sliding doors

'3 For vehicles with make year from December 2003

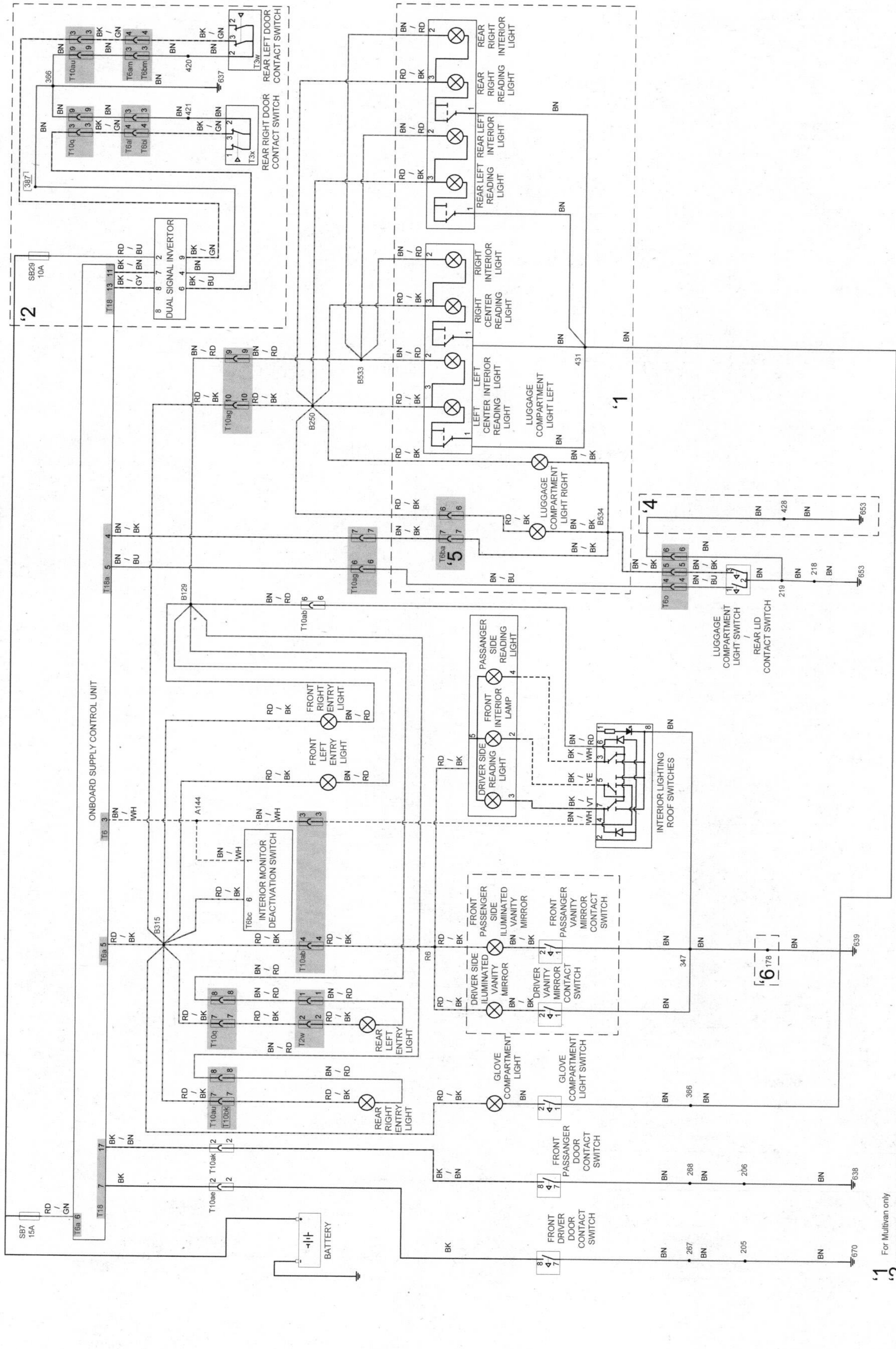
ONBOARD SUPPLY CONTROL UNIT
DUAL SIGNAL INVERTOR
REAR RIGHT DOOR CONTACT SWITCH
REAR LEFT DOOR CONTACT SWITCH
LEFT CENTER READING LIGHT
LEFT CENTER INTERIOR LIGHT
RIGHT CENTER READING LIGHT
RIGHT INTERIOR LIGHT
REAR LEFT READING LIGHT
REAR LEFT INTERIOR LIGHT
REAR RIGHT READING LIGHT
REAR RIGHT INTERIOR LIGHT
LUGGAGE COMPARTMENT LIGHT LEFT
LUGGAGE COMPARTMENT LIGHT RIGHT
LUGGAGE COMPARTMENT LIGHT SWITCH / REAR LID CONTACT SWITCH
FRONT RIGHT ENTRY LIGHT
FRONT LEFT ENTRY LIGHT
PASSANGER SIDE READING LIGHT
FRONT INTERIOR LAMP
DRIVER SIDE READING LIGHT
INTERIOR LIGHTING ROOF SWITCHES
INTERIOR MONITOR DEACTIVATION SWITCH
FRONT PASSENGER SIDE ILLUMINATED VANITY MIRROR
DRIVER SIDE ILLUMINATED VANITY MIRROR
FRONT PASSANGER VANITY MIRROR CONTACT SWITCH
DRIVER VANITY MIRROR CONTACT SWITCH
REAR LEFT ENTRY LIGHT
REAR RIGHT ENTRY LIGHT
GLOVE COMPARTMENT LIGHT
GLOVE COMPARTMENT LIGHT SWITCH
FRONT PASSANGER DOOR CONTACT SWITCH
FRONT DRIVER DOOR CONTACT SWITCH
BATTERY
SB7 15A
SB29 10A

'1 For Multivan only
'2 For vehicles without electric sliding doors
'3 Models with illuminated vanity mirror only
'4 For vehicles with make year from January 2005
'5 For vehicles with make year to Decembre 2005
'6 Only for vehicles with sliding / tilting sunroof
□ For vehicles with make year from January 2005
[ ] Only for vehicles with mechanical sliding door and anti-thief system make year from January 2005

Diagram 12 – Interior lights from February 2004

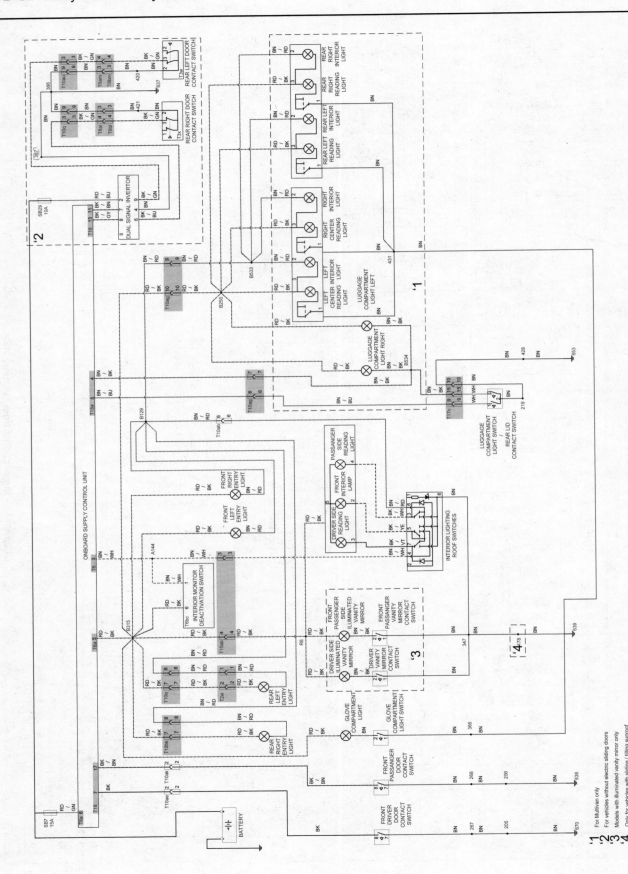

Diagram 13 – Interior lights from November 2006

*'1 For Multivan only
*'2 For vehicles without electric sliding doors
*'3 Models with illuminated vanity mirror only
*'4 Only for vehicles with sliding / tilting sunroof
[ ] Only for vehicles with mechanical sliding door and anti-thief system make year from January 2005

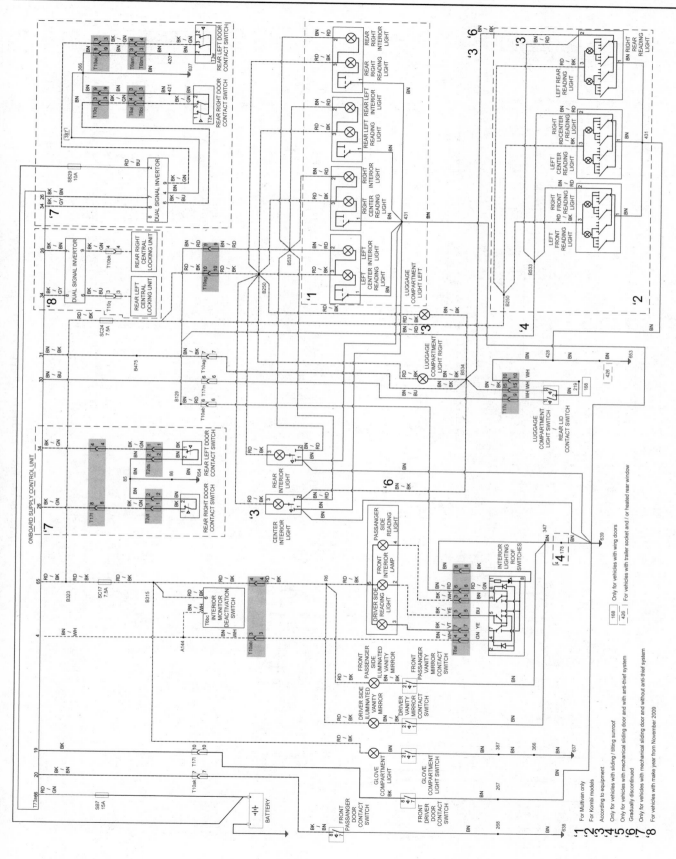

Diagram 14 – Interior lights from August 2009

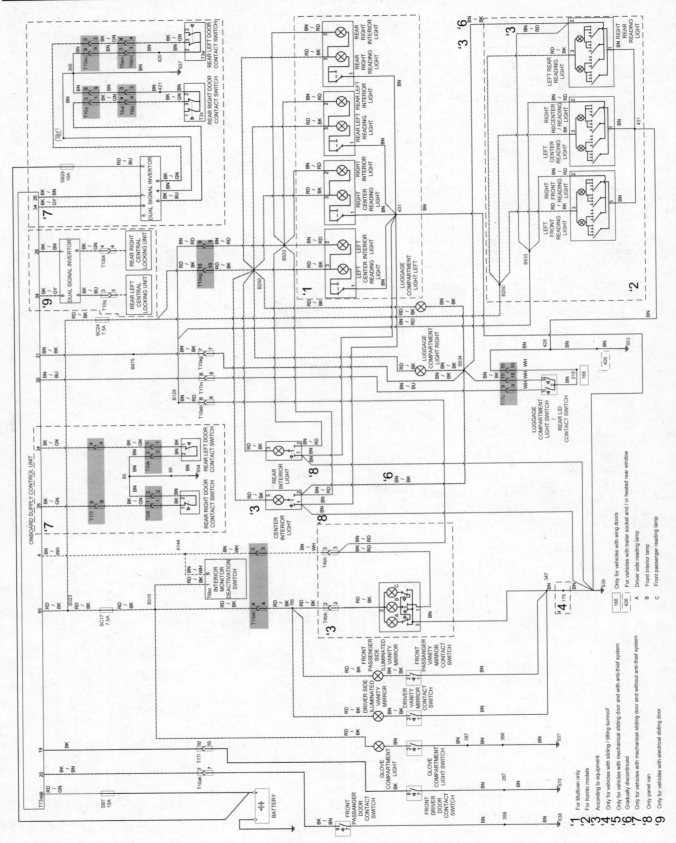

Diagram 15 – Interior lights from February 2011

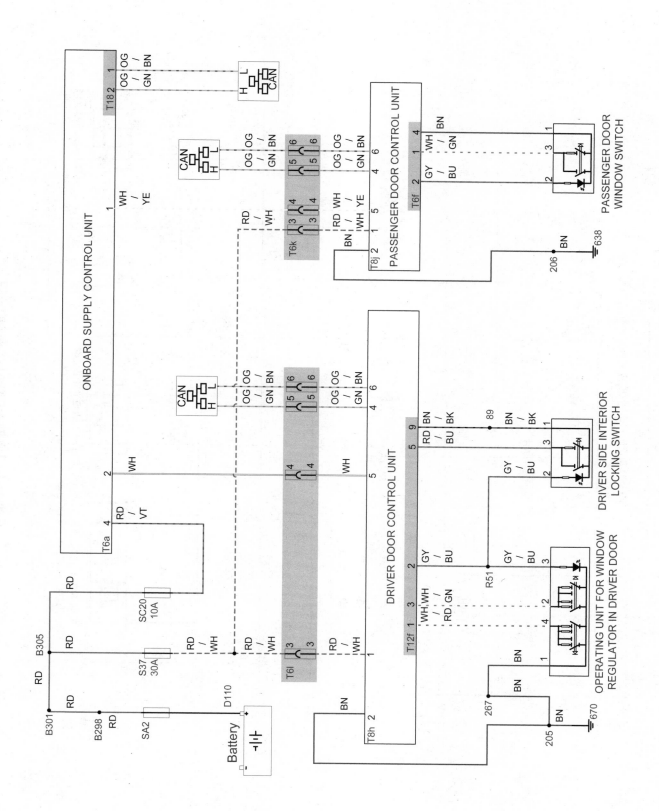

Diagram 16 – Electric windows from 2003

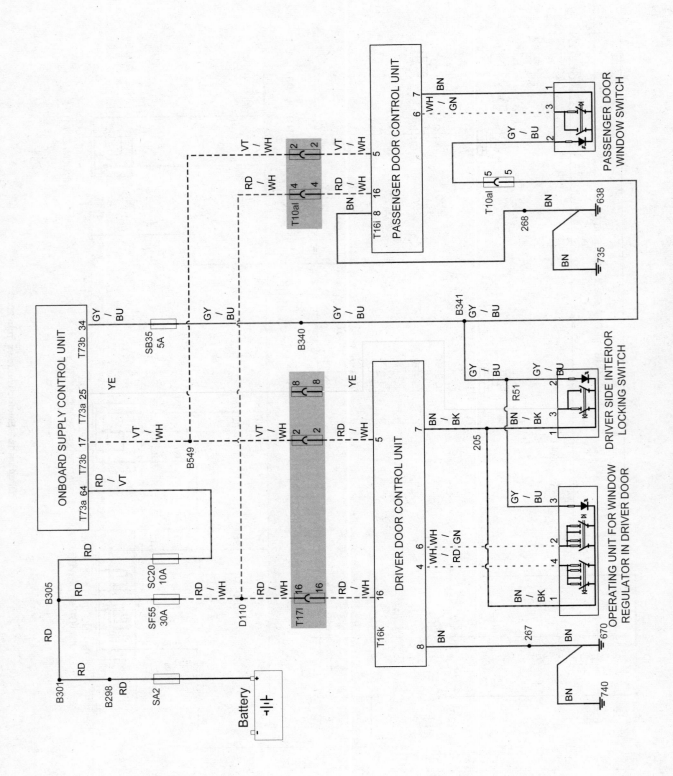

Diagram 17 – Electric windows from January 2009

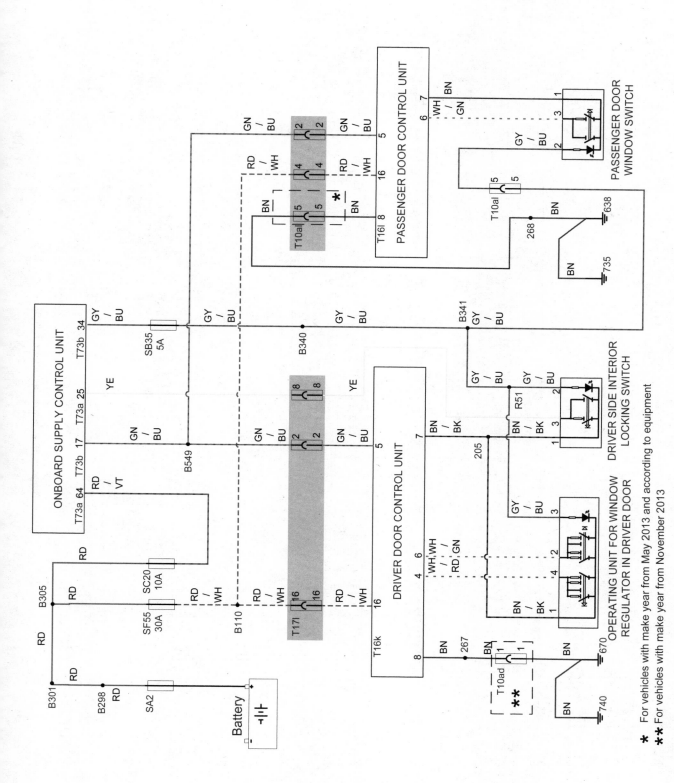

Diagram 18 – Electric windows from November 2012

* For vehicles with make year from May 2013 and according to equipment
** For vehicles with make year from November 2013

* For vehicles with make year from May 2013 and according to equipment
** For vehicles with make year from November 2013

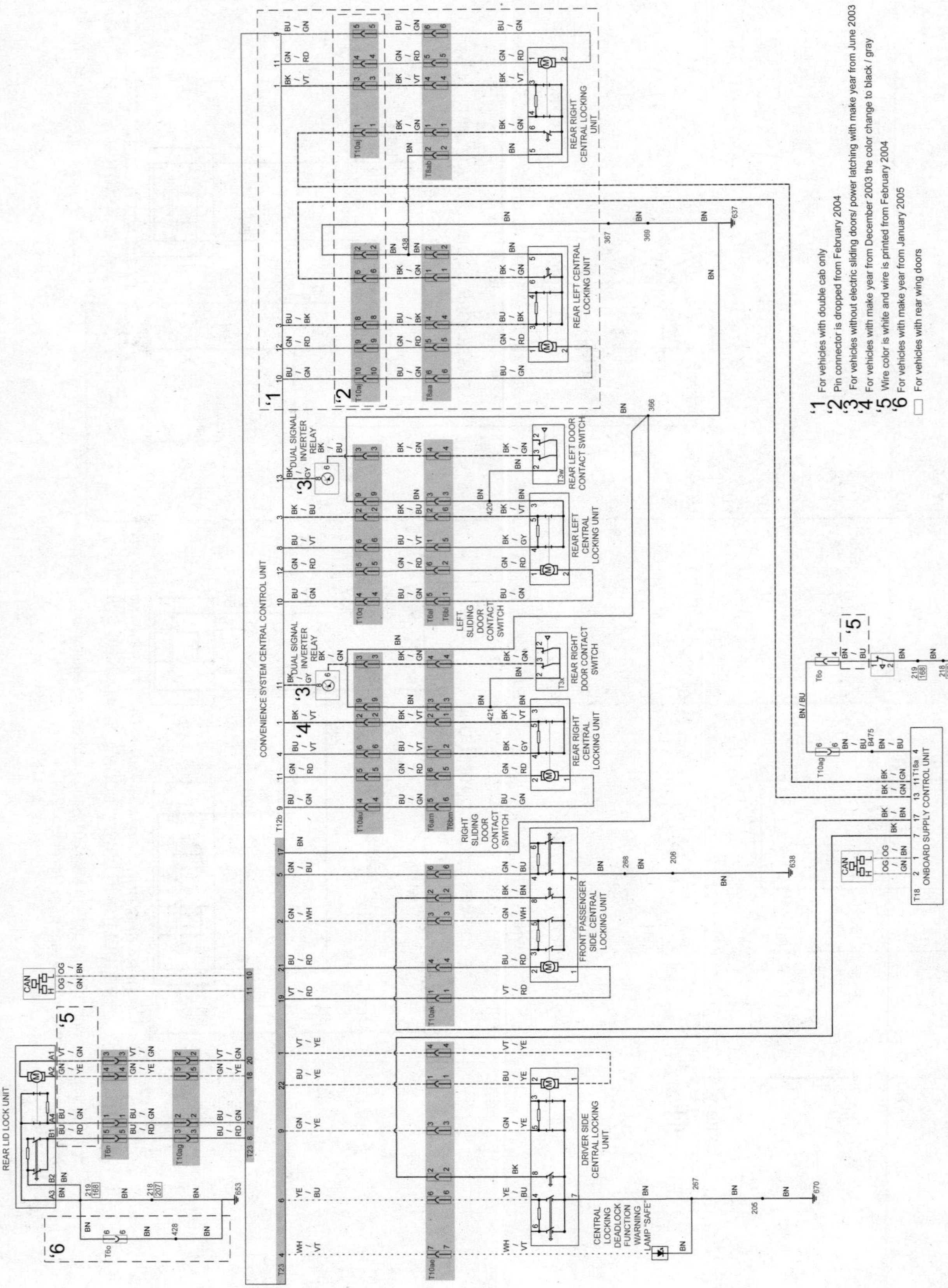

Diagram 19 – Central locking from 2003

'1 For vehicles with double cab only
'2 Pin connector is dropped from February 2004
'3 For vehicles without electric sliding doors/ power latching with make year from June 2003
'4 For vehicles with make year from December 2003 the color change to black / gray
'5 Wire color is white and wire is printed from February 2004
'6 For vehicles with make year from January 2005
□ For vehicles with rear wing doors

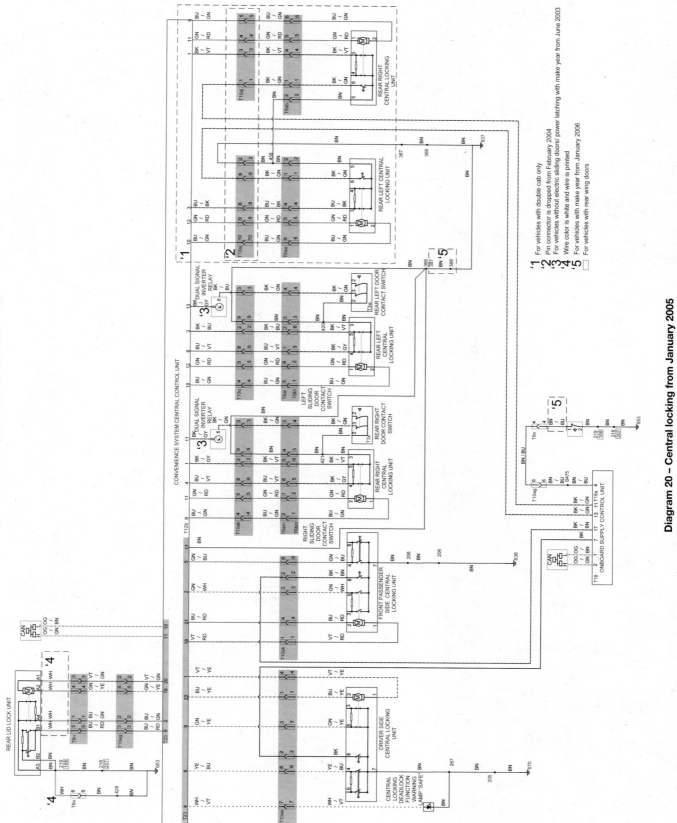

Diagram 20 – Central locking from January 2005

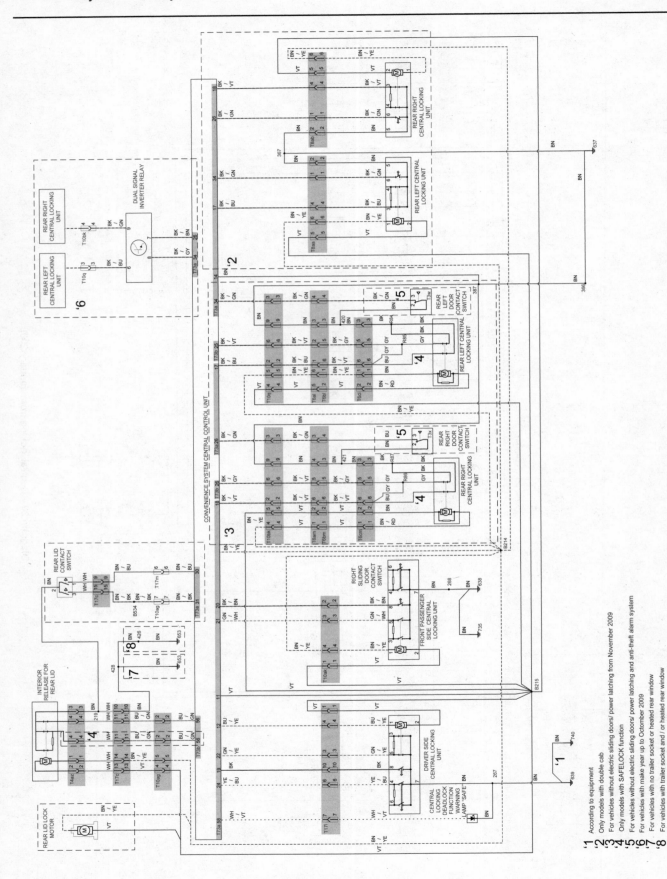

Diagram 21 – Central locking from January 2009

'1 According to equipment
'2 Only models with double cab
'3 For vehicles without electric sliding doors/ power latching from November 2009
'4 Only models with SAFELOCK function
'5 For vehicles without electric sliding doors/ power latching and anti-theft alarm system
'6 For vehicles with make year up to October 2009
'7 For vehicles with no trailer socket or heated rear window
'8 For vehicles with trailer socket and / or heated rear window

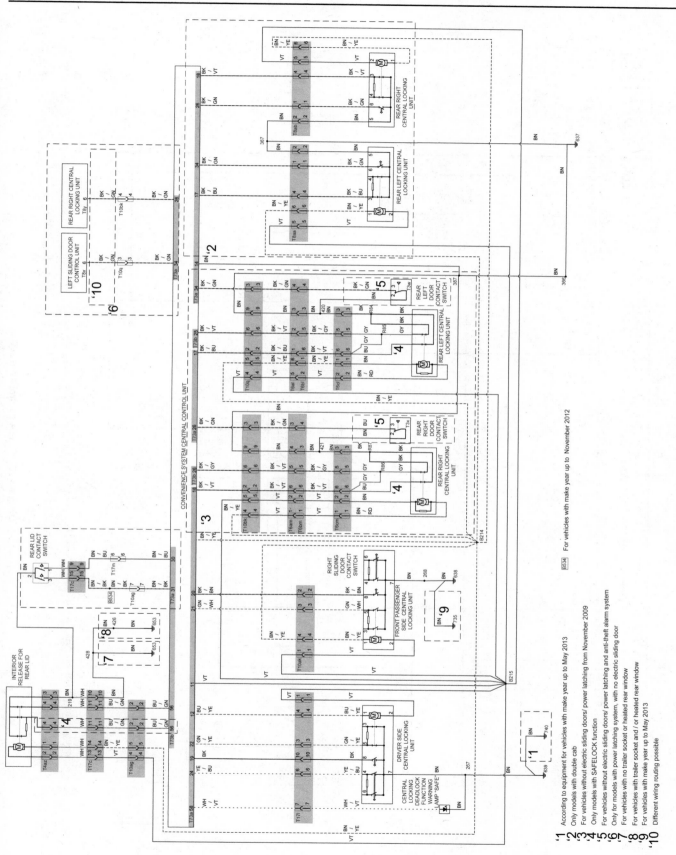

Diagram 22 – Central locking from November 2012

B534 For vehicles with make year up to November 2012

*1 According to equipment for vehicles with make year up to May 2013
*2 Only models with double cab
*3 For vehicles without electric sliding doors/ power latching from November 2009
*4 Only models with SAFELOCK function
*5 For vehicles without electric sliding doors/ power latching and anti-theft alarm system
*6 Only for models with power latching system, with no electric sliding door
*7 For vehicles with no trailer socket or heated rear window
*8 For vehicles with trailer socket and / or heated rear window
*9 For vehicles with make year up to May 2013
*10 Different wiring routing possible

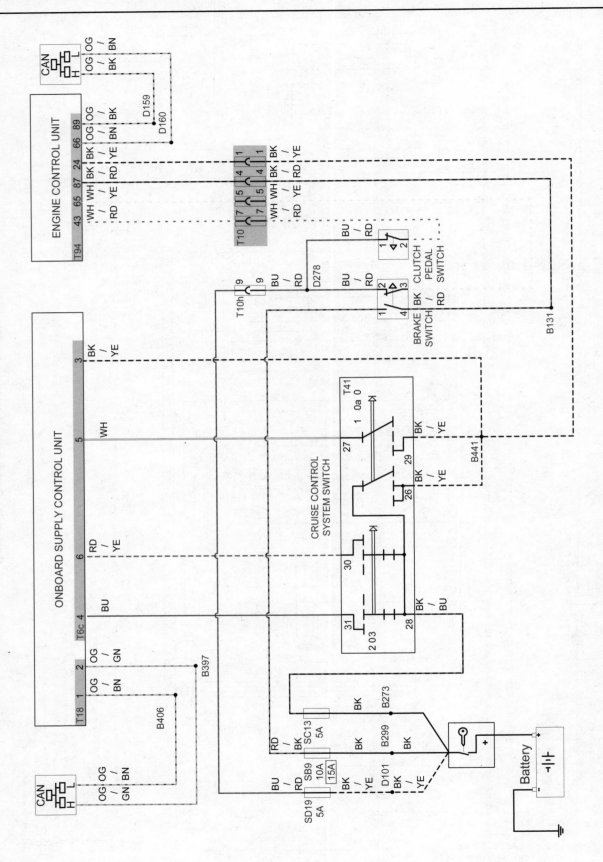

Diagram 23 – Cruise control from 2003

For vehicles with make year from September 2003

15A

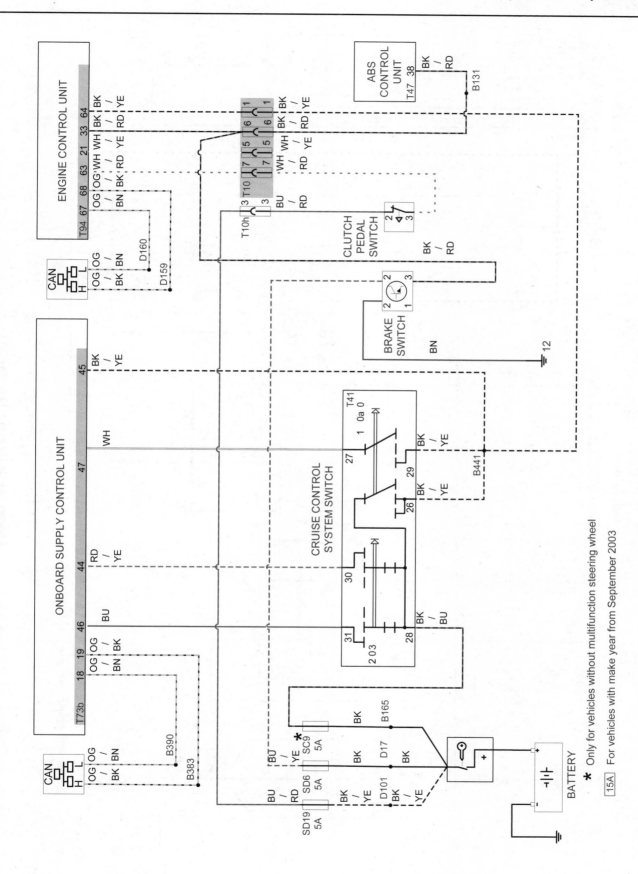

Diagram 24 – Cruise control from August 2009

* Only for vehicles without multifunction steering wheel

* For vehicles with make year from September 2003

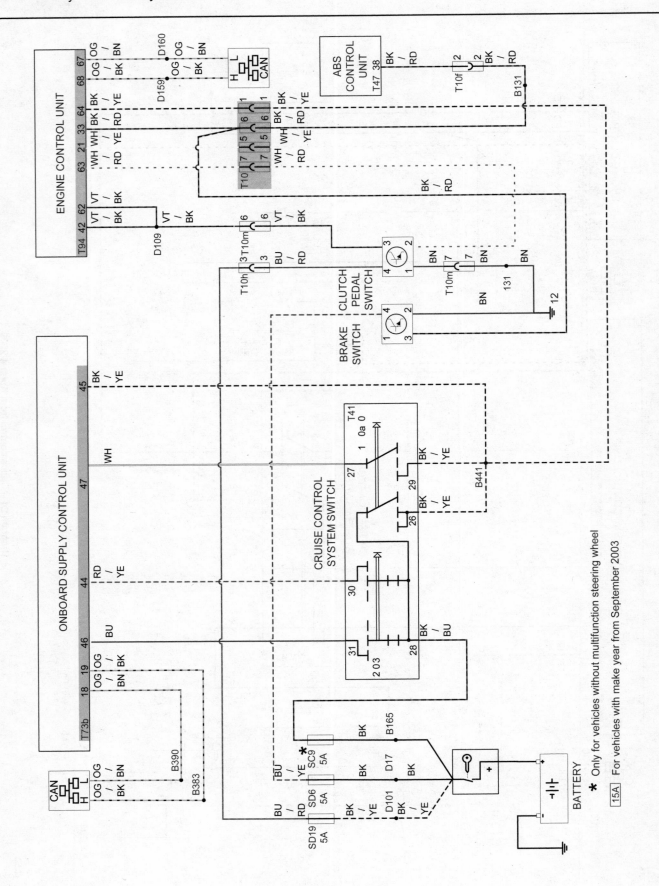

Diagram 25 – Cruise control from May 2011

* Only for vehicles without multifunction steering wheel

* For vehicles with make year from September 2003

15A

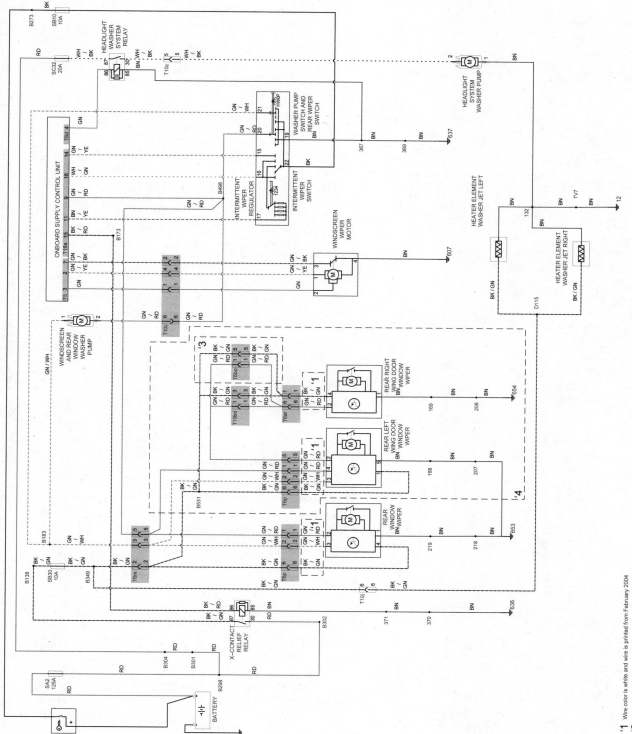

Diagram 26 – Wipers and washers from 2003

*1 Wire color is white and wire is printed from February 2004
*2 Wire color is black from June 2003
*3 Only for vehicles with make year from December 2003
*4 Only for vehicles with rear wing doors

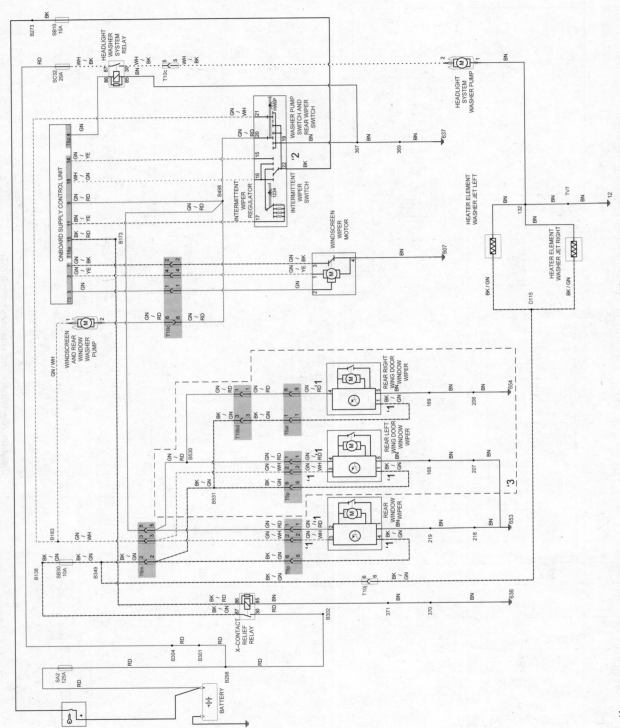

Diagram 27 – Wipers and washers from June 2006

*1 Wire color is white and wire is printed from February 2004
*2 Wire color is black from June 2003
*3 Only for vehicles with rear wing doors

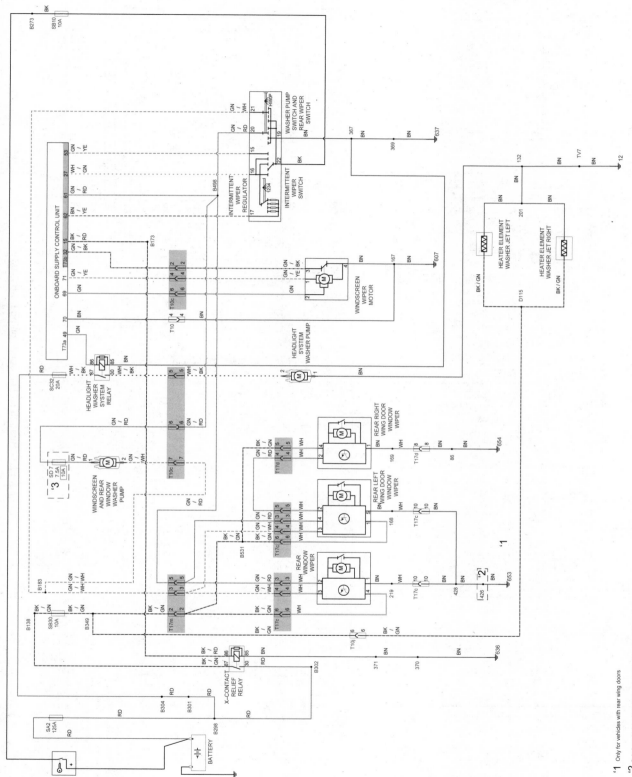

Diagram 28 – Wipers and washers from August 2009

*1 Only for vehicles with rear wing doors

*2 Only for vehicles with trailers socket and without heated rear window

*3 Only for vehicles with make year from June 2010 to April 2013

*3 For vehicles with make year from May 2012 to April 2013

10A

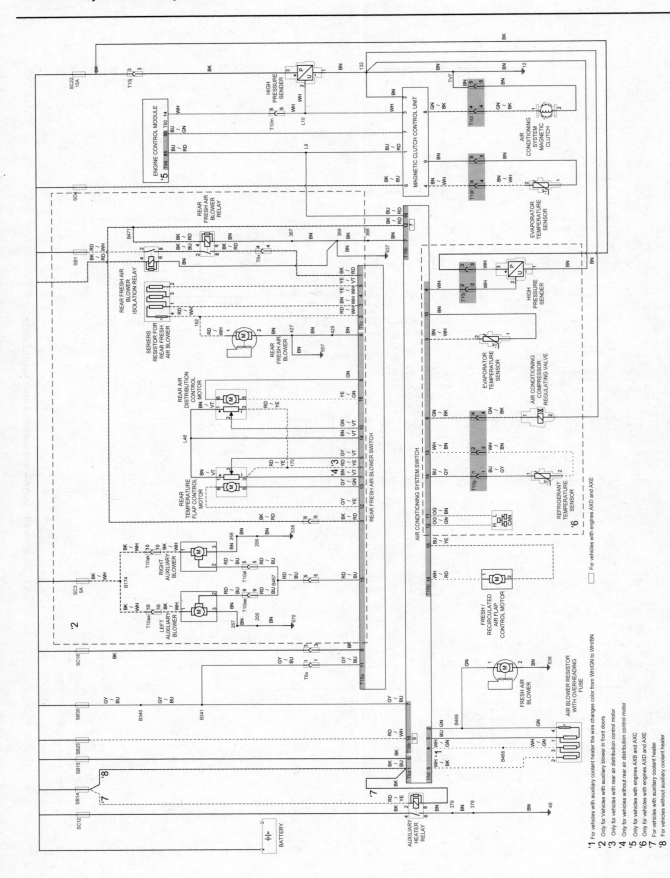

Diagram 29 – Heating and air conditioning from 2003

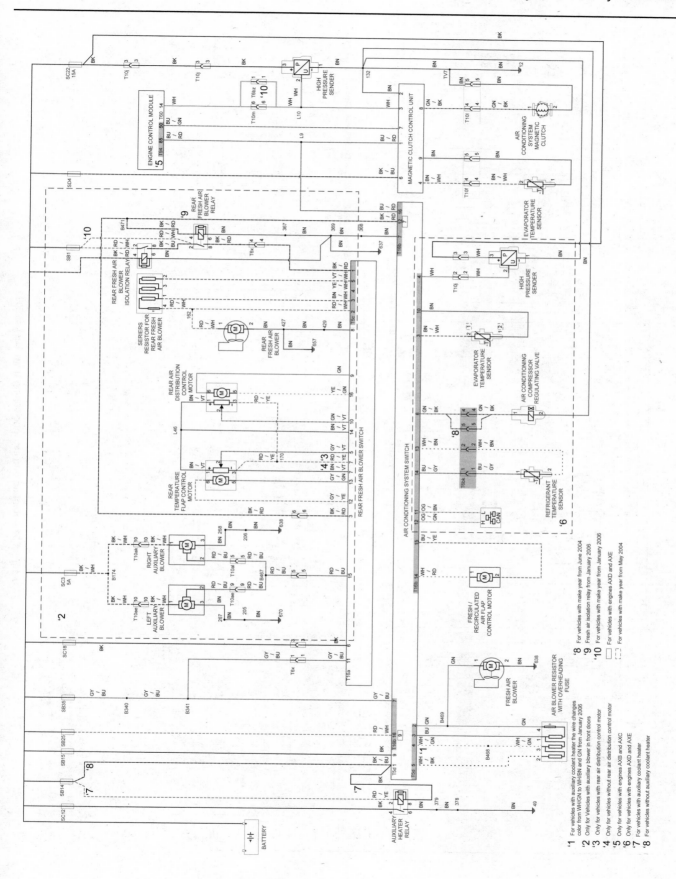

Diagram 30 – Heating and air conditioning from February 2004

*1 For vehicles with auxiliary coolant heater the wire changes color from WH/BN to WH/GN and GN from January 2006
*2 Only for Vehicles with auxiliary blower in front doors
*3 Only for vehicles without rear air distribution control motor
*4 Only for vehicles with rear air distribution control motor
*5 Only for vehicles with engines AXB and AXC
*6 Only for vehicles with engines AXD and AXE
*7 For vehicles with auxiliary coolant heater
*8 For vehicles without auxiliary coolant heater

*8 For vehicles with make year from June 2004
*9 Fresh air isolation relay from January 2006
*10 For vehicles with make year from January 2006
For vehicles with make year from May 2004

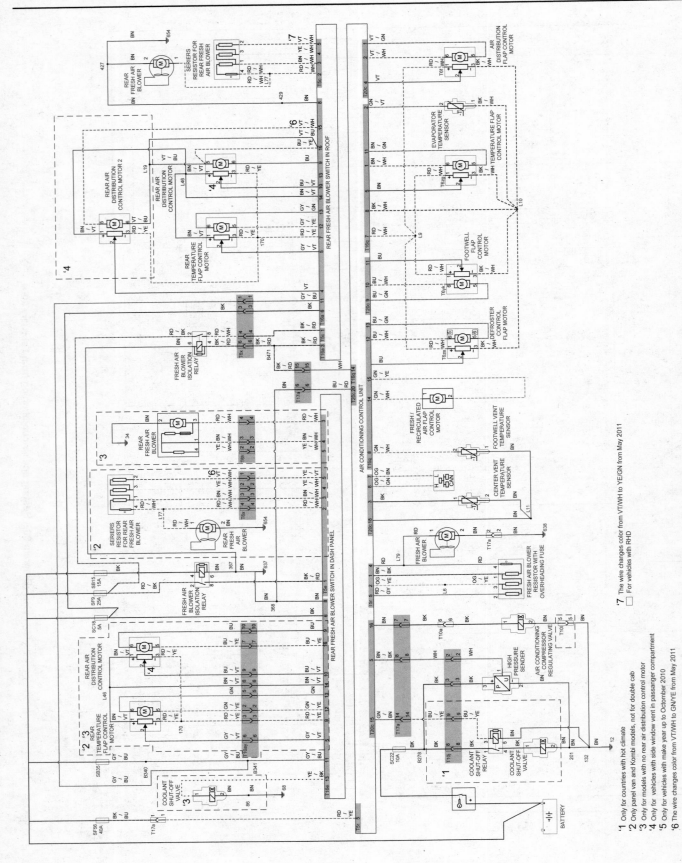

Diagram 31 – Heating and air conditioning from August 2009

'1 Only for countries with hot climate
'2 Only panel van and Kombi models, not for double cab
'3 Only for models with no rear air distribution control motor
'4 Only for vehicles with side window vent in passanger compartment
'5 Only for vehicles with make year up to Octomber 2010
'6 The wire changes color from VT/WH to GN/YE from May 2011

'7 The wire changes color from VT/WH to YE/GN from May 2011
□ For vehicles with RHD

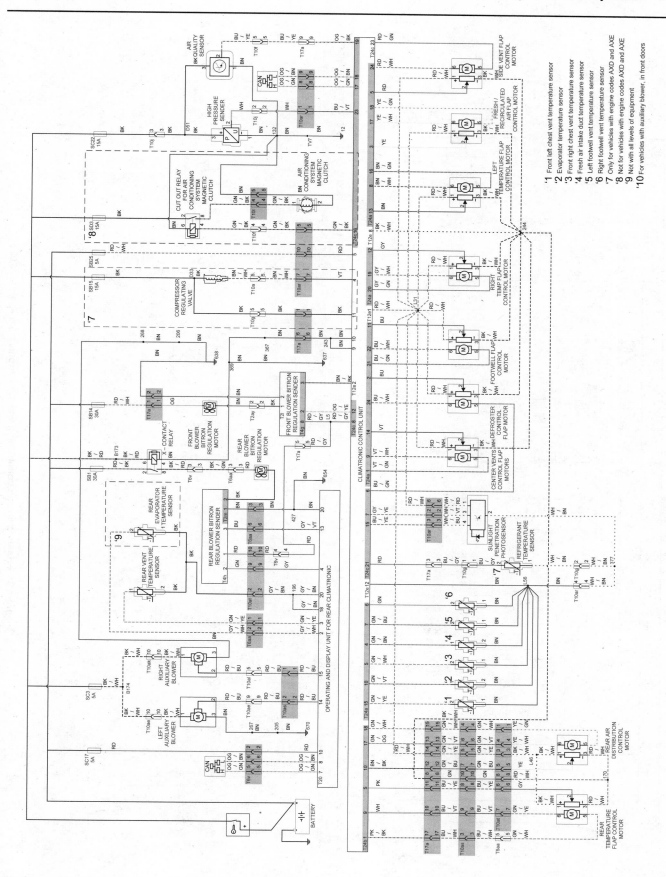

Diagram 32 – Heating and air conditioning with Climatronic from 2003

*1 Front left chest vent temperature sensor
*2 Evaporator temperature sensor
*3 Front right chest vent temperature sensor
*4 Fresh air intake duct temperature sensor
*5 Left footwell vent temperature sensor
*6 Right footwell vent temperature sensor
*7 Only for vehicles with engine codes AXD and AXE
*8 Not for vehicles with engine codes AXD and AXE
*9 Not with all levels of equipment
*10 For vehicles with auxiliary blower, in front doors

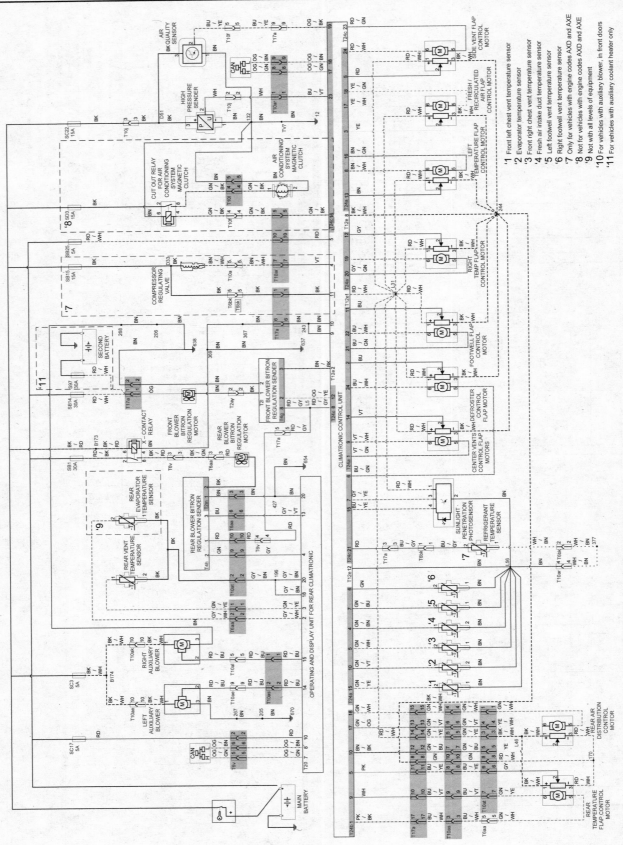

Diagram 33 – Heating and air conditioning with Climatronic from February 2004

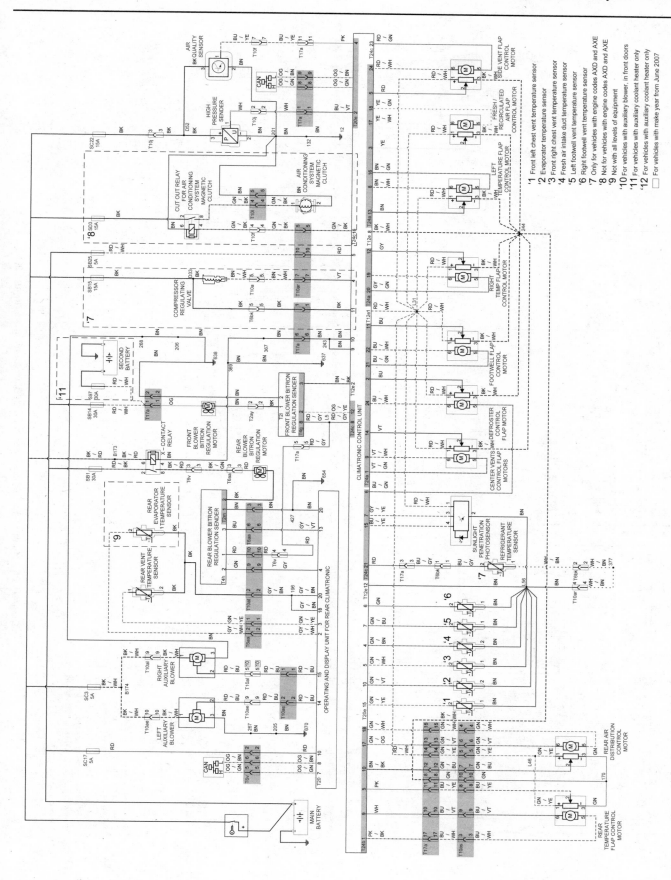

Diagram 34 – Heating and air conditioning with Climatronic from June 2006

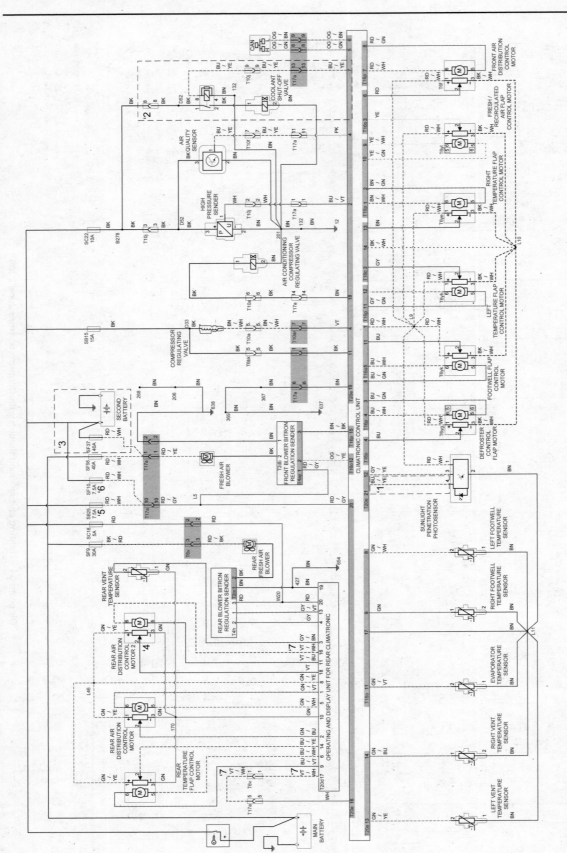

Diagram 35 – Heating and air conditioning with Climatronic from August 2009

*1 Only for vehicles with convenience dash panel
*2 Only for countries with hot climate
*3 For vehicles with auxiliary coolant heater only
*4 Only for vehicles with side window vent in passanger compartment
*5 Only for vehicles without start and stop system
*6 Only for vehicles with start and stop system
*7 The wire changes color from VT/WH to YE/GN from November 2011

☐ For vehicles with RHD

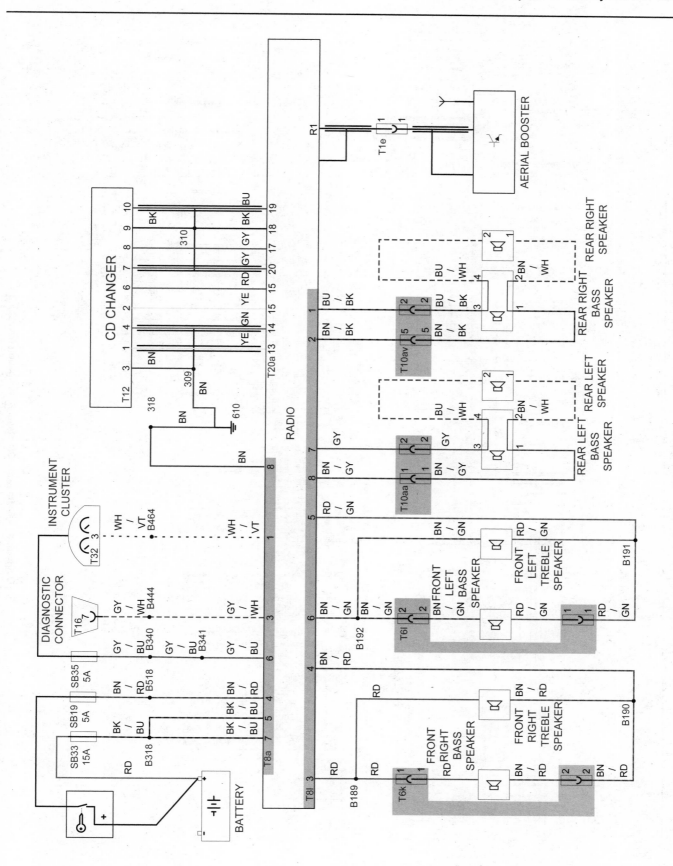

Diagram 36 – Alpha, Beta & Gamma radio/CD player from 2003

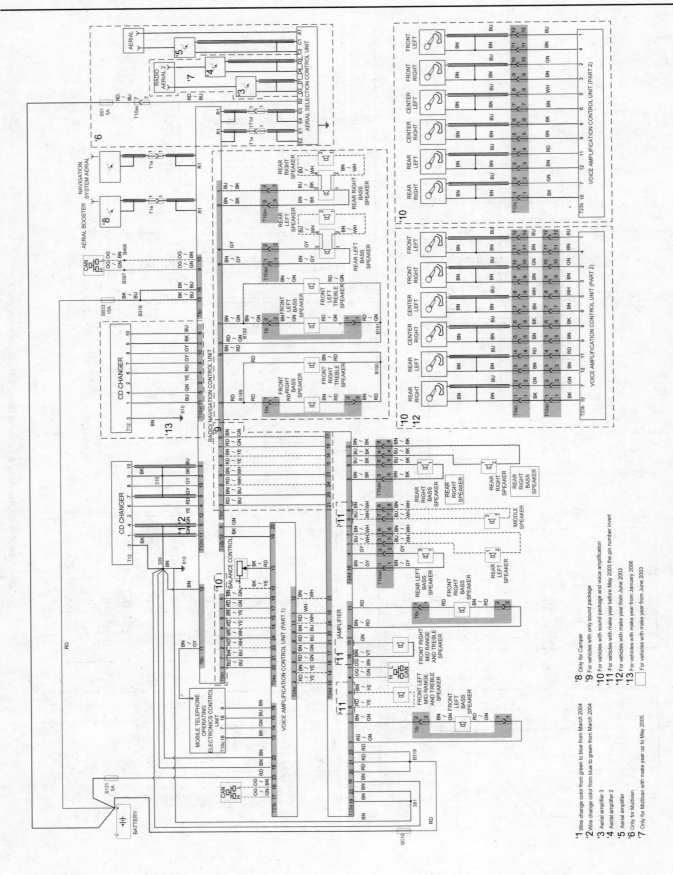

Diagram 37 – Delta radio/CD player & Navigation from 2003

*1 Wire change color from green to blue from March 2004
*2 Wire change color from blue to green from March 2004
*3 Aerial amplifier 3
*4 Aerial amplifier 2
*5 Aerial amplifier
*6 Only for Multivan
*7 Only for Multivan with make year up to May 2005

*8 Only for Camper
*9 For vehicles with only sound package
*10 For vehicles with sound package and voice amplification
*11 For vehicles with make year before May 2003 the pin number invert
*12 For vehicles with make year from June 2003
*13 For vehicles with make year from January 2006

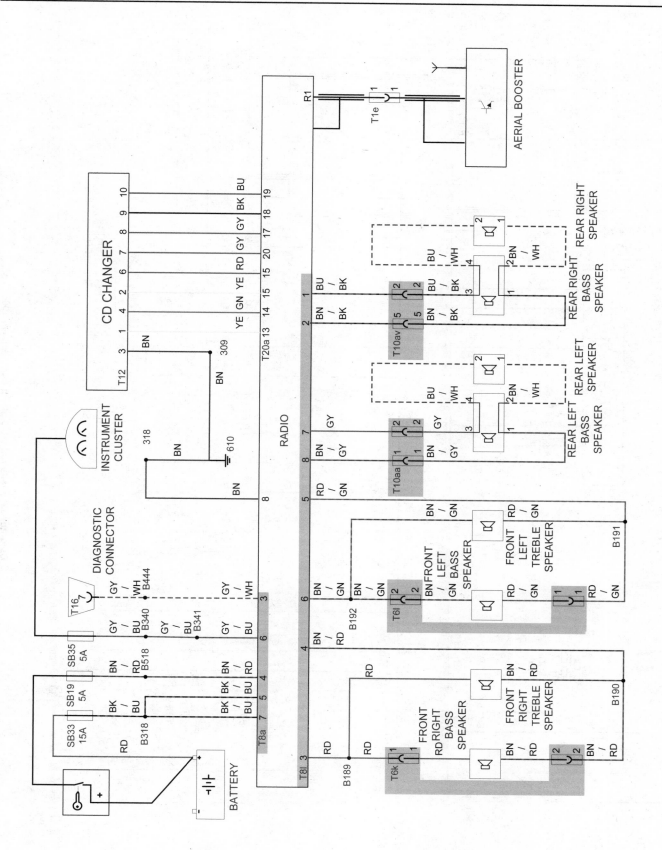

Diagram 38 – Alpha, Beta & Gamma radio/CD player from January 2006

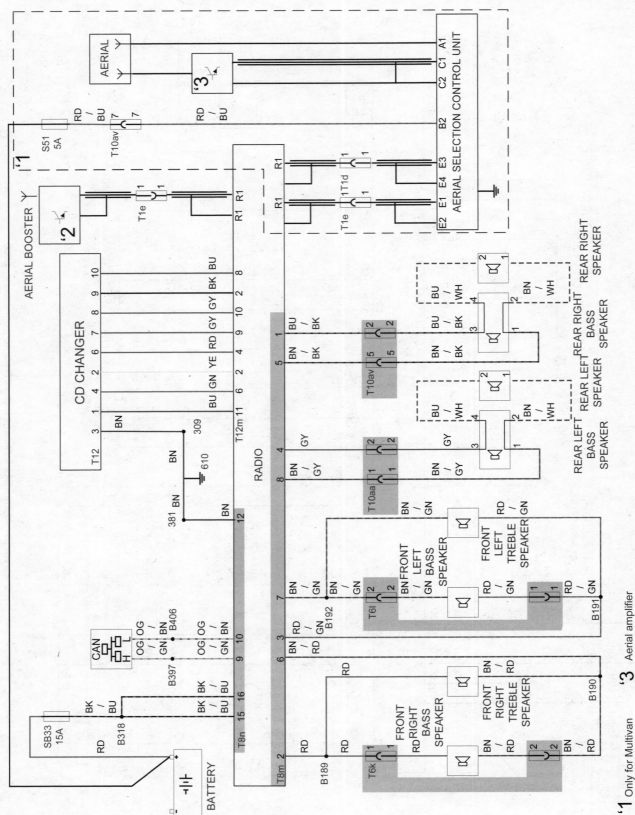

Diagram 39 – Delta radio/CD player from January 2006

'1 Only for Multivan
'2 Only for Camper
'3 Aerial amplifier

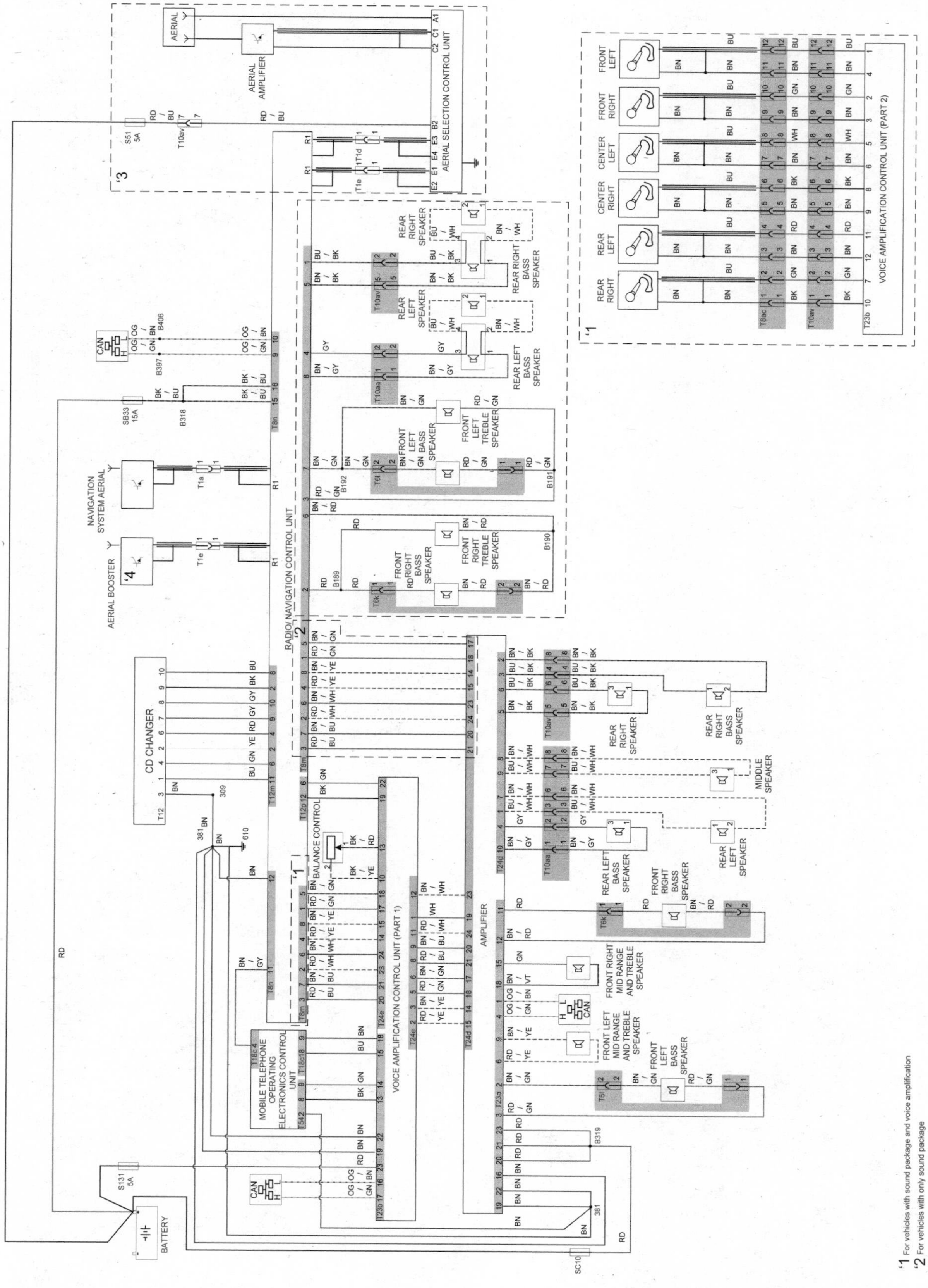

Diagram 40 – Delta radio/CD player & Navigation from November 2007

*1 For vehicles with sound package and voice amplification
*2 For vehicles with only sound package
*3 Only for Multivan
*4 Only for Camper

Dimensions and weights

Note: *All figures are approximate and may vary according to model. Refer to manufacturer's data for exact figures.*

Dimensions

Overall length:
  Van:
    Short wheelbase. . . . .   4892 mm
    Long wheelbase . . . .   5292 mm
  Chassis cab . . . .   5292 mm
Overall width (including door mirrors) . . . .   2283 mm
Overall height (unladen):
  Van:
    Standard roof . . . .   1990 mm
    High roof . . . .   2176 or 2476 mm
  Chassis cab: . . . .   1949 mm
Wheelbase:
  Short wheelbase. . . . .   3000 mm
  Long wheelbase . . . .   3400 mm
Front and rear track . . . .   1904 mm

Weights

Kerb weight . . . .   1905 kg to 2415 kg according to specification. Refer to manufacturer's documentation for latest information.

Fuel economy

Although depreciation is still the biggest part of the cost of motoring for most vehicle owners, the cost of fuel is more immediately noticeable. These pages give some tips on how to get the best fuel economy.

Working it out

Manufacturer's figures

Car manufacturers are required by law to provide fuel consumption information on all new vehicles sold. These 'official' figures are obtained by simulating various driving conditions on a rolling road or a test track. Real life conditions are different, so the fuel consumption actually achieved may not bear much resemblance to the quoted figures.

How to calculate it

Many cars now have trip computers which will

display fuel consumption, both instantaneous and average. Refer to the owner's handbook for details of how to use these.

To calculate consumption yourself (and maybe to check that the trip computer is accurate), proceed as follows.

1. Fill up with fuel and note the mileage, or zero the trip recorder.
2. Drive as usual until you need to fill up again.
3. Note the amount of fuel required to refill the tank, and the mileage covered since the previous fill-up.
4. Divide the mileage by the amount of fuel used to obtain the consumption figure.

For example:

Mileage at first fill-up (a) = 27,903
Mileage at second fill-up (b) = 28,346
Mileage covered (b - a) = 443
Fuel required at second fill-up = 48.6 litres

The half-completed changeover to metric units in the UK means that we buy our fuel

in litres, measure distances in miles and talk about fuel consumption in miles per gallon. There are two ways round this: the first is to convert the litres to gallons before doing the calculation (by dividing by 4.546, or see Table 1). So in the example:

48.6 litres ÷ 4.546 = 10.69 gallons
443 miles ÷ 10.69 gallons = 41.4 mpg

The second way is to calculate the consumption in miles per litre, then multiply that figure by 4.546 (or see Table 2).

So in the example, fuel consumption is:

443 miles ÷ 48.6 litres = 9.1 mpl
9.1 mpl x 4.546 = 41.4 mpg

The rest of Europe expresses fuel consumption in litres of fuel required to travel 100 km (l/100 km). For interest, the conversions are given in Table 3. In practice it doesn't matter what units you use, provided you know what your normal consumption is and can spot if it's getting better or worse.

Table 1: conversion of litres to Imperial gallons

litres	1	2	3	4	5	10	20	30	40	50	60	70
gallons	0.22	0.44	0.66	0.88	1.10	2.24	4.49	6.73	8.98	11.22	13.47	15.71

Table 2: conversion of miles per litre to miles per gallon

miles per litre	5	6	7	8	9	10	11	12	13	14
miles per gallon	23	27	32	36	41	46	50	55	59	64

Table 3: conversion of litres per 100 km to miles per gallon

litres per 100 km	4	4.5	5	5.5	6	6.5	7	8	9	10
miles per gallon	71	63	56	51	47	43	40	35	31	28

Maintenance

A well-maintained vehicle uses less fuel and creates less pollution. In particular:

Filters

Change air and fuel filters at the specified intervals.

Oil

Use a good quality oil of the lowest viscosity specified by the vehicle manufacturer (see *Lubricants and fluids*). Check the level often and be careful not to overfill.

Spark plugs

When applicable, renew at the specified intervals.

Tyres

Check tyre pressures regularly. Under-inflated tyres have an increased rolling resistance. It is generally safe to use the higher pressures specified for full load conditions even when not fully laden, but keep an eye on the centre band of tread for signs of wear due to over-inflation.

When buying new tyres, consider the 'fuel saving' models which most manufacturers include in their ranges.

Driving style

Acceleration

Acceleration uses more fuel than driving at a steady speed. The best technique with modern cars is to accelerate reasonably briskly to the desired speed, changing up through the gears as soon as possible without making the engine labour.

Air conditioning

Air conditioning absorbs quite a bit of energy from the engine – typically 3 kW (4 hp) or so. The effect on fuel consumption is at its worst in slow traffic. Switch it off when not required.

Anticipation

Drive smoothly and try to read the traffic flow so as to avoid unnecessary acceleration and braking.

Automatic transmission

When accelerating in an automatic, avoid depressing the throttle so far as to make the transmission hold onto lower gears at higher speeds. Don't use the 'Sport' setting, if applicable.

When stationary with the engine running, select 'N' or 'P'. When moving, keep your left foot away from the brake.

Braking

Braking converts the car's energy of motion into heat – essentially, it is wasted. Obviously some braking is always going to be necessary, but with good anticipation it is surprising how much can be avoided, especially on routes that you know well.

Carshare

Consider sharing lifts to work or to the shops. Even once a week will make a difference.

Electrical loads

Electricity is 'fuel' too; the alternator which charges the battery does so by converting some of the engine's energy of motion into electrical energy. The more electrical accessories are in use, the greater the load on the alternator. Switch off big consumers like the heated rear window when not required.

Freewheeling

Freewheeling (coasting) in neutral with the engine switched off is dangerous. The effort required to operate power-assisted brakes and steering increases when the engine is not running, with a potential lack of control in emergency situations.

In any case, modern fuel injection systems automatically cut off the engine's fuel supply on the overrun (moving and in gear, but with the accelerator pedal released).

Gadgets

Bolt-on devices claiming to save fuel have been around for nearly as long as the motor car itself. Those which worked were rapidly adopted as standard equipment by the vehicle manufacturers. Others worked only in certain situations, or saved fuel only at the expense of unacceptable effects on performance, driveability or the life of engine components.

The most effective fuel saving gadget is the driver's right foot.

Journey planning

Combine (eg) a trip to the supermarket with a visit to the recycling centre and the DIY store, rather than making separate journeys.

When possible choose a travelling time outside rush hours.

Load

The more heavily a vehicle is laden, the greater the energy required to accelerate it to a given speed. Remove heavy items which you don't need to carry.

One load which is often overlooked is the contents of the fuel tank. A tankful of fuel (55 litres / 12 gallons) weighs 45 kg (100 lb) or so. Just half filling it may be worthwhile.

Lost?

At the risk of stating the obvious, if you're going somewhere new, have details of the route to hand. There's not much point in achieving record mpg if you also go miles out of your way.

Parking

If possible, carry out any reversing or turning manoeuvres when you arrive at a parking space so that you can drive straight out when you leave. Manoeuvering when the engine is cold uses a lot more fuel.

Driving around looking for free on-street parking may cost more in fuel than buying a car park ticket.

Premium fuel

Most major oil companies (and some supermarkets) have premium grades of fuel which are several pence a litre dearer than the standard grades. Reports vary, but the consensus seems to be that if these fuels improve economy at all, they do not do so by enough to justify their extra cost.

Roof rack

When loading a roof rack, try to produce a wedge shape with the narrow end at the front. Any cover should be securely fastened – if it flaps it's creating turbulence and absorbing energy.

Remove roof racks and boxes when not in use – they increase air resistance and can create a surprising amount of noise.

Short journeys

The engine is at its least efficient, and wear is highest, during the first few miles after a cold start. Consider walking, cycling or using public transport.

Speed

The engine is at its most efficient when running at a steady speed and load at the rpm where it develops maximum torque. (You can find this figure in the car's handbook.) For most cars this corresponds to between 55 and 65 mph in top gear.

Above the optimum cruising speed, fuel consumption starts to rise quite sharply. A car travelling at 80 mph will typically be using 30% more fuel than at 60 mph.

Supermarket fuel

It may be cheap but is it any good? In the UK all supermarket fuel must meet the relevant British Standard. The major oil companies will say that their branded fuels have better additive packages which may stop carbon and other deposits building up. A reasonable compromise might be to use one tank of branded fuel to three or four from the supermarket.

Switch off when stationary

Switch off the engine if you look like being stationary for more than 30 seconds or so. This is good for the environment as well as for your pocket. Be aware though that frequent restarts are hard on the battery and the starter motor.

Windows

Driving with the windows open increases air turbulence around the vehicle. Closing the windows promotes smooth airflow and

reduced resistance. The faster you go, the more significant this is.

And finally . . .

Driving techniques associated with good fuel economy tend to involve moderate acceleration and low top speeds. Be considerate to the needs of other road users who may need to make brisker progress; even if you do not agree with them this is not an excuse to be obstructive.

Safety must always take precedence over economy, whether it is a question of accelerating hard to complete an overtaking manoeuvre, killing your speed when confronted with a potential hazard or switching the lights on when it starts to get dark.

Conversion factors

Length (distance)

Inches (in)	x 25.4	= Millimetres (mm)	x 0.0394	=	Inches (in)
Feet (ft)	x 0.305	= Metres (m)	x 3.281	=	Feet (ft)
Miles	x 1.609	= Kilometres (km)	x 0.621	=	Miles

Volume (capacity)

Cubic inches (cu in; in^3)	x 16.387	= Cubic centimetres (cc; cm^3)	x 0.061	=	Cubic inches (cu in; in^3)
Imperial pints (Imp pt)	x 0.568	= Litres (l)	x 1.76	=	Imperial pints (Imp pt)
Imperial quarts (Imp qt)	x 1.137	= Litres (l)	x 0.88	=	Imperial quarts (Imp qt)
Imperial quarts (Imp qt)	x 1.201	= US quarts (US qt)	x 0.833	=	Imperial quarts (Imp qt)
US quarts (US qt)	x 0.946	= Litres (l)	x 1.057	=	US quarts (US qt)
Imperial gallons (Imp gal)	x 4.546	= Litres (l)	x 0.22	=	Imperial gallons (Imp gal)
Imperial gallons (Imp gal)	x 1.201	= US gallons (US gal)	x 0.833	=	Imperial gallons (Imp gal)
US gallons (US gal)	x 3.785	= Litres (l)	x 0.264	=	US gallons (US gal)

Mass (weight)

Ounces (oz)	x 28.35	= Grams (g)	x 0.035	=	Ounces (oz)
Pounds (lb)	x 0.454	= Kilograms (kg)	x 2.205	=	Pounds (lb)

Force

Ounces-force (ozf; oz)	x 0.278	= Newtons (N)	x 3.6	=	Ounces-force (ozf; oz)
Pounds-force (lbf; lb)	x 4.448	= Newtons (N)	x 0.225	=	Pounds-force (lbf; lb)
Newtons (N)	x 0.1	= Kilograms-force (kgf; kg)	x 9.81	=	Newtons (N)

Pressure

Pounds-force per square inch (psi; lbf/in^2; lb/in^2)	x 0.070	= Kilograms-force per square centimetre (kgf/cm^2; kg/cm^2)	x 14.223	=	Pounds-force per square inch (psi; lbf/in^2; lb/in^2)
Pounds-force per square inch (psi; lbf/in^2; lb/in^2)	x 0.068	= Atmospheres (atm)	x 14.696	=	Pounds-force per square inch (psi; lbf/in^2; lb/in^2)
Pounds-force per square inch (psi; lbf/in^2; lb/in^2)	x 0.069	= Bars	x 14.5	=	Pounds-force per square inch (psi; lbf/in^2; lb/in^2)
Pounds-force per square inch (psi; lbf/in^2; lb/in^2)	x 6.895	= Kilopascals (kPa)	x 0.145	=	Pounds-force per square inch (psi; lbf/in^2; lb/in^2)
Kilopascals (kPa)	x 0.01	= Kilograms-force per square centimetre (kgf/cm^2; kg/cm^2)	x 98.1	=	Kilopascals (kPa)
Millibar (mbar)	x 100	= Pascals (Pa)	x 0.01	=	Millibar (mbar)
Millibar (mbar)	x 0.0145	= Pounds-force per square inch (psi; lbf/in^2; lb/in^2)	x 68.947	=	Millibar (mbar)
Millibar (mbar)	x 0.75	= Millimetres of mercury (mmHg)	x 1.333	=	Millibar (mbar)
Millibar (mbar)	x 0.401	= Inches of water (inH$_2$O)	x 2.491	=	Millibar (mbar)
Millimetres of mercury (mmHg)	x 0.535	= Inches of water (inH$_2$O)	x 1.868	=	Millimetres of mercury (mmHg)
Inches of water (inH$_2$O)	x 0.036	= Pounds-force per square inch (psi; lbf/in^2; lb/in^2)	x 27.68	=	Inches of water (inH$_2$O)

Torque (moment of force)

Pounds-force inches (lbf in; lb in)	x 1.152	= Kilograms-force centimetre (kgf cm; kg cm)	x 0.868	=	Pounds-force inches (lbf in; lb in)
Pounds-force inches (lbf in; lb in)	x 0.113	= Newton metres (Nm)	x 8.85	=	Pounds-force inches (lbf in; lb in)
Pounds-force inches (lbf in; lb in)	x 0.083	= Pounds-force feet (lbf ft; lb ft)	x 12	=	Pounds-force inches (lbf in; lb in)
Pounds-force feet (lbf ft; lb ft)	x 0.138	= Kilograms-force metres (kgf m; kg m)	x 7.233	=	Pounds-force feet (lbf ft; lb ft)
Pounds-force feet (lbf ft; lb ft)	x 1.356	= Newton metres (Nm)	x 0.738	=	Pounds-force feet (lbf ft; lb ft)
Newton metres (Nm)	x 0.102	= Kilograms-force metres (kgf m; kg m)	x 9.804	=	Newton metres (Nm)

Power

Horsepower (hp)	x 745.7	= Watts (W)	x 0.0013	=	Horsepower (hp)

Velocity (speed)

Miles per hour (miles/hr; mph)	x 1.609	= Kilometres per hour (km/hr; kph)	x 0.621	=	Miles per hour (miles/hr; mph)

Fuel consumption*

Miles per gallon, Imperial (mpg)	x 0.354	= Kilometres per litre (km/l)	x 2.825	=	Miles per gallon, Imperial (mpg)
Miles per gallon, US (mpg)	x 0.425	= Kilometres per litre (km/l)	x 2.352	=	Miles per gallon, US (mpg)

Temperature

Degrees Fahrenheit = (°C x 1.8) + 32   Degrees Celsius (Degrees Centigrade; °C) = (°F - 32) x 0.56

It is common practice to convert from miles per gallon (mpg) to litres/100 kilometres (l/100km), where mpg x l/100 km = 282

Spare parts are available from many sources, including maker's appointed garages, accessory shops, and motor factors. To be sure of obtaining the correct parts, it will sometimes be necessary to quote the vehicle identification number. If possible, it can also be useful to take the old parts along for positive identification. Items such as starter motors and alternators may be available under a service exchange scheme – any parts returned should be clean.

Our advice regarding spare parts is as follows.

Officially appointed garages

This is the best source of parts which are peculiar to your car, and which are not otherwise generally available (eg, badges, interior trim, certain body panels, etc). It is also the only place at which you should buy parts if the vehicle is still under warranty.

Accessory shops

These are very good places to buy materials and components needed for the maintenance of your vehicle (oil, air and fuel filters, light bulbs, drivebelts, greases, brake pads/shoes, touch-up paint, etc). Components of this nature sold by a reputable shop are of the same standard as those used by the vehicle manufacturer.

Besides components, these shops also sell tools and general accessories, usually have convenient opening hours, charge lower prices, and can often be found close to home. Some accessory shops have parts counters where components needed for almost any repair job can be purchased or ordered.

Motor factors

Good factors will stock all the more important components which wear out comparatively quickly, and can sometimes supply individual components needed for the overhaul of a larger assembly (eg, brake seals and hydraulic parts, bearing shells, pistons, valves). They may also handle work such as cylinder block reboring, crankshaft regrinding, etc.

Tyre and exhaust specialists

These outlets may be independent, or members of a local or national chain. They frequently offer competitive prices when compared with a main dealer or local garage, but it will pay to obtain several quotes before making a decision. When researching prices, also ask what 'extras' may be added – for instance fitting a new valve and balancing the wheel are both commonly charged on top of the price of a new tyre.

Other sources

Beware of parts or materials obtained from market stalls, car boot sales or similar outlets. Such items are not invariably sub-standard, but there is little chance of compensation if they do prove unsatisfactory. In the case of safety-critical components such as brake pads, there is the risk not only of financial loss, but also of an accident causing injury or death.

Second-hand components or assemblies obtained from a vehicle breaker can be a good buy in some circumstances, but this sort of purchase is best made by the experienced DIY mechanic.

Modifications are a continuing and unpublished process in vehicle manufacture, quite apart from major model changes. Spare parts manuals and lists are compiled upon a numerical basis, the individual vehicle numbers being essential to correct identification of the component required.

When ordering spare parts, always give as much information as possible. Quote the vehicle type, year of manufacture and vehicle identification and/or engine numbers as appropriate.

The *Vehicle Identification Number (VIN)* is visible from the outside of the vehicle, through the left-hand lower corner of the windscreen, and is also shown on a sticker on the engine compartment bulkhead on the right-hand side **(see illustrations)**.

The *vehicle data sticker* is located in the passenger compartment either on the right-hand footwell trim panel **(see illustration)** or on the driver's seat. The data sticker includes the Vehicle Identification Number (VIN), engine code, paint and trim colour codes and other additional vehicle information.

The *engine number and engine code* is stamped into the left-hand end of the cylinder block and is also given on a sticker on the timing belt upper cover. The engine code is also given on the vehicle data sticker.

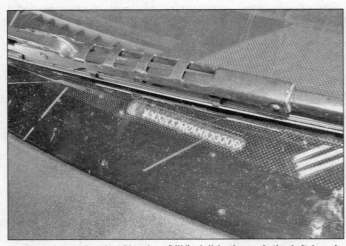

Vehicle Identification Number (VIN) visible through the left-hand lower corner of the windscreen

Vehicle Identification Number (VIN) shown on a sticker on the engine compartment bulkhead on the right-hand side

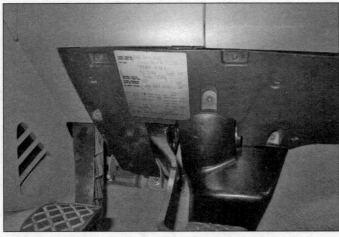

Vehicle data sticker located in the passenger compartment on the right-hand footwell trim panel

Vehicle data sticker information

1 Production control number
2 Vehicle identification number
3 Model code number
4 Model explanation/engine output
5 Engine and gearbox code letters
6 Paint number/interior trim code
7 Optional extra number

Whenever servicing, repair or overhaul work is carried out on the car or its components, observe the following procedures and instructions. This will assist in carrying out the operation efficiently and to a professional standard of workmanship.

Joint mating faces and gaskets

When separating components at their mating faces, never insert screwdrivers or similar implements into the joint between the faces in order to prise them apart. This can cause severe damage which results in oil leaks, coolant leaks, etc upon reassembly. Separation is usually achieved by tapping along the joint with a soft-faced hammer in order to break the seal. However, note that this method may not be suitable where dowels are used for component location.

Where a gasket is used between the mating faces of two components, a new one must be fitted on reassembly; fit it dry unless otherwise stated in the repair procedure. Make sure that the mating faces are clean and dry, with all traces of old gasket removed. When cleaning a joint face, use a tool which is unlikely to score or damage the face, and remove any burrs or nicks with an oilstone or fine file.

Make sure that tapped holes are cleaned with a pipe cleaner, and keep them free of jointing compound, if this is being used, unless specifically instructed otherwise.

Ensure that all orifices, channels or pipes are clear, and blow through them, preferably using compressed air.

Oil seals

Oil seals can be removed by levering them out with a wide flat-bladed screwdriver or similar implement. Alternatively, a number of self-tapping screws may be screwed into the seal, and these used as a purchase for pliers or some similar device in order to pull the seal free.

Whenever an oil seal is removed from its working location, either individually or as part of an assembly, it should be renewed.

The very fine sealing lip of the seal is easily damaged, and will not seal if the surface it contacts is not completely clean and free from scratches, nicks or grooves. If the original sealing surface of the component cannot be restored, and the manufacturer has not made provision for slight relocation of the seal relative to the sealing surface, the component should be renewed.

Protect the lips of the seal from any surface which may damage them in the course of fitting. Use tape or a conical sleeve where possible. Where indicated, lubricate the seal lips with oil before fitting and, on dual-lipped seals, fill the space between the lips with grease.

Unless otherwise stated, oil seals must be fitted with their sealing lips toward the lubricant to be sealed.

Use a tubular drift or block of wood of the appropriate size to install the seal and, if the seal housing is shouldered, drive the seal down to the shoulder. If the seal housing is unshouldered, the seal should be fitted with its face flush with the housing top face (unless otherwise instructed).

Screw threads and fastenings

Seized nuts, bolts and screws are quite a common occurrence where corrosion has set in, and the use of penetrating oil or releasing fluid will often overcome this problem if the offending item is soaked for a while before attempting to release it. The use of an impact driver may also provide a means of releasing such stubborn fastening devices, when used in conjunction with the appropriate screwdriver bit or socket. If none of these methods works, it may be necessary to resort to the careful application of heat, or the use of a hacksaw or nut splitter device. Before resorting to extreme methods, check that you are not dealing with a left-hand thread!

Studs are usually removed by locking two nuts together on the threaded part, and then using a spanner on the lower nut to unscrew the stud. Studs or bolts which have broken off below the surface of the component in which they are mounted can sometimes be removed using a stud extractor.

Always ensure that a blind tapped hole is completely free from oil, grease, water or other fluid before installing the bolt or stud. Failure to do this could cause the housing to crack due to the hydraulic action of the bolt or stud as it is screwed in.

For some screw fastenings, notably cylinder head bolts or nuts, torque wrench settings are no longer specified for the latter stages of tightening, "angle-tightening" being called up instead. Typically, a fairly low torque wrench setting will be applied to the bolts/nuts in the correct sequence, followed by one or more stages of tightening through specified angles.

When checking or retightening a nut or bolt to a specified torque setting, slacken the nut or bolt by a quarter of a turn, and then retighten to the specified setting. However, this should not be attempted where angular tightening has been used.

Locknuts, locktabs and washers

Any fastening which will rotate against a component or housing during tightening should always have a washer between it and the relevant component or housing.

Spring or split washers should always be renewed when they are used to lock a critical component such as a big-end bearing retaining bolt or nut. Locktabs which are folded over to retain a nut or bolt should always be renewed.

Self-locking nuts can be re-used in non-critical areas, providing resistance can be felt when the locking portion passes over the bolt or stud thread. However, it should be noted that self-locking stiffnuts tend to lose their effectiveness after long periods of use, and should then be renewed as a matter of course.

Split pins must always be replaced with new ones of the correct size for the hole.

When thread-locking compound is found on the threads of a fastener which is to be re-used, it should be cleaned off with a wire brush and solvent, and fresh compound applied on reassembly.

Special tools

Some repair procedures in this manual entail the use of special tools such as a press, two or three-legged pullers, spring compressors, etc. Wherever possible, suitable readily-available alternatives to the manufacturer's special tools are described, and are shown in use. In some instances, where no alternative is possible, it has been necessary to resort to the use of a manufacturer's tool, and this has been done for reasons of safety as well as the efficient completion of the repair operation. Unless you are highly-skilled and have a thorough understanding of the procedures described, never attempt to bypass the use of any special tool when the procedure described specifies its use. Not only is there a very great risk of personal injury, but expensive damage could be caused to the components involved.

Environmental considerations

When disposing of used engine oil, brake fluid, antifreeze, etc, give due consideration to any detrimental environmental effects. Do not, for instance, pour any of the above liquids down drains into the general sewage system, or onto the ground to soak away, as this is likely to pollute your local environment. Many local council refuse tips provide a facility for waste oil disposal, as do some garages. You can find your nearest disposal point by calling the Environment Agency on 03708 506 506 or by visiting www.oilbankline.org.uk.

Note: It is illegal and anti-social to dump oil down the drain. To find the location of your local oil recycling bank, call 03708 506 506 or visit www.oilbankline.org.uk.

The jack supplied with the vehicle tool kit should only be used for changing roadwheels – see *Wheel changing* at the front of this manual. Ensure the jack head is correctly engaged before attempting to raise the vehicle. When carrying out any other kind of work, raise the vehicle using a hydraulic jack, and always supplement the jack with axle stands positioned under the vehicle jacking points or structural members. The front jacking point is the reinforced area under the door sill approximately 80 mm from the edge of the wheel arch. The rear jacking point is the reinforced area around the rear suspension trailing arm outer mounting. The exact locations of the front and rear jacking points are indicated by notches in the door sills **(see illustrations)**.

When jacking up the vehicle with a trolley jack, position the jack head under one of the relevant jacking points, front subframe or vehicle structural members. Do not jack the vehicle under the sump or any of the steering or suspension components. Supplement the jack using axle stands.

⚠️ *Warning: Never work under, around, or near a raised vehicle, unless it is adequately supported in at least two places.*

The front jacking point is the reinforced area (arrowed) under the door sill approximately 80 mm from the edge of the wheel arch

The rear jacking point is the reinforced area (arrowed) around the rear suspension trailing arm outer mounting

Numerous systems fitted to the vehicle require battery power to be available at all times, either to ensure their continued operation (such as the clock) or to maintain control unit memories which would be erased if the battery were to be disconnected. Whenever the battery is to be disconnected therefore, first note the following, to ensure that there are no unforeseen consequences of this action:

a) First, on any vehicle with central locking, it is a wise precaution to remove the key from the ignition, and to keep it with you, so that it does not get locked in, if the central locking should engage accidentally when the battery is reconnected.

b) On vehicles equipped with an original equipment anti-theft alarm system, before disconnecting the battery, de-activate the alarm system, otherwise the alarm will be triggered.

c) If a security-coded audio unit is fitted, and the unit and/or the battery is disconnected, the unit will not function again on reconnection until the correct security code is entered. Details of this procedure, which varies according to the unit fitted, are given in the vehicle audio system operating instructions. Ensure you have the correct code before you disconnect the battery. If you do not have the code or details of the correct procedure, but can supply proof of ownership and a legitimate reason for wanting this information, a VW dealer may be able to help.

d) The engine management electronic control unit is of the 'self-learning' type, meaning that as it operates, it also monitors and stores the settings which give optimum engine performance under all operating conditions. When the battery is disconnected, these settings are lost and the ECU reverts to the base settings programmed into its memory at the factory. On restarting, this may lead to the engine running/idling roughly for a short while, until the ECU has re-learned the optimum settings. This process is best accomplished by taking the vehicle on a road test (for approximately 15 minutes), covering all engine speeds and loads, concentrating mainly in the 2500 to 3500 rpm region.

e) On all models, when reconnecting the battery after disconnection, switch on the ignition and wait 10 seconds to allow the electronic vehicle systems to stabilise and re-initialise.

Introduction

A selection of good tools is a fundamental requirement for anyone contemplating the maintenance and repair of a motor vehicle. For the owner who does not possess any, their purchase will prove a considerable expense, offsetting some of the savings made by doing-it-yourself. However, provided that the tools purchased meet the relevant national safety standards and are of good quality, they will last for many years and prove an extremely worthwhile investment.

To help the average owner to decide which tools are needed to carry out the various tasks detailed in this manual, we have compiled three lists of tools under the following headings: *Maintenance and minor repair, Repair and overhaul*, and *Special*. Newcomers to practical mechanics should start off with the *Maintenance and minor repair* tool kit, and confine themselves to the simpler jobs around the vehicle. Then, as confidence and experience grow, more difficult tasks can be undertaken, with extra tools being purchased as, and when, they are needed. In this way, a *Maintenance and minor repair* tool kit can be built up into a *Repair and overhaul* tool kit over a considerable period of time, without any major cash outlays. The experienced do-it-yourselfer will have a tool kit good enough for most repair and overhaul procedures, and will add tools from the *Special* category when it is felt that the expense is justified by the amount of use to which these tools will be put.

Maintenance and minor repair tool kit

The tools given in this list should be considered as a minimum requirement if routine maintenance, servicing and minor repair operations are to be undertaken. We recommend the purchase of combination spanners (ring one end, open-ended the other); although more expensive than open-ended ones, they do give the advantages of both types of spanner.

- [ ] *Combination spanners:*
  Metric - 8 to 19 mm inclusive
- [ ] *Adjustable spanner - 35 mm jaw (approx.)*
- [ ] *Spark plug spanner (with rubber insert) - petrol models*
- [ ] *Spark plug gap adjustment tool - petrol models*
- [ ] *Set of feeler gauges*
- [ ] *Brake bleed nipple spanner*
- [ ] *Screwdrivers:*
  Flat blade - 100 mm long x 6 mm dia
  Cross blade - 100 mm long x 6 mm dia
  Torx - various sizes (not all vehicles)
- [ ] *Combination pliers*
- [ ] *Hacksaw (junior)*
- [ ] *Tyre pump*
- [ ] *Tyre pressure gauge*
- [ ] *Oil can*
- [ ] *Oil filter removal tool (if applicable)*
- [ ] *Fine emery cloth*
- [ ] *Wire brush (small)*
- [ ] *Funnel (medium size)*
- [ ] *Sump drain plug key (not all vehicles)*

Repair and overhaul tool kit

These tools are virtually essential for anyone undertaking any major repairs to a motor vehicle, and are additional to those given in the *Maintenance and minor repair* list. Included in this list is a comprehensive set of sockets. Although these are expensive, they will be found invaluable as they are so versatile - particularly if various drives are included in the set. We recommend the half-inch square-drive type, as this can be used with most proprietary torque wrenches.

The tools in this list will sometimes need to be supplemented by tools from the *Special* list:

- [ ] *Sockets to cover range in previous list (including Torx sockets)*
- [ ] *Reversible ratchet drive (for use with sockets)*
- [ ] *Extension piece, 250 mm (for use with sockets)*
- [ ] *Universal joint (for use with sockets)*
- [ ] *Flexible handle or sliding T "breaker bar" (for use with sockets)*
- [ ] *Torque wrench (for use with sockets)*
- [ ] *Self-locking grips*
- [ ] *Ball pein hammer*
- [ ] *Soft-faced mallet (plastic or rubber)*
- [ ] *Screwdrivers:*
  Flat blade - long & sturdy, short (chubby), and narrow (electrician's) types
  Cross blade – long & sturdy, and short (chubby) types
- [ ] *Pliers:*
  Long-nosed
  Side cutters (electrician's)
  Circlip (internal and external)
- [ ] *Cold chisel - 25 mm*
- [ ] *Scriber*
- [ ] *Scraper*
- [ ] *Centre-punch*
- [ ] *Pin punch*
- [ ] *Hacksaw*
- [ ] *Brake hose clamp*
- [ ] *Brake/clutch bleeding kit*
- [ ] *Selection of twist drills*
- [ ] *Steel rule/straight-edge*
- [ ] *Allen keys (inc. splined/Torx type)*
- [ ] *Selection of files*
- [ ] *Wire brush*
- [ ] *Axle stands*
- [ ] *Jack (strong trolley or hydraulic type)*
- [ ] *Light with extension lead*
- [ ] *Universal electrical multi-meter*

Sockets and reversible ratchet drive

Brake bleeding kit

Torx key, socket and bit

Hose clamp

Angular-tightening gauge

Special tools

The tools in this list are those which are not used regularly, are expensive to buy, or which need to be used in accordance with their manufacturers' instructions. Unless relatively difficult mechanical jobs are undertaken frequently, it will not be economic to buy many of these tools. Where this is the case, you could consider clubbing together with friends (or joining a motorists' club) to make a joint purchase, or borrowing the tools against a deposit from a local garage or tool hire specialist.

The following list contains only those tools and instruments freely available to the public, and not those special tools produced by the vehicle manufacturer specifically for its dealer network. You will find occasional references to these manufacturers' special tools in the text of this manual. Generally, an alternative method of doing the job without the vehicle manufacturers' special tool is given. However, sometimes there is no alternative to using them. Where this is the case and the relevant tool cannot be bought or borrowed, you will have to entrust the work to a dealer.

- [ ] *Angular-tightening gauge*
- [ ] *Valve spring compressor*
- [ ] *Valve grinding tool*
- [ ] *Piston ring compressor*
- [ ] *Piston ring removal/installation tool*
- [ ] *Cylinder bore hone*
- [ ] *Balljoint separator*
- [ ] *Coil spring compressors (where applicable)*
- [ ] *Two/three-legged hub and bearing puller*
- [ ] *Impact screwdriver*
- [ ] *Micrometer and/or vernier calipers*
- [ ] *Dial gauge*
- [ ] *Tachometer*
- [ ] *Fault code reader*
- [ ] *Cylinder compression gauge*
- [ ] *Hand-operated vacuum pump and gauge*
- [ ] *Clutch plate alignment set*
- [ ] *Brake shoe steady spring cup removal tool*
- [ ] *Bush and bearing removal/installation set*
- [ ] *Stud extractors*
- [ ] *Tap and die set*
- [ ] *Lifting tackle*

Buying tools

Reputable motor accessory shops and superstores often offer excellent quality tools at discount prices, so it pays to shop around.

Remember, you don't have to buy the most expensive items on the shelf, but it is always advisable to steer clear of the very cheap tools. Beware of 'bargains' offered on market stalls, on-line or at car boot sales. There are plenty of good tools around at reasonable prices, but always aim to purchase items which meet the relevant national safety standards. If in doubt, ask the proprietor or manager of the shop for advice before making a purchase.

Care and maintenance of tools

Having purchased a reasonable tool kit, it is necessary to keep the tools in a clean and serviceable condition. After use, always wipe off any dirt, grease and metal particles using a clean, dry cloth, before putting the tools away. Never leave them lying around after they have been used. A simple tool rack on the garage or workshop wall for items such as screwdrivers and pliers is a good idea. Store all normal spanners and sockets in a metal box. Any measuring instruments, gauges, meters, etc, must be carefully stored where they cannot be damaged or become rusty.

Take a little care when tools are used. Hammer heads inevitably become marked, and screwdrivers lose the keen edge on their blades from time to time. A little timely attention with emery cloth or a file will soon restore items like this to a good finish.

Working facilities

Not to be forgotten when discussing tools is the workshop itself. If anything more than routine maintenance is to be carried out, a suitable working area becomes essential.

It is appreciated that many an owner-mechanic is forced by circumstances to remove an engine or similar item without the benefit of a garage or workshop. Having done this, any repairs should always be done under the cover of a roof.

Wherever possible, any dismantling should be done on a clean, flat workbench or table at a suitable working height.

Any workbench needs a vice; one with a jaw opening of 100 mm is suitable for most jobs. As mentioned previously, some clean dry storage space is also required for tools, as well as for any lubricants, cleaning fluids, touch-up paints etc, which become necessary.

Another item which may be required, and which has a much more general usage, is an electric drill with a chuck capacity of at least 8 mm. This, together with a good range of twist drills, is virtually essential for fitting accessories.

Last, but not least, always keep a supply of old newspapers and clean, lint-free rags available, and try to keep any working area as clean as possible.

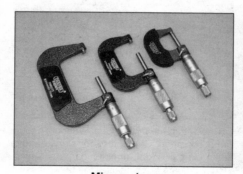

Micrometers

Dial test indicator ("dial gauge")

Oil filter removal tool (strap wrench type)

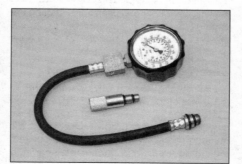

Compression tester

Bearing puller

This is a guide to getting your vehicle through the MOT test. Obviously it will not be possible to examine the vehicle to the same standard as the professional MOT tester. However, working through the following checks will enable you to identify any problem areas before submitting the vehicle for the test.

It has only been possible to summarise the test requirements here, based on the regulations in force at the time of printing. Test standards are becoming increasingly stringent, although there are some exemptions for older vehicles.

An assistant will be needed to help carry out some of these checks.

The checks have been sub-divided into four categories, as follows:

1 Checks carried out **FROM THE DRIVER'S SEAT**

2 Checks carried out **WITH THE VEHICLE ON THE GROUND**

3 Checks carried out **WITH THE VEHICLE RAISED AND THE WHEELS FREE TO TURN**

4 Checks carried out on **YOUR VEHICLE'S EXHAUST EMISSION SYSTEM**

---

1 Checks carried out **FROM THE DRIVER'S SEAT**

Handbrake (parking brake)

☐ Test the operation of the handbrake. Excessive travel (too many clicks) indicates incorrect brake or cable adjustment.
☐ Check that the handbrake cannot be released by tapping the lever sideways. Check the security of the lever mountings.

☐ If the parking brake is foot-operated, check that the pedal is secure and without excessive travel, and that the release mechanism operates correctly.
☐ Where applicable, test the operation of the electronic handbrake. The brake should engage and disengage without excessive delay. If the warning light does not extinguish when the brake is disengaged, this could indicate a fault which will need further investigation.

Footbrake

☐ Depress the brake pedal and check that it does not creep down to the floor, indicating a master cylinder fault. Release the pedal, wait a few seconds, then depress it again. If the pedal travels nearly to the floor before firm resistance is felt, brake adjustment or repair is necessary. If the pedal feels spongy, there is air in the hydraulic system which must be removed by bleeding.

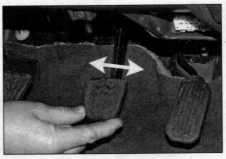

☐ Check that the brake pedal is secure and in good condition. Check also for signs of fluid leaks on the pedal, floor or carpets, which would indicate failed seals in the brake master cylinder.
☐ Check the servo unit (when applicable) by operating the brake pedal several times, then keeping the pedal depressed and starting the engine. As the engine starts, the pedal will move down slightly. If not, the vacuum hose or the servo itself may be faulty.

Steering wheel and column

☐ Examine the steering wheel for fractures or looseness of the hub, spokes or rim.
☐ Move the steering wheel from side to side and then up and down. Check that the steering wheel is not loose on the column, indicating wear or a loose retaining nut. Continue moving the steering wheel as before, but also turn it slightly from left to right.

☐ Check that the steering wheel is not loose on the column, and that there is no abnormal movement of the steering wheel, indicating wear in the column support bearings or couplings.
☐ Check that the ignition lock (where fitted) engages and disengages correctly.
☐ Steering column adjustment mechanisms (where fitted) must be able to lock the column securely in place with no play evident.

Windscreen, mirrors and sunvisor

☐ The windscreen must be free of cracks or other significant damage within the driver's field of view. (Small stone chips are acceptable.) Rear view mirrors must be secure, intact, and capable of being adjusted.

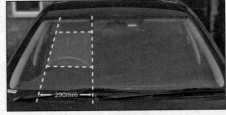

☐ The driver's sunvisor must be capable of being stored in the "up" position.

Seat belts and seats

Note: *The following checks are applicable to all seat belts, front and rear.*

☐ Examine the webbing of all the belts (including rear belts if fitted) for cuts, serious fraying or deterioration. Fasten and unfasten each belt to check the buckles. If applicable, check the retracting mechanism. Check the security of all seat belt mountings accessible from inside the vehicle, ensuring any height adjustable mountings lock securely in place.

☐ Seat belts with pre-tensioners, once activated, have a "flag" or similar showing on the seat belt stalk. This, in itself, is not a reason for test failure.

☐ The front seats themselves must be securely attached and the backrests must lock in the upright position.

Doors

☐ Both front doors must be able to be opened and closed from outside and inside, and must latch securely when closed.

Bonnet and boot/tailgate

☐ The bonnet and boot/tailgate must latch securely when closed.

2 Checks carried out WITH THE VEHICLE ON THE GROUND

Vehicle identification

☐ Number plates must be in good condition, secure and legible, with letters and numbers correctly spaced – spacing at (A) should be 33 mm and at (B) 11 mm. At the front, digits must be black on a white background and at the rear black on a yellow background. Other background designs (such as honeycomb) are not permitted.

☐ The VIN plate and/or homologation plate must be permanently displayed and legible.

Electrical equipment

☐ Switch on the ignition and check the operation of the horn.

☐ Check the windscreen washers and wipers, examining the wiper blades; renew damaged or perished blades. Also check the operation of the stop-lights.

☐ Check the operation of the sidelights and number plate lights. The lenses and reflectors must be secure, clean and undamaged.

☐ Check the operation and alignment of the headlights. The headlight reflectors must not be tarnished and the lenses must be undamaged.

☐ Switch on the ignition and check the operation of the direction indicators (including the instrument panel tell-tale) and the hazard warning lights. Operation of the sidelights and stop-lights must not affect the indicators - if it does, the cause is usually a bad earth at the rear light cluster. Indicators should flash at a rate of between 60 and 120 times per minute – faster or slower than this could indicate a fault with the flasher unit or a bad earth at one of the light units.

☐ Check the operation of the rear foglight(s), including the warning light on the instrument panel or in the switch.

☐ The warning lights must illuminate in accordance with the manufacturer's design. For most vehicles, the ABS and other warning lights should illuminate when the ignition is switched on, and (if the system is operating properly) extinguish after a few seconds. Refer to the owner's handbook.

Footbrake

☐ Examine the master cylinder, brake pipes and servo unit for leaks, loose mountings, corrosion or other damage. If ABS is fitted, this unit should also be examined for signs of leaks or corrosion.

☐ The fluid reservoir must be secure and the fluid level must be between the upper (**A**) and lower (**B**) markings.

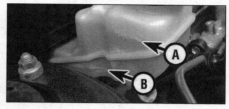

☐ Inspect both front brake flexible hoses for cracks or deterioration of the rubber. Turn the steering from lock to lock, and ensure that the hoses do not contact the wheel, tyre, or any part of the steering or suspension mechanism. With the brake pedal firmly depressed, check the hoses for bulges or leaks under pressure.

Steering and suspension

☐ Have your assistant turn the steering wheel from side to side slightly, up to the point where the steering gear just begins to transmit this movement to the roadwheels. Check for excessive free play between the steering wheel and the steering gear, indicating wear or insecurity of the steering column joints, the column-to-steering gear coupling, or the steering gear itself.

☐ Have your assistant turn the steering wheel more vigorously in each direction, so that the roadwheels just begin to turn. As this is done, examine all the steering joints, linkages, fittings and attachments. Renew any component that shows signs of wear or damage. On vehicles with power steering, check the security and condition of the steering pump, drivebelt and hoses.

☐ Check that the vehicle is standing level, and at approximately the correct ride height.

Shock absorbers

☐ Depress each corner of the vehicle in turn, then release it. The vehicle should rise and then settle in its normal position. If the vehicle continues to rise and fall, the shock absorber is defective. A shock absorber which has seized will also cause the vehicle to fail.

Exhaust system

☐ Start the engine. With your assistant holding a rag over the tailpipe, check the entire system for leaks. Repair or renew leaking sections.

3 Checks carried out **WITH THE VEHICLE RAISED AND THE WHEELS FREE TO TURN**

Jack up the front and rear of the vehicle, and securely support it on axle stands. Position the stands clear of the suspension assemblies. Ensure that the wheels are clear of the ground and that the steering can be turned from lock to lock.

Steering mechanism

☐ Have your assistant turn the steering from lock to lock. Check that the steering turns smoothly, and that no part of the steering mechanism, including a wheel or tyre, fouls any brake hose or pipe or any part of the body structure.
☐ Examine the steering rack rubber gaiters for damage or insecurity of the retaining clips. If power steering is fitted, check for signs of damage or leakage of the fluid hoses, pipes or connections. Also check for excessive stiffness or binding of the steering, a missing split pin or locking device, or severe corrosion of the body structure within 30 cm of any steering component attachment point.

Front and rear suspension and wheel bearings

☐ Starting at the front right-hand side, grasp the roadwheel at the 3 o'clock and 9 o'clock positions and rock gently but firmly. Check for free play or insecurity at the wheel bearings, suspension balljoints, or suspension mount-ings, pivots and attachments.
☐ Now grasp the wheel at the 12 o'clock and 6 o'clock positions and repeat the previous inspection. Spin the wheel, and check for roughness or tightness of the front wheel bearing.

☐ If excess free play is suspected at a component pivot point, this can be confirmed by using a large screwdriver or similar tool and levering between the mounting and the component attachment. This will confirm whether the wear is in the pivot bush, its retaining bolt, or in the mounting itself (the bolt holes can often become elongated).

☐ Carry out all the above checks at the other front wheel, and then at both rear wheels.

Springs and shock absorbers

☐ Examine the suspension struts (when applicable) for serious fluid leakage, corrosion, or damage to the casing. Also check the security of the mounting points.
☐ If coil springs are fitted, check that the spring ends locate in their seats, and that the spring is not corroded, cracked or broken.
☐ If leaf springs are fitted, check that all leaves are intact, that the axle is securely attached to each spring, and that there is no deterioration of the spring eye mountings, bushes, and shackles.

☐ The same general checks apply to vehicles fitted with other suspension types, such as torsion bars, hydraulic displacer units, etc. Ensure that all mountings and attachments are secure, that there are no signs of excessive wear, corrosion or damage, and (on hydraulic types) that there are no fluid leaks or damaged pipes.
☐ Inspect the shock absorbers for signs of serious fluid leakage. Check for wear of the mounting bushes or attachments, or damage to the body of the unit.

Driveshafts (fwd vehicles only)

☐ Rotate each front wheel in turn and inspect the constant velocity joint gaiters for splits or damage. Also check that each driveshaft is straight and undamaged.

Braking system

☐ If possible without dismantling, check brake pad wear and disc condition. Ensure that the friction lining material has not worn excessively, (A) and that the discs are not fractured, pitted, scored or badly worn (B).

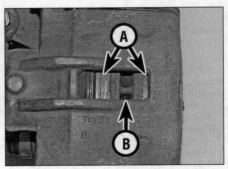

☐ Examine all the rigid brake pipes underneath the vehicle, and the flexible hose(s) at the rear. Look for corrosion, chafing or insecurity of the pipes, and for signs of bulging under pressure, chafing, splits or deterioration of the flexible hoses.
☐ Look for signs of fluid leaks at the brake calipers or on the brake backplates. Repair or renew leaking components.
☐ Slowly spin each wheel, while your assistant depresses and releases the footbrake. Ensure that each brake is operating and does not bind when the pedal is released.

☐ Examine the handbrake mechanism, checking for frayed or broken cables, excessive corrosion, or wear or insecurity of the linkage. Check that the mechanism works on each relevant wheel, and releases fully, without binding.

☐ It is not possible to test brake efficiency without special equipment, but a road test can be carried out later to check that the vehicle pulls up in a straight line.

Fuel and exhaust systems

☐ Inspect the fuel tank (including the filler cap), fuel pipes, hoses and unions. All components must be secure and free from leaks. Locking fuel caps must lock securely and the key must be provided for the MOT test.

☐ Examine the exhaust system over its entire length, checking for any damaged, broken or missing mountings, security of the retaining clamps and rust or corrosion.

Wheels and tyres

☐ Examine the sidewalls and tread area of each tyre in turn. Check for cuts, tears, lumps, bulges, separation of the tread, and exposure of the ply or cord due to wear or damage. Check that the tyre bead is correctly seated on the wheel rim, that the valve is sound and properly seated, and that the wheel is not distorted or damaged.

☐ Check that the tyres are of the correct size for the vehicle, that they are of the same size and type on each axle, and that the pressures are correct.

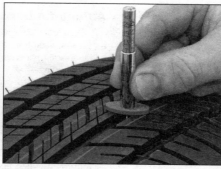

☐ Check the tyre tread depth. The legal minimum at the time of writing is 1.6 mm over the central three-quarters of the tread width. Abnormal tread wear may indicate incorrect front wheel alignment or wear in steering or suspension components.

☐ If the spare wheel is fitted externally or in a separate carrier beneath the vehicle, check that mountings are secure and free of excessive corrosion.

Body corrosion

☐ Check the condition of the entire vehicle structure for signs of corrosion in load-bearing areas. (These include chassis box sections, side sills, cross-members, pillars, and all suspension, steering, braking system and seat belt mountings and anchorages.) Any corrosion which has seriously reduced the thickness of a load-bearing area (or is within 30 cm of safety-related components such as steering or suspension) is likely to cause the vehicle to fail. In this case professional repairs are likely to be needed.

☐ Damage or corrosion which causes sharp or otherwise dangerous edges to be exposed will also cause the vehicle to fail.

Towbars

☐ Check the condition of mounting points (both beneath the vehicle and within boot/hatchback areas) for signs of corrosion, ensuring that all fixings are secure and not worn or damaged. There must be no excessive play in detachable tow ball arms or quick-release mechanisms.

4 Checks carried out on YOUR VEHICLE'S EXHAUST EMISSION SYSTEM

Petrol models

☐ The engine should be warmed up, and running well (ignition system in good order, air filter element clean, etc).

☐ Before testing, run the engine at around 2500 rpm for 20 seconds. Let the engine drop to idle, and watch for smoke from the exhaust. If the idle speed is too high, or if dense blue or black smoke emerges for more than 5 seconds, the vehicle will fail. Typically, blue smoke signifies oil burning (engine wear);

black smoke means unburnt fuel (dirty air cleaner element, or other fuel system fault).

☐ An exhaust gas analyser for measuring carbon monoxide (CO) and hydrocarbons (HC) is now needed. If one cannot be hired or borrowed, have a local garage perform the check.

CO emissions (mixture)

☐ The MOT tester has access to the CO limits for all vehicles. The CO level is measured at idle speed, and at 'fast idle' (2500 to 3000 rpm). The following limits are given as a general guide:

At idle speed – Less than 0.5% CO
At 'fast idle' – Less than 0.3% CO
Lambda reading – 0.97 to 1.03

☐ If the CO level is too high, this may point to poor maintenance, a fuel injection system problem, faulty lambda (oxygen) sensor or catalytic converter. Try an injector cleaning treatment, and check the vehicle's ECU for fault codes.

HC emissions

☐ The MOT tester has access to HC limits for all vehicles. The HC level is measured at 'fast idle' (2500 to 3000 rpm). The following limits are given as a general guide:

At 'fast idle' – Less then 200 ppm

☐ Excessive HC emissions are typically caused by oil being burnt (worn engine), or by a blocked crankcase ventilation system ('breather'). If the engine oil is old and thin, an oil change may help. If the engine is running badly, check the vehicle's ECU for fault codes.

Diesel models

☐ The only emission test for diesel engines is measuring exhaust smoke density, using a calibrated smoke meter. The test involves accelerating the engine at least 3 times to its maximum unloaded speed.

Note: *On engines with a timing belt, it is VITAL that the belt is in good condition before the test is carried out.*

☐ With the engine warmed up, it is first purged by running at around 2500 rpm for 20 seconds. A governor check is then carried out, by slowly accelerating the engine to its maximum speed. After this, the smoke meter is connected, and the engine is accelerated quickly to maximum speed three times. If the smoke density is less than the limits given below, the vehicle will pass:

Non-turbo vehicles: 2.5m-1
Turbocharged vehicles: 3.0m-1

☐ If excess smoke is produced, try fitting a new air cleaner element, or using an injector cleaning treatment. If the engine is running badly, where applicable, check the vehicle's ECU for fault codes. Also check the vehicle's EGR system, where applicable. At high mileages, the injectors may require professional attention.

Engine

- [ ] Engine fails to rotate when attempting to start
- [ ] Engine rotates, but will not start
- [ ] Engine difficult to start when cold
- [ ] Engine difficult to start when hot
- [ ] Starter motor noisy or excessively-rough in engagement
- [ ] Engine starts, but stops immediately
- [ ] Engine idles erratically
- [ ] Engine misfires at idle speed
- [ ] Engine misfires throughout the driving speed range
- [ ] Engine hesitates on acceleration
- [ ] Engine stalls
- [ ] Engine lacks power
- [ ] Engine backfires
- [ ] Oil pressure warning light illuminated with engine running
- [ ] Engine runs-on after switching off
- [ ] Engine noises

Cooling system

- [ ] Overheating
- [ ] Overcooling
- [ ] External coolant leakage
- [ ] Internal coolant leakage
- [ ] Corrosion

Fuel and exhaust systems

- [ ] Excessive fuel consumption
- [ ] Fuel leakage and/or fuel odour
- [ ] Excessive noise or fumes from exhaust system

Clutch

- [ ] Pedal travels to floor – no pressure or very little resistance
- [ ] Clutch fails to disengage (unable to select gears)
- [ ] Clutch slips (engine speed increases, with no increase in vehicle speed)
- [ ] Judder as clutch is engaged
- [ ] Noise when depressing or releasing clutch pedal

Manual transmission

- [ ] Noisy in neutral with engine running
- [ ] Noisy in one particular gear
- [ ] Difficulty engaging gears
- [ ] Jumps out of gear
- [ ] Vibration
- [ ] Lubricant leaks

Automatic transmission

- [ ] Fluid leakage
- [ ] Transmission fluid brown, or has burned smell
- [ ] General gear selection problems
- [ ] Transmission will not downshift (kickdown) with accelerator pedal fully depressed
- [ ] Engine will not start in any gear, or starts in gears other than Park or Neutral
- [ ] Transmission slips, shifts roughly, is noisy, or has no drive in forward or reverse gears

Driveshafts

- [ ] Vibration when accelerating or decelerating
- [ ] Clicking or knocking noise on turns (at slow speed on full-lock)

Braking system

- [ ] Vehicle pulls to one side under braking
- [ ] Noise (grinding or high-pitched squeal) when brakes applied
- [ ] Excessive brake pedal travel
- [ ] Brake pedal feels spongy when depressed
- [ ] Excessive brake pedal effort required to stop vehicle
- [ ] Judder felt through brake pedal or steering wheel when braking
- [ ] Brakes binding
- [ ] Rear wheels locking under normal braking

Suspension and steering

- [ ] Vehicle pulls to one side
- [ ] Wheel wobble and vibration
- [ ] Excessive pitching and/or rolling around corners, or during braking
- [ ] Wandering or general instability
- [ ] Excessively-stiff steering
- [ ] Excessive play in steering
- [ ] Lack of power assistance
- [ ] Tyre wear excessive

Electrical system

- [ ] Battery will not hold a charge for more than a few days
- [ ] Ignition/no-charge warning light remains illuminated with engine running
- [ ] Ignition/no-charge warning light fails to come on
- [ ] Lights inoperative
- [ ] Instrument readings inaccurate or erratic
- [ ] Horn inoperative, or unsatisfactory in operation
- [ ] Windscreen wipers inoperative, or unsatisfactory in operation
- [ ] Windscreen washers inoperative, or unsatisfactory in operation
- [ ] Electric windows inoperative, or unsatisfactory in operation
- [ ] Central locking system inoperative, or unsatisfactory in operation

Introduction

The vehicle owner who does his or her own maintenance according to the recommended service schedules should not have to use this section of the manual very often. Modern component reliability is such that, provided those items subject to wear or deterioration are inspected or renewed at the specified intervals, sudden failure is comparatively rare. Faults do not usually just happen as a result of sudden failure, but develop over a period of time. Major mechanical failures in particular are usually preceded by characteristic symptoms over hundreds or even thousands of miles. Those components which do occasionally fail without warning are often small and easily carried in the vehicle.

With any fault-finding, the first step is to decide where to begin investigations. Sometimes this is obvious, but on other occasions, a little detective work will be necessary. The owner who makes half a dozen haphazard adjustments or replacements may be successful in curing a fault (or its symptoms), but will be none the wiser if the fault recurs, and ultimately may have spent more time and money than was necessary. A calm and logical approach will be found to be more satisfactory in the long run. Always take into account any warning signs or abnormalities that may have been noticed in the period preceding the fault – power loss, high or low gauge readings, unusual smells,

etc – and remember that failure of components such as fuses may only be pointers to some underlying fault.

The pages which follow provide an easy-reference guide to the more common problems which may occur during the operation of the vehicle. These problems and their possible causes are grouped under headings denoting various components or systems, such as Engine, Cooling system, etc. The general Chapter which deals with the problem is also shown in brackets; refer to the relevant part of that Chapter for system-specific information. Whatever the fault, certain basic principles apply. These are as follows:

Verify the fault. This is simply a matter of

being sure that you know what the symptoms are before starting work. This is particularly important if you are investigating a fault for someone else, who may not have described it very accurately.

Don't overlook the obvious. For example, if the vehicle won't start, is there fuel in the tank? (Don't take anyone else's word on this particular point, and don't trust the fuel gauge either!) If an electrical fault is indicated, look for loose or broken wires before digging out the test gear.

Cure the disease, not the symptom. Substituting a flat battery with a fully-charged one will get you off the hard shoulder, but if the underlying cause is not attended to, the new battery will go the same way.

Don't take anything for granted. Particularly, don't forget that a 'new' component may itself be defective (especially if it's been rattling around in the boot for months), and don't leave components out of a fault diagnosis sequence just because they are new or recently-fitted.

When you do finally diagnose a difficult fault, you'll probably realise that all the evidence was there from the start.

Consider what work, if any, has recently been carried out. Many faults arise through careless or hurried work. For instance, if any work has been performed under the bonnet, could some of the wiring have been dislodged or incorrectly routed, or a hose trapped? Have all the fasteners been properly tightened? Were new, genuine parts and new gaskets used? There is often a certain amount of detective work to be done in this case, as an apparently-unrelated task can have far-reaching consequences.

Diesel fault diagnosis

The majority of starting problems on small diesel engines are electrical in origin. The mechanic who is familiar with petrol engines but less so with diesels may be inclined to view the diesel's injectors and pump in the same light as the spark plugs and distributor, but this is generally a mistake.

When investigating complaints of difficult starting for someone else, make sure that the correct starting procedure is understood and is being followed. Some drivers are unaware of the significance of the preheating warning light – many modern engines are sufficiently forgiving for this not to matter in mild weather, but with the onset of winter, problems begin.

As a rule of thumb, if the engine is difficult to start but runs well when it has finally got going, the problem is electrical (battery, starter motor or preheating system). If poor performance is combined with difficult starting, the problem is likely to be in the fuel system. The low-pressure (supply) side of the fuel system should be checked before suspecting the injectors and high-pressure pump. The most common fuel supply problem is air getting into the system, and any pipe from the fuel tank forwards must be scrutinised if air leakage is suspected. Normally the pump is the last item to suspect, since unless it has been tampered with, there is no reason for it to be at fault.

Engine

Engine fails to rotate when attempting to start

- [ ] Battery terminal connections loose or corroded (see *Weekly checks*)
- [ ] Battery discharged or faulty (Chapter 5)
- [ ] Broken, loose or disconnected wiring in the starting circuit (Chapter 5)
- [ ] Defective starter solenoid or ignition switch (Chapter 5 or 10)
- [ ] Defective starter motor (Chapter 5)
- [ ] Starter pinion or flywheel ring gear teeth loose or broken (Chapter 2A, 2B, 2C or 5)
- [ ] Engine earth strap broken or disconnected (Chapter 5)
- [ ] Engine suffering 'hydraulic lock' (eg from water drawn into the engine after traversing flooded roads, or from a serious internal coolant leak) – consult a main dealer for advice

Engine rotates, but will not start

- [ ] Fuel tank empty
- [ ] Battery discharged (engine rotates slowly) (Chapter 5)
- [ ] Battery terminal connections loose or corroded (see *Weekly checks*)
- [ ] Immobiliser fault, or 'uncoded' ignition key being used (Chapter 12 or *Roadside repairs*)
- [ ] Pre-heating system faulty (Chapter 5)
- [ ] Fuel injection/engine management system fault (Chapter 4A or 4B)
- [ ] Air in fuel system (Chapter 4A or 4B)
- [ ] Major mechanical failure (Chapter 2A, 2B, 2C or 2D)

Engine difficult to start when cold

- [ ] Battery discharged (Chapter 5)
- [ ] Battery terminal connections loose or corroded (see *Weekly checks*)
- [ ] Preheating system faulty (Chapter 5)
- [ ] Fuel injection/engine management system fault (Chapter 4A or 4B)
- [ ] Wrong grade of engine oil used (*Weekly checks*, Chapter 1)
- [ ] Low cylinder compression (Chapter 2A, 2B or 2C)

Engine difficult to start when hot

- [ ] Air filter element dirty or clogged (Chapter 1)
- [ ] Fuel injection/engine management system fault (Chapter 4A or 4B)
- [ ] Low cylinder compression (Chapter 2A, 2B or 2C)

Starter motor noisy or excessively-rough in engagement

- [ ] Starter pinion or flywheel ring gear teeth loose or broken (Chapter 2A, 2B, 2C or 5)
- [ ] Starter motor mounting bolts loose or missing (Chapter 5)
- [ ] Starter motor internal components worn or damaged (Chapter 5)

Engine starts, but stops immediately

- [ ] Fuel injection/engine management system fault (Chapter 4A or 4B)

Engine idles erratically

- [ ] Air filter element clogged (Chapter 1)
- [ ] Uneven or low cylinder compression (Chapter 2A, 2B or 2C)
- [ ] Camshaft lobes worn (Chapter 2A, 2B or 2C)
- [ ] Fuel injection/engine management system fault (Chapter 4A or 4B)
- [ ] Air in fuel system (Chapter 4A or 4B)

Engine misfires at idle speed

- [ ] Faulty injector(s) (Chapter 4A or 4B)
- [ ] Uneven or low cylinder compression (Chapter 2A, 2B or 2C)
- [ ] Disconnected, leaking, or perished crankcase ventilation hoses (Chapter 4C)
- [ ] Fuel injection/engine management system fault (Chapter 4A or 4B)

Engine misfires throughout the driving speed range

- [ ] Fuel filter choked (Chapter 1)
- [ ] Fuel tank vent blocked, or fuel pipes restricted (Chapter 4A, 4B or 4C)
- [ ] Faulty injector(s) (Chapter 4A or 4B)
- [ ] Uneven or low cylinder compression (Chapter 2A, 2B or 2C)
- [ ] Blocked catalytic converter (Chapter 4A, 4B or 4C)
- [ ] Fuel injection/engine management system fault (Chapter 4A or 4B)
- [ ] Engine overheating (Chapter 3)

Engine hesitates on acceleration

- [ ] Faulty injector(s) (Chapter 4A or 4B)
- [ ] Fuel injection/engine management system fault (Chapter 4A or 4B)

Engine (continued)

Engine stalls
- [ ] Fuel filter choked (Chapter 1)
- [ ] Fuel tank vent blocked, or fuel pipes restricted (Chapter 4A or 4B)
- [ ] Faulty injector(s) (Chapter 4A or 4B)
- [ ] Fuel injection/engine management system fault (Chapter 4A or 4B)

Engine lacks power
- [ ] Air filter element blocked (Chapter 1)
- [ ] Fuel filter choked (Chapter 1)
- [ ] Fuel pipes blocked or restricted (Chapter 4A or 4B)
- [ ] Engine overheating (Chapter 3)
- [ ] Accelerator pedal position sensor faulty (Chapter 4A or 4B)
- [ ] Faulty injector(s) (Chapter 4A)
- [ ] Uneven or low cylinder compression (Chapter 2A, 2B or 2C)
- [ ] Fuel injection/engine management system fault (Chapter 4A or 4B)
- [ ] Blocked catalytic converter (Chapter 4A, 4B or 4C)
- [ ] Brakes binding (Chapter 1 or 9)
- [ ] Clutch slipping (Chapter 6)

Engine backfires
- [ ] Fuel injection/engine management system fault (Chapter 4A, 4B or 4C)
- [ ] Blocked catalytic converter (Chapter 4A, 4B or 4C)

Oil pressure warning light illuminated with engine running
- [ ] Low oil level, or incorrect oil grade (see *Weekly checks*)
- [ ] Faulty oil pressure warning light switch, or wiring damaged (Chapter 2A, 2B or 2C)
- [ ] Worn engine bearings and/or oil pump (Chapter 2A, 2B, 2C or 2D)
- [ ] High engine operating temperature (Chapter 3)
- [ ] Oil pump pressure relief valve defective (Chapter 2A, 2B or 2C)
- [ ] Oil pump pick-up strainer clogged (Chapter 2A, 2B or 2C)

Engine runs-on after switching off
- [ ] Excessive carbon build-up in engine (Chapter 2A, 2B, 2C or 2D)
- [ ] High engine operating temperature (Chapter 3)
- [ ] Fuel injection/engine management system fault (Chapter 4A or 4B)

Engine noises

Pre-ignition (pinking) or knocking during acceleration or under load
- [ ] Excessive carbon build-up in engine (Chapter 2A, 2B, 2C or 2D)
- [ ] Fuel injection/engine management system fault (Chapter 4A or 4B)
- [ ] Faulty injector(s) (Chapter 4A or 4B)

Whistling or wheezing noises
- [ ] Leaking exhaust manifold gasket or pipe-to-manifold joint (Chapter 4A or 4B)
- [ ] Leaking vacuum hose (Chapter 4A, 4B, 4C or 9)
- [ ] Blowing cylinder head gasket (Chapter 2A, 2B or 2C)
- [ ] Partially blocked or leaking crankcase ventilation system (Chapter 4C)

Tapping or rattling noises
- [ ] Worn valve gear or camshaft(s) (Chapter 2A, 2B or 2C)
- [ ] Worn or damaged dual-mass flywheel (Chapter 2A, 2B or 2C)
- [ ] Ancillary component fault (coolant pump, alternator, etc) (Chapter 3, 5, etc)

Knocking or thumping noises
- [ ] Worn big-end bearings (regular heavy knocking, perhaps less under load) (Chapter 2D)
- [ ] Worn main bearings (rumbling and knocking, perhaps worsening under load) (Chapter 2D)
- [ ] Piston slap – most noticeable when cold, caused by piston/bore wear (Chapter 2D)
- [ ] Ancillary component fault (coolant pump, alternator, etc) (Chapter 3, 5, etc)
- [ ] Engine mountings worn or defective (Chapter 2A, 2B or 2C)
- [ ] Front suspension or steering components worn (Chapter 10)

Cooling system

Overheating
- [ ] Insufficient coolant in system (see *Weekly checks*)
- [ ] Thermostat faulty (Chapter 3)
- [ ] Radiator core blocked, or grille restricted (Chapter 3)
- [ ] Cooling fan faulty (Chapter 3)
- [ ] Airlock in cooling system (Chapter 1 or 3)
- [ ] Expansion tank pressure cap faulty (Chapter 1 or 3)
- [ ] Engine management system fault (Chapter 4A or 4B)

Overcooling
- [ ] Thermostat faulty (Chapter 3)
- [ ] Cooling fan faulty (Chapter 3)
- [ ] Engine management system fault (Chapter 4A or 4B)

External coolant leakage
- [ ] Deteriorated or damaged hoses or hose clips (Chapter 1)
- [ ] Radiator core or heater matrix leaking (Chapter 3)
- [ ] Expansion tank pressure cap faulty (Chapter 1 or 3)
- [ ] Coolant pump internal seal leaking (Chapter 3)
- [ ] Coolant pump gasket leaking (Chapter 3)
- [ ] Boiling due to overheating (Chapter 3)
- [ ] Cylinder block core plug leaking (Chapter 2D)

Internal coolant leakage
- [ ] Leaking cylinder head gasket (Chapter 2A, 2B or 2C)
- [ ] Cracked cylinder head or cylinder block (Chapter 2A, 2B, 2C or 2D)

Corrosion
- [ ] Infrequent draining and flushing (Chapter 1)
- [ ] Incorrect coolant mixture or inappropriate coolant type (Chapter 1)

Fuel and exhaust systems

Excessive fuel consumption

- [ ] Air filter element dirty or clogged (Chapter 1)
- [ ] Fuel injection system fault (Chapter 4A or 4B)
- [ ] Engine management system fault (Chapter 4A or 4B)
- [ ] Crankcase ventilation system blocked (Chapter 4C)
- [ ] Tyres under-inflated (see *Weekly checks*)
- [ ] Brakes binding (Chapter 1 or 9)
- [ ] Fuel leak, causing apparent high consumption (Chapter 1, 4A, 4B or 4C)

Fuel leakage and/or fuel odour

- [ ] Damaged or corroded fuel tank, pipes or connections (Chapter 4A or 4B)

Excessive noise or fumes from exhaust system

- [ ] Leaking exhaust system or manifold joints (Chapter 1, 4A, or 4B)
- [ ] Leaking, corroded or damaged silencers or pipe (Chapter 1, 4A or 4B)
- [ ] Broken mountings causing body or suspension contact (Chapter 1, 4A or 4B)

Clutch

Pedal travels to floor – no pressure or very little resistance

- [ ] Air in hydraulic system/faulty master or slave cylinder (Chapter 6)
- [ ] Faulty hydraulic release system (Chapter 6)
- [ ] Broken diaphragm spring in clutch pressure plate (Chapter 6)

Clutch fails to disengage (unable to select gears)

- [ ] Air in hydraulic system/faulty master or slave cylinder (Chapter 6)
- [ ] Faulty hydraulic release system (Chapter 6)
- [ ] Clutch disc sticking on transmission input shaft splines (Chapter 6)
- [ ] Clutch disc sticking to flywheel or pressure plate (Chapter 6)
- [ ] Faulty pressure plate assembly (Chapter 6)
- [ ] Clutch release mechanism worn or incorrectly assembled (Chapter 6)

Clutch slips (engine speed increases, with no increase in vehicle speed)

- [ ] Faulty hydraulic release system (Chapter 6)
- [ ] Clutch disc linings excessively worn (Chapter 6)
- [ ] Clutch disc linings contaminated with oil or grease (Chapter 6)
- [ ] Faulty pressure plate or weak diaphragm spring (Chapter 6)

Judder as clutch is engaged

- [ ] Clutch disc linings contaminated with oil or grease (Chapter 6)
- [ ] Clutch disc linings excessively worn (Chapter 6)
- [ ] Faulty or distorted pressure plate or diaphragm spring (Chapter 6).
- [ ] Worn or loose engine or transmission mountings (Chapter 2A, 2B or 2C)
- [ ] Clutch disc hub or transmission input shaft splines worn (Chapter 6)

Noise when depressing or releasing clutch pedal

- [ ] Faulty clutch release/slave cylinder (Chapter 6)
- [ ] Worn or dry clutch pedal bushes (Chapter 6)
- [ ] Faulty pressure plate assembly (Chapter 6)
- [ ] Pressure plate diaphragm spring broken (Chapter 6)
- [ ] Broken clutch disc cushioning springs (Chapter 6)

Manual transmission

Noisy in neutral with engine running
☐ Lack of oil (Chapter 7A)
☐ Input shaft bearings worn (noise apparent with clutch pedal released, but not when depressed) (Chapter 7A)*
☐ Clutch release bearing faulty (noise apparent with clutch pedal depressed, possibly less when released) (Chapter 6)

Noisy in one particular gear
☐ Worn, damaged or chipped gear teeth (Chapter 7A)*

Difficulty engaging gears
☐ Clutch fault (Chapter 6)
☐ Worn, damaged, or poorly-adjusted gearchange (Chapter 7A)
☐ Lack of oil (Chapter 7A)
☐ Worn synchroniser units (Chapter 7A)*

Jumps out of gear
☐ Worn, damaged, or poorly-adjusted gearchange (Chapter 7A)
☐ Worn synchroniser units (Chapter 7A)*
☐ Worn selector forks (Chapter 7A)*

Vibration
☐ Lack of oil (Chapter 7A)
☐ Worn bearings (Chapter 7A)*

Lubricant leaks
☐ Leaking driveshaft or selector shaft oil seal (Chapter 7A)
☐ Leaking housing joint (Chapter 7A)*
☐ Leaking input shaft oil seal (Chapter 7A)*

Although the corrective action necessary to remedy the symptoms described is beyond the scope of the home mechanic, the above information should be helpful in isolating the cause of the condition, so that the owner can communicate clearly with a professional mechanic.

Automatic transmission

Note: *Due to the complexity of the automatic transmission, it is difficult for the home mechanic to properly diagnose and service this unit. For problems other than the following, the vehicle should be taken to a dealer service department or automatic transmission specialist. Do not be too hasty in removing the transmission if a fault is suspected, as most of the testing is carried out with the unit still fitted. Remember that, besides the sensors specific to the transmission, many of the engine management system sensors described in Chapter 4A and 4B are essential to the correct operation of the transmission.*

Fluid leakage
☐ Automatic transmission fluid is usually dark red in colour. Fluid leaks should not be confused with engine oil, which can easily be blown onto the transmission by airflow.
☐ To determine the source of a leak, first remove all built-up dirt and grime from the transmission housing and surrounding areas using a degreasing agent, or by steam-cleaning. Drive the vehicle at low speed, so airflow will not blow the leak far from its source. Raise and support the vehicle, and determine where the leak is coming from. The following are common areas of leakage:
a) *Fluid pan*
b) *Dipstick tube*
c) *Transmission-to-fluid cooler unions*

Transmission fluid brown, or has burned smell
☐ Transmission fluid level low (Chapter 1)

General gear selection problems
☐ Chapter 7B deals with checking the selector cable on automatic transmissions. The following are common problems which may be caused by a faulty cable or sensor:

a) *Engine starting in gears other than Park or Neutral.*
b) *Indicator panel indicating a gear other than the one actually being used.*
c) *Vehicle moves when in Park or Neutral.*
d) *Poor gear shift quality or erratic gear changes.*

Transmission will not downshift (kickdown) with accelerator pedal fully depressed
☐ Low transmission fluid level (Chapter 1)
☐ Engine management system fault (Chapter 4A or 4B)
☐ Faulty transmission sensor or wiring (Chapter 7B)
☐ Incorrect selector cable adjustment (Chapter 7B)

Engine will not start in any gear, or starts in gears other than Park or Neutral
☐ Incorrect selector cable adjustment (Chapter 7B)
☐ Faulty transmission sensor or wiring (Chapter 7B)
☐ Engine management system fault (Chapter 4A or 4B)

Transmission slips, shifts roughly, is noisy, or has no drive in forward or reverse gears
☐ Transmission fluid level low (Chapter 1)
☐ Faulty transmission sensor or wiring (Chapter 7B)
☐ Engine management system fault (Chapter 4A or 4B)

Note: *There are many probable causes for the above problems, but diagnosing and correcting them is considered beyond the scope of this manual. Having checked the fluid level and all the wiring as far as possible, a dealer or transmission specialist should be consulted if the problem persists.*

Driveshafts

Vibration when accelerating or decelerating
☐ Worn inner constant velocity joint (Chapter 8)
☐ Bent or distorted driveshaft (Chapter 8)
☐ Worn driveshaft support bearing (Chapter 8)

Clicking or knocking noise on turns (at slow speed on full-lock)
☐ Worn outer constant velocity joint (Chapter 8)
☐ Lack of constant velocity joint lubricant, possibly due to damaged gaiter (Chapter 8)

Braking system

Note: *Before assuming that a brake problem exists, make sure that the tyres are in good condition and correctly inflated, that the front wheel alignment is correct, and that the vehicle is not loaded with weight in an unequal manner. Apart from checking the condition of all pipe and hose connections, any faults occurring on the anti-lock braking system should be referred to a VW dealer for diagnosis.*

Vehicle pulls to one side under braking

- ☐ Worn, defective, damaged or contaminated brake pads on one side (Chapter 1 or 9)
- ☐ Seized or partially-seized brake caliper piston (Chapter 1 or 9)
- ☐ A mixture of brake pad lining materials fitted between sides (Chapter 1 or 9)
- ☐ Brake caliper mounting bolts loose (Chapter 9)
- ☐ Worn or damaged steering or suspension components (Chapter 1 or 10)

Noise (grinding or high-pitched squeal) when brakes applied

- ☐ Brake pad friction lining material worn down to wear sensor or metal backing (Chapter 1 or 9)
- ☐ Excessive corrosion of brake disc (may be apparent after the vehicle has been standing for some time (Chapter 1 or 9)
- ☐ Foreign object (stone chipping, etc) trapped between brake disc and shield (Chapter 1 or 9)

Excessive brake pedal travel

- ☐ Faulty master cylinder (Chapter 9)
- ☐ Air in hydraulic system (Chapter 1 or 9)
- ☐ Faulty vacuum servo unit (Chapter 9)
- ☐ Faulty vacuum pump (Chapter 9)
- ☐ Disconnected, damaged or insecure brake servo vacuum hose (Chapter 9)

Brake pedal feels spongy when depressed

- ☐ Air in hydraulic system (Chapter 1 or 9)
- ☐ Deteriorated flexible rubber brake hoses (Chapter 1 or 9)
- ☐ Master cylinder mounting nuts loose (Chapter 9)
- ☐ Faulty master cylinder (Chapter 9)

Excessive brake pedal effort required to stop vehicle

- ☐ Faulty vacuum servo unit (Chapter 9)
- ☐ Faulty vacuum pump (Chapter 9)
- ☐ Disconnected, damaged or insecure brake servo vacuum hose (Chapter 9)
- ☐ Primary or secondary hydraulic circuit failure (Chapter 9)
- ☐ Seized brake caliper piston (Chapter 9)
- ☐ Brake pads incorrectly fitted (Chapter 9)
- ☐ Incorrect grade of brake pads fitted (Chapter 9)
- ☐ Brake pad linings contaminated (Chapter 1 or 9)

Judder felt through brake pedal or steering wheel when braking

Note: *Under heavy braking on models equipped with ABS, vibration may be felt through the brake pedal. This is a normal feature of ABS operation, and does not constitute a fault.*

- ☐ Excessive run-out or distortion of discs/drums (Chapter 1 or 9)
- ☐ Brake pad linings worn (Chapter 1 or 9)
- ☐ Brake caliper mounting bolts loose (Chapter 9)
- ☐ Wear in suspension or steering components or mountings (Chapter 1 or 10)
- ☐ Front wheels out of balance (see *Weekly checks*)

Brakes binding

- ☐ Seized brake caliper piston (Chapter 9)
- ☐ Faulty master cylinder (Chapter 9)

Rear wheels locking under normal braking

- ☐ Rear brake pad linings contaminated or damaged (Chapter 1 or 9)
- ☐ Rear brake disc warped (Chapter 1 or 9)

Suspension and steering

Note: *Before diagnosing suspension or steering faults, be sure that the trouble is not due to incorrect tyre pressures, mixtures of tyre types, or binding brakes.*

Vehicle pulls to one side

- ☐ Defective tyre (see *Weekly checks*)
- ☐ Excessive wear in suspension or steering components (Chapter 1 or 10)
- ☐ Incorrect front wheel alignment (Chapter 10)
- ☐ Accident damage to steering or suspension components (Chapter 1 or 10)

Wheel wobble and vibration

- ☐ Front wheels out of balance (vibration felt mainly through the steering wheel) (see *Weekly checks*)
- ☐ Rear wheels out of balance (vibration felt throughout the vehicle) (see *Weekly checks*)
- ☐ Roadwheels damaged or distorted (see *Weekly checks*)
- ☐ Faulty or damaged tyre (see *Weekly checks*)
- ☐ Worn steering or suspension joints, bushes or components (Chapter 1 or 10)
- ☐ Wheel bolts loose (Chapter 1)

Excessive pitching and/or rolling around corners, or during braking

- ☐ Defective shock absorbers (Chapter 1 or 10)
- ☐ Broken or weak spring and/or suspension component (Chapter 1 or 10)
- ☐ Worn or damaged anti-roll bar or mountings (Chapter 1 or 10)

Wandering or general instability

- ☐ Incorrect front wheel alignment (Chapter 10)
- ☐ Worn steering or suspension joints, bushes or components (Chapter 1 or 10)
- ☐ Roadwheels out of balance (see *Weekly checks*)
- ☐ Faulty or damaged tyre (see *Weekly checks*)
- ☐ Wheel bolts loose (Chapter 1)
- ☐ Defective shock absorbers (Chapter 1 or 10)
- ☐ Power steering system fault (Chapter 10)

Excessively-stiff steering

- ☐ Seized steering linkage balljoint or suspension balljoint (Chapter 1 or 10)
- ☐ Incorrect front wheel alignment (Chapter 10)
- ☐ Steering rack damaged (Chapter 10)
- ☐ Power steering system fault (Chapter 10)

Suspension and steering (continued)

Excessive play in steering

- ☐ Worn steering column/intermediate shaft joints (Chapter 10)
- ☐ Worn track rod balljoints (Chapter 1 or 10)
- ☐ Worn steering rack (Chapter 10)
- ☐ Worn steering or suspension joints, bushes or components (Chapter 1 or 10)

Lack of power assistance

- ☐ Broken power steering pump drivebelt (Chapter 1)
- ☐ Power steering system fault (Chapter 10)
- ☐ Faulty steering rack (Chapter 10)

Tyre wear excessive

Tyres worn on inside or outside edges

- ☐ Tyres under-inflated (wear on both edges) (see *Weekly checks*)
- ☐ Incorrect camber or castor angles (wear on one edge only) (Chapter 10)

- ☐ Worn steering or suspension joints, bushes or components (Chapter 1 or 10)
- ☐ Excessively-hard cornering or braking
- ☐ Accident damage

Tyre treads exhibit feathered edges

- ☐ Incorrect toe-setting (Chapter 10)

Tyres worn in centre of tread

- ☐ Tyres over-inflated (see *Weekly checks*)

Tyres worn on inside and outside edges

- ☐ Tyres under-inflated (see *Weekly checks*)

Tyres worn unevenly

- ☐ Tyres/wheels out of balance (see *Weekly checks*)
- ☐ Excessive wheel or tyre run-out
- ☐ Worn shock absorbers (Chapter 1 or 10)
- ☐ Faulty tyre (see *Weekly checks*)

Electrical system

Note: *For problems associated with the starting system, refer to the faults listed under 'Engine' earlier in this Section.*

Battery will not hold a charge for more than a few days

- ☐ Battery defective internally (Chapter 5)
- ☐ Battery terminal connections loose or corroded (see *Weekly checks*)
- ☐ Auxiliary drivebelt worn, incorrectly adjusted or faulty automatic adjuster (Chapter 1)
- ☐ Alternator not charging at correct output (Chapter 5)
- ☐ Alternator or voltage regulator faulty (Chapter 5)
- ☐ Short-circuit causing continual battery drain (Chapter 5 or 12)

Ignition/no-charge warning light remains illuminated with engine running

- ☐ Auxiliary drivebelt broken, worn, incorrectly adjusted or faulty automatic adjuster (Chapter 1)
- ☐ Internal fault in alternator or voltage regulator (Chapter 5)
- ☐ Broken, disconnected, or loose wiring in charging circuit (Chapter 5 or 12)

Ignition/no-charge warning light fails to come on

- ☐ Faulty instrument panel (Chapter 12)
- ☐ Broken, disconnected, or loose wiring in warning light circuit (Chapter 5 or 12)
- ☐ Alternator faulty (Chapter 5)

Lights inoperative

- ☐ Bulb blown (Chapter 12)
- ☐ Corrosion of bulb or bulbholder contacts (Chapter 12)

- ☐ Blown fuse (Chapter 12)
- ☐ Faulty relay (Chapter 12)
- ☐ Broken, loose, or disconnected wiring (Chapter 12)
- ☐ Faulty switch (Chapter 12)

Instrument readings inaccurate or erratic

Fuel or temperature gauges give no reading

- ☐ Faulty gauge sender unit (Chapter 3, 4A or 4B)
- ☐ Wiring open-circuit (Chapter 12)
- ☐ Faulty instrument panel (Chapter 12)

Fuel or temperature gauges give continuous maximum reading

- ☐ Faulty gauge sender unit (Chapter 3, 4A or 4B)
- ☐ Wiring short-circuit (Chapter 12)
- ☐ Faulty instrument panel (Chapter 12)

Horn inoperative, or unsatisfactory in operation

Horn operates all the time

- ☐ Horn push either earthed or stuck down (Chapter 12)
- ☐ Horn cable-to-horn push earthed (Chapter 12)

Horn fails to operate

- ☐ Blown fuse (Chapter 12)
- ☐ Cable or connections loose, broken or disconnected (Chapter 12)
- ☐ Faulty horn (Chapter 12)

Horn emits intermittent or unsatisfactory sound

- ☐ Cable connections loose (Chapter 12)
- ☐ Horn mountings loose (Chapter 12)
- ☐ Faulty horn (Chapter 12)

Electrical system (continued)

Windscreen wipers inoperative, or unsatisfactory in operation

Wipers fail to operate, or operate very slowly

- ☐ Wiper blades stuck to screen, or linkage seized or binding (Chapter 12)
- ☐ Blown fuse (Chapter 12)
- ☐ Battery discharged (Chapter 5)
- ☐ Cable or connections loose, broken or disconnected (Chapter 12)
- ☐ Faulty relay (Chapter 12)
- ☐ Faulty wiper motor (Chapter 12)

Wiper blades sweep over too large or too small an area of the glass

- ☐ Wiper blades incorrectly fitted, or wrong size used (see *Weekly checks*)
- ☐ Wiper arms incorrectly positioned on spindles (Chapter 12)
- ☐ Excessive wear of wiper linkage (Chapter 12)
- ☐ Wiper motor or linkage mountings loose or insecure (Chapter 12)

Wiper blades fail to clean the glass effectively

- ☐ Wiper blade rubbers dirty, worn or perished (see *Weekly checks*)
- ☐ Wiper blades incorrectly fitted, or wrong size used (see *Weekly checks*)
- ☐ Wiper arm tension springs broken, or arm pivots seized (Chapter 12)
- ☐ Insufficient windscreen washer additive to adequately remove road film (see *Weekly checks*)

Windscreen washers inoperative, or unsatisfactory in operation

One or more washer jets inoperative

- ☐ Blocked washer jet (Chapter 12)
- ☐ Disconnected, kinked or restricted fluid hose (Chapter 12)
- ☐ Insufficient fluid in washer reservoir (see *Weekly checks*)

Washer pump fails to operate

- ☐ Broken or disconnected wiring or connections (Chapter 12)
- ☐ Blown fuse (Chapter 12)
- ☐ Faulty washer switch (Chapter 12)
- ☐ Faulty washer pump (Chapter 12)

Electric windows inoperative, or unsatisfactory in operation

Window glass will only move in one direction

- ☐ Faulty switch (Chapter 12)

Window glass slow to move

- ☐ Battery discharged (Chapter 5)
- ☐ Regulator seized or damaged, or in need of lubrication (Chapter 11)
- ☐ Door internal components or trim fouling regulator (Chapter 11)
- ☐ Faulty motor (Chapter 11)

Window glass fails to move

- ☐ Blown fuse (Chapter 12)
- ☐ Faulty relay (Chapter 12)
- ☐ Broken or disconnected wiring or connections (Chapter 12)
- ☐ Faulty motor (Chapter 11)

Central locking system inoperative, or unsatisfactory in operation

Complete system failure

- ☐ Blown fuse (Chapter 12)
- ☐ Faulty relay (Chapter 12)
- ☐ Broken or disconnected wiring or connections (Chapter 12)
- ☐ Faulty motor (Chapter 11)

Latch locks but will not unlock, or unlocks but will not lock

- ☐ Broken or disconnected latch operating rods or levers (Chapter 11)
- ☐ Faulty relay (Chapter 12)
- ☐ Faulty motor (Chapter 11)

One solenoid/motor fails to operate

- ☐ Broken or disconnected wiring or connections (Chapter 12)
- ☐ Faulty operating assembly (Chapter 11)
- ☐ Broken, binding or disconnected latch operating rods or levers (Chapter 11)
- ☐ Fault in door latch (Chapter 11)

A

ABS (Anti-lock brake system) A system, usually electronically controlled, that senses incipient wheel lockup during braking and relieves hydraulic pressure at wheels that are about to skid.

Air bag An inflatable bag hidden in the steering wheel (driver's side) or the dash or glovebox (passenger side). In a head-on collision, the bags inflate, preventing the driver and front passenger from being thrown forward into the steering wheel or windscreen.

Air cleaner A metal or plastic housing, containing a filter element, which removes dust and dirt from the air being drawn into the engine.

Air filter element The actual filter in an air cleaner system, usually manufactured from pleated paper and requiring renewal at regular intervals.

Air filter

Allen key A hexagonal wrench which fits into a recessed hexagonal hole.

Alligator clip A long-nosed spring-loaded metal clip with meshing teeth. Used to make temporary electrical connections.

Alternator A component in the electrical system which converts mechanical energy from a drivebelt into electrical energy to charge the battery and to operate the starting system, ignition system and electrical accessories.

Ampere (amp) A unit of measurement for the flow of electric current. One amp is the amount of current produced by one volt acting through a resistance of one ohm.

Anaerobic sealer A substance used to prevent bolts and screws from loosening. Anaerobic means that it does not require oxygen for activation. The Loctite brand is widely used.

Antifreeze A substance (usually ethylene glycol) mixed with water, and added to a vehicle's cooling system, to prevent freezing of the coolant in winter. Antifreeze also contains chemicals to inhibit corrosion and the formation of rust and other deposits that would tend to clog the radiator and coolant passages and reduce cooling efficiency.

Anti-seize compound A coating that reduces the risk of seizing on fasteners that are subjected to high temperatures, such as exhaust manifold bolts and nuts.

Asbestos A natural fibrous mineral with great heat resistance, commonly used in the composition of brake friction materials.

Asbestos is a health hazard and the dust created by brake systems should never be inhaled or ingested.

Axle A shaft on which a wheel revolves, or which revolves with a wheel. Also, a solid beam that connects the two wheels at one end of the vehicle. An axle which also transmits power to the wheels is known as a live axle.

Axleshaft A single rotating shaft, on either side of the differential, which delivers power from the final drive assembly to the drive wheels. Also called a driveshaft or a halfshaft.

B

Ball bearing An anti-friction bearing consisting of a hardened inner and outer race with hardened steel balls between two races.

Bearing The curved surface on a shaft or in a bore, or the part assembled into either, that permits relative motion between them with minimum wear and friction.

Bearing

Big-end bearing The bearing in the end of the connecting rod that's attached to the crankshaft.

Bleed nipple A valve on a brake wheel cylinder, caliper or other hydraulic component that is opened to purge the hydraulic system of air. Also called a bleed screw.

Brake bleeding Procedure for removing air from lines of a hydraulic brake system.

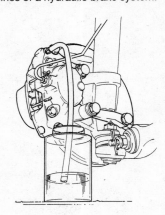

Brake bleeding

Brake disc The component of a disc brake that rotates with the wheels.

Brake drum The component of a drum brake that rotates with the wheels.

Brake linings The friction material which contacts the brake disc or drum to retard the vehicle's speed. The linings are bonded or riveted to the brake pads or shoes.

Brake pads The replaceable friction pads that pinch the brake disc when the brakes are applied. Brake pads consist of a friction material bonded or riveted to a rigid backing plate.

Brake shoe The crescent-shaped carrier to which the brake linings are mounted and which forces the lining against the rotating drum during braking.

Braking systems For more information on braking systems, consult the *Haynes Automotive Brake Manual*.

Breaker bar A long socket wrench handle providing greater leverage.

Bulkhead The insulated partition between the engine and the passenger compartment.

C

Caliper The non-rotating part of a disc-brake assembly that straddles the disc and carries the brake pads. The caliper also contains the hydraulic components that cause the pads to pinch the disc when the brakes are applied. A caliper is also a measuring tool that can be set to measure inside or outside dimensions of an object.

Camshaft A rotating shaft on which a series of cam lobes operate the valve mechanisms. The camshaft may be driven by gears, by sprockets and chain or by sprockets and a belt.

Canister A container in an evaporative emission control system; contains activated charcoal granules to trap vapours from the fuel system.

Canister

Carburettor A device which mixes fuel with air in the proper proportions to provide a desired power output from a spark ignition internal combustion engine.

Castellated Resembling the parapets along the top of a castle wall. For example, a castellated balljoint stud nut.

Castor In wheel alignment, the backward or forward tilt of the steering axis. Castor is positive when the steering axis is inclined rearward at the top.

Catalytic converter A silencer-like device in the exhaust system which converts certain pollutants in the exhaust gases into less harmful substances.

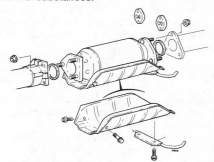

Catalytic converter

Circlip A ring-shaped clip used to prevent endwise movement of cylindrical parts and shafts. An internal circlip is installed in a groove in a housing; an external circlip fits into a groove on the outside of a cylindrical piece such as a shaft.

Clearance The amount of space between two parts. For example, between a piston and a cylinder, between a bearing and a journal, etc.

Coil spring A spiral of elastic steel found in various sizes throughout a vehicle, for example as a springing medium in the suspension and in the valve train.

Compression Reduction in volume, and increase in pressure and temperature, of a gas, caused by squeezing it into a smaller space.

Compression ratio The relationship between cylinder volume when the piston is at top dead centre and cylinder volume when the piston is at bottom dead centre.

Constant velocity (CV) joint A type of universal joint that cancels out vibrations caused by driving power being transmitted through an angle.

Core plug A disc or cup-shaped metal device inserted in a hole in a casting through which core was removed when the casting was formed. Also known as a freeze plug or expansion plug.

Crankcase The lower part of the engine block in which the crankshaft rotates.

Crankshaft The main rotating member, or shaft, running the length of the crankcase, with offset "throws" to which the connecting rods are attached.

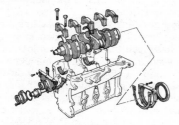

Crankshaft assembly

Crocodile clip See Alligator clip

D

Diagnostic code Code numbers obtained by accessing the diagnostic mode of an engine management computer. This code can be used to determine the area in the system where a malfunction may be located.

Disc brake A brake design incorporating a rotating disc onto which brake pads are squeezed. The resulting friction converts the energy of a moving vehicle into heat.

Double-overhead cam (DOHC) An engine that uses two overhead camshafts, usually one for the intake valves and one for the exhaust valves.

Drivebelt(s) The belt(s) used to drive accessories such as the alternator, water pump, power steering pump, air conditioning compressor, etc. off the crankshaft pulley.

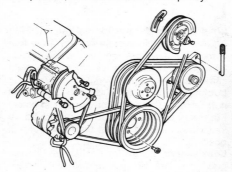

Accessory drivebelts

Driveshaft Any shaft used to transmit motion. Commonly used when referring to the axleshafts on a front wheel drive vehicle.

Drum brake A type of brake using a drum-shaped metal cylinder attached to the inner surface of the wheel. When the brake pedal is pressed, curved brake shoes with friction linings press against the inside of the drum to slow or stop the vehicle.

E

EGR valve A valve used to introduce exhaust gases into the intake air stream.

Electronic control unit (ECU) A computer which controls (for instance) ignition and fuel injection systems, or an anti-lock braking system. For more information refer to the *Haynes Automotive Electrical and Electronic Systems Manual*.

Electronic Fuel Injection (EFI) A computer controlled fuel system that distributes fuel through an injector located in each intake port of the engine.

Emergency brake A braking system, independent of the main hydraulic system, that can be used to slow or stop the vehicle if the primary brakes fail, or to hold the vehicle stationary even though the brake pedal isn't depressed. It usually consists of a hand lever that actuates either front or rear brakes mechanically through a series of cables and linkages. Also known as a handbrake or parking brake.

Endfloat The amount of lengthwise movement between two parts. As applied to a crankshaft, the distance that the crankshaft can move forward and back in the cylinder block.

Engine management system (EMS) A computer controlled system which manages the fuel injection and the ignition systems in an integrated fashion.

Exhaust manifold A part with several passages through which exhaust gases leave the engine combustion chambers and enter the exhaust pipe.

F

Fan clutch A viscous (fluid) drive coupling device which permits variable engine fan speeds in relation to engine speeds.

Feeler blade A thin strip or blade of hardened steel, ground to an exact thickness, used to check or measure clearances between parts.

Feeler blade

Firing order The order in which the engine cylinders fire, or deliver their power strokes, beginning with the number one cylinder.

Flywheel A heavy spinning wheel in which energy is absorbed and stored by means of momentum. On cars, the flywheel is attached to the crankshaft to smooth out firing impulses.

Free play The amount of travel before any action takes place. The "looseness" in a linkage, or an assembly of parts, between the initial application of force and actual movement. For example, the distance the brake pedal moves before the pistons in the master cylinder are actuated.

Fuse An electrical device which protects a circuit against accidental overload. The typical fuse contains a soft piece of metal which is calibrated to melt at a predetermined current flow (expressed as amps) and break the circuit.

Fusible link A circuit protection device consisting of a conductor surrounded by heat-resistant insulation. The conductor is smaller than the wire it protects, so it acts as the weakest link in the circuit. Unlike a blown fuse, a failed fusible link must frequently be cut from the wire for replacement.

G

Gap The distance the spark must travel in jumping from the centre electrode to the side electrode in a spark plug. Also refers to the spacing between the points in a contact breaker assembly in a conventional points-type ignition, or to the distance between the reluctor or rotor and the pickup coil in an electronic ignition.

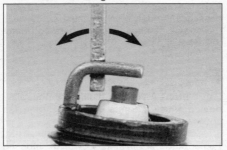

Adjusting spark plug gap

Gasket Any thin, soft material - usually cork, cardboard, asbestos or soft metal - installed between two metal surfaces to ensure a good seal. For instance, the cylinder head gasket seals the joint between the block and the cylinder head.

Gasket

Gauge An instrument panel display used to monitor engine conditions. A gauge with a movable pointer on a dial or a fixed scale is an analogue gauge. A gauge with a numerical readout is called a digital gauge.

H

Halfshaft A rotating shaft that transmits power from the final drive unit to a drive wheel, usually when referring to a live rear axle.

Harmonic balancer A device designed to reduce torsion or twisting vibration in the crankshaft. May be incorporated in the crankshaft pulley. Also known as a vibration damper.

Hone An abrasive tool for correcting small irregularities or differences in diameter in an engine cylinder, brake cylinder, etc.

Hydraulic tappet A tappet that utilises hydraulic pressure from the engine's lubrication system to maintain zero clearance (constant contact with both camshaft and valve stem). Automatically adjusts to variation in valve stem length. Hydraulic tappets also reduce valve noise.

I

Ignition timing The moment at which the spark plug fires, usually expressed in the number of crankshaft degrees before the piston reaches the top of its stroke.

Inlet manifold A tube or housing with passages through which flows the air-fuel mixture (carburettor vehicles and vehicles with throttle body injection) or air only (port fuel-injected vehicles) to the port openings in the cylinder head.

J

Jump start Starting the engine of a vehicle with a discharged or weak battery by attaching jump leads from the weak battery to a charged or helper battery.

L

Load Sensing Proportioning Valve (LSPV) A brake hydraulic system control valve that works like a proportioning valve, but also takes into consideration the amount of weight carried by the rear axle.

Locknut A nut used to lock an adjustment nut, or other threaded component, in place. For example, a locknut is employed to keep the adjusting nut on the rocker arm in position.

Lockwasher A form of washer designed to prevent an attaching nut from working loose.

M

MacPherson strut A type of front suspension system devised by Earle MacPherson at Ford of England. In its original form, a simple lateral link with the anti-roll bar creates the lower control arm. A long strut - an integral coil spring and shock absorber - is mounted between the body and the steering knuckle. Many modern so-called MacPherson strut systems use a conventional lower A-arm and don't rely on the anti-roll bar for location.

Multimeter An electrical test instrument with the capability to measure voltage, current and resistance.

N

NOx Oxides of Nitrogen. A common toxic pollutant emitted by petrol and diesel engines at higher temperatures.

O

Ohm The unit of electrical resistance. One volt applied to a resistance of one ohm will produce a current of one amp.

Ohmmeter An instrument for measuring electrical resistance.

O-ring A type of sealing ring made of a special rubber-like material; in use, the O-ring is compressed into a groove to provide the sealing action.

Overhead cam (ohc) engine An engine with the camshaft(s) located on top of the cylinder head(s).

Overhead valve (ohv) engine An engine with the valves located in the cylinder head, but with the camshaft located in the engine block.

Oxygen sensor A device installed in the engine exhaust manifold, which senses the oxygen content in the exhaust and converts this information into an electric current. Also called a Lambda sensor.

P

Phillips screw A type of screw head having a cross instead of a slot for a corresponding type of screwdriver.

Plastigage A thin strip of plastic thread, available in different sizes, used for measuring clearances. For example, a strip of Plastigage is laid across a bearing journal. The parts are assembled and dismantled; the width of the crushed strip indicates the clearance between journal and bearing.

Plastigage

Propeller shaft The long hollow tube with universal joints at both ends that carries power from the transmission to the differential on front-engined rear wheel drive vehicles.

Proportioning valve A hydraulic control valve which limits the amount of pressure to the rear brakes during panic stops to prevent wheel lock-up.

R

Rack-and-pinion steering A steering system with a pinion gear on the end of the steering shaft that mates with a rack (think of a geared wheel opened up and laid flat). When the steering wheel is turned, the pinion turns, moving the rack to the left or right. This movement is transmitted through the track rods to the steering arms at the wheels.

Radiator A liquid-to-air heat transfer device designed to reduce the temperature of the coolant in an internal combustion engine cooling system.

Refrigerant Any substance used as a heat transfer agent in an air-conditioning system. R-12 has been the principle refrigerant for many years; recently, however, manufacturers have begun using R-134a, a non-CFC substance that is considered less harmful to the ozone in the upper atmosphere.

Rocker arm A lever arm that rocks on a shaft or pivots on a stud. In an overhead valve engine, the rocker arm converts the upward movement of the pushrod into a downward movement to open a valve.

Rotor In a distributor, the rotating device inside the cap that connects the centre electrode and the outer terminals as it turns, distributing the high voltage from the coil secondary winding to the proper spark plug. Also, that part of an alternator which rotates inside the stator. Also, the rotating assembly of a turbocharger, including the compressor wheel, shaft and turbine wheel.

Runout The amount of wobble (in-and-out movement) of a gear or wheel as it's rotated. The amount a shaft rotates "out-of-true." The out-of-round condition of a rotating part.

S

Sealant A liquid or paste used to prevent leakage at a joint. Sometimes used in conjunction with a gasket.

Sealed beam lamp An older headlight design which integrates the reflector, lens and filaments into a hermetically-sealed one-piece unit. When a filament burns out or the lens cracks, the entire unit is simply replaced.

Serpentine drivebelt A single, long, wide accessory drivebelt that's used on some newer vehicles to drive all the accessories, instead of a series of smaller, shorter belts. Serpentine drivebelts are usually tensioned by an automatic tensioner.

Serpentine drivebelt

Shim Thin spacer, commonly used to adjust the clearance or relative positions between two parts. For example, shims inserted into or under bucket tappets control valve clearances. Clearance is adjusted by changing the thickness of the shim.

Slide hammer A special puller that screws into or hooks onto a component such as a shaft or bearing; a heavy sliding handle on the shaft bottoms against the end of the shaft to knock the component free.

Sprocket A tooth or projection on the periphery of a wheel, shaped to engage with a chain or drivebelt. Commonly used to refer to the sprocket wheel itself.

Starter inhibitor switch On vehicles with an automatic transmission, a switch that prevents starting if the vehicle is not in Neutral or Park.

Strut See MacPherson strut.

T

Tappet A cylindrical component which transmits motion from the cam to the valve stem, either directly or via a pushrod and rocker arm. Also called a cam follower.

Thermostat A heat-controlled valve that regulates the flow of coolant between the cylinder block and the radiator, so maintaining optimum engine operating temperature. A thermostat is also used in some air cleaners in which the temperature is regulated.

Thrust bearing The bearing in the clutch assembly that is moved in to the release levers by clutch pedal action to disengage the clutch. Also referred to as a release bearing.

Timing belt A toothed belt which drives the camshaft. Serious engine damage may result if it breaks in service.

Timing chain A chain which drives the camshaft.

Toe-in The amount the front wheels are closer together at the front than at the rear. On rear wheel drive vehicles, a slight amount of toe-in is usually specified to keep the front wheels running parallel on the road by offsetting other forces that tend to spread the wheels apart.

Toe-out The amount the front wheels are closer together at the rear than at the front. On front wheel drive vehicles, a slight amount of toe-out is usually specified.

Tools For full information on choosing and using tools, refer to the *Haynes Automotive Tools Manual*.

Tracer A stripe of a second colour applied to a wire insulator to distinguish that wire from another one with the same colour insulator.

Tune-up A process of accurate and careful adjustments and parts replacement to obtain the best possible engine performance.

Turbocharger A centrifugal device, driven by exhaust gases, that pressurises the intake air. Normally used to increase the power output from a given engine displacement, but can also be used primarily to reduce exhaust emissions (as on VW's "Umwelt" Diesel engine).

U

Universal joint or U-joint A double-pivoted connection for transmitting power from a driving to a driven shaft through an angle. A U-joint consists of two Y-shaped yokes and a cross-shaped member called the spider.

V

Valve A device through which the flow of liquid, gas, vacuum, or loose material in bulk may be started, stopped, or regulated by a movable part that opens, shuts, or partially obstructs one or more ports or passageways. A valve is also the movable part of such a device.

Valve clearance The clearance between the valve tip (the end of the valve stem) and the rocker arm or tappet. The valve clearance is measured when the valve is closed.

Vernier caliper A precision measuring instrument that measures inside and outside dimensions. Not quite as accurate as a micrometer, but more convenient.

Viscosity The thickness of a liquid or its resistance to flow.

Volt A unit for expressing electrical "pressure" in a circuit. One volt that will produce a current of one ampere through a resistance of one ohm.

W

Welding Various processes used to join metal items by heating the areas to be joined to a molten state and fusing them together. For more information refer to the *Haynes Automotive Welding Manual*.

Wiring diagram A drawing portraying the components and wires in a vehicle's electrical system, using standardised symbols. For more information refer to the *Haynes Automotive Electrical and Electronic Systems Manual*.

Note: *References throughout this index are in the form "***Chapter number***" • "***Page number***". So, for example, 2C•15 refers to page 15 of Chapter 2C.*

Note: *References throughout this index are in the form* **"Chapter number"** • *"Page number". So, for example, 2C•15 refers to page 15 of Chapter 2C.*

Preserving Our Motoring Heritage

< The Model J Duesenberg Derham Tourster. Only eight of these magnificent cars were ever built – this is the only example to be found outside the United States of America

Almost every car you've ever loved, loathed or desired is gathered under one roof at the Haynes Motor Museum. Over 300 immaculately presented cars and motorbikes represent every aspect of our motoring heritage, from elegant reminders of bygone days, such as the superb Model J Duesenberg to curiosities like the bug-eyed BMW Isetta. There are also many old friends and flames. Perhaps you remember the 1959 Ford Popular that you did your courting in? The magnificent 'Red Collection' is a spectacle of classic sports cars including AC, Alfa Romeo, Austin Healey, Ferrari, Lamborghini, Maserati, MG, Riley, Porsche and Triumph.

A Perfect Day Out

Each and every vehicle at the Haynes Motor Museum has played its part in the history and culture of Motoring. Today, they make a wonderful spectacle and a great day out for all the family. Bring the kids, bring Mum and Dad, but above all bring your camera to capture those golden memories for ever. You will also find an impressive array of motoring memorabilia, a comfortable 70 seat video cinema and one of the most extensive transport book shops in Britain. The Pit Stop Cafe serves everything from a cup of tea to wholesome, home-made meals or, if you prefer, you can enjoy the large picnic area nestled in the beautiful rural surroundings of Somerset.

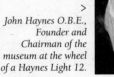

> John Haynes O.B.E., Founder and Chairman of the museum at the wheel of a Haynes Light 12.

< Graham Hill's Lola Cosworth Formula 1 car next to a 1934 Riley Sports.

The Museum is situated on the A359 Yeovil to Frome road at Sparkford, just off the A303 in Somerset. It is about 40 miles south of Bristol, and 25 minutes drive from the M5 intersection at Taunton.
Open 9.30am - 5.30pm (10.00am - 4.00pm Winter) 7 days a week, *except Christmas Day, Boxing Day and New Years Day*
Special rates available for schools, coach parties and outings Charitable Trust No. 292048